CUSTOMS

OF THE

MANOR

OF

WATFORD.

Common Field, Church Acre, Wiggen-hall Mead, Middlemore, Bushey Mead, Dagnell's and Moody's Alleys— all names of places now covered over with roads and houses.

The Customs are those by which all had to abide, or pay penalties, and date from 1621. Fences should not be damaged and sick animals should not be allowed in the fields.

Between the Town Mill and Hamper Mill the respective Landowners were expected to keep the river clear '5ft wide'.

The poster was 10¼ x 17½ inches in size and printed in 1820 by Perry, Printer, of Watford Market Place.

The quarter days are: Lady Day, 25th March; Midsummer Day, 24th June; Michaelmas Day, 29th September and Christmas Day, 25th December.

Reference to 'Candlemas Day' and 'Lammas Day' are Scottish terms for 2nd February and 1st August respectively.

Fences in the Common Fields ..
ALL those that have Lands in Watford Field, or Land in any of the Common Fields in or about Watford, shall make up their Fences belonging to their several Lands lying against the Lands adjoining, for their winter crop before Michaelmas; and for their summer crop before Lady-Day in every year, on pain of forfeiting to the Lord of the Manor twelve-pence per pole.

Court 9th. April, 1624. ......

Gate and Fence against Wiggen-hall Mead
The Occupiers of Church-Acre shall keep a sufficient Fence and Gate, at the end of Church-Acre, between Watford Field and Wiggenhall Mead, all the year long, (except between All-hallowed Tide and Candlemas; upon pain of forfeiting twelve-pence per week to the Lord of the Manor.

Courts 1621 and 1624. ......

Sheep ....
No Man shall put any Sheep in Common Meads, Wiggen-hall Mead, or Middlemore, before the first day of November, nor after Candlemas-Day following, on pain of forfeiting for every Sheep six-pence; half to the Lord of the Manor, and the other half to the Meadow Drivers.

1624. ....

1631. ....
No Man not holding Land in the Common Field, shall at any time put upon, or into, the Common Fields and Meadows above the number of Ten Sheep, on pain of forfeiting for every Sheep twelve-pence, so often as they shall be taken; half to the Lord and half to the Finder.

Batchelors. ......
No Batchelor (unless he be a Householder) shall put any Sheep in the Commons on the same forfeiture.

Foreigners. ......
No foreigners have any Right of Commoning in Wiggen-hall Meadow, Middlemore, or Bushey Mead, except they have Land in the Meadow, and in their own possession at the same time. And also, that none but Housekeepers have a Right of Commoning, except they have Land in the Meadow.

5th. April, 1703.
Also that the ANCIENT CUSTOM is, that all Cattle that are put in contrary to the Custom of the Manor, shall pay FOUR-PENCE per foot to the Meadow Driver.

Cattle in the Highways or Lanes.
No Inhabitant within the Town or Parish of Watford, shall keep above Two Beasts in the Highways nor then either, unless they have a Follower to keep them from breaking or hurting the Fences, upon pain of forfeiting twelve-pence to the Lord of the Manor, by them that shall keep above Two; or any Beast there at all, without a Keeper.— ☞ The fine twelve-pence each, half to the Lord and half to him that poundeth them.

Mares. ....
No Man shall put any Mare to feed in the Common Meadows, or Highways, or Lanes, in the Parish of Watford, upon pain of forfeiting twenty shillings for every Mare so found; half to the Lord of the Manor, and the other half to the Meadow Driver.

Diseased Horses ..
No Man shall put any Horse or Gelding that hath the Fashions (Farcy) or Mange into any of the Common Meadows, upon pain of forfeiting ten shillings for every such Beast so put in; half to the Lord and half to the Finder.

River Cleansing ..
The Landholders on both sides the River between the Town Mill and Hamper Mill, to clear the River 5 Feet Wide; on pain of forfeiting two shillings and six-pence per pole.

Shutting up the Meadows ....
Common Meadows to be shut up at Candlemas-Day; and any putting Cattle therein between that Day and Lammas forfeit three shillings and four-pence; half to the Lord, and the other to him who receives the Damage.

Geese, &c. ......
Neither Cattle or Geese to be put in the Common Mead before the Crop be off; but shall keep them from thence from Candlemas-Day until Lammas-Day.

Hogs. ....
Whoever have any Hogs go into the Common Fields and Meadows unrunged, shall pay for every Hog one shilling.

Passages into Watford Field ..
Dagnall's Alley and Moody's Alley, a Passage for foot Passengers into Watford Field, and a stile or Fence to be maintained by the Persons who own the Houses.

Extract of Court Roll. { EDWARD BOODLE, Chief Steward.
{ PHILIP COWLEY, Deputy Steward of the said Manor.

PERRY, Printer, Engraver, Bookbinder, Librarian, &c. Market-Place, WATFORD.
[Printer to The Earl of Essex, The Earl of Clarendon, &c. &c.]

J B Nunn

The Book of

Watford

2nd edition

Entrance Lodge to Cassiobury, c1835

The Book of Watford, 2nd Edition
J B Nunn

ISBN 0 9536918 1 0

October 2003

© J B & L V Nunn

Published by J B & L V Nunn, Malden Road, Watford, Herts, WD17 4EW,
Printed by Alpine Press Ltd, Kings Langley, Herts
2003

The Book of Watford
2nd edition

Main Photographs by
Whitford Anderson
Barry Anthony
George Bolton
William Coles
Frederick Downer
Greville Studios
Bob Nunn
Albert Warren
Harry Williamson

Text excerpts from
Evening Echo
The Review
Watford Illustrated
Watford Newsletter
Watford Our Town/Watford Today
The West Herts and Watford Observer
The West Herts Post

Contributors
Edgar Chapman B. A. (Hons)
George Lorimer
David Noades
Oliver Philips
to The Book of Watford 1987
Ted Parrish

Compiled by
J B (Bob) Nunn

Watford, from Bushey, c 1813

Contents

Conventions used in this work.

As far as is practicable the illustrations in this work are chronological though there are instances where a modern comparison is introduced. Page 45 is an example. Through the pages of the High Street panorama (pages 301 to 374, photographed in 1994/5) the history runs from 1960/61 to 1987, at places interspersed with items and photographs to link older times with the modern High Street. There are side-by-side comparisons as, for example, the 'Green Man' evolution on page 365. On some pages will be found pictures reprinted from earlier pages of the book of which the UDC Offices, Fire Station and Gade House on page 370 is an example.

From the very earliest days photographs were coloured to more match nature than black and white or sepia could and in this work that tradition has been carried on. Of the dust jacket, for example, that of New Street and the Church, The Odeon Cinema, the Park Gates, and the entrance to the Harlequin Centre were originally monochrome photographs.

In Watford's early days the road we know as High Street was the Main Street of Watford. When King Street was made the convention for naming streets was, e.g., King-street, Queen's-street. For captions here the current style, e.g., 'King Street' is used though the text uses that of the time. The war of 1914-18 was, until well past the 1950's, referred to as the 'Great War' and is so named here. The captions for the illustrations from 1914 'Watford Illustrated' are original, some being reset to match the original style of type.

Where text gives prices they are expressed in that of the time, hence £ s. d., until 1971. For those not conversant with old money there were 20 shillings to the £1, and twelve pence to one shilling. A penny was further divided into four farthings. It is fallacious to relate an old price to modernity, without knowing some form of conversion factor, and this is not done in this work. Two pennies would at one time buy a loaf, now costing 50p, the equal of 120 old pennies or 60x difference. This equates with an example on page 267.

Excerpts from newspapers, etc, are in the style of the orginal and carry details of the source and date. The abbreviations are:
EE – Evening Echo;   WN – Watford Newsletter;
WO – Watford Observer;   WI – Watford Illustrated;
WHP – West Herts Post;   WOT – Watford Our Town/About Watford

Watford: the origin of a name . . .

The origin of our town's name remains shrouded in mystery, and many possible solutions proposed, some, no doubt, by writers who had not journeyed to this place. That some writers missed a point is evidenced by their referring to the River Colne which 'makes two streams'. There were, indeed two streams, two fords, but one was from the man-made channel which fed the town mill, and it was the mill's tail-race rather than a natural river.

Contractions of names based upon Watling Street have been discounted, leaving Wata's and Waet, the first a leader's name, the second a description. The description has been derided by 'Not from the Ford's being wet for I never heard of of a dry one,' but in reality the wetness is in all probability not far from the truth.

To our modernity the topography of the land is a mystery, hidden by buildings and railway embankments but the unassailable fact is that the lower part of the town lies in a depression, much like a saucer or plate slightly tilted, and after prolonged heavy rain, fills and overflows.

The extent of flooding within recent memory is such that water extends for two to three hundred yards up our High Street. When that occurred in earlier times marshy land would be flooded from the Mundens, through the Bushey and lower High Street area, through Oxhey Park, and past Moor Park and Moor Lane to Rickmansworth, a distance of five miles or so. That distance would present a formidable barrier.

An illustration has been commissioned, *p13,* which shows the extent of the flood from the bottom of Clay Hill area, northward, based upon modern flood distances. When in spate, access was impossible. In 1915 troops were taken by train from Watford High Street to Bushey Station, the road being impassable.

Of all the photographs which exist of Watford and district there are those of the rebuilding of Two-bridges at Croxley; of rebuilding the Wiggenhall-road Bridge, and of that over the Colne at Bushey Mill-lane. There is a newspaper picture of building the bridge over the canal at Hunton Bridge which is near the 'Blue Star' garage, but of Watford Bridge—nothing.

There are, however, some reports which shed a little light.

Henry Williams remarks that c1840 a house near the ironworks had ground which sloped to the river, and was open from the street to the river. Cattle being driven along the street turned off onto this piece of land and into the river. A horse and haycart, with sleeping carter, turned off the road and into the river and had a narrow escape from drowning. He stated:

"The bridge over the Colne at this spot was built in 1770, and at that time may have been considered a wide and handsome structure, but it is quite inadequate to the traffic of the present day. The capacity of the arches for passing water in flood time is also inadequate and about three years ago (1881) when the Local Board of Health was laying a sewer across the bridge, the men came across another arch, at the upper end of the bridge, which must have been closed many years ago as no-one appeared to remember that it ever existed."

David Downer, later in his life, recalled the one street in about 1846:

"crossing the River Colne by a bridge, a much narrower one than the present one, and with a ford by the side for horses and carts to go through"

George Thomas Clark, General Board of Health, in examining Watford in 1849 notes that:

"at the lower end of the town the main street is crossed by the tail-race of the Town-mill and afterwards by the main stream of the Colne" thus firmly indicating that water crosses at road level.

An inhabitant, in 1887 states:

"If the Local Board intend to erect a footbridge by the side of the old one I must raise my voice against such tinkering; let our Board set to work to provide a new bridge at once."

Dr Brett, in his report for 1889, alludes to the:

"crumbling Colne Bridge"

W R Saunders, *1871-1938,* historian, in his 'History of Watford', 1931 notes:

"Proceed to the Townsend Bridge over the Colne near Bushey Arches. The ford by the side of the Townsend Bridge exists no longer"

Attributed to Dr Brett's persistence, over the years, to effect improvement "not only on account of its narrowness but of the arches detaining rotten weeds"—"He saw the day, in County Council, the proposal to build a new bridge, and afterwards used the present substantial structure in his daily drives". The bridge was finally re-built in 1893/4, by which time bicycles had pneumatic tyres and Karl Benz's motor cars were making an appearance.

From the various recorded recollections of the ford there would, for a great many years, be no more than a need for a footbridge. Horses, and horse and carts, would be happy to use the ford, of no great depth when not in flood–and the horses would be happy to quench their thirst. It may be conjectured that with the increase of use of the road by more gentile coaches and carriages—more civilisation—a 'road bridge' would be necessary; this would need the road to be raised at both banks, but as a bridge was provided for foot passengers the ford was still no great problem for vehicles and was deferred.

Of the nature of the land it was found to be soft and marshy. Great difficulty was experienced in the building of the railway embankment with slippage and loss of foundation materials. When works were being carried out in the construction of the gasworks some human and animal remains were found. It appeared the bones were of a traveller who had attempted to cross the ford and was caught in marshy land and drowned, The animal remains were bones of red deer which were at one time abundant in the area. Under bad conditions the flood plain could stretch from Bushey Mill to Hampermill, a distance of some three miles.

The name 'Waterfields', which Watford perpetuates into the 21st century, is not from fancy but long established fact.

A typical narrow-river bridge, Wiggenhall Road 1926

Preface

by

A. G. Dillingham, J.P.

As a boy I well remember walking the roads and knowing the shops of the time. That was in 1910 when I came to live in Watford. My life's work has been involved in and with Watford and Watford's people; my wife and I have memories stretching back and reaching to us from every turn.

The changes which span the past 80 years have been vast; places I knew well are, to others, just names. One day the younger readers too will be faced with youngsters asking about the past.

This book chronicles the happenings of the town, not for 50 or 80 years, but essentially for the 150 years since the coming of the railway. It succeeds admirably; it was with considerable pleasure that I was able to browse through it in advance of publication.

Watford is a fine town in which to live, work and play; it has achieved its present status through hardship and hard work and the town's popularity is a measure of that success.

For me the book captures the flavour and anxieties, hopes, joys, and, yes, some disappointments of the times. I know that every reader fortunate enough to own a copy will feel the same; for every Watfordian, young or old, 'The Book of Watford" will become an ever more valued and priceless possession.

A G Dillingham,

June, 1987

Albert Dillingham passed away in the summer of 2003 but his comments written in 1987, so full of prescience, have proved true. The book has become valuable but long unavailable. By libraries and museums it is used as a source of reference; by students for scholastic projects; by families to trace their forebears, and by many to evoke memories.

This work continues from, and overlaps, the first and I feel it appropriate to reprise his words, in the hope that this second edition will be as deserving of trust and respect as the first.

Bob Nunn, July 2003

THE BOROUGH ARMS

In the top third of the shield are the Arms of St.
Albans to commemorate the long association
between that city and Watford.
The 'harts' represent the Herts in Hertfordshire.
In the lower part of the shield occur two
escallop shells taken from the Arms of the
Earl of Clarendon, Charter Mayor. The wavy blue
and white lines represent the ford in Watford.
The fasces in the centre denote magisterial
authority.
The motto *'Audentior'* is a quotation from
Virgil's *Aeneid* VI, 95: 'tu no cede malis, sed contra
audentior ito, quam tua to Fortuna
sinct'. (Yield not thou to ills, but go forth to
face them *more boldly* than thy Fortune shall
allow thee.)

Introduction

"They have built a supermarket on my old man's allotments . . ."

Some towns grow old gracefully, blending new with old so that as the inhabitants age their town does not present culture shocks too great to bear. St Albans, our near neighbour, is one such. Watford, on the other hand, looked over its shoulder and saw vigorous and thrusting newcomer Hemel Hempstead as a major threat to Watford's supremacy as a shopping centre and felt that, at all costs, it had to compete.

With Watford's straggling High Street stifling progress the best minds battled with the problems of equating shop space with the increased traffic and congestion which would ensue.

There was much wasted space and undeveloped land in the lower High Street. In the 1950's and 60's to some property developers this seemed ideal but Councillors and planners surmised, wisely, that in the face of historical movement from lower High Street to upper it would not make sense to build a major shopping centre in a part of the town to which shoppers would not be willingly drawn.

Little of this was known when work was started in 1985 on 'The Book of Watford'. Queens Road was still trading, albeit under clouds of uncertainty. Road works seemed interminable as the various phases came and went. Conservationists were concerned that some ancient shop frontages should be preserved. Alarm bells really started ringing when Brent Cross opened which, as a new and undercover shopping experience, drew busloads of shoppers from far and wide, including, of course, Watford.

Watford's own shopping centre was in final stages of detail planning, including a leisure facility of swimming baths, and arguments were still raging when the book was published in 1987. Much of the hinterland, centred on Carey Place, behind the High Street had been cleared. Sainsbury's, trading from the rebuilt Technical School in Queen's Road and using cleared Charles Street and part of Clifford Street as its car park, had first to be rehoused. For this the last cinema in the High Street, the Odeon, was sacrificed and space found for the store, warehouse and car park. Closing the cinema played a pivotal role in the subsequent downfall of the 'Parade'. We weren't to know.

Sainsbury's moved and the Mars project could truly begin.

The bottom of the High Street, meanwhile, had many old shops cleared for road widening and still remained the town's unloved nether part.

In 1988 the Watford Camera Club, at their Annual Exhibition in the Library, featured a panel of seven photographs of aspects of the area which included Sedgwick's/Benskin's Brewery. The panel, by Barry Anthony, was succinctly headed *"They have built a supermarket on my old man's allotments"*. It was my first image of the Tesco building, but it was the heartfelt comment that stayed in my mind.

It led, indirectly, to photographing the backside of Harlequin which, when built, looked like a fortress wall. And the High Street, end to end. And from that, to this work, greatly revised from the 1987 book. This work includes a great many new illustrations, and, more importantly, a great amount of feedback, cordial help and good wishes from the many people who appreciate that this will update the charting of the progress of our town, and the High Street in particular, through an incredibly eventful four decades.

The High Street panorama starts on page 301, in textual time, at about 1958—and this is the date of the listing of shops and businesses of the High Street. Interwoven is the thread of the background news items unfolding and, in some places, an effort to illustrate parts of the 'old' High Street to its place so that, for example, 'Buck's' and other long-gone landmarks can be located.

This work, though, is not a history, but more of a reminisce, of recent times just before when all we knew was taken in hand, thoroughly shaken and dumped down for us to pick up the pieces. The engineering industries faded, banks retrenched, post offices disappeared, cars proliferated to reach the places that a bus can't, plastic became money and negative equity the result of too much plastic. Independent shops are a declining minority and buying many products involves no more than turning catalogue pages and trusting that the delivered article will live up to the glossy colour picture.

New terms enter the vocabulary of which 'Planning gains, Section 106', enhancement, brownfield sites, SRB, digital printing, spin-doctors, web-sites, Gatso cameras, mobile phones, text messages, 4 x 4's, school runs and couch potatoes are just a few examples.

If you lived in that earlier era you will recognise much of the content of this book.

From the plans announced, and in the pipeline, the next decade seems set to be just as interesting.

Bob Nunn

Part I

The pot-boilers.

The back area was not yet a garden; the house was new and the ground strewn with builders' rubble. The evening was cool and the sky starry and bright with little or no cloud.

What noise there was was of a dog yapping in the distance, and, though near a main road, there was little or no traffic and seventy years ago there were no aircraft to shatter the silence. This night was magical because we were entertained to a magnificent display of Northern Lights which danced over the horizon soundlessly for what seemed like ages. Then there was competition of bright flashes behind us. For that the explanation was more prosaic in that the electric trains of the LMS and Bakerloo lines set off brilliant sparks which flashed like lightning.

From the bottom of our road—Thorpe-crescent—one could see across the slight valley of the River Colne, across Riverside Road, to the high ground of Vicarage Road. Down Eastbury Road a little way was a stream which rose from somewhere beyond the Blackwell's lands at Oxhey and which trickled past the sewage settlement tanks (alongside which was Stinkpot Alley) and into the Colne.

Within yards of the spot where we were fascinated by the display of the Aurora Borealis an earlier family had spent their days digging and crafting flints, some 12,000 or so years earlier. Family, because the evidence pointed to flint workings, spanning a long period of time. Flint tools discarded covered a wide range of applications and could be considered as Watford's early tool manufactory and toolshop. Remains included 'pot-boilers'; early clay or earthenware pots could not withstand direct heat from a fire though holding water. A suitable sized and shaped flint could be heated in the fire and then plunged into the pot. By this means water could be heated and other ingredients of food could be cooked.

What must the scenery then have looked like?

Just after the last Ice Age our country was still joined to Europe by a land bridge; our flint workers, by the style of their handicraft, had travelled from the area we know as Belgium.

Were they "summer workers" making their tools for export back to their homeland or were they trading with local Britons? They left debris but no evidence of habitation, and had it not been due to a local archeaologist interested in the diggings for foundations of the then new houses their passing would have been unnoticed.

Dr Norman Davey, B Sc, A M Inst C E, was a Director of the Building Research Station, Garston and, on the land then in his possession he had been, between 1926 and 1930, searching for and discovering worked flints. The British Museum gave an opinion that they were of the accepted microlithic class assigned to the end of the Paleaolithic period and after. Further, of the two groups chiefly recognised, they evidently belonged to the broad-blade industry associated with the 'Tardenois' industry of Belgium and not to the narrow-bladed industry connected with the 'Asil' industry of France which is supposed to be the earlier.

The British Museum considered that the group of flints submitted was probably late in the series, which was supposed to cover one or two thousand years beginning about 10,000BC. Dr Davey had previously discovered evidence of a later Belgic settlement at Hampermill (but which was now under the lake). Many of the flints were annotated and photographed and the prints and notes deposited in Watford's then relatively new Library in Hempstead Road.

Dr Norman Davey, wrote "The site is upon an estate which is undergoing building development, in Eastbury Road, where the ground slopes away gently to the west to the river Colne, and near a tributary of the Colne which flows through Oxhey in a south-easterly direction.

"The soil was light, sandy with a subsoil of chalk.

"The implements ... include hammerstones, pot-boilers, cores and flakes, arrow and harpoon heads and borers. There is little doubt that the site was inhabited and that the manufacture took place upon it."

The flint site, Thorpe Crescent, gave firm indications that man had lived and worked there some eleven or twelve thousand years ago. The travellers would have walked from the Belgic area of the continent, there being no 'Channel' to cross. Flints were essential tools for dressing skin, carving bone, cutting and shaping wood, and for use as arrow and spear heads, etc.

Later, much later, man learned how to make tools from metal—bronze and iron—but flint still had uses in walls and buildings. In more modern times flints were found in the 17th century to be of use in firing muskets. The British Army used flints from Brandon mines until about 1850 when they were superceded by percussion locks.

Bronze-age tools found in West Watford . . .

Thirty years later, in 1960, workmen were preparing foundations in West Watford for a building on an industrial-site-to-be, when they discovered a large collection of bronze-age tools. The discovery was kept quiet for fear that numerous amateur archaeologists would interrupt the construction work on the site. News was later given and a photograph published in the local press. The tools are in the possession of Watford Museum.

After the Ice Ages had passed and our local landscape had settled into its present shape, the clay-capped Chiltern plateau with its forests, and the Colne and Gade valleys with their marshes, offered poor sites for human habitation at a time when men had scarcely begun to scratch the soil. Analysis of finds of artifacts reported to, and by, the Watford and South West Herts Archaeological Society in recent years suggests that Croxley, Moor Park, Tolpits, Oxhey and Abbots Langley were populated, albeit sparsely, from Mesolithic (Middle Stone) times. In the Celtic Iron Age the district came under the sway of the Belgic Catuvellauni, who had their centre at Prae Wood, near St. Albans. In Watford Parish they had a small settlement at Hamper Mill, now alas covered by the lake. Their Roman conquerors built a walled city at Verulam for their new cantonal capital, and several Roman villas (farmhouses) have been discovered and excavated in the district: Kings Langley, Munden, Sarratt and Moor Park are all sites where the long arm of Rome once reached.

The Belgic settlement at Hamper Mill was succeeded by some Roman buildings, discovered by Dr. Norman Davey. They too are under the water. The Romans wisely adapted some existing trackways to their use, but their own roads were built long and straight for their armies and merchants to travel. The nearest certain Roman roads were the Watling Street at Radlett, and Akeman Street at Two Waters; a road from Verulam to Silchester via Buck's Hill has also been described.

By 410 AD the majority of Rome's soldiers and administrators had been withdrawn, leaving the locals to their own devices. It has been argued that a Catuvellaunian remnant population held out against the incoming Anglo-Saxons in the Chiltern forests, with evidence from place-names; lack of pagan burial sites; and the dark hair and eyes of our nineteenth century villagers to support the contention. Christianity, widespread in the Roman Empire by the 4th century, may have persisted, so that King Offa, much later, was able to identify the site of Alban's martyrdom. Be that as it may, the popular belief that the early English invaded and conquered South East England has now been discounted in favour of long term immigration and integration.

The late arrival of Anglo-Saxons in the Watford area may be due, as has been suggested, to local Celtic resistance, but is just as likely to have been the result of avoiding terrain unwelcome to farmers. When they did arrive our English ancestors settled along the valley sides above the flood levels at Berkhamsted (Birch Farm), Hemel Hempstead (Farm in the cut-off valley), and Aldenham (Old Farm). They had already been Christianised and probably moved in when King Wulfhere of Mercia extended his realm southwards in 660 AD.

As the population grew it expanded into less agreeable sites, such as Rickmansworth (Ricimer's Paddock) a marshy spot; or up on the Chilterns at Chipperfield (Forest clearing used by traders). A prominent landmark was Cassio (Cay's Hoe or promontory hill) now the West Herts Golf Course. This hill would in time give name to: a) a nearby farm; b) the district or 'manor'; and c) as an alternative name to the administrative

Thirty years after the flint discovery, in 1960 workmen were preparing foundations in West Watford for a building on an industrial-site-to-be, off Greenhill Crescent, when they discovered a large collection of bronze-age tools dated to 1000-600BC. The find included many socketed axes, finely worked spear-heads, a knife blade and wood gouges.
The tools are in the care of Watford Museum and the few shown here include, left, the remains of a bowl, and a socketed axe. Above is a collection of spearheads and above right an unusual bugle-shaped strap toggle.

hundred of Albanstow. A successor of King Wulfhere, the great Offa, King of Mercia, friend of Charlemagne, founded an abbey in the 8th century on the site of the reputed tomb of the martyred Christian Roman soldier Alban. He endowed it with lands stretching south-west to Rickmansworth, including Cassio and Oxhey (Ox enclosure). The Anglo-Saxon Oxhey Charter of 1007 AD is the first mention of our Watford by name, but only as a boundary ford.

Despite recent suggestions that the first element is 'Wath' meaning hunting, this seems unlikely for two reasons: the Anglo-Saxon spelling ends in 't' not in 'th'; and all fords were used for hunting. Because this particular ford and another of the same name in Northants, were notoriously liable to flood in winter it seems more likely that the first element is 'Waet' meaning full of water. Watford is again mentioned just before the Norman Conquest in the will of Edwin of Caddington who owned Watford and regranted it to St. Albans Abbey, so by then it must have been a territorial name, although no house foundations older than the 12th century have been found. The abbey lands in Cassio and Oxhey were let to tenants on various

The ford was not always in flood and the artist's impression (top) shows how the ford may have looked nearly two millennia ago on an autumn day, c AD250. The man on foot is already in the water and once around the bend and into the distance he has to face a steep hill, (which we today know as Chalk Hill), leading to Stanmore and London.

The photograph, centre, shows the gasworks site cleared, in 1989. If the railway and its embankment were not in place there is really not much difference in the near two thousand years. An upright of the railway overhead power gantry may be seen towards the top left-hand corner. The road line is to the extreme right of the picture.

The bottom picture, again an impression, shows the river in spate, looking townwards. The footbridge is underwater with only the handrail showing. With such a flood of water the ford would be impassable and the track northwards to and from Aylesbury impracticable.

leases and the idea that monks did the farming of these outlying estates is due to a popular misconception, for in reality monks were confined to the immediate environs of the abbey.

The farms in Watford 'parish' were at Cassio Hall or Bury, and at Oxhey Hall. The primitive Saxon huts were often sunk into the ground for warmth, but the larger 'halls' were built of logs. As time went on the standard of housing slowly improved, but there are no known Saxon buildings or artifacts in the Watford area.

The Norman Conquest of 1066 changed the course of our history yet again, and a French-speaking aristocracy was imposed upon an English population. William and his forces headed north to Berkhamsted where a castle was erected. Twenty years later, by which time the English had been subjugated, commissioners were appointed to tour the country and survey it. 'Not even an ox, nor one cow, nor one pig, escaped notice.' When completed, but not seen by King William, it was used by William II, and his successors, for all available rural statistics were included for calculating feudal dues as was the intention.

The four watermills in 'Cassio' may have been Sarratt Mill, Grove Mill, Tolpits Mill and Oxhey Mill (later Rookery). In these, tenants had to have their corn ground into flour and pay the abbey for the privilege. 'Free' tenants held their lands by either military service (Oxhey Hall), or socage, which meant paying a rent or providing certain amenities or produce. 'Unfree' tenants or 'villeins' were tied to their pieces of land. When they died, or their children married, dues had to be paid to the abbey. Villeins were not allowed to leave the manors they lived on without the lord's permission, and they had to do compulsory unpaid work on the abbey's private estates or 'demesnes'. By the 12th century a village had grown up along the highway from Aylesbury to Stanmore, where the old Roman Watling Street was joined. The village was a little north of the Wat-ford and clear of the floodable area. Henry I granted to the Abbots of St Albans a Charter enabling Watford to enjoy the rights and privileges of weekly markets—a privilege which in no small part contributed to Watford's present-day position of eminence—and a church was built for their worship and, later, at Sarratt (whose name is of doubtful origin and may mean neck of land). Watford villagers had two open arable fields in furlong strips; "Westfield" from Colney Butts to the Colne; and "Powfield" from St. Albans Road to Loates Lane.

The demesne farm of Cassio was held either by stewards, or by farmers on short leases. Oxhey Hall, protected by a moat around the house, was held by military service on an inheritable tenancy. In addition to the common fields there were patches of manorial waste where the land was unfavourable for agriculture, such as Watford Heath, Commonwood, and Pen-mans Green. On these geese or cattle could be grazed.

Long distance roads or army paths came into being. On the Aylesbury road was our original Wat-ford, by now slowly growing in size and importance. Another road linked St. Albans to Rickmansworth via Cassio-ford (later-bridge). A third linked Watford to Pinner and Harrow (Pinner-road). Tolpits Mill became disused, after adapting to fulling (cloth-cleaning). New mills were made at Watford's main street and Hamper-mill (Waterhen Pool).

to page 16

Let all men know through us present that Edward, Earl of Rutland and of Corke has received from Hugo De Holes, Knight, two hundred and thirty and three pounds six shillings and eightpence in gold, by the hands of Thomas Gerberge, companion of Richard Whytyton, Citizen and Merchant of London, and William Gyles, appointed receiver of money in England: which the aforesaid Hugo owed us for the Manor of Oxhey Richard, with its appurtances, in the county of Hertford, which the said Hugo and another now have and hold for themselves and the heirs of the said Hugo forever: concerning which two

hundred and thirty and three pounds six shilligs and eight pence, we declare that the heirs of the said Hugo, and his executors after him, will be satisfied.

It is agreed by us present, and signed with a seal, given this eighth day of May in the third year of the reign of King Henry, the fourth after the conquest.

Deed presented to Watford Public Library by Colonel and Alderman Sir Charles Cheers Wakefield, Bt, C.B.E. Wakefield House, Cheapside, E.C. November 1929 referring to land sold in AD1402.

The Domesday Book

The Saxon Chronicles, compiled by monks, were started in the late 9th century and are a yearly record of events as:

1. Octavian reigned for fifty-six years and in the forty-second year of his reign, Christ was born. and, later,

200. The Holy Cross was found; followed by

286. Here suffered St Albans, martyr. etc

King William's reign is equally sparse of detail, the monks perhaps not wanting to arouse William's ready temper.

Earlier, King Alfred, the Great, achieved a measure of peace by introducing measures for civil law and order and—very importantly—a form of written English which could be understood more widely than the priestly Latin. He set up County and shire divisions and the system of law and justice based upon Hundreds and Tithings, and the Jury.

This, unwittingly, paved the way for King William's gathering of the Domesday Records, without which his task would have much harder. In 1081 the great work was started, taking six years to complete; commissioners were appointed to tour the country and survey it. 'Not even an ox, nor one cow, nor one pig, escaped notice', with further commissioners checking the work of the first. The tremendous work, collected, checked, and fair-copied, was called Domesday Book, (Law-Day Book). All rural statistics were included for calculating feudal dues. Engaged for two years protecting his realm in Normandy, rebellions broke out in England which were quickly and viciously repressed.

Earlier a vast area north of the Tees which was sacked, ravished and desecrated—and so Northumberland was not deemed worth recording in the Domesday record. Back in France William, being offended by some rude remarks of his corpulence, sacked the town of Mantes; his horse startled by the fire threw the King, he dying a few days later, 9th Sept 1087, at the monastery of St Gervas.

In the Hundred of Cassio were Rickmansworth, Cassio, Bushey, Aldenham, St Albans and Sandridge. Of Watford there is no mention. Sparsely populated Cassio returned data for 20 hides, a hide reckoned to be about 120 acres.

Cassiobury Park—as we know it—comprises about 120 acres. There are 640 acres to a square mile and modern Watford, with shrub and woodland cleared, has an area of about 5,275 acres, or, in old terms, 43 hides. Bushey was stated to have two mills, Cassio four, St Albans three, Hatfield four, Rickmansworth one and Hemel Hempstead four mills. King's Langley at 1½ hides was held from the Count of Mortain and had two mills.

The main landowner was the king—now William II—followed by the Archbishop of Canterbury, Bishops of London, Bayeaux, Lisieux and Chatteris, then by Counts, Earls and others.

Hertfordshire's 'Hundreds' as listed in the Domesday Book.

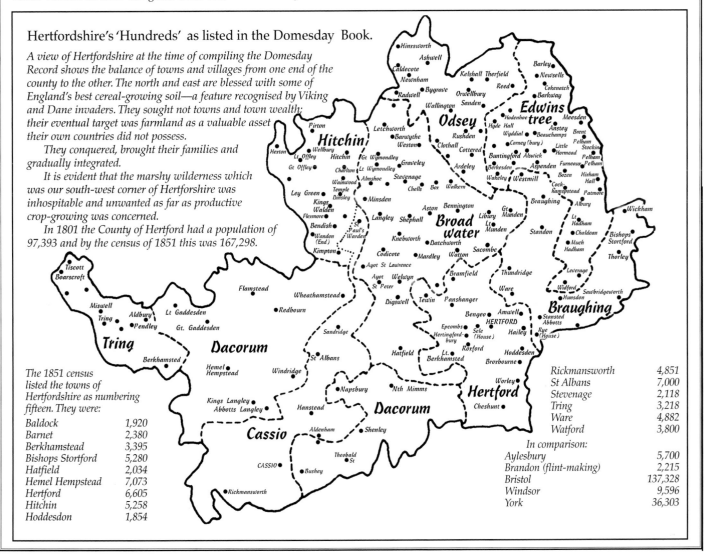

A view of Hertfordshire at the time of compiling the Domesday Record shows the balance of towns and villages from one end of the county to the other. The north and east are blessed with some of England's best cereal-growing soil—a feature recognised by Viking and Dane invaders. They sought not towns and town wealth; their eventual target was farmland as a valuable asset their own countries did not possess.

They conquered, brought their families and gradually integrated.

It is evident that the marshy wilderness which was our south-west corner of Hertforshire was inhospitable and unwanted as far as productive crop-growing was concerned.

In 1801 the County of Hertford had a population of 97,393 and by the census of 1851 this was 167,298.

The 1851 census listed the towns of Hertfordshire as numbering fifteen. They were:

Baldock	1,920
Barnet	2,380
Berkhamstead	3,395
Bishops Stortford	5,280
Hatfield	2,034
Hemel Hempstead	7,073
Hertford	6,605
Hitchin	5,258
Hoddesdon	1,854
Rickmansworth	4,851
St Albans	7,000
Stevenage	2,118
Tring	3,218
Ware	4,882
Watford	3,800

In comparison:

Aylesbury	5,700
Brandon (flint-making)	2,215
Bristol	137,328
Windsor	9,596
York	36,303

... villagers grew rich by trading in wool and leather.

Though some feudal rigidities were gradually loosened, life stayed the same for most folk until 1349 when the Black Death, the bubonic plague carried by black rats, struck. At Oxhey the old military family was replaced by Roger Louth, a Royal official, who made a park, or warren, on his estate. From now on Oxhey was held by rent instead of by military assistance.

Due to labour shortage villeins began to work for wages and to wander from manor to manor seeking more reward. Lords converted tillage to sheep-runs to save labour and some Watford villagers grew rich by trading in wool and leather. More and more neglected their land and became traders in the markets. It was men like these who marched on St Albans Abbey in 1381 to extort freedoms from the Abbot. The so-called Peasants' Revolt was instigated by a government 'Poll Tax', but the Watford men sought liberty to fish in the Colne and Gade, snare rabbits, and for the cessation of 'alepenny', a tax paid to the Abbey. They also wanted to grind their own corn. But the local leaders were executed and the new freedoms soon retracted.

Watford had its importance recognised by the institution under Richard II of a Court Leet which met in the town under the Abbey Steward as judge, and with a jury of free tenants. It settled disputes between landholders and fined people who had offended against the common good. It appointed constables to keep the King's Peace in the 'hamlets' or 'tithings' of Watford, Cassio, Grove, Sarratt, Oxhey, Garston and Munden. In Watford town aletasters and leathersellers were created. Richer townsfolk left wills recorded by the Abbey clerks or at Canterbury; such as Sir Hugh Holes of Oxhey Hall who died in 1415 and has a memorial brass in our church. Feudal dues were ignored or forgotten. Copyholders (villeins) began to consolidate their open field strips and enclose them with hedges. Tithes on crops supported the clergy. Houses were of timber, mud and straw with smoke from open hearths escaping through the thatch. Stone, apart from flint, did not exist locally and bricks were 'continental' until c1500. Only our church, built of flint and freestone, survives from the Middle Ages. Our present language, Anglo-Saxon at base but with French and Latin additions, had evolved by c1400 as a workaday tool.

National events passed us by but Walkelin of Oxhey fought at St Albans in the civil war in Stephen's reign, and William Troutbeck of Oxhey died at Blore Heath in the War of the Roses in 1459 fighting for Henry VI.

The Parish Registers, started in 1539, were the nearest we were to get to any form of news recording for over three hundred years. Recording births, marriages and deaths, they incorporate an occasional small amount of information of a day-to-day character.

It is co-incidental that what must be the second or third page of the first register starts off with October 1540, one burial, and to go through to the following June–nine months—with a total of 18 burials. Extended for a year this equals about 10 to 12 deaths per 1,000; a very respectable figure.

But in July 1541 the calamity of plague struck with force claiming 36 victims in the July, August and part of September. In that period there were only three 'normal' deaths recorded.

The keen-eyed reader will note that the 'January' still continues as 1540.

King Henry divided Watford town from Cassio Manor . . .

Modern times begin with Henry VIII's Protestant Reformation. The dissolution of the St. Albans Abbey in 1539 rang the death knell of feudalism whereby those holding land had been bound to render services to the owner. Those estates (demesnes) which had been under the direct control of the abbey were sold by the king as separate manors. They included part of Oxhey, called Oxhey Walrond or Wiggenhall, sold to a Londoner, James Joskins; and Cassiobury, sold in 1545 to a royal servant, Richard Morrison. Former villein holdings were now called copyholds as they were freed from all feudal dues except for payments which had to be 'copied' into the manorial books when a tenant died or sold his estate.

King Henry divided Watford Town from Cassio Manor and made it a separate manor of which he was the direct lord. In 1607 it was granted by James I to Lord Chancellor Egerton, and continued with his successors the Earls and Dukes of Bridgewater, who sold it in the late 18th century to the Earl of Essex. Watford now had the Court Leet for the entire former manor of Cassio and also a Court Baron for the copyholds within the town. Lawyers did well under the Tudors. One such, William Heydon, grandson of a Leavesden farmer, was of Lincolns Inn which he partly built, and Clerk to the Duchy of Lancaster. In Watford he built, on land acquired by his father in New Street, a mansion partly of the new brick. It became known as Watford Place and later as the Lecture House. Heydon's father and grandmother had built the south chapel of St. Mary's Church by 1505. Watford Place had two new features, chimneys and a porch.

Our parish register begins in 1539 and in it we can trace many of Watford's inhabitants up to the present. The Protestant Reformation, which started as a gesture by an aggrieved monarch against a pope who would not allow him to divorce, took on a special shape by Elizabeth's reign. The Morrisons and Heydons chose Watford's vicars and lecturers. Under their aegis the parish vestry began to exercise local government powers, and in particular was responsible for poor relief, and later for highway maintenance. The local gentry, as Justices of the Peace, took much of the work from the Royal judges. Within the Hundred or Liberty of St. Albans they kept the jail for minor malefactors. They controlled the village constables, and raised rates for administration. But all J.P.s, vestrymen and constables were unpaid except for necessary expenses.

From the late Middle Ages onwards into the 18th century the tenor of life scarcely varied. Watford was an agricultural market with a radius of from three to five miles and contained a fair number of rural processors; tanners, millers, bakers, maltsters, brewers and butchers. The richest townsfolk were mealmen (corn-dealers). The first brewer of note was Nicholas Colbourn in Elizabeth's reign and who died in 1630.

The Great Civil War had little impact on our life.

The gentry supported Parliament, and except for small scuffles there was no fighting in the district. The strict hand of Cromwellian control gave way to the more liberal sway of the Merry Monarch. In 1683 the Earl of Essex was arrested at Cassiobury and charged with complicity to kidnap the king for Whiggish purposes. He committed suicide in the Tower to save his family's property. His friend Monmouth, from Moor Park, was executed in 1685.

Some London citizens came to Watford to escape the epidemics of that crowded and insanitary city. Lawyers and government officials also settled here. Thomas Hobson, Bushey born, a government lawyer, built his new Watford Place south of the churchyard. His widow Elizabeth (*née* Chilcott) remarried a Mr. Fuller, and in 1704 built and endowed Watford's second 'free' school.

The Free School, near St Mary's Church, is one of Watford's two grade II* listed buildings.

In its early days it was inevitable that its small size would be unable to cope with rising numbers of scholars.

But Mr Jonathan Cox Lovett, of Holywell, had made a reversionary devise of certain of his estates, including Holywell Farm.

The devise, not being registered in Chancery, became void–had it been valid the income would have fully supported the school. The school closed on August 10th 1882 but preparations had been made to find ground and build a new school, in Derby Road.

The Free School building has recently seen a number of occupancies, mainly of firms of solicitors, thus keeping it in use.

Rookery Silk Mill opened in 1768, beginning our industrial age . . .

Nearby, at the vicarage gate, an older 'free' school functioned, founded in the mid 17th century by Francis Combe of Hemel Hempstead. Local gentry were educated by private tutors in their own homes or at the 'grammar' schools at Berkhamsted, St. Albans, or Aldenham. A few would proceed to Oxford or Cambridge, and more to the London Inns of Court and Chancery to become lawyers, a suitable preparation for J.P.s.

But most Watfordians would remain unlettered except for a few days at a dame school. Most marriage contracts were signed by 'marks', especially by the females. Baptists, who did a deal of Bible study in their private houses, (and after 1721 in their new meeting house), were somewhat more literate. Shops were often distinguished by signs, as were public houses. Houses in Watford, by 1760, were much improved with thatch often replaced by clay tiles. Most

houses had strong timber frames, proper fireplaces and chimneys. The richer owners built in brick, though sometimes they merely refronted timber houses. Drainage services, despite the Court Leet and their fines, were almost non-existent. Offal from tanyards and butchers polluted the streets and alleys. The town pump by the Market Hall and wells in the yards were the only source of water except for the river and the millstream. Disease was rife, though the town had its apothecaries and even medical doctors. Life expectancy was short and infantile mortality high, not least in the crowded courts which were springing up behind the High Street to house the growing population.

The 'town'—in reality an area stretching from present-day Leavesden to Rickmansworth—had about 2,000 people in 1760. They now had more varied food, including potatoes introduced in 1600, turnips since 1660, and, from Elizabeth's

In 1771 a map was drawn to support a proposal to realign the road (New-street) to increase the size of the burial ground. The Vicarage is the second of three. The first was on a site nearer King-street and was demolished in 1914—to make way for Woolworth's. This, the second, was demolished in 1915, the grounds cleared and shops built. The third Vicarage, was built in 1916 further back from the road and to the left and lasted until c1990 when it, too, was demolished and redeveloped. The Church Houses were demolished in 1822 and the ground added to the Vicarage grounds.

1) The Lecturer's House wherein lived a curate who gave lectures on the Protestant faith. The building was erected by William Heydon of Lincoln's Inn (d1545), and enlarged by his grandson when it became known as Watford Place.

2) Bedford Almshouses, built by Bridget Lady Bedford, wife of Sir Richard Morrison, in 1580

3) Almondwick barns used to store the tithe corn from the Earl of Essex's Estates.

4) Engine House for the Parish fire pump.

5) The Workhouse, built in 1721.

6) Mr Dyson's Yard in which he established his brewery in 1750, —later to be known as Ballard's Buildings.

7) The Market House, open underneath to give shelter in bad weather.

8) The Church Houses where Francis Combe's Free School was housed.

9) The Vicarage, built about 1630.

10) The Free School built by Dame Fuller in 1704.

11) Mr Whitfield's House. This was built in 1668-70 by Thomas Hobson, Dame Fuller's first husband, on the site of two previous buildings.

12) Mr Munn's houses, the cottages shown on p85

13) One of the wells remarked in water supply, p41

14) The existing road which was to be incorporated in the extended churchyard.

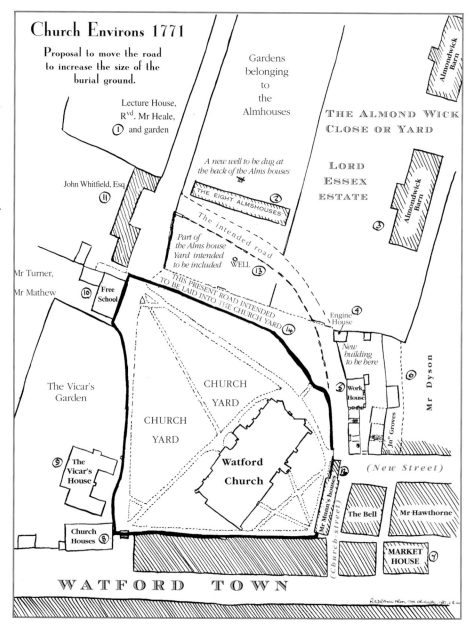

Church Environs 1771

Proposal to move the road to increase the size of the burial ground.

reign, the comfort of tobacco in clay pipes. Travel was slow and cumbersome over rutted roads. So it was in Watford when the Rookery Silk Mill opened in 1770, to begin our Industrial Age.

As the Elizabethan era ended the essence of a poor law emerged when national legislation required local magistrates to relieve the plight of the poor, under the jurisdiction of a com pulsory poor rate system. For many years bands of 'sturdy beggars' had been terrorising the countryside and something had to be done to curtail if not control their activities. The course of history would have been very different if Henry VIII had invested even a small proportion of the spoils acquired at the time of the Dissolution in the care and education of the common people. The long-term beneficiaries proved to be the gentry and not the crown. They were given the opportunity of buying monastic land with manorial rights at prices they could not refuse. The Morrisons and the Russells are local examples.

Tudor England came to realise that the presence of so many vagrants and beggars constituted a threat to the country, a threat which whipping would not cure. In the interests of the state and the church they should be gainfully employed and to that end the local Overseer of the Poor was directed to purchase a working stock of 'flax, hemp, wool, thread, iron and other stuff to set the poor to work' by the Statute of 1601. In 1535 Henry VIII had ordered all parish churches to keep registers of christenings, marriages and burials. Watford's earliest register covers the period 1539-1557 (and is kept at the County Records Office at Hertford). Between the years 1540-1541 fifty-four deaths from the plague are recorded. The second register spans the years 1558-1666. In the early years the entries were generally of an informal nature with marginal notes reflecting the personal touches of the recorder, a source of useful information to the researcher.

Contrary to the practice of many parish churches, the Churchwarden's Accounts were not maintained in a separate ledger but included with the reports of business conducted by the Vestry which acted in the capacity of a local governing body. Members included the Lord of the Manor, the Vicar, Churchwardens, Overseer of the Poor as well as the Parish Clerk. Their interests were many and varied but their main preoccupation was concerned with the Church and the role it played within the community. The bells and the bell-ringers assumed great importance. The condition of the structure, inside and out, concerned the churchwardens. The conduct of their parishioners also received the attention of the Vestry along with the apprenticing of children, the care of the poor and the infirm. Each meeting was reported to the Archdeaconry Court where the submission was examined in detail and the accounts checked. Occasional surprise visits were made by the Archdeacon to see for himself that all was well.

In the Vestry Records of 1681 an entry notes the fate of Richard Man who was whipped and with his wife and two children was sent by pass to Bishop Auckland for which journey 60 days was allowed. Another entry, two years later, notes:

"Jane Joyner, wife of Wm. Joyner, a sturdy vagrant beggar whipped according to the law, sent with her two children under 7 years by a pass, the nearest way to Taunton Dean in Somerset, where she confessed she was born."

but it was not to be for a further ten years before the next vagrant beggar was 'whipped and returned', this time to Lincolnshire. The manner in which the Vestry administered the Poor Law was absolute. In 1696 an entry reveals that

Map, left, *the Lecturer's house No. 1, Mr Heale, was built c1540 by William Heydon, demolished in 1822 and the above Almshouses built, the road later named Vicarage-road. These Almhouses were demolished for the ring road.*

From 96 High Street. The corner of New Street is cleared of the cafe and cottages and the Workhouse building has gone; the National School building remains. Almondwick beyond was later swallowed by the ring road and the area rebuilt as Watford's first multi-storey car park. The building on the right are the Public Conveniences behind the One Bell. See p126.

. . . the mobility of labour was upset . . .

those receiving Parish Relief 'shall wear on the right shoulder of their upper most garment a brass badge with the letters W.P. on it denoting them to be Watford Poor.' In the year of the Revolution (1688) roughly twenty per cent of the population (over one million) received at some time public relief through parish authorities. At the end of the seventeenth century the claim was made that the parish dole some times exceeded current wages and was sometimes so generous as to encourage people not to work, to drink the best ale and eat the 'finest wheat flour'.

None complained more bitterly than the ratepayers. This state of affairs, if correctly reported, came to an end with the Act of Settlement passed by Charles II's Cavalier Parliament. The Act, a reactionary piece of legislation, gave the parish and authorities the necessary power to evict a non-resident and send him back to the parish of which he was native so that he may not become a charge on the rates. Technically, few people were safe from arrest whether or not they were law-abiding or of excellent character. The Act, as well as causing untold distress, completely upset the mobility of labour to meet the needs of seasonal employment, as well as the peace of mind of many whose employment took them outside their native parish. In addition hostility was generated between local authorities, none of whom were adequately briefed, directed or controlled by a central organisation or body. Another factor to be taken into account was the resentment expressed by local tax payers at having to pay for the maintenance of roads and sanitation as required by the local magistrate. The Poor Rate was yet another burden levied without reasonable justification!

In the Justice of the Peace

was vested the necessary authority to determine the amount of the local rate to be raised and the purpose for which the revenue would be spent. In earlier times their appointment had been the prerogative of the Privy Council but now the Lord Lieutenant appointed them in the name of the Crown. Without a central control the J.P.s were relatively free agents inasmuch as they had local control over county life. Their functions included the administration of justice, the licensing of public houses, the maintenance of roads, bridges, workhouses and prisons to name but a few duties. Without a staff or adequate premises the J.P. went about his business as best he could without sympathy from the ratepayers who were content to encourage inefficient local government if the cost of efficiency represented a further charge against the rates! The surprise was that corruption was not rife although acts of favouritism and prejudice were not unknown. There was no remuneration for the post so Justices of the Peace were invariably landowners and of substantial independent means.

In common with most other towns in England, Watford had its workhouse, a purpose-built three-storey brick edifice of barrack proportions relieved only by a series of small windows at each floor level. For good reason the communal workhouse was erected, near the Parish Church, in Church

The Parish Church's naves, pillars and arches (south early English AD 1250, north, Perpendicular, AD 1430) were spurred out by weight and were repaired when the interior of the church was restored in 1848, the outside was rebuilt in 1871 being refaced in flint. Church services were meanwhile held in a 'temporary' iron church in the churchyard. When no longer required it was rebuilt in Sutton-road and formed the basis of St John's Church. The church is shown as about 1865–an early photograph–but the inset of the interior is earlier, the box-pews, galleries and sounding board being removed in 1848.

Street in 1721. Here the inmates, a motley mix of young and old, healthy and sick, law-abiding and law-breakers, were given shelter at the expense of the ratepayers. However, this captive workforce had a revenue-producing potential and it was accordingly exploited to the full by the Master and his subordinates by directing some of the inmates to provide the services with which to maintain the workhouse.

Alternatively, the poor were hired out to factory owners and one such, locally, was Mr Paumier of the nearby silk mill. The hire rate for the 'Poor's Labour' was between 6d and 1s. 6d. per day, and paid to the Overseers. A tilted wagon was sent to fetch the labourers every morning and send them home again at night, 'between 29th September and 25th March, and at such times as the floods render meadows unpassable without being wet-shod.' The inmates enjoyed at least one meal a day, a bed and, if they were lucky, some heating. The dietary, in 1777, included 'Coarse flour, pease whole and split, oatmeal, salt butter, cheese, beef, sugar 5d. a lb. Clothing of coarse materials,—good flaxen sprig, brown linsey and blue serge'—was also supplied. When they were not gainfully employed they were allowed to spend their time in the town, much to the annoyance of the residents.

The opportunities open to workhouse staff to line their own pockets were regarded as the perquisites of the job and as a result the wrong types achieved management and support status, the consequence being that priority of care was forsaken for personal gain. A Vestry report noted that 'the House

was filthy, and the Poor in an uncleanly state, resulting that the allowance of bread be augmented by 2ozs. and cheese by a half oz. and that some additions be made to the bedclothing in winter. Also that the fireplaces are insufficient for warming the rooms.'

The inmates became tools of the Master and the workhouse, as a provident institution, went into a temporary decline. Provision was made for the sick and an infirmary became an essential adjunct of the workhouse. When isolation of a patient suffering from an infectious disease, such as smallpox, was required, the pesthouse some distance away, as its name implies, served to accommodate him. By the end of the eighteenth century signs of improvement in the care of inmates became apparent. The feudal outlook of the latter day yeoman farmers, however, was still in evidence. The lot of the farm labourer was never a happy one. His staple diet was bread and cheese; meat was a luxury he or his family seldom enjoyed. His diet was no better than his low wages permitted, hovering at starvation level. In 1795 the magistrates of Berkshire, conscious of the conditions pre-

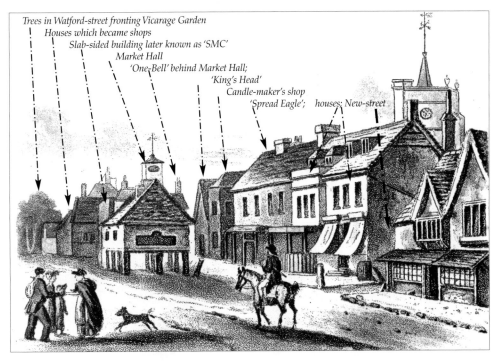

Market Place c1780. The candle-maker's premises burned down in 1828 taking with it the King's Head. The market dealings were done within the shadow of the Market Hall, or underneath. The cottages, right, have boundary stones to deter riders or wagons. There are no shop or public house signs though the Spread Eagle was established c1750, the King's Head c1600. The hamlet's population was merely 2,000 and this quietitude would continue for another sixty years, and then see the coming of the navigators, (who constructed the canal), followed by the Railway men. The drawing is contemporary with the proposals to alter the churchyard layout. The church clock, and the light, confirms that it is early morning. The man, carrying the ubiquitous bag of luggage slung over a shoulder on a stick, woman and child are talking to an older woman, and standing outside (or near) the Essex Arms–are they waiting for a stage-coach or is it just coincidence? The 1996 panorama is offered to show how very little our Hamlet centre's buildings have changed.

Trees in Watford-street fronting Vicarage Garden
Houses which became shops
Slab-sided building later known as 'SMC'
Market Hall
'One-Bell' behind Market Hall;
'King's Head'
Candle-maker's shop
'Spread Eagle'; houses; New-street

KINGS HEAD   Butcher   SPREAD EAGLE   House   House   New-street

This 1996 panorama shows the early usage of the sites . . .

...a new Union Workhouse...

vailing, called a meeting at Speenhamland near Newbury at which it was hoped to devise a sliding wage-scale based on the cost of bread at a time of widely-fluctuating prices. The J.P.s decided against such measures and opted for a sliding scale subsidy from the parish rates. The scheme was readily adopted by local county authorities who ignored its inherent dangers. In theory the labourer should have benefited by the move but in practice the employer paid him, but less the amount he would receive from the parish. He no longer earned even a living wage and though fully employed he was still forced to become a pauper. His problem was made worse when in 1815 the Corn Law was introduced which prevented the entry into the country of cheap grain. Even the middle-classes resented that the poor should need to spend their wages in buying bread, and the repeal of the Corn Law in 1846 was a decided victory of the middle-classes over the landed gentry. The close of the 18th century and beginning of the 19th saw up-welling of engineers and mechanics and from whom the adult education 'Mechanics' Institutions' sprang.

1801 saw the first census of Great Britain; and in 1829 the introduction of a 'catholic relief bill' intending to allow catholics to be eligible to seats in both Houses of Parliament. This passed through the Commons 320 to 142, and, eventually, on 10th April, through the Lords, receiving Royal Assent on 13th April. This cleared the way for re-establishment of catholic churches and worship. In 1836 a 'marriage act' brought a degree of church reform in that in was not any longer obligatory to comply with ritual of the established church, but could be contracted in the office of a registrar.

The lot of labourer and ratepayer was not improved by the new Poor Act of 1834, which made conditions so unattractive in the workhouse that it was argued that none would wish to avail themselves of its facilities. The Act ignored the plight of the aged,

children and the infirm who, as inmates, would suffer the same indignities as adults. The conditions of the workhouse were intentionally reduced to an intolerable low. At the other end of the scale three Commissioners were appointed at national level to represent central government and made responsible for the creation of rules for administering the Poor Law and the means by which they were enforced. The physical application of the Act through the Commissioners at local level was through a 'board of guardians of the poor' democratically elected through the ratepayers. The Justices of the Peace were no longer involved with the parish poor and despite their reputation their withdrawal from the scene was deplored by those who appreciated the personal touch.

Four years after the enactment, in 1838, the complex of workhouse buildings in Church Street was sold and towards the end of the century was occupied by the commercial interests, the Parish Clerk and others. In its place was built a brand new Union Workhouse in Vicarage Road and, later, an Infirmary and Chapel and separate schools for boys and girls, which together, through the Local Board of Guardians, continued to care for the poor and under-privileged.

The Union served a large area of the parishes of Watford, Abbots Langley, Aldenham, Bushey, Rickmansworth and Sarratt. Each parish was represented by *ex-officio* and elected members on the Board of Guardians. Officers of the Union included the Medical Officer, Relieving Officer and, as residents of the Workhouse, the Governor, Matron, two nurses, two teachers and the porter. After World War I and during the post-war days of unemployment and recession the Union Workhouse still had a role to fulfil by offering overnight accommodation to unemployed who walked from town to town in search of work.

By 1939 the roving unemployed had become a token force although the traditional tramp still used the facilities available.

Alongside: In Watford's earlier days water was obtained from two or three wells in the vicinity of the church. Men, and even women, might be seen with yokes and pails fetching water from the Colne at the bottom of Water Lane.

Right: Otter's Pool, 1797, near Munden, Watford.
An area named 'Little Otter's Pool' was where the Colne crosses Water Lane, but is now named, aptly, Waterfields.

Otter's Pool near Watford. 1797.

The life-line of canals

Road-making, as an enduring art, ceased when the Romans left the Britons to their own devices. Unmetalled roads became the norm placing a severe restriction upon carriage of goods, farm produce and livestock. Many parts of the country conducted trade by river. London, after the dark ages, with its sea highway, eventually regained eminence as a trading centre and, centuries later, it was in part to link with the Thames that the Grand Junction Canal was built. Started in 1793 it was designed to provide a waterway 100 miles shorter than the existing Birmingham to London canal, via Oxford.

The first section from Brentford to Tring, the summit, was completed by 1799 and the remainder of the 137 miles to Braunston by 1805. The canal was built without mechanical aids by gangs of navigators—from whence the term 'navvies'—under the supervision of some of the best civil engineers of the day. Unlike the later navvies who built the railway the originals caused none of the rowdy trouble that later plagued the hamlet. The canal passed through the estates of the Earls of Clarendon and Essex, the towpaths being built on the canal-side furthest from the stately homes—no mooring up or trespassing on their Lordship's grounds!

The fortunes of the industrial midlands were revitalised as pottery, coal, slate, bales of straw, clay and farm produce found new markets and ready buyers. The Company was soon operating in a profit situation using pairs of narrow boats pulled by horses. A narrow boat could carry ten tons, the larger barges 20 tons. The freight charges varied between a half-penny to one penny per ton/mile. Our local wharf was Lady Capel's Wharf, along the Hempstead road where the canal is nearest to the road. The carriage of coal beyond that point was at first prohibited, but permitted in 1805 when a resident tax collector allowed passage of coals to points south of Watford on payment of Coal Tax. Esparto grass and rags later helped keep Dickinson's Mills at work turning out fine papers–which in turn were carried from the Mills by barge. In 1823 an extension was made to the Paddington Basin in London.

During the canal's heyday John Dickinson was among those who had built their enterprises alongside the canal where barges brought coal and raw materials for his papermaking factories, and took away the finished products. The service may have been slow but for an age which superseded those when there was nothing except the laborious journey by horse and cart, over vile roads, the mass and bulk which could be delivered helped the prosperity of the towns and villages alongside. Despite the advent of the railway the canal enjoyed good business for many years, but by 1890 the duty was abolished by which time the railway companies were successfully competing for the boats' cargoes. As bulk carriers the Company survived until 1920 when business declined to such an extent that a merger was formed by the controlling company. Under the new title of Grand Union Canal Company long overdue improvements were made and to this end Lady Capel's Wharf was removed—only the name surviving.

The Watford Gas and Coke Company was formed in 1834 and in its first year had consumed 16fi tons of coal. Despite the advent of the London and Birmingham Railway the carriage of bulk goods did not take place for many years.

Canals restricted the main businesses to those with access to the waterside wharves; the railways were later restricted to servicing firms near a rail spur, and large enough to warrant sidings into large plants, such as Odhams and Benskins.

Only roads were eventually able to give impetus to other firms.

At a distance of near two-hundred years a horse drawn barge may seem a slow method of transport, but, in its era was a revolution when, for bulk transport of goods, there was no alternative. The roads sufficed for travel around a small radius but neither the road–unmade, pot-holed, dusty or muddy, nor the horse-drawn carts—could cope with carriage of coal over long distances. With the canal carriage of loads of coal, bales of straw, clay, paper and bulky goods were at last practical.
Upon the advent of the canal many canalside mills—mainly of paper but also of corn—developed, among them were Dickinson's Mills—Apsley, Nash, Home Park, and Croxley and were heavily barge dependent, especially for coal where there could be no rail facilities. This drawing by P Heseltine, March 1880, though long after the canal's coming, is almost timeless.

Cassiobury and the Grove

This drawing published, in 1707, shows the new garden lay-out of Cassiobury in 1698 as well as the general area..

The old Cassiobury House, (later rebuilt), and the grounds— here laid out as cultivated park and gardens— became the modern Cassiobury housing estate and the more open ground on the left is known to us as Cassiobury Park.

It is stated that this drawing shows the H-shaped house as complete whereas one stroke of the H was not built. But the garden Moses Cook designed and planted in the 20 or 30 years prior to 1697 is shown in detail; from this date the 2nd Earl employed George London as gardener. Behind the house the number of cottages and other buildings will be seen to amount to a small village in its own right; an illustration of the facade of the house is also shown next page.

The meandering lane (to the right of the drawing) leads from Cassio Hamlet at the bottom (Nascot Farm) on towards Langleybury village's houses on the hill just beyond the River Gade (top of the drawing).

From the house, the avenue leading from left to right, culminating in the apex of three avenues is almost exactly the line of our Langley Road, from the Park to Hempstead Road.

On the road, bottom right, the estate is shown gated; this is approximately the site of Little Cassiobury adjacent to the college buildings in Hempstead Road. This drawing is some one hundred and fifteen years before the map on the next page; here there is, of course, no canal. Beyond Cassiobury lies the Grove estate, the seat of the Earls of Clarendon, where, during reconstruction during the period 2000-2002 evidence was discovered of Saxon-type buildings and skeletons of a couple buried in graves marked with a large wooden post. This was thought to date to between AD 400 to 550.

Several sunken-floor buildings, perhaps store houses, were uncovered. Also discovered was pottery dating back to about 4000BC.

Not without reason is Cassiobury considered a desirable part of Watford!

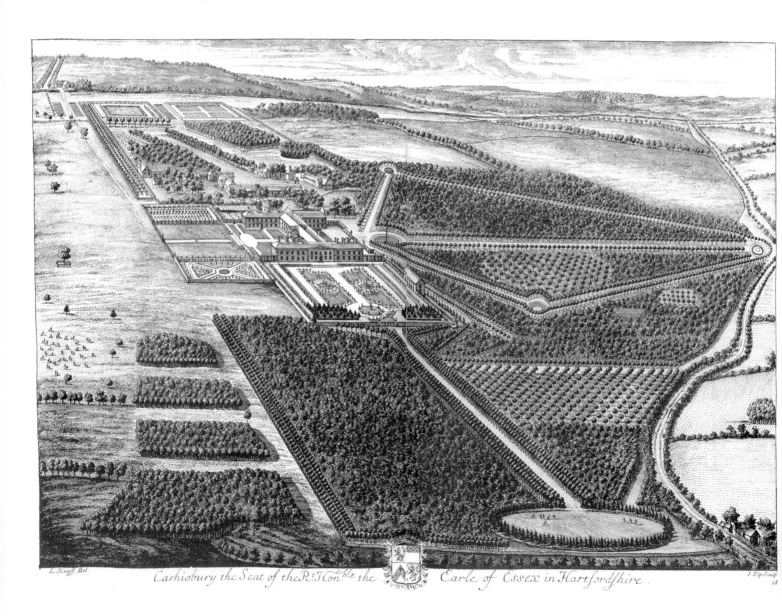

L. Knyff. Del.   *Cashiobury the Seat of the R.t Hon.ble the   Earle of Essex in Hartfordshire.*   *I. Kip Sculp.*
28

Two early printers

From Herts Sessions Books (Liberty Sessions) the following entries are of interest:

a) Declaration (under the Act 39 George III) by James Hugh Perry, late of Uxbridge, in the county of Middlesex, but now of Watford, that he intends to set up a printing press in Watford, and requires a licence therfor. 1816.
b) a refusal by Perry to re-accept an apprentice. 1827.
c) John Peacock applies for licence. 1827.

In the 1841 Census, John Peacock then aged 60, lived one house above Chater the chemist, near Carey Place (*Chater was No. 129*).

In 1851 he was in the 'Manor House' between Local Board Road and Farthing Lane. Prior to establishing a press at 15 Queen-street he was stated to have had a press at the site of the High Street Station. The Queen-street address was the fourth cottage or house past the Library when it was built (*see illustration on page 64*) and it was from this address that his son Samuel established the Watford Observer in 1863.

Below: *Arthur Capel, Earl of Essex, resumed residence at Cassiobury in 1670 when, over the coming years, he had Hugh May reconstruct the house and Moses Cook lay out the gardens in the style of Versaille. This house lasted until later rebuilt, by the fifth Earl, George Capel Coningsby c1800, with lodges and keeps, in the manner by which it was best known .*

Watford in 1822. Modern names are overlaid on panels. The sites of the flint and bronze finds are indicated. As the crow flies they are just under a mile and half apart. In the Grove Park remains of Saxon buildings were discovered as well as buried skeletons, dated to c500AD, and pottery to BC4000 Bushey Mill is noted as is the Silk 'Factory'–the number of streams crisscrossing the land is indicative of the drainage the land needed

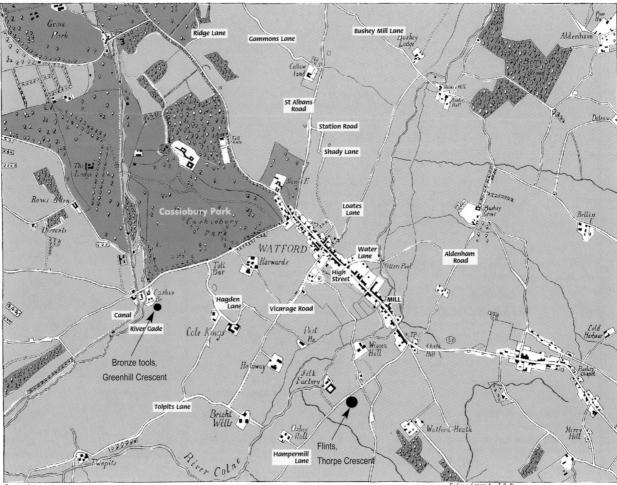

The manor of Cayshobury taken from the Monastery of St Albans

When, for a token sum, Henry VIII conveyed, together with other estates, the manor of Cayshobury on August 29th, 1545 from the Monastery of St. Alban to a grateful Richard Morrison, he acquired himself a dependable ally. Sir Richard became the owner of a large wooded estate.

Watford was an adjunct of Cashio at the time of the Domesday survey so it was probable that on the Normans' arrival there was a manor house occupied by bailiffs or agents of the Abbot at the abbey church of St. Alban. Sir Richard chose virgin land on which to build a 'fair and large house', situated on a dry hill, near a pleasant river park. Morrison chose to live in London during the period of construction of his new house but before its completion he was forced to flee the country because of Protestant leanings on the accession of Queen Mary. He died in voluntary exile in 1556 and his son Charles was left to complete the 'sturdy structure' in the contemporary style. Its size may be judged by the number of rooms, quoted as fifty six, including outbuildings as

assorted as stables, dairy and brewhouse. Charles was not a militant protestant like his father.

His mother, Bridget, Dowager Countess of Bedford, had survived three husbands when she died in 1601 at the age of 75, the widow of Francis Russell, 2nd Earl of Bedford. Although resident at Woburn she still retained her own suite of rooms at Cassiobury House. Evidence of her generosity to the widows of Watford, Langley and Chenies may still be seen in the form of the Bedford or Essex Almshouses built in Church Street, which then connected the High Street with what was later to become Vicarage Road. Knighted in 1588, Sir Charles, and his mother, followed the fashion of the times by providing for themselves a chapel in advance of their demise as an extension to the Parish Church (shown on page 28). Unexpectedly Charles predeceased his mother and died in 1599. In accordance with their own provision they were buried in what is still called the Essex Chapel. Then, in 1907, the monument to her, along with accoutrements of a military nature, was removed to Chenies while monuments to Sir Charles, his wife and sons, remain.

Dame Dorothy Morrison assumed control of Cassiobury until her son reached his majority. In 1606 young Charles married the daughter of Sir Baptist Hicks, a rich mercer, who helped his son-in-law to increase the size of the estate by acquiring peripheral farms and woods. He was made Deputy Lieutenant by the Earl of Salisbury and a baronet in 1625. Following the accession of James to the throne

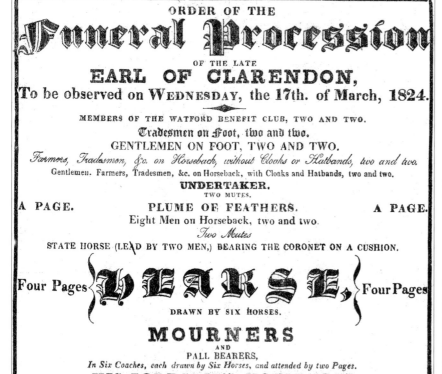

Portraits of the (5th) Earl of Essex, aged 10, and his sister, aged 13.

he was made a Knight of the Bath at his coronation in 1625. In 1628, representing the Shire of Hertford, he died after a short illness. The Morrison ladies also left their spiritual mark on Watford. His step-daughter, Dame Elizabeth Russell, set up a trust to provide for a lecturer to regularly preach at the Parish Church. Both infant sons of Sir Charles, named after their grandfather, Baptist and Hicks, died leaving a surviving daughter, Elizabeth. She married Arthur Capel of Little Hadham Hall in 1627, thereby introducing the family name to Cassiobury with which it is now synonymous. The family seat stayed at Hadham. As Lieutenant-General of Shropshire, Cheshire and North Wales he left for

Shrewsbury ostensibly to prevent Parliamentarian General Sir William Brereton from joining the forces already besieging Chester, with reasonable success.

His popularity and his future seemed assured in his task to protect the Prince of Wales, which duty should have divorced him from further military exposure to the Royalist/Parliamentarian conflict. When everything appeared to be resolving itself he involved himself again in 1648, this time at Colchester, but his luck ran out. He surrendered to Fairfax, who already held his son, Arthur, captive. The son survived but the father was beheaded at the Tower in 1649, and his heart, after his execution, was placed in a silver casket at the

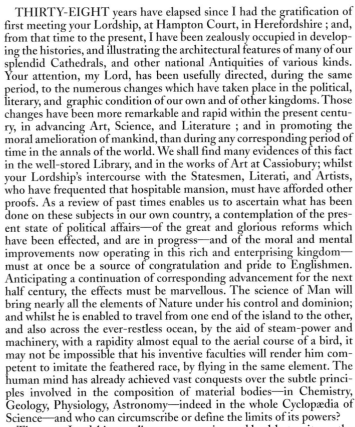

To the right Honourable THE EARL OF ESSEX

MY LORD,

THIRTY-EIGHT years have elapsed since I had the gratification of first meeting your Lordship, at Hampton Court, in Herefordshire ; and, from that time to the present, I have been zealously occupied in developing the histories, and illustrating the architectural features of many of our splendid Cathedrals, and other national Antiquities of various kinds. Your attention, my Lord, has been usefully directed, during the same period, to the numerous changes which have taken place in the political, literary, and graphic condition of our own and of other kingdoms. Those changes have been more remarkable and rapid within the present century, in advancing Art, Science, and Literature ; and in promoting the moral amelioration of mankind, than during any corresponding period of time in the annals of the world. We shall find many evidences of this fact in the well-stored Library, and in the works of Art at Cassiobury; whilst your Lordship's intercourse with the Statesmen, Literati, and Artists, who have frequented that hospitable mansion, must have afforded other proofs. As a review of past times enables us to ascertain what has been done on these subjects in our own country, a contemplation of the present state of political affairs—of the great and glorious reforms which have been effected, and are in progress—and of the moral and mental improvements now operating in this rich and enterprising kingdom—must at once be a source of congratulation and pride to Englishmen. Anticipating a continuation of corresponding advancement for the next half century, the effects must be marvellous. The science of Man will bring nearly all the elements of Nature under his control and dominion; and whilst he is enabled to travel from one end of the island to the other, and also across the ever-restless ocean, by the aid of steam-power and machinery, with a rapidity almost equal to the aerial course of a bird, it may not be impossible that his inventive faculties will render him competent to imitate the feathered race, by flying in the same element. The human mind has already achieved vast conquests over the subtle principles involved in the composition of material bodies—in Chemistry, Geology, Physiology, Astronomy—indeed in the whole Cyclopædia of Science—and who can circumscribe or define the limits of its powers?

That your Lordship may live many years in good health, to witness the realization and substantial effects of the national and moral reforms now in progress in this country, and continue to derive solace and pleasure from the beauties of Nature and Art, as well as from association with men of political integrity, moral worth, and mental attainments, is the sincere wish of

Your Lordship's Obedient servant,
    J. Britton.   Burton Street, London, July 9th 1837

The frontispiece to Britton's 'Cassiobury' is dated 1806 and depicts the fifth Earl of Essex in his prime when aged about forty-five. An introduction, alongside, presents Britton's reasons for taking so long to complete the work, and remarks upon the changes science and progress have wrought upon the face of the land. The Earl was well aware of the coming of the railway but with no stretch of mind could have forseen its progress; he died just one year after the railway was built and Watford Station opened.

feet of his dead King. The casket was kept at Hadham and not placed in the family vault until 1703. As a further penalty the Cassiobury estate was sequestrated. Lady Capel stayed at Kings Langley or Little Hadham until the restoration of Charles II.

Arthur Capel was created **Earl of Essex** by Charles II and as Viscount Malden and Earl of Essex, was appointed Lord Lieutenant of Hertfordshire. By 1670 he was again in residence at Cassiobury. Seven years later Arthur became leader in the House of Lords and a member of the Privy Council under Shaftesbury. Unhappily he was exposed to

the hatred and prejudice generated by a protestant parliament and a catholic James. He aligned himself with Monmouth and was promptly expelled from the Privy Council. Disillusioned, he returned to Cassiobury and transferred his attention to it. Lord Arthur had married Elizabeth Percy, daughter of the Earl of Northumberland. Of a family of seven sons, only two boys reached maturity.

He spent his time studying English history and involving himself in the reconstruction of the house, except for one wing which was retained. Hugh May was entrusted with the work and his head gardener, based at Hadham, laid out the Versailles-inspired gardens. He was accused in 1683 of involvement in the Rye House plot to kidnap King Charles on his way from Newmarket races and force him to disinherit his heir, brother James (a catholic). When awaiting trial, he was lodged in the same room in the Tower in which his father had been prior to his execution, thirty four years before. He was found dead, his throat cut. It was said by Whig propagandists that he had been murdered.

The second Earl, **Algernon**, born in 1657, served William of Orange in many capacities and Queen Anne as Lieutenant General of her army in Spain. He married Mary, daughter of William Bentinck, Duke of Portland, in 1692. She bore him two sons and one daughter. He died in 1710 and was succeeded by thirteen-year old

Above: From Britton's 'Cassiobury' this illustrates part of the old buildings which are shown as the row of terrace-style cottages in the illustration on page 24.

The Great Library, 54ft x 23ft, has bookcases all round and fifteen portraits of personages of the family above, and was drawn and coloured c1830 to accompany Britton's 'Cassiobury'.

Remarking upon the quality of the lodges provided upon the estate he contrasts "unlike the ragged wretched sheds and hovels too often seen by the road-side . . . were the mechanics and work-people of large manufacturing towns and peasantry (our "country's pride") provided with better and more comfortable habitation, the ruinous gin shops would be less frequented and ragged, impudent, children would not so constantly infest our streets and public roads."

William who also became a member of the Privy Council. His first marriage brought no male heirs. His wife Jane, daughter of Henry Hyde, Earl of Clarendon, died in 1724. He then married Elizabeth, daughter of the second Duke of Bedford. Their second son succeeded to the title as **William Anne**, fourth Earl of Essex. Algernon died in 1743 and was interred at Watford. William served George II and followed in the family tradition as Lord Lieutenant of Hertfordshire, and married twice. His first wife bore him a son and two daughters and the second, four sons.

The fifth Earl, **George Capel Coningsby** (family name of his maternal grandmother) was born in 1757 and for two decades served as a member of Parliament. He commissioned James Wyatt to remodel the house; ornamental lodges and cottages were carefully sited at points of access to the estate including Swiss Cottage and the celebrated Cassiobury Park Gates, all attributed to members of the Wyatt family. By the beginning of the nineteenth-century the work had been largely completed. At the age of 42 he met John Britton, a 'free-lance' historian, cataloguer and producer of high quality profiles of country homes and cathedrals. With Cassiobury nearing completion of the many works of transformation, it transpired that a work about Cassiobury was mooted. It took 38 years to produce but remains an enduring record of the house and grounds which later proved to such a pivotal part of Watford's history. His marriage to Sarah, daughter of Henry Bazet of St. Helena was less than successful and after her death in 1838, George, at the age of eighty two, married

The sixth Earl, Arthur Algernon, (1803-1892) succeeded the fifth Earl in 1839 when aged 36. He was responsible for selling much land, (leaving the Cassiobury estate intact), making possible Watford's growth.

Top: *One of the many cottages on the estate.*

Centre: *The 'Iron (or Navigational) Bridge' across the canal.*

Right: *The Great Cloister.*

Kitty Stephens, the toast of the aristocracy, a well-known singer and actress of her day as well as being an acknowledged beauty. She gave him a year's happiness; he died in 1839.

George died childless; he was succeeded by Arthur Algernon, eldest son of his half-brother.

The new Earl, **Arthur Algernon Capel**, eldest son of George's half brother, married three times, to Lady Caroline Beauclerk, Lady Caroline Elizabeth Boyle and Louisa, daughter of Charles Heneage and widow of General Lord George Augustus Paget. He found time to involve himself in local affairs as Lay Rector, President of the Watford and Bushey Volunteer Fire Brigade and the West Hertfordshire Agricultural Society. At the House of Lords he voted Liberal.

In 1880 he changed his name to the original version of 'Capell' by Royal Licence. Eton-educated Arthur brought to Cassiobury new outlooks and interests which included involvement of the manufacture of croquet sets, and the popularising of the game on a national basis.

Towards the end of the nineteenth century the old aristocratic families felt the pressures of a changing social and economic order. In 1846 Cassiobury House had been rented to Queen Adelaide, widow of William IV, who came to Watford to recuperate from an illness. Some weeks later Queen Victoria and Prince Albert travelled from Windsor to see her. Prince Albert took the opportunity of joining a shooting party bound for Callowland. After two years Queen Adelaide moved to Bentley Priory when she died in 1849.

Arthur Algernon had his pulse upon Watford's affairs

Top: From 'The Illustrated London News' of July 1855, the Watford Horticultural and Floricultural Society Show, held in the Cassiobury gardens, facing the east wing of the house.

The view, (above), drawn looking from the position of the golf course, over canal, River Gade and the park, to the house in the distance.

Right: The view from the southwest shows the stables and office, west porch with towered facade and long frontage to the dining room, drawing room and No. 1 library.

Next page, left: In the Park, an oak and elm. Right: the view is from the northeast. Also shown is a plan of the house. For clarity the annotations are modern but the 90° change in orientation is unchanged (though a compass rose has been included).

and from his early days of Earldom saw his land as the source of income. Unlike other landed gentry who were careful to retain ownership of their land, renting rather than selling, Arthur chose to sell. Consequently his income was quicker (and doubtless suited his agents who did not have the responsibility of thereafter managing the land on the Earl's behalf) but over the the years his realisable assets dwindled. Arthur did not appear to have income from Government or other services as had his predecessors. In that lay the seeds of gradual decay and dilapidations.

It was he who instigated the sale of the Nascott Estate, of some 150 acres, in 1857; it was he who, in 1890, offered eight acres of Harwoods Farm for the West Herts Sports Club ground, on a 21-year lease, at £100 per year, with a further option of 21 years, and an option of purchase during the first 21 years for £6000.

At this time the Cassiobury estate was still intact but was to change. Upon his death in 1892 the title of Seventh Earl passed to **George Devereux de Vere**, Vice-Lieutenant of Hertfordshire and Aide-de-Camp to the King (Edward VII). He served as the Seventh Earl with the Imperial Yeomanry in South Africa at the turn of the century. He had one son by his first marriage (Algernon George de Vere), and two daughters by his second marriage, to Adèle,

daughter of Beach Grant of New York. Adèle was a wealthy heiress whom he married in 1893; they were greatly fêted on their journey through the town, from the station to their mansion in the park.

They realised that 'no repairs had been done for about fifty years' and so started, in that year, the selling of paint-

31

The Essex and Watford association ends . . .

ings and treasures, whilst maintaining a lifestyle of lavish entertainment for the cream of society. The first sale of paintings—including Landseer's Cat's-Paw, and three Turners—was followed by one of porcelain, bronzes and furniture, and estimated to have raised some £40,000.

The upkeep and maintenance of the house and grounds was expensive, and their lifestyle vigorous. Cassiobury was famous for its parties, balls and entertainment generally. They were both lavish and costly. The aristocracy in general, and chosen guests, such as Churchill, Henry James, and John Sargent, in particular, were just some of the distinguished visitors who enjoyed the hospitality of the the fun-loving Essex family. Not always occupied, the house was from 1900 available to be let, furnished, for periods of months or even years. The last entry in the Mansion's Visitor's Book was in July 1913. Earlier, in 1897, Callowland Farm was sold for development and by 1908 parts of Cassiobury were being sold off, some being bought as a public park.

Further calamity was to follow. The seventh earl, **George de Vere**, was in 1916 knocked down and injured by a cab in London, later dying from his injuries. The Countess, now Dowager, had the task of overseeing the sale of the house, dying in 1922. The title of Eighth Earl

passed to **Algernon de Vere** but without connections with Cassiobury or Watford.

Cassiobury had been eulogised in a lavish work of art, but two miles away was the Silk Mill where conditions were very different. It must have appeared as a godsend when the mill at Oxhey turned to producing silk for it employed men, women and, especially, children all year round. Earning a living was hard; in an agricultural environment the weather dictated all, and builders, especially, were completely at the mercy of the seasons. The rule was devastatingly simple, if the weather was bad, then work stopped and so did the pay. At the mill the wages were low, the hours long, but for the sake of a few pence per week they were endured.

Accidents there were aplenty—"rarely more than the loss of the end of a finger, or fingers"—to be bandaged up as best possible and wait for nature (and perhaps some herbal ointment) to effect a cure.

The country's social conscience was awakening and in 1832 the House of Commons held an inquiry into the state of the mills. It was to produce a Bill to regulate the Labour of Children in the Mills and Factories of the United Kingdom. Many operatives from the Mill were summoned to appear before the committee, an invitation they declined for fear that they would lose their job as a reprisal for testifying . . .

Above: The 7th Earl, George Deveraux de Vere, died following an accident in London, in 1916; his widow, afterwards Dowager, oversaw the auction and sale of Cassiobury House in 1922.

Right: The Essex Chapel in the Parish Church, built for Sir Charles Morrison on a licence granted by the Archdeacon of St Albans in 1596. Bridget, Sir Charles' mother, Dowager Countess of Bedford, was buried here in 1601, but the monument and other Morrison connections were removed to Chenies in 1907. Many of the Chapel's monuments still remain.

... rarely more than the loss of the end of a finger or fingers ...

Extracts from a
REPORT
from the Committee on the
"BILL to regulate the LABOUR of CHILDREN in the MILLS and
FACTORIES in the United Kingdom"

Ordered, by the House of Commons, to be printed.
8 August, 1832

Mr. Thomas Daniel *(Rookery Mill)* called in; and further Examined.

HAVE you been employed in any other business in mills and factories besides cotton?—*In the silk mills I have been employed.*

Where both silk throwing and silk spinning have been conducted?—*Yes.*

In what departments were you in any such mills?—*I was a superintendent in throwing and spinning the silk.*

In both instances, therefore, you are competent to speak as to questions relating to that branch of business?—*I am.*

Is a great proportion of children employed in that manufacture?—*There is a great number.*

Does the proportion of boys or girls preponderate?—*They are girls principally.*

Do you think that girls are as well capable of sustaining long-continued exertion as boys?—*By no means.*

You have already mentioned that the labour of the children in the cotton factories has been considerably increased of late years?—*It has been very considerably increased.*

Will you state whether that is the fact in regard to the labour of children in silk mills?—*It is; their labour has been increased very much.*

Has the number of spindles that they have to attend to been considerably increased by recent alterations in the machinery?—*They have, more than one-half I should think.*

Do you consider that those improvements of alterations in the machinery have materially lessened their labour with respect to the same number of spindles that children had previously to endure?—*No, it has increased their labour very materially; they have as much labour again, thereabouts now, as they have to perform before.*

Have not the children in silk mills also to regulate, in some measure, their own labour, so as to be often in a state of considerable anxiety regarding the quantity of work that they produce?—*They have to be answerable for all the work that goes through their fingers, have the children in silk mills.*

So that they have a kind of responsibility upon them, as well as actual labour, to endure?—*They are responsible for all work that goes through their fingers.*

Does the mill system, as at present pursued, occasion many accidents among the hands employed?—*I know that it does produce those*

accidents inseparable from machinery. It is possible that, at a late period of the day, a state of languor and lassitude may be brought on, whereby they would be less able to guard against the accidents which would naturally occur in such large establishments, and with such machinery.*

It is sometimes said, that those accidents occur often at the termination of the day's labour, but generally at the termination of a week's labour, when the person becomes fatigued; does that consist with your experience?—*Yes, the latter part of it does; for on Saturday there was always a number of accidents, but generally trifling, being rarely more than the loss of the end of a finger or fingers; that is as far as relates to the cleaning of the machinery at the time specified; but I cannot say that these ever appeared to me to be connected with or produced by reason of the languor to which the question refers; although, as I have already observed, I can conceive that listlessness might deprive them of that caution which, with their full energies, they would exercise.*

Daniel Fraser, called in; and further Examined.

DID you bear a summons to George Montagu, of Watford?— *Yes, I did.*

To appear before this Committee to give evidence touching an inquiry respecting a Bill for limiting the hours of children employed in mills and factories?—*Yes, I did.*

Are you aware that an answer has been returned to that summons, stating that he is too unwell to attend?—*Yes.*

Do you know that, nevertheless, he worked on the day on which you delivered the summons to him?—*Yes; and I found him coming*

The road leads from Wiggen Hall to the silk mills and by now, c1900, has established the width and character of an unmade country lane.

Here, as a way to and from the mills, footpaths led through to Watford Fields, through the alley by the Fox Inn, to where there was a collection of shops. Much earlier the trek would have been to the Market Place.

With farmland on the left-hand side this view would see a quarter-century unchanged as, after the Great War, housing was needed for returning servicemen but, more importantly, to rehouse families who had been removed from slum areas as they were destined to be cleared.

... far rather have less wages, than see her children so tired at night ...

out of the mill when I delivered the summons.

Where you desired to summon others also?—*Yes, I was.*

Have you not found much disinclination to attend as witnesses on the part of those that would have been brought before this Committee, had it not been for their expressing their apprehension, that if they appeared they should endanger their interests, and, perhaps, lose their situations? —*Yes; I am sorry to see that this feeling is very deeply impressed upon the minds of the operatives in connection with the factories; otherwise they said they would give evidence with cheerfulness; it is my deep impression, that though very favourable to the passing of a Bill to limit the hours of labour to ten hours a day, they are afraid to express their sentiments upon this subject, lest it should affect their interests.*

What, speaking from your own knowledge, is the state of employment in the silk mills which you have recently visited, in respect of the number of hours; state, also, whether they work several of them by night, and the general condition and appearance of the hands employed, specifying the particular places that you have visited, with a view to collect information upon the subject, and to select witnesses to appear before this Committee?—*As far as I have had an opportunity of knowing, I find that there is very little difference between the number of hours that the children work in those various places which I have visited in Essex, Suffolk, and elsewhere, from those which I have already stated to the Committee, viz, twelve hours' actual labour a day.*

They work from half past 5 in the morning, at Braintree, in Essex, till half past 6 in the evening, and with the intermission for meals of one hour, half an hour for breakfast, and half an hour for dinner and the children there are fined a penny per hour for being absent.

I am quite confident that they would be glad of a regulation of the hours of labour, even if it was attended with diminished wages.

One woman, in particular, said "She would far rather have less wages, than see her children so tired at night;" and another thus remarked, relative to the health and morals of the children employed in factories, "That if a jolly girl goes into a mill, her countenance soon alters, and they become more unruly than they were before."

And another trait of the factory system is, that women and children do the work of men and grown-up people.

I observed one man kept to attend to the engine and to the repair of the mill, and females performed the rest of the labour along with children.

Have you inquired whether the children employed that length of time are beaten and chastised at the silk-mills as well as at the cotton and other factories?—*Yes, they are chastised; and it is found necessary under this system, to keep driving them on.*

The children are taken much earlier to the silk-mill than to any other mill, are they not?—*Yes; and when they are not tall enough, they find them little stools to stand upon, to reach their work.*

How old are some of them?—*Some of them turned 5, and at 6 years of age ...At Watford, in Hertfordshire, the mill is worked both day and night, the children go at 6 in the morning, and work till 7 at night; and they have one hour and twenty minutes intermission.*

Then the night hands go on at 7, and work till 6 in the ensuing morning?—*Yes, The Committee most likely will have some further evidence upon that subject; which will be able to state that more particularly. In this mill children were going in at 5 years of age; and those children have worked the usual hours.*

At this mill, if the children are not tall enough, stools are got for the infants; they have no Sunday-school, nor week-day evening-school at this village; it is a little village where this mill is.

I found that one of the children, Elizabeth Taylor, went to the mill at between 7 and 8 years old for 1/- a week at first; she is now nearly 15 years old, and has 3s. 6d. a week There are instances there, where the wife is working during the night; and the husband working during the day; the amount of their wages is 20s. a week; both their wages united, for working night and day.

Do you know whether the children are beaten up to their work there also?—*Yes; they are regularly urged to their work by beating; they use canes in that mill to beat the children.*

Have you seen any instances, in going round, of those children being chastised?—*Yes; I saw a boy of the name of Richard Love, for making a waste with a peg which is a thing that will very frequently occur in the silk business, by being thrown off the bobbin; I saw him standing in the midst of a group of little children, he had received a bleeding wound in the right side of his face, in consequence of making this peg waste.*

Are you able to say, whether that fault might not have been unavoidable, and whether it might not have been an accident?— *From the number of pegs they have to keep up, it is a thing that might occur with older ones than this*

The National Schools, in Church Street and facing the Churchyard, were built by members of the Parish Church in 1841. They provided elementary education for boys and girls (separate entrances as always) until 1922 when the building was taken into use as offices later becoming the Registrar's Local Office for Births, Marriages and Deaths.

This continued, through a gradually run-down environment not helped by the narrow street being used as a car park, until the Registrar's Offices were housed in 36 Clarendon Road. There they were together with the County's Divisional Careers Office and Probation and After-Care Service.

Demolition took place before 1970 was out, the land, with part of the Almshouses' gardens, Almondwick's Barns and land, was used to build Exchange Road and multi-storey car park.

... it is the rule; if we find children with books, to take them from them.

Richard Love. I dare say he might be from 12 to 15 years of age.

This was not inside the mill, was it?—*No.*

Is there not considerable objection made to yourself and other persons, that wish to observe upon the system of examining those mills?—*Yes, they do not allow any person to examine those mills except they have business; they fine the children at this mill: there is James Naylor, who has 2s. a week; he lost two hours one morning and he was fined for that 7d; his mother asked the reason of this deduction, and Mr. Roddick, the overlooker, simply replied, "That this was the "rule"".*

I found there was one female doing the work of three or four men in the throwing department, in taking charge of the silk which they wound. Thirty or forty children are the usual charge for a man.

This young woman had nearly 100 under her care, and the amount of her wages was 10s. a week; for which, as I calculate, she was doing the work of three men; and if the children had been properly attended to, they would have required more than three.

Had not several of the hands in those mills previously petitioned against the Bill now under the consideration of Parliament?— *Yes, all the hands in this mill had signed a petition, but neither old nor young, parents nor children, knew anything of the matter, all the infants signed with a cross.*

I am fully prepared to mention names, but refrain solely from a fear of injuring individuals. That petition was signed by the orders of their employer.

Did they sign it?—*Yes.*

And they told you that they knew nothing about it?—*They did; neither parents nor children, nor up-growing operatives in the mill, could give any proper account what it was, or for what purpose it was done, the masters possess so much power, I would almost say unconstitutional power, over the operatives.*

William Rastrick, called in; and Examined.

WHERE do you reside?—*At Watford.*

What age are you?—*Thirty-four.*

Have you ever been in a silk-mill? Yes.

At what age did you go into one?—*At 11 years of age. [1809]*

How young have you known children go into silk-mills?—*I have known three at 6; but very few at that age.*

In whose mill did you work at that period?—*Mr. Shute's, at Watford.*

What were your hours of labour?—*From 6 in the morning till 7 at night.*

What time had you allowed for breakfast, for dinner and for tea?—*Half an hour breakfast; half an hour dinner, but no tea time; at least not at that time.*

Was the mill worked at night?—*No, not then.*

Had you, or any of the hands, any opportunity of going to an evening-school, or of learning anything during that time?—*No, it was too far from the town; a mile from the town.*

Was there a Sunday-school in the town?—*Yes, two or three.*

Did those afford the hands, generally, the only opportunities they possessed of getting a little learning?—*The only opportunity.*

Were not the children very much disinclined to attend the Sunday-schools after having been thus employed during the week?—*Yes; in a great many instances they would absent themselves from the school and ramble in the fields, instead of going.*

You state that during the time you were in those mills, you had no opportunity during the week to obtain instruction?—*None whatever; it is always the rule in those mills, if we find children with books, to take them from them.*

And the only opportunity you had for obtaining instruction was in the Sunday-schools?—*Yes.*

Do they teach writing in those schools?—*No.*

There is no opportunity therefore for the children to learn to write?—*No; unless the parents can write, and set them to it of an evening.*

Do you think that many children can write?—*Very few.*

The system, then, has the direct tendency to deprive them of what may be now justly denominated a necessary part of education for a working person?—*Yes, it has.*

Did you find them particularly fatigued towards the evening?—*Yes, excepting some of them; there are some of stronger constitutions whom the labour does not affect so much.*

Have the children to stand at that employment?—*Yes.*

Was it not found necessary to beat children at that age, so as to keep them up to their employment?—*Certainly.*

Did the beating increase towards evening?—*Their strength relaxes more towards the evening, they get tired, and they twist themselves about on their legs, and stand on the sides of their feet.*

They begin then to neglect their work, being in a state, perhaps, of exhaustion?—*Yes.*

So that they have to be occasionally beaten to induce them to perform it?—*Yes.*

And in some cases with considerable severity?—*In some cases they are.*

Are those children under the control of the overlookers, or are they under the master?—*Under the control of the overlookers. The master comes in perhaps three or four times in the course of the day; he merely comes up and down the room a time or two.*

Does the overlooker hire or pay them?—

The master in that mill hires them and pays them.

Is it the case in all other mills?—*No, it is not.*

Have the children often to work over-time in those mills?—*Yes.*

How much over-time?—*Two hours.*

Making altogether fifteen hours of confinement?—*Yes.*

From your experience in mills, do not you think that a limitation of the hours of labour would be a great benefit to those employed at present in the silk-mills, especially if connected with an opportunity of giving them an education?—*Certainly it would.*

And that it would, notwithstanding the apparent opposition, that may be offered to such a legislative measure, meet with the ready concurrence, and gratify the earnest wishes of those who may be engaged in such pursuits?—*Yes, I am confident it would.*

Do you think that the children, and workmen generally, that work in those mills, are worse off than the agricultural labourers?—*Yes, they are, considerably.*

• *The Rookery Mill was built by Thomas Deacon of Wiggenhall c1770 and leased to Edward Crutchley. Later it was bought by Mr. Paumier (whose name is mentioned regarding the carriage of workers from and to the Workhouse) and by the 1820's it had passed to Thomas Rock Shute in whose ownership it was at the time of the Silk Mill Enquiry Report.*

The 'change of machinery' mentioned would be the introduction of steam-driven machines rather than powered by water-wheel.

The Enquiry led to the Factory Act of 1833 in which children under nine years of age were barred from textile factories; for 9-13 year-olds the hours were limited to forty-eight; young persons of 13-18 years, sixty-nine hours.

This restriction would also have the effect of curtailing mens' hours as, normally, their work was dependent upon the women and young persons being present.

It was laid down that every factory child should receive two hours schooling per day—a part of the Act usually ignored.

A further Factory Act of 1844 reduced children's hours still more, and controlled women's hours to the same as a 'young person', and stipulated that all dangerous machinery had to be fenced.

The name 'Rookery' was acquired from a rookery in nearby elms—the site is shown on the map on page 25 and the c1910 road from Wiggenhall leading to it on page 33.

The silk mill ceased as such in 1881, being used the Watford Steam Laundry in 1883 and after long service, as general manufactory including pianos and in the latter part of the 20th century electrical control gear; the premises were demolished in the year 2000.

The Silk Mill name is perpetuated in nearby roads as Silk Mill Road *and* Silk Mill Court.

... growth, beyond the power of the Vestry to cope ...

Even the quietest hamlets face problems of space. In 1771, Watford, with a population of just over 2,000, had a very pressing problem—the graveyard was overcrowded and it was becoming increasingly difficult to deal decently with burials. The Vestry thought that if the road past the Churchyard was moved nearer to the Almshouses the size of the Churchyard would be almost doubled. Accordingly an application was made for an Act of Parliament allowing re-alignment of the road and thus the road was moved to the line we know today. A further enlargement was made in 1843 and the enlarged Churchyard sufficed until the laying out in 1858 of a new burial ground in Vicarage Road. In 1771 the Workhouse had been established for some fifty years and Mrs. Fuller's Free School for nearly seventy years. The town's growth was static, though that of the country was not.

A slow migration to towns was taking place where the work in the new factories—however hard—offered a surer measure of food than work upon the land. More, the growth of population had a disastrous effect upon the country's woodland and forests as they were stripped for fuel and, for a great many, cold winters meant great hardship. As a response a network of canals came into being allowing the transport of coal to effect gradual relief and it was the Grand Junction canal which linked London and Birmingham.

The canal, when built, had relatively small direct impact upon the town, (not needing the small army of mechanics later needed for the railway), but by bringing the coal into the district it paved the way for the founding of the gas works and gave impetus to the paper-making mills at Apsley, Nash, Home Park and Croxley. It also allowed the steam engine and machinery to be installed in the silk mill leading to greater production and harsher working conditions. Far over the horizon, in the north of England, successful experiments with steam locomotives were taking place and in 1830 it was decided to build a railway line between Birmingham and London. Taking several years to plan and survey, the line was projected to run in the Gade valley, almost alongside the canal. Whilst the Earl of Clarendon and the 5th Earl of Essex were tolerant of the canal, and canal traffic at a speed of three or four miles per hour through their parks, they were less inclined to tolerate the rush, noise and smell of the new-fangled steam train. The projected line had to be resurveyed, and was moved somewhat to the north, necessitating the construction of a mile-long tunnel. The coming of a railway, in itself, would naturally bring a degree of growth, as happened to many other towns and villages countrywide. Watford, however, had three other contributory factors which greatly enhanced the impetus of the railway.

Firstly, the town had a degree of prominence resulting from the crossing of two turnpike roads and sited on the main track from London to Aylesbury. Secondly, it had a considerable degree of importance by virtue of the grant and right to hold weekly markets and thirdly, not long after the coming of the railway, Arthur Algernon Capel, Earl of Essex and Lord of the Manor realised the advantage of selling land he owned, a trend that other landowners followed. He had sufficient virgin land to keep pace with demand and its release enabled Watford to grow without the excesses of industrial connurbations. The town's growth, when it started, was beyond the power of the Vestry to deal with. A social conscience was awakening and the hard life of youngsters—in particular—who were employed at the Silk Mill, was the subject of a Government enquiry, and consequent reforms. Also, with growth, the hamlet was foul and stank; people were afraid cholera may strike and another enquiry was held.

On September 28, 1829, George and Robert Stephenson's locomotive 'Rocket', fitted with Henry Booth's patent multi-tubular boiler, arrived at Liverpool and on October 6th it drew the Liverpool & Manchester Railway directors' carriages from the crossing of the Huyton Turnpike to Rainhill where, from October 6 to 14, it competed for, and won, the £500 offered by the directors of the L & M R for the best locomotive power. Huge crowds gathered to witness the competition. The trial had proved successful; within two years the Liverpool to Manchester line was carrying upwards of 1000 passengers a day—profitably. In many other parts of the country, businessmen made haste to promote their own railway and a free-for-all system was the result. George and Robert Stephenson engineered the London to Birmingham line.

Next page: The two and half-mile long Tring Cutting where the soil was excavated and dragged up steep ramps in barrows by horse and rope. A breakage or slippage was feared! June 1837. A similar cutting was made (with mechanical power) during 2002 enabling the A41 to by-pass Aston Clinton.

During the Roman occupation their roads, metalled and solid, took their legions countrywide; and indigenous trade followed. During the dark ages everything Roman was spurned. Roads were used for as long as they stayed fit and when they deteriorated there was no knowledge or organisation to effect repairs. As the stone could be put to better use in building dwellings it proved to be a convenient and ready source of supply. At the time of the Viking and Danish invasions and occupancy the country's rivers were deeper, faster flowing and navigable further inland. The Roman towns were sacked, deserted and spurned and Augusta—London—was no exception. Our nearby St Albans, built apart from the Roman town of Veralum, is a case in point.

From the early 18th century the principal owners of Watford land were the Earls of Essex, Fellows of Merton College, Oxford, and the Church. Between our now Clarendon Road and the Pond were two large estates, that of Watford House, notable as the home of the County Historian, Clutterbuck (of which part became the site of Clements) and Monmouth House. Monmouth House was built in 1610 by Sir Robert Carey, Earl of Monmouth, as a dower house. Named the 'Mansion Houses' it had all the land called Great and Little Poa Fields which extended from the High Street to beyond where the railway was built. Upon the death of Sir Robert's widow, in 1640, the house and grounds passed into the ownership of William Carpender of Coleford, Gloucester and upon grandson John's death in 1771 the house was divided into two and the land belonging to the property was sold, the Great and Little Poa Fields being bought by Mr. Clutterbuck The two houses stayed within the Carpender/Cox family, and in 1865 the south house was named 'The Platts', the north 'Monmouth'. The

houses were finally sold in 1927 and a little later the north house was almost entirely rebuilt; using bricks from the demolished Cassiobury House, the south much altered, and the whole converted into the shop premises we know today.

The extensive grounds of Watford House included the area later known as Dudley's Corner which at that time (c1800), accommodated maltings. The maltings were removed to the rear of 66 High Street; cottages built in their stead, and the gates to the grounds removed and Clarendon Road cut through in 1864. This development heralded the end of Poa Fields.

The town's people used the Common Fields and Lammas lands which were small tracts of ground spreading to the rear of the Church, towards Colney Butts, southwards towards our present Watford Fields (which perpetuates the name) and, in part, bounded by the river Colne before the advent of both the Rickmansworth Railway and Electric Railway to London. Countrywide, between 1750 and 1820, 'enclosure' of open fields was carried out to improve farming methods although, of course, many ancient rights were lost in the process. The enclosure of the Watford Fields—which at that time was grazing and arable land behind the Crown Passage in the High Street— seemed more in the nature of acquisition for development. The ancient rights were sold in 1855 for compensation of £1698. A further £159 was received for two crops of grass and a further £507 17s. in 1862 when the Rickmansworth railway company put their line through the fields. Of the resultant £2991 7s., £161 12s. was later granted to the Library committee. The remaining £2,828 was invested and the income was devoted to help the upkeep of the Peace Memorial Hospital. Upon the implementation of the Enclosure Act part of the land was retained for public recreation ground—our present Watford Fields.

"A Railway?, What is a Railway?"

Through this tranquil and old-fashioned spot, rumour spread the intelligence that a railway was about to be constructed from London to Birmingham. What a railway was, and by what new and unheard-of evils it would destroy the repose of the country, no resident had any idea. Some of the readers of the few copies of the Times that passed through the post-office were aware that in the preceding year a bill for this purpose had been thrown out in the House of Lords, following the opposition of a noble Earl, (the fifth Earl of Essex) through whose park Robert Stephenson, following the line selected by Telford for the Grand Junction Canal, had proposed for the railway.

A second bill had been brought forward by which, at the expense of heavy works, the park and ornamental grounds of the Earl had been avoided, the line crossing the valley of the Colne by an embankment of what was, in those days, unprecedented magnitude, and thus boring beneath the woods, at a distance from the mansion, by an equally unprecedented tunnel of nearly a mile in length.

At last one or two strange faces appeared in the town, and men in leathern leggings, dragging a long chain, and attended by one or two country labourers armed with bill-hooks, were remarked as trespassing in the most unwarrantable manner over pasture land, standing crops, copse and cover, actually cutting gaps in the hedges, through which they climbed and dragged the land-chain. Then would follow another intruder, bearing a telescope set on three legs, which he erected with the most perfect coolness wherever he thought fit, peering through it at a long white staff, marked with unintelligible hieroglyphics, which was borne by another labourer, and moved or held stationary in accordance with a mysterious code of telegraphic signals made by the hand. The farmers, naturally indignant, ordered these intruders from their fields. The engineers, for such they were, took but little notice.

The next step in the the invasion proved a yet further aggravation to the farmers, although affording them the pleasure of retaliation. Loads of oak pegs, accurately squared, planed, and pointed, were driven to the fields, and the course of the intended railway was marked out by driving two of these pegs, one left standing about four inches above the surface to indicate position, and a smaller one driven lower to the ground a few inches off on which to take the level, at every interval of twenty-two yards.

It is obvious that the operations of farming afforded many an opportunity for an unfriendly blow at these pegs. Ploughs and harrows had a remarkable tendency to become entangled in them; cart wheels ran foul of them; sometimes they disappeared altogether. A mute and irregular warfare on the subject of the pegs was generally protracted until the last outrage was perpetrated by the agents of the company; the land was purchased for the railway.

The Railway Worker

The primary object in the application of steam to Railroad travelling being the economising of time, the inhabitants of Watford cannot be congratulated on enjoying the advantages of the discovery to its fullest extent, for the "line" here, after intersecting the houses at the eastern end of the town, proceeds onwards for nearly two miles, before it reaches the Watford "station," which is at a point where the western extremity of the town is one mile distant. We may remark that it has afforded an opportunity to compare Railway with Omnibus speed, and to call into action the rivalry of inn-keepers, and accordingly a choice of vehicles, from the "Essex Arms" and the "Rose and Crown" is offered to carry passengers into the town. This journey of a mile is not uninteresting. There is a small portion of the high road from Watford to St. Albans (which crosses the Railway) leading South, lined with elms, at the end of which, turning East, lies the town, on both sides of the road for about a mile.

In 1830 two lines were proposed; one by Sir John Rennie, via Banbury and Oxford, and the other by Mr. Giles, via Coventry. George Stephenson had, a little prior to this, been engaged by the parties who had chosen the Coventry line for the Railway, and as he also gave his opinion in favour of that route, it was finally decided that the London and Birmingham Railway should go via Coventry, and George Stephenson and his son were appointed engineers to the now united 'London and Birmingham Railway Company.'

The country between London and Birming-ham is a series of basins separated from each other by ridges of hills; the object to be gained was, therefore, to cross the valleys at as high a point as possible, and the hills at as low as one.

The low districts are the London basin—the valley of the Colne, extending from Brentford by Watford, to St. Alban's,—the lowland in the neighbourhood of Leighton Buzzard, on the Stoke Bruern,—the valley of the Nene, in which is Northampton,—and the basin of the Avon; which last, from its great depth, low level, and abrupt termination on the south, by the high ridge of hills on which Daventry, Kilsby, and Crick are situated, and on the north side by the Meriden ridge, required particular attention.

The high grounds which bound these districts are the county boundary between the London basin and valley of the Colne,—the Chalk ridge, at Ivinghoe, which rises between the Colne valley and the Leighton Buzzard district,—the Blisworth ridge, —and the Kilsby and Meriden ridges, forming the abrupt sides of the valley of the Avon.

No private bill was more strictly scrutinised than that of the London and Birmingham Railway; the opposition to it being confined more to the cross examination of the witnesses in its favour than in producing any direct evidence against it, which would have been rather a difficult task. There was not a single fact proved against, while its advocates clearly established in its support the following important points,—viz., that the exporting of goods suffered material loss and great inconvenience by the present slow mode of traffic,—that goods for the Baltic trade were often delayed by the frost for the whole winter, through a very short delay in shipping them,—that considerable orders were frequently lost from the impossibility of completing them in time,— that in fancy articles it is almost indispensable, orders being frequently sent subject to the condition of their being shipped in a particular vessel,—that returns of money were sometimes made in eighteen months instead of nine, through this delay in the shipment of the goods ordered,—that farmers would be able to send to London a different kind of produce altogether, better, particularly lambs, calves, dairy produce, &c., saving also a great expense in their carriage;—besides which, cattle driven till their feet were sore, and could go no further, were sold on the road for what they would fetch.

At about eleven and a half miles from the Euston Station, and immediately on the other side of the bridge which carries the road from

... farmers would be able to send to London better produce ...

Harrow to Harrow Weald over the Railway, we reach the HARROW STATION, being the first from London. Stations are classified into two kinds: the first class and mail trains stopping for passengers only at certain stations, called principal stations; whilst the second class, or mixed trains, take up and set down passengers at all the stations. Further along we enter the excavation through the first ridge which this Railway crosses; it varies from thirty to forty feet deep, and is composed of plastic clay and sand, in some parts very loose. There are two or three bridges in this cutting which present a bold appearance, and are elegant in their proportions; that, for instance which conveys Oxhey-lane over the Railway is formed of three fine segmental arches, the centre one springing from two very lofty piers at an elevation of twenty-five feet, and the two side arches abutting upon the slopes of the excavation; the parapets are about thirty-five feet above the level of the Railway, and the whole is composed of brickwork of a very superior description.

The trains as they pass through this bridge present a remarkably picturesque object. It was originally intended to have had a short tunnel through this ridge, but the soil was found of such a nature that a saving of expense was effected in adopting an open cutting. From the summit of the ridge a most extensive and delightful view is obtained of the surrounding country, more especially in the direction of Watford and the valley of the Colne, in which the course of the Railway may be traced for several miles in advance, and being on a curve, the trains are seen winding along for some time before they approach this spot.

The soil from this excavation amounted to about 372,000 cubic yards, and was conveyed partly to a spoil bank, and partly to form an embankment towards the town of Watford, of about three quarters of a mile long. Soon after entering upon it the Railway goes over the London road, by a brick viaduct of five arches, of forty-three feet span each; the centre arch is of an oblique form, in order that the course of the road should be preserved. The other arches are square with the line of the Railway; and at either end are retaining walls built into the embankment, making the total length of the viaduct three hundred and seventy feet.

The next bridge conveys the Railway over the river Colne. It consists of five semicircular brick arches, of thirty feet span each, with side walls, and having a stone cornice its whole length, the total length of the parapet walls being 312 feet. It has a light appearance; and viewed from the meadows appears very lofty, being fifty feet high. The construction of the bridge was a work of considerable skill and labour, the foundations being of the loosest material possible; in fact, almost a floating bridge, resting entirely on platforms of wood, having sheet piling to protect them. The cost of its construction was little less than £10,000.

The whole of the land in this spot is most precarious in stability; and the effects are clearly visible in the amazing 'slips' which have taken place in the embankment across the valley. Oftentimes, in a very few hours, the level of the newly-formed ground has sunk several feet, while the base of the embankment has widened out to an enormous extent, causing infinite labour to bring the level of the Railway back again to its original state, and to make it

solid enough for the passage of the trains. The length of this embankment is about a mile and a half, and is composed entirely of the finest materials for such a purpose, chalk and gravel.

On arrival at a very elegant skew bridge, which carries the road from Watford to St. Albans over the Railway, and at about seventeen miles and a half from London, we enter the WATFORD STATION: and here, every arrangement is made for the comfort and convenience of passengers. The first and second class waiting rooms are very commodious, and so is the departure yard, sheltered from rain by an elegant corrugated iron roof.

This is the first principal station, and where the engineers supply their tenders with water after leaving London; for which purpose a ten-horse steam engine is provided with suitable pumps and machinery. There is also an engine house for locomotives, and a carriage shed; in fact the arrangements of the whole are of the most perfect description, and no expense appears to have been spared in their construction. The entrance of the Watford Tunnel is composed of an arch, nearly semicircular, twenty-five feet high and twenty-four feet wide, with retaining walls on either side, extending to the slopes of the cutting; a blocking and cornice runs through the whole length of the front, and the arch is surmounted by a pediment.

In passing through the tunnel travellers will not fail to observe a wide opening or shaft formed through an accident which occurred here during the formation of the tunnel. At this spot one of the six working shafts was sunk, of about eight or nine feet diameter, and it had been nearly finished, when the whole mass of soil surrounding it gave way, com-

Man and dog by the trackside have no part to play in the running of the railway—that is left to the railway policemen, one of whom is standing by the steps from the station, and another person is at the top of the steps.

Just beyond, in front of the engine house another of the staff is awaiting the coming of a train and is perhaps getting ready to replenish the water in its tender.

From this small nucleus of engine and carriage shed and works spread, in future North Watford, an extensive 'railway-workers' community.

From this, and their Unions work, came many of the towns councillors, Mayors and a Freeman.

Here the bridge carries the rustic road from Watford Hamlet to St Albans, and was later to prove a danger spot not removed until 1962/3. See p298.

At every three miles will be observed a policeman . . .

pletely burying ten men who were at work below. They were engaged in fixing on of the iron rings, built into the top of the tunnel to support the brickwork of this shaft, and not one was spared to tell the tale. So swift was the accident, that one poor fellow was found, three weeks afterwards, standing perfectly upright, with his trowel in his hand. It was nearly a month before the soil that had given way around the shaft could be cleared out; when the opening was found to be so extensive, and the material so loose, that the idea of making a large ventilating shaft at once occurred.

At every three miles will be observed a policeman and each man has his beat and duties defined, and is provided with two signal flags, one of which is red and the other white; the white flag is held out when no obstruction exists; and the red flag indicates that there is danger, and that the train must not pass the signal till it is ascertained that the cause of danger is removed.

Each policeman, also, is furnished with a revolving lamp, to be used after dark, which shows, at the will of the holder, a white light when the line is clear, a green one when it is necessary to use caution, and the speed of the train to be

diminished; and a red light, to intimate the necessity of immediately stopping. The whole of the police department is under the able control and superintendence of Captain C. R Moorsam, RN. It is but justice to add that the police arrangements on the London and Birmingham Railway are more complete than on any other line.

Every station is furnished with an alarum, to give notice of the approach of each train, and to summon the whole of the men to their appointed places. These alarums are so con-

structed, that a weight is wound up after they have performed their office. On seeing the forthcoming train has reached the proper spot, the policeman stationed at them pulls a trigger, and the weight begins to descend, ringing a loud gong shaped bell by means of internal machinery. Bells are also hung so as, in a few seconds, to collect together the whole of the men belonging to the station for any required purpose.

Roscoe,
The London and Birmingham Railway. c1840

Above: *Looking towards Watford station from the tunnel; two main lines are provided, with a siding on either side. The building with the tall chimney is the engine-house which is used to pump water into the locomotive's tender.*

The station proper lies beyond the engine-house and the waiting room for it may be seen in front of the clump of trees. This part of the early Watford Station still exists and is listed Grade II. It forms part of a used-car lot which lies on the left-hand side of St Albans Road just past the bridge.

Left: *A Railway Policeman stands at the Watford end of railway line over the Bushey Arches and in the distance is the bridge carrying Oxhey Road over the railway.*

The railway 'intersected the houses at the eastern end of the town'; in the vale on the left—which gave name to Vale Stores, Grocers and Ironmongers, at 30 Chalk Hill—one road became Chalk Hill and the other, slightly higher, and beyond, Pinner Road. Nearby was situated the Watford Gas and Coke Company.

A Water Supply

Prior to the early part of the present century the quantity of water obtainable at Watford for domestic purposes was small and of very doubtful purity. The supply was obtained from two or three wells, and the River Colne. One of these wells was close to the old churchyard, and another very near to an old-established slaughter house. Men, and even women, might be seen with yokes and pails, fetching water from the Colne at the bottom of Water Lane, and not infrequently this heavy work was assigned to children.

A circular, of which the following is a copy, was issued on the 26th May, 1819, showing that a committee of the inhabitants had been formed for the purpose of erecting a public pump in the High Street —

VESTRY ROOM, WATFORD,
May 26th, 1819.

At a meeting of the subscribers to the fund for sinking a well and putting down an engine for public use, convened by notice given in the church on Sunday last, to examine the treasurer's accounts, it appears that the total amount of subscriptions is £312 16s., and the total amount of expenditure is £310 19s. 1d., leaving a balance in the hands of the treasurer of £1 16s. 11d., which accounts have been examined and approved.

It was resolved that it will be expedient to raise a fund to keep the engine in repair, and that the amount thereof be placed in the Watford Savings Bank.

Henry William's "History of Watford", 1884

● *The well was built and the old pump (engine) stood in the market place until the formation of the Local Board (1850) when it was later removed, having become much dilapidated from constant use, and a drinking fountain, purchased by subscription, raised on the site. (It was 'an unsightly piece of architecture' and soon removed). The pump had been used to draw water to fight a fire (c1828) in a candle-maker's shop next to the 'King's Head' when fat used in candle-making boiled over, destroying the house and the 'King's Head' and later (1853) in an attempt to save the Market Hall from being destroyed by fire.*

The well was forgotten until 1931 when it was rediscovered by workmen digging a trench for Post Office telephone works.

Discovered in Market Place

Brick-lined and four or five feet across, the well had a depth to the water-line of about 75 feet. There was about ten feet of water at the bottom. Apparently, when the well was built-in the brickwork was dome-shaped at the top, the top of the dome being only 12 inches below the street level.

For years this brickwork, under the thin layer of cobble and concrete, has withstood the weight of the market stalls and the cattle in the old days, political and religious meetings, and in more recent times the cars and lorries that have been parked above it.

WO (May, 1931)

Henry Williams

To Richard Williams, Beadle at the Parish Church, and his wife, was born a son, on 17th August, 1828. He was named Henry. Henry become Sanitary Inspector, Inspector of Nuisances, and author of the 'History of Watford' (1884).

Correctly, Watford Bridge, more commonly Five Arches—the bathers seem to be taking little notice of the modern wonder of their age though the railway has not long opened.

In 1848–the workhouse was transferred from Church Street to the now Vicarage Road. A small barracks-like building in the form of a square with a courtyard in the centre the rear looked out towards the Bushey Arches.

There were no houses in-between and the workhouse inmates passed time carving drawings of the trains they saw high on the embankment.

Later, their drawings were interspersed with names and dates of those who had died, mostly 1858—the date of the opening of the new burial ground.

Many names still exist; the drawings harder to find. See p336.

Part II   Cholera and the Board of Health

In Clutterbuck's county history the population for Watford in 1801 is given as 'Watford Town' 3,530; which includes Leavesden, Oxhey and Cassio Hamlets. In 1841 the Town Hamlet is recorded as 3,697. The London Gazette, of 21st October 1831, published details of precautions to be adopted to counter the Asiatic Cholera which had spread from Moscow to Hamburg. A Board of Health was to be set up in every town, of magistrates, clergy and the medical profession, to confer with the Board in London on the best methods of insuring cleanliness and free ventilation, etc, to be carried out.

The quarantine laws were evaded and a carrier landed at Sunderland where the disease took hold, after an initial attack dying down, returning in spring of 1832 with vigour through northern towns and attacking London. After three month's abeyance it returned again at the end of summer and then again abated. Believed to have started in Hindustan the epidemic spread through Europe and across the Atlantic to Canada and the United States thus encircling the globe. A report in 1842 acknowledged a grim state of affairs nationwide; without 'local government' there could be no improvement in conditions, and many land-owners would be against such improvements, believing they would be involved in heavy expense and increased rates.

No Board of Health was set up in Watford.

The epidemic passed the town by until, in 1848, a renewed threat spurred the Vestry to action—and they finally asked the Board of Health for advice. The request was timely, for 1849 saw countrywide outbreaks. In London it climaxed in the first week of September claiming 12,847 victims. By this time, added to by the growth occasioned by the railway, Watford was 'tired' and very dirty—perfect conditions in which the disease could take root.

Enquiry into the state of drainage

At a Vestry held on the 6th of October 1848 it was moved by Mr. Moore, and seconded by Mr. Vaughan, that a Committee be appointed forthwith to inquire into the defective state of the drainage of this parish, and the various nuisances which exist in it, and to report the same at the next Vestry. A Committee was accordingly appointed, consisting of the following gentlemen:—
R Clutterbuck, Esq., Mr. Young, Mr. F. Dyson, Mr. Lavender, Mr. C. Lewin, Mr. Capell, Mr. Catlin, Mr. Chater, The Surveyors, ex-officio.

They reported:

"The Committee appointed to inquire into the defective state of the drainage of the parish, and the various nuisances which exist in it, proceeded on the 9th instant to inspect the sanitary condition of the town. After a careful examination of the present drainage in

the main street, and the various courts and alleys leading into it, they have to report that they found both in a very unsatisfactory condition.

In a large proportion of the yards, the privies and pigsties are most offensive; whilst the open cesspools and manure heaps, loaded with decaying vegetable and animal matter, infected the atmosphere to such an extent as to be in many cases almost intolerable, and do more than justify the very general complaint made by the inhabitants of the prejudicial effect of these accumulated nuisances on their comfort and general health. The few drains carried under ground in the main street were choked at the gratings and gully-holes, and in a very filthy condition. The Committee would particularly call the attention of the Vestry to a cesspool placed in the footpath in the High-street, which receives the drainage from Wells'-yard: it is in a very filthy state, and covered with wooden flaps which are not airtight.

With regard to the condition of the courts and alleys it is noted that the houses they contain have, with hardly an exception, no means of disposing of the refuse matter, whether liquid or solid, except by throwing it either into open cesspools, on the manure heaps, or at once into the surface-drains, which lead into the open side-channels in the main street. So long as no efficient means are taken to remedy these serious defects, accumulations of filth and manure are indispensable evils. These various receptacles may in future be emptied more frequently, at more regular intervals, but under existing arrangements the accumulation of the nuisances described cannot possibly be entirely obviated. The Old Yard may be quoted as an instance of the injurious effect of an open cesspool, from which the inhabitants suffer severely. The cottages there command an increased rent in proportion as they are removed from the cesspool; that nearest pays 1s. 6d. per week, the next 2s., and those beyond 2s. 6d. In conclusion, the Committee beg to remark that the sanitary condition of the town, as detailed in this Report, appears to be so unsatisfactory as to have demanded immediate attention under ordinary circumstances. But at this moment, when the cholera is almost at our own doors, they would impress upon the attention of the rate-payers that they are now especially called upon to act cordially together, not merely for the purpose of abating existing nuisances, but to devise and adopt without delay such measures as may secure the permanent improvement of the town, and thus advance the real interests of its inhabitants.
Robert Clutterbuck, Thomas Young, James Capell, C. W Moore, F. Dyson, Thomas Lavender, John Sedgwick Hon. Sec."

Moved by Mr. Cotton, and seconded by Mr. Vaughan,—That the above Report be adopted, and entered upon the minutes of the Vestry.
Agreed to *nem. con.*

Moved by Mr Clutterbuck, seconded by Mr Sedgwick, and carried unanimously,—

"That the Report presented this day to the Vestry be printed and a copy sent to every rate-payer of the town and Cashio hamlet; and that at the same time notice be given that a vestry meeting will be held on the 3rd November next, at 11 o'clock in the forenoon, for the purposes of taking into consideration what measures may be desirable to adopt for the purpose of improving the present imperfect drainage of the town."

… the government, if such it can be called, is miserably unfit for the wants of the town.

The Vestry acted with commendable speed, if not fright. The General Board of Health responded with equal promptitude by sending Inspector Thomas Clark to prepare a report. In this he was willingly assisted by the parish officers and surveyors and the report, complete with four maps, was presented to the general Board of Health. A copy exists in the Watford Public Library's reference room and the report is here in an abridged form but with the complete summary.

The map which follows *(page 49)* has the main street redrawn on a larger scale and is annotated to name the main houses and courtyards of that date.

The original was compiled from the Parish Maps by Surveyor C. F. Humbert.

Public Health Act

Report to the General Board of Health, on a Preliminary Inquiry into the Sewerage, Drainage, and Supply of Water, and the Sanitary Condition of the Inhabitants of the Town of WATFORD.
By GEORGE THOMAS CLARK, Superintending Inspector, 1849.

MY LORDS AND GENTLEMEN,
London. 25th April 1849
In obedience to your instructions I proceeded, on the 26th of February last, to inspect the town hamlet of Watford, and so much of the contiguous district as it seemed necessary to include within one administrative area. I held public sittings at the Rose and Crown Inn, on the mornings of the 26th and 27th, and employed the rest of those days and the 28th in carrying on the inquiry, and in framing this Report.

Although the petition proceeded only from the town hamlet, which forms, though by much the chief part, yet but a part of the town of Watford, I found it necessary to include the whole town in my examination.

Watford is composed of a principal street, about 1½ mile long, built along a sort of ridge sloping southwards to the river. On either side, and communicating with this street, are numerous courts and alleys, composed of small tenements, in which the bulk of the population is lodged. There are scarcely any cross streets, and the town is nowhere above 440 yards, and seldom above 200 yards broad. The London and Birmingham Railway passes about a mile from the top of the town. About the station, and along the road leading to it from Watford, houses have recently been built.

GOVERNMENT—Watford has grown up gradually into a town, and still retains its old village and manorial institutions. The parish is composed of the hamlets of Watford Town, (the hamlet petitioning), Cashio, Oxhey, and Leavesden, the three former of which enter into the composition of the town, of which, however, the first constitutes by much the chief part. The northern extremity of the town, in Cashio, is known as Nascott. The lord of the manor levies market tolls, and holds manor courts. The rate-payers in vestry annually elect parish officers, including two surveyors of highways, for the town hamlet, and one for each of the other hamlets, five in all; they also elect inspectors under the General Gas Act. The above government, if such it can be called, is miserably unfit for the wants of the town.

The expenditure is in consequence high in proportion to the quantity or quality of the work done. Persons ignorant of road-making are appointed surveyors of highways, and there is fostered a strong party spirit fatal to all improvement.

MORTALITY. – Mr. Ward, surgeon to the Union, produced a list of 62 fever cases attended by him in the town between April, 1848, and February, 1849. Out of these there were 13 deaths; 23, or above 37 per cent of the cases were children, of whom 8, or nearly 35 per cent. of those attacked died. It appears from a statement from the Registrar-General, that the current mortality of Watford is 23.33 in the 1,000; that of the surrounding rural districts being 20 in the 1,000. Here I may quote an extract from a Report made to the Board of Guardians by the Messrs. Pidcock, as medical officers to the Union, in 1838, upon the state of Watford, and which has been put into my hands by Mr. Clutterbuck—

"The most unhealthy localities in the town are found to be Meeting-alley, Dyson's (now Ballard's) buildings, Red Lion; Chequers, and Old-yards. The confined position of the former, and the open drains and deposit of ordure in the latter, at once account for this unhealthy condition. Few dwellings in these yards have escaped the visitation of disease and but few of the inhabitants of them can be said ever to enjoy robust health. Those yards, which have blind extremities, such as Dyson's, are in the worst condition; having no thoroughfares, little publicity is given to the habits of the cottagers, and thus a principal stimulus to cleanliness is wanting."

This was in 1838, and it will be seen that the 10 or 11 years which have elapsed have produced no improvement, nor indeed, under the existing system of government by vestry officers, is any likely to be produced. Around the

The Parish Church, St Mary's, c1851.
On the previous page the church is shown in its setting of houses fronting it and abutting the street. That drawing, by Buckler, is a companion to that of the Market Hall, next page.

Market-place, the oldest part of the town, the nuisances are very numerous.

In the words of the Report (already cited), as applied to the town generally, *"the privies and pigsties are most offensive, whilst the open cesspools and manure heaps, loaded with decaying vegetable and animal matter, infected the atmosphere to such an extent as to be in many cases almost intolerable, and do more than justify the very general complaints made by the inhabitants of the prejudicial effect of these accumulated nuisances on their comforts and general health."*

Ballard's-buildings, otherwise in a credible state, has a very narrow passage on its south side, blocked with privies, open cesspools, and night soil, upon an unpaved surface. On the north side of the churchyard, a block of poor houses is closely shut up between the church-yard and the narrow street with no back yard or privvies whatever. Close by, against the churchyard wall, is a heap upon which the refuse of these houses is thrown.

Meeting-House-Alley, a place in which the fever cases are very numerous, form a cluster of houses set close together, badly built, and approached through very narrow passages. The privies are very offensive, and in one part is a slaughter-house. At the back of these is Grove-circus, the refuse from which is led through iron piping under the road in front of the houses into an open stagnant ditch, running alongside a thoroughfare which is much frequented. In Chequer's-yard are three houses, without a privy, and with an open dung-heap and a slaughter-house.

At the Post-office, a newly-erected building, the garden slopes towards and drains upon the house. The drainage of the back yard

is led into the street by an iron pipe, laid between the ceiling of the kitchen and the floor of the room above. In this house last year seven children were all attacked with fever, and three died. Mr. Smith, surgeon, states, *"I am of opinion the disease was produced and the symptoms rendered more severe in consequence of bad drainage; so that the filth was coming into the cellar through the wall".*

Red Lion-yard, Boot and Pump-yard (both fever localities), and Water-lane, contain pigsties, dung-heaps, privies, overflowing cesspools, dirty gardens, and badly paved passages. Since this Report was drawn up the following extract from the district medical-relief-book has been transmitted to me: *"There have been four cases of fever at Brown's, in the Red Lion-yard and two have died. The drainage is most defective, and cannot be otherwise than extremely prejudicial to the health of the inhabitants residing in the cottages in the neighbourhood".*

Thos A. WARD
.

At the lower end of the town the main street is crossed by the tail-race of the Town-mill, and afterwards by the main stream of the Colne.

The land on each of these water-courses, including the island between them, is very low and swampy, and though thickly built over, utterly undrained. On the island may be mentioned the Old Tan-yard, is occasionally flooded. Old-yard lies near the Colne. Here a cesspool in the corner, though much improved, is still a considerable nuisance.

Fever was recently prevalent here.

WATER SUPPLY. – Watford is supplied with water chiefly from wells worked with buckets, varying from 10 to 60 feet deep. There is a

public well in the main street fitted with Braithwaite's pump. Samples of this water shewed 60° of hardness, and of another well 26½°. Besides these waters, which are much too hard to be used for washing, rain water is largely collected from the roofs, and stored in butts and tanks or pans. It appears that the rain water storage of a cottage lasts from one to three weeks, seldom longer.

When the butts run dry, the people either purchase water from a neighbour, or fetch it from the river. In the former case the price is about 1d. for seven gallons, in the latter it varies according to the distance, but is not less than 1d. per week on an average per family of those using it. The consumption of soap and soda is unusually great, 6d. or 7d. per week does not appear an extraordinary payment per family for these articles, and it is stated by several poor persons engaged in washing that the use even of river water adds about one-fourth to their consumption as compared with rain water. In rainy weather, when the waters of the Colne, though turbid, are much softer, the water is not needed by the people.

Sir James M'Adam, in a report upon the main road or street of Watford, in 1843, comments upon the want of system in proceedings of the way-wardens:—"The paved water channels in many parts being higher than the centre of the turnpike-road, and the outer paving-stone, forming a shoulder, so as effectually to prevent the surface water finding its way into the water channel."

In 1845, upon the renewal of the Sparrow's-Herne Turnpike Trust, £400 was laid out upon the turnpike-road in the town, under Sir. James M'Adam. The road was left in good repair, and a comparatively small sum judi-

The flagstone pavement is cleared but the roadway is of rutted snow; Mr Buckler, in 1832, had to be up early on a cold, but bright, morning to draw this view. On from the view on page 21 the 'Spread Eagle' sports a sign and the hamlet has a pump in front of the Market Hall. As a sign of the times there is protest at parking coach and wagon wheels on the pavements by the fitting of boundary posts. On market days there would have been childish delight for youngsters to gather and note the bustle of the market; but not for the youngsters employed six days a week at the silk mill . . .

Although later in the century (c1900), as evidenced by the telegraph poles, the unmade road is timeless of earlier days. 'Old Ricky Road' is one of Watford's main arteries and, apart from pavements and lighting, in 2003 is little changed–except for the modern traffic. This is just past where the Park Gates were and looking towards Shepherd's Lodge (now Shepherd's Road, and the Boys' Grammar School).

Insets: Cassio-bridge Lodge in Gade Avenue (1986) and road works putting a throttle upon evening traffic (November 1992).

ciously spent from time to time, would have sufficed to keep it so.

The road has, however, been neglected, and has now fallen into nearly the same condition as that described by Sir James five years ago. It was pointed out to me that the highway in front of the surveyors' houses was in far better order than elsewhere, and it seems to be admitted on all hands that this was a sort of legitimate perquisite of office.

The report went on, at length, to describe the high cost of gas—there being no competition—the nuisances of slaughter yards and the practice of killing pigs in their styes—the lack drainage of the marshy land, and above all, lack of fresh water.

SUMMARY. – In conclusion I have to state,–

1. That it appears by the appended statement of the Vestry Committee, as well as from what is advanced in this Report, that the town of Watford is in a very filthy condition indeed; and that existing arrangements are quite insufficient to remedy the evils.

2. That the mortality of the town is considerably above that of the surrounding district, that epidemics and febrile diseases have recently prevailed extensively in the worst drained and filthiest quarters; and that such diseases are mainly attributable to a want of drainage and of the means of cleanliness.

3. That cottage property in the town has suffered depreciation in great part from the want of proper drainage; that the highway rates are high, and the roads ill kept, and that

the direct expenses incurred by the poor in the use of hard water, or the purchase of soft water, far exceed the whole probable cost of the remedies.

4. That the requisite remedies, that is to say, a proper water supply and drainage, the removal and filling up of all cesspools, and the construction of a proper surface in the courts, can be supplied for a very moderate expense, or for a general rate of 13d. in the pound, and a special private improvement rate upon cottage property, according to its need of the remedies.

5. That the proposed rates will be in reduction of existing charges.

6. That the circumstances of the town admit of its sewage being employed profitably as a source of revenue, under the form of fluid manure, and that, with this view, it is desirable that special powers should be given to commence the application of it upon the common lands below the town upon the river.

7. That in the case of Watford, it is in a peculiar degree essential to the cheap and effectual execution of the sanitary works recommended, that the General Board should be fully convinced that the plans finally agreed upon provide for the complete removal of the evils, that they are extended over the whole of the town, and that they embody all the various improvements and economies in house drainage which are now carrying out by the Metropolitan Board of Sewers.

GEO T CLARK.
The General Board of Health

To be disposed of by Tender,

THE LEASE AND FIXTURES OF

Bushey Mills,

WATFORD, HERTS.

30 Years of the Lease to come from Michaelmas day next, at a low Rent, at which Time it may be entered upon, the proposals to be delivered Sealed up to MR. STEVENS, on the premises, on or before the 28th; day of July next, where Letters directed Post paid, or any application made, further information will be given: and no proposals will be attended to which are offered after 12 o'Clock, on the above day.

The above named Mills are exceeding advantageously and pleasantly situated, 14 Miles from London, 2 from the Navigation, and only a few Miles from several respectable Market Towns; the Mills now consists of a one Vat paper Mill, with all its gear-work, Presses, Engine, and all other requisites for making paper.

Also a Corn Mill with two pair of Stones, 4 dressing Mills, and other tackling will be included in the above disposal, both Mills are worked on the same head, and capable of great improvement, having a strong stream of water equal to drive two powerful Wheels, carrying 6 Engines or 6 pair of Stones, and at no time of the Year is short of water, and near 7 Feet fall; the whole may be converted into a Paper or Corn Mill as may be required: in addition to which there is a Beautiful spring of clear water which produces the finest colours.

A modern built House, a large Barn, Stable and sundry other out-buildings, a Pleasure ground and Kitchen garden well stocked with Fruit Trees, and upwards of Eleven Acres of meadow Land, with the right of Fishing belonging to the said Mills·

*** ROUGH TIMBER FOR REPAIRS WILL BE FOUND.

The Term will be extended to 60, Years if required, the Lessee finding their own materials for building.

N.B. The parlour has got a door

Seale and Bates, Printers, 160, Tottenham Court Road

Population
At the time of the opening of the London and Birmingham Railway, Watford's population was around 2000. 18 years later in 1855, it had grown to 3800. By comparison: (1855)

Bushey	2675
St. Albans	7000
Kings Langley	1600
Berkhamsted	2943
Tring	3218
Aylesbury	5700

Just one year after the railway had opened, and more than thirty since the opening of the canal, Bushey Mills are up for sale.

When the mills went out of use the name was perpetuated in our locality with 'Bushey Mill Lane'. The land is still farm land though cut in two by the M1 Link Road which extends from Berry Grove to Watford's one-way ring road, and the Lower High Street.

Note the sales-message footnote of "The parlour has got a door."

Here for the ale and beer . . .

The Celts are usually accorded blame for introducing Iron Age man to real ale, with the Germans adding bitter hops in the 16th century. For two thousand years man diligently perfected the art of brewing in the home. By the seventeenth century many innkeepers had set up their own operation on the premises for direct sale. The earliest known large scale common brewer selling to other public houses in Watford, was Nicholas Colbourne (died 1630). His nephew continued until 1662. The first John Dyson was the grandson of a miller-baker, John Pope, who brewed in Pope's Yard (later Dyson's Yard and later Ballard's Buildings, now Church car park) from 1715 to 1722. Sarah Pope, widowed, continued until 1749 when John Dyson took over. The second John Dyson bought a mansion with attached grounds at 194 High Street; and moved his brewery behind it in 1812. The house had been built by a Londoner, Edward Dawson, for his wife, in 1775. The third John Dyson extended the brewery and by his time the family owned or rented a large number of pubs in the district. This last John Dyson was a bachelor and his executors sold the brewery, by then Cannon Brewery, to Joseph Benskin, a retired London publican in partnership with Mr. Bradley, a Watford draper, in 1867.

Later, Bradley dropped out; and after Joseph's death his widow carried on. Later still Benskin's became a limited company, and at the turn of the century rebuilt their premises on a more grand scale. In 1897 Benskin's bought Groome's of Kings Langley, in 1898 they bought Healey's and in 1923 they bought their long-time rival, Sedgwick's. In 1957 they were themselves bought by Ind Coope, and they in turn were part of Allied Lyons by 1963.

Samuel Smith, miller at the Grove, in partnership with Robert Shackell, a distiller, bought a disused malthouse and yard at 223 Watford High Street in 1753. Here he started brewing and began to buy up pubs in the district as outlets. When he died his son William continued, but sold out to George Whittingstall, son of a Hitchin miller, in 1790. On George's death in 1822 his brewery went to a cousin, Edmund Fearnley, a cattle dealer, who assumed the surname of Whittingstall. His son George sold the business in 1862 to W. F. Sedgwick of a local farming family. The brewery was now known as Watford Brewery with Robert Ashby as the manager until 1890 when he retired to be a developer of working class estates in Watford in 1927. Sedgwick's buildings were converted to maltings and demolished by 1966.

In 1763 Thomas Meadows, a Watford corn dealer, in partnership with Thomas Clutterbuck snr., land agent to the Earl of Essex, bought a small brewery on Stanmore Common. The business expanded under further Clutterbucks; and they had another brewhouse at Hunton Bridge. The business, with 83 pubs, was sold to Cannon Brewery, Clerkenwell, in 1923. and in 1930 merged with Taylor Walker. Ind Coope bought them in 1960. The old brewery still stands on Stanmore Hill.

By c1750 Stephen Salter was brewing in Rickmansworth to be followed by his nephew Samuel who died in 1829. Salter had a partner, Job Woodman, of Watford. Another partner, Thomas Fellowes, then ran the brewery with William Capel. It contin-

ued, as a public company, until 1924 when it and its 76 pubs were bought by Cannon of Clerkenwell. The Groome brewery in Kings Langley was started by the Goodwin family by 1720 and in 1768 passed to Thomas Groome. The brewery, with 32 pubs, was bought by Benskin's in 1897. A malting remains as a parish room.

Samuel Roate commenced brewing in about 1845 near Watford Station, at 147 St Albans Road, on the corner of the later Church Road. By 1874 Fred Cocks had the business, by then called Victoria Brewery. In 1891 Healey's bought it; brewing ceased. The house remains (as a shop) but the brewhouse has been demolished.

Joseph Healey, a Londoner was for many years the manager of Whittingstalls. His son George set up in Watford as a grocer and wine merchant; after acting as brewer's clerk to George Whittingstall it was his son Charles who bought the stable block of the former Watford Place estate in George Street and King Street; and converted it to a brewery in 1852. Colonel Charles Healey sold out to Benskin's in 1898 for a seat on the board. He was son of the founder, who died prematurely in 1863. As Colonel Charles was only seven at the time his mother ran the business, called King Street Brewery. The badge was a primrose.

Ralph Thorpe was a Lincolnshire farmer who settled in Watford in 1889. Buying land in St. Albans Road, he opened his brewery for business in 1890. In 1913 the brewery was greatly extended, with plant and methods the most up-to-date in the area. It was known as Wells Brewery because of the deep wells in the chalk subsoil, though with a trade mark of a red lion, it sometimes took the name of Red Lion Brewery. Ralph Thorpe had acquired 20 pubs by 1925 and, after his passing in 1929 the business continued until bought by Benskins in 1951. Benskins ceased brewing in Watford in 1969 (high costs and difficulty of road access being among the reasons given) though bottling carried on until final closure in 1972. Watford lost its reputation as a 'brewing' town, the processes perfected throughout the centuries, and the expertise acquired by generations of employees. This labour-intensive industry, like so many others, had become a victim of the age of rationalisation.

Edgar J Chapman, 1987 & 2003

Top: *Virtually the last of the Benskins buildings to be demolished, in 1983. The site, destined for housing, was instead used for the short-lived Watford Springs swimming complex. In 2003 the site is empty.*

The Local Board formed

Arising from the town's disquiet was the formation in 1850 of the Watford Local Board of Health, with Mr. C. W Moore elected as Chairman, a post he held for 22 years. The first rate raised, in July 1851, was of 6 pence in the pound. From being founded to deal with improvements to water supply and sanitary conditions, as well as paving, road-making and lighting the Local Board of Health was set upon a course to become the future local government

In 1854 the rate income of the Local Board of Health was £603. This was budgeted for in the following manner:

Clerk	£ 30
Surveyor and Inspector of Nuisances, and Collector	£100
Road Officer	£ 25
Rental of Board Room	£ 8
Stationery & adverts	£ 25
Labour for roads	£100
Material for roads	£100
Repairs of pavements	£ 25
Watering street	£ 50
Incidental expenses	£ 80

Rateable values:
Rookery Mill £288 10s. 0d.;
One Bell £ 13 0s. 0d.;
the Brewery £287 0s. 0d.;
Gas Light Co £100 0s. 0d.; and
the railway (for 1 mile 6 furlongs) £41 13s. 6d.

The report to the General Board of Health noted that "About the station, and along the road leading to it from Watford, houses have recently been built".

(The map produced, for the Board of Health report, extended to the station but was not included with the 'courtyard' depiction *(next page)* for to have done so would have rendered the scale too small to include the courtyard names *(as done for this book)*, and so is shown here separately.)

"Beyond the Station" was the first road and later took the name Bedford-street. Back-road was next and took the name Church-road when St Andrew's church rose in 1858. This 1849 map shows the nucleus of buildings along the road to St Albans and by this date a few pubs and a brewery are established. They are:
From the town the first is
The White Lion, *c1850*
Roate's Brewery, *c1850*
The Railway Arms, *on the right hand side of the road, 1839*
The Leviathan, *1839*
The Stag, *c1850*
The Queens Arms, *on the right hand side of the road, over the railway bridge, 1839 (No. 4 on the map)*
The Roate's Brewery was on the corner of Church-road/St Albans-road and ownership passed to a Mr Cocks in 1874 and the name changed to the Victoria Brewery, passing to Healey's in 1891 and later to Benskins.
There are no other roads, the fields still in cultivation and the boundary hedges indicated. These hedge-lines would, later, be taken for roads as was common practice. Age-old ditches provided ready-made drainage trenches.

Nascott Park is still intact—but for not much longer as Lord Essex would, in a few year's time, instruct Mr Humbert to sell for housing.

Already he has allowed building along the road to St Albans, and through the middle a boundary line crosses. This would become the future Langley-road, (1), on the one side, and Station-road on the other (5) *(when the station was moved in 1860)*; other future roads:

Park-road (2) and Alexandra-road (7); Stratford-road (first called Upper Nascot-road) (8); Church Road, established, (3); the Queen's Arms (4) (with the Leviathan and Stag opposite and further along); Station Hotel (6) (later renamed Clarendon Hotel when it, too, moved into Station-road). Adjacent to the hotel was a cattle-pound to which all strays would be taken. The footpath (9) is the line of the subsequent Leavesden-road. On the northern side of the railway, right-hand side of the road to St Albans, stands the Station Master's House, a building which stood until it fell into dereliction and was demolished c1985.

Local Board Road's water supply

Local Board Road gained its named by being host to the 'Local Board' (of Health) formed in 1850; prior to that date there was no local 'government' as such—the Board being founded to effect improvements in the town's water supply and sewage disposal and general cleanliness.

Offices were established in Local Board Road in 1854. The Board gave way to 'Urban District Council' in 1895. In 1891 the town's population numbered about 16,000 and, typically, eight or nine board members would attend to deal with the town's affairs.

Local Board Road is notable for housing the beam pump which first supplied Watford's water. (The Board meetings were held in one of the pump house upper rooms).

The supply was pumped from a depth of about 50 ft and carried the length of the High Street via a 6 inch main to a reservoir in what is now Stratford Road. All the courtyards off the High Street were supplied via 2 inch branches; a 6 inch branch supplied the church-yards and on to the Union House (Shrodells). By 1868 an additional 8 inch main was laid and this was in turn increased in 1881 to a 12 inch. Pumping operations were transferred to a new pumping station at Watford Fields c1915; the original pump house building remained and is now part of the 'Pump House Theatre.'

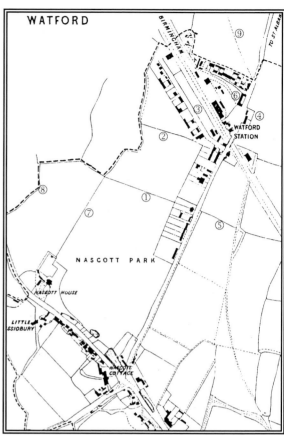

Above: *(see notes, left)*

Next page: *Watford Hamlet c1848. By this time the railway had been established some ten years or so and house construction in 'Nascot' area signalled the beginning of a population growth. Houses in the town were unnumbered, an exception being a handful of houses 'beyond the station'.*

The courtyards, by common usage, carried the names of the owner(s), frequently changing and leading to confusion. To overcome this problem Henry Williams, Sanitary Inspector, introduced 'Court Numbers'—with a blue and white enamelled plaque affixed to each courtyard entrance. Watford at this time was self-contained, both Water Lane and Loates Lane led across fields to Aldenham. A lane went to the Union House but there were no other roads in or out of the Hamlet excepting the two turnpike roads crossing at the top end. To provide a good supply of water to the mill the banks of the Colne were built up, and a straightened course of about one mile made, the work is attributed to 'the monks', for the natural meandering course of the river was further south.

The original map was drawn to accompany the Board of Health's Report; the annotations are modern; see page 58 for the courtyard list.

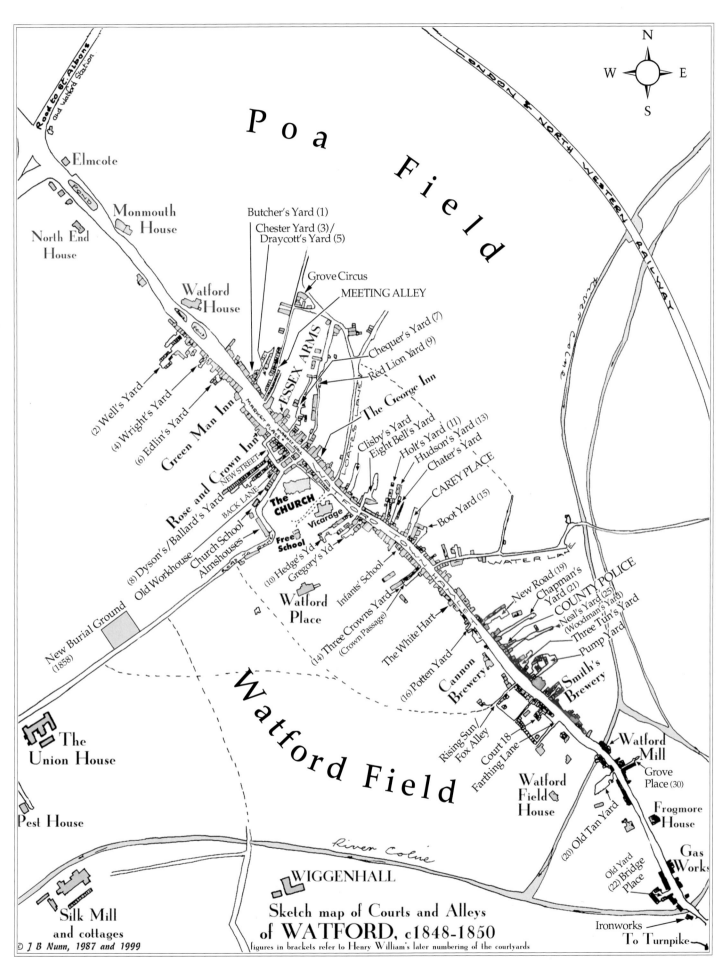

N
W   E
S

Poa Field

Elmcote

Road to St Albans

(to Watford Station)

Monmouth House

North End House

Watford House

Butcher's Yard (1)

Chester Yard (3)/
Draycott's Yard (5)

Grove Circus
MEETING ALLEY

Chequer's Yard (7)

Red Lion Yard (9)

ESSEX ARMS

The George Inn

(2) Well's Yard

(4) Wright's Yard

(6) Edlin's Yard

Green Man Inn

Clisby's Yard
Eight Bell's Yard

Holt's Yard (11)

Hudson's Yard (13)

Chater's Yard

CAREY PLACE

Rose and Crown Inn
NEW STREET

BACK LANE

The CHURCH

Vicarage

Free School

Boot Yard (15)

(8) Dyson's/Ballard's Yard

Old Workhouse
Church School
Almshouses

(10) Hedge's Yd
Gregory's Yd

Watford Place

Infants' School

New Road (19)
Chapman's Yard (21)

COUNTY POLICE

Neal's Yard (25)
(Woodman's Yard)

Three Tun's Yard

Pump Yard

New Burial Ground
(1858)

(14) Three Crowns Yard
(Crown Passage)

The White Hart

(16) Potten Yard

Cannon Brewery

Smith's Brewery

Watford Field

The Union House

Pest House

Rising Sun/
Fox Alley

Court 18
Farthing Lane

Watford Field House

(20) Old Tan Yard

Watford Mill

Grove Place (30)

Frogmore House

River Colne

WIGGENHALL

Old Yard
(22) Bridge Place

Gas Works

Silk Mill
and cottages

Ironworks

To Turnpike

© J B Nunn, 1987 and 1999

**Sketch map of Courts and Alleys
of WATFORD, c1848-1850**

figures in brackets refer to Henry William's later numbering of the courtyards

London & North Western Railway

Water Colne

WATER LANE

Watford's industrial age gathers pace . . .

The growth started by the railway, and the railway town growing up adjacent to the station, exerted pressure on the main street and the forty or so courtyards. The 'industrial age' started by the silk mill had tentacles in other directions. There were more people to feed and farm implements to be made and the smithies were a very active part of daily life as were leather tanners, meal-men and corn dealers.

Mr Tidcombe's iron works by the river at the far end, founded in 1827, won an important order to provide machinery for pumping water from the Board's first well; they earlier played a substantial part in construction of the Gas Works gasholder. Engineers and labourers built a reservoir in Stratford-road and laid water pipes through the street to it. Over the years the pipes were relaid and enlarged to cope with growing demand.

Streets were laid out on the Watford Place grounds and, gradually the new builders realise the opportunities; they would be active in a few years time and would need timber which Rogers' sawmills—started in 1777—near Meeting Alley would supply. At the other end, near the Station, Mr Tom Turner, having completed fourteen years of woodwork, blacksmith, wheelwright, etc on the Cassiobury Park, removed his business to Cassiobury Mills in 1876. (In doing so he established an 'industrial estate' which lasted 124 years until 1990).

The people who fuelled this growth were not local—the population growth could not have kept pace—and many were drawn from outlying districts and London. Watford was a 'new' manufacturing town without the disadvantages of the grimy northern industrial centres. The breweries were large employers of labour and their growth was owed to the purity of the water brought up from the brewer's wells. Not far distant were Mr Dickinson's Mills; paper at Croxley, Fine paper at Home Park and Pulp Board at Nash—they competed with the Railway for labour.

The streets were springing up across the parish; in pockets among the houses were large back-yards; builder's yards, coach-makers and the like soon filled them. The main street's courtyards and alleys survived the century and it was not until the early part of the 1900s that social conscience saw that most had lack of facilities causing them to be classed as slums and needing removal.

The Vestry, from looking after two or three thousand people to several times that number, had their capabilities overtaxed; they were outstripped by growth and were hard pushed to cope with the problem of providing decent pavements and roads. If they had problems so did elements of the populace who argued

Particulars and Conditions

OF

The Sale of Eligible

Business Premises,

IN THE HIGH STREET,

WATFORD, HERTS.

AT THE

ROSE & CROWN INN, WATFORD,

ON

Tuesday, the 21st day of January, 1851,

At 3 o'Clock, by

MR. HUMBERT,

Mr Henry Kingham was the highest bidder at the sale in the sum of one thousand one hundred and fifty pounds (£1,150). Philip Cowley Snr, and Charles Francis Humbert acted as agents for the vendor, on January 21st 1851. Elizabeth Kingham opened a small shop in the High Street c1790 dealing in provisions and groceries.

LOT 1. Comprises a most Commodious

SHOP AND DWELLING- HOUSE,

situate opposite the Market House, on the best side and in the best part of the main Street of Watford, Copyhold of the Manor of Watford, and subject to the customs thereof (the usual fine on death or alienation an heriot, which on the death of the present owner's Father was compounded for at £5. 5s. 0d.) and a Quit Rent of 7s. 4d.

WITH A LARGE GARDEN

a portion of which was granted to Joseph Rogers on the 10th of April 1844, by the Lord of the Manor of Watford, at a Quit Rent of 3d. per annum, upon condition that he his Heirs and Assigns, did within six Calendar months from that period, well and sufficiently enclose the same on the North West and North East sides, and within the same time make a proper and sufficient cesspool under or upon the said piece of ground, . . . thereafter keep the said cesspool in good repair, and sufficiently emptied and cleansed, this is not leased but is in the same occupation as the House and Premises, which are let under a Lease dated 24th June, 1831, and terminating the 24th of June, 1852, to Mr. William Phillips, Chemist and Druggist, (late Henson) a most desirable Tenant, at a

Rental of £73. 10s. 0d. Per Annum

for the whole, the Tenant is bound under the usual Covenants to sustain, uphold, support and keep in good repair the said Premises. The Premises including the Carriage Entrance, have a frontage of about 35 feet.

INVESTMENT OR FOR OCCUPATION

Her eldest son, Henry inherited the business in 1835. Note that the street is described on the document (left) as High Street but in the details (right) as 'the main Street of Watford. The 'best side' is that which is warmer from midday sun and the 'best part' is that almost opposite what is now St Mary's Square

that 'education in trades' should be denied to those most in need.

Back in 1851 Mr Humbert was selling a very desirable 'Copyhold' property in the centre of the town and, at the same time Watford Place estate was being cut up; a new road—the first ever off the High-street, King-street—was being laid out, and from it another road, Smith Street and yet another, George-street which went to link up with Church-street. On the corner of George and King-streets Charles Healey bought a site and founded a brewery.

'Copyholds' in the Manor of Watford were those properties once held by mediaeval villeins from the Abbey of St. Albans. In more modern times the Lord of the Manor was the Earl of Essex and his steward, a local solicitor; had to enter in the Manor Books all changes in copyhold ownership, whether caused by sale to another, death and inheritance, or regranting to the Lord if no heir was found. It was also possible for a copyholder to sell to somebody for a term of years only, at the end of which it would revert to the proper copyholder, in this case William Phillips, who wished to pass its ownership to someone else. Transactions of this nature needed a 'licence' from the steward and a 'fine' was payable. By the early 20th century, all copyholds were converted to freeholds, and are now registered with the National Land Registry.

Nine years later, 1860, stable yards next the 'Eight Bells' in the High-street became the entrance to Watford's next new road—Queen-street. Soon after, Mr Peacock removed his plant and office into No. 15 Queen-street from the premises which, lower down the High-street, had been demolished to make way for the station for the Rickmansworth branch line of the LNWR.

Ralph Thorpe came from Norfolk to Watford and started a brewery, in St Albans Road, in 1890; next door were Paget Prize Plates (photographic). In Callowland Dr Tibbles started a Cocoa and Chocolate factory in what became Sandown Road—another industrial estate of the future. In the late 1890s the foundations of Watford's print era of big league players were laid down by Andre and Sleigh in Hall-road, Bushey, and Waterlow's in Milton Street.

This diversity was to play a huge part in the War when it started in 1914; Watford was by now a growing manufacturing town and yet it had easy access to parkland—good for training troops—and access to a main railway line. Much later, Dr Tibble's factory—with new ideas in looking after employees' welfare—did not survive an economic disaster, and during the late 1930s part was turned into a Government Training Centre attracting to it potential trainees from all over the country, many of whom settled in Watford.

Tidcombe's iron foundry and works laid the foundation for a continued presence on the site for an engineering works, eventually as the Watford Engineering Works. Whether by association with the local mills or not the WEW were paper-makers' engineers specialising in paper strainers and in the background, right, is a large cylindrical strainer in final stages of construction or checking. This is c1900.

... two fire engines sent from Euston . . .

When the Market Hall Was Destroyed

On Thursday (last week) a fire broke out in the town of Watford, which reduced to a heap of ruins the old building used as the Corn Exchange and Market-house. On the alarm being given, it was recollected that about 23 years since, every house opposite the premises on fire was destroyed by a similar misfortune; and the Market-house was then partially destroyed.

The authorities, fearing the recurrence of a like calamity, and profiting by proximity to the L. and N.W. Railway, sent an electric telegraph message to London for the aid of the Fire Brigade engines. Two engines were, by order of Mr. Braidwood, the superintendent, despatched to Euston-square, for the purpose of proceeding by a special train to the scene of the conflagration.

Notwithstanding this precaution, at noon next day, the ruins were still emitting sheets of fire, and some hours elapsed before the fire was wholly extinguished. The damage done may be thus described: The Market-house burnt down; the contents, consisting of 90 quarters of wheat, 100 quarters of oats, and a considerable quantity of barley and other produce, destroyed. The premises of Mrs. Taylor, the 'King's Head' Hotel, much damaged by fire and water. 'The Spread Eagle', kept by Mr. Coulson, had the windows demolished and the shutters burnt. The premises of Mr. Hollingworth, a butcher, were also much burnt, as were those belonging to Mr. Brent, also a butcher and Mr. Flaxman, a corn-dealer. The origin of the fire is not precisely known, but there is strong ground for supposing that it was the work of incendiarism.

The sketch by Mr. Henshew from a window of the 'King's Head' Hotel, shows the Market-house, a low-pitched building of considerable age, now a mass of black ruins.

Illustrated London News, June 4th, 1853

More Details of the Fire

"This building, which was about 100ft. long by 24ft. wide, was built principally of wood, and had lofts and corn stores standing on numerous strong wooden columns about 18ins. or 2ft. square; it was open at the bottom, and round the columns were shambles and stalls, on which goods were exposed for sale at the annual fairs and on market days; corn was also pitched in the open space on market days.

Two or three days after one of the fairs the fire broke out, and it was thought a spark from one of the lights used at that fair having settled in some crevice, set the wood on fire, which smouldered until it burst into a flame.

The parish engine was brought round, and plenty of willing hands being present, it was speedily set to work, and water thrown onto the burning building but it was soon found that from the inflammable nature of the material of which the building was composed, it would be labour in vain to try to save it with the small quantity of water available, so attention was given to 'The Kings Head' public house and other houses on that side. Several times the window sashes caught fire, but were extinguished by the water thrown from the engine, which was worked willingly by the inhabitants in relays.

In the exigency, a number of men and lads were called together and placed at intervals from the Market House to a pump in the 'Essex Arms' Hotel yard, from which water was supplied and handed from one to the other in the parish leather buckets and several pails lent by the inhabitants, and the engine thereby kept at work. The Market House, left a prey to the fire, soon became a vast body of flame, and great was the excitement of the thousands of persons present when the bell-turret, with tinkling bell that had been rung at the opening of the corn market each week for years previously fell with a loud crash on the road. The Market House was entirely destroyed."

WHP (July, 1928)

Drawn by a correspondent of the 'Illustrated London News' the morning after the fire, the scene shows the chaos remaining at the end of a long tradition of the Town's Market Hall. Corn sales were later conducted a new 'Corn Exchange' next to the Essex Arms across the road. The bow-fronted window is of Henry Kingham's new shop, and the site now is of Pearl Assurance Chambers and shops under, Nos. 77 and 79. The same shop front is shown in a photograph in 1902, p110, but after the Great War Kingham's were in occupancy of buildings slightly further along the street, just past Red Lion Yard.

The inset shows a 'fire-engine' of the period; a manually-drawn hand-pump into which water is poured by buckets, with one or two men at each end of the handle pumping up and down.

... one hundred and fifty acres; Lord Essex has allowed it for building purposes ...

In February 1857 Mr Humbert awoke to a fright that the Watford Station was to be moved—to Bushey. He wrote a strong letter to the London and North Western Railway Company instancing that many important personages would have an extra three-quarters of a mile to travel, and that they would have to travel in their conveyances along the main street *'narrow, & much encumbered with vehicles'* and further *'there is a turnpike with a toll of 4d for a vehicle with single horse'*.

He instanced the Earl of Essex, the Earl of Clarendon, Lord Rokeby. Chas Pearser, Esq, George Roper, Esq and others.

He then went on to the main and most serious point: *"But Lord Essex is deeply interested in another respect—He is the owner in fee of the Nascott Estate, a fine tract of land comprising about one hundred & fifty acres, lying between the Railway & the high road to Hemel Hempstead, on which it has a frontage of about 1600 yards. Its nearest point to the Watford Station is 1/5 of a mile & its most distant is 1 mile.*

"Upon my strong recommendation Lord Essex has consented to allow me to dispose of this for building purposes, for which it is in all respects most eligible. I have made the ground plans & am about to lay out the streets with the view of immediately bringing the matter before the public. As there is ample space for some hundreds of good houses, I need hardly remark that the land is now very valuable; but if the Watford Station is moved as proposed I shall abandon the idea of selling it for building purposes. The nearest point to the Bushey Station being within a fraction of a mile & three quarters, whilst the

The new Watford Station, 1860

farthest is two miles & a half.

"If this is the only application made to the Board on the subject, I beg to assure you that the cause is that the landowners & residents have not thought seriously upon it, even if the report has reached them.

> *I have the honour to be Sir*
> *Your most obedient servant*
> *C F Humbert"*

He was, of course, quite mistaken. The intention was to move the station a mere 150 yards or so (to its present position) so that lines to St Albans, and Rickmansworth, were facilitated.

"The valley of the Colne from Bushey Mill to Hamper Mill is much flooded each year during the winter and spring months. A few years ago a sudden thaw, with rain, after a deep fall of snow, flooded the meadows, and before the water subsided a severe frost set in and a thick sheet of ice was formed all over them beyond the Loates Lane arch.

When the water went down, this sheet of ice was left on the grass, forming a splendid skating ground on which thousands indulged in the healthful pastime of skating; tents were erected in which ladies put on their skates and articles of dress were left.

Each night the ice was lit with torches, and the scene, as viewed from the banks of the railway, was very grand. This continued but a short time as the uneven nature of the ground under the ice caused it to crack and become dangerous ..."
Henry Williams, "History of Watford"

...a newspaper, and photography...

Watford's first recorded photographer was not, as may be imagined, Frederick Downer, but Henry Williams, of Hudson's yard, 1859-1864, and then of King-street, before passing the business on to a Mr Dixon. Hudson's Yard was a little to the north of Chater's Yard; a geographical location would be just about under Harlequin's food court and a little towards Trewins.

Frederick Downer started in 1861 a studio at the rear of his father's stationery shop at 97 High-street. He worked from the house near Loate's-lane where he had an outdoor studio. Photography was still very new and primitive to master.

John Peacock started a printing business in premises in Lower High-street, about where the station is. Queen-street was cut through from the main road in 1861 and shortly afterwards Mr Peacock moved the business to No. 15 Queen-street, four or five doors down from the cabbage patch upon which the library would be built and opened in 1874.

In 1863 John Peacock's eldest son, Samuel, decided that Watford needed a newspaper, and that he could provide it—and this duly happened. It was a four-pager, with three of the pages printed in London, and the remaining page being written, typeset and printed in his works. There was a wedding in the air—very eagerly awaited, a comprehensive programme was drawn up to give the schoolchildren a treat, though the distance they had to parade through the town meant they had to earn their tea and cake. Food parcels were distributed to the poor and of the day's events the Observer reported:

"The Marriage of the Prince of Wales, on March 10th, 1863, was celebrated at Windsor by order of the Queen, rather than at Westminster Abbey:

"The spring morning saw a warm sun shining on a town gay with bunting and flags. In 800 poor homes there was a festive dinner to be prepared by a special gift of meat and groceries. The children were washed and dressed and wearing red, white and blue rosettes and waiting impatiently. At half-past twelve the 'Smithies' cannonaded a Royal Salute from their anvils, followed by thundrous cheers from the crowd. At one o/clock the bells rang out their joyous peals. More than 1,100 schoolchildren assembled four abreast in the Market Place and proceeded to the Parish Church for a short service. Afterwards, they marched back to their respective schools where they were treated to a feast of tea and cakes. Several hundred children belonging to no school were separately entertained at the Corn Exchange. In the meantime there was a cricket match, games, races, rural sports, such as climbing the greasy pole for a pig and a leg of mutton, for their elders. In the evening, the Recreation Ground in Watford Fields was illuminated, a great fireworks display organised and the bonfire lit, traditional to

MARRIAGE OF HIS ROYAL HIGHNESS THE
PRINCE of WALES.
Watford, Tuesday March 10th, 1863.
PROGRAMME.

The CHILDREN of the various Schools will assemble at their respective School-rooms at 2 o'clock.

The MANAGERS of the different Schools will marshal the Children to the MARKET PLACE, opposite the Corn Exchange, at half-past 2 o'clock, where the General Committee will meet them.

The Children will then proceed into the CHURCH four a-breast, where a short Service will be held, and the NATIONAL ANTHEM sung. The Committee earnestly hope that no person will attempt to occupy a Seat in the Church till all the Children are accommodated.

At the conclusion of the Service the Children, attended by their Managers, will again form in the Market Place, and proceed 8 a-breast (headed by the RIFLE CORPS BAND, who have kindly offered their services,) to Mr. Rooper's, at Nascott, and then down the Town to the Railway Arch near Bushey Station, from thence returning to their respective School-rooms, where they will partake of TEA and CAKE.

All OTHER CHILDREN between the ages of 5 and 14 years, will assemble in the Corn Exchange, at 3 o'clock, and there receive Refreshments under the direction of Mr. Urlwin, and Mr. Wm. Rogers, who have kindly undertaken that duty.

Tickets for MEAT and GROCERY will be given to every deserving Poor Family, on Monday the 9th instant, at their own homes, by the following

DISTRICT COMMITTEES—viz:

Mr. MOORE, Dr. BRETT, Mr. W. ROGERS,	From Mr. Moore's House to Nascott, and outlying parts of Cashio Hamlet.	Mr. HUMBERT, " HUTTON, " ROATE, " LONG, — The St. Andrew's District.

WEST SIDE OF THE TOWN.		EAST SIDE OF THE TOWN.	
The Rev. R. LEE JAMES, Mr. J. SEDGWICK, " G. STONE, " CAMFIELD,	From Mr. Moore's House to The Church Gates.	Mr. J. A. SMITH, " KINGHAM, " JOHNSON, Dr. WILSON ILES,	From Dr. Brett's to Loats Lane.
The Rev. C. BAILHACHE, Mr. CHATER, " LINTON, " BALLARD,	From The Church Gates to The Turnpike.	Mr. C. CHILD, " URLWIN, " PEARKES, " COOK, " JAS. CAPELL,	From Loats Lane to Colne Bridge.
The Rev. A. GURNEY, Mr. W. SHUTE, Silk Mills, " J. G. SMITH, Hamper Mill,	Oxhey Hamlet.		

The Committee will thus expend all the means placed at their disposal.

BY ORDER,
JOHN SEDGWICK, Hon. Sec.

N.B.—It is understood there will be a display of Fireworks on the Recreation Ground in the evening, followed by a Bonfire.

S. PEACOCK, PRINTER, "OBSERVER" OFFICE, WATFORD.

Left: *Albert, Edward, Prince of Wales, was Queen Victoria's eldest son, born at Buckingham Palace in November 1841.*

Widely travelled, and very popular, he was aged 24 when he married the Princess Alexandra, eldest daughter of Christian IX, of Denmark, in March 1863. Their combined popularity led many towns and villages to name roads and streets after them.

Queen Victoria came to the throne in 1838 and married in February 1840 the Prince of Saxe-Coburg and Gotha, bearing him four sons and five daughters. The early death of the Prince-Consort in 1861 led the widow to seclusion.

She survived to Jubilee, and Diamond Jubilee in 1897

The wedding of the Prince of Wales relatively soon after his mother's widowhood was seen by the population as cause for great rejoicing and in this Watford needed no further encouragement. The Prince assisted in promoting the Royal College of Music and provided the suggestion for the Imperial Institute.

Next page, top: *The prominent three-storey building was once a Royal Mail coaching house until Mr Rogers acquired the premises for his corn, timber and salt business in 1771. It would be more familiar in later years as Rogers & Gowlett. Mr Roger's original Coal office stood to the left of arch sign, and adjacent to Meeting Alley which is just visible between the two buildings. The small two-storey cottage, and Meeting Alley, are now an entrance to Charter Place.*

Inset: *Market Place, May 1987.*

Bottom: *The childrens' procession, to which the poster refers.*

the British on holiday. Watford had seen nothing like this in its history."

Young Downer had jumped at the opportunity to photograph the return procession on its way to Nascott. Some days earlier he had set up his camera and made a trial exposure of a corner of the Market Place *(right)*–and though some fifteen years after the Board of Health report the area still looks grim. To take his picture he would have to prepare his photographic plate and coat it with liquid light-sensitive emulsion and, with the wet plate in the camera, make the exposure, which appeared satisfactory.

If the big day dawned a little sunny it didn't last and by about three-thirty he'd be worried that the light would hold. The lens of his 12 inch by 10 inch camera would be focussed upon the near ranks of children and at a given signal nearly all of the children stayed still and held their pose; not so the onlookers, for their perambulations continued. A half second exposure; perhaps as long as two, but more he dare not risk.

At any rate his result was a veritable tour-de-force.

Police, Turnpike Trusts and new estates . . .

The main shepherds of the crowd were the committee members of the Local Board but no doubt the police were as interested as the next person. Early police were established on a village basis of Parish Constable, appointed annually at the Watford Manorial Court Leet without regular pay, being paid by result. For each prisoner brought to quarter sessions a fee could be charged. Early constables had various duties ranging from suppression of drunkenness to checking weights and measures. Over and above the Parish constables were 'head' or 'chief' constables responsible for an area of a 'hundred'. Robert Peel—made Home Secretary in 1822—was dissatisfied with the public's confusion of the roles of 'police' and 'military' particularly after the military, in trying to suppress a meeting at Manchester, charged the crowd, killing eleven and injuring hundreds. Peel's early action was to dress the police in a manner totally unlike the army, and so the dress of the "Peelers", with top hat and frock coat came into being.

Watford's early Parish Constable (from 1832 until the coming of the County Police in 1841) was James West. In addition, the Watford Subscription Police force was founded in 1829, this costing a few inhabitants £1 annually for private watching *(Clarke's report, 1849)*. In 1841 a County Police presence was established at 193 High Street with Superintendent Captain Kelly and a constable.

Premises were later obtained in the then new Estcourt Road. Arising from the early duty of checking weights and measures it was appropriate that the Estcourt Road premises would become the local office of the Inspector of Weights and Measures, food and drugs, petroleum and explosives, and fertilisers and feeding-stuffs for the county of Hertfordshire (Western Division), until well past the 1939-45 war.

There were two turnpikes passing through Watford. The first was the Hatfield Trust which set up Toll Houses in North Watford and Hagden Lane. Collection of tolls started in 1757 and ended in 1881. The second, the Aylesbury to Bushey Heath turnpike, was operated by the Sparrow's Herne Trust with local Toll Houses at Bushey Arches and near Ridge Lane on the road to Hemel Hempstead. Opened in 1762, the turnpike tolls were last collected in 1872. These trusts repaired the roads they controlled by collecting tolls from road users and so maintained them as 'long-distance' routes in a better state than when they had been repaired by parish labour.

Milestones were set up by these Trusts. From 1770 onwards, coaches were able to travel at faster speeds on these roads and after 1800 they were further improved by engineers such as Mc'Adam, employed by the Trustees. The two roads crossed by the 'Elms' or Pond Cross Roads.

Before 1757 the Rickmansworth Road was called New Mill Lane, then sometime Coach Lane. In 1887, at the time of the tree-planting ceremony outside the 'Elms' it was called the 'Park Road'. It was said that the Hatfield Trust was set up by the Earl of Salisbury to give the family a good road to Bath and their west country properties. The laying out of an estate or the making of a road was a process spread over a long period of time.

There was rarely a start or finish date. In the early days the building of a town needed no planning permission. The only public announcements would be those of the Auctioneer announcing the sale of the plots *(as for Market-street; seen later)*, and made on bill-boards outside the Rose & Crown and other local inns in the Market Place. In any event such happenings could be seen daily by the town's inhabitants and in the mid 1860's and 70's would not be news to the Watford Observer.

The role of a newspaper in this period can be defined as 'having ears with which to report' but; lacking means to print photographs, had no 'eyes'. Reports of learned society's meetings, Literary and Local Board; Flower Shows, Music and Drama

Left: *Watford Police of 1863. The County Police Station was then in a small house/shop at 193 High Street, almost opposite the Watford Museum. For many years, prior to demolition, the shop was occupied by H A Swann, leather merchants–carrying on the last vestiges of what had been an essential business in the 'horse' days. Around this time building had started in Estcourt Road and premises near the top of Meeting Alley and Grove Circus were chosen for the new station.*

Right: *The Watford Volunteer Rifle Brigade c1868/70, are posed on a piece of land next to where the Baptist Church stands in Clarendon Road. The then new Estcourt Road is featured in the background; on the left stand Drs Iles and Brett. Dr Brett had joined the Volunteers when they were formed in 1859.*

meetings, Yeomanry, etc., were at extreme length as befitted a journal tailored exactly to the readers who, in most part, would be the gentry, businessmen and farming community spread over a wide area, an area which included St. Albans, Hendon, Edgware and Rickmansworth.

The 'eyes' would come gradually, first in the form of drawings or engravings from photographs and then, much later, blocks made directly from a photograph.

Mr Humbert's prospectus for the sale of property (p54) describes the premises—in glowing terms—as in the "main Street", but on the cover the London typesetter has used the adjective "high" as a noun thus turning it into a name.

King-street was opened just after 1851 and Queen-street was started in 1860. Also at the start of the 1860's, land owned by Thomas Henry Sutton Sotheron Estcourt between Clarendon-road and the railway was developed; resulting in Estcourt and Sutton-roads, etc, followed a little later by Derby-road. The Clarendon-road was laid out in 1864. The Estcourt-road estate ran off Beechen-grove, (in which a Meeting House existed since 1707), and which in turn was connected to the High Street by narrow 'Meeting Alley'.

The next street out of the High Street was not to be made for 26 years, in 1890 (pages 72-76).

Near the Railway Station, Church-road and Bedford-street had been in existence since soon after the coming of the railway, although un-named for many years. From the letter of Mr. Humbert in 1857 (p53) will be seen the intention to develop the Nascott area,—this eventually included Denmark-street and Alexander-road; so named because of the feeling of affection and respect following the wedding of the Prince of Wales to Princess Alexandra of Denmark in 1863. George-street and Smith-street were established soon after 1851.

Before these streets had been built in the now 'central area' of Watford a compact development had already taken place at 'New Bushey' (Oxhey) and which consisted of Villiers and Capel-roads.

The workhouse opposite the church was in disuse of its original purpose, a new workhouse having been built in 1838 at Colney Butts (Vicarage-road). The cemetery was started in 1858.

From the Mother Church, St. Mary's, had grown St. Andrews in Church-road (1855); the Baptist Church was still in Beechen-grove, and other places of worship included the Town Mission at Farthing-lane, a Primitive Methodist Chapel in Carey-place and Wesleyan and Beulah Chapels in Queen-street. Watford, as such, to the north along the road to St. Albans, did not exist. There was a lane (later Leavesden Road) leading to Leavesden, further along still was the lane to Bushey Mill and beyond that were fields to St. Albans.

There was another problem in the town. It was of the ownership and naming of the courtyards and alleys. In the slower pace, when growth was static, the inhabitants could remember whose name their abode owed allegiance to.

But with growth, new inhabitants who did not know previous history the changes in name, as ownership changed, was confusing. Henry Williams, one-time correspondent to the *Buckingham Advertiser,* and one-time photographer, had taken on the post of Sanitary Inspector and he—living earlier in Hudson's Yard—saw the solution as numbering the lesser courtyards and alleys and retaining the names of the major.

Despite these efforts many names continued in common useage until the main slum clearance orders took effect between 1920 and 1939. Henry Williams' task of overseeing the town's sanitary arrangements would not have been easy in dealing with landlords reluctant to spend money on improvement for which they, personally, would derive little or no benefit. Many old names persisted, resistant to change and it is the

The courtyards are numbered . . .

whereabouts of such as Woodman's Yard, Holt's Yard, Draycott's and Butcher's Yard, Meeting Alley and the like that are key places for many people seeking the homeplaces of their forebears, while Briden's and Rodwell's yards, and probably many others, using a 'local name' for a few years, have long since disappeared without trace.

Sanitary arrangements were:
1852	Comprised cesspools.
1852-75	Sewer system without ventilation.
1875-87	Incomplete system of chiefly road ventilation.
1871	Storm water partly diverted from the sewer system.

St. Andrews
The ecclesiastical district of St. Andrews, an area of 1200 acres which included Callowland, was formed in February 1855 and a temporary church built.

Building of the present church was started in 1857.

Literary Institute
A library was opened in 1854 in Carey Place. The Literary Institute had a library, a reading room and also accommodation for classes and lectures.

In 1855 the Public Library Act allowed a ld in the pound rate to be collected, once per year, which the Local Board added to a general and water rate.

Time-line
1803	Buonaparte's adventures following Robespierre's reign of terror after the French revolution of 1789 cause alarm. A British army of 50,000 reserve of is raised, followed by a volunteer corps of 300,000 men.
1839	'Penny postage' introduced
1850	Telegraph cable laid to Calais.
1851	Window Tax repealed; house tax introduced.
1858	Telegraph cable laid to Newfoundland.
1882	Invention to make printing blocks from photographs.
1888	In Germany Karl Benz has produced a saleable petrol-driven motor car.
1888	John Boyd Dunlop produces a pneumatic bicycle tyre with separate air-filled inner tube.
1899	Boer war started.

Population 1838, 2,960

Names not altered and New Names	Old Names
Court 1	Butcher's Yard
Court 2	Well's Yard
Court 3 and 5	Two small Courts in Meeting Alley
Court 4	Wright's Yard
Court 6	Edlin's Yard
Court 7	Chequers Yard
Court 8	Ballard's Buildings
Court 9	A Court in Red Lion Yard, *formerly Water-butt Sq.*
Court 10	Hedge's Yard
Court 11	Holt's Yard
Court 13	Hudson's Yard, *leading out of Chater's Yard*
Court 14	Top of Crown Passage, *formerly Clark's Buildings*
Court 15	Boot Yard
Court 16	Between Nos. 184 and 186 *(on map as 'Potton Yd')*
Court 17	In Water Lane
Court 18	In Farthing Lane
Court 19	New Road
Court 20	Old Tan Yard
Court 21	Chapman's Yard
Court 22	Old Yard
Court 23	Malting Yard
Court 25	Neal's Yard
Court 30	Grove Place
Albert Street	Chater's Yard
Crown Passage	Three Crowns Yard;
Chapel Row	Chapel Row, in Water Lane
Watford Field Road	Farthing Lane

Unchanged were:
Meeting Alley, Bell Alley, Red Lion Yard, Fenn's Yard, Water Lane, Pigg's Alley, and Swann Alley.

Henry Williams, Sanitary Inspector.

Salter's new Almshouses

More than four centuries ago (1454) Thomas Beaumont Esq. gave to the company a hall, in Bread-street, and six alms-houses adjoining. And, in 1578, Sir Ambrose Nicholas, Lord Mayor in 1576, gave an alms-house, in Monkwell-street, for twelve women.

The original premises were burnt down in the Great Fire of 1666, after which the company rebuilt the almshouses which, later, had become so dilapidated as to require reconstruction. When the Master, and Wardens, and Assistants—trustees for all time—instead of rebuilding the refuge for their decayed brethren in Monkwell street, chose the neighbourhood of Watford for their new location. The new almshouses, a view of which is engraved from a photograph by Mr. F. Downer of Watford, have been erected at a cost of £8000 exclusive of the expense of the site and adjoining grounds in a pleasant part of Watford about ten minutes' walk from the railway station.

The buildings present three sides of a square, or a centre and two wings, the principal portion resting on a raised terrace. The interiors are planned with careful regard to sanitary considerations and the domestic accommodation of the inmates—the Almswomen from Monkwell-street and the Almsmen from Salters'-rents, Bow-lane. The architect is Mr. John Collier of Putney and the builder Mr. King of Shefford, Bedfordshire. The Salters flourished in the times when salt fish formed part of every meal, and the use and consumption of salt fish in the ancient Catholic periods was amazing. In short, it formed part of the allowance of the King and nobility, of monastic establishments, and the custom is even commemorated in modern times, in the 'King's Maundy', which was, in great part, composed of salt fish.

Illustrated London News, July 30th 1864 (the Almshouses, in Church Road, were refurbished in 1989/90)

Bushey Station, the ford and the toll . . .

The area around the River Colne where it crosses the High Street is low-lying marshy ground, as floods in 2000 and 2001 witnessed. In the very early days, probably long before Domesday, it would be recognised as an extremely unpleasant and wide ford to cross especially after heavy rains, hence the derivation of 'Wet'-ford from which Watford gets its name.

In the 1830's there was a small thriving community centred around the ironworks and the trades catering for travellers who perforce had to halt for a while before or after going through the toll. The view from Watford towards Bushey was uninterrupted except for tree-clad slopes. This changed quite dramatically when the railway builders took over. From the north, a massive embankment and from the south, a huge bridge; wonders of engineering the like of which was unknown to Watfordians. But, at one stroke, Watford was enclosed with a physical wall which one entered or left via the toll and from that day to this the 'Bushey Arches' marks a tangible boundary between the town and all to the south. Following the building of houses in "New Bushey"—which we know as Oxhey—a station was built at Bushey with the entrance from the Kingsfield side of the track.

The date suggested for the Bushey Station photograph (top) is 1869 and this may the earliest railway photograph of our area. This is after the construction of the third track on the embankment and through the single Watford Tunnel. There were then four lines into Bushey from London, and which were reduced to three carrying on northwards.

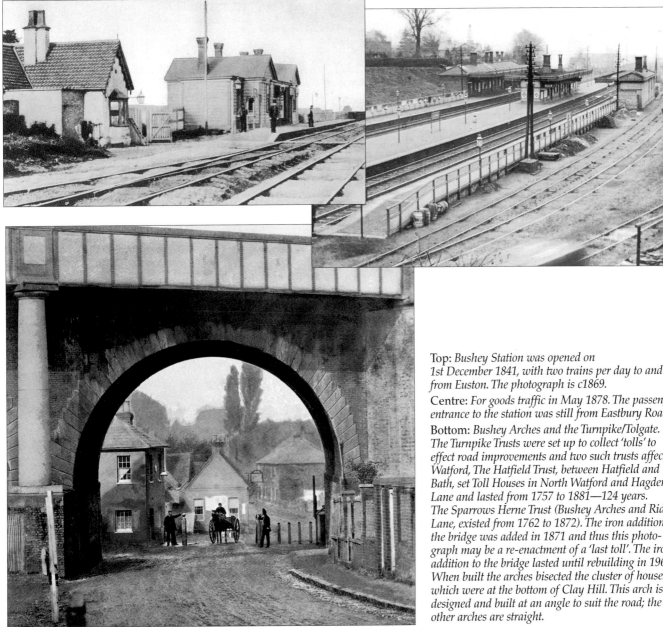

Top: *Bushey Station was opened on 1st December 1841, with two trains per day to and from Euston. The photograph is c1869.*

Centre: *For goods traffic in May 1878. The passenger entrance to the station was still from Eastbury Road.*

Bottom: *Bushey Arches and the Turnpike/Tolgate. The Turnpike Trusts were set up to collect 'tolls' to effect road improvements and two such trusts affected Watford, The Hatfield Trust, between Hatfield and Bath, set Toll Houses in North Watford and Hagden Lane and lasted from 1757 to 1881—124 years. The Sparrows Herne Trust (Bushey Arches and Ridge Lane, existed from 1762 to 1872). The iron addition to the bridge was added in 1871 and thus this photograph may be a re-enactment of a 'last toll'. The iron addition to the bridge lasted until rebuilding in 1963. When built the arches bisected the cluster of houses which were at the bottom of Clay Hill. This arch is designed and built at an angle to suit the road; the other arches are straight.*

Taken to the fields to glean the corn . . .

No man in Watford's civic circles has a more interesting tale to tell than Alderman William Tucker, the first "Father of the Borough", who has watched Watford grown from little more than a village of 5,000 inhabitants to a thriving town of 55,000.

Fields where he used to play have disappeared and in their place have sprung up houses and shops—thousands of them! Winding lanes and paths where he used to roam have become wide open streets and thoroughfares.

Quiet meadows where only the song of birds broke the early morning silence now resound with factory hooters, and where once upon a time the only sign of life was a man behind a plough, thousands of people now earn their daily bread.

And after all this transformation. Alderman Tucker, at the age of 77, still remains one of the most active men engaged in local public work today. He was prevailed upon to tell his life story to a "Post" reporter. William Tucker was born in Chesham, Bucks, in 1852.

As a baby in arms he was carried by his mother into Watford and has lived here ever since. For years not a single new house appeared in Watford—nothing happened that gave any hint of its future growth. Almost the first thing he remembers doing as a boy was gleaning in the fields picking up corn which had been left by the reapers.

The farmers allowed people to do this, and it was not an uncommon sight to see mothers take their children out at five o'clock in the morning to pick up the precious grains. The children, once they had stopped yawning and blinking, thought it great fun. Then the mothers would take their little harvest to the mill at the bottom of the town and have the corn ground into flour. Few people trouble much about education in those days. The prime concern was getting a boy to work as soon as possible, for a few pence were always a welcome addition to the purse of the hardworking housewife.

William Tucker was eight years old when he commenced work as a wage-earner. He worked in a silk mill at the Rookery for seven hours each day, commencing at six o'clock in the morning and was paid 1s. 6d. a week. In the afternoon he used to go to the Old National School in Church Street, for which his parents had to pay a penny or twopence a week.

When he was 14 years of age, William Tucker was apprenticed to a carriage builder, and received one of Dame Fuller's £10 grants, which were given to boys of good character, towards their apprenticeship.

Many people still preferred to go to London in horse-drawn vehicles rather than trust to the "new-fangled railway." The branch line to Rickmansworth helped to modernise their ideas though.

The traffic through Watford was confined mostly to farm waggons, though occasionally a handsome "four-in-hand" or a gallant-looking pair would gallop through.

The lords and ladies who lived in the neighbourhood were frequent visitors in their carriages, and used to do their shopping in Watford. Later on, when William Tucker started in business on his own as a carriage builder, he did a lot of work for Lady Ebury, Lord Essex and Lord Clarendon. This business, which he started in Sutton Road, began to flourish, and he moved into larger premises in Queen Street. Ultimately, he came into the High Street, and stayed there until motor cars began to arrive, and then he handed the business over to his sons.

WHP

THE WATFORD CARRIAGE WORKS
QUEEN'S ROAD AND PRINCES STREET.

W. TUCKER, Proprietor.

Carriages Warehoused, Bought and Sold on Commission. Carriages of every description kept in stock, including the Basket Car and Rustic Cart on Cee Springs.

Carriages called for and taken home if required—distance no object.

When Emma Oliver produced this evocative drawing of Watford Market Place of 1868 William Tucker, whose story starts above, would have been sixteen years of age, and have served two years of his apprenticeship. William Tucker's carriage business was handed over to his sons at the dawning of the motor age and carried on in St Albans Road, as Tucker Bros. Ltd until works for the underpass caused its cessation.

The Parish Church is rebuilt . . .

The Parish Church

"The Tower", said Miss Helen Rudd, in a talk to the Herts Archaeological Society, "was 15th century. The width of the walls showed Norman origin and were probably built upon the original foundations.

"Upon restoration of the walls in 1871, 12th century stones and broken pieces of a Norman font were found embedded. In 1270 the Chancel Arch and adjacent walls were built together with the Rood Loft and winding staircase—still to be traced.

"That was the origin of the church. The 13th century church had to be enlarged in the 15th century and so the walls and the clerestory were raised. The 15th century builders were to be thanked for the beautiful timber roof from which the plaster was removed in 1841.

"In the 15th century the south aisle was restored and three of the pillars were found to be too weak; three new 15th century pillars were inserted. The pulpit had been assigned to 1670, the carving being like that of Grinling Gibbons who was at that time working at Cassiobury, but in an old Vestry Book she found a note that "The Pulpit was erected in 1714 by Richard Bull at a cost of £55".

"It was felt that Richard Bull was either a very good imitator of Grinling Gibbons, or else his pupil. The reredos dates from 1871; before that there was a very heavily carved oaken altar piece in the style of carving of Charles II, which almost hid the 15th century east window. She remarked that Vicar Capel and Vicar James had shared the pulpit for over a century, from 1799 to 1915."

(WO, June 1926)

The Fig Tree

Countless burials had taken place around the church, many without benefit of coffins, with the result that earthwork grew so high around the church that the parishioners had to step down some three or four steps to enter the building.

This, of course, caused both considerable dampness and inconvenience. During the lowering of the churchyard rows of skeletons were uncovered which appeared to have been buried side-by-side and were very probably remains of those who died in a period of plagues, (in 1540 some 47 burials between July and September, and in 1592, 1594 and 1625).

It was at this time that the 'Fig-tree' tomb, famous as an old legend that a fig tree had grown from the buried atheist lady's heart, was accidentally opened. It showed that the roots of the fig tree were not in the vault but in the crown of the arch, some four or five feet above where the lady's heart must have been. The outer walls of the church were of rough cast, which was removed, and replaced by a casing of flint.

The entire roof was releaded and large stone 'pine-apples' removed and the top turreted to lighten the weight as the top of the tower was of solid stone.

Somewhat later, around 1880, alterations were being made to underground premises of Mr. Edmonds, ironmonger; when the workmen, in removing the earth, exhumed a number of human bones, which led to the supposition that at one time the churchyard extended to the High Street, from the church gates, to Church Street, and that under the feet of the occupants rest the bones of many of the former inhabitants of Watford.

William's 'History of Watford'

● *No. 98 High Street; prior to rebuilding in 1959/60, was the shop of Spurriers, bakers, prior to which it had been that of Mr. Edmonds, ironmonger, who was established in 1798.*

Top: *The Bushey Lime Kilns were located adjacent to Bushey Arches on the north side of Chalk Hill. The chalk used in the kilns was obtained locally and the process of burning converted the chalk to quicklime which was spread on fields as a fertiliser, especially on acid and clay soils. It could also be used for making lime-based mortars for bonding bricks or for plastering walls. Thinner solutions provided whitewash and the church and workhouse would have been among its users.*

Left: *The Parish Church has been rebuilt and the top of the tower has been castellated and the large corner stones—'pineapples'— removed to lessen the weight upon the tower's foundations. The cladding has been refaced with flint and cement and ends centuries of dilapidation. This drawing, probably from the yard of the property between the workhouse and Dyson's Yard (Court 8/ Ballard's buildings) is enigmatic in showing workmen taking what may be a lunch break, their spades indicating building or clearance work. The building in front of the church is most certainly the back view of the old workhouse, which by this date had been converted to a shop and a house.*

. . . a ford, for horses and carts to go through, by the side of the bridge . . .

In later life Mr David Downer wrote of earlier days:

"The Market House was built on wood pillars with a loft over. Corn was not sold by sample, but in bulk and the sacks of corn unsold were stored in the loft until the next market day. The 'stocks' were under the side of the market house, facing the High-road.

The town pump was at the end and was a large iron box, worked by turning a wheel with a handle projecting from the rim. People fetched pails of water by carrying them by wooden yokes on their shoulders.

About 1846 Watford had only one street — commencing at the Toll Gate near the railway arches, and crossing the River Colne by a bridge, a much narrower one than the present one, and with a ford by the side for horses and carts to go through, and I expect the town took the name from it of Wet or Watford.

For passing through the toll gate 6d was charged for a horse and cart, and 3d for a man on horseback.

At the end of the garden of Frogmore House ran a narrow lane (generally full of water) which was the entrance to Bushey Meads. There was also an entrance by the side of the pawnbroker's shop, to the Mill Stream, so that anyone could fetch water or take horses down. Most houses in the area had two or three steps to their doors on account of the floods, and also there being no drainage, the storm water ran down and over the gutters.

Most of the pavement was Denner Hill blocks of stone [sandstone] and only near the shops. York paving about six feet wide, was laid by the Local Board from 1860, and any owner of property wishing to make up his frontage had to do so at his own expense.

Where High Street Station now is were three small houses, one occupied by Mr Poulton, a leather breeches and gaiter maker; and on the other side Mr Draycott, maltster, had a yard in which a blinkered horse used to go round under a beam to grind malt.

All the cattle coming to market had to pay toll; the sheep pens were opposite the 'Rose & Crown'; the cattle cows and calves stood in herds up by the 'Green Man Inn'; and the pigs in pens on the piece of ground in front of Meeting Alley.

The Town Cryer used to charge a shilling and ring a bell and 'cry' anything that was lost or strayed. Where Clarendon Road begins, was a large barn, and a cottage occupied by the bailiff to Mr R Clutterbuck, [County Historian] who farmed all the fields at the back, and who had a rick yard where now stands the Clarendon Hall [now under Palace car park].

A little way along St Albans Road was the 'pound', a wood paling enclosure, in which straying cattle were kept until the fine was paid. Where Essex and Malden roads are now was Nascot Park and Mr Greenus' Forest nursery grounds. On the right hand side were no houses—all fields—only the 'Railway Arms' at the corner of the bridle path. The Railway Station was over the bridge, on the left hand side, approached by steps down into the Station Yard. The 'Clarendon Hotel' was the house now attached to the Coliseum Picture Palace and where the Coliseum is were

the hotel stables. Women and children, after harvest, went into the field 'leesing', that is, gathering up what corn was left; and once a week were allowed by Lord Essex to go into Cassiobury Park and gather up fallen wood.

The entrances to most courts and yards of High Street were under gateways, with a room over. Across the entrance to the present Market Street was a butcher's shop, with a room over the entrance, by the side of the 'Compasses' Inn. This entrance led up to a path by the side of the Malting, and went across fields, out into Rickmansworth Road, opposite Shepherds Lodge. The path was called Monks Folly. Most houses had pig sties in their back garden. King Street was the carriage drive to Watford Place, and the public house on the corner [Kings Arms] was part of the old lodge.

Where the entrance to Queen Street now is was the stable yard of the 'Eight Bells' public house. In the stable yard at the 'George Hotel' where is now a club room [No. 91, Marks and Spencer's main store] were large stables with a wooden balcony along the front, and it was said that soldiers were billeted there during the Great Rebellion."

W R Saunders, History of Watford, 1931

Above: The pair of early shops, Nos. 48 and 50. Many a householder in the main street started selling goods from their parlour; home-cooked sweetmeats and produce, tinware and ironware, etc. In 1868 Mr Buck started a baker's businesss at No. 48 and acquired No. 50 in 1872, when, left, a double shopfront was installed, making an early 'big' shop. Very much later he bought Nos. 52/54, creating a restaurant and ballroom above.

No. 52, to the left of the photograph, is the home of architect C. P. Ayres whose designs included Mr Fisher's home (1889), the Cottage Hospital (1885) and the Fire Station (1900).

The horse and cart is leaving court No. 6, Edlin's Yard. Note the frontage paved as described by Mr Downer.

Free school—Endowed schools—Grammar schools; 'Old Fullarians' all.

The picturesque Queen Anne building, which is still called the Free School, sited in the south-west corner of St. Mary's Churchyard, has close associations with Dame Elizabeth Fuller, one of Watford's many past benefactors. The School is now a Grade II listed building, which gives it special protection, in recognition of its architectural merit and unique historical association. For many years it was a popular meeting place for many local organisations with direct access to the nearby St. Mary's Church Hall. In the 1960s the Free School was converted to offices and in this capacity the fabric of the building neatly dovetails into the environs of the Church at the same time serving the needs of Watford's commercial growth.

The building bears the inscription:

"Anno Dni 1704. This Free School was built and
endowed for the teaching of poor children at
the proper cost of Mrs. Elizabeth Fuller of Watford Place."

To trace the grass roots relationship of the School with the Watford Grammar Schools it is necessary to go back as far as the late seventeenth-century when religious conventions subscribed to propriety rather than piety. In those remote pre-evangelistic days the plight of the poor was not considered to be a moral issue except to an enlightened minority who believed that poverty was neither a natural phenomenon nor God's will. To combat this problem in practical terms the Society for Promoting Christian Knowledge initiated the 1699 'Charity School'.

Mrs. Elizabeth Fuller found herself wholly in accord with the ideals of the movement as it conformed with her own interpretation of the Christian faith. Moved by the ignorance of the poor and in empathy with this wind of change she acquired part of the Vicarage garden and graveyard on which to build her new school for Watford's deprived children. By 1704 the building was completed, endowed and occupied. Forty boys and fourteen girls were initially accommodated in large and light classrooms. There they received a basic education and religious instruction. Children were accepted from the age of seven and required to leave on reaching fourteen.

In 1709 at the age of sixty-five, Dame Elizabeth Fuller, who had survived three husbands, died. She was buried in the Churchyard of St. James' Parish Church, Bushey, but even in death she had provided for the financing of her Free School. Notwithstanding her generosity, changing circumstances in later years only served to increase operating costs, forcing the Trustees to appeal for financial assistance. Many local people responded, not least Queen Adelaide, who was familiar with the town as a resident of Cassiobury House as well as Bentley Priory. The Trustees monitored the progress of the pupils for over one hundred and fifty years, until 1870, when examinations were introduced in conformity with the requirements of the Education Act of the same year. The problem of funding the School from its own resources increased each year. The endowments and gifts could no longer sustain its operation as a Free School and although strict economies were applied there was no way in which it could be made viable unless fundamental changes were made.

At that time Dr. Brett, who was a Trustee, in searching for a solution to this apparently insurmountable problem, discovered that the school may qualify for a grant from the Platt's Charity of Aldenham. Application was made, and the Trustees were informed that Consols to the value of £13,333 6s. 8d. would be conditionally assigned to Watford when 'a scheme for the management of Watford Charities should be found'. After considerable research a scheme was duly presented to the Charity Commission in 1881 in which scholarships would be offered to a certain number of boys and girls. The package was well prepared, researched and presented. The application could not fail!

"The Endowed Schools in Derby Road. The head master's salary to be £100 per annum, with a payment from the capitation as may be fixed from time to time by the governors, at a rate of not less than £1 or more than £3 a year for each boy in the school.

The salary of the head mistress to be £50 per annum, with proportion of capitation grant; each to have a residence, and to sign a declaration of their willingness to discharge their duties to the best of their abilities. The school to be open to all boys and girls of good character and sufficient health, residing with their parents and guardians or near relatives within an area to be fixed by the governors."

A later adjunct to the school was a building in which the science and craft of cooking could be taught to girls. This was a hard-fought battle which the Revd. Newton Price supported and saw to a successful conclusion.

A Board of Governors was appointed and then a search made for a suitable site. A consensus supported the Derby Road location where a single building would be erected. Although under the one roof each school would have its own entrance. The new Derby Road School for Boys was opened by the Earl of Clarendon on April 21st 1884, and on the next day he opened the Girls' School. On the occasion of his second speech he apologised for having omitted to give credit to Dr. Brett in his first speech for having initiated the project and bringing it to a successful conclusion. The new-look Endowed Schools were regarded as a highly successful venture and in 1903 the names were changed to the Watford Grammar Schools, thus diminishing the connection with Dame Elizabeth Fuller and the old Free School of 1704. The euphoria was short-lived as success brought its own problems.

The Education Act of 1902, amongst other things, specified a space of not less than 18sq. foot per pupil excluding hall or assembly areas, a requirement that could not be met because of the ever-increasing number of pupils. A proposal to place an extra storey on top of the existing building was considered only to be rejected. An alternative proposal was adopted in which the Girls' School moved to new premises and the Boys' School took possession of the building.

In theory this was an ideal solution but unfortunately the necessary funds were not available to the Trustees. They were obliged to go cap-in-hand to the local and county authorities for financial assistance. As soon as the appeal became public knowledge there was an immediate adverse reaction. The question was asked whether public funds should be used to support the historically sectarian nature of the Schools' curriculum. The reconstitution of the Board of Governors to include representatives of local authorities and the introduction of denomination safeguards appeared to placate if not wholly sat-

isfy a very sensitive public.

A site was found not far from the Watford District Hospital in Vicarage Road and St. Mary's Church which enjoyed a panoramic view of the Colne Valley and the wooded hill beyond. Charles Brightman of Watford was appointed general contractor and by 1907 a two storey building designed to accommodate two hundred and fifty girls had been completed. Because feelings were still running high the new accommodation was quietly occupied without being officially opened. There was no ceremony and as little as possible attendant publicity. The move was deliberately planned as a low-key exercise that would not further exacerbate the feelings of the protesters. Ironically within five years of the departure of the Girls' School, the Derby Road premises could no longer house the ever-increasing number of boys. By 1908 there were 267 boys attending school with classroom space for only 240 pupils. Inspectors of the Board of Education recommended a new building on a larger site. The Governors lost no time in negotiating with the Earl of Essex and acquired a little over twelve acres.

Included in the deal was Shepherds Lodge, which for

many years had guarded a minor entrance to Cassiobury House from Rickmansworth Road. The new school premises were completed in 1912 and the official opening was arranged for the 20th March with Lord Clarendon again presiding. On this occasion the Headmaster, W. R. Carter, is reported as saying 'My greatest ambition is to make the School a great and important institution of the town and I hope all the boys here now will be proud some day to say they were among the first to be educated within its walls.' That his dream was realised there is no doubt, although sadly in the space of two years both the Earl of Clarendon and Mr. Carter died.

Ambitious parents in the middle ages sent their sons to the Abbey of St. Alban to be educated. If their social status or economic circumstances did not permit such indulgence the local Parish priests were asked to undertake a form of tuition. The first intimation of a school in Watford is to be found in an entry for the year 1595, making reference to 'George Redhead, schoolmaster' and to Nicholas Hall who was 'licenced to keep a Grammar School'. This school may have been located on the upper floors of two cottages, close to the Vicarage, which were demolished in 1821. The location to which the school was transferred is not known although records indicated that it was still in existence in 1832. The foundation of the London University in 1827 was the materialistic inspiration of secularists and nonconformists for whom there was no place at Oxford or Cambridge where traditionally a classical curriculum offered a ticket to ride to the establishment of the Church of State.

Numerically the Dissenters were in a minority but their militant voices were nevertheless heard in matters of education. Public money was available to promote education facilities but only, claimed the Church, if grants and disbursements were deployed under the protection of the State religion; terms which were abhorrent to all Dissenters. In defiance they raised money by voluntary contribution to finance the building and running of their own day schools and Sunday schools. Under the patronage of the Whigs the British and Foreign School Society was formed as a viable alternative to the Church School. In response the Church founded the National Society for the Education of the Poor according to the principles of the Church of England. In deference to the proper title the name 'National School' was adopted and by the same token the Dissenters Schools were called 'British Schools'. The National Schools dominated the scene in cities, towns, villages and hamlets aided by a modest grant that was made available from 1833.

Perhaps as a result of the grant some of the members of the Parish Church decided to raise by subscription an amount sufficient to acquire the site of the notorious 'Nag's Head'* beerhouse in the High Street—notorious because it became the meeting place of the body snatchers—and build there a new infants' school. At the time the Earl of Essex maintained what became known as 'My Lord's Schools' in Rickmansworth Road, at his own expense, for children of the working classes in Watford of any denomination. The school closed on his death in 1839. Then there was the private sector ranging from 'minders' of children on a daily basis to reputable establishments attracting the children of local tradespeople, merchants and others of adequate means. In 1841 members of the Parish Church subscribed towards a new National School in Church Street for boys and girls which served in that capacity for the next eighty one years until it was closed in 1922 when it became better known as Almond Wick.

One of the first areas to receive the attention of the developer as a direct result of the arrival of the London and Birmingham Railway, and because of its convenience to the

A Model Public Library

In Vestry assembled, in November 1871, inhabitants adopted the Public Libraries Acts of 1855, 1866 and 1871. A committee was organised and an appeal made to the public for funds, the most liberal contributor being Mr Thos. Clutterbuck, of Micklefield Hall, who gave the greater part of the site, the cottage at the rear, and £100. The building (Architects Messrs Sedgwick & Son), has a frontage of 80ft and a depth of 47ft and in the two floors there is an area of about 7,500 ft. On the ground floors are two spacious reading rooms communicating with library or book-room, and news-room, committee room and apparatus-room.

On the first floor are two good science classrooms, convertible into one, and capable of holding some 250 persons; also a set of rooms for art teaching, namely elementary painting and modelling rooms, with room for art master.

"A penny rate was stated, in 1881, to have brought in £144 2s. which small amount developed around it an expenditure of £700 a year. Ten distinct sections are worked, the accounts of each shown in a separate balance-sheet each year. The sections are:

Section A, the Library proper, contains about 7,000 volumes; a payment of three shillings a year, or fourpence per month, is required for taking the books home to read. The yearly issues amount to about 12,000. The only free part of the library, the reading room, shows a similar use of books and is patronised chiefly by young men in the winter time.

Section B, is the School of Science and Art, the latter division showing clearly that the Public Library at Watford by no means attends to the wants of the industrial classes only, for non-government pupils may pay six guineas a year for drawing only. This section includes science teaching, organic chemistry, botany, principles of agriculture and shorthand also.

Section C is Entertainments, set going or stopped as occasion offers.

Section D in the Youths' Institute, supported by special honorary subscribers and one penny a week paid by its members for admission to the reading room, *because without that the room was too full.*

Section E is the Private Subscription room, supported by 100 members who subscribe ten shillings each per year.

Section F is a School of Music where some of the best masters obtainable in London are engaged. Nine different classes of lessons, again not free, are available to those who wish them. It is now supported by 160 students.

Section G is the nucleus of a Museum, and how treasures of local interest to a town for want of such a nucleus in trustworthy hands, the writer knows well!

Section H, the English Literature Club, meets weekly through the winter, at the library rooms, adding greatly to the care with which books are read. A very small subscription pays its, no doubt very small, expenses.

Even needlework in elementary schools has its head centre in a committee of the Watford Public Library."

Nature, August 25 1881,
from Henry Williams "History of Watford"

main station, included Church Road. There, in 1860, a Church School was erected to accommodate boys and infants. The school for girls was in Sotheron Road. In common with other Church and National Schools religious instruction was in accord with the doctrines of the Church of England.

The Dissenters (noncomformists) taught their first pupils in cottages near the old Baptist Chapel in Beechen Grove until the accommodation proved inadequate for an ever-increasing number of children. A larger custom-built school was erected in 1859 for boys and girls but even these premises proved unsuitable after a very short time and the boys were transferred to the old Baptist church premises. Victorian politicians disagreed about most things but on one aspect they were unanimous, that it was in the national interest to provide education facilities for the masses; a matter so important as to override religious intolerance and allied issues. In a climate of sectarian zeal and religious ardour the reconciliation of all these factors to achieve a kind of unity presented a problem so imponderable as to defy an acceptable solution.

W. E. Foster of Quaker origin, against all odds, cut the Gordian knot without compromising Gladstone. The immediate impact of the Education Bill of 1870 was to double State grants to all church schools, including those of the Roman Catholics, and so bring them into line within a common system. Any short-fall in the educational cover was to be made good by introducing a new Board School, each governed by a locally elected board and funded by a direct charge on the rates. The Act avoided the major pitfalls and created some degree of parity between Church and Board schools. Long overdue, a primary education system had been created, at least in principle. In practice, hamlets and villages, the population of which could only sustain one school, were obliged to stay with the old established Church

School. of which the National School serving the hamlet at Watford Heath is a prime example. There were other problems, some incidental to the enactment. In twenty years the number of children attending school increased nationally by one hundred per cent and costs in the same proportion. The new schools' prescribed function confined their curriculum strictly to a primary level. The School Board was, by its very nature, parochial in outlook, having little regard for events and developments beyond its influence. The induced pact between Church and Dissenter was sometimes infringed and occasionally broken but, undeniably, tremendous progress had been made in bringing together those of different persuasions.

The implementation of the 1870 Act was not effected in Watford until 1883. For thirteen years those eligible to pay rates had enjoyed the doubtful benefit of the local schools having to operate without a School Board and so saved on the expenses they would have otherwise incurred. The long period of grace may have suited the pockets of the town's rate-paying citizens but the School Authorities, without additional State aid, had difficulty in collecting sufficient subscriptions to meet the cost of teaching ever more children. The British (Dissenting) Schools ran into debt. To place so many infants was beyond the financial means of all school managers and so they called a meeting of all ratepayers. Mr. C. E. Humbert, Chairman of the Local Board of Health and the Hon. Richard Capel, one of the managers at St. Mary's School, explained to a disinterested audience the statistics and the facts pertinent to the problem of providing schooling for local children. Of 1,724 parish ratepayers only 250 helped maintain the schools by voluntary subscription. The meeting agreed to circularise all ratepayers recommending a voluntary increase of 6d. in the £.

Not unexpectedly there was so little response that the mat-

· WATFORD DISTRICT COTTAGE HOSPITAL ·   Charles. P. Ayres. Architect
WATFORD.

The Cottage Hospital was built in Vicarage Road in 1885 with a nine-bed accommodation. To mark the 1897 Diamond Jubilee of Queen Victoria a new six-bed ward and an operating theatre were added.
Five years later two additional six-bed wards, plus dining rooms and staff accommodation saw the total capacity increased to hold 27 patients.
The original building cost £1,700 and was opened by Lady Clarendon in 1886. The building still exists.
The hospital was supported by an infectious diseases house much further along Vicarage Road, but the 1902 additions were quickly found to be inadequate when casualties started flowing back from the battlefront from 1914 onwards.
Larger properties in the surrounding countryside were pressed into duty as convalescent homes and this fact shamed the town into finding a better hospital . . .

ter was shelved. To avoid a stalemate and provoke action the Education Department was requested to order the formation of a School Board.

The outcome, in the pursuit of efficiency and economy, was the uncontested election of the original school managers of the National, Church and British Schools who duly formed the first Watford School Board. After its formation the boys of Beechen Grove Baptist School were transferred to the Victoria Senior Boys' School. Other schools built in this era included Watford Field, Chater, Callow Land, Parkgate, Alexandra and Oxhey. The shortcomings in the 1870 Act were largely remedied in Balfour's Act of 1902. The era of the School Boards ended with the transfer of their near absolute power to County Councils at both primary and secondary levels, through the media of Education Committees. For two decades the schools founded or acquired by the Board and the Council served the ever-growing population until the development of farmland still surrounding the town into housing estates. This forced the South West Herts Divisional Executive to provide a series of new schools conforming to an enlightened design concept and which included Leggatt's Way in 1934 followed by Kingswood, Knutsford and Oaklands. These new schools in turn coped with the ever-changing, but always increasing population during the town's phenomenal expansion during the inter-war years including the development of the Tudor, Bradshaw, Kingswood, Leavesden Green and Harebreaks estates.

The growth of the town had been inexorable; where possible the existing courtyards were further built upon or extended; more cottages built in Loates Lane, New Road and Chapel Row in Water Lane and it would not be long before the land sold just a few years earlier would have plots built upon. Slowly at first but with gathering momentum.

Once King Street was cut out of the High-street, followed by Queen-street, the houses started to appear. Small in Carey Place and Charles Street; small in Estcourt and Sotheron Road. Though small—front room for best, living room and scullery, two, or sometimes three, small bedrooms—they had piped water with a tap over the sink. Though the W.C. was outside it, too, had piped water and could be flushed, and there was the additional convenience of piped gas for lighting. Those travellers by train could not fail to see, over the fields, the smart clean brick fronts of the houses in the then new Sotheron Road, shown in the drawing on p58. The west side of the road, was quickly filled, including the St Andrew's School for Girls. That the houses were small suited the artizan class for whom they were designed. Merton Road followed soon after, again with terraces of small houses. It was in Nascot that development proceeded most swiftly; Church Road, a mix of terraced cottages and larger houses in their own grounds, Park Road, a few large houses; Stamford Road of smaller terraced cottages and the remainder of Nascot was laid out—Essex-road with larger plots, Malden-road with varying sizes but mostly smaller. Denmark-street and Alexandra-street were large plots and, in consequence, took much longer to find buyers.

When Clarendon Road was cut through to the junction the plots allowed for carriage-drive fronts and very extensive gardens behind the houses. By 1870 the town's 40 or so courtyards and alleys had grown by the addition of nearly forty new roads. The overall progress must have gratified the Local Board that their town was proving so popular—but the popularity was attended by problems. One such was the thorny question of how to pay for paving and this occupied the Local Board's time for many meetings until a solution was found of having paving laid, and paid for on the 'never-never'!

The larger houses as, left, St John's Road c1900, would have bathrooms and WCs, but many of the very first houses would have had a privy at the bottom of the garden without running water for flushing. The (disused) example above was photographed in 1975 in St Albans Road.
Later, most of the earliest terraced houses, and some semi-detached, would have the privy attached to the outside rear of the house.

Over the fields, in the distance, a row of new houses...

Bedford Street was the town's first new road, closely followed by Church Road. The roads which followed were:

Albert Place
Alexandra *laid out only*
Beechen Grove Rd
Bedford St
Carey Place
Charles St
Church Rd *part*
Clarendon Rd *10 large laid out only*
Cross St
Derby Rd *part*
Denmark St
Essex Rd *laid out only*
Earl St
Estcourt Rd *1/3rd*
Fearnley St
Franklin Rd *laid out only*
George St
King Street
Langley Rd *part*
Local Board Rd

Malden Rd *laid out only*
Nascot Rd
Nascot Place
Nascot St *8 houses only*
New Rd
Park Rd
Queen's Road to Duke St, *1/3rd*
Smith Street, *1/3rd*
Sotheron Rd, *1/3rd*
St Johns Rd *14 houses only*
Stamford Rd
Station Rd, *laid out only*
Upper Nascot St *laid out only (later renamed Stratford Road)*
Vicarage Rd, *no houses*
Water Lane
Weymouth St *1/3rd*
Weymouth St Nth *laid out only*
Woodford Rd *to St Johns Rd*

Top: *The world's first petrol-driven car. This was designed and built by Carl Benz in 1885. The horizontal single cylinder engine developed a half horsepower. Five years later Carl Benz made his first four-wheeled car. Prior to this success a number of steam powered vehicles had been made since c1827, many beset with problems with inefficient boilers until design and manufacture gradually improved. Progress was swift; from 1898 a Wagonette bus service ran in Watford for a brief time (p100). Early car progress is summed up on page 89.*

Centre: *This drawing illustrates the scene of a Russian Nihilist scare, in 1881, when dynamite was found by a railway foreman of plate-layers alongside the track. It was believed to have been placed to wreck an Irish mail train from Euston in which a Russian Grand Duke was expected to be a passenger. When the parcel of dynamite was found there was no fuse upon the rail and so danger was averted. It is interesting to note that Water Fields are depicted as being flooded. The houses stretching from the left hand side are of Gladstone Road, with Shaftesbury and Ebury Roads abutting the railway line. To the right of the railway is the distinctive 'tower' of the Orphanage (page 124).*

Bottom: *A carefully posed 'working group' at the rickyard at Harwood's Farm, west Watford, September 1887. Note the horse-drawn farm steam engine.*

School of Music Examinations

Sir.—Has the idea ever occurred to the managing committee of the above excellent institution that the time allowed on an average for the study of vocal and instrumental pieces selected for competition at their annual examinations is scarcely sufficient for the thorough preparation of such works for instance as 'Voi che capate' (Mozart), or Beethoven's 'Sonata Pathetique.'

Works of such a high standard surely require more than three weeks' study to fit them for an examiner's ears. The committee are probably cognizant that the Royal Academy allows three or four months, and Trinity College likewise.

If you will kindly publish this plea for intending candidates at the next examination you will be sincerely thanked by

An Old Student. WO March 1887

Her Majesty's Jubilee

At 9 o'clock there was a large assembly at the north end of the town to witness the planting of a tree by the Countess of Essex. The tree, a fine young oak from Cassiobury, was placed in position on the piece of green at the junction of the Park-road with High-street, and on the Park side of the drinking fountain.

The Royal Standard was mounted near.

Her Ladyship, accompanied by the Earl of Essex, arrived punctually on the ground, and was met by Mr. Humbert, the Chairman of the Committee, the Vicar of Watford, the Chairman of the Local Board, and the members of the Committee. The Vicar, in welcoming Lady Essex, said that she joined with them heart and soul in the proceedings of that day, and they had to thank her very much for her presence. He had merely to announce that Lady Essex would go through the formal ceremony of planting the tree which they saw before them, and to express the wish that great success might attend these efforts to perpetuate the memory of our noble and gracious Queen's reign. (*Cheers.*) It was with extreme pleasure that they saw such unanimity and cordiality throughout her extensive dominions. They did not wish to be behind others, and therefore Lady Essex had acceded to the united wish of the parish that she would plant that memorial, of the day, and might God grant his best blessing on this and other ways in which they tried to celebrate the occasion. (*Cheers.*) Mr. Humbert then handed to Her Ladyship a silver spade, with which she proceeded to place mould around the tree amid the cheering of the spectators, and the Band played 'God save the Queen.'

WO June 1887

To celebrate Queen Victoria's 50 years reign, the town's people were involved in many suggestions as to suitable and befitting monuments. Architect C. P. Ayres suggested demolishing the houses and shops from the 'One Bell' to the Vicarage. thus exposing to view St Mary's Church, and widening the road.

The Earl of Essex suggested an extension to the library or building and endowing some almshouses. Insufficient interest and money was raised and celebrations were limited to planting a tree and giving the children a good feed and a fireworks celebration.

Her Majesty's Jubilee

The arrangements were—and they were carried out as nearly as possible according to the programme—that the Union children, preceded by their band, should march to New-street, and there fall in with the National School children, that the Union band should then proceed down High-street to meet the Bushey children; that the London Orphan Asylum Band should meet the boys from the St. Andrew's School in front of the Watford Railway Station, and proceed by way of Woodford-road to the Sotheron-road Schools, where the St. Andrew's School girls should join the procession, and the Beechen Grove school children fall in at the top of Sutton-road, and go by way of Queen-street to the Market-place. Having assembled there in good order, they marched with their teachers, who entered thoroughly into the arrangements of the day, to the Agricultural Hall.

After the tea the schools were again formed outside, and headed by the band proceeded to Cassiobury Park. Safely arrived in the park, the children dispersed to find amusement.

WO June 1887

Jubilee Committee

The following is the balance sheet—Receipts: from subscriptions, £332 17s.

Expenditure:

Mr. Buck, for dinner, tea, &c., £200 2s. 8d; bands, £18 10s.; medals and favours, £14 11s.; sports committee, for prizes, £44 16s; fireworks, £15; expenses for planting the tree, £3 18s,; refreshments for committee and the police, £5 11d.; Mr. Peacock, for printing, &c., £14 8s.; postage and stationery, £5 6s. 7d.; labour, £5 13s 9d.; Mr. Grant, for collecting, £5 6s.; total, £332 17s. Audited and found correct by Messrs. H. S. Allen and G. Heath.

WO November, 1887

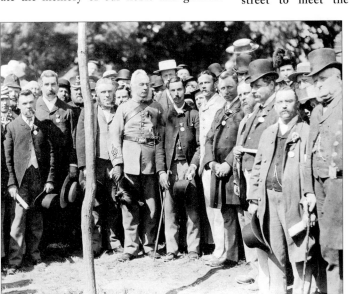

Above: *An 'Arch of Welcome' across the High Street (from where modern Woolworth's is across to 'Moon Under Water').*

Left: *The oak tree so carefully planted grew well and survived until 1938 when the island was removed for the new roundabout in place of the erstwhile crossroads. (See p213).*
Most of the men of of importance were at the ceremony; in uniform is Dr Brett, then C P Ayres, and next to him, in the light suit, Lord Clarendon; passing to the bowler hat may be C R Humbert and at the extreme right is the Earl of Essex. The Vicar, Reg Capell, and most of the members of the Local Board were in attendance.

The Bridge Over the River Colne

To the Editor of the Watford Observer.

Sir,—Let me endorse every word your correspondent 'An old Inhabitant" writes on the subject of the bridge over the river Colne. If it really be the case that our Local Board intend to erect a foot-bridge by the side of the old one, I for one must raise my voice against any such 'tinkering.' Let our Board look the matter boldly in the face and set to work to provide a new bridge at once. The cost would be nominal, with assistance from the County Authorities, which we might expect—a three-farthing rate would be ample.

May I also ask when the sewer ventilators are to be removed? I understood the Board had arrived at a determination to this effect; if so, the delay is unpardonable. I would advise your readers particularly to avoid the gratings opposite Oxhey Church, the stench from these is abominable and undeniably dangerous to the number of people, particularly young children, who attend that church.

I am sir, your faithfully, Another Inhabitant
Watford, November 15th 1887.

Dinners for Poor Children

To the Editor of the Watford Observer.

Dear Sir,—During the winter of 1886-7 I was enabled through the benevolence of various donors to give dinners, at the school of cookery, for such children at the elementary schools as appeared most in want of nourishment, and whose parents were not in a position to provide them with sufficient food. The amount received was £20 19s. 6d. I have a balance of £1 0s. 8d. in hand. I propose to recommence what I look upon as a good charity as soon as I can make the necessary arrangements, and I shall be glad to receive subscriptions at the address below.

I should like to add that preference is given to those children whose parents do not dissipate their earnings in drink, and that last winter we were enabled to provide nearly 2,000 dinners.

Faithfully yours, Reg. Capell
Little Cassiobury, Watford. December 13th.

Allotment Gardens

Dear Sir,—I hope in the course of a week or so to mark out for allotment gardens a portion of the farm on the left of the St. Albans-road, now in the occupation of Mr. A. Johnstone. The land is in good heart, and the rent will be to the tenants 6d. per pole, and the plots will be of about 10 poles each. Before finally settling with Mr. Johnstone, it is desirable I should know how many plots are likely to be taken up; and Mr. T. Turner (Cassiobury Saw Mills), has been so good as to say that applicants may register their names, etc., at his office.

I subjoin the rules which have been in force in regard to the allotments on Harwoods Farm. They have worked well, and I propose to adopt the same for the Callow Land Allotment Gardens. Each tenant will have a copy, and will be required to sign a book, agreeing to abide by them.

Yours faithfully, REG. CAPELL.

(1). The rent of the allotments shall be at the rate of 6d. per pole per annum. All rents to be paid on the 25th March, 24th June, 29th September, 25th December in each year. Any tenant not paying his rent within seven days of the times stated shall be fined 3d.; if not within 14 days 6d., after which he shall be liable to be expelled, and to forfeit all crops on the ground.

WO, January 1888

• *In 1887 an Allotment Act empowered local Sanitary Authorities to provide allotments for the labouring classes—partly as a means of providing self-help for the unemployed. Sunday work on allotments was not to be allowed.*

Dr. Brett wrote

"We the undersigned, being registered Parliamentary electors, residing in the Watford Urban Sanitary district, beg respectfully to submit to your Board that circumstances of the Urban District of Watford are such that it is the duty of the Authority to provide allotments for the inhabitants of the district"

and appended signatures of 38 other gentlemen. The two questions to be answered were (a) was there a demand and (b) would allotments be found by voluntary arrangements.

Vicar Reg Capell was successful in obtaining land and 'labouring classes' was taken to include sedentary and shop workers so that these, too, could enjoy an 'open-air' activity.

Tenders for the new Police Station

Hazelgrove, W., Luton	£6475
Andrews & Sons, Watford	6275
White, John, Bedford	6185
Marriott Bros, High Barnet	6162
Grist, S, Aylesbury	6058
Ellwood & Son, Sandy	5990
Rhodes, W. A., London	5850
Willmot & Son, Hitchin	5846
Turner, Thos. Ltd., Watford	5839
Judge & Eames, Watford	5796
Miskin, Christr., St Albans	5700
Bunting, Arthur, Fenstanton	5694
Dabbs, M. W., London	5580
Bonnett, S. T., Watford	5492
Waterman, G. & J., Watford	5396
Dupont, F., Colchester *(accepted)*	5185
Jarvis, Edwin, Banbury	5000

WO, March 1888

Left: *"It is seldom that one comes across, within twenty miles of London, such a quaint old market town as Watford, or meets with such diverse types . . . and pity is taken upon the poor girl, looking longingly at the silk handkerchief, who wishes she had money to invest in such finery." c1885/6 from a pencil drawing by W. Borough Johnson, published in a Christmas issue of the "London Illustrated News", c1890. It is drawn in the corner near the King's Head and looks towards the Green Man.*

Right: *Hertfordshire Yeomanry parade in the Market Place, outside the King's Head and Spread Eagle. The shop with the blind is a butcher's, burned down in 1828 and rebuilt, as was the King's Head. The two-storey building 'East', another butcher's, is Nos. 74 and 76, Mr Fisher's, to be demolished.*

Far right: *A livestock market day, with the Auctioneer on his stand outside the Compasses. The large building, right, houses the offices of Sedgwick, Turner and Walker; to its left, the Compasses and beyond is the butcher's shop doomed for demolition to make a new road. Beyond is the 'Rose & Crown'.*

The right to hold a weekly market was a privilege to be respected, and that of the Lord of the Manor, the Earl of Essex, and incumbent upon his lessee to run it for him. Their sales of land and the increase in population had made the street cattle market an anachronism and the Board devoted much time to solving the problem.

Behind the 'Rose & Crown was a sort of general-purpose hinterland having upon it playing fields and being used as short cuts from the High Street to Merton and Vicarage Roads. Rumour would have it that Mr Fisher was contemplating knocking down a small shop—a butcher's—and cutting through a new street. The opening of Market Street would be an event of considerable importance as it could provide an eventual link to Croxley, as well as a new street, or streets, of houses and perhaps new shops. Speculation is not reported in the local paper but the conversations reported in 'Moving the Market', below, give some indication of expectations. In due course several roads were laid out, and the plots allowed for including Catholic and Board schools. It would also pave the way for a livestock market and a new Catholic Church.

As an aside, Mr Fisher's new building–home and shop–was then the first modern premises to built in the High Street. This was followed shortly by the rebuilding of the Bucks and Oxon Bank across the road.

Tenders.

The following tenders have been received for pulling down Nos. 74 and 76, High-street Watford, and erecting new house, shop, and slaughter-house for Mr. Francis Fisher.

Mr. Charles P. Ayres, 52, High-street, Watford, architect—

Brightman, C.	£2699
Judge and Eames	£2687
Andrews and Sons	£2678
Dove, H. M.	£2575
Turner, T. (Limited).	£2447
Neal, W. B	£2397
Waterman, G. & J. (accepted)	£2337

WO May, 1888

Watford Market

To the Editor of the Watford Observer.
Dear Sir,—Can you, through the medium of your paper, inform me who is responsible for the obstruction to trade and a nuisance to the people in upper High-street, on market days?

Yesterday there was a large flock of sheep from 12 until 4 o'clock all over the road and on the pavement in front of my steps, close to the windows.

It was impossible for vehicles to get near, and also most difficult for foot passengers to pass. I spoke to the owner of the cattle, and he, in a very abrupt manner said "I pay toll for them," and that I could have my remedy.

Is the Lord of the manor, the Local Board, or is Mr. Humbert responsible for this nuisance that is taking place every Tuesday?

I maintain that those who receive the tolls should be compelled at once to find a proper place for the cattle; and not to be the means of sending customers away on market days.

I am sir, respectfully yours,
Walter Allen.
Watford,
Wednesday, October 31st, 1888

Herts Yeomanry Cavalry

The annual training of the Yeomanry, which began on Wednesday in last week, was hampered considerably by the heavy thunder showers which prevailed for several days. On Friday morning the regiment paraded in the Market place at 10.45, and marched to Cassiobury Park, but heavy rain came on and very little drill was got through. There was an improvement in the weather, however, on Saturday, and various evolutions with outpost duty, were undertaken in the Park until luncheon time, field movements, sword exercise, and a march past finishing the day's work.

WO (May, 1890)

Moving the Market

The Chairman: In case we are compelled by the authorities to remove the market we may have certain compulsory powers; but you see that our idea as to what may be done is very vague.

... the Board of Health ought to make the town attractive, a residential place ...

Mr. S. Martin: I am in favour of removing the market, because it will remove the present nuisance. Outside the market place the beasts and sheep brought in are an abominable nuisance. Yesterday there was a flock of sheep along Dr. Brett's wall; there were more along the path for two hours outside Dr. Brett's house, and a flock outside my office, and the paths today are all left in the state they were when the cattle left. That I think shows the necessity for the removal of the market. I asked the question because I thought that if it were decided to buy this piece of land the remedy we wish to arrive at will be effected.

The Chairman: We cannot say the remedy will be effected until we get the power to remove the market, but if the Board had the premises and likewise the power to act as regards the market, we should of course issue rules for the regulation of it and prevent cattle and sheep, and what not, straying all over the place.

Mr. S. Martin: Then there is another question. What is the price asked for the land in question?

The Chairman: I do not think we need go into the price to-day, because when we come to the price we shall have to apply to a ratepayers' meeting of the whole Local Board district.

The Chairman: I can instance another place—the market at King's Lynn. They have there a very admirable cattle market, about 11/2 acres, with iron pens, and in an adjoining square dry goods and other things. I went through the cattle market a day or two after the market, and there was no smell whatever.

Mr. Austin: I do not think we require more room than we have already, if we find room for the cattle. I think we should spoil the trade of the town if we do not keep the rest of the market where it is now. Would Mr. Humbert move his cattle to his own land?

The Clerk: The difficulty would be this. If Mr. Humbert did move his sale, and the local Board had not acquired the rights, there would be nothing to prevent anyone else coming and selling in his place.

Mr. Austin: If the Local Board take it, cannot they be the master, as Mr. Humbert is?

The Clerk: Mr. Humbert is not the master. Mr. Humbert can take the toll of any person who comes into the market, but he has no exclusive right of selling. If an auctioneer claims a space he must find room for him.

Anyone can go with a flock of sheep and claim a right to sell them in the market.

The Chairman: Mr. Hoy asks the value of the tolls. According to the information given before the Commissioner they amount to £40 or £50 a year. He also asks what it will cost us for the market generally. It may surprise you to learn that it will cost about £5,000, taking it all together. That is not saying anything about the site, but the general figure. Either we must make a friendly arrangement with Lord Essex or wait until we have compulsory powers. We

Left: Mr Fisher's new house, shop and slaughter house is complete; his recently purchased butcher's shop now demolished and the way clear to start laying out the new roads.

The passageway between No. 78 and Fisher's shop is the entrance to New Street leading to Ballard's Buildings and Church Street; and now the foot entrance to Church Car Park.

Top: A 1995 view of the same section of the Market Place

... good gravel well laid, pleasant to walk upon ...

have the lord to deal with and the lessee also.

Dr. Brett: I would rather hear other people speak their minds, but as I am called upon I will say something. I am old enough to recollect Smithfield, where they used to have a cattle market, and it was found to be an intolerable nuisance to the London people; in our small way this is a second Smithfield.

It is a nuisance from the cattle coming in, the smell, and the noise. I saw ladies rushing into Buck's shop yesterday, and I had to stand by while the cattle passed me. The beasts and flocks of sheep stand in Clarendon-road, and the stench they leave is not desirable. If there were more room in the market-place trade would be increased; there really is not room for the beasts and cattle. I think that the quadrupeds ought to be removed to some more convenient place where there is room for them.

It is cruel to the poor animals, and I am sure that it is a nuisance to health, and the smell remains from week to week. Though the place is washed down, you can see pools of coloured liquid, apparently stinking urine. Mr. Williams and I do not quite agree as to the cause of the nuisance: he will tell you presently, if he is asked, that it is owing to horses. I am not skillful enough to tell the difference, but I know that the result of the accumulation of the droppings of swine and other animals is very bad.

If you have cattle, you should have material, which can be washed down like a slaughter house and leave no remains whatever. If you look at the Market place you see big stones which you could put your thumb between, and the urine and excreta get between them.

Mr. Humbert said that he had put 15 loads of gravel down lately. But if you make a farmyard with a gravel bottom, whenever you wash it you wash it further in. I think that the Board of Health ought to aim to make the town attractive—make it a residential place.

There is no doubt that Watford might be made a place that people would think it an honour and privilege to live in. We have the country; every day in the week you can walk into a fresh park. We all agree that to have a market in a town like this is of very great value to us; it brings many people to the town. No one wants to do away with the market, but the trade has increased so much that there is not space enough to do the business. If you have space for ten times as much the business of the market would be ten times as big, and bring ten times as many people to increase the trade of Watford.

If you get rid of the quadrupeds in the street you will have more business done. It will improve the old market-place, and I think after first buying it you will make it pay, because when you get the tolls you can charge sufficient to compensate for the outlay.

The Clerk: I was asked as to the power of the Local Board with the view to acquiring the market I think that it will be convenient to answer it to this extent at the present

moment—that the Local Board can only acquire the market by consent, but I think we have every reason to believe that they will have compulsory powers within a very limited time.

I think the question is this. If it is thought generally desirable to remove the cattle and sheep from the market place, is it not desirable before the opportunity passes to get a piece of the only land in the immediate neighbourhood of the market? If you can get it on fair terms, is it not desirable to get it? If then, going to Lord Essex and Mr. Humbert, they do not see their way to give you terms which are reasonable, you will only have to wait one or two sessions, when the Local Board, or the District Council it may be, their successors, will have power to take the market on fair terms.

Perhaps I may state that Mr. Fisher—I am not divulging anything by saying this—has given us the refusal of the property until the 31st October. *(Applause.)*

I think that we should move rapidly and make up our minds.

WO October, 1888

The Roads and Footpaths

To the Editor of the Watford Observer.

Sir,—I beg you will afford me a small space in your paper for what I venture to term a public grievance in Watford. I am referring to the state of the public roads and footpaths in the town, and am in hope that the members of our Local Board will themselves look into these matters and remedy the defects which so painfully force themselves upon our notice.

When a road is relaid or repaired, the system, or want of system, in Watford, seems to be to spread over the surface a thick layer of stone, chiefly pebbles and flints—very good material for road making,— and then leave it to its own devices, or to be trodden and worn down by general traffic.

The stones are never properly broken, numerous lumps are left as big or bigger than a large man's fist, which always remain as stumbling-blocks.

It may be noted also that the centre of the road is hardly raised higher than the sides, and the ordinary traffic quickly pushes the loose stones from the centre to the side, so that by the time the road is worn a little smooth, its centre is on a level or even lower than the sides.

It is said that the Local Board possess rollers and even use them, but one seldom has the good fortune to see them in this part of the town—St. Andrew's district.

The stones are left loose on the roads for days and weeks and if eventually the roller is employed it is too late, for the ballast has been displaced to the sides and the road is hollowed out in the centre and can never become either good or lasting. Everyone knows that the stones should be broken to a suitable size, and that directly they are laid, if there is no rain, they should be well watered

and at once rolled, and it would pay well to use a steam roller.

Now for the footpaths, which are if possible worse than the roads. I would not myself wish to see pavement of asphalt, except in the main streets where there are shops, as gravel looks nicer, and good gravel well laid and properly rolled makes a good smooth path and pleasant to walk on, as one has in one's own garden, but the paths in Watford are infamous, and it is simply cruel to ask people to use them.

They appear to be of a sort of coarse shingly gravel, at least this is what always appears on the surface, and when laid they are neither watered nor rolled, and are either a surface of loose rough stone in dry weather, or of soft mud in wet. The badness of the roads and paths in Watford is a bye-word, and they are a disgrace to a civilised community. Our money is being wasted, and not only have we to put up with disgracefully bad roads, but they last half as long as they would if properly made, and are far more expensive in the long run. In the interests of the public, of their cattle, and of their poor feet, I call upon the Local Board and agents to mend their ways.

Yours faithfully, A Long-Sufferer.
Watford, October 10th, 1888

THE South of England Telephone Company offer to connect their subscribers with a central office in Watford for £10 per annum. Mr. Henry Rogers, whose advertisement appears in the present issue, will supply telephones for short distances, including erection, at £3 17s. 6d., and for greater distance at £10, without any further payment whatever, this being at the same rate for the entire purchase as the Telephone Company charge annually. Mr. H. Rogers has recently fitted up telephonic communication between the central building at the St. Pancras schools and the Infirmary and other outlying offices, and is now engaged in telephonic work at Marlborough, Ballyclare, and other places.—

[ADVERT] WO September, 1888

a new road to be opened out of the High Street . . .

The Coat-of-Arms For Watford

Dear Sir,—As we have now a coat-of-arms for Watford, I thought it might interest your readers to know the history of the movement. The idea of having a coat-of-arms for Watford originated with the Committee of the Library about seven years ago, so we cannot be accused of being rash and precipitate.

When I was Chairman to the Library for the first three years, my years of office were rewarded by seeing the foundation stone of the Library building laid with Masonic honours, and the opening of it by the Lord Lieutenant, the Earl of Verulam. I am anxious that my second chairmanship shall be distinguished by clearing off two works that have been on the stocks many years—namely, the coat-of-arms for Watford, and the enlargement of the Library. We have obtained the first, and I trust we shall accomplish the second as soon as the turmoil of the

County Council election is over. I should like to be permitted to explain why I have had to take a prominent part in this matter. I saw how desirable it would be to have some device for our work in the Library, in our certificates of merit, and for our books.

The same is wanted much for the Endowed Schools. The Committee requested me, some years since, to obtain the opinion of those who were learned in heraldry or in mottoes, or who had artistic taste. I should like to mention that thanks are due for suggestions and for information to the following among many others:—The members of the Library

Committee in general, and the Rev. Newton Price in particular, who is sponsor for the motto, "Audentior"; the Earl of Essex; the Earl of Clarendon; the Master of the Rolls (Lord Esher); the Hon. Arthur Capell; Mr. John Evans (the Treasurer of the Royal Society); Mr. Thomas Woods, of Durrants Farm; Mr. Henry Finch, J.P., Red Heath; Dr. Puckett, our Art Master, who took great trouble; the Vicar; Mr Charles Healey the First, Mr. Clement Heaton, and many others.

The above are not responsible for the design at last adopted. I hope some day to send to your Notes and Queries columns an explanation of the coat-of-arms when time permits.

I remain, your obedient servant,
ALFRED THOMAS BRETT.
WO, December 1888

Below: *Charles Ayres, holding the roll of plans, and standing next to Mr Fisher, has designed, and had built, Watford's most imposing commercial building, so dragging Watford's High Street out of the agricultural era. It is against this backdrop that many traders and shoppers are irked by the cattle markets. The Rose & Crown shows the remains of the demolished buildings which allowed Market-street to be cut through. This photograph and bottom p72 are by William Coles.*

A new Wesleyan church consecrated . . .

The Story of Watford Methodism.

There is no record of any visit of John Wesley to Watford. Methodism was mainly introduced to the town from St. Albans, where there was a vigorous Society. On or about the year 1814, Methodism in Watford was represented by a few godly folk who were content to meet in each other's houses, and traditions exist of their gatherings in Hedges Yard, Rodwell Yard and Briden's Yard.

It was owing to the generosity of a Mr. John Wood of Holywell Hill that the Methodists were able to build their first Chapel. He bought a plot of ground near to Water Lane and presented it to the Methodist Connexion. On this land the first chapel was built. This first chapel soon became too small and was succeeded by one in Farthing Lane.

As late as 1862, the population of Watford was only 7,415, and only four clergymen and two nonconformist ministers were resident in the town. The Wesleyans were worshipping in Farthing Lane Chapel, the Independents in the older Water Lane Chapel and the Primitives in Woodman's Yard. The Baptist Church in Beechen Grove was founded in 1707, the present edifice being opened in 1878.

This Farthing Lane Chapel was afterwards sold to the trustees of the Watford Ragged School and is still used by them.

Owing to the liberality of Mr. W. H. Petty and the help of the Rev. E. Day, a commanding site was secured in Queen's Road and a school chapel, now used as a school, was built. This was opened in 1869 and the church membership at the time was 71.

Mrs. Petty, a Portuguese lady, gave the greater portion of the site, and her monument is still to be seen in the cemetery at Watford. During the ministries of the Rev. W. P. Peck and the Rev. F. Holmes Smith, the project of building the present fine structure was started;

and during the ministry of the Rev. Daniel Pearson, building operations were commenced.

The new church, the cost of which was £8,800, and the seating accommodation 1,100, was consecrated on Wednesday, January 16th, 1889, and the first sermon in it preached by the late Rev. James Stuart. The organ was the generous gift of the late Mr. E. Clifford, other friends meeting the cost of accessories.

Wednesday, October 14th 1914, was the hundredth anniversary of Methodism in Watford and was celebrated at the Wesleyan Church, Queen's Road, in a very enthusiastic manner. It is interesting to note that according to an old circuit plan, Watford Methodists were attached to the Luton Circuit from October 24th, 1812, to April 3rd, 1814.

Watford Illustrated
(October 1914)

Below: *The light-coloured line above the heads of the crowd listening to Mr Sequah's band is that of the newly laid-out line for Percy Road. Beyond are the houses in Merton Road with a small clump of bushes at the right being the site of the Empire Cinema in 1913. The name 'Merton' perpetuates that of Merton College, Oxford, whose land it was. Sequah was a travelling salesman of potions–claiming to cure rheumatism–and extractor of teeth; here giving a farewell concert of live music from his carriage in May 1890. The photograph is interesting in that it is by Mr Downer who first published it in his illustrated weekly paper in February 1916.*

. . . the principal street laid out, named Market-street.

Result of Auction
MESSRS. HUMBERT, SON & FLINT
Mr. Humbert first put up the shop plots, pointing out their value, being in the centre of the town and close to the Market-place. The plots were small to suit purchasers, and it had been said that they were too small, but if they were two could be had. Four plots might be bought and three houses put upon them, or three plots and two houses built; but, he said in answer to a query, three plots would not be sold to put four houses on.

There was no other building land for sale in Watford, and the last sold, only a few weeks ago, fetched a very high price, £9 a foot frontage. Messrs. Andrews, who were always lucky, for whatever they touched seemed to turn to gold, were about the only holders of building land in the neighbourhood. No doubt they would want £5 or £6 a foot if they were asked. (Mr. John Andrews: We have none to sell). Therefore the only land for sale was the Rose and Crown Estate.

The first bid for the shop lots was £70, then £80, the amount afterwards rising by biddings of £1 to £91, and lots 4 and 5 were taken at that price; the next two at £85; the next two at £88; lot 10 at £89; lot 11, £88; 12 and 13 at £87; 14 and 15 at £95; 16 at £92; 17 and 18 at £96; 19, 20, 21 and 22, at £85; 23 and 24 at £86.

At lot 38 biddings were slow, and Mr. Humbert announced that though the price required was £88 a plot £80 would be taken for that day only up to lot 45. Proceeding then to the plots abutting upon Stone's-alley, the whole, from 93 to 103 were soon disposed of at about £90 each. The number of plots sold was 47, the total sum realised being £3,096, the average being £83 per plot.

Rose and Crown Building Land
THE first offer by public auction of the freehold land on the Rose and Crown estate, belonging to Mr. Francis Fisher, took place on Tuesday, after the market. It is many years since land so near the centre of the town has been offered for building. The principal street laid out, which has been named Market-street, opens directly from the Market-place, by the removal of the premises formerly occupied by Mr. Fisher (and in years gone by Mr. G. Stone) as a butcher's shop. The opening has on one side the Rose and Crown Hotel, which is being in great part rebuilt, and on the other the Compasses Inn.

Turning out of Market-street, which continues in a straight line until it opens into Merton-road on the far side of the estate, is, first, Marlborough-road, which, turning to the left, and running almost parallel with the old way known as Stone's-alley, runs into the old way across Monks Folly, or the continuation of Merton-road, leading to Park-road. Percy-road comes next, connecting Market-street, at somewhere about half its length, with Francis-road, a street which leaves Market-street near the Merton-road end, and goes parallel with the old way to Marlborough-road.

Mr. C. R. Humbert has purchased a good piece of the land between Stone's-alley and Marlborough-road for his sale yard, and a smaller piece adjoining is held for a similar purpose by Mr. H. B. Didsbury.

Between Marlborough-road and Percy-road a site, with a frontage also to Market-street, has been purchased for a Roman Catholic church. The sale took place in the Corn Exchange, in consequence of the building going on at the Rose and Crown Hotel.

WO June, 1889

The New Catholic Church
The tender of Messrs. T. Turner, Limited, has been accepted for the erection of the new Catholic Church, which is to stand in Market-street, with return frontages in Marlborough-road and Percy-road, Mr. John F. Bentley, of John-street, Adelphi, being the architect.

The Post and Sorting Office was built upon the corner of Queen Street and Derby Road in 1885. From here the horse-drawn mail coach left every night for London, until 1908 when it was superseded by a motor van. In the background, behind the house, is the larger building of the Beechen Grove School in Red Lion Yard.

... technical instruction, is it for the benefit of the working man?

The church will be in the late perpendicular style, and its outer walls will abut directly upon the three streets, without an intervening fence.

The exterior facing will be of dressed flint, with stone quoins, windows, buttresses, &c. The main roofs will be tiled, and twin turrets springing from the chancel piers will surmount the whole. The plan shows a chancel 35 feet long, a nave 65 feet long by 25 wide, three chapels, two transepts, three aisles and a baptistry, of which rather more than half will be built now at a cost of just over £4,000.

There will be a rood and rood loft, and its treatment, as well as that of the baptistery, the pulpit, and a double arcade and tritorium round the chancel, will be very picturesque. The tracing in the windows will also be noticeable. A clergy house will be erected next to the church, and behind this will stand the schools, while close by, the sisters, who undertake the education of the children, have secured a site for their house.

It is expected that Cardinal Manning will shortly lay the foundation stone, and Messrs. Turner have undertaken to finish their contract by the end of February, so that the church may be consecrated upon Lady-day, 1890.
WO, July 1889

The part-finished church opened in September 1890 and Messrs T Turner Ltd, of Cassiobury Saw Mills of St Albans Road went on to complete the church by 1897 at a cost of £20,000, and between £30,000 and £40,000 including the presbytery and school.

The benefactor was Mr Stephen Taprell Holland who, with Drs Wilson Iles and Brett, served in Watford Rifle Volunteer Corps.

The Technical Instruction Act

A letter to the board:

Watford, 31st December, 1889. Gentlemen,—In response to the invitation to the ratepayers, I for one would protest against the adoption at present of this Act.

Watford is not a manufacturing town, or noted for any special industry, and therefore the trade of the place would not be more prosperous if you could train up a few special local workmen, however dist-inguished they might become.

It would, I submit, be an act of injustice to tax all the ratepayers for the benefit of a few. In a leader in the Times a few days ago it was said, 'Polytechnics are excellent things, but it is not certain that they will succeed when they are directed exclusively by a class above the persons who use them. Mechanics' institutions of the latter kind are a declared failure because they were managed not by the mechanics, but for them, while on the other hand the self-governing institutes and clubs in Lancashire and Yorkshire, in which the men, women, and boys feel their personal honour to be involved are a conspicuous success.' Let those who want Technical

At a distribution of prizes of the Literary Institute in 1871 Stephen Camp (above) broached the subject of establishing a Public Library and Reading Room; the sequel was that a Building Committee was appointed by the Institute and this led to the building of the Public Library and School of Science and Art in 1874.

Education in Watford pay for it. If they could get it for nothing they would regard it generally as worth what it cost.

Whether you get many communications or only a few on this subject, depend upon it there will be a great outcry, as there was against the adoption of the Libraries' Act, if the Board in the exercise of their powers make a penny rate or apply a sum equal thereto for the purposes of the Technical Education Act.

Increased rents and increased rates are a burden which some of the tradesmen in Watford may find it difficult to cope with, and the Local Board will not contribute unnecessarily to the latter.

Yours obediently,
Stephen Camp.

Technical Instruction Act

Watford House
Gentlemen,—I wish to thank you for allowing me and other ratepayers to express an opinion upon the desirability of our adopting this Act in Watford. I am strongly in favour of adopting the Act because I think it is capable of doing great good (if properly managed), and it may in the end decrease our rates. It is not quite clear to me how best to carry out the Act.

It seems that the Science and Art Department is charged with it. I find that there are two institutions in Watford working

---

Printing photographs

In 1882 an invention made possible the printing of copies of photographs by letterpress printing. By having a special glass plate with finely engraved lines the tones of a photograph could be broken up into very fine 'dots' each varying in size according to the darkness or lightness of the original. Hitherto, illustrations had either to be hand-engraved in steel or copper, or of 'woodcuts' or 'lithographed' from drawings upon stone.

The new police station in King Street—one of the few woodcuts printed, by the Watford Observer, of buildings newly erected. Opened in January 1889 the building has, since 1962, been the Robert Peel public house. A suggestion, in 2001, that the Robert Peel be demolished and rebuilt as a hotel has yet to mature.

... inclined to favour Technical Education ... if our Surveyor would become a pupil ...

Local Board Meetings, in a room at the pumping station in Local Board Road, were invariably concerned with 'street' affairs—paving, cleanliness (or lack of), drainage, lighting, etc. This report is therefore little different to many others with the Market-place, and lighting, being prominent.

The Medical Officer of Health's report, which follows, is in its brief entirety and deals with the town's health very succinctly. It is also quite typical.

in conjunction with South Kensington—the Watford Public Library and the Endowed Schools.

I am informed that the grant obtained last year from South Kensington by the Endowed Schools (Boys) was £86 12s., I think by the Library £9, so that the boys schools do ten times the science work of the library, at least they got ten times the reward.

Under these circumstances, as I presume the governors of the Endowed Schools would be represented in the new Board of Management of the Technical Instruction Act, if the Governors could assist in carrying out the Technical Instruction Act for the benefit of the town, I think I may say they would willingly do so. Some plan might be devised that would obtain the help of both the educational institutions—the Watford Endowed Schools and the Watford Public Library. I enclose you a list of the subjects taught at the Endowed Schools.

I remain, Your obedient servant,
Alfred T. Brett.
N.B.—*The above remarks are made as a private ratepayer. I alone am responsible for the opinions.*

WO January 1890

Technical Instruction

To the Editor of the Watford Observer.
Sir,—I think the thanks of the ratepayers and the working men are due to our townsman, Mr. Camp, for his outspoken letter to the Watford Local Board.

As to technical instruction, there is no doubt that it would be a great hardship to many. Supposing it could be carried out as it has been in Germany, what would it do?

Cheapen the price of labour and so become a curse to the working man. If a trade is worth learning, it is worth paying for. Is it for the benefit of the working man?

No, most certainly not, it is for the middle and upper classes. When the Public Library was first talked about, it was said what a good thing it would be for the working man. What do we hear now about the working man?

Nothing, what we want is a public meeting in the Corn Exchange, not at the Liberal Club or at any other club.

This is not a political question, it is a question of pounds, shillings and pence.

Yours, &c., A Ratepayer
(Who has paid to learn his Trade). Watford.
WO January, 1890

Local Board

The usual meeting of the Board was held on Thursday. There were present Mr. E. J. Slinn (Chairman), Mr. C. P. Ayres, Mr. J. Weall, Mr. H. Thomas, Mr. E. Mead, Mr. J. C. Benskin, Mr. E. Clifford, and Mr. J. Andrews.

The Market Place

A letter from Messrs. Humbert, Son, and Flint, said that they had considered the request by the Local Board that they should pay 6s. a week for cleansing the Market-place instead of the sum they now pay. Inasmuch as paying for the cleansing at all was purely a voluntary act, they hardly thought that the Board should have requested them to pay a further sum.

However, as the Board had done so, and they were anxious to fall in with their views, they would agree to pay the 6s. a week from the 26th March next. But they would like it to be understood that it was a voluntary matter on their part; they did not admit their liability to contribute towards the cleaning of the Market-place.

The Board received the following letter.—

Elmleigh, Watford, January 28th, 1890.
"Dear Sir,—There is an old saying that "lookers see most of the game," and I trust you will allow me to bring to the notice of the Board a few matters that I think if properly attended to would conduce most materially to the comfort and convenience of the inhabitants of Watford.

In the first place crossings are absolutely needed in very many of the streets and roads, particularly at the crossing of the St. Albans-road at the end of Langley-road, in the neighbourhood of Queen's-road, Sotheron-road, &c., which is a much used thoroughfare into the town, three or four are required, and I have no doubt there are several other places where they are wanted.

I hear that two or three 'carriage people' do not want them, as they say the springs of their conveyances suffer, but even if they did, surely the convenience of the few should not prevail against that of the many? But I have yet to learn that crossings, if properly laid down in the first instance and kept in good repair do occasion any appreciable damage or inconvenience even to the few, and if the Surveyor to the Board cannot keep them in order it is time that there should be someone who can.

A great portion of the benefit derived from our new paths is done away with, when having to cross the road in wet weather you have to do it through a sea of mud. It is a source of

amusement to me to see the manner in which green stone is put on the roads, and then scraped up again in the shape of mud a few days after. Surely if we must have gravel roads there is some place where it can be exposed to the action of the sun and air before it is laid on. Strongly as I am opposed to adding to the rates for the new fad of technical education, I should be inclined to favour it if I thought that our Surveyor would become a pupil and learn the art of practical road and path making.

Before closing this letter, I should like to ask when the residents in Church and Park-roads are likely to get their new paving? The first of these roads is very thickly populated, and the residents have, together with those of Park-road, paid rates and taxes for the last 25 or 30 years, yet I see mushroom streets that have only been called into existence the last two or three years have got their pavements, whilst these two are out in the cold. By all means let new streets be properly paved, but do not neglect the old ones because they have no one on the Board specially interested in them. I trust that we shall not be put off again on the ground that the money will be wanted in the shape of a technical education rate.

Yours truly,
Josceline F. Watkins.

Mr. Clifford: That's a scorcher!
Mr. Thomas: But with a good deal of truth in it.
The Surveyor: And there is a good deal that is not true. We have not been putting "green" gravel on the roads.
The Chairman: Then we refer the Surveyor's report and Mr. Watkins's letter to the Highway Committee?
Mr. Mead: I propose that it should be dealt with to-day. Mr. Benskin seconded.
Mr. Thomas said that it was a question for the future, not for this year, and he moved that it be referred to the Committee. Mr. Ayres seconded and Mr. Thomas's amendment was carried.

Numbering Houses

A letter from Dr. Brett was read asking the Board to have the houses in the different streets properly numbered, and pointing out the inconvenience of the present irregularity of numbering some streets. It was resolved to instruct the Inspector to report.

The Lighting at Watford Junction

A letter from the London and North-Western Railway Company in reply to one from this Board was read, stating that enquiry had been made into this matter, and it was found that the Company had five gas lamps in front of the station, which were amply sufficient for all purposes in connection with the railway.

Doubtless the open space in front of the station was inadequately lighted when the lights of the Malden and Clarendon Hotels were extinguished, but that was a question for the Local Board to deal with, and there were no grounds for calling upon the Company.

the sooner we get lanterns and hang them on the lamp-posts, the better ...

The Public Lighting

A letter from Mr. J. C. Binyon was read, asking whether we were really to go through the winter without light at night, if not, the sooner we got lanterns and hung them on the lamp-posts the better. Watford was supposed to be a flourishing town, and yet was compelled by this Board to go back to the days of the curfew to save a few pounds.

The Chairman said that in putting out the lamps he thought they had begun at the wrong time of the year, it would do perfectly well in May, June, and July. Mr. Clifford said that he could see that now, and he thought it desirable to make an alteration, that six weeks before and six weeks after the longest day they should not light the lamps at all. The Chairman said that the saving from not having the lamps lighted would be very small indeed, but he thought that instead of at once proposing that they should not light them for six weeks before and six weeks after the longest day, they should use the time between now and next May in thinking out the best way of acting. He thought it was certainly the wish of the town that the lamps should be lighted now; the feeling was certainly in favour of continuing the old scale. Mr. Clifford said that a lot of people were in favour of putting out the lamps early, and they asked him not to let the new arrangement be altered; but there were many people whose business began early in the morning who felt very great inconvenience, and so, having considered the matter further, he thought they ought to have the light.

Mr. Savill said that the memorial to the Board was signed by 157 inhabitants, most of the tradespeople. Mr. Clifford said that people were asked to put down their names to that memorial whether they were ratepayers or not. What reply had been received in answer to their letter to the Gas Company?

The Clerk said that they had had no reply.

The Chairman said that looking at the number of personal applications he had, he thought that they ought to deal with the matter at once. Mr. Benskin said that so far as he was concerned, he had a great many more come to him and express themselves in favour of his resolution, than he had people expostulating with him for it.

The Chairman thought they must be people who went to bed early and got up late.

Mr. Benskin said that he was told by a gentleman who goes up to London at 8 o'clock in the morning that all the clerks who go from Bushey agreed with his proposition.

Mr. Benskin said that from figures he had obtained from Mr. Rowell, the secretary to the Gas Company, he found that the total amount expended by the Board on gas in the six months of the summer of 1886 was £159, and the total amount in the two winter quarters was £447. Last year they carried out a proposition he made that the lamps should be extinguished at 1 o'clock, and this year, he not being present at the Board meeting, they went back to the old scale, and spent £113 6s. 9d. in three months.

They could only save about £20 in the summer months if they put the lamps out for three months, on the figures of 1886, whereas in the winter months, if they put them out as they did at Rickmansworth and Hemel Hempstead, they could save upwards of £200.

Paving

Mr. Andrews said that he believed loans for Hobman's paving had been made for ten years.

He thought that they ought to have a more lasting paving in the streets where the traffic was greatest. After further conversation, the Chairman put the motion, when there appeared—for, 2; against, 8. It was then decided to go into the matter *de novo*, and try to bring it to a settlement.

Mr. Andrews then said that seeing that a 6d. rate only produced £1,200 a year, and the paving in the roads that had been named, only about a fifth or a sixth part of the paths of the town, would amount to more than that sum— say £1,500, he considered that it was almost an absurdity to think of raising the money required by a rate. If the paving were undertaken in that way, it would take five or six years to do any satisfactory amount, and by that time the existing paving would require to be

Aubon's shop, on the corner of Water Lane in the High Street, has a display of prize-winning carcases following the 1892 South West Herts Agricultural Show. The road shows the rough surface and one of the the road crossings complained of as being uncomfortable for riders in carriages. The crossings would be muddy in winter. The 'steel' age is reflected in the growing use of corrugated iron, which is the material for the canopy extending over the pavement.

A loan to be raised to pay for paving . . .

repaired or renewed, so that an annual rate of 6d. in the pound for paving would be established.

He wished to avoid this by the adoption of permanent paving where the wear was hardest, so that no money would be required for constant repairing. Then besides the streets named in the report, Beechen Grove-road had been mentioned, and St. Albans-road, about which they had a petition. King-street also must be done on one side at least, also from Station-road to St Andrew's Church, and from the Bushey viaduct to the Bushey Board school, and perhaps to Bushey Station.

That would expend nearly a rate and a half. These and the others named, taking the cost at 2s. 3d. a yard, would come to £2,300, or even £2,500, so that it was totally impossible to do it under two rates. The 6d. rate would bring £1,200, so that they must agree with him that it would do only a fourth or sixth part of what it was desired to do. He might mention that Denner-hill stones could be taken up at certain places and permanent paving put down, and the Denner-hill stones more fittingly used for other purposes. At St Albans the brick paving was done by a loan of £6,000, and he could not hear that there had been a single dissentient voice.

He was prepared to propose that this Board should proceed in a similar way. He thought at first that the amount should be £3,000, which, borrowed for 15 years, would cost £290 yearly, or 4¾d. per head on a population of 15,000,

But he would go further, and suggest that the loan should be £5,000 or £6,000, for as long a time as possible, say 20 years, for the best and most permanent paving. Mr.Clifford said that he would second Mr. Andrew's motion. Mr. Andrews submitted his resolu-

tion as follows:- "That money be raised by loan for paving the town with some permanent paving."

Mr. Clifford seconded, and the resolution was carried.

Medical Officer's Annual Report

"Gentlemen,—I beg to submit to you my seventeenth annual report, for the year 1889.

"Vital Statistics.

"The population in 1881 was 12,162; the estimated population of your district in 1890 is 16,300. The number of houses is 3,335. The number of new houses in the year is 63. The number now empty is 73. In 1889 the new houses were 114, empty 79.

"Births.—The births were 457, giving a proportion of 28.03 in the thousand against 466 in 1888, and a proportion of 29.1 per thousand.

"Deaths.—The deaths were 237, that is 57 less than last year. In the Workhouse 24, that is 10 less than last year. Fifteen did not belong to the district. There were 80 under 5 years of age, 76 above 60; there were 17 above 80 −5 males, 12 females; three were 90 or above; one in the Union House 95. Twenty-eight died of lung disease, 25 heart. The proportion of deaths per 1000 13.6. In 1888 it was 17.2.

"Marriages.—There were 44. Two males under 21, four females under 21. Ten were married at the Registry Office.

"Health of Paupers.

"In the Workhouse Infirmaries there was 246 cases, 114 acute, 132 chronic; 147 medical, 99 surgical. In 1888 there were 248 cases.

"Out-door Paupers.—New cases, 533. Surgical 99; medical, 434. Acute 151; chronic, 382. In 1888 there were 541 cases.

"Zymotic or Infectious Diseases.

"Deaths—Measles 12, Scarlet fever 3, diphtheria 1, croup 4. This gives a percentage per thousand of 1.6. Smallpox and Vaccination.— No case of smallpox in 1889. In 1888 we had 10 cases and 2 died. The history of these cases showed the benefit of good vaccination.

"Re-vaccination.

"All children should be re-vaccinated before they leave school, with as much regularity as in infancy.

"Remarks from my Journal.

"Register of Applications.—I have had 79 applications made to me on the following subjects:—Supposed smallpox, diphtheria, and supposed diphtheria, scarlet fever, typhoid fever, three cases (two in one house, the other imported), croup, nuisance from slaughter houses, w. c.'s out of order, want of water, houses not fit for human habitation, diseases of swine, rabies, overcrowding. I have sent you reports on typhoid fever, two on rabies, on diphtheria, and on the combined Isolation Hospitals.

I have had consultations with you on the enlargement of your Public Library, and on the adoption of a coat-of-arms for Watford; you adopted both. Also consultations with your Hospital Committee and with Dr. Thomson. I have sent 30 notices to disinfect, and made 120 visits to houses and places.

Hospital Accommodation for Watford and District

"The Cottage Hospital continues to do useful work. There were 73 cases, against 56 last year, 34 males, 39 females; 30 surgical, 43 medical. Nine patients at present.

"The Guardians' Isolation Hospital.—One typhoid fever, 4 scarlet fever, 4 measles, 12

Left: A London-bound train emerging from the Watford Tunnel.

Right: When the Watford to Rickmansworth line was opened the crossing at Loates Lane was a level crossing but was later converted to a road under a bridge– Radlett Road, (and known locally as 'the Death Trap')

Far right: LNWR's Dreadnought Class 'Versuvius' over water troughs at Bushey with an up Belfast Mail/Boat train. The first coach is for mail sorting and has automatic equipment for dropping off mail at a station into a safe-net, and for picking up mail from a suitable 'hung-out' device.

mumps, 10 itch, 2 syphilis, in all 33, against 32 last year. No deaths. In 1888 there were 10 cases of smallpox and 2 deaths from it. "The Joint Isolation Hospital for the Six Parishes of the Union for Private Patients.— We have had 54 cases, against 30 in 1888. Sixteen Urban from your district, 38 out of your district, Rural Two diphtheria, 51 scarlet fever (two of these had whooping cough afterwards).

"Our Paths
"During the year some of the paths have had asphalte laid down. The High-street, especially the defective and varied (six sorts) paving in the Market-place, demands attention.

"Gas.
"The gas has been above the legal standard in pressure, purity, and illuminating power. I often see it burning after 12 o'clock during light moonlit nights.

"General Remarks
"The death-rate has never been so low, and the zymotic death-rate is very small. The general health was good. There are many buildings in a very dilapidated state, and although I cannot say they are injurious to health, yet they should be repaired for the credit of the town.

I allude among others to the crumbling Colne Bridge; houses just outside the Churchyard, and one inside the Churchyard walls. The approach to Watford from London might be improved, Aldenham-road East made wider, the corner by the Board School rounded. The Market-place requires Val de Traver cement, as in London.

There is more smoke than there should be from manufactories.

"I remain, gentlemen, Your obedient servant, Alfred Thomas Brett, Medical Officer of Health for the Watford Urban District"

Watford & West Herts Post

"The above newspaper is founded and printed and published at its offices at 42 High-street", and claimed its circulation of 2,000 was more than any other paper in the area.

The "Watford Observer" rebuffed the claim stating that its circulation averaged 3,000 and was up to 4,000 on special occasions.

The Fearful State of St. Albans Road

Mr. Goss, jun., wrote to call attention to the state of the St. Albans main road, now in the district of the Watford Local Board. He supposed that nothing would be done until the Chairman or some other member of the Council were drowned.

People had to go and lodge in hotels. Mr. Clifford asked why a state of things was allowed to exist here and not allowed to exist 100 years ago? There was a lake 120 feet long, across the road.

The Clerk suggested that they should write to Mr. Judge; the Chairman admitted that the road was in a shameful state.

Mr. Clifford: Are the public to put up with it

Gustave Doré illustrates the bustle of a London station of the 1870s—the early workmens' trains were the commuter trains of the day. The early trains offered first and second class for those who wanted to reach their destination with more promptitude and in more comfort, the third class being the slower 'stopping' trains. For those travelling to or past Watford the image of clean fields and new houses would be an imagined paradise after London's sulphurous fumes.

The Watford and West Herts Sports Ground . . .

month after month? The road, I repeat, is in our district. It is simply disgraceful.

Mr. Coles: It has been all right for 100 years—until the building commenced there.

No motion was come to.

Watford Time

To the Editor of the Watford Observer.

Dear Sir,—Please allow me through the medium of your journal—only it is a weekly—to call attention to the discrepancies between the several prominent clocks in Watford. The other day I had the curiosity to compare my watch with the following clocks:—Morse's, Sims's, Judge's, and the outside and inside of the Post Office.

Not one of them coincided. The time at which I did this was just after 10 o'clock, at which time I believe the clocks are supposed to be set. This is the result in a tabulated form:—

By Judge's I was 3 minutes slow
By Morse's I was 2½ minutes slow
By Sims's I was 2¼ minutes slow
By Inside Post Office I was ¾ minute slow
By Outside Post Office I was ¼ minute slow.

That is to say that at 10 by my watch the mean time by these clocks was 1¾ minutes past. The difference is in some cases not very great, but as 'an inch is a good deal on a nose,' so is a quarter of a minute to train time.

I have several times missed trains by a quarter of a minute, just because I was relying on one clock. Can anyone suggest a remedy for this?

I should think that if the clock owners were to have a meeting every morning there might be some chance of, say two, coinciding, but that is hardly practicable.

Yours in doubt as to what the time is,
Tempus, Watford, July 18th, 1889.

The Lighting of the Station Yard

To the Editor of the Watford Observer.

Sir,—In your account of the last meeting of the Local Board, I am reported to have stated that the Hon. Holland Hibbert had informed me that, in addition to paving a piece in the centre of the Station-yard, the London and North-Western Railway Directors would put up a good lamp column provided the Local Board would light the lamp.

This is hardly correct, as what I said was that Mr. Hibbert was of opinion, or thought it possible, that the Directors would erect the lamp post, if the Local Board would provide the gas and light it.

I do hope the Boards, separately or conjointly, will arrange to light the yard in some way, as now, after dark, it is a disgrace to the town, and dangerous to the public.

Your obedient servant,
52, High-street, Chas. P. Ayres.
Watford, January 29th, 1890.

West Herts Sports Ground

Proposed Cricket and Football Ground

At the Public Meeting held in the Corn Exchange, Watford, on Wednesday, the 26th February, it was resolved that the generous terms offered by the Earl of Essex and Lord Capell for securing the 8 Acres of land on Harwood's Farm for this purpose should be accepted, as follows:—

"To lease the land for a term of 21 years at a rental of £100 a year, with the option of a further term of 21 years, at a rent to be fixed, and with the option of purchase at any time during the first of 21 years at the price of £6,000."

It is estimated that the cost of laying out the ground, turfing, planting, fencing, building a pavilion, &c., will be about £1,200.

At a later public meeting it was made clear that an original proposal to form a Limited Company, to manage the new ground as a profit-making concern, would not be agreed to. The plans were changed to manage the grounds as a non-profit-making venture . . .

"Chas. R. Humbert, Esq.
In this letter I have only wished to express my hearty concurrence in and willingness to support this project, but have neither wished nor endeavoured to suggest any details as to how it should be carried out; those I leave to the judgment and decision of the trustees and committee, when appointed, who will be much more competent to the task than I feel myself to be.
"Yours faithfully,
"Essex.

That goes plainly to show that Lord Essex never had the remotest intention or idea of letting the town of Watford have land considerably less than its worth to rent, undoubtedly less than its worth to purchase, with the view of a limited liability company being formed and profit being made out of it.

Although I have not had an opportunity of seeing Lord Essex since the last meeting, I have seen his solicitors, and they emphatically endorse all that Lord Essex has said. So, if the company idea is persisted in, you will not have this land for the purpose of playing your cricket or football. Before going any further, perhaps you will expect to hear from me exactly what steps I took after the meeting on Thursday last.

It appeared to me abundantly clear that it would be absolutely impossible that this scheme should take place if a company were formed, and in consultation with Mr. Turner and others I proceeded to send out circulars asking whether the subscriptions might be considered as donations, and if any profits accruing should be considered as belonging to the scheme itself, to be handled by the trustees, and dealt with for the further development of the land or its eventual purchase.

The meeting being on Thursday, I sent them out on Saturday night, and by Monday morning I had received letters to the effect

that out of £1347 promised before the meeting on Thursday £1305 were to be considered as donations. *(Loud cheers.)*

That goes further, gentlemen, and shows that it was never the intention of the principal part of the subscribers to join in any company, in fact, many men who had been good enough to give their money for this purpose have taken the trouble to write me a little note on the form they have sent back, and nine-tenths of them have said, 'If any company is formed, please consider my subscription as withdrawn.'

Professor Attfield then said: My Lord and 'gentlemen, I have much pleasure in moving "That the resolution passed at the meeting of subscribers held at the Masonic Hall, on the 10th of April, 1890, in relation to the formation of a limited liability company, be rescinded.'

Now with regard to that meeting, although some good work, I think, was done, I suppose most of us will be of the opinion that a very large amount of time of a number of gentlemen was wasted *(hear, hear)*, and when a great many men waste an hour or a couple of hours apiece it is apt to make them as angry as when one man finds he has wasted some 100 or 200 hours; they are all in the position of Matthew Mears. I do not know whether you are all acquainted with the history of that gentlemen, which is summed up in the following rhyme:—

"There was a man of Kirkcudbright,
His name was Matthew Mears;
He wound his clock up every night
For six and forty years.
But when that clock an eight-day clock
Was clearly proved to be,
A madder man than Matthew Mears
You'd seldom wish to see."
(Laughter...)

Professor Attfield, referring to the question of adopting a name for the ground, expressed the hope that such a name be chosen as would spread the interest in it over a wide area around Watford, so that more subscriptions might be available.

The Chairman, humourously remarking that 'Elysium' and 'Promised Land, had crossed his mind, asked whether 'West Herts County Ground' would be acceptable.

The Hon. R. Capel suggested 'Watford Cricket and Football Ground,' which met with general favour.

Dr. Berry then proposed that Mr. E. J. Slinn should be appointed hon. treasurer. Mr. W. L. Smith seconded, and the resolution was carried unanimously. Mr. Slinn briefly returned thanks, and promised to do all he could.

Mr. G. Rooper, in eulogistic terms, proposed Mr. H. M. Turner as hon. solicitor.

Mr. R. Ashby seconded.

Mr. Turner, in his reply, expressed the hope that they would stick to the title of 'Watford and West Herts Cricket and Football Ground,' Watford being the capital of West

Stealing a pocket-knife—a fortnight's imprisonment . . .

Herts, and the centre of a large area from which they could provide the funds necessary for the support of the ground. The Chairman, having made some remarks with reference to the last meeting, proposed Mr. Humbert as hon. secretary—a proposition that was received with continued cheering.

Mr. W. Pearkes seconded.

Mr. Humbert, in his reply, referred to the disheartening effect of the last meeting, and said that it had caused him to take off the twenty men and seven or eight horses and carts from their work of turfing and ground and to pull up the stakes. The work should now be pushed on as fast as possible, for if this were done and the grass not sown in April, they would not be able to play football upon it next season. Though he might not long be able to occupy the position of hon. secretary, he hoped that when he gave it up the affair would be a successful one.

A meeting of the committee was then appointed for Tuesday next, at 6 p.m.

Votes of thanks concluded the meeting.
WO April 1890

To the Editor of the Watford Observer.

Sir,—In the large and earnest meeting in the Masonic Hall last night we heard many interesting speeches. I refrained from speaking, being afraid of prolonging the meeting.

If I should not be considered impertinent, I should like to make a few remarks.

(1). We did not sufficiently express the obligation we are under to Mr. C. R. Humbert for the part he has taken. I do not know any other man who could have got in £1400 in so short a time.

Whether we are managed by trustees or by a company, I hope Mr. Humbert will continue to give us his valuable aid, so that the scheme so well conceived is fairly born and able to run alone.

(2). I hope the directors will meet at once and approve of the works already begun by the Earl of Clarendon in buying turf—I mean in getting it for nothing—and the other works.

(3). That they will continue them so as to save a year.

(4). The company should raise enough capital to buy eventually, and only call up as much as is necessary.

(5). We need not discuss how to spend the dividend till Christmas. It is prudent not to count the chickens before they are hatched.
Your obedient servant,
A. T. Brett.

Watford, April 11th

The Case of the Boy Sutton

Dear Sir,—The case of the boy Sutton, who was sentenced last week by the magistrates to a fortnight's imprisonment for stealing a pocket knife, is one which calls for more than passing notice, since it brings before us the fact that there is a class of boys in the town who are being allowed to grow up in vicious ways through no fault of their own, but simply because they are too poor for anyone to care at all about them. Clubs, institutes, classes, and amusements do not reach such as these. Ragged, untidy, rough, unrestrained in word and deed, their presence would soon end in driving all the other members away.

Often, especially in winter, dependent for food upon what can be picked up in the streets, they frequently go the whole day with nothing to eat and (as I know was the case with Sutton last winter) sometimes have nowhere to sleep in at night.

It is pitiful to see them struggling against their fate, trying hard to obtain work and being refused, owing to their untidy, suspicious appearance, or losing it through some trivial offence. About twelve months ago I was induced to form a number of them into a class for instruction and amusement, but unfortunately my health completely broke down and I was compelled to give it up.

I have, however, kept myself acquainted with many of them since, and they frequently ask me to resume the work. I write this, therefore, in the hope that someone may be induced to come forward and carry it on. The lads are extremely grateful for any simple act of kindness, and generous to any who are worse off than themselves.

An instance that came under my notice was that of a little Italian boy whose means of livelihood, an accordion, had been stolen from him. The child was kept in food by a number of them (including Sutton) for nearly a week, and the money, fourpence a night, contributed between them for finding him a bed.

The Bench would have done an act of real kindness if they could have sent the boy Sutton to a reformatory instead of inflicting the penalty of 14 days' hard labour upon him for stealing a knife, thereby ruining his chances of obtaining honest employment on his release.
Yours faithfully,
C. H. Finmore. 8, Sutton-road, Watford.
WO, July 1890

The window above the 'Market Street' name-plate was discovered when the adjoining building was demolished and retained after the Compasses was rebuilt, and remains to this day. The poster-covered flank wall is of the Green Man Inn and between it and the three-storey business premises is Mr Horton's Swan Iron Works; the three-storied building houses the offices of Sedgwick, Turner and Walker (Registrar's Offices). Henry Morten Turner was Chairman of the Local Board and UDC from 1882-1910.

Lighting—a man has to strike a match to find the next lamp post . . .

THE WATFORD OBSERVER
SATURDAY, JULY 5TH, 1890.

IT must be a gratification to the lovers of the manly sports to feel that though they may lose something through the stormy weather of the present season, it is a great factor in preparing for them the ground which is to be the future centre for Watford and the neighbourhood.

When in the dry days of the spring the long desired land was secured and the levelling begun, there were fears no doubt that the turf and springing of the seed might not be such a success as was desired. Thanks, however, to the great determination and energy of Mr. Humbert, who had pledged himself to carry the matter through, we see the ground in such a state, by the aid of the copious showers, that cricket might by played on it at the present moment The levelling has been admirably done, the splendid oak fencing is in a forward state, and this, we feel, is an earnest of the work being completed thoroughly.

The land was in general estimation the best suited for cricket and football of any near the town, and its application to the purpose shows more and more how thoroughly well adapted it is. Time only is needed to make it one of the most delightful spots in the neighbourhood, and the belief that it is sure to be adequately supported will, we think, not turn out to have been unfounded.

The Lighting of the Town
A committee had had before them complaints as to the number of lamps in the town which were not burning at all, and they recommended that a man should be engaged to attend to them. They also fixed a day and hour to meet to look at the lamps, but it seemed that no one attended.

Mr. Benskin said he saw that Hertford was going in for electric lighting.

The Chairman: Ah, they have a river.

Mr. Benskin: So have we.

Mr. Ayres said it would be as easy at Watford as at Hertford.

The Chairman: They have the use of water power at Hertford.

Mr. Ayres: Could we not have the use of water power?

The Chairman: You would have to pay for it.

Mr. Mead said that a paper was read the other day to a meeting of engineers and others on the use of gas engines for generating electricity for lighting, and a deputation from Hertford had been over to his place to see his engines. Mr. Clifford thought the Gas Company ought to take this question up seriously. Mr. Mead's mill would be a good station for electric lighting.

Mr. Ayres: Well, we pay now £1,000 a year for darkness; we might pay a third more and have light. Our public lighting is useless. A man going down the Clarendon road has to strike a match when he leaves one lamp post to find the next (*Laughter.*)

Chairman: That is a romance. *(Laughter.)*

Mr. Wilson said the lamps did not give any light when one was near them, and they certainly did not when they were far away.

The Chairman said the lamps were too high. They seemed to have been erected to light people to bed. They were three feet too high.

Mr. Wilson: We used to burn rushlights when I was a boy.—Mr. Ayres: And they were better than our lamps. *(Laughter.)*

The Chairman: Mr. Ayres is not a shareholder in a gas company.

This discussion seemed to be much enjoyed by the members.

WHP January 1893

The Roads
A report of the Highway Committee stated that on a report submitted to them by the Engineer, they recommend that 500 yards of broken hand-picked flints should be procured. A specification by the Engineer gave the amount of material required as 730 cubic yards. Mr. Benskin asked the Engineer if he thought the flints would be more economical than granite.

The Engineer said he thought so, on the present gravel roads, and it was then resolved to advertise for flints.

The Engineer said that he had put 400 tons of granite on the roads, and asked for 200 loads more, also granite chips. The Committee recommended that 200 tons of granite and 50 tons of granite chips should be procured.

The Board approved.

WO January 1893

SATURDAY, OCTOBER 17, 1891.

Fire Brigade
In 1867 an advertisement in the Watford Observer led to the formation of a 'volunteer' fire brigade on November 23rd. A new engine was purchased from funds, amounting to £148, raised by public subscription. The engine, named 'Vesta', was horse-drawn and the pumps worked by hand. With 200ft of delivery hose it was capable of pumping 140 gallons of water a minute to a height of 130ft; delivery of the engine was taken in March 1868. The Volunteer Fire Brigade remained an independent unit until 1898 when it was taken over by the W.U.D.C.—but members were still unpaid.

Fire in Langley Road
A fire, which at one period threatened to involve a great part of Langley-road, occurred on Wednesday evening. At half-past four information was received at the Volunteer Fire Station of a fire at Mr. Suttle's oil shop in Langley-road, and not many minutes afterwards both the Volunteer and the Local Board Fire Brigades were on their way to the scene of the conflagration. The Watford Brewery Fire

CORN EXCHANGE, WATFORD.

Under the patronage of the Right Hon. the Earl of Clarendon, the Hon. Reginald Capel, and E. Henry Loyd, Esq.

TWO ENTERTAINMENTS
ON
EDISON'S WONDERFUL TALKING MACHINE,
THE PERFECTED PHONOGRAPH,
Will be given
On THURSDAY, OCTOBER 16th, 1890, at 3 and 8 o'clock,
BY
MR. CHARLES E. GIRARDOT.

The Entertainments, which will be preceded by a brief explanation of the working of this marvellous apparatus, will consist of the Reproduction of Loud Records of Speech and Music, and of the Voices of Animals, which will be heard simultaneously by the whole audience; and of Low Records, which will be heard by a limited number of persons at a time. Of these records some will be Reproductions of Musical Solos and Concerted Pieces played in England, Ireland, and America.

Records of Speech and Music will be made and reproduced in the presence of the audience.

TICKETS—Front Seats (numbered and reserved), 3s.; Second Seats, 2s.; Admission, 1s.—to be had of Mr. A. Spicer, High-street, where a plan of the room may be seen; also of Mr. W. J. Elliott, Music Warehouse, Queen's-road; and Mr. H. L. Barrett, St. Albans-road.

THE NEW BOARD ROOM OF THE WATFORD LOCAL BOARD.
From a Photograph by F. Downer.

Above: *An advert for technology to come–the gramophone.*

Left: *First Photograph? In the Watford Observer of 17th October 1891, was published, without comment, a photograph of "The new Board Room of the Local Board" showing Dr. Brett and Mr. Slinn . This is the first noted use of a photograph in an Editorial context (some advertisements had previously used a halftone block) and was followed by a series of head and shoulder portraits of local notables.*

. . . land being offered on the easy-system of payment . . .

Brigade, which did not receive the call until after the others, lost little time in proceeding to the spot with their steamer.

The stock which was almost entirely composed of combustible materials, took fire. The flames shot across the road and made it impossible to get near the premises, a plate glass shop window on the opposite side of the road soon cracked, and the flames began to lick the wooden door of the side entrance to the private house opposite. The explosion when the barrels of oil caught fire was tremendous, and the firemen soon found themselves unable to cope with the flames. The stock in the shop, consisting of oils, firewood, glues, paints, etc., blazed furiously, and the services of the steamer were soon afterwards called into use.

Under Superintendent Taylor a good pressure was got up, and the steamer supplying the three hydrants, a diminution was at once apparent.

There seemed, however, a strong probability that the whole block of four shops with dwellings above would soon be ablaze. However, after a time, the fire in the lower part of the house eventually succumbed to the strong jets of water, and attention was next directed to the upper rooms and roof.

Several long ladders were sent for, and two having been planted in the front the flames were partly reached from that direction. Several firemen got from the ladders on to the roof, and with the aid of hatchets attempted to arrest the progress of the flames by breaking the slates.

Cheer after cheer from the large crowd assembled below greeted these attempts. It was soon evident that the united efforts of the three brigades, greatly assisted by the Watford Brewery steamer, had obtained some mastery

over the flames, although not quite able to prevent them spreading on to the next roof.

After an hour's hard work it was evident that the further progress of the flames had been arrested and at a quarter to eight Captain Ashby and his men left with their steamer, leaving Supt. Geo. Urlwin and the Volunteer Fire Brigade in charge.

It is not known how the fire originated.

WO 1893

Sale of Properties in Watford

Messrs. Humbert, Son and Flint offered by auction at the Rose and Crown Hotel, on Tuesday afternoon, two freehold residences, known as *Colne View* and *St Ronan's*, situate in Queen's-road, and sold for £1220.

The Sale room then rapidly began to fill, and some excitement was evident so soon as the first of the 51 plots of building land, situ-

ate on the Rose and Crown estate, were offered. This is the second sale of land on this estate, and lot 36, which comprised the first piece offered, has a frontage of 18 feet to Market-street, and a depth of 106 feet. This, together with the remaining similar lots, and two others, were sold at the sum of £840. The next two lots formed a corner plot, with frontages to Market-street and Merton-road, for which the bidding was keen, and Mr. W. B. Neal bought these subsequently, together with the next lot, for £214. The sale altogether was a very successful one, and from the number of enquiries made of the auctioneer there can be but little doubt that a good deal more of the property was sold by him privately before he left the sale-room.

The land being offered with the option of purchasers paying for the same on the easy system of payment, for five years, naturally was a great inducement to make small investments. The amount realised for the land sold amounted to about £2,500.

Old Cottages in Church-street

The Highway Committee recommended that tenders should be invited for pulling down the old cottages in Church-street.

The Engineer was instructed to prepare a specification.

WO January, 1893

Colney Butts estate

Messrs. Humbert Son & Flint offer for sale by public Auction, at the Rose and Crown Hotel, Watford, early in February, 1893, upwards of 150 PLOTS of most eligible and advantageously placed FREEHOLD BUILDING LAND, with suitable and important frontages to the Vicarage, St James's, and Cardiff-roads, and to other roads in course of construction, and with depths of from 100 to 150ft. The Colney Butts Building estate is within easy distance of the centre of the town and Market Place, within 500 yards of the High Street Station, and adapted to the erection of private houses, shops, and business premises, for which there is an unlimited demand in Watford.

The new roads, sewers, gas, and water supply will be forthwith constructed and laid on.

WO January, 1893

Top: *Old cottages in Church Street adjoining the High Street. Modern-day location would be under the new St Mary's Square (Town Square).*

Left: *Activity in the despatch bay of Charles Healey's Brewery in King Street, 1893.*

School of Music

The Rev. Newton Price said that a concert had been arranged to take place at the Agricultural Hall on the 20th April. They were obliged to take this building because they had 100 performers, but unless they were well supported the concert would result in financial loss.

Mr. Benskin suggested that the people should be admitted to the galleries at 3d. The Rev. Newton Price said they would not go below 6d. unless Mr. Benskin wanted them to pay the people to go in.

Dr. Brett said that he was at the County Council on the previous day, and he was told on the highest authority that music had been recognized as a technical subject. Schools of music in other parts of the county were going to apply to the County Council for money, and it had been suggested that Watford should communicate with the other schools of music with the object of making this a sort of joint question.

Watford School of Music was much more developed than other schools of music in the county, and he suggested that it should apply for £50. The committee was of the opinion that the Watford School of Music should act independently in the matter of application for grants.

WO March, 1893

Watford National Schools

Dear Sir,—For the information of the subscribers to the above schools will you please insert the following Government reports, and oblige
Yours faithfully,

REG. CAPEL

BOYS' SCHOOL.—"This is a well disciplined school, and the boys are taught with intelligence and considerable success. The reading and recitation of the upper standards are admirable, the handwriting is uniform and neat, the problems in the III. and IV. Standards are praiseworthy. History has made an excellent start. Geography is good except in the lower standards, and some very creditable maps were drawn. The points requiring attention are the composition of the VI. Standard, the arithmetic of the V. and VI. Standards (especially the latter), and the work generally of the I. Standard, which no doubt suffered from the weakness of the staff in the autumn."

GIRLS' SCHOOL.— "The discipline and general tone are excellent and Swedish drill and singing by note (both now taken for the first time) are admirable in every way. The elementary work is taught with thoroughness and intelligence, problems (especially in the VI. Standard) being worked with unusual success. Recitation is said with marked expression, and despite some weakness in the composition of the VI. Standard, and the arithmetic of the V. Standard, and in the intelligence of the reading, the highest grant is well deserved. Needlework and English show further improvement, and deserve special praise."

WO March, 1893

Bricklayers' Strike

There is no change to chronicle with regard to the bricklayers' strike, nor can there well be any if one side or the other does not give way, and it only remains to be seen which will hold out the longest. The T. Turner Company hav-

"NEW ELLIS" LADY'S.

PRICE £14 14s., WITH TRANSPARENT GEAR CASE.
Or by easy gradual payments by arrangement.

Left: Mr Ellis, at the 'Vicarage Cycle Works' in the High Street (pic p120) introduced his 'New Ellis' range c1895 when pnuematic tyres were relatively new. This model was fitted with the best Dunlop tyres, having a 5-inch tread, and braking by a direct action brake-block upon the front tyre. A man's racing bike with drop handlebars cost £13. The lady's model, with black gear case at £14 equates to near £2000 at 2003 prices. In a few year's time factory-made bicycles would fall in price.
In 1914 a mason's weekly wage was £1 15. 0d.

Death of Mr. Henry Williams

Mr. Henry Williams died on 28th October, 1893, aged 65 years.

He began his business career as a photographer—but his liking and aptitude for newspaper work led him to change his vocation and he became a reporter, as representative in Watford and the surrounding district, on behalf of the "Buckingham Advertiser."

Later, he became Sanitary Inspector at Watford, and, presumably, followed his bent for writing in his spare time. Sometimes he wrote absolutely for the amusement of his friends; then, the humorous element came very much to the top.

His "History of Watford"—the first history of its particular kind—gave him a double dose of work. When he had passed the proofs and they and the original "copy" were at the printers, the printing works was destroyed by fire and he had to re-write the manuscript
J. W C.

WHP (August, 1928)

Left: The Post Office staff of 1890 with Postmaster Mr J. Morley and proudly showing their bicycles.

... the re-erection of the bridge over the Colne is half done ...

ing signed the bricklayers' rules, the latter are of course bound to them, while the other masters in Watford hold to the amended rules they submitted to the Bricklayers' Society. What work there is in progress is being done quietly with a little outside help.

WO, June 1893

Watford Bathing Place

The hot weather has caused a large number to use the Bathing Place this year. The largest number in one day was 560—last Saturday.

WO, June 1893

Smallpox, Scarlet Fever

The INSPECTOR reported that all the cases of smallpox had been discharged, and he was cleansing the Pest House under the direction of Dr. Berry. The Board awarded the nurse, in addition to a testimonial, £5 5s. for extra services. The Chairman said that scarlet fever had been put an end to at Croxley Green and the schools reopened, but a child was sent home from the Isolation Hospital and in three or four days the fever broke out again in the same house. There seemed to be something radically wrong, and it was destroying the advantages of isolation.

WO, July 1893

Marriage at Westminster

ON Thursday afternoon, at the handsome church of St. Margaret's, Westminster, the marriage was duly solemnized of the Right Honourable the Earl of Essex (George Devereux de Vere Capell) and Miss Adele Grant.

The Bridegroom traces his descent from Mr. Arthur Capell, who was Member of Parliament for the county of Hertford, in the Long Parliament, and was created 'Baron Capell of Hadham,' and for his loyalty to the 'Royal Cause' was beheaded in 1649. He was succeeded by his son (second baron), who was created 'Viscount Malden' and 'Earl of the county of Essex' (peerage of England, 1661).

He was appointed Viceroy of Ireland, 1672-1677, and for some time First Commissioner of the Treasury, but being accused with Lord Russell of connection with the "Fanatic Plot" was committed to the Tower, where he was found dead in 1683. His son, the second earl, was a lieutenant-general in the army, and Constable of the Tower of London, and died in 1709, and was succeeded by his son William, as third earl, who died in 1743.

His son, William Anne, the fourth earl, died in 1799. The fifth earl, George, 'D.C.L.' who assumed the name of 'Coningsby,' died in 1839, and was succeeded by his nephew, Arthur Algernon (son of the Hon. John Thomas Capell, second son of fourth earl), who was sixth earl (and grandfather of the present peer), who on his death last year in September, was succeeded in the family estates and titles by the present peer, who sits in the House of Lords as '7th Earl of Essex.'

The Bride, the charming and accomplished Miss Adele Grant, is a famous American beauty, and eldest daughter of the late Mr. Beach Grant, of New York, and Mrs. Beach Grant, of 35, Great Cumberland-place, Hyde Park, London, W., and granddaughter of the late well-known General Stewart, of America, and niece of the late Mr. Thomas A. Scott, a former President of the Pennsylvania Railway Company.

WO, December 1893

Reception of the Earl of Essex

LORD and Lady Essex arrived at Watford Junction at a quarter to 6. Number 1 platform, at which the train stopped, had been specially and appropriately decorated under the superintendence of Mr. Braide, of the Permanent Way Department. One company of Volunteers formed at the Station-yard under Major Lake, and had proceeded to keep the Park gates, while another company formed at High-street, under Major Humbert, and proceeded to the Station-yard, and marched after the carriage behind the torch-bearers. The Malden and Clarendon hotels were illuminated, and the scene was made more brilliant by the coloured fire.

As soon as the procession turned the corner of Queen-street coloured fires were lighted on the front of some of the houses in High-street, and in the market-place, the beacon fire upon the triumphal arch having been previously set ablaze. The carriage passed on its way up the High-street towards Cassiobury. There were the same signs of welcome all along the route, indeed the inhabitants seemed to vie with each other in the demonstration of their goodwill.

From the almshouses to the Cassiobury entrance there was a chain of fairy lights on the side next the West Herts Ground, also fairy lights on the almshouses and along the space to the entrance. At the gateway itself the windows of the lodges were outlined with fairy lights of different colours, and the carriage proceeded through the park to the mansion.

WO, December 1893

Marriage of the Earl of Essex

Sir,—I should like through the medium of your columns to tender, on behalf of Lady Essex and myself, our most sincere and heartfelt thanks to the people of Watford and the neighbourhood for the most cordial and unanimous reception which they accorded us on our arrival here last week.

It was one, the remembrance of which, will, I know, never fade; and will be a continual reminder to us of the good feeling which exists, and which I hope will not only ever exist but will grow stronger as time goes on between the House of Cassiobury and the people of Watford.

Yours faithfully, ESSEX.

WO, December 1893

Year End Summary

As to improvements in Watford, we are pleased to record that the re-erection of the bridge over the Colne is half done. To Dr. Brett, no doubt, who for many years, year after year, pointed out the necessity of this alteration, the first thanks must be given, then also to the gentlemen who have pursued the matter to its present stage.

Another improvement which ought not to go unrecorded, is the widening of Church-street. The year has also seen the completion of the church of St. John, which was consecrated in July, adding largely to the church accommodation of the town.

A step has been taken by the proprietors of what has up to a few months ago been known as the Agricultural Hall to make that building of greater general utility and consequently a better investment. The name has been changed, and as "Clarendon" Hall it is hoped that it will become the general meeting place for large gatherings. The best, possibly, has been done with that object.

A cherished institution, the Watford District Cottage Hospital, is always to be remembered, and in saying anything at this time, the Society for Improving the Condition of the Poor must not be left out of sight.

WO December 1893

Care of Market Place

THE Clerk stated that he had had an opportunity of considering the matter, as to who was liable for keeping the Market Place in order, and the opinion he had arrived at was this— the whole of the Market Place, from house to house, was clearly dedicated to the public, subject to the rights of the lord of the manor to hold his market there on Tuesdays, and possibly, to a limited extent, on Saturdays.

Therefore, as the place was to be treated for the purpose of a highway, he thought it was the duty of the Board to prevent its being dangerous, and to make it passable for her Majesty's subjects.

If through the use of the place as a market, it was necessary that a portion should be treated differently from a highway, he thought the duty rested with the lord of the manor, and where it was so treated, it was clearly his duty to keep it in repair.—

Mr. Andrews believed the lord of the manor paid for the cleansing of the place, and he presumed he was also responsible for the repairing.—

The Chairman said he thought the path the public were complaining of now was where the old fountain stood.—

The Clerk said they might call upon him for that.

After some discussion, it was decided to give notice accordingly.

WO December 1894

Watford, the most scientific town in Herts ...

Local Government in 1894

The initiatory steps towards the new order of local government was taken by the County Council who at their meeting had before them the report of the special committee appointed to bring into operation the Local Government Act, and under their directions a local enquiry was held by Mr. J. C. Earle, barrister-at-law, on the 27th June, respecting the division of the parishes of Watford Union.

The effect of the Act on Watford was that the parish was divided into two parishes, that part which was within the district of the Local Board being the 'Urban Parish,' and the residue the 'Rural Parish.' A similar division took place in the parish of Bushey.

During September the School Board made provision for the erection of new schools at Leavesden-road for 480 boys, and the first annual meeting of the Committee appointed under the Technical Instruction Act showed a distinct advance in organised education work.

At this meeting Dr. Brett bore testimony to the great success of Watford with regard to technical instruction, which, he said, took the lead as the most scientific town in Herts.

The great advance made in respect of the Public Library was shown by the Committee at their annual meeting. Twenty years ago the income was only £80 a year; now the rate money is more than four times that, namely, £320 a year.

The Local Board, Rural Sanitary Authority, and ex-officio Guardians ceased to exist, the latter authority being succeeded by the Rural District Council, comprised solely of representatives of the rural parishes in the Union.

The Urban District Council takes the place of the old Local Board, the election for which was marked by great interest.

The newly constituted Boards in town and district enter on their work for the year with great possibilities, and judging by preliminary meetings held already give promise of realizing many of the hopes entertained of them.

WO, December 1894

Building

	1891	1892	1893	1894
Houses	96	418	264	328
Other erections	67	55	96	77

New Streets—The Board have during the past year approved plans for making and sewering 7 new streets:—Garfield-street, 173 yards long, Shakespear-street, 190; Parker-street, 158; Milton-street, 208; Cecil-street, 208; Judge-street, 193; Ridge-street, 188. Total, 1318 yards. The whole of the above streets are in the Callow Land district, and some are now in course of construction. Private Streets—Great progress has been made during the year in completing the works required to be done to private streets before being made public, under Private Street Works Act, 1892. Works of sewering, metalling, channelling, kerbing, paving with 2in. indurated stone slabs, and lighting have been carried out in the following thirteen streets, and the whole, except Victoria-road, have been declared public:—

	Yards long	Cost £ s. d.
Percy-road	158	276 3 6
Ebury-road	111	320 13 6
Shaftesbury-road	157	422 6 4
Stanmore-street	130	206 17 0
Copeswood-street	286	439 1 1
Leavesden-road	275	466 13 8
Lowestoft-road	130	258 6 6
Grover-road	316	778 14 7
Oxhey-street	132	280 16 9
Westland-road	200	349 16 8
Wellington-road	137	245 11 5
Canterbury-road	123	222 18 6
Victoria-road estimate	225	500 4 11
Total yards	2,380	£4,768 9 0

Street Improvements

Upton-road—This street has been completed by paving the footpath with indurated stone slabs 2in. thick, and declared a public highway.

St Albans-road—One side of this street has been completed by kerbing and channelling from Bedford-street to Leavesden-road, and paving the whole from the railway to Regent-street with 2in. indurated stone slabs. By arrangements with the owners of the property the water troughs in front of the Stag and Leviathan public houses have been moved to the edge of the footway. The corner of Leavesden-road has been widened, the land having been given by Messrs. Benskin and Co., and the L. and N.W. Railway Company.

Vicarage-road—In consequence of building operations near the Union House, it was found necessary to ask the builder, Mr. T. Clark, to set back his frontage line to get the road 36 feet wide. The piece of land was purchased by the Board.

Numbering of Streets—Progress has been made in numbering the new streets in the Callow Land district, and the other new streets are now receiving attention. The following rule is being adhered to—Odd numbers on the left, even numbers on the right, begin at the end nearest the Central Post Office, or nearest the main road. One number to be left for each vacant plot of ground.

WO January 1895

Above: *Court No. 18, Farthing Lane, Lower High Street. The two girls are standing outside the entrance to the 'Ragged School'.*

Right: *The Beechen Grove Baptist Church in Clarendon Road takes its name from earlier churches built and used in nearby Beechen Grove. The gates to the Clarendon Hall grounds mark the present position of the ring road which passes nearby.*

Emancipation—the Red Flag Act is repealed.

It is apposite to digress to take stock of developments to date of powered road vehicles. A search for a faster vehicle than that of the horse-drawn carriage was the goal. Frenchman Captain Nicholas Joseph Cugnot made a steam powered vehicle in 1770, had room for four passengers and reached a a speed of 2½mph over a fifteen minute run. The boiler was poorly made and the steam escaped. A Cornishman, in 1827 built a steam coach using coke as the fuel. His second model made a run of 84 miles from Melksham, Wilts, to London, in ten hours including stops. In 1831 a regular passenger carrying service plied four times daily between Gloucester and Cheltenham, a distance of nine miles at an average 12mph.

Unofficial opposition came from systematic road obstructions—and the opposition soon became official and powerful.

Between 1827 and 1838 several steam road coaches were running between Paddington and the Bank. Rival horse 'bus drivers, aided and abetted by powerful financial interests, tried to wreck the venture. Bad roads, light loads and high overheads caused the venture to fail.

The farmers and landowners had seen the trend.

They opposed it as destroying peace, beauty and because of alleged dangers to Human Beings. A series of Bills were passed imposing punitive restrictions, from six to twelve times than of horse drawn vehicles. Heavy tolls were crippling, further legislation enforced patent laws by which 'any development carried out by individuals in public became the property of the public *unless* a patent had been obtained which covered every aspect of the vehicle.' Legislation to change the situation failed and for many years development was stifled. In 1861 three more Acts were passed; one fixed the width of the iron or steel tyres, depending upon the load, and ensured that if a bridge were damaged by a mechanical road locomotive the damage had to be made good by the vehicle owner. Other traffic would be free of this imposition even if they added to any damage!

Another Act (1861) legislated that mechanical vehicles could not be used for more than eight consecutive hours in the 24—forcing night-time use, which the busybodies also complained about. A later Act of 1865 introduced the rule which allowed local authorities to compel a vehicle driver to have a man walking 60 paces in front and carrying a Red Flag—2mph in town and 4mph in certain other places. (Previously, where they were allowed at all, it was at five or 10mph). Various Acts added minor irritations, and in 1878 the Red Flag was deemed unnecessary, but the walker, still required, was permitted to proceed only 20 paces in front.

A further Act specified that damage to a road must be repaired. In many instances this 'damage' was merely a wheel mark in the gravel—this lead to the development of the (solid) rubber tyre in 1871, but the cost of the rubber and manufacture was too heavy for widespread use at that time.

1881 saw Dunlop's first pneumatic bicycle tyre . . . but in Britain the progress of the development of the motor vehicle was clouded by oppression, litigation and prejudice. For the first time since the progress of Britain's Industrial Revolution the major advances would be from Germany and France. In

Germany Gottlieb Daimler built his first car in 1886 with a single cylinder air-cooled 1½hp engine; his third model, a few years later, featured a twin-cylinder in a V-formation—a decisive step in the progress of Daimler's cars. They were handled, sold and developed in France by Panhard and Levassor, and they realised that no car could be successful unless designed as a unit, rather than attaching an engine to a converted horse carriage.

Warwickshire-born F R Simms acquired the Daimler agency; made improvements to the engine, and attempted to overturn the restrictive laws, with little success. By 1895 the motor car was attracting public attention—but little support; that year the magazine *The Autocar* was founded.

The man who produced Britain's first car was F W Lanchester. He was, first and foremost, an engineer, and made his car by 1896. Fitted with a 5hp engine, and specially made 2½inch Dunlop pneumatic tyres, the model achieved a speed of 16mph. The engine was not powerful enough and the next was of 8hp, giving a speed of 20mph. Of Lanchester's car it has been said that of the 36 primary features of a modern car (1950) Lanchester had been responsible for eighteen of them.

In 1896 a small Exhibition was held at the Imperial Institute, at which a procession of four cars, preceded by a child carrying a Red Flag, moved through the Institute. Lawson, the organiser, had special police permission to put on a run to Hurlingham—without infringing the Red Flag Act.

The Locomotives on Highways Act was made law on November 14th 1896 and motor cars up to 1½ tons unladen were allowed to travel at speeds not exceeding 12mph; 8mph if between 1½ and 2 tons, and 5mph if more than 2 tons.

This was celebrated by an Emancipation run to Brighton.

By 1899 Lanchester had made several models of his cars but attracted no press publicity until the two-seater Phaeton won a Gold Medal for design and performance. Lanchester is reported as saying; "We were not attracting publicity for the good reason that we were not manufacturing cars for sale."

One huge service he later did was to write and publish a treatise on 'Driving for Lanchester Customers'; there was then very little knowledge of what driving involved and the learning process was haphazard and dangerous to people as well as vehicles. At the onset of the Great War, 1914-1918, development of cars, trucks and lorries made great progress. Many were the servicemen who realised the potential and were later to embrace the 'future'. Watford already had coachbuilders and cycle-makers turning to the motor-car, or servicing them; more were to follow. In the meanwhile speed restrictions still throttled development.

The permitted lorries weights were understandably rigorous given the crude road surfaces. A 1903 Bill became law. It introduced registration of a car, specified two number plates; a five-shilling driving licence, and a car speed limit of 20mph.

In 1922 Lieut-Colonel A G Scammell DSO founded Scammell Lorries Ltd, to market and develop the Scammell Articulated Six Wheeler, a 7½ ton solid-rubber tyred model.

The Scammell story is continued in 1922.

...gas engine, dynamo for lighting – and high-quality block-making...

Frederick Downer has been established 33 years, during which time he has photographed almost everyone of note; every newsworthy occasion, and almost every new building. From the time when his photographic equipment verged on the primitive, coating his plates before he could make his exposures, he now has at his command better lenses and better plates.

So far without serious competition, he now faces the threat of Mr. Coles, recently established in Queens Road—who quickly builds up a business of quality to become a serious rival. A newish American firm called Kodak has made a film which anyone can load into a suitable camera; and furthermore, has designed a device by which the film may be processed in daylight. The new cameras can be used *in the hand* without the erstwhile cumbersome tripods.

Block-making of photographs has been possible for a number of years but editors of newspapers have not yet realised that their readers would appreciate more photographs to support the text, and Frederick Downer with his sons, enters the craft of 'process engraving' and has some surprises to spring, surprises which have preserved Watford in images available from no other source. In a short while he would have finely-printed postcards on sale, and, later, go on to print a news sheet.

Entering the studio, the eye is first attracted by the numerous photographic pictures adorning the walls, including portraits of celebrities and other familiar faces.

Mr. Downer has had the honour of sittings from many of the nobility and gentry both in and beyond the County.

Here are lifelike presentiments of the Earl of Clarendon (Lord-Lieutenant of the County) and the late Countess of Clarendon, the Lady Edith Villiers (in the pose and dress of Millais' well-known picture, 'Cherry Ripe'), the late Earl of Essex, the present Earl and the Countess of Essex, Lord Maldon, Professor

Herkomer, R. A., &c, &c. Mr. Downer's high standing in the County as an expert and artistic photographer being well-known, a special account must be given of his new enterprise.

Mr. Downer is now justified in styling himself a Photo-Engraver and Photo-Etcher. He cannot only furnish a photographic print, but also a reproduction of it in metal, suitable for book illustration, and examples of his work will be found in the present article as well as in previous numbers of the Hertfordshire Illustrated Review.

The engraving department is under the management of his eldest son, Mr. Fredk.

Downer, who is assisted by his two brothers, Edward and Arthur. His second son, Harold, an electrician by profession, is partly responsible for the installation of the electric light in the studios and show rooms, and for the fitting-up of necessary appliances.

The art of reproducing paintings, drawings, and photographs is known as "Process" engraving, and a brief account of the method by which nearly all the illustrations in the Hertfordshire Illustrated are produced will probably prove interesting to my readers.

'Process' is a comparatively recent development, for it was only a few years ago that the means were discovered of applying the principles of printing through the agency of light.

The original picture is first photographed, the camera being mounted on a sliding platform, by means of which the difficulty of focussing is minimised. The electric light is generally used even during the day at Watford, as it is always ready to be switched on, and supplements the strength of the natural light.

The plate glass for the negative is prepared in the usual manner, and after the necessary exposure in the camera it is conveyed to the 'dark-room' to be developed. The negative is next taken to the printing-room, and placed in a wooden frame in front of a highly-polished zinc plate which has been sensitized by means of a specially-prepared solution.

Miss Lucy Kemp-Welch, one-time pupil of Professor Herkomer, and now with her own art studio was well noted for her paintings of equestrian subjects and here Mr Downer has recorded her at work on one of her larger canvases.

The glazed front of the frame is now exposed to the light, which, for several minutes, is directed through the negative and upon the sensitized surface of the zinc. The metal plate, after sufficient exposure, is removed from the frame, but nothing is visible upon it until it has been rolled up with transfer ink and developed in a bath of water, when, by rubbing with cotton wool, those portions of the sensitized film are removed which have not been fixed by action of the actinic rays of light, the parts so fixed being a replica of the original picture— in fact, a photograph of it. The plate, after being again rolled up with ink in order to give the lines a firm acid resist, is transferred to the etching-room, and the large surfaces which will appear white when printed are painted out with a preparation consisting of shellac in solution. When this is dry, the plate is placed in a bath containing diluted nitric acid, which eats* away those parts not protected by the acid resist.

When the plate is sufficiently etched, a proof is taken, and, if satisfactory, it is mounted on oak to make it 'type high'—that is to say, after the plate has first been punctured for rivets and the superfluous margins cut away. At this stage the engraving is called a 'block' which must be trimmed and touched up with the graver before it is ready for the printing-press. It is a remarkable fact that such a block will yield about 50,000 impressions before exhibiting an appreciable amount of wear and tear.

The above description similarly applies to the reproduction of 'line' work (that is, all drawings executed in lines) and to 'half-tone' work (drawings in wash, or photographs), the latter, how ever, being the more delicate operation, requiring greater skill.

There is one feature of 'half-tone' engraving that should be mentioned. Those who examine with a powerful glass any such reproduction of a wash drawing or photograph will observe that the various degrees of light and shade are made up of minute square dots. This peculiar texture is obtained by means of a screen formed by two sheets of glass attached to each other, each having upon its inner surface a series of minutely-engraved parallel lines; on one plate these lines are vertical and on the other horizontal, or they may be engraved diagonally, to the right and left respectively†.

It will be easily understood that when such a screen is inserted in the camera between the lens and the negative, the engraved lines (sometimes numbering 200 to the inch) cut up into minute squares the image of the picture as it appears on the negative, except in those parts which are solid black. After the negative is printed on the zinc plate, the latter goes through several acid baths, between each of which it is dusted with an acid-resisting powder. On closely inspecting the plate one can detect the effect of the glass screen in the minute squares of metal which form the picture in relief.

From the above it will be seen that the art of 'Process' engraving is not so simple as it might at first sight appear. It obviously means great pecuniary expense, as well as steady perseverance in overcoming difficulties and disappointments, before success is assured, and Mr. Downer is to be congratulated in having achieved such results as those he has already attained in so short a time.

Here, in Loates Lane, he has made the most of the accommodation at his command, this being necessarily somewhat limited. A 51/2 nominal horse-power Otto high-speed gas-engine and a brush dynamo machine generate the electricity and motive power required for the various operations. In the photographic studio connected with the engraving department are two arc lamps (Brockie-Pell), each affording light equal to 2,000 candles, and, in addition, there are a number of glow lamps for purposes of general illumination.

† These screens, being very difficult to produce without a flaw, are very expensive, even those of moderate size costing as much as £60.

*The word "etch" is from the Dutch word etzen, to eat.

Hertfordshire Illustrated Review, 1894

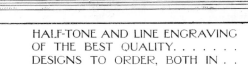

HALF-TONE AND LINE ENGRAVING OF THE BEST QUALITY. . . . . . DESIGNS TO ORDER, BOTH IN . . LINE AND WASH. . . . .

Above: *Frederick's son supervises the smooth running of the five-and-a-half horse-power gas engine driving the dynamo, with gas-meter and regulator on the wall, and a fire-extinguisher to hand.*

Left: *An advertisement for his services and abilities; Mr Downer is proud to put 'Watford' above his own name, together with the town's coat-of-arms, in the top-left-hand corner.*

A carters' service station . . .

The Local Board (of Health) had its offices at the bottom of the High-street among the breweries, water works, tan yards, gas works and engineering works, in Local Board-road opposite the Watford-mill, then a wooden structure. The Board was among the corn dealers, hay merchants and just yards from the highway and the local industry. It was the highway which, for two hundred years or more—long before the railway—carters had travelled between the farms and the London markets.

The Watford High-street was a sort of carters' service station. There were numerous public and beer houses for their refreshment and the tail-race of the mill, and river, would provide water for the horses—this would be their first watering stop after the 'Dog' and 'Horns' on the road to Hemel Hempstead. Their loads would be hay and straw. London had no means of providing its own food and necessities. In primitive times, when there was only the one bridge—London Bridge—there were three roads. Watling-street went through Newgate and two roads, one towards Suffolk and one to Essex, left through Bishopgate. To London's south, over the bridge, the Watling-street led to Kent and Canterbury, following the old Roman Road.

For the carter, in Watford, refreshed, the toll-gate and Clay Hill had to be faced and then a mile or so further, Chalk Hill, 'Up this hill, at all seasons, and in all weathers lines of wretched horses toil painfully, dragging huge loads of hay and straw for the London market. At the steeper part of the hill, the poor animals, always overladen, struggle with panting

Going down the High Street, Bottom: A coachmaker's premises next to International Stores and the Fox and Fox-alley adjacent.

Centre: The Holly Bush and Rising Sun are on the right and on the left are the Brewer's Arms and Leatherseller's Arms. On the right-hand side of the road Farthing Lane is just beyond the white cottage.

Top: On the left the white-fronted building is the Angel pub (about where George Ausden's now is); the shop on the right, a clothing, outfitters and boot store, survived until c1960.

sides, wealed with the cruel blows of their brutal drivers.' On the return journey the carts carry night soil, manure, or soot to be used by farmers as 'fertiliser.'

One beer-house was aptly named, the "Horse in Chains" as being able to provide last-resort-assistance when needed. In addition to this 'through-traffic' there was, of course, a not inconsiderable amount of trade generated by Watford's mill, adding to the busyness and congestion of the narrow street. Bushey Station was opened in 1849 but did not have a goods yard until 1878 and so, until at least that time, the coal for the gasworks was carted along the High-street, probably from Lady Capel's Wharf on the canal, about three-quarters of a mile from modern Hunton Bridge. When coal was carted from Bushey Station it was by horse and cart long into the motor era.

With the removal of the Board to Upton House, at 14 High-street, (upon the change of status to Urban District Council) there followed the inevitability that the 'Lower-High-street' would be run-down and forgotten. Not so much a case of out of sight, out of mind, as the sheer amount of other matters which needed attention.

Telephones had been accepted and now electricity was being asked for!

Railway Bridle Path

Sir,—I am glad to see by your report of the proceedings of the Urban Council that Mr. Ayres is not going to let the action, initiated by himself and Mr. Pridmore some little time ago, with reference to the state of the bridle path from the St. Albans-road to the Station, drop.

I took some little trouble four or five years ago to get the Railway Company to open up a continuation of that path direct to the Station, thus saving a longer and less pleasant route round the 'Clarendon,' and I have incessantly since then pointed out to the late and present Chairman of the Council the state of their path as described so truthfully by Mr. Ayres, but wholly without effect. Binding gravel or granite chips properly rolled and kept rolled with the steam roller is all that is required, if a proper drain is placed at the head of the path in the St. Albans-road to keep the water from washing the mud down from the road on to the path.

We have suffered for years from unjustifiable neglect on the part of the authorities in this respect, and I hope Messrs. Ayres and Pridmore will not rest until the path is put into proper order.

Yours obediently,
JOSCELINE F. WATKINS
Stratford Lodge, Watford, August 31st, 1896.

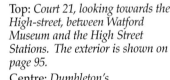

Top: *Court 21, looking towards the High-street, between Watford Museum and the High Street Stations. The exterior is shown on page 95.*

Centre: *Dumbleton's display of prize-winning carcasses, c1900. The road crossing on the left extends across the High Street from Farthing Lane; the other across Farthing Lane's entrance.*

Bottom: *Looking to the Town Mill. The shop with the sun blind is Dumbleton's. The pubs, farriers, and corn merchants around the mill area were the old town's commercial powerhouse. All is now under the front of Tesco's site.*

HENRY J. ROGERS,
THE WATFORD ENGINEERING WORKS

Will allow 10 to 15 per cent. discount for cash off

AGRICULTURAL IMPLEMENTS.

H. J. R. having any amount of MACHINERY and thoroughly COMPETENT MECHANICS can execute REPAIRS promptly and economically.

FURNACE BARS, 6s. per cwt.   GENERAL CASTINGS, from 8s. per cwt.
STEAM & GAS ENGINE REPAIRS.   ELECTRIC LIGHTING.
PUMPS of all descriptions made on the premises.   Several Second-hand Engines in Stock.
GAS WORKS remodelled or renovated.   GAS RETORTS, £7 per ton.

Christ Church, Callow Land

SATURDAY was a day of rejoicing in the parish of St. Andrew's, the occasion being the dedication and opening for divine service of the new temporary church at Callow Land, by the Bishop of St. Albans. The new church has been erected on the land given some years ago by the late and present Earl of Essex for the purpose, adjoining the St Andrew's Parish Room, on the St Alban's road.

The church is lofty, and consists of nave with side aisles, the nave having clerestory windows. The ventilation is on modem principles, and the lighting by incandescent gaslight. Tenders were obtained from various iron church builders, and that of Messrs. Harbrow, of Bermondsey, for an iron church to accommodate 400 persons, at a cost of £508 was accepted, exclusive of furniture and fittings. Towards the cost of the new building £616 has already been subscribed, and £220 for endowment.

The furniture and fittings are at present incomplete, but kneelers will be provided for all the seats. The interest taken in the new church may be seen from the fact that much of the furniture has been given, and some of it made, by members of the church. The pulpit, which is not yet finished, is the gift of Mr. J. S. Daw, one of the churchwardens of St Andrew's, and the choir stalls, are the gift of St Andrew's congregation.

WHP 1896

Population 1838,	**2,960**
Population 1871,	**7,461**
Population 1891,	**16,819**

Right: *The pubs are the Anchor and the Hit or Miss; the later rebuilt Hit or Miss carried on till the M1 Link Road took its toll nearly a century later.*

Above: *Old Yard shortly before being demolished under a slum clearance order. It, and Old Tan Yard, were earlier cited as being among the worst fever spots of the then very dirty town. The area between the tail race of the mill (which was then a ford), and the river, was described in a Board of Health Report as being 'an island' between stream and river.*

Top: *Mr Rogers took over the business started by Mr Tidcombe and, with his sons, has changed the firm's name and greatly extended their sphere of activity. Though steam and gas engine repairs would seem most natural the firm are also pioneers in lighting using high-capacity batteries to light interiors of meetings places.*

Left: *The High Street Station. The line from the Junction to Rickmansworth is a one-track, steam powered, service. A very important function is that just a short distance away is the siding and tracks into Benskin's Brewery, essential for their London and general trade.*

Right: *To the left is the parapet of the railway bridge and, part-hidden by the near lamppost, Mr Oatley's shop at 181 High Street. The arched courtyard is the entrance to New Street and the two ladies are looking into the window of a baker's and confectioner's, No. 183. The courtyard on the right is No. 21, Chapman's Yard.*

Below: *A 17th century timber-framed house flanks the Railway Tavern which is next to the station. The station entrance is via the canopied stairway down to the platform.*
Halted, on the left, is the Board's street-watering cart.

Public Library, with science and art classes, grew into the Watford College of Science

For much of his working life in Watford Dr. Brett worked closely with colleagues Dr. Wilson Iles and the Reverend Newton Price; they were a formidable trio, constantly crusading on behalf of the working class, the poor and the town in particular. Dr. Iles held almost as many posts as did Dr. Brett and between them they forwarded plans for building Watford's first hospital. Dr. Iles did not see the plans come to fruition, dying in 1883, aged 49. He had performed a tracheometry operation during which he suffered a small cut to a finger. This became infected and he died of the resultant blood-poisoning.

Dr Brett lived to the age of 68; he came to Watford in 1850 aged 22 and served the town for 46 hard and troublesome years, helping transform the filthy country-market-town into a healthier and desirable-to-live-in thrusting town.

Watford mourns this week one of the most prominent of its oldest inhabitants, Alfred Thomas Brett, M.D., of Watford House, who died on Saturday morning last.

Dr. Brett's health had been failing for some time; he suffered from chronic Bright's disease; about eighteen months ago he had an attack of influenza and bronchitis, and in December last, pleurisy. Being only 68, he lived to the physicians' age, and bears all the honours of the aged, for his years were full of work; he had done much for the inhabitants of the town to which his footsteps were led early in life.

Dr. Brett was born in Hinde-street, Manchester-square, London, in 1828. His professional education was received at Guy's Hospital, where obtained all the appointments open to students. Dr. Brett was on the

Council of the Society of Medical Officers of Health, and a member of the Volunteers' Medical Staff Association.

He was Hon. Secretary for more than thirty years, Treasurer, and since President of the West Herts Medical Association.

That society was formed in 1849, and he attended nearly every meeting since its formation.

The public offices Dr. Brett held in connection with his profession were—Medical Officer of Health for the Watford Urban District, Medical Officer for the Union and Parish of Watford, Public Vaccinator, Certified Factory Surgeon, Hon.

Surgeon to the Watford District Cottage Hospital, Medical Officer of the London Orphan Asylum, Watford, and Surgeon London and North-Western Railway.

Dr. Brett married the daughter of Mr. Reeves, of Chalk-hill, Watford, and had four daughters, also a son who died in infancy. Dr. Brett will be remembered as one of the most earnest promoters of the growth of Watford institutions. When building became general, when new streets were laid out, and Watford began to assume the character of a suburban town, the necessity for institutions such as the locality had not before possessed became apparent, at times assuming such an urgent aspect that except to the most sanguine the provision of funds by voluntary means seemed almost impossible.

But this did not deter Dr. Brett.

Before the establishment of the Public Library, he was a supporter and Chairman of the Science and Art Classes in connection with South Kensington: for he was always enthusiastic in regard to the acquisition of knowledge in science, art, and indeed in literature.

Above: *Mr Horton relinquished ownership of the George Inn at 91 High Street in 1887 to further his Swan Iron Works, next to the "Green Man", then an old-established inn offering refreshments, stabling and hire of horses and traps; and catering for 'bicyclists and tricyclists' in the corner of Market place.*

Next page: *a plan of the Watford House grounds and, alongside, a view of Dr Brett's house.*

He joined in the proposal to substitute the Public Library for the more private Mechanics' Institute with all his heart. The Public Libraries' Act was adopted in 1871, and the foundation of the present building was laid in 1873. For the first three years Dr. Brett was chairman of the institution, and again occupied that position in 1888, when enlargement was in progress. It was at that time, by his influence, that the coat of arms for Watford was adopted for the Library.

He pushed forward the schemes for Technical Education, leading the way with those gentlemen who had made it more particularly their study. It is a matter of gratification that he lived long enough to count up in some measure his successes. The establishment of the Public Library as a library and reading room, with science and art classes, grew into the Watford College of Science, Art, Music, and Literature, and he rejoiced over each success, marking the standing of the Technical branch in 1894 by congratulating the Committee that Watford was still taking the lead.

But the connection of Dr. Brett with the Public Library is the history of that institution.

Twenty-three years ago Dr. Brett became the first Medical Officer of Health for the Urban District of Watford, upon the passing of the amendment of the Public Health Act establishing that office. In order to take that position he resigned the seat on the Local Board which he had filled for many years.

The commencement of his work could not have been pleasant; there was a great deal to be done in improving the sanitary condition of the town, and the prejudices to be contended with were not few. It will be safe to say that even what were regarded as his whims and fancies have to a great extent been carried out.

Year after year in his reports he was persistent in recommending different improvements, one being the alteration of the bridge at the lower part of High-street, not only on account of its narrowness, but the annually recurring nui-

sance of rotting weeds that the arches detained in their course down the Colne. He saw the day when he was able to support in the County Council the proposal to build a new bridge, and afterwards used the present substantial structure in his daily drives. With regard to this office it will be remembered that he bore the burden of the beginning, he resigned only a few weeks ago. "Sanitation; public health; all means to improve the physical, and moral condition of the people." were the ideas that he carried with him to the County Council, and we find him, while supporting general matters, bringing forward a proposal for the supervision of the rivers and water-ways of the County.

One of the movements which he took up with great earnestness was that for the provision of allotments. Summing up the result of this movement, he remarked that (including the previous provision of allotment gardens) there are now five fields set apart for the purpose, with 600 cultivators.

Dr. Brett joined the Watford Company of Hertfordshire Volunteers when the movement began, in 1859, as, he used to say, 'a full private.' He became surgeon to the Company, and time brought him the rank of Surgeon-Major, the Queen's medal for 32 years' service, and the addition of Lieutenant-Colonel to his title.

It would be difficult to sum up such a life as that of Dr. Brett if it had not been lived before the people; not indeed for applause, but because the work that was done could not be hidden. He found his pleasure and reward in what he did for the good of the community. He gained esteem, respect, reverence, for he had a faith in the ultimate success of his endeavours that sustained him against opposition, and with it, unbounded geniality.

WO, July 1896

Sale of Dr. Brett's House and Land

THE first part of this was described in the particulars as highly valuable freehold residential property, adjoining the High-street of Watford, 800 yards from the station, and close to the centre of the town and Cassiobury Park, possessing an extremely valuable building element. The property includes the commodious old fashioned family residence known as Watford House, which is approached by a carriage drive and well removed from the road, standing in the midst of lovely old-fashioned garden. The land has an area of 3a. 2r. 22p.

The corner piece of the property, on which stands the surgery, was reserved.

The next property that I have to bring before you, said Mr. Humbert, is Watford House, where our old friend Dr. Brett lived a vast many years of his life, and I do not hesitate to say that in course of my career in Watford I have never had such a saleable thing through my hands—I have never had to deal with an estate which can be bought and developed without the expense of a single shilling. The roads exist—the High-street and Clarendon-road—and are made up; there is nothing to pay for road-making.

You can sacrifice the house if you are so disposed, and sell the whole of the frontage on

the High-street in about half-an-hour, in fact, I will undertake to do it. Apart from that you have the old-fashioned house—a charming old place which has taken many years, all Dr. Brett's life and his predecessor's, to make it what it is. I am not going to wade through all the particulars, because you have all been to look at the property and know its capabilities, and whatever I say you will take no notice of.

Bidding began for Lot 1 at £3,000, and went on rapidly up to £4,250, but then began to drop off. It stopped at £4,320, and the lot was knocked down to Mr. W. Judge. "Will you take the field?" asked Mr. Humbert.

"The whole," replied Mr. Judge; so that he takes the whole of the property for £7,320.

WO, October 1896

Ground plan of Dr Brett's home. Developed by Mr Judge into 'The Parade' the resultant shops were held in high esteem until part was sacrificed for the ring road flyover in 1972. From then decline was gradual, and rapid after the opening of the Harlequin Centre. In 2003 plans were mooted to demolish the Clements block. See p308.

Part III

Stirrings of Industry

An era ended with Dr Brett's death, but the progress he started did not stop. More importantly his vision of teaching the sciences to pupils began to bear fruit, as industry gradually became dominant. The larger factories, such as the paper mills, made full use of steam power for both heating and powering engines to drive machinery by shafting, pulleys and belting but the smaller factories, rather than install steam engines, relied on the alternative power plant of the single-cylinder slow running stationary gas engine with its distinctive 'pop, pop, pop' which could be heard emanating from many sheds and yards. Gas engines powered plant at Bemrose Dalziel, Acme Tone Engraving Company and at the Paget Plate Company.

Mr. Downer, as did the Paget Prize Plate Company, used the gas engine to generate electricity. In the meantime the Urban District Council, which had grudgingly accepted the telephone, belatedly acknowledged that a municipal electricity generating undertaking could prove remunerative to operate. Some public functions had been electrically lighted many years earlier by lamps strung across a hall and powered by batteries loaned by Henry Rogers. The generating plant was conceived to provide light as substitution for gas, and principally for street lighting. When the Cardiff Road plant was operational street lamps were soon changed, though not without justified criticism.

Five men now enter Watford's history, each in their own way to have as much impact as did Dr Brett, Dr Wilson Iles, Revd. Newton Price and C. P. Humbert.

Ralph Thorpe was a Lincolnshire farmer who came to Watford in 1890. Brewing was his interest and this he started in St Albans Road. Unmarried, he was interested in sport, the fire brigade and politics. He was asked to stand as councillor, but with Watford just one big ward, came last. At the next election, when Watford had been divided into wards, he won Callowland, and never lost an election thereafter. He first comes to our notice when, as a member of the Urban District Council, he asks some searching questions about the state of the town's fire brigade, which, at that time was very out-dated

and antiquated. He is not content with talking. He acted, in his interest, but more importantly, the town's interest. He strides across the pages for nearly forty years passing away, aged 74, in 1929.

Charles Brightman was born in 1853, in Luton, and established his business in Watford in 1870; he comes to our notice as unsuccessfully tendering to demolish and rebuild Mr Fisher's premises in 1888. He later complained that a builder in Aylesbury was, in his opinion, unfairly quoting for building the Watford Field Schools. He later teamed up with Robert Ashby and achieved great success as a speculative developer; he died in 1933. Robert Ashby, born in Bushey in 1842, died 1928, was employed at Sedgwicks Brewery for fifty years, much of the time as manager. In the early 1900s he joined partnership with Charles Brightman to start a trail of development and building which was to transform Watford. Their paths merged with Thorpe's and were to cause a not small degree of antagonism.

David Greenhill was not a builder or politician; a printer's engineer would be nearer the mark. In achieving several ambitions he led the way for Watford to become the print town of the country and his inventions achieved world fame. His restless drive also involved him in several building projects both in Garston and the town centre. He died in 1949.

The fifth person remains an enigma. Dr Boisellier was manager of Dr Tibbles' Vi-Cocoa. There is no doubt that there was a Dr Tibbles. He lectured upon the efficacy of his products–some of which contained a fair amount of cocaine–but the firm, and the name, were owned by a group comprising a newspaper publisher, wholesale grocer, wholesale tea dealer, an editor of 'Great Thoughts', and a printer and newspaper proprietor. They brought good business to Callowland; they also, at the Government's bequest, turned much of North Watford into a Great War munitions arsenal, under the name Watford Manufacturing Company Ltd. It is to these five that we owe much of the basic structure of the town; the Park, the roads and bricks and mortar of the houses survive but David Greenhill's masterwork of the printing industry was squandered.

Highway Offences

David Edmonds, of Chiswell Green, was charged with riding asleep on the cart of which he was in charge, at Watford, on August 7th.

Police-constable Hadder found the defendant asleep in the bottom of another man's cart in company with the other man. The second cart ran into a barrier placed in the street where a new crossing was being put down.

The man in charge of the barrier said that he led the first horse past the barrier, but the second horse being tied to the first cart, the second cart came in contact with the barrier. The Chairman said that the Bench would adjourn the case for the attendance of the man who was in charge of the barrier. Edmonds pleaded guilty, and he was fined 2s. 6d.; costs 6s. Allowed a week to pay.

Charles Gibbs, the man in charge of the second cart, pleaded guilty. Fined 2s. 6d.; costs 6s. Allowed a week to pay.

Watford Electric Lighting

Although the question of electric lighting has been before the Urban District Council on several occasions, it was not till June of 1896 that any serious move was made, and it was then decided to advertise for a consulting engineer to advise the Council generally on the matter. As a result, the Council placed the drawing up of a report in the hands of Mr. W. C. C. Hawtayne, who presented a long report in October of the same year, in which he advised the Council that the establishment of municipal electricity supply works should prove remunerative. The system recommended was the high tension alternating current transformer system with distribution at low pressure, and the scheme was estimated to cost £19,000, if the buildings could be combined with new sewerage works that the Council were about to construct at the old sewerage sites, which are distant about a mile and a quarter from the centre of the town, or about

£21,000 if the two undertakings were not combined.

As an indication of the rapid growth of Watford, it may be mentioned that whereas the number of public lamps set out on the plan was 414, the actual number now being connected to the mains is exactly 800.

It was originally intended that a number of arc lamps should be placed in High-street and Queen's-road, but the Council afterwards decided that they would rather go in for incandescent lighting throughout, except in the Market-place, where three arc lamps are to be installed, and in the railway station approach, where there will be one. Separate mains are laid throughout for the public lighting, which is controlled from six switching-on points.

The high tension mains are connected to transformers at a ratio of 2000 volts to 400 volts, from which the low tension mains run to the groups of Street lamps, each lamp-post being fitted with two 200 volt 8 c.p. or two 16 c.p. lamps in Series across the 400 volts in all the streets with the exception of a few in the centre of the town, where two 20 c.p. lamps are to be placed in each lamp-post Existing posts are being adapted in the majority of cases, but in the centre of the town new lamp-posts are being erected.

The installation has several features of interest. In the first place, taking the last census as the guide, there are but two Municipal installations in England with a smaller population to serve, namely Taunton and Whitehaven, and but one in Scotland, Ayr. We are not therefore surprised that Mr. Hawtayne, the consulting engineer, originally advised the adoption of small units, namely, three of 75 K.W. each and one of 25 K.W. for day load.

Before the contract was definitely placed, however, Mr. Hawtayne recommended two 150 K.W. sets and one 30 K.W. set for day load. The station has been designed to take a third 150 K.W. set before the temporary cable requires to be removed, and we are glad to learn that this space is not likely to remain long unoccupied, owing to the rapidity with which premises of all kinds are being wired for connection to the mains.

It is a most business-like combination, and the way in which it performed its 6 hours' full load test leaves nothing to be desired. Not only were the bearings "stone cold" at the end, but almost the same could be claimed for the armature and field coils of generators and exciters. In no case did the temperature exceed

40 degrees F. The engine has but a single crank, the vertical compound cylinders being arranged tandem. Each cylinder is in itself single acting, but the H.P. piston is active upwards, and the L.P. downwards, so that the crank receives two impulses per revolution.

The two large engines develop 250 I.H.P. at 300 revolutions per minute.

WO May, 1899

Water Supply, Wells & Co

Messrs. Wells and Co.'s application—from Messrs. Wells and Co., stating that they desired to extend the water laid on to the stables at their premises, to a portion of the brewery.

The Committee recommended that the application be acceded to on the following terms:—
(a) the costs of the necessary pipes and meter to be paid by the Company. (b) An agreement relieving the Council from all liability in the event of the supply being at any time deficient, and empowering either party to determine the arrangement on one month's notice to be entered into. (c) That the charge for water supplied be at the rate of 1s. per 1,000 gallons, with an annual minimum payment of £10.

Water Supply, Dr Tibbles

Application from Dr. Tibbles' Vi-Cocoa (1898), Ltd.—A letter dated 26th inst. from Mr. R. W. Price, was read, stating that this Company, having purchased 50 acres of land

bounded by St. Albans-road, Bushey Mill-lane, and the branch line from Watford to St., Albans, were about to construct two roads on the lower portion of the land and to build a factory, and enquiring whether the Council would be prepared to lay water mains before the roads were made, and on what terms they would supply the factory with water. The matter was referred to the Engineer for consideration and a report.

WO July, 1899

Below: *The centre of the High Street in 1897; on the left the houses (of page 42) show their conversions into shops. On the right hand side of the road the small premises of Gardiner's (printers of the 'Leader' newspaper), (in ownership of Mr C H Peacock since 1896) becoming Mr Peacock's printing works. Later he took over the next-door premises (Lipton's) and the firm continued occupation of both until the buildings were demolished in 1961, at which time they moved a few doors along Loates Lane to restart. 'Langley' is the shop on the corner of Loates Lane and just beyond is the tall town house (No 97) once the shop of David Downer. At this time Frederick Downer's offices and show gallery were across the road at No 110; his studios were in Loates Lane. This shows decorations ready for the celebrations for Queen Victoria's Diamond Jubilee in 1897. The building on the right, with the very tall chimney, is where Marks and Spencer's now is but in 1897 was the 'George Hotel'.*

... the town was totally unprotected against fire ...

Above: An 1896 Observer advert suggests their founding as pre-1796, and gives their address by the earlier name of Queen Street.

The Fire Brigade

Mr C. H. Peacock, writing in answer to a letter from the Council asking if he would drill the firemen at Callow Land, said he was quite willing to drill the men when there were any. (Laughter.) If the Council would provide outfits for about six men, they could soon be picked out. He added that he should be glad to see the application for tenders for the new fire station at Upton House. Mr. Thorpe said that he had received a fire engine at Callow Land that day. It was a very ancient one, somewhere over 50 years old. He should like to know whether they were to have a more powerful engine.

The Chairman: This one used by the Volunteer Brigade will find its way there when a small repair has been carried out.

Mr. Thomas enquired when the plans would be ready for the fire station. If the obsolete engine mentioned was a sample of their fire protection it was quite time they took the matter thoroughly in hand.

Mr. Ayres: I shall be able to have the plans ready, and the estimates in, in about a month. The engine spoken of is not the engine we use in the town. There is a better engine ready.

Mr. Pitkin asked if there was really a fire brigade of any description existing, and if so, whether the men ever practised? He pointed out that they must consider not only Callow Land, but the requirements of the whole district.

The Chairman: That question can be raised on the reference to the Committee of Mr. Peacock's letter, and the Committee can bear in mind there is a strong feeling in the town that the present provision is inadequate.

Mr. Thomas: There is a great amount of dilatoriness and drifting at present.

Mr. Ayres said that he was advised it would take 12 months at least to get an engine, and he proposed it should be an instruction to the Committee to consider the advisability of at once ordering an engine.

Mr. Pitkin pressed his question as to whether there really was a fire brigade. He had been told by men who should know something about it that they had a new fire escape, but that it was perfectly useless, as they had not a man who knew anything about it. Mr. Thomas said that the town was totally unprotected against fire. The arrangements were quite inadequate for a place half the size of Watford.

Mr. Trew said he had a very short time of the committee, and he thought Mr. Peacock was the man who was more thoroughly up in the matter than anybody on the Council. However, Mr. Waterhouse had made every preparation for extending the water mains, or rather increasing their size and doing away

Above: Watford Engineering Works could lay claim to being one of Watford's earliest motor dealers; in 1990 monetary terms the £35 motor cycle equated to some £1,750!

Left: The Waggonette bus service operated between Callowland (water trough, Gammons Lane) and Bushey Arches in 1898. With driver G. J. Bence and a conductor, four passengers were carried for a fare of threepence each for a single journey. Popularity led to frequent over-loading and consequent breakdowns and the service was withdrawn and the 8hp Daimler was taken into service by the Standard Range and Foundry Co Ltd. The route to Junction was otherwise worked by a horse-drawn double-decked bus.

with a number of dead-ends, so that they would have a certainty of a good supply for any emergency. They had the same advantages and same fire engines as they always had, and Mr. Peacock was, he believed, still interested in the work.

Mr. Thorpe asked whether Mr. Peacock was really acting as captain or not, because some time ago he resigned from the Volunteer Fire Brigade, and now was rather uncertain whether he was acting under the Council or not.

Mr. Trew said they understood Mr. Peacock was still acting as captain, but he would see him and get something definite from him.

The whole matter was then sent to the Committee, who, it was understood, would consider the purchase of a new engine.

WO June 1899

Fire Station at New Bushey

Mr. Pitkin brought forward a motion of which he had given notice with regard to the provision of a fire brigade station at New Bushey. He had understood that the question was to be dealt with all over the district and a thorough scheme of protection against fire adopted.

At Callow Land a station had already been provided, and what he asked for was a similar one at New Bushey. The expense would not be great, or he should have considered seriously before bringing this forward. They had two manual engines, one of which had gone to Callow Land, and he suggested that the other should be sent to New Bushey.

WO July, 1899

New Fire Engine

It was reported by the Water Supply and Fire Brigade Committee:— "The following tenders for the supply of a fire engine capable of throwing 350 gallons per minute, with accessories, were received and opened—Messrs. Shand, Mason and Co., £362 10s.; Messrs. Rose and Co., £375; Messrs. Merryweather and Co., £435. The Committee recommend that the tender of Messrs. Shand. Mason & Co. be accepted subject to the Engineer being satisfied with the specification."

In reference to Mr. Pitkin's motion, the report stated- "The Committee considered Mr. Pitkin's motion for the establishment of a fire station at New Bushey, and resolved to recommend that a hose reel be obtained for New Bushey."

WO August, 1899

Firemen's Suits

Tenders were opened for the supply of eight fireman's suits, consisting of trousers, tunic, and cap. They were as follows:—
Messrs. Shand, Mason and Co., £19; Mr. Austin, Watford, £16 16s.; Mr. J. P. Taylor, £2 17s. 6d., £2 14s. 6d., and £2 7s. 6d. per suit.

Mr. Austin's tender was accepted.

The Fire Station

Tenders for the erection of the Fire Station at Upton House were opened as follows:—

	£
H. Martin, Northampton	2020
Clifford and Gough, Watford	2037
George Wiggs. Watford	2011
H. V. Watkins. Watford	2085
Henry Brown, Watford	2298
Clark Bros., Watford	1928
R. L. Tonge, Watford	2099
F. Dupont and Co., Watford	2228
H. M. Dove, Euston-road	2237
G. and J. Waterman, Watford ...	2267

The approximate estimate was £2,250.

Mr. Cossham moved that the tender of Messrs. Clarke Bros. be accepted. Mr. Longley seconded.

WO October, 1899

The Fire Brigade

The time fixed for the trial was half-past six, and a few minutes after that time the new engine, which is very smart in appearance, was driven up. Unfortunately the weather was bitterly cold.

Mr. Trew lit the fire, and in 6 mins. 45 secs. steam of 100 lbs. pressure was registered. Those present were able to check the time for pressure at 5, 10, 20, 30, 60, and 100lbs., on cards which were handed round for that purpose. The engine was started by Mr. Trew when the 100 lbs. was reached.

Interesting tests followed. First with 60 feet of hose a 1½ in. jet was thrown to a height that would command any building in Watford; then two deliveries, with ¾ in. nozzle, were put on 160 feet of hose; after that two breechings of one into two, giving four ⅝ in. jets were worked, 360 gallons per minute being thrown; and last the biggest spray possible was shown with two lines on, breeching of two into one, with 1½ in. jet.

The result of the trials was regarded by those competent to judge as most satisfactory. The absence of oscillation in the engine was remarkable considering the work done.

Above: *After many years of buying their own suits (or not) the new Urban District Council have provided the crew with new suits. The fire-engine "Vesta" was at this time some 31 years old, having been bought in 1868. The new machine on order is horse-drawn, with steam powered pump.*

Left: *A Test Call in about 1910, to Hunton Bridge; Molly and Tommy did the run in 11 minutes flat. The photo shows the crew and appliance returning from this test call and about 200 yards north of the Dog public house in Hempstead Road. The crew comprised: 2nd Officer Graham Neill, Fm Dick Wise, Bill Hilliard, Charlie Crawford, Chief Officer Thorpe, Fm Dan Fountain, Dick Hatton, and Freddie Heath. All the men here except the C/O and Fm Wise were Council employees.*

... police bicycles ... each trip to be fully documented ...

When she was working at top pressure the body and wheels were perfectly steady, and there was not the slightest signs of rocking. The weight of the engine, it may be mentioned, is 32 cwts., the hose bringing it up to two tons.

In each of the four ⅝ in. jets referred to was obtained the same power as could be got from the old manual at full pressure with 22 men at the levers, and this with, of course, only two men working, the stoker and driver.

With the adoption of a new call-bell system, which is under favourable consideration by the Council, there will be, what has not been the case for many years, adequate fire protection for the town. That is a fact which it is most satisfactory to record.

In order to celebrate in an informal way the opening of the new Fire Station adjoining Upton House, the Brigades taking part in the Whit-Monday procession, were entertained to dinner on the new premises, by permission of the Urban District Council, by Mr. C. H. Peacock, captain of the Town Brigade.

About forty sat down, the company including the members of the Town Brigade, Sedgwick's Brigade under Deputy-Captain Harold Sedgwick, and Croxley Mills Brigade.
WO June 1900

Police Christmas Boxes

By Colonel Daniell's time (1880-1911) public relations had improved somewhat, but this improvement itself created problems. From around 1888 onwards the citizens of Watford began at Christmas to offer gratuities out of appreciation for the work of the police.

However, by Christmas 1897 the police had fallen into the practice of calling round to the houses of various residents in the borough and, while not specifically asking for a Christmas box, making it quite clear what they had called for.

A certain Mr. Moore wrote to the Chief Constable and complained of this practice. Colonel Daniell, naturally, was furious. Captain Wymer, the commander of Watford Division and Deputy Chief Constable of the county, was forced to resign, but only after Daniell had threatened to dismiss him summarily from the force.

Wymer was turned out of his house at Watford police station in spite of appeals for a stay of execution on account of his family's health. The inspector of the division retained his job only after a pathetic letter begging for clemency on account of his wife's nervous ill-health. The £26 that had been collected was offered back to the donors. It is perhaps indicative of the state of the relations with the public that out of the £26 only £5/11/6d was received back by the donors. Daniell followed up this action with the following general order on February 7, 1898:

"All the officers and constables stationed at Watford are aware that from the point of view of the Secretary of State in the Home Department, with whose opinion every chief officer of police must be in absolute accord, a very grave breach of the regulations concerning the police has been committed by local police at Watford going round private residents and places of business collecting Christmas boxes.

"Nothing can be more destructive to the morale and discipline of the force. How would it be if a constable in the witness box were asked in cross-examination *'Did you go into the plaintiffs (or defendant's) house for a Christmas box?' 'Yes.' 'Did he give you one?' 'No.'*

"Would not counsel immediately make a point that the police were against his client on having been refused a Christmas box? If anyone sends money to the police station as a Christmas box for the men the sum so received will be divided, but there must be no collecting."

In 1892 the first full-time plain-clothes officer had appeared at Watford. He was supplemented by a second officer in 1894.

This move was designed to cope with the growing liaison between Watford and London and the consequent increase in crime.
'The Story of Hertfordshire Police'

Cycles—Hertfordshire Police

Daniell was very concerned with the new forms of personal transport being developed.

Bicycles came into general use after one had been bought as an experiment in 1893 in Watford. In 1895 Daniell ordered that 'names and numbers of officers of all ranks competent to ride bicycles are to be sent into this office, and names of officers are to be sent in as they learn to ride a machine.'

By 1896 there were eleven county-owned cycles in use by the Hertfordshire Police. In June of that year Daniell announced that officers could use their own cycles for police work with an allowance of 3d. per hour (this high allowance was given because Daniell regarded cycling as a very dangerous occupation).

Early introduction of cycles on a fairly large scale was one of the reasons why the mounted section of the force was never very strong.

Characteristically, Daniell surrounded police operations on two wheels with a mass of paper work. Each cycle trip had to be fully documented. In 1899 the magazine 'Cycle' reported the proposed setting up of a cycle corps in the Hertfordshire Police, which the magazine feared would be extremely hard on speeding cyclists or 'scorchers.' The fears were not entirely unfounded, for many speeding cyclists were caught by the corps.

These officers, who operated largely on the Great North Road, were distinguished by the wearing of a forage cap instead of a helmet.
'The Story of Hertfordshire Police'

War Fund

Now, at the end of nine months, the company are still in the field. The have done hard campaigning work, have lost a few of their number in battle, and more through disease.

When they return they are assured of a great

Summer 1900, the new fire station, next to the UDC offices in the High Street, completed and open for business!

welcome from Watford townspeople, a committee of whom have all the arrangements for the home-coming in hand. While on this subject, it may be mentioned that a War Fund, started by the 'Watford Observer,' was responded to most liberally, and reached a total of £282.

Also, it should be added, that Major the Earl of Essex was invalided home, and was on a bed of sickness for weeks after his return from South Africa, his recovery being regarded with the greatest pleasure by everyone in the town.

Lieut.-Colonel Healey, too, who went out in command of the South Wales Borderers, came home, broken in health, to receive a cordial welcome from the people amongst whom he lives.

WO February, 1900

New Masonic Schools at Bushey

An escort of Yeomanry attended the Prince from the railway station to the Market-place, where from a covered stand, on which stood most of the public men of the town, an address of welcome to his Royal Highness was read. In his reply, the Prince referred to the growth of the town, which, he said, he had visited in 1874 with the 7th Hussars. He also expressed his gratification at the loyalty of the inhabitants.

As he drove away the crowds broke into lusty and prolonged cheers. The route to the new schools was lined with people. The ceremony connected with the new institution was notable in many respects.

With such of the ritual of Freemasonry as could be gone through before the eyes of the uninitiated, the Prince laid the stone well and truly, to the honour of the Craft and the glory of God. The building, which is to cost nearly £100,000, is now proceeding apace, the site being on the Bushey Grove estate.

WO May, 1900

The Relief of Mafeking

Like the rest of the country Watford celebrated the relief of Mafeking with great enthusiasm, the scenes in the streets both on Friday and Saturday evenings being unparalleled in the history of the town. The decorations which had been used the previous week to welcome H.R.H. the Duke of Connaught came in most handy. High-street, Queen-street, and the Broadway were in gala-day garb. The

festoons of Chinese lanterns which were so effective on the 12th along the Broadway were again lighted and were again admired.

But it was not only in the main thoroughfares that flags were displayed. Away in side streets tiny banners peeped from the windows or were waved by youngsters in the garden—the same youngsters who had on Thursday night been drawn up in the school playground and had cheered for Baden Powell, and been given a day's holiday because Mafeking had been relieved. It was about half-past ten on Friday evening when the news arrived, and in less than half-an-hour from that time a dense crowd blocked the thoroughfare.

The good news so eagerly awaited had come. Men did not stop to ask whence it had come, or whether it were official. Someone was certain of its authenticity, and that was enough.

The loyal and patriotic residents of Watford rushed from their homes on hearing the first shouts and the first cheers. They swarmed into the High-street, where, with unrestrained enthusiasm, they woke up echoes in the little back streets. All the town, or very nearly all, knew the great news before midnight. Everywhere it was received with joy. The people who had given the Herts Yeomanry a magnificent send-off two months ago were just the people from whom one could expect a great outburst over the end of the sufferings of heroic Mafeking.

As time passed the uproar grew.

The heaviest sleepers in the neighbourhood were awakened, and as it dawned upon them that the noise meant the arrival of the news for which they had waited with such feverish impatience for days that seemed weeks, they rushed, half dressed and cheering lustily, into the street.

The Artizan Staff Band turned out, and the

singing of "Rule Britannia" and the National Anthem, now led by the band, rose louder and louder. Women, looking on from the windows above, waved flags and now and again joined in with treble notes that could be distinctly heard above the bass roar of the crowd. A number of people carried torches, and that old-time expression of jubilation—the bonfire, was not lacking. The police did not interfere but kept a watchful eye on the bonfires.

WO, May 1900

A Charter For Watford?

The important subject of Incorporation was again put on the agenda, and once more did the Council decide in favour of seeking a charter.

The necessary steps, however, towards obtaining it remain to be taken, though there seems to be lacking a public man sufficiently interested in the matter to see it carried through.

WO, December 1900

Above right: Colonel Healey returned from the Boer War in bad health, leading to the sale of the King Street Brewery to Benskin's who then wanted to liquidate the assets of the site and premises. The 'restrictions' would be 'no brewing'.

Right: Mill End, looking to Rickmansworth, 1905.

This map covers some of the Cassiobury and central area of the 1822 map on page 25.

The area was surveyed in 1870-71 and this map is a revision dated 1896. Wiggenhall, St James, Cardiff and Liverpool Roads are laid out and partly built upon. The Rickmansworth Railway line crosses Wiggenhall Hall Road by level crossing (as at Radlett Road). The Bushey Lime works are a feature and in Bushey Hall Road a printing works was noted (that of Andre and Sleigh).

Watford Mill is still in existence and the area at the bottom of Water Lane Hill is noted as 'Little Otter's Pool'.

Much of the land above Clarendon Road, fronting the High Street is open; Dr Brett's Watford House, and Monmouth House further along, are the only houses before reaching the Pond. Abutting the Pond was a large garden nursery. Clarendon Road shows houses in large grounds, spacious, and unbeknowing, very suitable for redevelopment several times in the decades to follow.

Back in the High Street the tail-race of the Mill is now underground but the small stream before Wiggenhall Bridge is still crossed as a ford. The raised pavement is still testimony to the frequent flooding which occurred.

The Silk Mill premises houses the Watford Steam Laundry and Dye Works; the adjacent fields being known as the Rookery.

The perimeter of Cassiobury shows Swiss Cottage, Cassiobury Lodge, Watford Lodge (the gates), Lodge near Nascot House, and the Garden Lodge, in Hempstead Road.

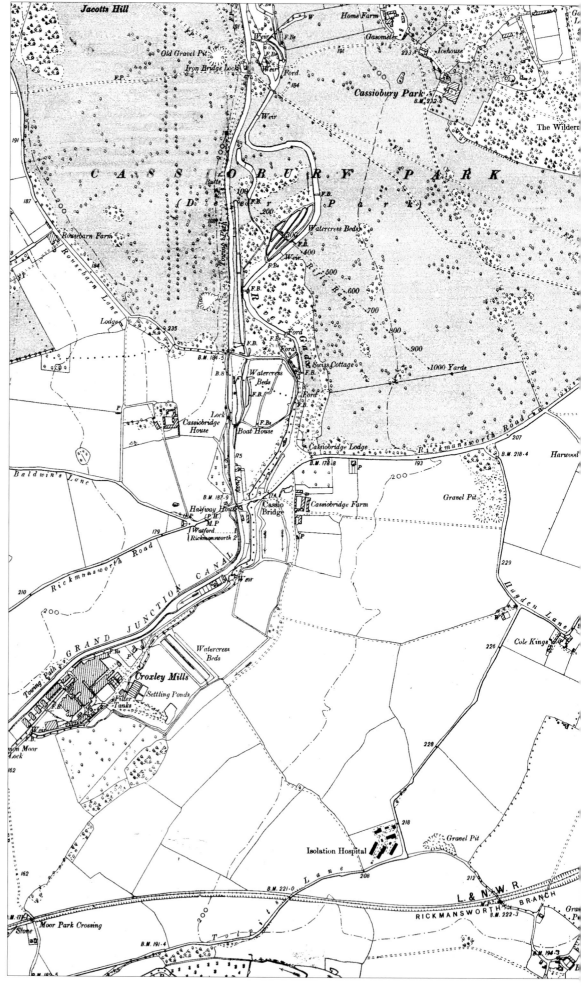

Save Mills
Engine Shed
Cattle Pens
Watford Junction
Goods Shed
Infirmary
LONDON
ORPHAN ASYLUM
Chapel
Lodge
Hotel
L.B.
Subway

Scotts Wood

Boat House
Gravel Pit
Nursery

Reservoir
(Watford U.D.)
Post
Nascott House
Lodge

CASSIO HAMLET
The Elms
B.M. 246
B.M. 247.8
Little Cassiobury
Nursery
Sun. Sch.
Posts
Chap.
B.M. 244.5
B.M. 237.5
Ch.
Chap.
Watford Ho.
Sch.

Icehouse
Icedale Wood

Almshouses
Northend House
B.M. 241.7
Ch.
U.D.
Offices
Watford Lodge
St. Albans
M.P. Rickmansworth 3
L.B.
West Herts
Club & Ground
Pavilion
Berkhampstead N.M.
B.M. 242.6
STONES ALLEY
Sch.
Chap.

Hall
Nursery
Lodge
B.M. 233.3

WATFORD
River Colne
Swimming Baths
Colne Bridge
S.P.
Obelisk
Printing Works

Pumping Shed
B.M. 177.4
Bushey Sewage
Pumping Shed

Bushey Grove
B.M. 236.3

School
240
Almshouses
Sch.
237.8
Ch.
Vic. Sch.
Busheymead
House
Little Otter's Pool
S.P.
B.M. 233.9
Mort. Chap.
Receiving House
Mort.
Chap.
Hospital
B.M. 235.6
Court
Watford Place
High St. Sta.
S.P.
F.B.
B.M. 185.4
WATFORD CEMETERY
B.M. 229.1
Watford Brewery
Colney Butts
Paddocks Hill
Benskin's Brewery
Almshouses
B.M. 194.1
B.M. 182.0
Watford Mill

Colne Valley
Water Works
201

School
Chapel
Watford
Union Workhouse
Infirmary
School
COLNEY BUTTS
Watford Field
(Recreation Ground)
Watfordfield House
School
Watford
Field Crossing
M.P.
WATFORD
FIELDS
Water Works
(Watford U.D.)
B.M. 177.1
Dalton
House
Pumping Station
Eyemore
F.B.
Condensing
Pond
Chalk Pit

Gravel Pits
Infectious Wards
WATFORD URBAN
Acres 1169.447
Watford Sewage
Pumping Station
Ford
F.P. 170
Boat
House
Watford Gas
Works
Watford
Bridge
Foundry
Boat House
Bushey Lime
Works

Penthouse Lane
Post House
Wiggenhall Bridge
Ford
Colne
Weir Tumbling
Bay
Wiggen Hall
178
Post
196
Ford
F.B.
200
235
Kingsfield
The Dell
Cliff
Villa
St. Matthew's Church
Vicarage
Bushey Station
Subway
Sch.
Chap.
B.M. 233.9

NEW BUSHEY
BUSHEY URBAN
Acres

River Colne
Watford Steam Laundry
& Dye Works
THE ROOKERY
F.B.
Tommy Deacon's
Hill
Meth.
Chap.
Berkhampstead 12
London 14
Crooked
Brick Wo

Oxhey Farm
218
Bushey Sewage
Outfall Works
Sewage Tank
Filter Beds
F.B.
200
222
Green Lane
Reservoirs
L.&N.W.R.
Pumping Station
Reservoir
(Watford U.D.)
B.M. 300

186
246
The Roughs
U.D. By.
Lodge
B.M. 273.4
Watford Heath Farm
Watford Heath
Spring

... photographic plate business, practically destroyed ...

A Soldier's Letter

Private S. Dolamore, writing from Kroonstad, on June 28th to his mother at Watford, says:—
"I dare say you have been worrying about me not writing for so long, but I could not write before as we have had such a lot to do since we left Bloemfontein to go to Pretoria.

I must tell you that it was very hard marching, and plenty of fighting, but not so much as we expected there would be; and I am very glad to tell you that my regiment, the 5th Mounted Infantry, was one of the first regiments to enter Pretoria.

We had a fight outside of Pretoria on the 4th of June, and marched past Lord Roberts and on through Pretoria on the 5th, and camped the other side. We stopped there two days, and then came back through to this side.

Then my regiment went on to try to knock Botha out. I was left behind because my horse died. I was there for three days, but I did not write because I was waiting to hear if there were any orders about coming home. I have not heard anything about it yet.

Then I was sent down to Johannesburg to get some horses, but we could not get any there, so we had to come down here to Kroonstad to get some. We came by train, and were nearly blown up by De Wet, and delayed for three days because the line was torn up.

It was at the same place that De Wet captured our mails and burnt them, but we found several letters all intact.

We had Mr. Winston Churchill and the Duke of Westminster on the train.

WO July 1900

Paving

The paving of the town has been taken in hand, and about £15,000 is being spent on it. Towards half of this sum the County Council contributes two-thirds. During the year the Council added another to their officials by appointing a building inspector, whose duty it is to see that the byelaws are adhered to, and that no "jerry building" goes on.

WO, December 1900

Paget Company's Premises Gutted

Soon after 2 o'clock on Thursday morning a fire broke out on the premises of the Paget Prize Plate Company, Limited, Callow Land, with the result that one block, that in which the photographic plate business is carried on, was practically destroyed.

The Company have been established in Watford some twelve years, and employ a considerable number of hands mostly girls, some 50 or 60 of whom found on arriving at their work on Thursday morning that, owing to the fire, they had to return to their homes. The outbreak turned out to be one of the most serious that the Brigades have had to contend with in the town for years.

The fire started in the engine room. An employee named Samuel Brooks was on duty, and it appears that while he was in the boiler-house his attention was called to a bright light in the engine room near by. He soon discovered that this particular room was in flames, and at once gave the alarm.

The Callow Land District Brigade, under Lieutenant R. A. Thorpe, turned out with promptitude, and, after connecting their hose with the hydrant, they ran out a length of over 300 yards and tackled the flames by breaking entrances through the windows.

The town Brigade, led by Captain C. H. Peacock, and Messrs. Sedgwick's Brigade,

Above: *Rickmansworth Road–once known as the "Park-road"– in about 1900. This is looking towards our underpass; the building by the elm tree on the left is where our Colosseum is. The rustic house on the right is near where the Rosslyn Road opens on to Rickmansworth Road; here the garden is full of geese!*

Right: *Cassiobury Park Gates and Lodge and the railings which fronted the Almshouses, (shown on the next page).*

under Captain Harold Sedgwick, followed in quick time. It should be added that the London and North Western Railway engineers also assisted with a couple of lines of hose from the railway supply.

The police, under Superintendent Wood, also rendered considerable assistance. At half-past 2 the reflection from the flames could be seen in the sky for a long distance. Immediately the nature of the fire was known, instructions were sent out to the pumping station for the best possible force to be put on, and by this means sufficient water was obtained to keep the steamer well supplied.

The block in question was the original one in which the Watford business was commenced, the other premises being extensions. The fire burnt with great fierceness. In the engine room ventilating fans were at work,

and these accelerated the progress of the fire, which had a clear run along the roof of the block, owing to a false ceiling.

The two six-horse power engines for driving the electric dynamo were much damaged. The other rooms in the department were given to photographic plate work, and the stock and machinery burnt is of considerable value.

The cause of the fire is probably connected with the electric wiring. The firemen deserve great praise for their efforts.

Every man was wet through to the skin, and considerable risk was run through the falling roof, iron shafting, and cisterns of water.

WO April 1902

Electric Street Lighting

Dear Sir,—I should like to recommend any of your readers, who desire an object lesson, to walk down High-street to the new showrooms of the Watford Gas Company, and compare the town electric lamp and the gas lamp of the Company.

Being an electrical engineer myself I can hardly be accused of holding a brief for the Gas Company, but I am very anxious that the matter should be carefully gone into, and the Council urged to make their electric street lamps a better advertisement for their undertaking than it is at present. As a ratepayer I am also anxious that we should get the best system of lighting at the least expense.

The following figures may interest those who consider that the matter at all affects their pockets as ratepayers. The gas lamp outside the Gas Company's showrooms, I am

Top: *Cassiobridge Lodge; at this time, c1900, a small path led across the ford of the Gade and into Rousebarn Lane. To the right of the ford (where there is now a footbridge) was Swiss Cottage for which Cassiobridge Lodge is frequently mistaken.*

Above: *Shepherd's Lodge, one of the several of the Cassiobury Estate, on the corner of Shepherd's Road and the boys' Grammar School site.*

Left: *between Cassiobury Drive and the Park Gates – the Almshouses.*

informed, gives 700 candle power, and consumes 20 cubic feet of gas per hour, this, at 3s. per 1000 feet (the price the Company are charging their customers) costs about three farthings per hour.

The ordinary incandescent electric lamp absorbs about 31/2 watts per candle power, and at the price of 5d. per unit, about one farthing (the price charged by the Council), 700 candle power absorbs about 2,450 watts, at a cost of about one shilling per hour.

Again, the two eight candle power electric lights in the street lamps absorb about 56 watts per hour, costing 5d. per unit, about one farthing per hour, against a 50 candle power incandescent gas burner consuming about three cubic feet per hour, at 3s. per thousand, burning over two hours for one farthing.

With these figures it certainly behoves us to either turn over the street lighting to the Gas Company, or cast-about for some method of improving matters. I do not know why electric arc lamps are not used more than they are in Watford, for instead of absorbing about 31/2 watts per candle power, the arc lamp gives about three candle power per watt, or ten times the light for the energy absorbed.

I beg to remain, dear sir,
Yours faithfully,
H. Cecil Hodges.
WO November 1902

[The gas showrooms referred to was a small shop at 96 High Street, now under St Mary's Square; see advert p121.]

Fire Brigade
Lt. R.A. Thorpe became Captain of the Watford Fire Brigade upon the resignation of C. H. Peacock later in 1902.

Right: *Church Road, Mill End with the Rose and Crown on the corner. 1905*
Above: *Bedmond Village's main road, 1910*

Top: *Bushey Village, c1910.*

Electric Lighting?

The Editor, Watford Observer,

Dear Sir,—Having noticed several letters in your valued paper from those who seem to be (according to their own views) competent to judge as the value of electric lighting, I would like to draw your attention to my case, which I am sure must be very similar to that of other sufferers. At some considerable expense I had the electric light laid through-out the premises I occupy, and thought any other illuminant superfluous, but since then have found that I can only have light when it suits those in charge. This, surely, is not as it should be. Unfortunately the light in a room (which I do my reading and writing) only penetrates through another apartment facing the front and the electric light is not available today (Bank Holiday).

There are, furthermore, other holidays for 'the powers that be', such as Sundays, &c, when I can only obtain the light in the evening, arrangements which to say the least, are unsatisfactory and dangerous.

I am, dear sir, Yours respectfully,
ONE IN PERIODICAL DARKNESS.
WO April 1902

Coronation Postponed

So advanced were the arrangements for the carrying out of the festivities in Watford that some reference to the indefinitely postponed programme may be made.

The celebrations promised to be on a scale in every way worthy of the reputation of the town. Our readers hardly need reminding that the permanent local memorial of the great occasion will take the shape of a new district hospital, towards which already over £3,000 has been subscribed, and for June 26 itself an excellent programme of festivities had been arranged, the cost being estimated at £800, and the money now in hand being approximately £700.

WO June 1902

Riots in Watford

ON Thursday evening scenes which were an absolute disgrace to Watford occurred in its main Street. It appears that among a certain rowdy element the postponement of the fes-tivities for the Coronation was regarded as a grievance. The Town Committee, over which presided Mr. F. Fisher, as chairman of the

Top: *Dr Tibble's Vi-Cocoa works, Callowland.*

Centre: *H. R. H. the Princess Henry of Battenburg (Queen Victoria's daughter) and Lord Hyde, with an escort of the Herts Imperial Yeomanry, on their way to lay the foundation stone of the Royal Caledonian Schools, Bushey, 17th May 1902, passing Chater's at 129 High Street).*

Bottom: *The throng following the procession down the High Street, here just north of Queens Road .*

... two shops sacked ...

Council, met on Tuesday evening, immediately after the official news of the King's dangerous illness was received. The committee unanimously decided to postpone all the festivities.

On Wednesday, however, a number of roughs were heard to express their determination to cause trouble on the following night.

On Thursday morning Mr. Fisher, who seems to have been especially singled out by the rowdies, was hissed as he went about the town. As the day wore on, the rumour that riotous conduct was expected drew large crowds into the streets. A feeling of subdued excitement prevailed, but at 8 o'clock the police had matters well in hand.

At 11 o'clock there was a huge crowd in the High-street, including about 50 or 60 of the lowest characters in the town, who were determined to create disorder. Stones began to fly, a number of windows were broken, and an attempt was made to fire the shop of Mr. F. Fisher. Two shops belonging to Mr. G. Longley were sacked, and considerable damage was done to the shop and residence of Mr. Fisher. A few mounted police proved unequal to quelling the disturbance, and it was not till a large number of special constables were sworn in that a semblance of order was restored.

Police Court proceedings followed, no fewer than 62 persons having been apprehended on charges of riotous conduct and larceny. Of these 56 were summarily convicted, three were committed to the Quarter Sessions, one was dismissed, and two cases were withdrawn. The prisoners sent to the Quarter Sessions each received terms of imprisonment. The claims which had afterwards to be paid by the County Council to tradesmen whose property had been wrecked amounted to over £1,000.

WO 1902

The Coronation

EARLY on Friday the town began to assume a gay appearance, and by the evening most of the decorations were completed. Crowds paraded the main streets, and between 7 and 10 o'clock the High-street and Queen-street were in parts almost impassable, owing to the density of the people. It is not too much to say that the decorations were on as elaborate a scale as they would have been had the Coronation taken place on the date originally fixed.

Across the narrower portions of High-street hung lines of flags and bunting, and in some instances the designs worked out with lights were very striking after darkness had set in.

One saw such patriotic sentiments as 'God save the King' and 'God bless our Queen.' on every hand, the words being either in red, white or blue.

Though the Coronation Festivities programme for Watford was necessarily on a smaller scale than it would have been on June 26th, thousands of people found enjoyment on Saturday in Cassiobury Park, so kindly lent for the occasion by the Earl of Essex and the Hon. Mrs. W. Peel. The weather was fortunately beautifully fine. There had been in the morning a special service at the Parish Church, and the streets from 12 till 2 o'clock were full of people, rejoicing right loyally. At half-past 2, throngs passed through the Park gates.

Inside on the left of the main path were roundabouts, all the side shows, and further across the green sward were stands around which a Pierrot banjo team and a company of comedians drew small crowds.

Top: *The Prince of Wales was proclaimed King and the Coronation date given; he fell ill and the postponement of the celebrations led to riots in the town centre and,* bottom left: *the convoy of convicted rioters upon their return from sentencing at St Albans. They are passing Mr Longley's shop which is having its windows boarded up following the damage. Note Henry Kingham's bow-fronted shop.*

Next page: *Mr Longley's shop awaiting repairs.*

WO, August 1902

Watford Camera Club

Another successful meeting of this club was held at headquarters on Thursday evening, the 5th inst, when representatives of Kodak, Ltd., gave an interesting exposition of their specialities. Mr. W. Coles, who presided, referred to the revolution hand cameras and their specialities had created, some of which they would have the opportunity of examining. He was pleased to see so many members present, and as he understood that a portion of the evening would be devoted to the consideration of members' work and other difficulties experienced he was certain that a club formed on such exquisite lines must prove successful.

The lecturer then proceeded to demonstrate the advantages derived by the use of the new pelloid films and the daylight developing machine, and some excellent prints were also made by gaslight on Dekko paper. A number of interesting slides, all made from negatives taken by Kodak hand cameras, were next shown.

WO February 1903

A contemporary Vi-Cocoa advert.

Vi-Cocoa factory gutted . . . 550 workers . . . a week's wages and notice to leave . . .

Vi-Cocoa works gutted

THE largest fire that has ever occurred in Watford broke out between 7 and 7.30 o'clock on Saturday evening in the factory erected in the Callow Land district by Dr. Tibble's Vi-Cocoa Company.

The extensive block of buildings, which was put up some three years ago, stands on an eminence on the confines of Callow Land, and runs alongside the St. Albans branch of the London and North-Western Railway Company.

At the factory are employed nearly 600 hands, two-thirds of whom are young girls, the rest being men and boys. Although the premises are known as the Vi-Cocoa factory it is understood that the business is confined to the preparation of chocolate in various forms. The resident manager is Mr. Boisselier, and almost without exception all the employees live in the town. The alarm of fire seems to have been given in the first instance by one of the workmen named Eames, who lives in the Balmoral-road near by.

No one was on the premises at the time, the factory having closed at one o'clock on account of Saturday, but a night watchman was on duty, and to him the alarm was given by Eames. The hooter was promptly blown, and this was followed very quickly by the pulling of the fire-bell outside the residence of Captain R. A. Thorpe. Captain Thorpe, who was then at dinner, rushed out, and, with the nearest men available, hurried to the scene with the escape, the steamer and men, under Superintendent Butler, following from High-street. Soon, Messrs. Sedgwick's Brigade, under Super-intendent Taylor, were on the spot, and then the Bushey, Rickmansworth and Croxley Brigades.

The fire had evidently broken out in the basement of the south corner and fanned by a fairly-stiff south-west breeze was carried over the greater part of the several wings which complete the factory and which cover more than half-an-acre of land. The roofs of the several departments were well alight before the fire brigade could get to work.

Quickly a connection was made with four-inch main and Capt. Thorpe directed the Brigade to try and save the engine rooms and also the boiler sheds, a step which met with the approval of Mr. Boisselier, who had arrived upon the scene. This the Brigade did, Supt. Butler and others taking to the roof of the building for that purpose.

To the ordinary spectator the work of the steamer and the brigade seemed a waste of time. But it proved otherwise. At the time the fire broke out a steady trade was being done in the town in the many places of business, but the way in which the town was illuminated by the fire some two miles away was the means of completely clearing all the shops and denuding the main streets of people, who hurried off to witness the spectacle on the Vi-Cocoa Estate.

The crowd increased and it was estimated that no less than 20,000 or more persons were congregated in the locality. They came from all parts of Watford, Bushey, Hendon, Uxbridge, St. Albans, Rickmansworth, Hemel Hemp-stead, Kings Langley, Boxmoor, Chesham, and from localities even further afield than Uxbridge.

On the St Albans branch of the Railway it was doubtful whether it would be possible for trains to safely pass the burning buildings. This doubt was entertained with regard to the train which leaves at 7.55 for St. Albans. To settle the point, a pilot engine was sent to try the experiment, and the trial being satisfactory the passenger train was allowed to depart. The work of the Brigade in saving the large engines and boilers has been spoken of, but also the huge heaps of coals, representing scores of tons and had the boiler-houses gone, there is but little doubt the coal heaps would have vanished also.

Not only that but a little way beyond the same spot were some huge stacks of timber, cut and shaped ready for use in the room set apart for carpentry and which is of the value of £4,000. All this was saved. Then too, at the rear of the boiler-houses and engine room, or rather on the other side of them running parallel with the line was what we may describe as the carpenters' shop. This is some 40 to 50 yards in length and contains a large number of steam saws, a large quantity of timber and boxes already manufactured and ready for use. It seems a marvel how this was saved, especially when it is pointed out that the fire extended right up to the partition wall of this part of the factory. All this was saved in connection with the factory proper. The fire brigade therefore accomplished some most valuable work. The men generally and likewise Capt. Thorpe and Supt. Butler, the responsible officers, worked with the greatest enthusiasm and time after time ran no small degree of personal risk, but happily each time escaped unhurt

The workers in all number about 550. The great majority were girls, but there were also a number of men and boys and the number of unemployed in the town is already unpleasantly large. In many cases we know girls employed there were the sole support of their homes, and it is feared there will be much distress as an outcome of the conflagration.

On the Monday morning the following notice was pasted up:— "We regret that owing to the extensive damage done by the fire, the works will be compulsorily closed, and in consequence all will receive a week's wages and notice to leave our employment. It is proposed to start rebuilding immediately, and Mr. Boisselier would like to speak to the hands in their mess-room on Monday morning between nine and twelve. A registry will be made of names and addresses, any change to be notified to the office.—

(Signed) Vi-Cocoa Ltd."

WHP February 1903

The scene of desolation on the morning after the fire.

... ten classrooms, each to accommodate 60 pupils ...

Vi-Cocoa Poor Relief Fund

Dear Sir,—Mr. Gorle, in his letter to the "Leader" of the 17th inst. entirely ignores the fact that the Society for Improving the Condition of the Watford Poor has 33 visitors in Watford, all of whom have been distributing relief to the unemployed since the middle of November.

They had, up to the end of January, given away to applicants for relief 1,051 tickets, varying in value from 1s. to 2s., besides having given upwards of 5,000 to 6,000 dinners to poor children. It is quite unnecessary to have a multiplicity of funds, as the persistent cadger will by this means obtain relief from many sources, which is the form of relief most to be deprecated.

The Committee of the Vi-Cocoa Relief Fund has, very properly, placed itself in communication with the heads of the factory, with the object of avoiding this overlapping of relief.

I invite Mr. Gorle to let our society and Vi-Cocoa Fire Relief Committee know the names of those whom he is assisting, and to what extent. It would also be interesting to know the names of the unemployed "who have helped to make Watford what it is," and in what way they have achieved the result.

Donations may be sent to any of the banks at Watford, or to any of the Committee.

Yours truly, HENRY J. ROGERS.
Hon. Secretary.

WO February 1903

Victoria Boys' School

On Saturday afternoon last the new Victoria Boys' School, Watford, which has recently been erected to meet the growing scholastic requirements of that part of the town in which the present block of buildings named after the late Queen are situate and more especially that part known as Harwood's Estate, were formally opened by Mr. E. M. Chater, the chairman of the School Board.

Mr. R. A. Thorpe, as chairman of the Works Committee, first gave an official description of the new building, the points enumerated being as follows:—The school is arranged on the central hall system to satisfy the requirements of the Board of Education for 600 children. The central hall is 73ft long by 33ft wide having a gallery 53ft wide across the south end. The class rooms are ten in number each arranged on the Board of Education scale to accommodate 60 pupils, being 24ft x 24ft 8in and are entered from the central hall. They have six ranges of deal desks. The four back rows are on stepped platforms and a space is provided behind the last row to allow the teacher to pass.

WO February, 1903
[The schools had been in use since 1897.]

Cameras and Clubs

After preliminary meetings in October 1902, at the Library in Queens Road, the inauguration of the Watford Camera Club was not without incident. Disagreements about the premises and the degree of involvement in the educational aspect of the Library caused a split and the formation of two organisations, the Camera Club and the Watford Photographic Union. At the first meeting of the Watford Photographic Union, Whitford Anderson, ARIBA, spoke of the need to make and preserve a complete record of the changing face of Hertfordshire.

The two clubs continued in rivalry until 1910 when a merger was successfully negotiated and the original name, Watford Camera Club, adopted. With the outbreak of the Great War the Club was closed, to be restarted in Autumn 1919 with Mr. L. H. Haines as President.

Trial 'Bus Service

The trial trip of a motor 'bus service between Edgware, Stanmore, Watford, Rickmansworth, St. Albans, Dunstable, Luton, and Harpenden was run at the end of November.

A company is being formed in connection with the undertaking.

WO 1904

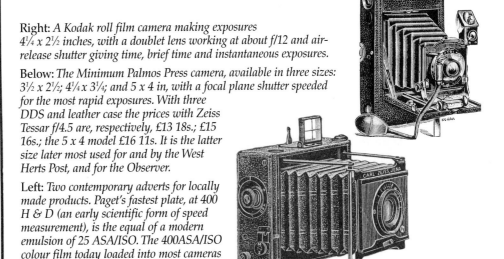

Right: A Kodak roll film camera making exposures 4¼ x 2½ inches, with a doublet lens working at about f/12 and air-release shutter giving time, brief time and instantaneous exposures.

Below: The Minimum Palmos Press camera, available in three sizes: 3½ x 2½; 4¼ x 3¼; and 5 x 4 in, with a focal plane shutter speeded for the most rapid exposures. With three DDS and leather case the prices with Zeiss Tessar f/4.5 are, respectively, £13 18s.; £15 16s.; the 5 x 4 model £16 11s. It is the latter size later most used for and by the West Herts Post, and for the Observer.

Left: Two contemporary adverts for locally made products. Paget's fastest plate, at 400 H & D (an early scientific form of speed measurement), is the equal of a modern emulsion of 25 ASA/ISO. The 400ASA/ISO colour film today loaded into most cameras would have had an unheard of rating of 6,000 H & D!

Printing—Caxton

The art of printing was introduced to this country by William Caxton, late in his life, setting up a press at Westminster Abbey. Born in Kent, 1424, in an area largely populated by descendants of Flemish clothworkers, and apprenticed into the Company of Mercers, he went on to serve in the 'Domus Anglorum', in Bruges, then the principal market of Western Europe. The 'Domus Anglorum' was a sort of merchant embassy and it was at Bruges that he learned of, and about, 'printing'. Following Gutenberg's invention of moveable type in about 1438 and the printing of the Bible in Latin, c 1450, the invention spread. At Bruges was a printer, Colard Mansion, who printed and published twenty-two works of which two were in English for Caxton. One was a *Recuyelle of the Historyes of Troie*, this the first book printed in the English language, and the *Game and Playe of Chess* another early publication. Having 'served his time' for thirty years in protecting English interests at the 'Domus Anglorum' he returned to set up a Press in London. This he could not do in the City as any trader had to be a member of the appropriate Merchant Guild—and printing was not yet a trade. The Strand, then a suburb of the city, was hardly ideal, Caxton wanted a town, with patrons and customers, and Westminster seemed suitable. His house, known by the sign of the Red Pale, was outside, but near, the Abbey, in the Almonry, from which the *Dictes and Sayings of the Philosophers* (1477) is the first book proven to have been printed in England.

Caxton undoubtedly thought there would be a demand for printed books, being cheaper. They were at first similar in style to those hand lettered, with similar ornaments and woodcuts.

The cheaper versions were at first spurned because they looked cheap. Further, he had made a miscalculation in that he had forgotten that there would be a vested interest in continuing to hand-letter and make books, and stocks still to be sold.

He knew that printing was an enterprise full of danger—he had seen his friend Collard, printer of Bruges, flee the city in poverty and debt; seen Melchoir of Augsburg dying a bankrupt, heard how Sweyheim and Pannarts in Rome had petitioned the Pope for help. Enjoying the patronage and friendship of some of the chief men of the time his work was diligent in translation and execution. He died in 1491, in harness and was buried in St Margaret's, Westminster. Had he lived he would have found that printing was a dangerous occupation; it could be seditious and had to be controlled. Printers were licenced, everything printed had to bear the printer's imprint.

In the early 1800s Watford had two printers applying for licences, James Perry, of Uxbridge, in 1816, and John Peacock, of Watford, in 1827, of whom John Peacock achieved ascendancy, his son later founding the Watford Observer.

Early inventions in photography were bedevilled with arguments about patents, having the effect of increasing costs and holding up progress. Fox Talbot had invented the method of making a camera negative, and from it a paper print. The negative was also of paper, needed a long exposure and the coarseness of the paper precluded fine definition.

Dickinson's Apsley Mills, in 1904, 100 years after their founding, employed nearly 1,500 people; by 1914 the total had exceeded 2,500 with many workers from Watford using the LNWR Boxmoor/ Watford omnibus service.

Above: Upon the sale of Cassiobridge Farm the (top) trackway would soon become Whippendell Road, and a Mr G. W. Jones would have a book printing factory built.

Right: c1885, a double cylinder, or perfecting, press. The first working Koenig and Bauer perfecting press, powered by steam, could produce 1,100 copies per hour, and was first used to print the "Times" of November 29th 1814. The speed of later machines was increased to 20,000 to 30,000 copies per hour.

In the perfecting press, below, the blank sheet of paper a is hand fed from the stack and caught by a series of endless tapes and held in position round the large revolving cylinder b, under which is run the forme or types previously inked by rollers cc. By means of the smaller intermediate cylinders dd the half-printed sheet is passed to second large cylinder e, when its other side is printed and the perfected sheet is delivered between the two cylinders f.

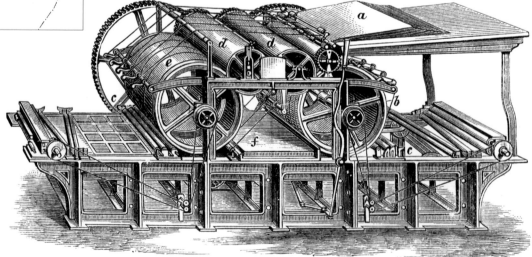

Making paper—Dickinson

John Tate is credited with setting up the first English paper mill, in Hertford, in 1490. Rags were the prime substance, and when reduced to a pulp, by water and grinding, the resultant mix or 'stuff' was spread and shaken into a wire-griddled box allowing water to drain away. The sheet was then tipped on to a piece of felt, a pile produced, and tightly pressed. The semi-dry sheets of pulp would then be taken from the felt and hung to dry. The size was limited to that of the former, and rate of making very slow. This was so for the following three hundred years and several inventors tried to find a mechanical method of making paper. Henry and Sealy Fourdrinier and Brian Donkin, with patents from Nicolas Louis Roberts, made a machine at Frogmore Mills in 1803*, near Hemel Hempstead. Mills at Two Waters and Apsley were nearby, the latter a converted flour mill. Paper was made at Frogmore, but failed by 1810.

A paper merchant, John Dickinson, experimented with a machine and with partner George Longman, purchased the Apsley Mill. At about that time there were in the country some 760 vats producing an annual average of 21 tons of paper each; a combined total of about 16,000 tons. Six machines made 91 tons each and were clearly the future. Dickinson was inventive, hard-working and his machines successful; problems there were aplenty; the canal was taking water from the Gade, rags imported from the continent were of poor quality and in short supply, his steam machines were troublesome and financial problems never far away. He bought Nash Mills (ear-

In 2003 it is reported that Frogmore Mill is to be preserved as a historical working example of the country's first paper mill, where paper was made by mechanical means.

lier a corn mill); and introduced steam power. In 1818 a small mill at Batchworth was bought. His machines, by which paper was drawn off in a continuous web, were efficient, and output ranged from bible papers, duplex boards, sized papers to forge-proof paper with threads running through. In 1824 he negotiated with Lord Essex for the purchase of some land at Home Park—where he had another mill built, mainly producing cards required for Jacquard weaving, and wrapping papers. In 1826 he bought land at Croxley (a little way from the small market town of Watford) from Caius College. By 1830 the mill was built and working, and by 1838 producing fourteen tons of paper a week.

For the mails postage had to be paid by the recipient, and was a very costly four-pence (for a sheet of paper which was folded and sealed by wafer or wax seal) for up to 15 miles, to a shilling for between 230 and 300 miles. But although the population was increasing post revenue was falling. Rowland Hill, in 1837, proposed a flat rate of one penny for each half-ounce, regardless of distance. This led to the introduction of envelopes in which the letter could be placed, and a flap sealed, and later, a gummed stamp to be affixed to the envelope, with a conse-

Above: *Croxley Mills c 1873, were reliant upon the canal for bringing in coal and raw materials and for taking out the finished product. A spur track was later introduced from the Watford to Croxley rail link adding greater transport flexibility.*

Left: *The Grand Junction Canal between Hunton Bridge and Lady Capel's Wharf, c1906. Dickinson's mainly used long-boats, a pair of which would carry 64 tons of coal. Handling was manual until steam-powered grabs and conveyor belts came into use.*

Photographic plates—Frederick Scott Archer

quent explosion in demand. The difficulty of obtaining rags kept prices high and output low. Successful experiments were made using esparto grass—but demand outstripped supply—and in America pulp was made from soft wood; eventually it was decided that using Apsley to convert paper into stationery, and envelopes especially, was more profitable. Paper-making there ceased.

Official postcards, sold by the Post Office since 1872, used card not made by Dickinson's but in 1895 the Post Office allowed private postcards to be used with adhesive stamps; giving a huge boost for production of this card by Nash Mills. Croxley was the sole mill of the group to make paper and was extended between 1887/90. This included lighting the plant, by 1890, with 950 'incandescent' lamps powered by two Mather and Platt 450-'lamp-power' dynamos and one Siemens dynamo of 12,000-'lamp-power' and in further improvements the whole plant was electrified by 1913 including two 750kw Parsons turbo genera-tors. Not unlike Tibbles' Vi-cocoa, Dickinson's realised the importance of workers' welfare, and though the wages were not high, conditions were better than in most manufactories.

A Bishop Stortford butcher's son, Frederick Scott Archer, (1813), was apprenticed to a silversmith. His interest was led through engraving to photography and, finding the drawbacks of Talbot's Calotype process, sought something better.

Experimenting with collodion—a mixture of ether and gun-cotton—he discovered that if it were spread upon glass, instead of paper, it would make the perfect support for the light-sensi-tive emulsion. Thus was born the wet-plate process c1870. For some altruistic reason he gave the invention to the public, though Fox Talbot, whose own patents were a stranglehold upon advancement, claimed it, but was rebuffed. Collodion wet-plates shortened camera exposures dramatically and were to become the preferred negative material for the next thirty years or so until gelatine dry-plates became commonplace. With no income from his invention Scott Archer died, aged 44, virtually penniless and his contribution to photography little known.

Around the time the Dr Tibbles company started a factory off Bushey Mill Lane in Callowland, the nearby housing estate was the continuation of the development of Leavesden Road and its side streets: Regent St, Parker St, Lowestoft Road, Victoria Road, Diamond Road, Jubilee Road, and others of the same era. Milton Street, Copsewood Road and Acme Road back onto, or were near the railway. The railway was to be of no direct service but the land was useful. Acme Road housed the Acme Tone Engraving Co; Copsewood Road housed Bemrose and Dalziel—Bemrose and Sons plus Dalziel Foundry. There a print-ing business was established. Next to the Police Station in St Albans Road was the firm of Paget's Prize Plates. In Bushey Hall Road another print works had started—Andre and Sleigh, com-mercial block-makers as well as printers. Other firms just start-ing the locality included G W Jones' printing factory in Whippendell Road; Nicole Nielsen, also in Whippendell Road, making watches.

Most of these had one fact in common and it was that they were large and specialised employers of girls and women, unlike the previous male bastions of brewing, sawmills, build-ing, engineering and railway work. The preponderance of print-ing came about by firms migrating from the grime and smoke of

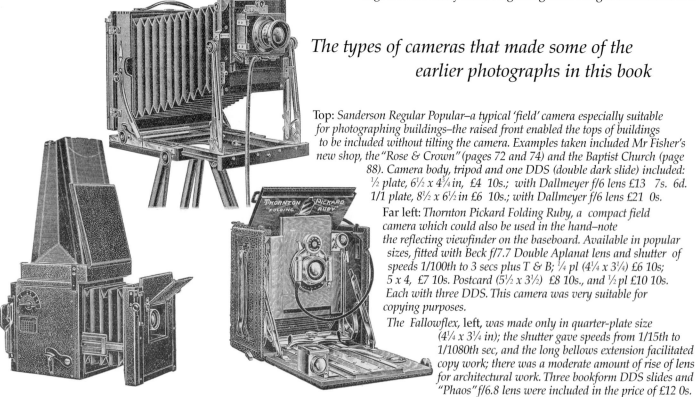

The types of cameras that made some of the earlier photographs in this book

Top: *Sanderson Regular Popular–a typical 'field' camera especially suitable for photographing buildings–the raised front enabled the tops of buildings to be included without tilting the camera. Examples taken included Mr Fisher's new shop, the "Rose & Crown" (pages 72 and 74) and the Baptist Church (page 88). Camera body, tripod and one DDS (double dark slide) included: ½ plate, 6½ x 4¾ in, £4 10s.; with Dallmeyer f/6 lens £13 7s. 6d. 1/1 plate, 8½ x 6½ in £6 10s.; with Dallmeyer f/6 lens £21 0s.*

Far left: *Thornton Pickard Folding Ruby, a compact field camera which could also be used in the hand–note the reflecting viewfinder on the baseboard. Available in popular sizes, fitted with Beck f/7.7 Double Aplanat lens and shutter of speeds 1/100th to 3 secs plus T & B; ¼ pl (4¼ x 3¼) £6 10s; 5 x 4, £7 10s. Postcard (5½ x 3½) £8 10s., and ½ pl £10 10s. Each with three DDS. This camera was very suitable for copying purposes.*

The *Fallowflex*, left, *was made only in quarter-plate size (4¼ x 3¼ in); the shutter gave speeds from 1/15th to 1/1080th sec, and the long bellows extension facilitated copy work; there was a moderate amount of rise of lens for architectural work. Three bookform DDS slides and "Phaos" f/6.8 lens were included in the price of £12 0s.*

Callowland growth

London, to the clean country air of Watford, with clean newly-built houses nearby. The manufactories were near the workers and for the majority travel was of little problem. At the beginning of the century the open market and the many shops lining the High Street served to attract the local population and visitors of every social level. There were nearly three-quarters of a mile of shops from Benskin's to Clements. The majority of shoppers' requirements were then more mundane but their shopping expeditions for food during hot weather were frequent since homes were not equipped to keep perishable food for more than two or three days; the only 'cold place' being a marble slab in a ventilated larder.

For clothing and domestic needs Saturday afternoon/evening was the traditional time for shopping. Shop staff hours were long, a 60-hour week normal. The central area was heavily populated and for many residents the facilities of a shopping centre were little more than a walk away.

Queens Road grew as a competitive shopping area. With the Library at the High Street end, the General Post Office in the middle on the corner of Derby Road, and interposed by a large number of shops, it could best be described as an artisans' shopping centre. The accent was on value for money, serviceable, rather than ostentatious. Queens Road traders offered clothing as well as footwear, bicycles and accessories, tools of all descriptions, household wares and drapery—the basic requirements of families whose breadwinners would most likely be employed in building, labouring, brewing or printing

Watford New Town—as the name suggests, was a self contained, if not self-sufficient, town which grew up in the area centred around the section of St. Albans Road from Langley Road/Station Road to the railway bridge. Here a community of independent shopkeepers—bakers, butchers, fishmongers, grocers, sweet shops, household hardware, bicycle shops and a dairy—grew to cater for the needs of the workers of the railway, the brewery, the Cassiobury Sawmills and the nearby homes of Nascot. The founding of Leavesden Road, Callowland, and the Bradshaw estate saw more shops established between the railway bridge and Balmoral Road, larger and with greater road space where carts could unload their deliveries. Balmoral Road led as far as the railway bridge, and then by a footpath through the fields to the river. Bushey Mill Lane, with Parkgate Road and Southwold Avenue off, was flanked on the north side by farmland.

Despite the new factories there was still hardship among those who had no work and the destruction of Dr Tibbles' factory made a bad situation worse.

Had the town expanded too quickly?

Above: *St Albans Road, looking from Station Road to the railway bridge.*
Left: *The shops on the left of this stretch of St Albans Road are on the corner of West Street, and would later become a garage—Darley's—and, later still, a tyre and exhaust fitting centre.*

Watford in 1904

During the year which has just drawn to a close the town of Watford has not stood still. There has been a steady increase in the population, and although building operations have not been so extensive as was the case five or six years ago, houses are still being erected on the outskirts of the Urban District, and the town is steadily pushing its way into the surrounding country, especially to the west and north.

The rates now stand at 8s 11d, in the £, made up of 4s 3d. general district rate, 3s 8d. poor rate, and 1s. for the water. A prospect has recently been held out by the Finance Committee of the Urban Council that their rate may be reduced next year to 4s.; on the other hand, the poor rate, which is made to cover school expenditure, shows a tendency to increase rather than go down. The two largest schemes which have been brought forward this year concern the electric light and the water supply, and the expenditure on the former work will be about £26,000 and on the latter £27,000.

A proposal to alter the name of the Callow Land district has not met with much success. Many of the residents in that locality hold an objection to the name, but historical research has shown that it has existed for centuries.

Last winter there was considerable distress in the town, and a number of unemployed were found relief work in levelling the Vicarage-road recreation ground. This winter a Joint Conference on the Unemployed has been sitting, and the Urban District Council have provided work at the gravel pits. Fortunately there has not been, so far, any long stretch of severe weather.

WO December, 1904

New Railway Schemes

THE projects remind us that a petition has been signed extensively in Watford during the past few days asking the Metropolitan Railway Co. to obtain powers to construct a line into Watford, with a station in the vicinity of the Harwoods Estate. This they can do very easily, as we have pointed out on previous occasions, as they already have a line which runs nearly to Croxley Green. The Metropolitan Railway Co. have before now had an eye upon Watford, and about a dozen years ago a deputation visited the town to go into the very scheme now proposed. The Company will certainly be received with open arms by Watford, as another railway in the town is absolutely necessary.

A connection with the Metropolitan could be effected in about two miles, and with a station near the West Herts Enclosure, and a thickly populated district. The Junction on the L. and N.W. is on the opposite side of the town, and as a matter of fact there is plenty of room for the successful working of a loop line as above described, by which passengers could run straight into Baker-street Station.

WHP December, 1904
The 'Met' line was opened in Watford in 1925.

Top right: After a storm and heavy rains, in mid-June 1903, Bushey Hall Road and Water Lane are impassable except by cart.

Above: The LNWR horse bus has a full load and is doing a task in flood conditions which would, in later years, stop motor vehicles.

Right: From the railway embankment the fields looking towards Water Lane and the town look like a placid lake. Sixty-two years on a George Stephenson college on stilts occupied part of the site and before the end of the century almost all became Tesco's.

Above: In 1892 Mr. Oatley assisted John Ellis and his brother to inaugurate the Lantern Mission in the Corn Exchange. These entertainments were later transferred to the Clarendon Hall where as many as 1,500 people would attend each Sunday evening. Collections raised hundreds of pounds for charity. Fred Oatley had three shops; that at No. 177 dealt in boys' and youths' suits and juvenile outfits; that at No. 179 sold mechanics' clothing, hats, caps and hosiery and No. 181 undertook High Class Tailoring (and is

featured on p95, centre). His shop, here, c1907, has been given a make-over, and the old gas lamps (the two very large lanterns) had given way to modern electric lights, of which Mr. Oatley had two installed rather higher up and, in addition, a globe in the porch and many lamps in the windows.

A few years later, 1911/12, the railway was widened for the Croxley line, and electrification to London, and the shop demolished. The alley at the right-hand side became New Road, opposite High Street Station.

Left: The projector could be powered by a gas burner, an acetylene burner or limelight. Limelight used a ball of lime upon which a jet of hydrogen and of oxygen was directed and burned, giving a brilliant light. Electric arc-lamp illuminants were just coming into favour.

Plans for a new girls' school receive opposition . . .

The New Girls' Grammar School

A scheme to build a new Grammar School for Girls on a site of seven acres at the Crescent, Watford, towards which the County Council decided to make a grant of £10,000 to the Governors of the foundation, aroused considerable opposition from the Watford Urban District Council and the Watford and District Free Church Council.

At the meeting of the Urban District Council on February 1st the Free Church Council wrote stating that the scheme contained objectionable features, and asking that it should be given the very fullest consideration, in order that no provisions unfair to the ratepayers of the district should be imposed.

On February 15th, on the motion of Mr. S. J. Ellis, seconded by Mr. E. B. Staples, a resolution was passed—Mr. J. C. Benskin alone opposing—setting out in detail the Council's objections.

On April 19th it was agreed to ask for a local enquiry by the Board of Education. The subject was next heard of at a meeting of the County Education Committee in June, when Sir John Evans moved that a sum of £10,000 should be borrowed, half of the instalments of principal and loan to be charged on the parishes of Oxhey and Watford Urban. This motion was adopted.

On July 24th Mr. W. C. Fletcher, senior inspector under the Board of Education, conducted an enquiry in the Council offices. The Urban District Council and the Free Church Council were legally represented; but many of the former's objections were cut away by the Inspector ruling at the outset that the financial aspect of the matter was outside the scope of the enquiry.

A conference during the luncheon interval resulted in the Urban District Council withdrawing their opposition on the understanding that they should appoint eight Governors instead of six, and that the County Council would not charge exclusively upon Watford for any part of the annual grant it was suggested should be given to the school to make up for loss of income consequent upon selling stock to purchase the land for the erection of the school buildings.

The Free Church Council submitted that a denominational basis for a public school was unfitted to present-day requirements.

The scheme was ultimately passed.

WO, 1906

Trams?

The Light Railway Commissioners sat at Watford on July 2nd, to consider an application from the County Council for an order to authorise the County of Hertford (Watford) Light Railway, and to extend the time for the Bushey Light Railway Order.

Opposition to the scheme was forthcoming on the ground that Queen's-road, which formed part of the route, was too narrow for a tramline, and until the gap at Stanmore was filled, linking-up with the Middlesex lines was impossible.

The order and the extension were granted.

WO, July 1906

Above: *King Edward VII, His Majesty the King passed through Watford, on his way to Mentmore, in his motor, on Saturday, July 7th, and was loyally received. His Majesty also passed through on his return to London on the following Monday.*
(WO July, 1906)

The photograph (above) was taken from the upper window of the lighted shop on the corner of the entrance to St Mary's Churchyard, seen at the right of the photograph alongside.

Left: *Mr Ellis would within a few years add garage facilities to his business. This, though, is no royal occasion but an early workaday morning—a gentleman carrying his newspaper, a lady, (going to the shops perhaps), being pulled in a handcart, and a bowler-hatted cyclist. If it were not for the newspaper and the fact that the shops are open one could be forgiven for thinking that they were parishioners on their way to church.*

. . . introduced the teaching of cooking into elementary schools . . .

Death of Rev. Newton Price

With great regret we have to record the death of the Rev. Newton Price, vicar of Oxhey, who passed away on Saturday afternoon. The rev. gentleman was 73 years of age.

The Rev. Newton Price was a B.A. of the University of London and also of Trinity College, Dublin, and was ordained deacon in 1866 and priest in 1867. For ten years, from 1858 to 1868, he was headmaster of Dundalk Grammar School, and afterwards held various clerical appointments.

He was appointed Minister of Oxhey Chapel in 1872, by the Right Hon. W. H. Smith. It was mainly through his efforts that Oxhey Parish Church was built. He rallied many friends round him in raising the necessary funds. He became the first vicar upon the consecration of the church in 1880, and his ministry has been continuous for the last 27 years.

The rev. gentleman's activity was not confined to his parish. He had the distinction of being the first man in England who adopted the teaching of cookery in elementary schools, though he only achieved this end after a protracted conflict with the Education Department of the day. This was in the seventies. The late Mr. William T. Eley built a kitchen at the old church school at Watford Heath, but the Government stopped the grant when the matter came to their knowledge. In the end the teaching of cookery became recognised as a legitimate adjunct to the curriculum of elementary schools.

But it will be for his work in connection with the Watford Public Library that the Rev. Newton Price will be chiefly held in grateful remembrance in Watford. Enthusiastic as he was in promoting a love of literature and science, being secretary of the Science and Art Classes in Watford, the rev. gentlemen saw in the Public Libraries Act, an opportunity for the education advancement of the people which was not to be missed. With the late Dr. Brett and others he secured, in 1871, the calling of a Town's Meeting and a resolution was passed adopting the Acts, Watford being the first Board in the country to take this course.

From this time, up to 1895, he devoted all his great abilities to laying the foundation of the institution as it exists today. His work on behalf of the Library was incessant, no detail was too small to secure his attention; he was the moving spirit week in and week out for 24 years. Either as chairman or hon. secretary he had charge of the educational department, and by rotation presided over the meetings of the Library Committee. The School of Music was founded by him, and the University Extension Lectures were started at his instigation. In the history of his own parish he was naturally deeply interested, and to his friends he was fond of showing a copy of a charter of 1007, of Oxangehaeg, the original form of "Oxhey." This charter was discovered among waste paper by accident in Ireland, and now lies in the Bodleian Library. The chapel is believed to have been founded by monastic settlers in 790. The present building dates from 1612.

During his career it is estimated that Mr. Price was successful in raising for Church purposes and public institutions no less a sum than £70,000.

WO 1907

Watford Public Library School of Music

Instruction is given in Pianoforte, Singing, Violin, Violoncello, Viola, Clarinet, Theory and Harmony. In addition there is a Ladies' Choir, Orchestra, and Choral Union under the conduct of the Principal.

On the Staff, are two Professors of the Royal Academy of Music, one of the Royal College of Music and other exceptionally qualified Instructors. The Fees for separate instruction range from 15/- to 105/- a term, and for the Classes 3/- to 21/-.

Goodrich "Guide to Watford"

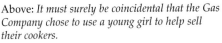

Above: *It must surely be coincidental that the Gas Company chose to use a young girl to help sell their cookers.*

Left: *The nearest pair of houses on the left were the school at Watford Heath where the Revd. Newton Price first had girls taught cooking. When cooking was established as a subject an extension was added to the Girls' Endowed School in Derby Road for that purpose.*

Road Crossings

A letter, dated 18th ult., from the Superintendent of the Line (London and North-Western Railway), was read, asking whether the Council can see their way to dispense with the crossings, one opposite the Green Man Inn, in Market square, the other opposite Three Crowns Inn, High-street. The committee recommend that these crossings be removed when the road is repaired, and also that all other road crossings in the town be taken up as the different roads in which they are now situate are repaired with granite.

Mr. Andrews said he had no objection to the two crossings complained about by the London and North-Western Railway Company being taken up, but he objected to the recommendation 'that all other road crossings be taken up.' Did this mean that the continuations of the footpaths were to be taken up?

Mr. King: It means take them all up.

Mr. Andrews: That would be the greatest mistake you could possibly make. I cannot imagine the Council will do such a thing. I have never been into a town where the footpaths are not continued with these crossings.

Mr. King said they had received so many complaints about the crossings that the committee thought it best for them all to come up. Now that the roads were made of granite and well rolled these crossings were not required.

Mr. Brydges said it was agreed some time ago that they should all come up, but it had never been done. These crossings were quite dangerous for horse and other traffic, and for foot passengers they were quite as dirty as the roads.

Mr. Tucker said he agreed with Mr. Brydges that the crossings were quite as dirty as the roads, and they might as well be taken up.

Mr. Thorn said he drove about the town a good deal, and he found these infernal crossings a great nuisance, especially to people who had weak backs, like Mr. Andrews.

Now that they had plenty of sweepers their roads were kept nice and clean, and he thought it would be safer, cleaner, and better if the crossings were taken up.

WO November, 1907

Top: *Green Lane, Oxhey, leading to Blackwell's Farm.*

Centre: *A horse-drawn bus at the Half-Way House next to the canal at Cassio Bridge.*

Left: *Pedestrian road crossings from pavement to pavement were cobbled and generally placed at main street junctions or other busy crossings, and have featured strongly in this book so far. Roads surfaced with coarse gravel were gradually improved until by this time (1907) they were given a hard compacted granite surface. Here such a surface, at the corner of High Street/Clarendon Road is being repaired.*

Many photographs show such roads with smooth surfaces thus conveying a deceptively modern appearance. The unbound granite surface became the norm for many years. The Hertfordshire County Council contributed, in the form of a small grant, towards the cost of tarmacadaming the St Albans Road and Rickmansworth Road in 1919.

The omnibus . . .

The earlier 'wagonette' service did not last long; the early Daimler was not up to the demands placed upon it and reliance was again placed upon horse drawn vehicles plying between Station and Town. Railway companies had been experimenting with motor buses for a few years and locally the LNWR took the plunge in April 1906 when they started a service between the Station and Croxley Green. An hourly service was provided at a fare of fourpence. Later in the year another service was started from the Station to Harrow and Wealdstone Station, via Bushey Arches

In 1907 the Croxley Green service was extended to Callowland and on 12th May 1913, further extended to the 'Three Horse-shoes' at Garston. On 1st September 1913, a new route was established to Hemel Hempstead calling at Hunton Bridge, Kings Langley, Apsley (for Apsley Mills) and Boxmoor.

The garage was in Leavesden Road, next to St Albans Road and this later became the base for the LNWR Road Motor Engineers Department. In 1914 the London General Omnibus Company ran a service from South Harrow Station to Watford as route 173 but this lasted only a few months.

From April 1915 all services except workmen's services between Watford and Boxmoor were withdrawn, the reasons variously given as 'vehicles being requisitioned for war use' and (by Downer in Watford Illustrated) that 'the services would cease owing to shortage of drivers and conductors so many having joined the colours'. The Watford to Boxmoor service ceased in 1917 and no further services were provided until 1919, one year after war's end.

Callow Land To Go?

A letter from the Callow Land Ward Association appealed to the Council to use its best endeavours to remove the name of the Callow Land district, and re-name it North Watford. The matter was referred to the Town's Improvements Committee.

The Council decided to send to the Postmaster-General a copy of another letter from the Callow Land Ward Association which complained of the altogether inadequate Postal facilities in that district.

WO, 1909

• *The name Callow Land gradually went out of use after the title 'North Watford' was adopted in 1916.*

Above: Market *Place opposite Market Street. The bus is a 24hp Daimler-Milnes, carrying 24 passengers, taken into service in March 1906 on the route between Watford Station and Croxley Green.*

Right: *The Horns in Hempstead Road showing the cottages near the Elms on the corner of Rickmansworth Road—later demolished for the building of the Town Hall. The haycarts may be making local deliveries but could be 'long distance', i.e. making the journey into London, where they would have to face both the Chalk and Clay Hills.*

Cassiobury Park: Arthur, 6th Earl of Essex died in 1892 and George de Vere Devereux succeeded to his title; within a short period parts of Cassiobury Estate were being sold piecemeal. In 1900 Cassiobury House was available on a letting basis; George and Adele were living in London. In 1908 Ashby and Brightman purchased 184 acres for housing development. They offered a large area to the Watford U.D.C. for use as a park but this move aroused considerable controversy in the town with the 'Watford Newsletter' taking a strong 'anti' stance.

A ballot resulted in a majority vote against the purchase but despite public feeling the U.D.C. eventually purchased 65 acres in 1909. A further 25½ acres were acquired in 1912 by the Watford District Council and in the autumn of 1932 the purchase by Watford Borough Council of the West Herts Golf Course for £24,500, was completed.

The Old and the New. The Watford to London Parcel Coach, which has been running every week-night during the last 23 years, has now been superseded by the modern Motor Van. A good crowd saw the Coach leave for the last time at 9.15 last Thursday evening, and a still larger assembly watched the new service start at 10.10 the following night.
The horse coach was remarkable for its punctuality, and may be said to have been slow but sure. On Tuesday evening the new Motor failed, and stood in the Lower High Street all night. The parcel mails had to be conveyed by train.
WN May 1908

London Orphan Asylum

In order to relieve to the utmost the very large number of candidates seeking admission to the institution, the managers have resolved to receive fifty orphans at the approaching January election. Contributions in aid of this enlarged and costly effort are very urgently needed. An earnest appeal is therefore made for generous contributions at this season, the need being especially felt of an increased number of regular annual subscribers. Five hundred orphans are now in the institution, and upwards of 9,300 have already received the benefits of the charity.

Subscriptions and donations will be very gratefully received by the secretary, Mr. James Rogers, 21 Great St. Helens, E.C.

A Free 'Paper'

The 'Newsletter,' now in its third month of publication, came out with no great flourish of trumpets. We left the 'flourishing' to the Watford public, the members of which have most kindly and efficiently performed that part of the business. At the same time, we now find it necessary to explain away certain misapprehensions which have arisen concerning the methods adopted by us to guarantee that

4,500 Watford homes—and, therefore, practically the whole population of Watford—receive a copy of the paper weekly.

The method is by free distribution.

The distribution scheme is of the completest character, streets necessarily omitted one week being covered the next, the actual number of houses in each street being supplied on lists to the distributors who have a corresponding number of copies. These facts, together with a certificate of the circulation, can be respectively proved and obtained by all interested, if they will favour us with a visit at The Printing House, 8, King-street, Watford..

Watford Newsletter, March. 1908

Centre: *One of the girls' dormitories at the London Orphan Asylum School.*

Left: *The Asylum was founded in Watford in 1872 to accommodate 600 orphans. After post-WWII use as offices for the Ministry of Pensions and National Insurance the later dormant site was part redeveloped for industrial office blocks (1998/9) and the remainder developed/converted into residentiual apartments.*

Purchase of Cassiobury Park

SIR,—I am directed by the Local Government Board to state that they have had under consideration the Report made by their inspector, Mr. Willis, after the inquiry held by him with reference to the application of the Urban District Council of Watford for sanction to borrow £16,500 for the purchase of a portion of Cassiobury Park for purposes of public walks and pleasure grounds and £1,200 for the widening of Rickmansworth-road.

The Board learn from the Inspector's Report that by the price proposed to be paid by the Urban District Council for this land the vendors would obtain £60 more per acre than was recently paid for it by them. It would further appear that, if the land is acquired by the Council for purposes of public walks and pleasure grounds, the vendors will be relieved from an obligation~to contribute half the cost of constructing a road 50 feet in width and a mile in length, with lamp posts, sewers, drains, &c., while adjacent land belonging to them will certainly be increased in value.

In these circumstances the Board are of opinion that the Council are being charged too high a price for the land.

I am, Sir,
Your obedient servant,
H. C. MONRO.

THURSDAY, SEPTEMBER 10, 1908.

The Watford Poll Committee.

POLL OF THE TOWN.
re Cassiobury Park.

This Committee has been formed for the purpose of taking a Poll of the Town in order to decide whether the town, as a whole, is in favour of purchasing a portion of Cassiobury Park for a People's Park and pleasure ground, or not, at a cost of £16,500 The Committee have resolved to take the poll on the method previously decided upon by the Urban District Council's Poll Committee, which is as follows :—

To every elector resident in the district upon the 1907 Register of Voters, being the Register now in force, will be addressed an envelope containing a voting paper and an addressed envelope, in which to cover the return of the voting paper.

The voting papers are being delivered to-morrow, Friday, September 11th, and will be collected on Monday, September 14th. Any person on the Register of Voters referred to above, who by reason of removal or otherwise does not receive a voting paper by noon to-morrow, Saturday, September 12th, is invited to call at the Committee Room, Lime Tree Hotel, High Street, Watford, either on Saturday, September 12th, before 6 p.m., or on Monday, September 14th, not later than 10 p.m., and then and there to record their votes.

No voting paper will be received under any circumstances after Monday, the 14th September, at 10 p.m.

By order of the Committee.

J. B. RYDER,
Chairman of the Committee and Returning Officer.

Watford Poll Committee Room,
Lime Tree Hotel, High Street, Watford.

THE WORRIES OF CITIZENSHIP.
What's the matter wid yer, Bill? Yer looks worried.
Yus, it's this ere park. Blowed if I knows whether to buy it or not.

Top left: *Notice of a poll to decide whether or not the Council should purchase the Park on behalf of Watford people.*

Centre left: *The mill on the Gade (site adjacent to the lock and barges shown in the two pictures). Originally a corn mill but later used to pump water to the mansion. The mill became derelict in the mid 1900s and, as a dangerous structure, was demolished in 1956.*

Bottom left: *Two working long boats raised in the lock and ready to motor northwards, c1920.*

Above: *A converted long boat as a pleasure craft, during the summer of 1998.*

... relief work; many homes saved ...

Watford Camera Club

Candidly, we were surprised and delighted at the quality of the exhibits in the Show, opened by the President of the Watford Camera Club (Lord Hyde) last evening, at Buck's Restaurant

Mr. S. J. Ellis presided at this inaugural function, there being also on the platform, in addition to Lord Hyde, Mr. Arnold Ward, Mr. Eric S. Hervey, and others.

Lord Hyde congratulated the Club on the exhibition, and the congratulatory remarks in the Judge's report. His Lordship said many felicitous things, as did also Mr. Ward, and the company forthwith proceeded to make a tour of the charming room, in which Messrs. Couper Matthews' (of the Parade, Watford) magnificent photograph of the noble President, was conspicuous. The requirements of getting to press early, and the crowded state of the room last evening, prevented our reviewing the show, but we hope to have the pleasure of publishing a notice next week.

The exhibition remains open until ten o'clock to-night *(Thursday)*.

November, 1908

A Lavatory?

Mr. Ryder said that having in view the poor property of old buildings which stood on one portion of the Market Place he thought that the time had arrived when it would prove a good investment to the Council were this property purchased by them, some handsome premises erected on the site and the land at the rear used for the public conveniences, a double set of the latter, of course, the main street to be reached by an ordinary subway. There could be a Central Hall and the first and second floors would find ready tenants to use them for office purposes. Further, the Council would have a chance of erecting buildings which would be at once an ornament and credit to the town, thus setting an example to the builders of Watford. (Hear, hear and laughter.)

Mr. Trewin said that objections would be raised, as before, to the use of the Market-place for this institution, and, speaking for himself, he knew that if he possessed premises there he should most strenuously oppose the scheme tooth and nail.

Mr. Gorle asked Mr. Trewin or anyone else to suggest a better alternative site.

There would be objection wherever the conveniences were placed, and seeing that the matter had hung about for so long, he urged that it be dealt with straight away, in spite of the likes or dislikes of those property owners and others of whom Mr. Brightman and Mr. Trewin had spoken so much.

Mr. Thorpe endorsed the remarks of Mr. Gorle. The best site was the Market-place. The matter must be dealt with quickly.

Mr. Oxley said that all questions of usage or prejudice must be set aside in this case. The necessities of a growing and important town could not be ignored, and therefore proposed that the Council at once proceed to acquire powers to purchase a Market-place site and proceed with the work.

Mr. George said he had been very quiet, but desired to say a word on that question. (Laughter). He was strongly opposed to the spending of any more of other people's money by that Council. They were always spending something. (Loud laughter). The matter was eventually referred to Committee.

In moving the adoption of the Relief Works Committee, Mr. Staples said the total amount which had been spent amounted to £628 17s. 6d. 290 tickets had been issued, employing an average of 100 men per day. It was pleasing to record that the work had been performed by the men satisfactorily, and that many homes had been saved in Watford by the Relief work provided. They were doing as much as possible.

WO November, 1909

The 'Public Lavatories' (Ladies upstairs, Gents semi-basement) were duly built and served the town well for many years. They feature in a picture on page 19.

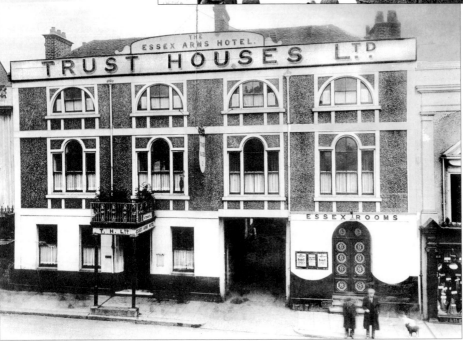

Following the burning down of the Market Hall in 1858 the new 'Corn Exchange' was established alongside the Essex Arms. Much later it served as lantern lecture hall, cinema and dance hall. Top, shows the result of the 1906 election being announced (Lib defeated Con). Left, The Essex Arms (here c1924) had only six years to go before being demolished and shops rebuilt. They, in turn, lasted until c1970 before being demolished to make an entrance to the then new Charter Place.

The High Street c1905-10.

Top: *The Crystal Palace beerhouse, No. 121, doubled as a greengrocers until 1908 (with a corset maker next door)—the yard entrance is to Court 11, Holt's Yard.*

Centre, above: *The entrance to the Red Lion Yard, until Charter Place was built. A modern 'dead-end' passage exists next to BHS.*

Above: *The Red Lion pub, originally Healey's, and later Benskins.*

Top right: *A charming camera study by F W Haines and, right, from a coloured postcard of the High Street c1908.*

By rail Watford was less than thirty minutes travelling time from the Metropolis. By road the journey was beyond contemplation, except to the privileged few who would enjoy the convenience, if not reliability, of the motor car, which was then coming into vogue.

The prospect of escaping from the smoke, smells, grime and sulphur-laden fogs during the long winter months and the unremitting heat in the summer attracted the Londoners, many of whom lived in terraced houses or flats, to the green fields, orchards and wooded countryside of Watford. Without question Watford was a desirable place in which to live. With the ever-increasing availability and efficiency of electric power Watford was also viewed as a desirable place in which to set up business.

As early as 1908/9 the Watford Urban District Council was confident its utilities and other essential services could meet any demand made upon them. With the major obstacles overcome the Council was convinced, with some justification, that by attracting new, non-traditional, industries, the town's rateable income could be increased without burdening the existing ratepayers. In a contemporary brochure these boun-tiful attributes were short-listed as progressive steps towards that end. The Urban District Council operated the Municipal Electricity Undertaking which at that time had no less than 670 consumers taking a supply of current. From a service, designed for the provision of lighting, emerged the first power station generating sufficient power to drive electric motors to the extent of 'several hundred horsepower'.

Statistically the town was exceptionally healthy with a death rate of 10.3 per 1000 population; lower than many acclaimed 'health spas'. The Municipal Water Works supplied particularly good and pure water. Additionally the same authority attracted engineers and observers from all parts of the world to view and inspect the efficient and well-run sew-erage disposal works. The town's drainage system had been designed to take storm-water to natural water courses while sewerage was treated at Holywell and Cassiobridge Farms. The fields on which the effluent was discharged produced excellent crops of mangolds, oats, rye grass and clover. Those which were 'resting' produced maize and vegetables; the farms operated at a profit.

As an adjunct collected refuse was burned by a refuse destructor; at an average of 27 tons a day the heat generated was used to provide power to pump the liquid sewage. The unburnable residue—clinker—was sold, again at a profit, at prices from 1s. per ton, ex-works. The refuse destructor was stated to be one of the Council's most profitable investments. With the town's affairs so well organised the Council wisely decided to publicise the benefits of moving to Watford by publishing a 68-page brochure. It was profusely illustrated with photographs taken by Frederick Downer and Sons and printed from blocks made by them. The blocks were 150 and 170 screen and the printing by Bemrose Dalziel.

The list of new industries, though relatively short, repre-sented a promising mix. Included were such undertakings as Paget Prize Plates (photographic materials); Vi-Cocoa (food products); Blyth and Platt (Cobra/Wren polishes); Nicole Nielsen (watches); White's (Bushey laundry); G. W. Jones (printing); as well as the 'newly arrived' International Health Association (Granose Foods). The municipal utilities, roads, market, housing, factories, schools, churches and excellent rail facilities in a clean-air environment made Watford an exciting and appealing town in which to live and work.

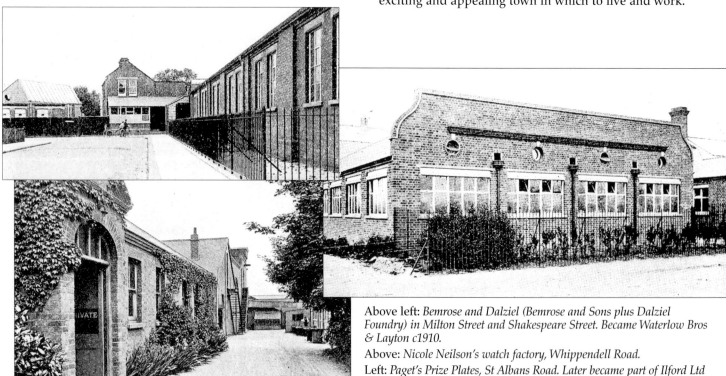

Above left: *Bemrose and Dalziel (Bemrose and Sons plus Dalziel Foundry) in Milton Street and Shakespeare Street. Became Waterlow Bros & Layton c1910.*

Above: *Nicole Neilson's watch factory, Whippendell Road.*

Left: *Paget's Prize Plates, St Albans Road. Later became part of Ilford Ltd photographic works. The entrance was almost exactly opposite Leavesden Road, and is shown next to the Police Station on page 275.*

This potential for production and expansion would be unexpectedly and fully utilised five or so years later in 1914.

In 1908/9, the majority of houses in Watford were new, or nearly new, with the exception of the High Street with its timber-framed houses and shops, and numerous medieval courtyards. Overall the quality of housing was of an acceptable standard although some sub-standard properties existed. Residents generally lived in conditions that would have been the envy of many Londoners. The design of many central buildings conveyed the age in which they were built, and the same may be said of the terraced houses built by Clifford and Gough in the late 1860's in the Sutton, Sotheron, Estcourt, Stanley, Derby Road area. It could also be said of the terraced houses built by the same company in the 1880's in Oxford, Souldern and Aynho Streets. To satisfy demand while using the area of land available, and to allow a low letting price, the units were compact and relatively inexpensive.

Charles Brightman, 'developer of Watford' was, in 1890, complaining that Aylesbury builders, – with wage rates some 20% lower than Watford, ought not be tendering for Watford work. His business had been established some twenty years earlier; Board Schools in Watford Fields were now to be built. Mr Robert Ashby, born in Bushey in 1842, worked for Sedgwick's Brewery and joined partnership with Brightman to develop the Bradshaw estate when it came on the market in 1896. The houses they built were larger than Clifford and Gough's of nearly forty years earlier, but were also in the form of compact terraces.

After this they bought 35 acres of Callowland Farm, (previously belonging to Fellows of Merton College, Oxford, from about 1380, and acquired by the Earl of Essex in 1881 who in turn sold off parcels of land of varying size to speculative builders) and working class residential roads were laid out, including Parker Street, Copsewood Road, Milton Street, etc. The properties were small having unit costs as low as £80 each. Shortly afterwards, plans were made for houses to be built near Dr Tibbles' new works. These roads were Parkgate, Windsor, Sandringham, etc. It was stipulated that no semi-detached house should cost less than £175, and detached £275. Ashby and Brightman were not involved in this scheme. Around 1900 they purchased Harwoods Farm, which extended to Hagden Lane, from the Earl of Essex, and laid out the estate upon which they, and other builders, built the houses. They later purchased Cassiobrige Farm, extending from Hagden Lane to Cassio Bridge and laid that out including Whippendell Road.

Though these estates were not fully filled-in, further parts of Cassiobury came up for sale and they acquired them by 1908. This was a very large acreage and Ralph Thorpe persuaded the Council to buy part as a park. This was duly done, after much acrimonious slandering of the 'A B C syndicate', which by now included Mr Camp. 65 acres were sold to the Council in 1909, and a further 25½ in 1912. This gave Ashby and Brightman opportunity to develop the remaining part of Cassiobury, for which they adopted a higher value approach for the proposed road, Cassiobury Park Avenue, of houses costing not less than £300 each, a considerable contrast to their earlier houses.

The anomaly of all these transactions is that although Robert Ashby finished as a manager for Sedgwicks the Brewers; all estates laid out by Ashby and Brightman carried a covenant that no alcohol should be sold thereupon, i.e., no 'off-licences' or public houses. The 'Hertfordshire Arms', in St

Above: Andre and Sleigh's premises in Bushey Hall Road c1906, later became home of Ellam's Duplicators, until destroyed by fire.
Right: In Whippendell Road, the Menpes Press of G W Jones, colour printers and photo engravers. This building and facade, built c1904, lay disused for the last decade of the 1900s and was finally demolished in the summer of 2002. The story of the 'Sun', and Robert Maxwell's catastrophic impact, will be retold later.

Albans Road, 1935, was the town's first new public house since 1873. The brochure 'selling' the town concentrated upon health and business opportunities but stirring in the wings were the new media of entertainment, first of black and white and coloured lantern slides and then the kinematograph—moving pictures. The Lumiere Brothers showed at the Library (Queens Road) in January 1898, for three evenings, a short—60-seconds—animated film of everyday movement, passing trains, processions, etc. For the latter part of 1800s and into the early 1900s Watford's entertainment venues were the rooms in the Corn Exchange/Essex Arms and the Agricultural hall, later renamed the Clarendon hall. During the early years of the century touring showmen exhibited short films at the Clarendon Hall.

Space between the Clarendon Hall and the Baptist Church (1888) was utilised with a large marquee acting as

Below: The Wheatsheaf near Bushey Arches in 1912. In the background the electric railway from the Junction to London is under construction (and at this time the level crossing in Wiggenhall Road was replaced by a hill and bridge over the lines which were to be electrified).

In front of the viaduct is the Watford Engineering Works and at the bottom, right, the Wheatsheaf. Beyond the buildings of the engineering works ran the river Colne, popular for evening and weekend walks. In one of the buildings adjacent to, or behind, the Wheatsheaf it is stated that itinerant actors and players would perform thus making the venue one of Watford's earlier entertainment centres.

skating rink. In the meantime the Palace Theatre was built and opened in 1908; short films were shown there, later at the Corn Exchange and at the first purpose-built cinema opened in the High Street in 1911, by which the length of show had increased to around two hours.

Following the opening of the Palace the temporary rink closed, was replaced by a circular shaped building, which in turn was converted into a cinema–the Super–in 1921. It was renamed the Carlton in 1930 and closed in 1980. The premises was rebuilt as substantial offices with a 'Green Room' facility adjacent to and adjoining with the Palace. The Green Room is to the left of the Palace, shown on the next page. The Palace Theatre, a 'palace of varieties', was successful and remains so to this day, being refitted before the advent of the theatre's century. The popularity of cinema shows could not have been foreseen; nor could the eventual demise of town centre cinemas, but the theatre remaining. The story of cinemas will be recounted later but in 1908 the Palace takes the stage. At this point are introduced the main players in the story of Watford's print industry with Andre & Sleigh in Bushey Hall Road (1890), Bemrose and Dalziel in Copsewood Road and G W Jones in Whippendell Road. Employed by Bemrose and Dalziel was a young engineer: David Greenhill.

It was he who, in time, welded several disparate firms into the giant Sun Engraving, and Sun Printers.

Watford Newsletter
THE Advertising Medium for Watford and Neighbourhood.

Guaranteed Circulation · **6,000 Weekly.**

THURSDAY, DECEMBER 10, 1908.

NEW PALACE THEATRE, WATFORD.

Above we reproduce a sketch made from the Circle of Watford's theatre, which opens on Monday next. Without making any pretensions as regards the exterior the architect, Mr. Brown, has lavished his constructive and decorative ability, on the interior, which is very pleasing indeed. We cannot here give any details; let it suffice to say that in the matters of safety, comfort, elegance and uninterrupted view of the stage, the building is as near perfection as any we have ever entered. Fitted with handsome tip-up plush seats in almost every part, with floors covered with rich-coloured carpets—even the "gods" having warm cork-lino—the whole scheme marks a new era, so far as Watford is concerned.

Top left: *A contemporary announcement from the Watford Newsletter.*
Top right: *Photographed in the spring/summer of 1909 the Palace is playing"The World, the Flesh and the Devil"; beyond the Palace is the tent of the Palace skating rink 'temporarily closing on August 7th' –rebuilt and lasted until converted to a cinema in 1921.*
Above: *The set of 'Kindertransport' 1996.*
Right: *The Palace facade c1992 (to its left, the 'Green Room').*

The Palace was built as a vaudeville theatre where intimicy was the norm. In time the lack of stage space became restrictive upon the type of plays produced. During late 2002 and through 2003 the theatre has undergone a massive 'rebuild' costing £7.5 million which promises greatly improved comfort for patrons, and better facilities for stage hands, sets, and players. Funded by local enthusiasm and grants, plus Lottery Funding, the 'Palace' will soon see a successful 100th birthday.

Printing, as originally invented, is virtually dead yet printed words and pictures on paper thrive as never before. But not by the same processes.

As with so many other trades the last person to leave the office turns out the lights, shuts the door and gives vent to an expression. It may be a sigh of regret, of dismay, or happiness that a long chore has ceased but the last thought is to set down an account. Keeping the records, material for an archive, is some else's job . . .

'Printing' from reverse image wooden blocks can be traced to the Chinese cAD600, as did the making of paper; the knowledge of both spreading westward. Where there was civilisation there were scribes copying, laboriously and remorselessly. Into this era Johann Gutenburg experimented and first printed from wooden type. His inventions which earned him his place in his-

tory was that of employing master die-engravers to make matrices from which to cast metal type, and, later, to formulate an ink which would adhere to the metal type and transfer part to paper under pressure against the type.

The first books were designed to look as books always had; there was an aversion to change which only gradually evolved over the ensuing decades. His 'moveable' type, cast as individual characters, had to have a body length enough for fingers to pick up and assemble into lines of words. His press, by modern eyes, was slow and cumbersome, needing considerable effort to make the impression. Though slow, it was infinitely faster—and more accurate–than the labours of a scribe. His style of press endured for more than 300 years; the early press which local firm Peacock used is, though more ornate, of the same principle. It may be viewed, in good condition, in Watford's Museum, in

Right: *An illustration of a Columbian Press showing raised the Tympan upon which the sheet of paper would be placed, and the Frisket above with protective tapes to keep clean the non-print area of the paper. Note that eight pages are shown as print areas.*

Above, right: *In the Gutenberg Museum in Mainz a practical layout of the typefounder's working area, with a typecase behind.*

Above, top: *A facsimile of Gutenberg's press showing, above, the type bed with the Tympan open ready to take paper for closing over the type.*

the High Street not more than a hundred yards or so from where it may have first been used in Peacocks early workshop.

Watford's first printer appears to have been J H Perry with work of c1820 and an item dated 1824 as in the specimen on page 26 (somewhat smaller than the original). A provincial printer would be concerned with posters, handbills, notices and, for a gradually increasing form of business, bill heads and stationery. Perry also lists his trade as 'bookbinder' for, at this time, it was the custom to take loose separate sheets of printed matter from the printer to a specialist in bookbinding to sew them together and cover the pages.

An invention (1866) which speeded the work of composing was a machine which fed single items of type from a type holder via channels or tapes, according to

The specimens of wooden poster type could well be collectors' items. The figure '6' is 5 inches high and the '52' just over 2fi inches.

duce four or five copies a minute, depending up size of machine. Later, machines were belt driven from overhead shafting, and later still, with their own motor built in. The Heidelberg original shown next page dates well back into the 1900s and was in use until the end of the 1900s (though at that time not so much printing as scoring, creasing card, perforating and numbering multi-part sets). The Heidelberg has automatic feed of the sheets of paper and a printing rate of approx 750 cph. It is against this background of embryonic development of machinery that David Greenhill, at Andre and Sleigh, endeavoured to produce colour printing of magazine covers. There was the problem of separating the colour of the original into the three process colours of red (magenta), yellow and blue

pressure of keys not unlike a typewriter, to a form of composing stick. Later, 1886, a machine used brass matrices which formed a line of characters into a mould against which lead was force fed to make a 'line o' type'. A skilled hand composer could manage up to 2,000 letters per hour; the Linotype, and later, Monotype, tripled this output. Unlike the earlier invention the Linotype and Monotype output could be dissed and reused. The earlier type, though assisting in composing, had to be hand distributed back into its case. On the next page is a photograph of a Linotype machine, of venerable age, which was used in Watford until about 1975, together with a slug produced.

Jobbing presses evolved in which the type forme was held vertically; the paper to be printed was inserted onto a moveable bed against locating stops (frequently dressmaking pins) and by pedal power the bed and platen were closed to make the impression. The forme was inked by rollers actuated by a lever as the platen opened and closed. An adroit worker could pro-

(cyan). In the early days colour work did not use black as a fourth colour.

The difficulties faced were the inadequacies of the inks, and the lack of precision of the machines thus precluding consistent close register of the three impressions.

These difficulties were slowly overcome.

Colour Barrier

In 1890 a Mr. Andre started a small business which specialised in half-tone engraving at Bushey, then took in his two nephews Wallace and Arthur Sleigh.

In 1895 Cassells bought the firm of Andre and Sleigh and built the premises in Bushey Hall-road, later acquired by Ellams and burned down, where a new building stands today, for the adventure into colour work.

"Arthur Sleigh took me into his confidence," Mr. Palmer recalls. "I was the only one besides himself and his brother who took part in the experiment because they did not want anybody to know about it until such time as they had made it a success." By 1896 they had come to be able to produce the three primary colours—yellow, red and blue. After further efforts they managed to blend in black with the work to give depth and a finishing touch.

"It was a very difficult job in those days," said Mr. Palmer. Negatives were very poor and it was a long time before we could get screens and filters to pick out the colours.

"Precision was the most important factor because otherwise the four blocks overlapped and made a sort of blurred pattern. And we had to leave the colour from each block a whole day to dry instead of running on each colour while wet as nowadays."

The great year of triumph was 1899. By that time the pioneers had brought the new process to the practical printing stage.

"We took on small printing orders," recalled Mr. Palmer "which would probably amount to about 5,000 in those days because there were hardly any printing machines able to print colour work on account of precision, or register. But the makers soon began to improve the

machines altogether." The first machine which satisfied the requirements of colour half-tone was the Miehle.

In 1913 Mr. Edward Hunter bought the firm of Andre and Sleigh from Cassells and it has become the world famous Sun Engraving Company. In the early 1900's there was a number of colour printers in the town, chief of these being Messrs. Bemrose Dalziel, of North Watford, Andre and Sleigh—a first rate process house and one of the first of its kind—and the Mempes Printing and Engraving Company in Whippendell-road.

At that time there was in Watford a brilliant young engineer who had already made his mark with Bemrose DalzieL His name was David Greenhill, a name which afterwards became synonymous with the "Sun."

In 1909 the famous printing house of

Cassells, owners of Andre and Sleigh, formed a new company known as Bushey Colour Press and young David Greenhill was appointed manager. He also became assistant manager of Andre and Sleigh and subsequently the whole of the process works of the two companies came under his supervision and management

A printing exhibition in London in the Spring of 1914 brought about the first moves that led to the birth of Sun Printers Limited. Some fine quality colour work was shown at the exhibition by Andre and Sleigh and Mr. Edward Hunter, chairman of the Anglo Engraving Company, who were also exhibiting, realised that under Mr. David Greenhill's management Andre and Sleigh were likely to be keen rivals with his own firm competing for quality work.

Mr. Hunter started negotiations for the takeover by Anglo Engraving of Andre and Sleigh and the subsidiary company of Bushey Colour Press, and after several meetings this was arranged for August 1, three days before the outbreak of War.

Upon the outbreak of war in 1914 the British Government recalled the gold coinage and Mr. Greenhill, by now recognised as an expert in printing, was called in for consultation by the Treasury and asked to act in an advisory capacity in the printing of treasury notes.

He soon found that it was easy to forge the first monochrome attempts at paper currency and between 1914 and 1916 he took an active part in the experiments to produce a banknote that would not be easy to forge. With this end in view he linked up with another Watford printing house, Waterlow Brothers and Layton—afterwards to become Waterlow and Sons Ltd, (Milton Street, North Watford).

Often David Greenhill worked right through the night at his home to perfect a note that could not be copied and after many setbacks the answer was found in a combination of the three major printing processes—letterpress, lithography and gravure—which neither colour filters nor other photographic methods could successfully copy.

Waterlow's got the contract for printing the new notes, and it was the part played by Anglo Engraving Company in developing the notes

that lifted them to a prosperous establishment able, in 1918, to take over the Mempes Printing and Engraving Company.

On this amalgamation the four companies, Andre and Sleigh, Bushey Colour Press, Anglo-Engraving Company and the Mempes Press, were renamed the Sun Engraving Company, with Mr. David Greenhill as a director and general manager.

Mr. David Greenhill's

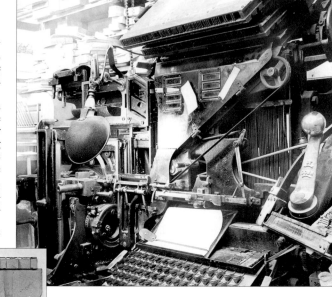

nephew, Mr. Gordon Greenhill, was appointed managing director of the new Rembrandt works in Whippendell-road. One of the earliest and perhaps largest orders he undertook at this time was the reproduction of a series of Poster Stamps in photogravure for St Dunstan's, using a series of bright single colours to give variety to a monotone production. There was not at that time a suitable photogravure machine in existence which could be adapted for such a formidable job. Under his guidance one of the Sun machines was subsequently converted to print two colours on one side of the paper with mono-

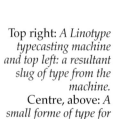

Top right: *A Linotype typecasting machine and top left: a resultant slug of type from the machine.*
Centre, above: *A small forme of type for an invoice , and above: a case of large sized printers type for leaflets and small posters.*
Right: *a Heidelberg platen press.*

tone on the reverse to test the possibilities of printing colour work on a rotary press from a reel of paper. Many of the experts considered such an undertaking was not practical, but Sun went ahead with an inset to a large publication and cylinders were etched for two colours to print from a reel. The experiment proved a great success and resulted in a demand for this class of work far greater than the facilities Sun Engraving had to offer.

Having overcome the difficulties for two colour printing, Mr. Greenhill turned his thoughts towards three or even four colours on each side of the paper by rotary printing.

An English firm of engineers was approached to build a small machine to print four colours on one side of the paper and one colour on the reverse. They refused to accept responsibility for making a machine they did not believe would work. Undaunted, Mr. Greenhill and Mr. J. A. Hughes, another

Printing by letterpress is done by taking an impression from inked raised type, or blocks, to the paper. The principle of gravure is substantially different. The text and pictures are exposed onto the surface of a cylinder and the exposed areas etched to a shallow depth. The cylinder is rotated so that the surface is coated with a liquid ink and then rotates past a rigid blade which squeegees ink off the surface, leaving ink only in the sunken image area. It is this ink which is transferred to the paper. The process is eminently suitable for high speed magazine production including high quality monochrome and colour illustrations.

director, went to Germany to try and get engineers there to build the rotary they needed for the Sun. Again they were unsuccessfuL They failed to convince the Germans that such a machine was a practical proposition and had to return to England empty handed.

David Greenhill did not lose faith in his idea and eventually he persuaded the firm of Messrs. John Wood, of Ramsbotham, to build the machine. They would not guarantee that it would be capable of four colour printing and said it was up to Mr. Greenhill to make it work.

Sun took the risk and pushed ahead. The great day arrived when the machine was installed at Watford and trial runs showed that very little adjustment was needed to produce sheets printed in four colour one side with monotone on the reverse.

David Greenhill's brainchild had become a reality.

He had produced the first colour sheet printed by Rotary Gravure. This machine was the prototype from which many more were built and incorporated with larger machines so that complete magazines with pages interspersed throughout could be produced.
(WHP July, 1957)

Top: *The process department of Sun Engraving c1930 showing the retouching benches.*
Centre: *Gravure cylinder preparation.*
Bottom: *This hall of large-sized letterpress machines shows printing's roots before the Sun had fully mastered printing colour gravure from the reel.*

. . . a new line to Euston . . .

The Watford to Euston line, with a branch to Croxley, was a further major work of construction for the town, carving a route behind Gladstone Road houses and under the High Street, for which several properties were demolished. Construction of the viaduct over Oxhey Park is shown on page 126. The layout to Bushey Station was altered to permit an entrance to the new line from the Oxhey side of the tracks. A further mixed blessing took place in Loates Lane near Queens Road, and Wiggenhall Roads where the earlier Rickmans-worth line crossed the roads with a gated level crossing.

The electrification of the line to Euston and Croxley by ground-level third 'live' rail meant that the Wiggenhall Road level crossing would have to be replaced by a bridge, approached from either side by a steep hill, and in the new Radlett Road, by a short tunnel. Radlett Road earned the nickname of 'Death-trap'.

In the early days of advancing mechanisation of lorries they, limited to a speed of 12 mph, were an irresistible source of a 'free lift' up Wiggenhall Road hill by adventurous boys hanging on to the lorry's tail-board. For some reason the road junction with Lammas Road was to be the site of several accidents involving cars and cyclists in the 'crazy era' of inexperienced road behaviour and unawareness of road dangers.

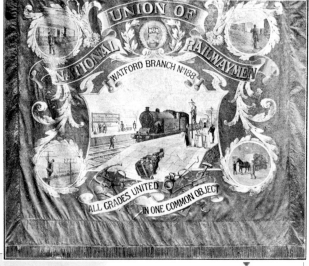

Croxley Branch Line

Of the works of building the Watford— Euston electric line, the section between Harrow and Willesden, and Watford to Croxley is complete.

The Watford—Croxley branch will open on June 15th. For the first few months North London carriages will be used, the handsome electrically propelled trains being put into service when the line is electrified. The public

will, of course, appreciate the policy which decided that, rather than keep the public from the convenience provided by the new line, old coaching stock has been got out and well prepared for temporary use pending electrification.
Watford Newsletter, June 6, 1912

Top and centre: *Just 15 miles from Euston, a junction for lines to Rickmansworth and St Albans, the railway was increasingly serving the needs of factories in the area from Benskin's and Sedgwick's in the High Street, Well's and Vi-Cocoa in North Watford, to Dickinson's at Croxley and the power station.*
The Junction platform photograph formed the basis of the design for a new banner for the Watford Branch of the N. U. R. The banner was designed and made in 1914 and dedicated in January 1915 to the Orphan Fund.

Bottom: *Twelve workmen stout and true; gangers and train crew believed to be working on the Croxley/Euston extension.*

The dawn of the movies . . .

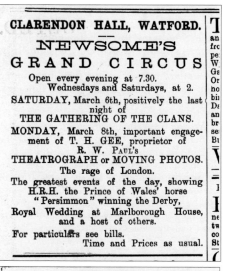

CLARENDON HALL, WATFORD.

NEWSOME'S
GRAND CIRCUS

Open every evening at 7.30.
Wednesdays and Saturdays, at 2.
SATURDAY, March 6th, positively the last
night of
THE GATHERING OF THE CLANS.
MONDAY, March 8th, important engage-
ment of T. H. GEE, proprietor of
R. W. PAUL'S
THEATROGRAPH or MOVING PHOTOS.
The rage of London.
The greatest events of the day, showing
H.R.H. the Prince of Wales' horse
"Persimmon" winning the Derby,
Royal Wedding at Marlborough House,
and a host of others.

For particulars see bills.
Time and Prices as usual.

Public Notices.

WATFORD ELECTRIC PICTURE PALACE, LTD.

MARKET PLACE.

Continuous Show Daily 2.45 till 11.   Tuesdays, Evening only, 6 till 11.
Special Children's Matinee every Saturday at 11 a.m.   Under 12. 1d.

Monday, November 3rd, to Wednesday, 5th—
FANTOMAS, THE MAN IN BLACK.
A Marvellous Production.   One hour of mystery, excitement and sensationalism.
And seven other pictures, all specially selected.

Thursday, November 6th, to Saturday, 8th—
THE FALL OF POMPEII.
The Latest Great Success.
MACBETH.
Another Fine Production.
A LEAP OF DESPAIR.
A long two-part Drama. A magnificent picture story.
And several others, all great successes.

PRICES—Reserved Seats, 1s. and 6d. (Children under 12 half-
price).   Front Seats, 3d. (Children 2d.)

*Newsome's circus show of animated pictures
was in March 1897; Downer brother's Bi-Pics
were 1909-1910 and the Watford Electric
Picture Palace 1913. The first purpose-built cinema was the Palace Cinema, May 1911, in the
lower High Street (right), near to King Street.
(The house and corner shop were demolished in
1912 and Barclay's bank built.) The Electric
Coliseum, in St Albans Road, followed in
October 1912; the Empire in Merton Road in
November 1913 and the Central Hall in King
Street in December 1913. The old Empire no
longer looks like a cinema and the Central Hall
is a Bingo Hall.*

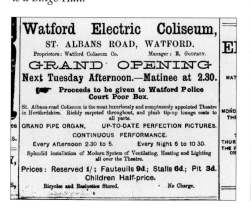

Watford Electric Coliseum,
ST. ALBANS ROAD, WATFORD.
Proprietors: Watford Coliseum Co.   Manager: E. GODFREY.

GRAND OPENING
Next Tuesday Afternoon.—Matinee at 2.30.
☞ Proceeds to be given to Watford Police
Court Poor Box.

St. Albans-road Coliseum is the most luxuriously and sumptuously appointed Theatre
in Hertfordshire. Richly carpeted throughout, and plush tip-up lounge seats to
all parts.
GRAND PIPE ORGAN.   UP-TO-DATE PERFECTION PICTURES.
CONTINUOUS PERFORMANCE.
Every Afternoon 2.30 to 5.   Every Night 6 to 10.30.
Splendid installation of Modern System of Ventilating, Heating and Lighting
all over the Theatre.
Prices : Reserved 1/; Fauteuils 9d.; Stalls 6d.; Pit 3d.
Children Half-price.
Bicycles and Bassinettes Stored.   ·   No Charge.

NOW OPEN.

CINEMA PALACE
134, HIGH STREET, WATFORD.
GRAND . .

OPENING CEREMONY
THIS DAY,
AT 3 P.M.

This spacious and luxuriously furnished Theatre will run a
continuous performance each day from 3 p.m. until 10.30
p.m., and the Management beg to announce that everything possible will be done for the comfort of their
patrons. The pictures will be up-to-date, and a special
feature of each week's programme will be the current
week's topics and happenings.

TEAS PROVIDED.   ORCHESTRA.

Prices of Admission—Pit, 3d.; Pit Stalls, 6d.; Fauteuils, 1s.
Children admitted HALF-PRICE to 1s. Seats.

Special Film of Unveiling of Queen Victoria's
Statute, and Kaiser's Visit to London.

CONSERVATIVE CLUB ANNEXE,
CLARENDON ROAD, WATFORD.

EACH EVENING at 6.15 and 8.15.
DOORS OPEN 5.45 and 7.45.
MATINEE EVERY SATURDAY, 3.30.

"BIPICS LTD" MOVING
PICTURES

POPULAR PRICES 1/-, 6d. & 3d. Children 6d., 3d. & 2d.

BIPICS
Animated PICTURES
Support Local Enterprise.

THE
EMPIRE
PICTURE HALL.
MERTON ROAD, WATFORD.

Opening Date
NOVEMBER 6th, 1913

By W. F. GOODRICH, Esq., J.P.
(Chairman Watford Urban District Council).

Proceeds of Opening Performance will be
given to Watford Hospital.

FULL PARTICULARS SHORTLY.

GRAND OPENING
OF THE

CENTRAL HALL
PICTURE HOUSE,
KING STREET, WATFORD,
ON

Wednesday, December 17th, 1913.

Under the distinguished patronage of the Committees of the
Watford Hospital and the Hertfordshire Nursing Association.
Special Prices of Admission for this night
☞ 1/-, 9d, 6d. & 3d.
Doors open at 7.30.   Commence at 8 o'clock.

The entire proceeds will be divided between
the above Charities.

Seats may be booked, and Tickets purchased from Garfield House, King Street,
Local Tradesmen, or at Office of this Paper.
ALL SEATS NUMBERED AND RESERVED.

... 25 acres more of park purchased for £7,000 ...

1912 Retrospect

The opening of the Harrow-Watford section of the new line from Euston in February.

The waiting-rooms, offices, and platform of Croxley Green Station were burnt down by Suffragettes in March, and in April a similar outrage destroyed Roughdown House, Chorleywood.

During the year a lot more has been heard of the tramway scheme of the County Council. A difference of opinion arose between the Urban District Council and the County Council as to the widenings which were necessary in High-street. The Light Railway Commissioners sanctioned the proposals of the County Council, and at the same time made the suggestion that a larger scheme of widening was necessary to carry out a town improvement

They indicated that if the U.D.C. would favourably consider this suggestion, they would be prepared to direct that the County Council should hand over £2,000 towards the cost. The idea did not commend itself to the Urban District Council. In connection with this matter, the "Observer" pointed out that the opportunity should not be lost to so improve Church-street as to obviate the great danger arising from such a narrow turning into the chief thoroughfare.

The bad condition of the Watford roads led to severe criticism of the Council's methods in this department of their work, of making up with gravel instead of granite such roads as are used by heavy traffic. The Council were moved to action and a fresh Chairman of the Highways Committee was chosen at the annual meeting, the Surveyor's department under went re-organisation, and a new highways surveyor was appointed.

The result has been an improvement, but a good deal still remains to be done.

The Council have acquired powers over Watford Heath, and—after a very long delay—over Cassiobridge Common.

Water Field Recreation Ground, which, owing to its proximity to the railway and its generally neglected appearance, was well described as "one of the worst advertisements the town could have," is to be taken in hand, a suggestion that a landscape gardener's advice should be sought having been adopted.

After prolonged discussion, a housing scheme has been adopted by the Council On allotment land near Pest House-lane, off Vicarage-road, 16 cottages at 4s. and six houses at 4s 6d. a week rent are to be erected.

In November the Council came to a decision to exercise their option to purchase an additional 25 acres of Cassiobury Park at a cost of £7,000. The vendors, Messrs. Ashby and Brightman, reduced their price by £500.

WO 1912/13

Are The Trams Dead?

Rumours have been current in the town lately that the proposal to bring the trams to Watford from London—and which has been the subject of the debates in the Urban District Council for a space of 13 years—has definitely been abandoned. Incidentally to this suggestion, another has been existence for some time, viz., that the London General Omnibus Company were contemplating running a service from Charing Cross to Watford, on similar lines to the one they inaugurated from London to St. Albans some time ago. Among these statements is one that the fare to Watford was to be 8d.

We enquired this morning of the London General Omnibus Company, as to what the position of affairs is, and they inform us that the matter is certainly under consideration, but the time is not ripe for the publication of any details. The Company has been running trial buses lately, and this explains why people have seen so many busses of a different kind to those usually seen in Watford.

WN December, 1912

Bad roads stop trams?

Electromotive power saw the upspring of trams in many towns and cities. For nearly 80 years rail travel had been swift; the trams promised an equal advance.

The tram routes suggested were from Stanmore into the town and from the Junction, along Queens Road, the High Street Market Street and out to Whippendell Road.

The problems of very narrow roads proved stumbling blocks and before they could be overcome the Great War halted such proposals. At war's end motor cars and lorries started their ascendancy and the tram proposition was dead.

The Coliseum, St Albans Road, later to be renamed the Plaza and demolished in 1956/ (the site is now that of a tyre and exhaust fitting centre opposite Homebase).

Top: *The High Street, with its horse-drawn buses and unhurried leisure, c1910,–which permits a young girl to play with her hoop!*

Centre: *From the photograph (p137) showing King Street corner Barclays Bank premises is rebuilt. Ellis Cycle Makers, at 122 High Street, have moved with the times and have turned their site, and skills, into servicing the motor car. After 1920 Peter Ellis established a motor garage in Rickmansworth Road, near Cassiobridge Common. This lasted until post-1945 when two further partners formed the firm of Lewis, Ellis and Foster, selling and servicing motor cycles. A 1961 advert for Lambretta and Triumph appears on page 316. Christmas, lower down the High Street on the other side, were originally coachmakers and turned to the motor car; and another just below High Street Station. The yard alongside Dixey's (late Tipple's), Butchers, is Gregory's/Tipples yard, and next to the game dealer that of Hedge's Yard/Ellis' Yard. Just two or three years later the small shops from Dixey to A E Smith (together with the old Vicarage behind) would be demolished to build Woolworth's new store in 1914/15.*

Bottom: *Door-to-door by road train, c1910/11.*
The tractor is a Wallis and Steevens 4¼ ton compound motor tractor. The brakeman atop the wagon, essential to control progress down hills, would have an unenviable task in inclement weather.

Brightman and Ashby's plans . . . large plots, no danger of being built in.

In August last the Metropolitan and Great Central Railway Company completed the purchase of 51/2 acres of the Park estate for their terminal for passengers and goods traffic, and this fact, combined with the already existing extension of the LNWR at Watford West and Cassiobridge, had facilitated the development for building purposes of part of the Cassiobury Park Estate, which for rural charm is not to be surpassed in the whole county of Hertfordshire.

The plan on this page shows where the new station will be erected, and where the new roads and approaches from Cassiobury Park Avenue and Rickmansworth-road are to be constructed.

Messrs. Ashby and Brightman incurred a considerable outlay in the formation of roads, and in passing, the fact may be noted that certain stipulations as to building values have been made, with a view to not only protecting those who have already built, but adapting the remaining the remaining plots and frontages

Harwood estate had been developed for some time though few houses were yet built along the Rickmansworth Road. There were a number of houses in Cassiobury Park Avenue.

The site of the Swiss Cottage is shown, but is now no more. At the time of writing (2002/3) a considerable amount of new housing is being built on the 'Met' estate and together with '124' Rickmansworth Road, and the 'Sun' site, making a total of near 900 units in west Watford, this equals a quarter of Watfords total number of houses in 1890.

to suit residential and business purposes without prejudice to either. The land will doubtless become more valuable as soon as the railway is started. Plans have been passed by the Watford Urban District Council for the main roads and sewers, and the work of laying the sewers will proceed as quickly as possible. The new road from Shepherds-road through the estate to Rousebarn-lane has already been marked out.

It is hoped that Swiss Cottage and grounds will be kept as a pleasure resort. As the town extends it would be desirable to keep such a charming little bit of rural Watford intact so that we may retain a local beauty spot and a quiet retreat.

Seventy-five acres of the estate have been acquired for a Public Park, and to-day no one regrets that the purchase was made. In the development of the remaining portion of this most desirable estate, no effort will be spared to make it worthy of the town as one of the most attractive and desirable places to live in near London.

Whippendell Road, which is 45 ft. in width, will eventually become a very busy thoroughfare owing to the proximity which it will enjoy to three railway stations as soon as the Great Central and Metropolitan is constructed in the Cassiobury Park Estate.

We already have the Speedometer Works at the corner of this road—a most successful enterprise with such a largely increasing business that the owners have secured more land for further extensions. The Menpes Printing

Factory at the lower end of the road, is another growing concern employing a large number of hands, and there is also Messrs. Kasner's Engineering Works, which provides work for a number of mechanics.

It will, therefore, be noticed that only desirable factories have been introduced, providing work for high-class workmen. The greatest care has been taken to keep out any business that is objectionable. Builders and others who have done business in Harwoods and other estates opened up by Messrs. Ashby and Brightman have no cause to regret their dealings with the firm and the present time is most opportune for further dealings as there is a considerable demand for houses of almost every class.

Messrs. Ashby and Brightman have spent large sums in the development of these estates and have full confidence in the future, as they had nearly 14 years ago when they started at Cassio-road. Every information, together with Plans and Particulars, may be obtained of the Vendors, or of Messrs. Humbert & Flint, Surveyors, Watford.

Many of the plots in this new road are from 140 to 190ft deep—quite an old fashioned depth for a garden—and they are suitable for detached and semi-detached cottage residences from £300 upwards, with no danger of being built in and at a price within the reach of a thrifty working man, every facility being given by easy terms for him to become a freeholder.

Extracts from prospectus published in WO March, 1914

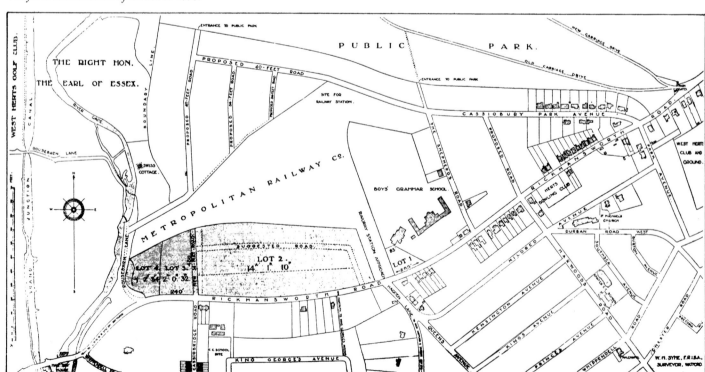

The Assassination of Archduke Franz Ferdinand, heir to the Austrian throne, in Sarajevo in June 1914, sparked a domino-effect which was to embroil most of the world. The quarrel between Austria and Serbia drew in Russia in support of Serbia; this signalled an attack by Germany against France, Russia's ally. Britain, and later Italy, Bulgaria, Japan, Turkey and the United States would all become involved.

The steam and industrial ages added massively to the complexity and effectiveness of new weapons of war. Germany, with shorter lines of communications and extensive rail systems could, and did, move troops more swiftly than the Alliance. Progress of the motor vehicle, of the aeroplane—and its use of photography for aerial pictures—and the improved arsenals of war in making munitions, tanks, and the means for chemical warfare followed. It was prodigious in expenditure of human life. Soldiers, of both sides, were expected to charge across shell-pocked and barbed-wire strewn fields after intensive barrages. Frequently the barrages did not hit their targets (means for accurate prediction were to come later) and the defenders easily mowed down the attackers. Casualties and killed were numbered in their thousands. It was not long after hostilities started that ammunition started to run out and with a great deal of urgency new munitions factories were built.

Early in the war a munitions factory at Silvertown, on the north bank of the Thames, almost opposite Woolwich, suffered an explosion. The factory disappeared leaving a hole in the ground and windows were broken as far away as St Albans, the sound travelling considerably farther. Strict censorship prevented details from being printed but the story spread by word of mouth.

Munitions factories were established in various parts of the country with local successful businesses given the task of setting them up. In Watford we had the successful Dr Tibbles' Vi-Cocoa enterprise and it was they who were given the task to set up our local munitions works. One, fairly near the junction, and with siding to the St Albans Railway, (extended from the railway to present-day Devon Road), was officially H M Filling Station No 24. No. 25 Filling Station, at Bushey Mill Lane, was hut-

ted and filled mortar and other bombs from 20 pounders to 3 hundredweights. In February 1917 a fire broke at the No. 24 Station, and the works' firemen worked to contain the blaze which was adjacent to a packing room containing tons of high explosives. Watford's Fire Brigade men worked with them and assisted in carrying out cases of T N T from the burning building. It was afterwards revealed that 'if the fire had extended it could have been disastrous to the whole town'. Works fireman Thomas Luther Butt received the Edward Medal at the King's hand in Oct 1917, but the town's Superintendent Pratchett, and Firemen Fountain, Driver and Wise, though publicly thanked by Lord Clarendon, received no other acknowledgement until 1920 when they were each awarded the O B E.

In West Watford Mr. North's enlarged works were producing speedometers and later became better-known for making magnetos essential for vehicle and aeroplane engines.

Troops, billeted in large numbers among local families, used the local parks and grounds for training. Later they suffered considerable inconvenience from the grave shortage of hospital accommodation. Conscription took all able-bodied men in ruthless 'combouts' with 'exemptions tribunals' sitting weekly. Hardship followed as men were called to the colours— the greater the number of men from a family, the greater its 'patriotism'. Instances of overcharging and of selling adulterated milk became commonplace soon after war's outbreak. Food shortages occurred in 1917/18 for which the local population was quite unprepared. In some respects social conditions for the remaining men and womenfolk improved with, for example, shorter hours for shop staff,

The war saw Mr. Downer's last, and biggest, venture—that of producing a weekly illustrated newspaper. Troop movements in the town were considerable, and without censorship they were photographed and printed with full unit details. Printed on a good quality paper, the newspaper gave a graphic account of one aspect of the time over four pages. However, unlike the

In the distance Mr Judge's parade of shops has been erected. The turret of Clement's dates the photograph as post 1898 and the pond, only partially railed, puts the late date as pre- 1914/15. After that time the pond was railed all round to prevent accidents during black-outs after threats of Zeppelin bombing raids.

Observer and Post—both of which carried masses of advertising and reported meetings, etc., at voluminous length, the "Watford Illustrated" carried extremely little news and, beyond perhaps five or six adverts, no other advertising. For 52 issues this continued then censorship put a stop to reporting troop details. From then on one platoon looked the same as dozens

before; Downer's reason for sale had been taken away. At issue No. 80 the reason for closing was given as cost and shortage of materials but, as the other papers appeared unchanged, it must have been that; without advertising revenue, failure was inevitable and so "Watford Illustrated" closed. For nearly 60 years his cameras had recorded Watford's transition from hamlet to a bustling thriving industrial town in an incredible show of photographs. However, as will have been noted from pages 90 and 91, Mr Downer and his sons were extremely competent block-makers and almost all of their general interest and news photographs they quickly printed as postcards. Economical of price the card on which they are printed does not have the longevity of photographic paper and so surviving copies are scuffed and invariably difficult to reproduce.

Further, a great number of his photographs of 1914/15 are only seen in copies of 'Watford Illustrated', and rarely as actual photographs.

Top: *Dr Brett's house and land have been sold (pages 96/97), and Mr Judge's parade of shops built. Two prominent businesses to open in 1898 were those of Clements & Co, and grocer J Sainsbury; the photograph shows a throng of ladies awaiting the opening of Clement's store on a sale day.*

Centre: *A reminder that Watford is a market town and sheep have to be taken to market, passing Sainsbury's delivery trike.*

Bottom: *A few years later and this view is only one of many of troops marching back and forth from billets in the town to the drill and firing ranges in the park.*

Watford Territorial Infantry

The Watford Territorial Infantry were the first of the three arms to mobilize for active service.

The men paraded at the Clarendon Hall early on Wednesday morning, August 5th, and proceeded to the Headquarters at Hertford.

They had just undergone a week's training under canvas at Ashridge Park, Berkhampstead, and certainly looked very fit with their tanned faces. It was not until 5 o'clock on Monday morning that the Battalion had the order to strike camp, which order was very quickly executed, and the Watford men were home by mid-day, with instructions to hold themselves in readiness and await further orders.

The Company was under the command of Lieut. V. H. Palmer, with Lieut. Lemare and Capt. H. A. Rudyard (R.A.M.C., attached), and numbered one hundred non-commissioned officers and men. Capt. Scott Gatty took over the command of the Company, on arrival at Hertford. In the ranks of the Company we noticed Private Webb, who served in the Volunteer Company sent out from the Battalion to the South African War. On Saturday, August 8th, they left Hertford for Romford.

The Watford Artillery and Yeomanry were occupied on Wednesday and Thursday in selecting and buying suitable horses. They left the town on Saturday. Major G. R. Holland was in command, and under him were Capt. E. A. Horsman Bailey, Lieut A. G. Agnew, and 2nd-Lieut. R. C. Foot, with one hundred and seventy-four non-commissioned officers

Top: *The first bus operators were, paradoxically, the railway companies. They saw the need for 'feeder' services to get people to and from the stations to use their trains and from this grew the networks of bus services. In this group the destinations are Harwoods Road, Croxley Green, Boxmoor, Garston and Bushey Arches. There was, at that time, no service up the 1 in 8 Scots Hill, nor the hills into Bushey. The buses, l to r, are: 1911 Leyland, 1914 Daimler, 1911 and 1912 30hp Leylands. They already show a marked advance upon the bus shown on p123 by having an upper deck but it would be many years before Traffic Regulations would permit the covering and enclosing of that deck. A memory of the arc lamp recalls; "When I was a youngster we'd watch the lampman wind down the lamps to replace the carbons. The ends were thrown out and we'd scramble for them. The arc lamp was turned off at about 11 pm and the two smaller lamps used; but they were quite dim".*

Bottom: *Close proximity to an excellent rail-head, ample park area for training and houses for billeting meant that Watford would become a busy military depot. In the High Street, passing the Eight Bells, September 1914, (see p318).*

WATFORD ILLUSTRATED.

NUMBER 1. THURSDAY, AUGUST 13th, 1914. PRICE ONE PENNY.

This Illustrated Publication is issued by the Watford Engraving Company, Limited, as a Local Historical Record of the crisis through which the country and the world at large is passing.

Billeting Party, at Garston

Buying and Branding Horses for the Herts Yeomanry and Artillery at the Rose & Crown Yard

and men. They, like the Infantry, had only just returned from a camp suddenly broken up, for it was only on Saturday, August 1st, that they went into training at Bellingham, Northumberland, and they were back in Watford on Monday night. To see the excellent way in which they marched through the town, one could scarcely believe that the horses had had practically no training in running in teams of six. The Yeomanry, at full strength, under the command of Major H. J. Wyld, with Lieut. Arnold Ward, M.P., Lieut. L A. J. G. Ram, Lieut. R. F. Barnett, and 2nd-Lieuts. Holland-Hibbert and W. Holland-Hibbert, followed closely on the Artillery in the march to active service.

They have gone at their King and Country's call, willingly and uncomplainingly, a unit in a mighty army standing and fighting for justice; and whatever duty they are called on to perform, Watford is confident that they will acquit themselves as soldiers and men, and from her heart wishes them "God's Speed."

The Watford Post Office have lost twenty-six of their staff of Postmen, who have either been called up to the Regular Forces or have gone with the Territorials

About one hundred Special Constables were sworn in at the County Court on Saturday after noon last by Mr. J. F. Watkins, Mr. W. F. Goodrich (Chairman of the Council).

The Watford Voluntary Aid Detachment are holding working meetings in St. John's Hall for the purpose of making uniforms. On the afternoon of our visit we found about fifty ladies hard at work. The Countess of Essex has offered Cassiobury House to the Detachment for a hospital.

Four private wireless installations have been sealed at Watford by a Government official.

It is with regret that we have to mention that the Earl of Clarendon, the Lord-Lieutenant of the County, is ill and has been forbidden to transact any business. The Earl of Essex is acting temporarily as his Deputy-Lieutenant and will attend to official and county duties.

A disturbance took place in the Market on Sunday evening about 9 o'clock. The Socialists were holding their usual meeting when one of the speakers made disrespectful remarks with regard to the King and Lord Kitchener, at which the large crowd took offence and finally upset the platform. The speaker was escorted to the Police Station and detained till it was safe for him to leave, which he did by a back way.

The Watford and District Master Builders' Association held a meeting on Friday and decided not to work more than three-quarter time on general work in order to provide labour for the greatest number.

WI, August 1914

Killed in action

The first Watford man to lose his life for his country in the present war, so far as is known, is Sergeant Horgan. He was in the 2nd Batt. Royal Inniskilling Fusiliers.

The only intimation which the father, Mr. Michael Horgan, of 20, Westbury Road, has had from the War Office, is to say that his son had been killed in action in France.

Mr. Horgan and his family have Watford's sincerest sympathy in their loss.

WI, September 1914

Top: *The mast-head of the first edition of Mr Downer's venture into the newspaper world, but in reality a medium for selling photographs of the troops he'd snapped.*

The Countess of Essex, President of the Watford Div. of the Soldiers and Sailors Families' Association, taking a keen interest in looking after servicemen's families.

The Late Earl of Clarendon

The Earl of Clarendon, P.C., G.C.B., G.C.V.O., M.A., whose death, which we very much regret to record, took place at The Grove, Watford, on Friday, October 2nd. His lordship was the fifth Earl, and was born in London, February 11th, 1846. He was A.D.C. to the King, Lord Lieutenant of Hertfordshire since 1892, formerly Lieut. Col. Commanding and afterwards Hon. Col. of the Herts Yeomanry; Lord-in-Waiting to Queen Victoria, 1895-1901; Lord Chamberlain of the Household, 1900-05; President and Chairman of the Herts Territorial Association, a County Councillor for Watford (Rural) Division of Herts, a Magistrate for Warwickshire and Hertfordshire, Deputy-Lieutenant for Warwick-shire and Chairman of the Board of Governors of the Watford Grammar School.

He was educated at Harrow and Trinity College, Cambridge, unsuccessfully contested South Warwickshire in 1868, and sat as M.P. for Brecon (L.), 1869-70. He succeeded his father, the fourth Earl in 1870, his elder brother having died in infancy. The estate consists of about 5,000 acres (The Grove, Hertford-shire, and Kenilworth, Warwick-shire).

The late Earl married in 1876, Lady Caroline Elizabeth Agar, who died in 1894; eldest daughter of the third Earl of Normanton, and in 1908, Emma Mary

Augusta, daughter of the late Lieut.-Gen. George Cliffe Hatch, C.S.I., and widow of the Hon. Edward Roden Bourke. He had two children by his first marriage, Lord Hyde who now becomes the new Earl, was born in 1877; and married in 1905 Adeline Verena Isabel, sister of the sixth Baron Somers. There are two children, George Herbert Arthur Edward Hyde (who now becomes Lord Hyde), and Nina Joan Edith Virginia. Lady Edith, born in 1878, married in 1911 Viscount Valletort, only son of the fourth Earl of Mount Edgcumbe. His lordship had been ill since the beginning of August, but after two weeks in bed he was able to go away for a change, on his return he was still far from well

He was present and was sworn in as Hon. Chief Commandant of the Special Constables, at the Clarendon Hall, on Tuesday, September 22nd, although he was too ill to address the parade. This was his last public appearance in Watford, but on the following Tuesday he motored to St. Albans and witnessed the review of troops by Lord Kitchener. On Wednesday evening he took to his bed, and gradually became worse, passing peacefully away at 3.30 on Friday afternoon.

He took a great interest in the welfare of Watford, and was closely associated with its public work. His death came as a very sudden shock to the town and the loss of his genial personality will be greatly felt.

The funeral took place on Thursday, at 12 o'clock, in the Grove Park, in a private vault which has been specially built and consecrated. The spot is in a beautiful part of the park, in what is called Heath Wood, and just behind the gardens. The service was quite private.

WI, October 1914

• *Lord Hyde, Earl of Clarendon, later assisted in obtaining the Borough Charter in 1922; he became the Borough's first mayor. His son, George Herbert Lord Hyde, died in 1935 of accidental shooting.]*

Recruits

During the past week, nearly 150 recruits have been enrolled at the Clarendon Hall, making a total of about 400. This is a great improvement, but others are wanted, and next week we hope to be able to state that more than double this number have offered themselves.

It is true that Watford has so far supplied as many men as all the rest of the County, but this is not sufficient. Let Watford be far and away at the top, and it will be an incentive for other towns in the County to follow and strive to do better.

WI, September 1914

Watford's Fire Protection

We are indebted for the following account of the Watford Fire Brigade to the courtesy of Mr. R. A. Thorpe (Hon. Captain) and Superintendent H. M. Pratchett, and from what we have seen and heard, Watford may well be proud of her organization for dealing with outbreaks of fire.

In the first place, we will deal with a "call."

Immediately the handle is pulled, an indicator drops down on the switch board at the fire station, showing the name of the street from which the alarm came, and a bell continues to ring for some minutes.

If the call is given at night, the whole of the ground floor of the building is illuminated automatically and a second bell rings in the Superintendent's bedroom. He at once jumps out of bed and, by moving one switch, rings up all the men of the Brigade at their houses. He can if he wishes communicate with each one separately, so that should he only require two or three, he can call them up without disturbing the others.

Each man's name is written on a tablet above the bell push which rings in his house. Should the alarm be given by telephone, the same thing happens with regard to the lighting of the building, but of course information as to the whereabouts of the fire will have to be

London Scottissh Marching along St Albans Road, en route for France.

"I realised a great ambition and spent 24 hours in the trenches."

received over the wire, and while this is being ascertained the men will have already been warned.

The Brigade consists of 24 men, three of whom, including the Superintendent, are paid firemen, the remainder are Council employees. They all live within easy reach of the station, and can turn out in a very few minutes after a call has been received; in fact, they have done so in as short a space of time as half a minute. At the fire at Mr. Luckett's shop, in Queen's Road, just recently, they were actually playing on the fire in four and a half minutes from the time they received the call. Those men who are not present when engine starts, follow on bicycles, for instructions are always left behind as to the destination.

Now for the engines.—These consist of two 60-h.p. motors with turbine pumps, propelled and pumped by the same power, so that all that it is necessary to do on arrival at a fire is to switch over from the driving gear and use the motor for pumping.

No. 1 Engine, which is for town use, carries 1,000 feet of hose; and No. 2, for use outside the Watford area, 2,000 feet. They will both throw 350-400 gallons of water per minute, to a height of about 150-160 ft with one inch jets. No. 1 has a 55 feet escape mounted on it, which can be immediately run off, for directly the wheels touch the ground it clears itself.

No. 2 Engine, instead of the escape, carries a 35-foot extending ladder, and can attain a running speed of 39-miles per hour, the speed of No. 1 being rather less, 37 miles per hour. The brigade is supplied with what are known as "hand controlled branches," which are the nozzles of the hose and which are held to direct the jets of water. With these branches, the damage by water is reduced to a minimum, for the fireman directing the hose has complete control of the water supply.

Further than this, by a simple arrangement, a spray of water can be formed in front of the fireman, which protects him to a great extent from heat and also tends to drive the smoke from him, so that with this appliance he can approach nearer to the flames than he would otherwise be able to do.

No. 1 machine is fitted with what is known as a "first aid tank" of 35 gallons capacity, and supplied with 180ft of one inch tubing, This is for use in extinguishing fires in early stages, when a small jet of water is only required, and being fitted with the hand controlled branch it can be at once shut off, and saves needless damage by water.

Superintendent Pratchett was Station Officer in charge of the Central Station of Tottenham Fire Brigade before he came to Watford, and served 12 years with that Brigade. He was during that time recommended three times for life saving, and was awarded a certificate from the Society for the protection of life from fire.

Tottenham were the first Brigade in the United Kingdom to adopt motor machines, and Supt Pratchett was a driver for six years, and it was then that he saw the great advantage they were over the horsed machines, and it is in some measure due to him, that Watford is at the present time in proud possession of two of the finest machines it is possible to obtain, and to his initiative that it has such an excellent staff to man them.

WI, October 10th 1914

Capt. R. A. Thorpe

Ancient and Modern Engines and Uniforms

Top: *Capt Thorpe, as a brewer with the responsibilities of safeguarding his brewery, expressed great interest in the town's firefighting abilities.*

Centre: *One of the new motor fire engines with Watford's pump of 100 years earlier alongside.*

Right: *It is just over 14 or so years since Watford bought its horse-drawn steamers ...*

The Watford Fire Engines turning out

Last Wednesday morning we went out trench digging, we were in France then, and at about 11.30 a.m. the order was suddenly given to pack up. We had a five to six-mile march home again, and on arriving found about forty motor buses waiting to take us to the front. Of course we were all rather excited, but when we had spent almost eight hours on the top in the pouring rain and bitter cold, I can tell you our excitement soon died away.

It was past 9 o'clock before our journey ended at a town some six miles from the firing line, and then we had to march there. It was a march too. We could hear the big guns blazing away and several times we saw small houses on fire, but that was nothing to what was to come.

As we marched through a large town, the whole place was in ruins and houses were burning, while the Germans were still shelling the place. We had a near shave, one of two of their shells bursting over our heads; but we reached our destination in safety. Our quarters were some distance away from the actual fighting and consisted of small "dug-outs" covered with straw and leaves. We stayed there until yesterday, when we had more orders to advance to relieve another regiment in the trenches.

Yesterday, a German aeroplane gave the enemy the range of our homes and we had to clear out in quick time. The shrapnel simply rained down, but only one or two were hit and they were not badly injured.

Received Nov. 23rd.

. . . As you want to know where we are at this time, I will tell you straight out.

It is the Front.

Yesterday I realized my great ambition and spent 24 hours in the trenches.

The Germans attacked twice in the night. Our trench was protected on both flanks by Regulars. Excitement!—we couldn't see any Germans, we could hear the attack and several bullets struck our shelter. In the morning we had the first real sight of a battlefield, and it was not very nice to see the dead lying about, but we soon got used to it. At the present time we are under shell fire, and one of our chaps has just been hit by shrapnel.

Letter from Sergt. Kempster, of the 1st Herts Regt. to his sister at 17 Langley Road, Watford.

428 Sgt G. H. Kempster "D" Company,
1st Battalion Territorials
British Expeditionary Force

Sunday, Nov. 2nd 1914.

Just after I sent you the last letter we were ordered up to the trenches, and marched two or three miles through inches of mud and slush and miserable rain. Half the Battalion went into the trenches Saturday night till Sunday night, and our Half Battalion Sunday night till Monday night, when we were relieved by the Troops. When we went in, we relieved the Infantry.

It was a wearisome time: we had nothing to do, only watch and wait, but no Germans came. In front of our wire entanglements laid dead Germans all over the place, not a very pleasant view. We left there Monday night, and went back to our dug-outs: they are holes dug in the ground for anything from two to twelve men to get in, and covered with sticks and straw and then earth on top, to be shrapnel-proof.

We were shelled for a week by "Jack Johnsons," tremendous shells, but not one hit us, but one landed in a farm yard, where our headquarters and stores were, and killed one man and wounded several others and smashed our grub, worse luck. Needless to say, they soon shifted the headquarters into our wood. You see, we have to keep out of the sight of aeroplanes.

Last Wednesday or Thursday, E Company were in the trenches and had several killed and wounded. We get rum served out every night and plenty of smokes and food. Friday night, we left the dug outs at 10 p.m. and marched away to where we are now, right away from the fighting. We were on the road from 10 p.m. till 5 a.m. Saturday morning, then stopped about an hour and had some hot tea and rum, and then continued our journey. We passed Billy How's sons and several we knew from round Watford.

The Battalion arrived here at 11 a.m., after thirteen hours on the road. Some came a good

Trooper ALAN C. AVERY, marked with a X, of the Herts Yeomanry, at Cairo. Trooper Avery was Assistant Scout-Master of Kings Langley Contingent, and is the son of Mr. and Mrs. Avery, of Hunton Bridge.

6th Battalion City of London Rifles marching into the Park, Watford

Watering Horses at the Pond

"Poor Belgium. Their country is absolutely ruined."

distance out of_____ into_____. It was a glorious sight, for there is snow all over here, and it is bitterly cold. We are in billets here. I am with five others in a nice little house, a bootmaker. . I made him understand Dad was a bootmaker.

They look after us splendidly. Last night the daughter was making pillow lace, just like mother does. She was quite excited when I let her know Ma made it. It was a treat to sleep under a roof after being out in the woods, for the cold is rotten and we had wet feet, and plastered with mud for over a week. You ought to have seen me when I got here yesterday, no shave for ten days and no wash for a week, so you can guess I looked very pretty. I was very pleased to get your letter during the week; they are worth their weight in gold. Keep bright, it is much better for all of you. It is bad enough for us out here; but for those at home it is worse, wondering all the while where we are.

You ought to see where the fighting has been, it is awful. Poor Belgium. Their country is absolutely ruined. We have been to where all the severest fighting has been. The fields are all cut up with trenches and shells, the woods chopped up and smashed, their towns burnt down and shelled down, simply awful: it will cost millions and millions of pounds to put right again if ever they can. We went through one town you have read about a lot lately, and it was terribly smashed up, simply heaps of ruins and single walls standing. Near where we were was a big farm, and a "Jack Johnson" caught it fair and set it on fire; next day, just a heap of ruins was left. Every night we can see

fires all round caused by shells. We have seen as many fires as a fireman sees in a lifetime. It is terribly hard out here: what with the war and the weather, a day's hard work in England is child's work compared with this. It is awful, and I shall be more than glad to get home, and so will every one. I would prefer to be a practical plumber than a fighting soldier. No one can realize the hardships of a soldier's life, only those who go through it. But I am very glad to think you are all safe at home. I would rather be out here fighting for you than be at home with war in England and be a civilian and everything smashed up. Now we are here, we are going to do our bit, but I am looking to the finish of it, for I have had quite sufficient of it. How is the old cat? Give him a stroke for me and keep him all right till I get back.

WI, December 1914

The latest "Domesday."

We cannot remember anything in English history exactly like the national registration which is now taking place. Of course the census comes along periodically but that differs in many respects, for example, in its whole object and purpose, from the present Register.

Most people will by this time have supplied

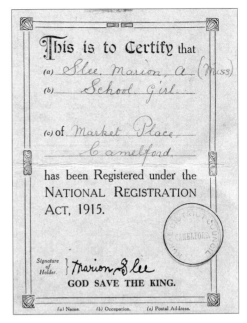

the information the Government requires. The young man of military age, who has not yet done his bit for his country, will have had to acknowledge that fact.

2/14th County of London Regiment (London Scottish) in Bushey Mill Lane

The Parish Church Gates, Watford where its proposed to cut a New Road

Artillery passing through Bushey on Sunday

The workhouse Christmas Dinner . . .

Possibly his form may also suggest some reason and justification for his holding back. But at any rate, among other advantages of the Register, the Government will get to know exactly the number of men of military age who are not yet drawn into the fighting forces, and also the numbers in the still more select circle of those who are not serving, though of military age and unmarried, neither martial nor marital, if we may so speak.

A good many ladies, again, who shrink from specifying the exact number of summers they have seen, will have had to set it down with precise and painful accuracy. But these and other susceptible folk may trust to the loyalty of the local authorities and their helpers not to make this public, or state information a matter of private gossip.

The Register is a big and important business and should help considerably towards a better national organisation directed to the one great end of victory in the present war.

WI, August 1915

In the issue of Watford Illustrated dated 24th April, 1915, is was reported that "The London and North Western Railway Company have been obliged to stop their motor bus services in the town, owing to so many of their drivers and conductors joining the Colours."

The Workhouse.

A very happy Christmas day was spent by the inmates of the Watford Workhouse, owing in the main part to the untiring efforts of the Master and Matron, Mr. and Mrs. Hurst, assisted by the Staff and to many generous gifts by members of the Board of Guardians, Tradesmen and others. The Rev. W. H. Littlebury (Chaplain) held a celebration of the Holy Communion and preached at a service in the Chapel in the morning.

Gifts were distributed in the different wards by the Master and Matron during the morning, sweets and other presents for the women and children and tobacco for the men.

The Christmas dinner consisted of good old English fare—roast beef, plum pudding and mince pies with fruit for dessert.

Some of the members of St. Michael's Church Choir paid a visit to the Institution in the afternoon and sang carols, and in the evening a concert was held, at which Mrs. Hurst officiated at the Piano; Mr. Hurst contributed some excellent songs, as also did Mr. Yandell; Dr. Kirkwood played a violin solo, and two members of the Civil Service Rifles who sang comic songs were much appreciated by the audience. During the concert, the Master and Matron, were presented with a silver syphon holder from the Infirmary Staff.

At the conclusion of the concert the Master, in a short speech, expressed his thanks to the donors of Christmas gifts, and thanked the staff for the way they had worked, and after cheers had been given for the Master, Matron and Staff, the day's celebrations came to an end.

WI, December 1914

Upper High Street

The Parade, Christmas Eve 1914

Troops unable to cross the floods waiting to take the train to Bushey at High St Station

Queens Road Corner

The Vicar

The Watford Parish Magazine of January, 1912, said of the Rev. Richard Lee James, LLB., B.C.L, Vicar of Watford 1855-1915:

"It would be impossible, even if we were able, to give any adequate outline of the work done by the Vicar during his Vicariate; but it may be safely said that he was the first to place the Services of the Church upon a proper footing, and to awaken Church life in Watford.

"He, too, has seen the restoration of the Parish Church (a work which has only recently been completed), in every part of which may be seen some evidence of his loving care for the building, or his generosity as to its furniture: for example, the beautiful oak in the Vestry, which, alike with other things, in the church, bears testimony to his love for the classics.

"Then there is the beautiful church of St. John, in the building of which he took so lively an interest, and which is a splendid example of careful building.

"But perhaps the greatest debt of gratitude which churchmen in Watford owe to their Vicar is the way in which he saved the Church Schools at the time of the passing of the Education Act. Happily they are still efficient and vigorous, and had his people the same courage as their Vicar, they might be enlarged and filled to overflowing. We believe nothing would give the Vicar greater pleasure than to see this done.

"When the free school, erected and endowed by Mrs. Fuller, was incorporated with the Grammar Schools, the purchase of the beauti-

The Royal Field Artillery (T. F.) in Cassiobury Park

DEPARTURE OF TROOPS ON WEDNESDAY FROM WATFORD GOODS STATION

Rev. Richard Lee James, LLB., B.C.L.,
Vicar of Watford 1855-1915

ful old school was effected by the Vicar, by subscription, and placed under trust as the Church House of the parish, and is valuable, as the Guilds and Societies in it find a home. An effort is now being made by a representative committee to erect a large Parish Hall, the site for which was secured by the Vicar (on lease), the present hall not being large enough for present requirements..

"It would be interesting to know how many couples he has married, and how many children he has baptized during his long term of office; for they must almost be a record.

"The Parish Hall mentioned above has now been erected and was opened only last month. The venerable Vicar attended the service at the Parish Church on Sunday morning and pronounced the Blessing and, considering his age, he is still quite active."

WI, February 1915

The Volunteers . . . had an enjoyable war game

The Bushey and Watford Volunteers.

The Bushey and Watford Volunteer Companies had an enjoyable war game last Sunday. The Watford Company was supposed to be invading London via Stanmore, and the Bushey men were detailed to attack them as they came along the main road or in the Woods to the left.

The Bushey commander threw out his patrols among the brushwood and trees, and good practice was made in the art of taking cover. About twelve o'clock, the grey uniforms of the Watford Company were descried coming along with equal care and skill.

The Bushey men were not instructed to resist to "the last ditch," and they fell back in good order. It is difficult to say which of the two sides won, but Watford certainly managed to mislay two of its platoons who turned up some time after all was over.

The two companies were afterwards drawn up on the cricket field and addressed by Major Seaton, the recruiting officer for the Watford District. A very pleasant and instructive morning it was, and a good many more of the same sort would be welcome.

WI, May 1915

Economize

A "Banker" writes of the necessity for economy during the war. We have to import enormous quantities of material for the war, as well as raw materials for our industries, and our exports, by which we pay for our imports, tend to fall greatly owing to so much of our labour being absorbed in the making of munitions. We have also to find vast sums of money for the financing of our Allies, so that the burden on this country will be enormous before the war is over. The banker's conclusion:

"We are brought back again then to the paramount necessity to our Country of economy, such economy as is being practised today by the German people. We import nearly £300,000,000 a year of food, about the same amount of raw materials, and nearly £200,000,000 of manufactured articles.

Every pound's worth of food wasted, of meat, petrol, rubber, tobacco, or any other article which we can economize, unnecessarily consumed, means a pound's worth more import and a pound more in the bill against us. We should import only absolute necessities and produce everything in this country that we possibly can. To import what is superfluous means to reduce by so much the money available for Government loans, contributes by so much to the difficulty of keeping our gold reserve and system of credit intact, and makes it by so much more expensive to obtain our vital supplies of munitions and raw materials."

It is to be hoped that our people, and especially our working classes who are getting high wages, will take these warnings to heart.

WI, June 1915

Shells, Shells and more Shells.

The country seems to be settling down in good earnest to the production of shells and guns in an ever-growing -volume. Everywhere workers and machinery are being diverted to the manufacture of these instruments of destruction.

Mr. Lloyd George has just informed a correspondent that he has 714 firms producing munitions under Government control. The profits to employing firms are in all these cases strictly limited, so that there is no profit-mongering going on. The men on their part have agreed to suspend all rules and practices which tend to restrict the output of material.

There is no doubt that we owe the military stalemate at the front, not to the want of men, but to the failure of munitions. Our present duty is to make up for lost time and to see that the valour and efforts of our troops are not prejudiced through any failure in arms and munitions.

The men are alright. They are perhaps the finest human material ever recruited for any war in history. The more shame it will be if they are not supplied with weapons in suffi-

The Bushey and Watford Volunteers

Above: In the early days of the war Defence Volunteer forces were raised.
To avoid confusion with the army their uniforms were of a different pattern and colour (grey is mentioned in the story above).
No badges or insignia were authorised and ranks were courtesy. It was later realised that many volunteers could possibly avoid war service and by mid- to late-1916 the volunteers were gradually incorporated into the army.

No. 4 Company Queen's Westminsters. parade at Victoria Schools for pay.

Munitions . . . orders for six million pounds in London and district . . .

cient and even overwhelming measure.

The Parliamentary Secretary to the Minister of Munitions has just told us that munition orders to the value of over six million pounds are now being placed in London and district.

The need for more workers, skilled and unskilled, is urgent. Forty to fifty thousand skilled workers will be wanted at once and many more later on. We trust that every available man, who is not "doing his bit" in any other way, will throw his strength into this all-important work. It may not be so exciting as actual warfare at the front, but it is quite as important, and the man helping in the munition factory may know that every ounce of muscle and effort he gives, is so much contributed to his country's triumph and the course of ultimate peace.

Our fighting men will turn all these weapons to the best account, if only they can get them. The recent dastardly Zeppelin raids and the murder of innocent non-combatants ought to stiffen our backs and clinch our resolve to exact, as soon as possible, a full and just retribution.

WI, June 1915

The Scots Hill Fatality.

The Deputy Coroner, Mr. J. K. Riggall, held an inquest on Monday last at the Fire Station, Rickmansworth, on the body of George Henry Wymant, aged 15½ years, of Caroline Street, Boston, Lincs, who was killed on August 27th through the overturning of a road traction engine on Scots Hill.

It appears that the engine, which belonged to Mr. J. H. Kent, of the Maud Street Mills, Boston, was drawing a trailer laden with machinery down Scots Hill. The engine shot forward, and though the driver reversed engines and tried to steer the engine as well as he could, the weight of the trailer behind proved too much and turned it right round and finally fell right over, completely crushing the boy who was on the trailer applying the brakes.

The jury brought in a verdict of accidental death, expressing their opinion that the driver, George Hallam, of Hospital Lane, Boston, was in no way to blame, but that the owner should be written to and told that, in their opinion, the weight of the load on the trailer was too heavy. Great sympathy is felt with the boy's mother, Mrs. Wymant, who is a widow.

WI, September 1915

Formation of the Hertfordshire Corps

Mr. Feilden stated that the movement which was being started in Herts was one of really national importance. The Central Association Volunteer Training Corps had authorised the formation of a mobile force for home defence, transport and other general military purposes throughout the country, and with this object it had been decided to organise all available motorists and motor cyclists, who will be known as the National Motor Volunteers.

It was sought to bring together into a highly organised and efficient body the motorists of the country, thus completely co-ordinating all voluntary motor and motor cycle activities. It was proposed to have the motorists, motor cyclists, and cyclists throughout Great Britain formed into battalions; trained in military duties; and ready, at a moment's notice, to place their services and the services of their cars, motor cycles, and cycles at the disposal of the Regular, Territorial or Volunteer troops.

But it was necessary, said Mr. Feilden, that this Force should get organised and equipped as quickly as possible. Nothing, however, could be effectively done without the ready response of every man—and every woman—in the county, who owned a motor car or a motor cycle. Those who possessed commercial motor vehicles also were asked to join up, as

The start for a 5-mile run on Saturday afternoon, for Soldiers, from "The Dog", Hempstead Road.

Female Ticket Collectors at Watford Station

The Watford Team. The Champions of the Southern League. 1914-15

Hennigan, photo, Watford

Mr Theo Feilden
Organising Officer
HERTS NATIONAL MOTOR VOLUNTEERS

Downer, photo.

Voluntary workers dealing with the National Registration Papers in the Watford Council Chamber.

The Recruiting Caravan in Watford

such vehicles might be of great assistance to the Corps. Other counties were going ahead and in Lancashire, he believed that 200 motorists with their cars had already been enrolled. He was sure that the County of Herts would not be put to shame in this connection and that it would hold its own, and he appealed to all who were able to give their services and the use of their cars to become active members of the organisation.

WI, May 1915

Recruiting on Wheels.

Most Watfordians will have noticed the recruiting van which has taken its stand in the Market Place. It is under the charge of its owner and builder, Mr. Alan McDonald, who has a roving commission from the War Office to gather and swear-in recruits. Mr.

McDonald built the car single-handed for sketching purposes, but some three months ago he offered his services to the War Office and has since then been travelling through Huntingdon and parts of Bedfordshire and Herts. His car contains a sitting room, ten feet by seven, provided with fireplace and very comfortably furnished; a kitchen with oven, and a lavatory. Six can sleep and eight can dine

in the car, but it is occupied at present by only three, Mr. McDonald and his two sergeants.

This little house on wheels is driven by a steam engine and does an average ten to twelve miles an hour, though fifteen is practicable, and costs to run about 1½d. per mile.

Some two hundred recruits have been gathered in through this agency, which has thus thoroughly justified its utilization. Mr. McDonald proposes to stay for a few days in Watford and then continue his progress through the 16th recruiting area. He tells some rather amusing stories of his experiences. At one point, a number of agricultural labourers were stricken with a sudden panic, thinking that the caravan was a Government armoured motor car, which had "come to fetch them" by force.

They dropped their tools where they stood and quickly disappeared. Elsewhere, an old lady had been observed for some time standing near the war car and apparently waiting for something. It turned out she thought the car was a peripatetic chapel and that service would soon begin. When told that "war service" was the only sort in which the caravan was concerned, she asked why, then, they bore the religious sign. It is imagined that the good soul mistook O.H.M.S. for I.H.S.

WI, August 1915

... dropped six bombs–the airship exploded, turning the Morane upside down ...

V.C. for a Local Hero.

AIRMAN'S MAGNIFICENT FEAT.

Flight Sub-Lieutenant Reginald Alexander John Warneford, V.C., R.N., who has secured the honour of being the first Airman to destroy a Zeppelin, is the step-grandson of Mrs. Warneford, of Oxhey, with whom he has made his home, and is also a nephew of Mrs. Nightingale, of Kings-field Road, Watford.

He is a member of an old Wiltshire family dating back to the reign of King John, who, in payment of money lent, made the founder of the family Lord of the Manor of Bibury and Sevenhampton, in which latter parish they built Warneford Place, where the head of the family resided until some few years ago, when the property was bought by Sir Frederick Banbury, M.P., for the City of London. Lieutenant Warneford was born at Kuch-Behar, in India, Oct. 15th, 1891.

His father, the late Mr. R. W. H. Warneford, who died about eleven years ago, was Engineer to the Maharajah of Kuch-Behar. His mother is a daughter of the late Captain Campbell, C.S.I., of the Indian Marines. His paternal grandfather was the Rev. T. L.J. Warneford, Chaplain to the Forces in India for 25 years. He was Chaplain on Sir Donald Stewart's staff through the Afghan Campaign of 1879-1881, was mentioned in despatches, and won the medal with clasp for the battle of Ahmed-Khel. On retirement he was given the living of Satley, Co. Durham, by the Lord Chancellor.

Lieutenant Warneford was brought to England at the age of seven, and educated at King Edward's Grammar School, Stratford-on-Avon, and at the age of 13 he entered the Mercantile Marine. He enlisted into the Sportsman Battalion during the early part of the war, on the understanding that he should be transferred to the Royal Naval Air Service on the occasion of a vacancy. This occurred in February. He trained at Hendon under Flight Lieutenant Merriam, and obtained his certificate with a Bristol biplane under Flight Commander Porte on Feb. 25th. Soon after, he left Hendon for Eastchurch, where he went through a further course of instruction, and from thence proceeded to the Front in April, becoming fully qualified in May.

While in the initial stages of his instruction, he was severely reprimanded for rising in the air before he had obtained mastery of the machine. On another occasion, when descending, he found that he would strike the ground too sharply, so to avoid an accident he looped the loop, and was thus able to plane smoothly down.

For this he was reported to the Admiralty.

Here he was asked why, being only a novice, he should do such a risky thing; and his reply was that he did it to save himself. He was then asked if he would like to go to France to amuse the Germans, and he promptly said that that was what he was dying to do.

The result is that at 3 a.m. on Monday, June 7th, he attacked a Zeppelin in the air, between Ghent and Brussels, at 6,000 feet. He dropped six bombs, and the airship exploded, fell to the ground, and burnt for a considerable time.

The force of the explosion caused the Morane monoplane to turn upside down. The pilot succeeded in righting the machine, but had to make a forced landing in the enemy's country. However, he was able to re-start his engine, and returned safely to the aerodrome.

Everyone will be delighted to hear that the King has sent a telegram to Flight Sub-Lieutenant Warneford, conferring upon him the Victoria Cross for this gallant act.

It is also announced that, on the proposal of General Joffre, the French Minister of War has decided to confer on Flight Sub-Lieutenant Warneford the Cross of the Chevalier of the Legion of Honour, in recognition of his brilliant exploit.

WI, June 1915

National Motor Volunteers, Herts Corps.

The Herts National Motor Volunteers continue to do very good service with their cars in connection with hospital work. Last Sunday, the 3rd inst, members of the Corps took out 22 wounded men, together with a nurse and the matron from the Red Cross Hospital, Rickmansworth, for a motor drive through Chesham, Berkhamsted, Kings Langley, and thence to High Elms, Bushey, the residence of Mr. and Mrs. Thomas, by whom they were entertained to tea. The day was happily fine and the men thoroughly enjoyed themselves, being brought back to the hospital about six o'clock.

Until the advent of the Herts National Motor Volunteers, there was no organised means of conveying wounded soldiers to and from the hospitals to partake of hospitality extended to them, but now the difficulty appears to have been met, and we can only wish the Herts Corps of the National Motor Volunteers a wide extension of their valuable activities.

WI, July 1915

Herts Volunteer Motor Corps assembling in Stratford Road, Watford

The Grove, Watford.Nov. 10th, 1915.
The Editor, "Watford Illustrated," Loates Lane,
Watford.

Lord Derby's Recruiting Scheme.
Dear Sir,
Will you be good enough to grant me the courtesy of space in your valued paper to give publicity to a request that the members (active and honorary) of the National Motor Volunteers (Hertfordshire Corps) all over the County, should without delay put themselves in touch with the Recruiting Officer in their district to see what assistance they can render in this our last endeavour to raise a Voluntary Army sufficient to meet our present needs.

Lord Derby has explained his scheme so fully that there is nothing left for me to say about it; but it is now my pleasant duty to urge all members of the Hertfordshire N.M.V. to make every endeavour to help.

Owing to the urgency of the matter, and the short time left us, all such work must be done independently of the Squadron Commanders, but I would particularly ask that a complete record of all services rendered should be sent to the Chief Executive Staff Officer, Corps Headquarters, Stratford Lodge, Watford, so that it may be registered under the good work our Corps is rendering the Country.

Trusting this appeal will receive very hearty support.
Yours truly,
CLARENDON, Commandant N.M.V.
Hertfordshire Corps.

Messrs. Peark's burnt out Store in High Street. Supposed to be the oldest building in the town.

Watford Post-women starting out on a round

Sheep Sale on Tuesday in Marlborough Road Sale yard

C and D Companies, the Suffolk Regiment

Railwayman brother taunted with white feathers . . . did not return before his first leave.

An early adventure out in 1904, although at just a few weeks old I didn't know anything about it, was to Landon's studios in Queens Road where my parents had a group portrait made. We were living in Queens Road and a few years later I started at St. Andrews Girls School opposite the Church [St Mary's]. There were four classes for boys and four for girls and boys and girls had their own entrances. Girls were upstairs, boys down.

I well remember the bustle of weekday market, but my mother had told me to hurry home and not dilly dally round the market. Just past the umbrella maker (near where the Green Man was) was a clairvoyant who always seemed to frighten me—anyway I always hurried past, and across to Meeting Alley.

I left school at 13 because we moved out of Watford for a short while; but when we came back I got a job at the Penny Bazaar, in the High Street, and soon rose to be first-hand on ironmongery. I stayed for about three years but on a day when some men were not in, I and a friend were asked to unpack some cases in the yard. Being first-hands we refused at first, thinking others should do the job, but eventually we gave in and did the job.

We received our cards at the end of the week!

Soon after we had returned to Watford the Great War was on; we had a soldier and sergeant billeted on us and they shared a room: we children had to share rooms together.

My brother was a lampman on the railway; a responsible job, but the taunts of the soldiers on the trains and them constantly showing him white feathers made him volunteer. He was killed just before his first leave. My other two brothers were called up and returned safely.

I did not find it easy to get work after I was sacked and I cycled all over the place trying to find a job—I got one eventually at Delectaland, foil wrapping chocolates. I was there only nine weeks when my mother died and I had to leave to look after the family. At 17, the youngest, and perhaps rather spoiled, I had a lot to learn, quickly. During the war my

sister worked at Waterlows as checker, my other sister at the Munitions Factory as examiner and my mother also worked there for a while as powder filler, but when my brother was killed, she left.

She'd have no more to do with it.

Shortly after my mother's death my father came into a largish legacy, around a hundred pounds or so; which, in those days, was a lot of money. Discussions were held and it was felt that mother would have liked something sensible done, and so father decided to use the money as deposit on a house.

He soon found one he liked, in what is now described as 'Nascot Village', and it cost £275 and of course the balance was on a mortgage which, at times, was a bit of a struggle to pay.

But it was worth it; it is now my home in my old age.

Mrs. Wilkins, Church Road, 1987

Earl of Essex hurt in an ccident
George Deveraux de Vere 7th Earl of Essex, was knocked down in London by a cab, dying in 1916 from his injuries. Adèle became Dowager Countess of Essex. Together with Algernon, who inherited the title of 8th Earl, she would later organise the break-up and auction of Cassiobury House.

At the time of recounting these memories in 1987 a house in the same terrace was advertised for sale at over £60,000. For comparison purposes an average North Watford 1900 terraced house is currently marketed at £60,000, and still rising! By 2002 the price had risen to around £130,000.

Part of the Watford that Mrs Wilkins knew as a young girl.
Top: *Grove Circus at the town end of Estcourt Road between there and Meeting Alley,*

Right: *Meeting Alley (looking townwards) leading into the Market Place.*

Callow Land Halt

We have had several requests from readers, who either reside or work in Callow Land, to try and induce the L. & N.W.R. Co. to stop more trains which now pass through Callow Land Halt.

It has been pointed out to us that very little time would be lost to the trains between Watford and St. Albans, and that now the 'buses have stopped running, the people of Callow Land would greatly appreciate a more frequent service.

We feel sure that the Railway Company will note the requirements of this growing district, and that the increasing number of workers near Callow Land Halt will receive every consideration. Trains suggested to us that might be stopped with advantage are the 6.55 a.m. and 1.34p.m. from the Junction, and the 8.40a.m., 1.58p.m., and 5p.m. from St. Albans.

WN, August 1916

Appeals

G. A. P. Warren (36), Gladstone-road, painter and decorator, appealed on the ground of domestic hardship. Passed for "C2."—Conditional on remaining on work of national importance.

F. Marland (33), Sandringham-road, munition worker, sole support of invalid father. Other domestic reasons. This case was adjourned for medical examination. Applicant had passed for active service—Dismissed.

E. Lavender (18), Brightwell-road, butcher's assistant, was appealed for by his mother, who said that he was the only son left at home. She had three sons in the Army, and a fourth had been killed.

The employer of E. Lavender also put in an appeal.—The mother *(crying)*: "It seems hard to lose them all. I lost one in South Africa. I have been left a widow twice."—The Chairman: "We don't want to be hard upon you. You can retain your boy until June 1st."—The mother: "I hope, please God, the war will be over before then."

R. H. Roberts (18), Brightwell-road, brush trimmer, was appealed for by his mother, who said that she had four sons in France, one of whom had won the Military Medal. This young boy was the only one left—Adjourned for medical examination.

WO, February 1917

1st Herts Recruiting Detachment at Watford on Tuesday

1st Herts Recruiting Detachment at Bushey on Tuesday. Meeting in front of Bushey Church.

The Bookstall

The Munitions Factories

Two local areas were selected as suitable to accommodate munition factories; Bushey Mill Lane and Station Estate better known as Imperial Way, Balmoral Road.

In accordance with national practice, local industrialists were asked to manage such factories. The Watford Manufacturing Company Limited, previously known as Dr Tibbles Vi-Cocoa, was approached to this end.

H.M. No. 1 Factory (Imperial Way) was described as "making 20lb and 50lb bombs" and the plant in Bushey Mill Lane (Greycaine) as H.M. No. 2 Filling Factory. Both establishments were engaged in all engineering aspects of the manufacture of mortar bombs, grenades, smoke cannisters, small arms magazines and other auxilliary equipment.

On 6th February, 1917, an Examiner in the Department of Munitions did not panic when he saw a mortar bomb which had ignited. With great presence of mind he grabbed the bomb from a pile and threw it out of the building For this act of bravery he was awarded the Edward Medal of the Second Class.

A week later, Tuesday 13th February 1917, a fire occurred which could have been disastrous for the Town, and about which the strict censorship has prevented the full details being generally known except as excerpts in isolation.

A young lad helping with grocery deliveries recounts:
"At that time Balmoral Road was only a lane and really finished at the little bridge. I was only a young boy and had been helping with some grocery deliveries to the factory, to earn some pennies. The alarms went and we were chased off the premises; our horse and cart had just got to the bridge when we had to quickly pull aside to let the galloping horses and fire engine pass through."

A. R. Green recounting his recollection of the 1917 Munitions fire (Oct 1986).

The West Herts Post reported:

Great Fire Prevented

Soon after eleven o'clock on Tuesday morning, the Watford Fire Brigade and other Brigades were called to a serious outbreak of fire at some works just beyond Watford Station, which threatened to involve many adjacent buildings.

The factory, which employs hundreds of girls, caught fire, and the flames spread so rapidly that, but for the exceedingly prompt action of the firemen on the spot, the Brigade from the Victoria Works, the Council Brigade, and Messrs. Sedgwick's, disastrous results might have had to be recorded.

The girls were marshalled off the premises, and people living in the vicinity were warned that the fire might assume alarming dimensions.

A large body of constables and "specials" were soon on the spot controlling the traffic and assisting in various ways.

Unfortunately, two succumbed in the District Hospital, to burns, and several persons were injured, but the management is to be congratulated on the fact that an outbreak of such inflammable material was so ably coped with.

February 1917

And later in the year, a rider:

Great Fire Prevented

On February 13th a big fire broke out at a large local factory, and only the promptitude of the various brigades and their remarkable skill in dealing with the blaze prevented the most disastrous conflagration. Two workers were unfortunately burned to death, but the

Watford Manufacturing Company's Employees listening to an address on "Business" on Friday April 30th, 1916

Above: The earliest of Watford's three vicarages this is on the site of the shops opposite Queen's Road and was demolished in 1914 to make way for a new branch of Woolworth's, which lasted 85 years.
Through the arch is seen a hoarding masking the building of a store for Boots (now the entrance to the Harlequin Centre).

Right: The young lad (in frock) giving cigarettes only learned in later life that these soldiers lost their lives when their troopship was sunk.

...the greater part of Watford would have been destroyed.

loss of life would undoubtedly have been great had it not been for the magnificent work of our firemen. So splendid did they act that Lord Clarendon and other public men called them together in the Council Chamber and publicly thanked them for the splendid bravery displayed by one and all.

S144   *December, 1917*

Apart from the public thanks the Watford Fire Brigade men received no other acknowledgement until after the war's end. Meanwhile, the Works' Brigade fared rather better:

The London Gazette of 22 June 1917 announced the award of the Edward Medal of the Second Class to Thomas Luther Burt, Chief of Police at HM Factory, Watford, with the following brief citation:

"On 13th February last an outbreak of fire occurred at the Watford factory at which explosives are manufactured. Burt, who was on his round of inspection at the time, at once rushed into the building, which was burning fiercely and full of suffocating smoke.

He carried out Mixer Price and immediately returned to rescue Mixer Morecroft, the smoke by then being so dense and the heat so great that he was compelled to crawl along on his hands and knees before he could reach Morecroft.

Afterwards he worked hard in assisting in the removal of explosives from the burning building,"

And in February 1920 the 'Watford Observer' reported:

Mr. Burt, who was formerly a sergeant in the Herts Constabulary, received the Edward Medal at the King's hands in October, 1917. He also received the Carnegie certificate, and £20, as did also the following:—Messrs. S. Poultney, P. O'Keefe, W. R. Knight, N. Hill, R. Swift, and R. Blanc (son of the general manager).

The 'Watford Observer' also reported:

We understand that the Home Office have intimated that they are prepared to award three O.B.E.'s to the Watford Fire Brigade in connection with gallantry shown at a fire at the local Munition Works in February, 1917.

but as a mix-up occurred regarding names submitted for these honours the awards were increased to four...

"At the time the fire occurred, so strict were the regulations of D.O.R.A., that no details of the circumstances under which two men lost their lives was allowed to appear in the Press. The official announcement simply stated that "a small fire took place on Wednesday at a factory in Hertfordshire. Although little damage was done, two workmen unfortunately lost their lives."

These men were Charles Moorcroft, a licensed victualler, of Harpenden, and William Pride, a shopkeeper in Percy-road, Watford. On Tuesday, February 13th, 1917, they were in No. 2 mixing house at the factory, mixing an explosive powder in a mixing machine. Suddenly there was a flash, but no loud explosion. The foreman of the department stated at the inquest that he was near the deceased, and was blown into one of the doorways. He was dazed, and knew nothing of what happened to the other two.

Thomas Luther Burt, Chief of the Factory

Police and Fire Superintendent, gave interesting evidence. About 11.20 a.m. he was on a round of inspection when he heard a slight booming noise, and saw smoke rise from No. 2 mixing house.

He immediately ran out two lines of hose. He saw the foreman stagger out of the packing house, which adjoined the mixing house. Through the door witness saw Pride, who was practically in a nude condition. Witness got him to his feet, and he walked to the door of the packing-room.

Returning, witness saw Moorcroft on his knees, trying to get to the door. The smoke was so dense that witness also had to get on his knees to assist Moorcroft outside. The mixing house during the whole of the time was one dense mass of smoke, and was very hot. Evidence was also given as to the machinery being lubricated, and the bearings not over heated. Both men were terribly burned, and died in the District Hospital from shock. The verdict returned was "Accidental death."

The Works Fire Brigade did fine work until the arrival of the local Brigades. In the packing room adjoining the mixing house were stocked tons of high explosives, and had the flames reached these the effect would have been terrible. In all probability the greater part of Watford would have been destroyed.

How narrow an escape the town had on this occasion was only fully realised by a few. It is therefore, fitting that those who played an heroic part should be rewarded, though in the case of the Watford firemen the recognition is somewhat belated.

S138   *WO, February 1920*

After the Armistice local authorities and others responsible for fire brigades were invited to submit recommendations for the Medal of the Order of the British Empire [approximately equivalent to the present day Queen's Gallantry Medal]. The recommendation covered only the fire on 13 February, 1917, and was on the following terms:

Both factories were 'filling factories'; neither employed women under the age of 21. Officially No. 24 and 25 they were known locally as No. 1 (Station Estate) and No. 2 (Bushey Mill Lane). They filled such weapons as rifle grenades, trench mortar bombs, red and white phosphorus and other 4" bombs, plus 25 and 50lb bombs.

Every chestnut is wanted to help provide a surprise packet for Fritz.

"On arrival the brigade found a building used as a powder mixing room on fire. Superintendent Pratchett was informed that he must stop the fire from spreading to adjoining buildings at all costs. Superintendent Pratchett and his men, with Mr. Brace, acted with the utmost coolness and promptitude.

They soon had the fire completely under control and extinguished although the roof required a considerable amount of cutting away. if the fire had extended it could have been disastrous to the whole town.

Superintendent Pratchett himself carried out the first case of T.N.T. from the burning building and all the men got to work removing it assisted by the works brigade. There is no doubt that all present faced an appalling disaster which was only averted by their own courage and devotion and the skill of Superintendent Pratchett".

(P.R.O. HO. 45/11016/377171)

Examination of this recommendation by the Home Office showed that Superintendent Pratchett, Firemen Fountain and Wise and Driver Robinson were first on the scene, followed shortly afterwards by the other men; and that they had carried the branch into the burning mixing room and succeeded in damping down the material inside sufficiently to prevent an explosion.

Superintendent Pratchett and his three colleagues received their medals from the Lord Lieutenant of Hertfordshire, Brigadier- General Viscount Hampden, at a ceremony in Clarendon Hall Yard, Watford, on 10 November 1920.

At the same ceremony W. J. Foxen received the Medal of the Order of the British Empire. His name appears in the same 'Gazette' as the four firemen with the citation:
"For great courage and devotion to duty at a filling factory, particularly on the occasion of an explosion which caused a great deal of damage. His control at the time was consid-ered to have prevented a most serious loss of life".

The 'Watford Observer' of 14th February 1920 carried the following story:

In October of the same year another explosion, in which three lives were lost, occurred at the Factory, and, in this instance, too, no publicity could be given to the facts. There were three victims—Clara Frost, Henry Frederick Turner, and Charles F. Tolfrey, all of Watford.

At the inquest the Coroner told the jury that in the afternoon of October 4th the deceased woman was engaged in soldering a box containing propellant charges, and the two deceased men were standing by to move the box when finished. A report was heard, and a witness saw the place in flames.

Assistance was at once obtained, and the three were got from the building. Unfortunately the injuries they had received were so severe that they afterwards succumbed.

The evidence showed that the accident occurred in the Trench Warfare Department. The fire was extinguished very quickly, the hydrant being at work in less than a minute. There was no direct evidence as to what caused the explosion. The deceased woman had been on the same work for some months.

The jury returned a verdict of "accidental death," and expressed their appreciation of the efficient way in which the fire was extinguished. A sixth medal was due to be presented but the recipient, R. A. Boyle, was absent abroad. His medal was also gazetted on 7 July 1920 for great courage in continuing to work in a poisonous atmosphere although repeatedly burned and gassed. Again, it is not clear whether Boyle worked at the Watford factory.

Medal award details: WO and Major J. D. Sainsbury T. D., courtesy of 'Medals and Awards' issue November 1980.

Horse Chestnuts for Munitions

Sir,—We have always looked upon horse chestnuts as of no commercial value, and they have been the perquisite of the boys for the noble game of "Konkers."

This war has taught us many things, and amongst them that it is possible to extract a spirit from these chestnuts, which is of use in the production of high explosives. A ton of chestnuts saves 10 cwt. of barley, so that it is easy to see how valuable they are to the country.

Every chestnut is wanted, and it is hoped to secure 250,000 tons this year. I have been entrusted by the Herts County War Agricultural Committee with the duty of organizing their collection, and I want to enlist the help of the schoolboys in the County schools; but I now appeal to all landowners, householders, and farmers who have chestnut trees to be good enough to have the chestnuts all picked up as they fall and reserve them.

If they will kindly send me a postcard, saying about what weight they have on hand, I will send them word what to do with them. I hope to have a local receiving agent in every village and district, who will take in small quantities; but in the case of those who can collect a ton or more, I should then notify the Ministry of Munitions, who will send a motor lorry for them as soon as possible.

I hope that Herts will do all it can to help provide "surprise packets" for Fritz.
Yours, etc.,
COLIN TAYLOR, C.C., J.P.

August 1917

Banknotes

To replace the withdrawn one and half-sovereign coins, £1 banknotes are to be introduced.

These are to be printed by Messrs. Waterlow Ltd. in Milton-street, Callow Land.

Superintendent Pratchett, Firemen Robinson, Hatton and Fountain shown with the medals won in February 1917 and presented in November 1920.

Far right:
A sketch map showing the location of the two munitions factories. The By-pass is indicated but was not then built.

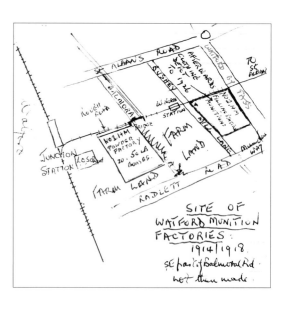

Captioned 'Munitions Factory, Station Estate, 1914-18' . . .

Subsequent enquiries pieced together the stories of the fires and dangers. It would appear that this photograph, showing about 380 people, is of the staff of H.M. No. 24 Factory.

The photograph includes Thomas Luther Burt wearing his Edward Medal, presented to him by King George V in October 1917.

The hutted buildings of the complex occupied a very large extent of the land between the new Imperial Way and Radlett Road.

The building behind the group had connections with the munitions works but it is known that the height of the top floor exceeded the level of the water reservoir which supplied the area and so there was no water on the top floor either for manufacturing or firefighting.

At one time, after 1920, it was used for furniture manufacturing, later becoming the works of T. H. Lewis for repairing and overhaul of Express Dairy vehicles.

It was then used from c1964 for about 20 years as a 'temporary' sorting office for the Post Office before they vacated it for larger premises at Ascot Road. Empty for two or three years, it was demolished in 1986 and site redeveloped as small industrial units.

Inset: Chief of Factory Police and Fire Superintendent Thomas Luther Burt.

A letter of complaint

2.7.17. Watford, Herts.
Mr Levey/ Sir you have a yellow powder you are now using at your No 2 filling Station Watford which staines the hands and face very much and i am medicaly informed tenders to shorten the lives of the girls working in it I understand that it is your wish that one and all shall take thire turn in working in it so that one shall not do more of it than another now this system unbeknown to you is not being carried out there being girls in it at present working for weeks and weeks and likely to remain there others who appear to be bits of favourits with the matron who up to the present have not soiled their hands with it and this is causing great discontent if this is not at once seen into and rectified I shall place myself in communication with the government Inspector and the minister of munitions to see if something can not be done in the matter (let one and all take her share)

I am Yours Truly
An Interested Party
[Mr Levi was General Manager of the H M No. 25 Factory; "Yours truly" had a valid complaint as the girls were supposed to rotated on filling work–but the outcome of his complaint is not known.]

L & N W Electrification

"The chief reason for deferring the running to Watford of the electric trains has been the want of suitable rolling-stock. Instead of constructing the necessary vehicles at their Wolverton Works, the London and North-Western Railway ordered the trailer and motor coaches of a private firm, and for some reason or another the vehicles are not yet available, nor does there appear any immediate likelihood of the vehicles being ready in the near future.

The coaches for working the through service need to be of a special design, because of the difference in the height of the platforms on the new Watford line and those on the Baker-street and Waterloo Railway. Every thing else being ready for electric working, the Baker-street and Waterloo Railway made experiments with trains composed of trailer cars of the Great Northern, Piccadilly, and Brompton Railway, and motor coaches of the Central London Railway, and by an ingenious arrangement these coaches have been made suitable.

Passengers alighting at the stations on the Watford new line will merely have to step up from the carriage on to the platform, and when entraining they will step down."

Shortage of labour and materials, due to the war, have delayed construction between Willesden and Euston. The service starts during mid-April.

WO April 1917

Death of Mr. F. Fisher

It is with great regret that we have to record the death, which occurred early on Saturday morning, of Mr. F. Fisher, of Roseberry, Hempstead Road, Watford, in his 68th year. He had been in poor health since he had a slight seizure three years ago, but he was not taken seriously ill until a fortnight ago. The end came very peacefully.

Born in 1849, at Aylesbury, the son of Mr. William Fisher, farmer, dealer, and wholesale meat salesman, the deceased, one of a family of 11, was educated at Howard House Academy, Thame. He married the eldest daughter of Mr. Edmund Keen, of Hemel Hempstead. He commenced business at Kings Langley, and came to Watford in 1877, purchasing the business of Mr. George Stone, at 70, High-street A few years afterwards he bought the Rose and Crown estate and developed it, building himself, at 74 and 76, High-street, new premises and abattoirs, with every modern improvement, including one of the finest private cold storages in England. He also built up a large connection at Deptford. As time went on his keen business instinct led him to buy and develop land on the Bushey Hall Estate and other large estates in Essex. In 1903 he retired, and went to reside at Roseberry.

He left the Watford business in the hands of

161

his son, Mr. F. E. Fisher. A second son, Mr. Arthur E. Fisher, is a wholesale meat salesman at Luton a third, Mr. William Fisher, is farming in Buckinghamshire; and a fourth, Mr. Percy Fisher, is an officer in the Northumberland Fusiliers. There are also two married daughters.

The deceased was held in great public esteem in Watford. He was a member of the Urban District Council for eight years, and Chairman in two very eventful years—1901-2 and 1902-3. He gave a memorable banquet at the Clarendon Hall to the Herts Yeomanry on their return from the South African War. His official position necessitated his taking a leading part in the local arrangements for commemorating the Coronation of King Edward. It was in connection with the postponement of the festivities, on account of the sudden and serious illness of King Edward, in June, 1902, that the town was brought into unenviable notoriety by rioting.   T h e Council had no option but to postpone the dinner to the aged and deserving poor and the distribution of money to school children, but a disorderly element obtained the upper hand on the night of July 26th, and created disturbances.   Damage was done in the town which cost the county over £1,000 in compensation. Of 62 persons who were apprehended on charges of riotous conduct and larceny, 56 were summarily convicted. No one felt the stigma which had been cast on the town more deeply than Mr. Fisher, and it was very unfortunate that his term of office was marred by such a lamentable occurrence, especially as he had thrown himself into his public duties with remarkable zeal and devotion.

When he retired from the chair of the Council high praise was bestowed upon his work by his colleagues, but Mr. Fisher never had the same taste for public work afterwards. He continued, however, to be a member of the school authority. He was made a Justice of the Peace in 1906, and attended the sittings of the Bench fairly regularly.

WO August 1917

No Football This Season
Owing to the fact that they have been excluded from the London Combination, and also that the West Herts Club and Ground have declined to continue to rent them the ground, the directors of the Watford Football Club have decided not to make any fixtures this season, and to give football a rest until more propitious times.

The Executive Committee of the West Herts Club and Ground sent the following surprising letter to Mr. W. Swain, secretary of the Watford FC.
"That in view of the fact that there has been some loss of subscriptions and opposition to professional football, the Committee regretfully decided that they could not entertain an application to re-let the ground for that purpose."

WO August 1917

Shorter Shopping Hours
Darkened streets, and fear of possible air-raids, combined with the withdrawal of nearly all the male assistants from the shops have brought about considerably shorter hours in retail businesses, and this is all to the good.

Before the war the average number of hours for a shop to be open in the week was about 72, and war-time conditions have conclusively proved that these were much longer than necessary. The Early Closing Association, which has done wonderful work in the past to improve the lot of those employed in shops, is now pressing for a 48-hour week (exclusive of

Below: Troops on parade during the war on the Hossacks fields–but which following a name change we know as Harebreaks (see above). At the top right is Russell Lodge which stood at the corner of Longspring and St Albans Road until demolition c1960.

This is just a part of the 130 acres upon which a Council-designed housing estate was to be built–with houses costing £1,000 each to build compared with terrace houses of twenty years earlier costing £80 and target prices for Rickmansworth Road of £300 to £400.

The arrival of the Sherwood Forresters, in Cassiobury Park Avenue, to be under canvas in Cassiobury Park.

meal times) and there is very little doubt that when the "boys" return from the front they will expect and deserve working hours of this description, as they remember only too well the few opportunities they had in the past for open air exercise and enjoyment

WO November, 1917

Big Blaze at Victoria Works

Soon after 9 o'clock on Thursday evening the Watford Fire Brigade was called to an outbreak of fire which occurred at Victoria Works.

A store-room containing dried milk, nuts, advertising literature, and a consignment of Vi-Cocoa about to be dispatched to the troops, was ablaze, and the nature of the contents of the building soon made possible, and even probable, the prospect of the disastrous consequences of Feb., 1903, when the greater part of the works was destroyed.

The night was pitch dark with occasional flashes of lightning illuminating the heavens, while a gusty wind favoured the conflagration.

The reflection of the flames on the low banks of cloud made the fire seem more serious than it actually was, and hundreds of people rushed over to Callow Land to witness the blaze, although really little could be seen, for the Works Brigade, under Captain Brace, with the Watford Council Brigade, under Captain Thorpe and Supt Pratchett, were assisted by the Croxley Mills Brigade, Messrs. Sedgwick's, and Bushey Brigades, and the whole of these firemen worked like Britons, getting the fire well under control within an hour, and by superhuman efforts saving the Freeman Factory and the main building adjoining from destruction

Two or three firemen were slightly injured by falling debris, and Captain Thorpe fell from a landing-stage, bruising his face and straining his wrist. But apart from having a black-eye, Mr. Thorpe looked little the worse for his accident the next morning. The Works Brigade continued on duty for 15 hours without a rest, and so well did all the Brigades work that on Friday morning every employee was able to go on as usual, and there was not the slightest disorganisation.

WO September, 1917

Food Rationing

For a foil to his comfortable, well-fed grumbler our artist pictures the wasted frame of a man who has been immured in the German camp for civilian prisoners of war at Ruhleben. Many hundreds of Englishmen have been detained there for three and a-half years, and those who have lately returned to England all tell the same story—that they had very spare living indeed and had to depend for food to keep body and soul together almost entirely on parcels sent to them from England.

Did they grumble about their lot? Not a bit of it. On the contrary, they accepted the fortune of war cheerfully and "kept their tails up" all the time. The sailors who guard us on the seas, the soldiers who are fighting our battles in France, have times of difficulty about rations.

Do they grumble? Not a bit of it. They growse, but growsing is different from ill-conditioned grumbling, and their letters home always declare they are "in the pink." We at home, thanks to the sailors and soldiers, have food enough for all if it is evenly shared, and rationing is the only means by which even distribution can be assured. Here and there the machinery of rationing may work irregularly at first, and where there is such mischance let everyone approach the difficulties in the spirit of making the best of it and setting the irregularity right without a fuss. A little patience, plenty of goodwill—these are ways in which we may all manifest a real patriotism.

The story of the Ruhleben internment camp shows the value of a rationing system well organised and well administered. The camp leaders there saw to it that the parcels from England were shared out so that all had food even if the quantities were spare. The Germans provided only a daily ration of potatoes for their prisoners, and the parcels from England alone saved the situation. There was not a man there who called the system of sharing the parcels "a dashed nuisance."

All were in the same boat, and all shared alike. One result was that many Germans in Berlin envied the English prisoners, and Mr. E. L. Pyke, who was lately released, says that the Prussian authorities more than once had fears that the mob would attack Ruhleben in order to get at the English parcels!

WN April 1918

The British Tradition

HE sat in a pool of water, with his hands before his face. He was almost the colour of the mud; hands, face, clothes, all stained and caked with it. His shrapnel helmet has a large dent in the side and under the rim of it a bandage tinged with red. Now and then, at some concussion greater than usual, he shuddered. The air was alive with death all round him, and from time to time a fresh deposit of mud and sandbags would hurtle into the trench.

By all the rules of the game he was a "casualty," but you could not have made him realise that He was badly shaken, and had been almost unconscious when his "pals" delved him from a collapsed dug-out But he was glad no officer had been present to order him to the aid-post He knew that the Germans would counter-attack presently, and he waited. That is the British tradition.

He was right in his surmise. The bombardment died down and the counter-attack began.

He rose unsteadily to his feet to take his place with his comrades on the fire-step. His lips were dry and swollen, and he moistened them with his tongue, while he pressed home a clip of cartridges in his rifle. For half-an-hour those obstinate men in grey tried to force their way into the trench, but the British stood firm, and the man who was the colour of mud stayed at his post, firing steadily into the grey mass.

When the German attack was finally broken up, and an exhausted remnant of field-greys surrendered, the little band of British lit their cigarettes and sat down again in the water, nursing their rifles.

It was unpleasant sitting in water, but they were too tired—far too tired—to stand. Many of them were casualties, but they still waited.

That is the British tradition.

The man who was the colour of mud dug his

STOUT PARTY: These rations cards are dashed nuisance.
THIN PARTY: Are they? We didn't have any where I've come from.
STOUT PARTY: Please name that place, sir!
THIN PARTY: Ruhleben--a prison camp in Germany.

teeth into his lips for fear the others should see his pain.

The Platoon Commander did not see many casualties when he came down the trench. They turned wounded arms and legs away from him, they pulled their helmets further down on their heads to hide bandages; men who were too hurt to sit up lay against the wall of the trench and sang and made a show of cleaning their rifles, trying to control the trembling of their hands.

They thought another effort might be wanted from them, and they knew how much their officer cared for their wounds, and how he would have sent them back instantly as casualties. So they hid their pain and waited, according to the British tradition.

When they were relieved, the man who was the colour of mud laughed. It was a dry, rather shaky laugh, but there was a smile with it.

"Rest," he said.... "bit done up... good fight, though.. . bloomin' good fight... Thank Gawd they dug me out in time for it."

They passed down the communication trench laughing and every man who could speak sang; the others smiled, and left cigarettes for those who had to be taken on stretchers; and the man who was the colour of mud carried his exhausted chum's rifle That, again, is according to the British tradition.

WN March, 1918

Watford's Rally Round the Tank

Watford lived up to its fine reputation for responding to every appeal made in the interests of the nation, and last week the Tank Bank had such a busy time that when the final figures were announced on Saturday evening, they were a source of pride and gratification to every towns man.

In the four days that "Julian" stayed in the

Market-place, £162,020 was invested in War Bonds and Certificates, and the crowds that collected each evening, especially on Saturday, were almost unprecedented.

On Thursday evening, Mr. W. Pearkes again presided on the Tank and appealed for the money to help to win the war.

Mr. Dennis Herbert said the appeal from the Tank was an appeal to one and all, no matter to which class they belonged. The best they could do for the men at the Front was to deny them selves. He felt certain that without the big money already subscribed it would be easy to raise Watford's total to £150,000 before Saturday by means of small amounts.

WN May, 1918

How Watford Celebrated Peace

The great news of the signing of the armistice between the Allies and Germany was received on Monday forenoon with jubilation. Every hooter in the district sounded, and the majority of factories closed for the day. Flags and bunting were immediately displayed, and the streets soon thronged with joyful crowds of citizens. In the evening the arc lamps in the Market-place once more brightened up the town.

The Market-place was simply packed throughout the evening, and young people gave vent to their feelings. There was some singing but no rowdyism, and the Deputy-Chief Constable, Mr. W. Wood, reported to the Magistrates the next morning that there was not a single case of drunkenness or disorderly conduct.

At the Churches thanksgiving services were held, and there was a general spirit of deep relief sobered by the thoughts of those who will not return to enjoy the blessings of peace.

WN November, 1918

A request

No. 25 National Filling Factory, Bushey Mill Lane,

Watford.
14th November, 1918
Brigadier General Milman, C.M.G., R.A.,
28 Northumberland Avenue,
W.C.

Dear Sir,
The Armistice being signed, the work for which I originally came forward, namely Production, is at an end. Under these circumstances I should be grateful if I could be released to go back to my own business.

During my tenure of office of nearly three years, I have been supported by a truly loyal staff, and in particular have I been fortunate in the services of my two Superintendents, Mr. H.C. Spratling at No. 24 Factory, and Mr. F. Stanley at No. 25., and I should esteem it a great personal favour if you would appoint them respectively, to take charge of the 'winding up of' these two factories.

They are naturally conversant with all details, and are, I know, fully competent to carry the responsibilities attaching to this work. You can also rely on my placing my assistance at their disposal, should they feel they need it.

May I take this opportunity of tendering my most earnest thanks for the great courtesy and consideration which I have received at your hands, and from every member of your staff with whom I have come in contact.
Believe me,
Yours sincerely,

•*The copy of the letter was unsigned, but the General Manager was Louis Levi.*

The war has dragged on; money is needed and so a savings drive, lasting four days, is held and an army tank driven into the Watford Market Place as a morale booster. This tank 'Julian' may have been a prototype before being developed into the British MkV Armament with one 6-pounder gun in each side-sponson (but not in evidence on this particular tank).
The crowd looks a little more restrained and serious compared to the 1915 recruiting drive—but £162,020 was raised. 1918

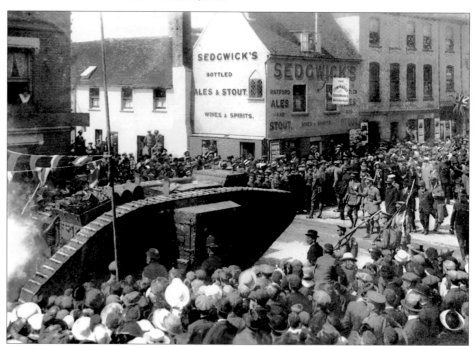

The Coal Position

The Coal Controller most emphatically warns the public that in consequence of the cessation of hostilities there must not be any relaxation of the effort to save coal and light, and to win coal from the mines. The demands of our Allies, France and Italy, must for some time continue to be of a very exacting character.

The fuel situation in this country is still precarious, and the demand for coal is far from being met. It will be impossible to materially alleviate the coal situation in the immediate future. The public are requested, in the national interest, to continue exercising the utmost economy in the burning of fuel and light at the present time as they so loyally did under a condition of war.

WN, December 1918

Wages of Council Employees

The Urban District Council held a special meeting on Monday, Dec. 16th, to receive an application from the Council's workers for an increase of wages. Mr. R. A. Thorpe presided, supported by Mr. G. Longley (vice-chairman), Messrs. Andrews, Staples, Trewin, Clark, Pearkes, Long, Oxley, Southam, Poultney, Moffat, Tucker, Julian, Gorle, with Mr. W. Hudson (Clerk) and Mr. D. Waterhouse (Surveyor).

Mr. Palmer, who represented the Workers' Union, spoke very earnestly on the men's behalf, pointing out that the abnormal increase in the cost of living justified the demands which had already been laid before the Council, and unfortunately turned down. He urged upon the Council to reconsider the matter, as feeling was very strong among the workers, and failing compliance a strike was imminent. He asked for an increase of 4s. a week for all employees, and 12 ½ per cent. on earnings of all men of 21 and upwards. Even this would leave them below the amount which the Committee of Production adjudged as providing a living wage, this amounting to 28s. 6d. additional per week.

Mr. Longley read a table showing the present increases to date as follows:

Employees	July, 1914			Dec. 1918		
	£	s	d	£	s	d
Carpenters	2	4	9	3	15	0
Blacksmiths	1	12	0	2	14	0
Strikers	1	7	0	2	3	0
Lamp-cleaners	1	2	0	1	18	0
Masons	1	15	0	2	11	0
Labourers	1	5	0	2	5	0
Other Labourers	1	5	0	2	1	0
Park-keepers	1	5	0	2	1	0
Sweepers under 60	1	4	0	2	0	0
Sweepers over 60	1	4	0	1	16	0
Destructor Stokers	1	12	0	2	8	0
Dust Van Assistants	1	5	0	2	1	0
Dust Van Drivers	1	18	0	2	17	0
Engineers Drivers	1	5	0	2	11	0
Engineer Stokers	1	10	0	2	1	0
Farm Carters	1	5	0	2	1	0
Sewage Destructor Men				2	1	0

Some general idea of the increase could be gained by realising that two or three rises had been given during the war, and it amounted to an average 16s. for unskilled and 20s. for skilled labour.

WO, December 1918

Death of Mr. F. Downer

We regret to record the death, which occurred early on Monday morning, of Mr. Frederick Downer, the well-known Watford photographer, aged 78 years. He had been in falling health for some little time, and passed away in his sleep after a paralytic stroke.

Deceased was born in Watford, where he lived all his life. He commenced his career as a clerk in a lawyer's office, but being very fond of drawing, he used to get up early in the morning and attend classes in London, at Lee's Artistic Studio, returning to take up office work at 10 a.m. When photography became popular he bought a camera.

He erected a studio at the back of his father's offices at 97, High-street, and later had a shop at 110, High-street, eventually he built up the premises in Loates-lane, where he had of late years carried on business. He had an extensive connection.

It is hardly too much to say that Mr. Downer's camera had been seen at every important local function for the past 50 years. Deceased took no active part in public affairs.

He was keenly interested in the Volunteer Fire Brigade, which was formed in 1867, being on the committee and a pioneer. Later he became a member of the Brigade for a few years.

WO January 1919

Lack of Hospital Accommodation

During the past four and a half years the situation at Watford with regard to accommodating wounded soldiers has been almost pathetic and would have been serious but for the heroic efforts of such kind-hearted people as Mrs. Morten Turner, Mr. Pierpoint Morgan, Mr. Barton-Smith, and other devoted ladies and gentlemen.

When the first big return of our wounded boys necessitated the help of practically every town in the kingdom, and the Watford Hospital was viewed as to its capacity for assisting the military authorities, we had to confess that our hospital was scarcely large enough to deal with all the private cases that came along, and it was not to our credit that we were unable to meet a demand such as condi-

As with other tailors in the town, Albert Ashwell was a gentleman's outfitter and tailor. With shop premises in the Market Place the firm's heyday was during 1914-18 when they were to make many officers' uniforms. Their workshops were situated in the courtyard nearby, just behind the Midland Bank premises (HSBC), in Chequer's Yard (Court 7), but by the early 1920s the buildings had run their span of practical life. A place was needed to remove the street market from where it hindered traffic in the High Street. Chequer's and Ashwell's Yards were cleared and, in 1928 the Market was relocated.
The men are standing on what is now the entrance to Charter Place, from the High Street.

...Hossacks estate, with site for a public hall, public baths and a public library ...

tions at that time required.

But think for moment what might have been if the town had possessed a fine spacious hospital such as is suggested by the Peace Memorial.

If we had been foresighted enough to offer our pennies, our shillings, and our pounds towards a building that would have done the community credit, we might have welcomed many hundreds more suffering lads and given them comfort whilst healing their wounds.

The troops who passed through the town in the very early days, and billeted round about, are almost unanimous in their praise of the treatment accorded them; and, indeed some of the Norfolks and Suffolks became very much attached to their Watford friends, and many a landlady spent days of anguish when the Norfolks were reported missing in Gallipoli, and no trace could be found of most of the men who left Watford to join in this unsuccessful fight for Constantinople. How much more then have the wounded who have been attended to at Lady's Close, Wall Hall, or the Croxley V.A.D. felt when they had gone back to their regiment or to their homes, that the kindness extended to them at Watford would never be forgotten, and that the town would be a remembrance to them of happiness.

It is our great opportunity at this moment to say whether we desire a cheap hospital for a Peace Memorial, or whether we would wish Watford to erect a building with the most up-to-date appliances. Even shillings make a difference, and a bigger difference than many of us imagine, because a multitude of shillings given by those who can only spare so small an amount soon mount up to the price of erecting an extra ward, and also show the breadth of appeal and the interest taken in our hospital.

WO January, 1919

National Factory For Sale

It is announced that the Government have decided to dispose of munition factories at Watford, Trafford Park (Manchester), and Dudley (Worcestershire). The first two have been used for the manufacture of explosives, and the third has been a projectile factory. The Watford factory stands on a site of 33 acres, and the buildings cover 124,100 square feet.

It is understood, says the "Daily News", though the Ministry of Munitions on Tuesday declared that no official announcement can be made on the point at the moment—that the decision to dispose of these three factories will probably be followed as rapidly as possible by the sale of many other of the Government factories which have been erected during the war.

The sale of the three factories named above will have to be by tender. A large number of enquiries have been made about them.

WO January 1919

•*This refers to No. 2 Factory in Bushey Mill Lane (later known as Greycaines).*

German War Trophies

A letter was read stating that it had been decided to offer to the town as war trophies a damaged German machine gun, an ammunition box, and ammunition belt, carriage forward.

The Clerk: Just about what I expected.

Mr. Mills: Are they worth troubling about? I will propose that we ask them to hold them over until we have formed a museum to put them in. *(Laughter.)*

On the motion of Mr. Batchelor, seconded by the Chairman, it was agreed to accept the trophies.

Mr. Mills: I will move that the proposer and seconder be appointed trustees to take care of them. *(Laughter.)*

The Chairman: We could have an auction sale and make more of them than the carriage will cost.

WHP February 1919

•*Two German field guns were sited just inside Cassiobury Park Gates on the greensward facing the toilets They were elevated to aim above the toilets but elevation and traverse wheels on both guns had rusted solid and the wooden handles were splitting. This was in the early 1920's*

Anonymous boyhood memory, 1987

Land For New Houses

THE Watford Urban District Council have decided to purchase, subject to the sanction of the Local Government Board, 130 acres of the Callowland estate, for housing purposes. The price is £27,500.

The Council were of the opinion that they have made a good bargain, and there was no opposition to the purchase. The scheme, if it should go through—and it is probable that the Local Government Board will bestow upon it a speedy benediction—will mark an important step in the development of Watford.

The growth of the town was to be expected to the north and west, particularly to the north. The Watford Manufacturing Company recently bought 210 acres of the Garston House estate. The Government intend, so it is stated, to adapt part of the munition works as a clothing factory.

It is apparent, therefore, that, apart from the existing demand for houses, building operations on a large scale will be necessary in the near future in Callow Land. The Council are pledged to the erection of 280 houses, a number which the local Labour Party ask should be increased to 500.

The Watford Council have all along shown that they are aware of the urgency of the problem, and anxious to do what they can to relieve a situation which becomes more serious every month. In the meantime they are not disposed to be dragged into the Greater London scheme of the London County Council. We entirely agree with the advice tendered to them by the Herts County Council on this point.

If the Watford Council allowed themselves to be swallowed by Greater London, they would be abrogating power of local govern-ment and practically admitting inability to settle their own affairs; it is almost certain, too, that the expense to the ratepayers would be very much greater.

WO February 1919

Snow Clearing

A letter was read from the Secretary of the United Builders and Labourers' Union stating that members of the society had been offered 6d. per hour for clearing the snow away from the streets, and the Union considered that that was not enough, considering the present cost of living The men did not want help, only work.

Mr. Julian: Was anyone taken on at 6d. an hour?

Mr. Trewin: No.

WO February, 1919

Housing Hustle

The way the Housing Sub-Committee of the Watford Council is moving is calculated to take away the breath of some of the older Councillors, who have never been accustomed to anything in the nature of hustle. The official intimation that the Local Government Board are paying the cost of housing schemes above a penny rate has warranted the adoption of a policy to meet local requirements to the fullest extent.

There is now no excuse for doing things by halves.

Enquiries have shown that there are two or more families in eight per cent. of the houses in Watford. Over three hundred applications, mostly from men who have served or are serving in the Forces, have been received by the Council for new dwellings. Last week an advertisement in the "Observer' of a 10s. 6d. house to let at Oxhey, was answered in a few hours by over 150 people. In view of such facts as these, the Council cannot be accused of overstepping the mark in approving a scheme for 750 houses. By their purchase of the Callowland and Wiggenhall Estate for £27,500 and £14,000 respectively, they are already in possession of the necessary land.

WO March, 1919

Property De-requisitioned

The Clerk reported that he had received an intimation from the officer commanding the troops in this district, that the military proposed to retain North End House, Clarendon Hall, the Skating Rink, Beechen Grove School House, and Halsey Hall.

It was stated that Little Nascot and Chater Schools would be vacated

WO May, 1919

County Council's Road Programme

The Highways Committee reported: Road Reconstruction.—Road and Bridge programme, 1919-20.— The Surveyor submitted correspondence with the County Surveyor upon the above subject, and reported that the net result of the negotiations with the County

Council was that they were prepared to make a grant of £9,752 towards the cost of re-surfacing with tar macadam St. Albans and Rickmansworth-road, the estimated cost of the work being £25,678, and that no grant was proposed to be made in respect of any of the other roads, the subject of the Council's applications.

WHP, June, 1919

Atlantic Flown

Alcock and Brown left Newfoundland in an open cockpit converted Vickers Vimy twin-engined bomber which had a cruising speed of 90 mph. The attempt was to cross the Atlantic to win a Daily Mail prize of £10,000. After sixteen hours and twenty seven minutes flying—during which Brown had to climb on the wings to chip ice from the carburettors—they crash-landed in an Irish bog.

The Magnetos, made at North's Factory in Whippendell Road, had performed faultlessly.

WN, June 1919

Peace—And After

So far as can be gathered, there was not a single untoward incident to mar the success of the Peace Celebrations in West Herts on Saturday. It is true that a drizzling rain fell in the evening. but this perversity of the weather had hardly any appreciable effect on the spirits of the holiday-makers.

Every town, village, and hamlet gave vent to its feelings in a carnival of rejoicing.

There has never been seen such a wealth of decoration. From church tower and public buildings floated the Union Jack; business premises were almost hidden in flags and bunting streamers and fairy lights hung in countless gardens, and from the windows of humble cottages small flags added to the wonderful glow of colour.

The Peace Celebrations in Watford July 19th were upon a large scale, and proved very successful On the Sunday prior to the 19th a united service of thanksgiving was held on the West Herts Ground. On the 19th there was an imposing procession through the town, a fete was held in the Park, and tea was given to the wives and children, to the number of 3,900, of ex-Service men.

A series of dinners was afterwards arranged for ex-Service men in the Clarendon Hall, and the number who attended these dinners, which were held on five separate evenings, was 2,150.

The money for the celebrations, £1,378, was all subscribed, so that no call was made upon the rates.

WO, July 1919

Atlantic Flight for £10,000 Prize.

NORTH & SONS. Ltd., Watford,

Right: *The procession into the Park is led by ex-servicemen, followed by a Regimental Band, and Army Officers and Other Ranks. To the right of the picture the caravans of the fun fair, just inside the Park Gates, may be seen.*
Below: *Part of the crowd listening to the band.*

The site . . . a bargain; the hospital for "all time" . . .

Peace Memorial Hospital Site

Mr. S. J. Attenborough read the report of the Sites Committee (Messrs. R. A. Thorpe, George Langley, Henry Brown, C. H. Peacock, and S. J. Attenborough, and Mrs. Schreiber), which stated that, in considering the question of a site, they had had the following principles in their minds, viz, :—

That the site selected should be in a prominent position in the town and worthy of the memorial to be erected upon it, that it should be free from building or other restrictions; that it should have no buildings upon it, that a sufficient area of land should be acquired so as to render the Hospital capable of enlargement in the future if rendered necessary by reason of the growth of the town and district.

The committee had found a site, viz., the "Elms" paddock in the Rickmansworth-road, of about three acres, having a frontage of 390ft in the Rickmansworth-road and a depth of 820ft, which they thought complied in all respects with the principles enunciated above.

Apart from the question of price, the only difficulty which arose was that the "Elms" paddock could not be acquired unless a purchaser could be found for the house and gardens, to which it is appurtenant.

A purchaser, however, should not be difficult to find, having regard to the price for which the committee had secured the option to purchase the property. By the contract the committee had by payment of £200 secured the option to purchase the "Elms" estate at any time on or before the 31st December, 1919, for the sum of £12,250.

This £200 has been found by Messrs. Arthur Kingham and Stanley J. Attenborough in equal shares, and these gentlemen will bear the loss of it in the event of the option to purchase the estate not being exercised, while the £200 is to be treated by the vendors as paid on account of the purchase-money in the event of the option to purchase being exercised, in which event the £200 would, of course, be repaid to the two gentlemen who had found it.

The "Elms" estate is of a total area of 10a. 1r. 9p., and consists of a house, outbuildings, gardens, and orchard, and six cottages, together with the paddock, which paddock the Sites Committee recommended the Executive Committee to acquire as a site for the erection of Watford's Peace Memorial.

With the exception of four of the six cottages, the estate is freehold, the four cottages being copy-hold of the Manor of Watford. The house, with the stabling and other outbuildings, gardens, and orchard, are subject to a tenancy agreement for three years from August 9th, 1918, at a rent of £300 per annum, the cottages bringing in addition about £50 per annum.

The paddock has been requisitioned by the Watford Urban District Council as garden allotments, for which they paid 6s. a week. The Committee hoped it would be possible under the scheme to obtain the Elms Paddock for £5,000.

Mr. R. A. Thorpe said that the Committee thought five acres were necessary. He knew it had been suggested that three acres would be sufficient, but they were looking forward to the time when the town would be double the size it is, and the Sites committee and Executive Committee were of opinion that the five acres should be acquired.

The Chairman: That will give plenty of room for expansion.

Mr. Thorpe thought the General Committee would be well advised to take the five acres. It was generally agreed this was the most suitable site.

Mr. W. Hudson pointed out that they had that liability wherever they bought land in the town. After all it was only a matter of an additional acre and a half between Mr. Holland-Hibbert's estimate and the Executive Committee. They were putting this hospital up for all time.

Everyone who signed the report earnestly hoped that they would use every endeavour to secure the Elms Estate for the benefit of Watford, and the paddock for the Peace Memorial for Watford and District. It was thought five acres was ample for hospital accommodation. This was the cheapest site that had been offered in Watford.

WO November, 1919

A Good Bargain

The estate known as "The Elms," standing at the corner of Rickmansworth and Hempstead roads, Watford, is to be acquired by the town. When the Peace Memorial Hospital Fund was started the paddock of "The Elms" was regarded as an ideal site for a new Hospital, and the Sites Sub-Committee were enterprising enough to secure an option to purchase the whole property for £12,250.

They decided to offer the Urban District Council the benefit of the contract, on the understanding that the Hospital site should be retained at a price of £5,000. The Council thus had an opportunity of securing the house, cottages, orchard, gardens, and grounds, an area of about five acres, for £7,250, and at their meeting on Tuesday evening, they unanimously decided to close with the offer.

Some two or three months ago we pointed out that the Council ought not to allow the opportunity of acquiring this property to slip. The Council's administration has suffered in the past from a lack of foresight and failure to grasp the possibilities of the growth of the town.

Otherwise there would have been years ago municipal offices worthy of Watford, the patchwork additions to Upton House would have been avoided, and proper accommodation would have been available for recent developments in the Public Health

Taken about six years after the war this shows the Vi-Cocoa/Watford Manufacturing Co's complex, but with the addition of their new multi-storey factory which, at this time was empty, unused.
The subsidiary buildings between Parkgate Road and Sandown Road and Parkgate School are prominent. Across the other side of Bushey Mill Lane can be seen the sprawl of the remains of HM No.25 Munitions Works, now in civilian use.

Department, and such new departments as those devoted to Infant Welfare Work and War Pensions.

The purchase of "The Elms" on such advantageous terms will materially assist in solving a problem that might have given the Council great trouble in a few years' time. When all the details are settled and the sanction of the Local Government Board obtained, the Council will no doubt consider whether it would not be a good financial move to sell the property on which the existing offices stand, and remove to "The Elms" site.

WO January, 1920

Hertfordshire and Road Transport

The Herts County Council are applying for a Parliamentary Bill enabling them to own and run motor omnibuses. We take it that they are adopting this course for two reasons—first, because they desire to protect Hertfordshire from the encroachment of other counties.

Both the London and Middlesex County Councils are promoting Bills which give them power to run motor 'buses over a wide area, including the Metropolitan Police District.

When these schemes were put forward, the Herts County Council sent representatives to conferences with various Councils round London. At the same time they submit a solution—which neither the London nor the Middlesex Bill contains—of the transport question for Greater London They ask for the setting up of a Joint Committee of the Councils interested in the provision of motor omnibuses. Broadly speaking, what it is hoped to effect by this arrangement is that each county, while absolutely preserving its own rights, shall have running powers, where desirable, in adjoining counties. Thus the services would be planned according to the needs of localities, and there would be no stopping and changing at geographical boundaries.

The Hertfordshire County Council, in the proposals they put forward, show that they are alive to the future. Some such action was inevitable if they were not to stand supinely by while the first step was taken in the encroachment on Hertfordshire by Greater London.

The danger of this encroachment has greatly increased in recent years. Places like Bushey and Watford have the strongest objection to being swallowed up in the vast agglomeration of the County of London. A moment's reflection will show how desirable it is for all the Hertfordshire local authorities to join together in thwarting the new Metropolitan policy.

WO January, 1920

Street Watering

Mr. Woodstock inquired why the streets were not being watered. The Chairman replied that it was a question of horses.

The Surveyor said that if the streets were watered they could not tar them, and it was also a question of traction Mr. Woodstock said they wanted the streets watered, so let them get horses.

Housing—£1,000,000

Before the war the mere mention of such a sum for any local scheme affecting a population of 50,000 would have been regarded as a symptom of municipal lunacy; now it passes without a word of comment from any Councillor, being looked upon as, perhaps, rather a heavy item, but really quite unavoidable, and, therefore, not worth worrying about.

It will be found, we imagine, much easier to talk of a million than to raise it. There are suggestions of mortgages, bonds, and the issue of County Stock.

Nobody seems quite clear what will eventually be done, although housing has been the most important problem in domestic politics for well over a year.

No decision has been reached on the question of rent, which must enter into any discussion on the financial soundness of housing undertakings, the fact being that a £1,000 house ought to fetch twice or three times as much rent as the local authorities will dare ask.

It is all a muddle.

The Ministry blame other people, and other people blame the Ministry. There are fine promises—1,000 houses for Watford this year, for instance—but little performance.

Much of the difficulty has arisen from the initial mistake in practically shutting out the private builder, who met all past needs, instead of giving him every encouragement.

In the mean time the Watford Council are sending deputations to the Ministry, appointing officials, discussing types of houses, arranging loans where possible, and generally immersing themselves in detail.

They have started on a few houses, and have arranged with a local firm to erect 813 houses on Harebreaks Estate "subject to the money being available." There are now over 1,200 applicants in Watford for new houses. Possibly the Council can give a more or less reasonable explanation why the housing eggs have not been hatched after a year's sitting.

It is not an unfair conclusion to draw, that if the Council majority had been constituted differently from what it is to-day, we should have had some wild denunciation at the forthcoming municipal elections.

WO March, 1920

Harebreaks

The area we know as Harebreaks was previously 'Hossacks'. A tireless and energetic worker in seeing the Harebreaks scheme to fruition Mr F H Gorle also took responsibility for naming the estate and many of its roads. The estate name 'Harebreaks' was taken from an old ordnance survey map.

In 1871 the woods alongside the road to St Albans, opposite Lea Farm were then named Harebreaks. (The wooded area is now the site of Spring Gardens and Holland Gardens) and Mr Gorle thought the name 'Harebreaks' more suitable than 'Hossacks'.

From a talk given in Watford by Mr Gorle after his retirement.

Retrospect of 1919

For the first time in the history of the town, Labour has had a majority on the Urban District Council, the Party, thanks to good organisation and to the apathy of their opponents, winning eight seats at the March election.

In January it was announced that the Watford Munition Works, standing on a site of 33 acres, with buildings covering 124,100 square feet, was for sale. Later the works were adapted as a clothing factory by the Government.

In March the Watford Rural City Society Ltd., purchased, as a Public Utility Society, 17 1/2 acres of land adjoining Gisburne House, their scheme being to erect four houses to the acre. In April it was reported that 556 applications for houses had been received, over 300 of the applicants having served in the Forces.

In May instructions were given for the "lay out" of the Hossack Estate, with sites for a public hall, public baths, and a branch library. By this time 739 applications for houses had been sent in.

In May, Mr. George R. Bolton, Sub-Librarian of Stoke Newington, was appointed Librarian at a salary of £250 a year. In July it was announced that a site in King-street for a new Library had been presented to the town by Mr. S. H. Timms.

In August it was announced that to recognise the services of the Hertfordshire Regiment during the war, and the attachment formed between that Regiment and the Bedfordshire Regiment, owing to the enlistment into its ranks of many Hertfordshire men, the name Hertfordshire Regiment was to be altered to Bedfordshire and Hertfordshire Regiment

In September it was suggested that open markets should be established in Watford. Mr. W. Hurst Flint, the owner of the market rights, stated that he had no objection if open markets would be for the good of the town, but asked where it proposed to put them, and what about the collection of the tolls.

It transpired in the course of correspondence with Mr. Flint that he would not oppose the acquisition of the Market rights providing it was in the interest of the town to acquire them.

WO January, 1920

Part VI

The false dawn

The veterans who had avoided death in the trenches returned home with the promise of a land 'fit for heroes to live in'. Their expectations could not be fulfilled over night and the reality of the dream was indecision and delay. The shattered economy could not be switched easily to the demands of peace, although Watford had embarked on an expansive and costly housing programme the size and quality of which exceeded all earlier projects. Watford's biggest shame was that the town did not possess a decent hospital—and within a couple of years plans were drawn that took shape in bricks and mortar as the 'Peace Memorial Hospital'.

The nation mourned the loss of its sons and did not disguise its abhorrence of the cost in human terms as the wounded, disturbed and permanently disabled ex-servicemen and women returned home. Social conditions had irrevocably changed and men found their places taken by the new civilian army of women workers, especially in shops and stores.

Before the war the suffragettes had campaigned, with little effect, for greater freedom. Ironically the war gave them the opportunity of proving the point that they had been making as they successfully undertook all manner of employment previously thought to be the prerogative of the breadwinner of the family.

The right to vote was given to men on reaching the age of maturity (21) and to wives of householders as well as women over 30 (reduced to 21 in 1928). The opening hours of shops were drastically reduced. The men who had faced death on land, sea and in the air had to adjust to these new and unfamiliar conditions.

The long term prospects of trade and commerce were bright, to make good the deficiencies of a society deprived of all luxuries and many necessities. Motor transport was beginning to take over from the 'horse-age', which had largely determined the speed of progress, and this led to job opportunities for returned drivers and mechanics as new garages were opened. Light trucks and vans replaced the erstwhile horse and cart.

In much the same tradition as the 1865 Red Flag Act which discouraged the early development of steam-powered road transport, the post-war era applied severe weight and speed restrictions on motor cars, buses and lorries. Mechanical transport had made excellent progress prior to 1914, progress which accelerated with the demands of war.

Road construction and maintenance did not follow suit.

Little changed, and for the most part roads had deteriorated—few were tarmacadamed; between towns and villages the majority were still rutted dirt and gravel. In towns they were generally of rolled and compacted granite. No surface could successfully resist heavy vehicles with solid tyres carrying excessive loads at the maximum speed allowed of ten or twelve miles per hour. Gradually a programme of road improvements took effect. An enterprising ex-serviceman named Scammell conceived a means of overcoming part of the restrictive 'weight' problem by designing an innovative articulated vehicle. In later years the same firm developed the famous and ubiquitous Mechanical Horse which successfully replaced the horse and cart for the movement of goods in town and city.

A generation of men and women had matured and aged before their time. Work was available if not too plentiful.

Inflation had forced up prices and wages were not far behind, but the future augured better living conditions, even prosperity.

It was not to be.

The Pond Cross Roads, here c1922, with an AA man on point-duty controlling the traffic, has the island site upon which was planted an oak tree in 1887 to commemorate Queen Victoria's Jubilee (p69).

The building behind the AA man is the Halsey Masonic Hall and the house to the left of the trees became Faircross House—of shops and flats.

The island, and tree, was removed in 1938 when the cross roads (which crossed dog-leggedly), were realigned and a roundabout built.

How "Shrodells" Got Its Name

Sir,—I am told that the numerous references to Shrodells in your columns this week are causing considerable comment and curiosity among those of your readers who are ignorant of the origin of this charming old name, and I am glad to be able to enlighten them.

When working at my history of the Parish

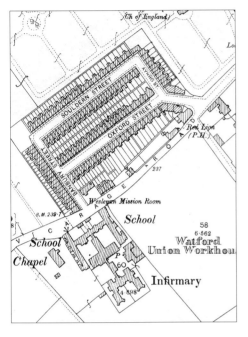

Church, I came across an ancient list of "gardens, meads, etc., in Watford Town" and among them I saw Shrodells. As this word is not recorded in any dialect dictionary, nor in any collection of archaic words, we may safely regard it as having belonged exclusively to Watford, and it was undoubtedly associated with the adjacent woods of Whippendell.

When I was asked to suggest a name for 60, Vicarage-road (something descriptive of that locality in olden days), I was glad to recall Shrodells from the echoes of the past; and it is pleasant to know that this long-forgotten name will survive among the annals of Watford when many other links with the past have been completely destroyed.

Yours, etc.,
HELEN RUDD

WHP (April 1932)

Watford Athletic Ground

Lovers of sport in Watford have always been haunted by the fear that sooner or later the West Herts ground would fall into the hands of the builder. Hence, there will be great gratification at the announcement that through the generosity of Mr. Dodwell the ground is to be purchased and conveyed to a central committee for the benefit, in perpetuity, of sport in the town.

To all intents and purposes Mr. Dodwell makes a gift, of the value of over £8,000, to Watford. Apart from any question of sport this is one of the most considerable benefactions the town has ever received.

The West Herts ground has been a great asset to Watford for nearly 30 years. It has been the local centre for the two national pastimes of cricket and football, and there, also, lawn tennis and hockey have been regularly played. With the rapid growth of the population its facilities have been more and more appreciated. To replace the ground would mean an expenditure of many thousands of pounds, and more-over no site equally central is available.

Messrs. Benskin, who bought the ground some time ago, and were coming into possession on the expiry of the Club lease, have acted very handsomely. They made the purchase in order to ensure the continuance of first-class football, and, with a commendable spirit, readily fell in with the scheme of Mr. Dodwell.

Mr. R. A. Thorpe, who financed the Football Club in the past, has generously waived a claim for an old debt standing, it is said, at something like £2,000. The Watford Athletic ground, as it is now to be called, has excellent prospects.

A central committee, on which all sections have representatives, with the Trustees as ex officio members, will govern its affairs. The difficulties which often arose through the conflicting claims of cricket and football ought now to disappear.

WO May, 1920

60 Vicarage Road was to most Watfordians for many years the 'Workhouse'. The chalk-pit like depression became the football ground in 1922. Towards its left, (in the photo), and abutting the road, is the quadrangle of the original workhouse and next to that the chapel. Behind the workhouse was built an infirmary and, over time, the various extensions to cope with growing need. This 1921 photograph shows the long 3-storey 'I' and 'H' block facing the open ground upon which, eventually, the Watford General Hospital would be built. The low bungalow-type building with the two ornamental gardens in front was for many years the TB ward.

Watford in 1920

The chief feature of the year has been the alarming upward tendency of public expenditure. The rates have reached an unprecedented level. In Watford they now stand at 18s. 4d. in the £, and a further increase is probable when the new budget is made.

Several reasons have been adduced for the additional burdens thrown on the ratepayers. The County Council claim that their hands are forced by new schemes which the Government call upon them to undertake. The Urban Council have been faced with increases of salaries and wages and the dearness of materials. The cumulative effect has been a demand for economy—a demand so strong that it cannot be resisted, so that in the near future it may be expected that local authorities will exercise the most rigid economy.

The most important subject which has engaged the attention of the Urban District Council during 1920 has been that of housing

The estimated number of new dwellings required is roughly 2,000, including 500 to replace houses in insanitary areas. Four separate schemes are in hand—at Harebreaks, Callowland, Willow-lane, Sydney-road, and Wiggenhall.

The first named scheme provides for 1,000 houses; the land alone cost £27,500, and the making of roads and sewers involves the outlay of over £100,000.

The houses will cost, roughly speaking, £1,000 each. The total expenditure on housing in Watford will, it is anticipated, eventually reach the huge total of two millions.

It may be interesting to take the events connected with the schemes in something like chronological order.

In January it was reported that the sanction of the Ministry of Health to the Harebreaks Estate loan had been received. The same month, at a meeting held in the Clarendon Hall, it was stated that the Council had given an undertaking to build 1,000 houses this year. A resolution was passed protesting against any reduction in the standard of houses.

In February this question was discussed by the Council, and a protest entered against the abandonment of plans drawn up by architects engaged by the Council, and the substitution of plans provided by the Ministry of Health. In March it was decided to inform the County Council, who were proposing to issue county stock for housing that the amount required for Watford was £1,000,000.

A contract was accepted with Messrs. Brightman and Sons to erect 813 houses at a cost of £980 per house on the Harebreaks Estate. Further contracts were entered into

Left: The Pond in what must be its last days of rusticity—as the photographs on page 175 show.

Below: Elizabeth Kingham opened a small shop in the High Street c1790 dealing in provisions and groceries. In 1835 her eldest son, Henry, inherited the business and henceforth traded as 'Henry Kingham'.

He purchased the freehold of the shop in 1851 (pic. p110). His five sons took an active part in the

by now widespread business and in 1911 a private company was formed to manage the firm's affairs after their father died, with son, Arthur, as Chairman and Managing Director. Arthur maintained an active interest until his death at the age of 80 in 1941.

Prior to 1913 the firm relied upon horse transport (and were noted for the excellence of their stabling), but in that year they hired a Foden steam wagon. During the early days of war their valuable horses were requisitioned and more Fodens were brought to replace them. This photograph shows their fleet of Foden wagons in 1921 or 1922. The last vehicle in the parade is a Thornycroft petrol engined lorry.

Henry Kingham & Sons Ltd. were retail and wholesale grocers, their specialities being tea and coffee blending and bacon curing. They packaged many products under their 'Larkspur' label. By 1951 they had 455 employees engaged in supplying retail outlets throughout Hertfordshire, Bedfordshire, Buckinghamshire, Cambridgeshire, Essex and parts of North London and Middlesex.

Next page: New Street, c1914-20, runs from the Market Place in the High Street to Church Street (and now houses the pedestrian entrance to Church Car Park).
The eating house and the two cottages would last about another 50 years before being demolished to make way for the car park, but Court No.8 (Ballard's Buildings), the entrance of which is shown, was demolished in 1926 under a slum clearance order.

with the same firm to put up 40 houses in Gammons-lane, at £850 each. In March it was stated that the amount allocated by the County Council from the issue of County Stock was £615,000.

In April the Clerk of the Council reported that the Ministry had sanctioned the borrowing of £32,400 for the 40 houses in Gammons-lane, and a loan of £100,500 for street and sewerage works on the Harebreaks Estate.

In June the rents of the houses in Willow-lane and Sydney-road were fixed at 12s. 6d. each, with 4s. 10d. rates, making a total of 17s. 4d. The Ministry of Health paid for the abandoned plans made by the Council's architects, the cost being £6,239 16s. At the same meeting the Council made an application to the County Council for a loan of £100,000 from the County Stock.

In July, at a special meeting of the Council, the rent of the new houses was discussed, and a resolution was proposed asking the Ministry of Health to reconsider the amount fixed for the Willow-lane cottages, as "it is considered that no tenants should be called upon to pay more than one-sixth of his wages." This resolution was lost by the casting vote of the Chairman.

In July it was suggested that the men engaged on the scheme should be asked to work an extra hour a day, so as to expedite building. The men, on a ballot, refused; it was stated that they would probably work an extra hour in the morning, but objected to working an hour longer in the evening.

In August the Ministry sanctioned a loan of £12,400 for the erection of 10 houses in Rickmansworth Road.

In November Messrs. W. King and Sons offered to put up 68 houses at a cost of £1,185 per house, and the Council wrote to the local Master Builders' Association with a view to other builders following suit. The rents originally fixed were decreased as the result of a deputation to the Ministry of Health, the figures being 16s. 3d., 19s. 4d., and 22s. 4d., these sums including rates.

At the Council meeting in December, it was stated that some 50 houses were occupied and more were nearly ready for occupation.

In October it was reported that five acres had been secured in King's Ward, which would provide 70 or 80 permanent new allotments, while in Harebreaks Estate 200 new allotments had been staked out.

In November, the sale of Church property in Watford by the Church Lands Charity, realised £7,000, the High-street Infant School fetching £3,100, and the Vicarage-road recreation ground £2,300.

In December, Mr. R. A. Thorpe resigned his position as Captain of the Fire Brigade, after 20 years' service, and the Council passed a vote of thanks to him for his services.

In January it was announced that the Watford Conservative Club premises, High-street, [corner of Clarendon Rd], had been sold to Messrs. Dudley, for conversion into shops, and that North End House had been purchased for the Club. The new premises, which were redecorated and renovated, were opened in July, and re-named Halsey House.

WO December 1920

New Motor-Bus Service

The restoration took place on Wednesday by the London General Omnibus Company of the motor bus service formerly worked by the North-Western Railway between Garston and Croxley, via Watford Junction station.

Running at 15-minute intervals during the busier hours of the morning and evening and at 30-minute intervals during the other periods of the day, the new service connects at Watford Junction with the electric trains working between that station and the Metropolis.

The journey time between the Garston terminus, the Three Horse-shoes, and Watford Junction is 14 minutes, the fare is fourpence; between the Croxley Green terminus, the Sportsman, and the Junction the time is 27 minutes and the fare sixpence.

The through fare between Garston and Croxley Green is tenpence. The new daily service between Bushey station and Boxmoor is at hourly intervals and the fare for the through journey being 1s. 1d. This service, No. 145, is a welcome augmentation of the weekend service, No. 146, recently started by the General Company between Golder's Green and Boxmoor.

The intention of the L.G.O.C. to develop its motor bus services in the Watford district is shown by the Company's recent opening of a garage at Leavesden-road, from which a large number of the motor buses working on local routes will be operated and which, incidentally, should provide employment for Watford workers. The Company hopes to be able to install motor bus services to such places as Rickmansworth, Berkhampstead, Hemel Hempstead and St. Albans.

WO August 1920

Football in Watford

A party of journalists were invited by the directors of the Watford F. C. to inspect the new Vicarage-road football ground on Friday evening.

The area of the ground is 6½ acres, and the total estimated accommodation is 33,000, for 5,000 of whom cover is provided. The grand stand will hold about 1,400, and there are two other stands.

Commodious dressing-rooms are provided, together with bath-houses (including shower baths); there are also a directors' room, cashier's room, referee's room and bath, a bar, and store rooms, and—as auctioneers say—the usual offices.

WO, August 1922

New Librarian

When librarian George Bolton was appointed, in 1921, the Watford Library occupied purpose-built premises in Queens Road. The facilities offered by the library were renowned but although the building had already been enlarged, space was again at a premium.

In an age, some 60 years or so before modern photocopiers made their mark, the only means of copying a rare document was photographically. In fact, many earlier plate cameras were well-designed, with long bellows extension, to get near and focus accurately.

George Bolton was keenly interested in photography and used his equipment to very good purpose in making copies of such items as church register pages and rare, fading, photographs. From this work; and probably inspired by men such as Whitford Anderson—who was prolific in photographing places and antiquities of Hertfordshire for posterity—he saw the wisdom of starting a local collection

This has survived and has been added to from that date. Much of George Bolton's work is among the collection, but difficulty exists in definite identification. Whilst the local professionals used plate cameras—and would do so for many years to come—George Bolton was a relatively early exponent of the use of both cut-film and roll-film, which meant lighter and more portable cameras.

He recorded progress of road changes, for example, the Cross Roads, bridge building at Wiggenhall Road, reconstruction of the High Street; and rebuilding of Cassio Bridge.

Some of his photographs of the years 1921 to 1939 are used in this book, of which that on page 182 shows Queens Road corner when the High Street was in course of reconstruction in 1923. New foundations were laid and the road given a tarmac surface and the High Street was, at last, suitable for modern traffic.

JBN 1987/2002

New Football Ground Opened

The Watford Association Football Club's new ground in Vicarage-road was opened on Wednesday evening by Colonel Charles Healey prior to the match with Millwall Athletic.

There was an attendance of over eight thousand when Mr. F. W. Jeffs asked Colonel Healey to perform the ceremony.

Those present who knew the ground five months ago could hardly realise the transformation that had taken place. It was now a beautiful area covered with lovely and very fine turf.

Mr. F. W. Jeffs presented Colonel Healey with a silver key, and also the silver lock and chain from the gate.

The padlock bore the following inscription:— "Presented to Colonel Charles Healey, C.M.G., on the occasion of the opening of the football ground, Vicarage-road, Watford, 30th August, 1922."

WO September, 1922

Solid tyred and limited by law to 12mph (and with an open cab) the motor lorry was a more functional load carrier than a horse and cart. Ausden's started in Fearnley Street and this was photographed in market Street, near the Rose and Crown stables.

Rebuilding Hunton Bridge

Messrs. K. Hoist and Co., London, are now engaged in rebuilding Hunton Bridge, which was not considered strong enough to carry modern traffic.

The structure will be of reinforced concrete and consist of a centre arch having a span of 31 ft. 6 in., leaving a roadway 26ft. wide and a footpath 5ft. in width. The amount of the tender was £4,050 and the Ministry of Transport have agreed to make a grant of 50 per cent. towards the cost.

WO September, 1922

• *For the reconstruction of the High Street and London Road; the tender of Mr. Chas. Ball of Letchworth amounting to £25,630 was accepted.*

Centre right: Jarvis's almost modern looking cut-price store has hitherto baffled local book compilers as to its whereabouts; "incorporated into Woolworth's from a people's yard in the High Street", and "St Albans Road" are two choices.

The view from a postcard, above, of the Pond c1926, shows a forecourt opposite of goods for sale, not seen on pre-1914 photographs.

Right: With the entire Pond area given a facelift and a service road, the Plaza cinema built, and Faircross House shops and flats, in 1934, one of the shops carries the name 'Jarvis Stores'. It is possible that the small store was started post-1919 to supply the people in Cassio Hamlet and nearby lower St Albans Road.

The AA man is on duty; the house on the far side of the Cross Roads, shrouded by trees, is the 'Elms' about which councillors frequently complained and eventually became the site of the Town Hall.

Cassiobury is to be sold . . . the sale will start on June 12th for ten days.

After George Devereux de Vere died following an accident in London in 1916, Adele became Dowager Countess of Essex and she, together with Algernon who had inherited the title of Eighth Earl of Essex, organised the auction and sale of property in 1922.

The estate comprised some 870 acres. At the auction, in 1922, the mansion and grounds, of 100 acres, and a valuable building estate, making over 433 acres, were purchased by a local syndicate of several men for about £55,000; the West Herts Golf Course, with its 5,000ft of road frontage, was taken in at £10,500.

Four months later the Mansion was stripped of furniture and left; as an unoccupied building, and with no semblance of previous history or glory, it remained so until it was demolished in 1927 and the grounds incorporated into the Cassiobury Estate of roads and houses. The West Herts Golf Club was founded in 1890 and obtained the lease of a course in 1897.

The present course, of about 260 acres, was bought by the Council in 1931 for £24,300, from the Earl of Essex, and let to the Club on a 25-year lease at £900pa, 15 acres being retained for building purposes. In 1935 162 acres of Whippendell Woods were further purchased for a sum of £16,500, with Herts County Council contributing £2,500, thus concluding the sale of the Estate.

Cassiobury House from the north-west

Why was the house not kept? The period following the Great War did not permit the luxury of buying large houses because 'they were there'; there was then no National Trust and, if there were, it would have been doubtful if they could have been interested in the house without the grounds in which it should have been situated. As can be seen from desultory prices realised by the sale, little interest was shown.

The way it finished meant that Watford, in the long run, had the better bargain.

RUSSELL FARM LODGE.

Sale of Cassiobury

CASSIOBURY, a Royal domain from the days of the Cassii tribe, with which the whole history of Watford is bound up, is one of the last of the stately Homes of England marked down for sale by auction, on June 8th, unless previously disposed of.

It touches a sad chord and marks the sign of the times to see these historic mansions come under the hammer. Messrs. Humbert and Flint, the estate agents who for years have had the Essex properties in their care, are offering (in conjunction with Messrs. Knight, Frank, and Rutley) the freehold estate in seven lots, if not sold as a whole.

Lot 1 and 2 will be offered together, they consist of the noble residence and 100 acres, the home farm, &c, and a valuable building estate, making together over 433 acres; Lot 2 is LITTLE CASSIOBURY, over 2 acres; Lots 4 and 5 are pasture land; Lot 6 is the West Herts Golf Course; and Lot 7 Whippendell Wood.

SWISS COTTAGE.

THORN COTTAGE.

RUSSELL COTTAGE.

Many other events happened in 1922 which changed forever many aspects of Watford's future. Meanwhile those who cared were sad that Cassiobury House had been empty for some years and no buyer found. A group of local men could see a disaster looming if the wrong type of purchaser bought at the auction. The estate was auctioned in seven lots and the local syndicate bought much land to be turned into the Cassiobury Estate of houses. Lots 1 & 2 comprised the home and 100 acres, and a building estate making together 433 acres. Lot 2 was Little Cassiobury, Lots 4 & 5 were pasture lands, Lot 6 the West Herts Golf Course and Lot 7 Whippendell Woods. The house was left empty after the contents were sold.

In just over a quarter of a century the late Earl had sold Callowland, Harwoods Farm Estate, Cassiobridge Farm Estate and extensive tracts of Cassiobury Park, of which the Council were wise enough to buy 75 acres.

Meanwhile, downturn had hit trade and a buyer could not be found for the Watford Manufacturing Co's new large factory; the firm was wound up, as was Mr North's Magneto works in Whippendell Road. On the brighter side a new firm called Scammell started in Watford with a workforce of 60, and the Watford to Euston line started running electric trains. (The line had been completed for a few years but was worked by steam trains.) The Council were excited about the rosy future that would attend its plans for prosperity, for the town was on the threshold of being granted Borough Charter status. This was an event which would greatly increase the status of the town, though meaning little to the average resident.

Radio was new with the starting of station '2LO' of the British Broadcasting Corporation, (an association of wireless apparatus manufacturers), who had received a licence to broadcast. A tender of £25,630 was accepted to rebuild the High Street, and Watford Football Club got its Vicarage Road new ground upon the site of an old gravel pit. Mr Brookman established a Motor Garage in St Albans Road, (later Tuckers, who moved from 134 High Street, ceased 1970/71).

Unsold, Cassiobury house was demolished in 1927.

The Watford Manufacturing Co's building bankrupted the owners and stayed empty for years until taken over by an American firm to make rubber hose (tubing). In due course the block of single-storey buildings (p168, bottom left) would be taken into use as a Government Training Centre in the 1930s, attracting from all over the country workless men for retraining with engineering skills. Many stayed on in the locality in employment causing resentment that 'they were taking jobs from local men'. The munitions factory in Bushey Mill Lane, which after war's end was part turned to manufacturing clothing, later become fragmented and let into units as the 'Greycaine's' estate.

The Hendon to Hunton Bridge by-pass was built in 1926-28 to take traffic away from the town centre and for a few years the number of vehicles which used it may have made a slight impression upon the town centre. However, gradually and imperceptibly, the reverse happened. The road attracted building estates, then industrial estates. The residents and workers needed to live, and shop, in the town and, far from easing congestion, within ten years the situation was immeasurably worse than hitherto.

Watford could see no end to the prosperity it thought it was creating, and many years later, when strong measures were needed to alleviate problems, there was never any money in the kitty.

We believe some members of the Royal Family came from Windsor last week for a private view. Would that the whole property, with its valuable and historic contents, its paintings, staircase, Grinling Gibbons' carvings, could again become the home of royalty.

The sale of the contents of the Mansion will start on the 12th June for ten days. There are some 3,000 lots to dispose of.

WO April 1922

Cassiobury Sold

We understand that the greater part of Cassio-bury Estate, together with the mansion, has been sold to a local syndicate.

Though the names of those comprising the syndicate have not been made public, it is rumoured that it consists of no fewer than nine members, of whom two are members of the Watford Urban District Council.

No information is available as to the price, but in business circles the figure is put down

CASSIO-BRIDGE COTTAGE.

RIDGE LANE COTTAGE.

GREAT BEECH TREE COTTAGE.

ENTRANCE LODGE.

with the end of war . . . manufacturer's expected good trade . . .

some where in the neighbourhood of £55,000.

Cassiobury was put up for auction by Messrs. Humbert and Flint, in conjunction with Messrs. Knight, Frank and Rutley, in London, in June. It was then stated that 11½ acres of pasture had been sold privately. Mr. W. Hurst-Flint suggested an opening bid of £90,000, and came down to £50,000, but no offer was made.

For Little Cassiobury £1,000 was offered, but on a final bid of £3,600, the property was bought in at £4,000. Since that time, however, it has been privately sold to Mr. G. Blake. Mr. Flint suggested at the sale that the estate could be adapted as a lido, country club, or public institution, but expressed the hope that some wealthy man would preserve it in its present character.

Referring to the noted Grinling Gibbons carvings in the mansion, he stated that he had had them valued, and it was estimated that they were worth anything from £14,000 to £20,000. The West Herts Golf Club's Course, embracing about 261½ acres, and having over 5,000 feet of existing road frontage, leased until 1932, at £600 per annum, was taken in at £10,500.

Since the auction, it has been known that attempts have been made to form a syndicate, and at first three or four names were mentioned as being interested.

Others apparently joined them, and the deal was arranged at the end of last week. The land purchased is bounded on the west side by the river Gade and Grand Junction Canal, and on the east side by Hemel Hempstead-road. The intention of the syndicate is to develop the estate for building. What will be done with the mansion remains to be seen.

A report appeared in a London paper to the effect that the Watford Urban District Council had acquired 50 acres "of the lower picturesque portion of the ground, through which the river Gade flows and which adjoins the present Park allotments, representing a portion of Watford Park proper."

At the June meeting of the Council Mr. G. Blake suggested that the question of securing an extension of the Park should be considered, and a sub committee, consisting of Messrs. T. R. Clark, G. Blake, R. A. Thorpe, and H. B. Watkins was appointed to deal with the matter.

The End of Cassiobury

The announcement made this week that the greater part of the existing Cassiobury Estate has been sold privately to a local syndicate means that the final step has been taken in the disintegration of the historic home at Watford of the Earls of Essex.

The intention of the purchasers is to develop the land as a new building estate. The mansion, now that all the furniture has been sold, stands as an empty shell. From a sentimental point of view, this is a matter of no inconsiderable regret. The town would have been a very different place from what it is to-day had the Cassiobury Estate remained intact.

It is just a quarter of a century since the late Earl made the first of a series of sales to Messrs. R. Ashby and C. Brightman—two men to whose enterprise and foresight the development of Watford in recent years has been largely due. They started with purchases in Callow Land, and followed these by the acquisition of the Harwoods Farm Estate, Cassiobridge Farm Estate, and extensive tracks of Cassiobury Park. From them the Council were wise enough to buy 75 acres to make the public Park.

On land which formed, a little over two decades ago part of the ancient estate, are now miles of streets. Judge-street, Victoria and Chater Elementary Schools, the Boys' Grammar School, St. Michael's Church, and other places of worship were erected as the new areas filled up with private dwellings.

The growth of Watford during this period put the town far ahead of any other place in Hertfordshire, and strengthened its claim, now happily conceded, to larger municipal powers.

If the late Earl had been able and disposed to say that the rural character of his inheritance should remain unchanged, Watford would have remained confined to comparatively small boundaries, and its development would have been stifled. As it is, the break-up of the estate coincided with the creation of new urban needs, and the final disposal of the mansion and adjoining land has been inevitable for some time.

There remain the West Herts golf course, Whippendell Wood, and a portion near the river Gade, which is being offered to the Urban Council as an extension of the public Park. That prospective purchase, by the way, is

Swiss Cottage by the Gade was thought to have been pulled down after neglect had made the structure unsafe.
But a letter to the Watford Observer Nostalgia page in Feb 2000 carried a confession. "As a little boy I used to play in the old Swiss Cottage. We were playing one day and were pulling at the beams, the whole place started to creak and crack; we ran as fast as we could and watched aghast as the whole building fell to the ground. That was around 1945, when we were about 12 years old."
That left Watfordians with the puzzle of 'where was it'.
Before the development of Gade Avenue Rousebarn Lane crossed the Gade by means of a ford and entered Rickmansworth Road where Gade Avenue now is. The map on page 140 shows the locations.

a matter which ought to be thoroughly discussed in open Council meeting. The price mentioned in this connection, £4,100 for 59 acres, would, of course be very low if the land were, like the other portion, suitable for building. It is a matter of some satisfaction that the syndicate referred to are all Watford men, and therefore are more likely than outsiders to have due regard to residential and other amenities. Cassiobury is now only a name in local history.

Watford, which has absorbed it, has history yet to make.

WO August 1922

● *At the same time as Cassiobury was being sold, the recession and down-turn in trade was hitting local industry; the Watford Manufacturing Company—in process of having a large new factory built at Delectaland—was in trouble.*

Watford Manufacturing Co. Ltd.

An extraordinary general meeting of the Watford Manufacturing Company, Ltd., was held at the Cannon-street Hotel, Cannon-street, London, on Monday, for the purpose of considering, and, if thought fit, passing a resolution to wind up the Company voluntarily.

The Chairman said he regretted that they were meeting that day in accordance with a resolution of the directors conveyed to them in the Company's circular dated August 24th, 1922. The proposal that the Company should be wound up voluntarily was no doubt a great disappointment to every individual shareholder, particularly to those who had been for so many years associated with the Company.

Naturally they desired to know the reasons why the directors were asking them to take the course proposed. In one word, it was the direct result of falling market prices. For the past twenty-four months manufacturing companies throughout the world had been experiencing conditions of which they had no previous experience or even precedent.

The cessation of hostilities created an unprecedented demand for goods, and there was no doubt that almost every individual manufacturer expected that demand for replenishing war depleted stocks to be still greater during 1920 and 1921; instead of which the years 1920 and 1921 were possibly the worst years for demand experienced, owing to the inability of the world, especially Central Europe, to finance the replenishment of their depleted stocks.

The huge readjustments which had been necessitated in many of the largest manufacturing and trading companies had unfortunately resulted in the fact that business under those altered conditions could only be carried on at a serious loss. It would not be right, nor would it help them, to refer by name to the number of other companies who had suffered enormous and unprecedented losses during that period.

Fortunately for them, most of them had been able to weather the storm by drawing on their reserves to liquidate their losses.

Unfortunately their Company had no reserves to fall back upon with the exception of its capital. The ordinary shareholders of the Company came forward last year, and agreed

to the sum of £225,000 being written off their ordinary shares, but they would see from the accounts that further heavy losses had been made.

That naturally had resulted in a weakening of confidence of the bankers of the Company, and they had become increasing insistent in their demand for repayment of their overdrafts. At the present moment they owed their bankers about £450,000 in round figures, and other creditors about £83,000, a total indebtedness of £533,000.

The simple fact, therefore, was that their creditors were insisting, not unreasonably, upon the complete liquidation of their overdraft, and it was that position which had given their directors no option but to ask the shareholders to attend that meeting. and, with their consent, to carry the resolution on that agenda paper.

Mr. Banks said that the Chairman had stated that the loss was mainly bought about by falling markets. Could he state the amount due to the bank on account of the new and unfinished factory?

The Chairman said that it was rather hard to reply specifically to that question because the bank overdraft did not necessarily mean money expended on building. The new building and plant purchased for it approximately amounted to £350,000 and the building was not yet completed.

WHP August, 1922

The Palace Theatre (bottom left) and St Mary's Church are identifiers to this overview of the medieval-like market town of Watford. A Saturday market is taking place in the Market Place and at the centre, extreme right, is Humbert and Flint's cattle market at Stone's Alley/ Marlborough Road.
At the top, centre are two tall building–on the left the dome of Boots' store and on the right the imposing edifice of Barclay's Bank on the corner of King Street, and in- between the remnants of the town's courtyards off the High Street.
1922

The Borough Charter

The Incorporation Campaign

IT is well over 30 years since Incorporation was first discussed at Watford, and it is probable that but for the war a Charter would have been obtained six or seven years ago.

Leaving out of account the persistent advocacy of Incorporation by the Observer, the body which has played a greater part than any other in the movement was undoubtedly the Watford Tradesmen's Association.

In 1910 they appointed a special committee to visit a number of boroughs of similar size to Watford, and were hoping to complete their campaign by arranging for a "petition of inhabitant householders," when the outbreak of war put an abrupt end to their activities.

Prior to that, however, it had been made clear that Incorporation was regarded as desirable by practically all parties and classes in the town.

Here and there were to be found opponents, but their number was always negligible.

Above: *The leading car of the procession is that of Watford's MP, Dennis Herbert, who has handed to Watford's Charter Mayor, the Earl of Clarendon, the Charter of Incorporation at the Borough Boundary of Haydon Road/London Road.. Among those who recorded the scene was Mr W Coles on his step-tripod-ladder with his plate camera. This picture is from a roll-film negative and may have been by George Bolton.*

Left: *The procession illustrating Watford's progress travels through Woodford and Queens Roads to the High Street.*

Below: *To the Council Offices in the High Street where the Proclamation will be formally read out.*

Charter Day Arrangements

THE programme of Watford's Charter Day celebrations on Wednesday next is now practically complete. The order of the procession was given in our last issue. The official timetable is as follows: 12 noon.—Reception of the Charter at the Borough boundary at the corner of Haydon-road and Chalk-hill. Mounted and walking detachments are requested to be ready to take up their positions at 11.15 a.m., and conveyances at 11.30 a.m.

12.10 p.m–Start of procession.

1.30 p.m.–Procession forms up in the Market place for Proclamation of the Charter.

1.45 p.m.–Luncheon to invited guests at Buck's Rooms.

3 p.m.–Public meeting in the Palace Theatre.

1.30 to 5 p.m.–Free cinema performances for school children at the Super-Cinema, Central Hall Picture House, Electric Coliseum, and Empire Cinema.

7.30 p.m.—Grand firework display in Cassiobury Park.

WO October, 1922

The New Borough

Watford has every reason to be proud of the wonderful success of the Charter celebrations.

It was the day of days in the town's history, and the scenes in the streets will long be remembered. The presence of the Lord Lieutenant of the county, the High Sheriff, the Mayors of Hertford, St. Albans, and Hemel Hempstead, and the Bishop, assured the pomp and dignity of the ceremonial of the reception of the Charter.

The procession was worthy of the occasion.

Hitherto, the town has been merely an urban district, with no municipal status above places with a thousand or two of population, and claiming only the passing interest of its neighbours; now the Borough of Watford, comes into its own, rising at once to a new status.

WO October, 1922

Euston and Watford Electric Line

The new electric line between Watford and Euston was opened for passenger traffic on Monday.

The section between Willesden and Harrow was opened for steam driven trains in June, 1912, on which date the Watford to Croxley Green branch was also opened for steam traffic.

In February, 1913, the extension from Harrow to Watford was opened, steam still being the motive power. During the years to 1915, the Bakerloo tube was extended from Paddington to Queen's Park, and opened early in that year. In May, 1915, electric trains from Elephant and Castle ran through to Willesden, and in April, 1917, onward to Watford. At the same time the electric service between Watford and Broad Street was inaugurated.

WO July, 1922

Scammell

In an era of post-war weight- and speed-restriction on commercial vehicles, Lieut-Colonel Alfred G Scammell, with his brother James, designed and built a revolutionary articulated vehicle which could be registered as a single vehicle. This was shown in 1920, was permitted to travel at 12mph rather than be restricted to 8mph and to carry a legal payload of 7 tons.

The reaction to the prototype led to further machines being built and exhibited at the 1921 Olympia Motor Show, where firm orders for 50 vehicles were taken.

The modest premises in London would not support production on the scale needed, and so ground in Tolpits Lane, West Watford was used to build a factory where, in 1922, a workforce of some 60 men was employed to start production.

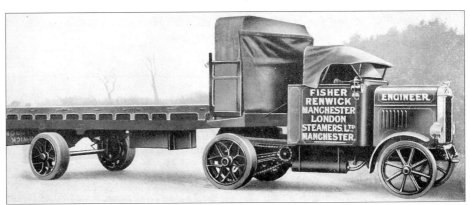

Top: *Scammell's early articulated lorry (1922/3) and centre left, a frameless tanker of 1926.*

Centre right: *Otto Brookman came to Watford in 1922 looking for a site upon which to start a motor garage and the top photograph is one of several showing a possible lower St Albans Road location. The site must have pleased Mr Brookman for the following year his album showed his garage open. Named the 'Nascot Motor Works, Brookman and Co' the business was later to be that of Tucker Bros, after they moved from their site in Lower High Street, just below King Street. (The early Tucker story is given on page 60). Brookman's garage started with the 'Singer' car agency. To the left of the Nascot Motor Works was built the Oddfellows Hall and both survived until road widening in 1970/71 when they were demolished along with many other properties, including the Park Gates.*

Lord Leverhulme's Offer

A meeting of the creditors of the Watford Manufacturing Co., Ltd., was held on Friday at the Cannon-street Hotel. The chair was occupied by Mr. F. D. Arcy Cooper, the liquidator in the voluntary liquidation of the Company, who submitted a statement of affairs, which disclosed liabilities of £538,653.

The assets were estimated to realise £427,709, or a deficiency of £110,944. The principal asset consists of the properties, which stood in the Company's books at £622,506, but which had recently been valued at £307,000.

The Chairman stated that he had received an offer from Lord Leverhulme to purchase the assets of the Company, as a going concern, for a sum of £543,000, payable in cash.

Lord Leverhulme desired that in the event of his offer being accepted, the liquidator would obtain the approval of the Court to the sale of the assets. This approval was given.

WHP October, 1922

Wiggenhall Houses

In reply to an enquiry, the Housing Committee had informed the Ministry of Health that of the houses erected or being erected at Wiggen-hall, 50 are for general applicants, and 74 for people removed from property scheduled for closing.

The Public Health Committee reported as follows: "Ballards Buildings, etc.— Demolition Orders—The Medical Officer and the Sanitary Inspector reported that all the new houses at the Rookery had been allocated, and that all the tenants selected by the Tenancy Sub-Committee had removed from Ballards Buildings, New street, and Lamb Yard. The Sanitary Inspector reported that every house in Lamb-yard was empty, but in Ballards Buildings a few houses were still occupied."

The Medical Officer reported that the next areas to be dealt with were the following:— Meeting-alley, 30; Butchers'-yard, 11; Watford Fields and Fox-alley, 6; Lower High-street, 6; Woodman's-yard, 3; Water-lane, 2; Carey-yard, 2; Wheatsheaf Cottages, 2; Tibbles'-yard, 1; Cassio Hamlet, 2; total 74.

WHP February, 1924

Sub-Letting on Harebreaks

The complex problem of sub-letting in Council houses was the subject of a debate introduced by Councillor Mansfield, who drew attention to a paragraph in the report of the Tenancy Sub Committee of the Housing Committee, instructing the Housing Official to commence proceedings for the possession of three houses at Harebreaks, where overcrowding was alleged.

Councillor Mansfield said that in these cases there were in the respective houses 10, 12 and 10 people. His point was that if the Council took action to turn the sub-tenant families out of those municipal houses, they would simply force those families to overcrowd other houses, where the conditions were less tolerable than at Harebreaks. If overcrowding in present conditions had to exist, it was better it should exist at Harebreaks where there were, at least, baths and air space, than in the conditions prevailing in some of Watford's dreary side streets.

WO February, 1924

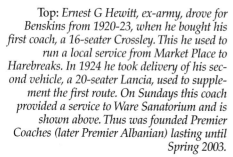
Top: *Ernest G Hewitt, ex-army, drove for Benskins from 1920-23, when he bought his first coach, a 16-seater Crossley. This he used to run a local service from Market Place to Harebreaks. In 1924 he took delivery of his second vehicle, a 20-seater Lancia, used to supplement the first route. On Sundays this coach provided a service to Ware Sanatorium and is shown above. Thus was founded Premier Coaches (later Premier Albanian) lasting until Spring 2003.*

Centre: *The corner of Queens Road and High Street where the High Street is undergoing reconstruction to take modern traffic.*

Right: *Wiggenhall Road looking to the bridge over the River Colne and towards the town. The railway carriage sheds on the left were built in 1914/15 (and demolished June 1987), and in the background, beyond the tree, Benskin's Brewery.*

Christmas & Co, established in 1827, were in business as coachbuilders at 141/143 High Street, (right) where Harlequin now is, two doors up from Boots' entrance (here c1922/3 after having moved to Clock House).

Far right: Clock House (p366), in the High Street was built in 1923 where the facilities seemed ideal. However, the bad access from and into the High Street against the increasingly heavy traffic made life difficult. Later the same problem was to affect Benskin's in a similar and more dramatic manner, contributing to the firm, and brewing, leaving Watford.

Below: This is the Cardiff Road/Holywell Farm/Riverside Road triangle of Watford. In the top right of A is the white flank wall of the Ice Works and just below is the chimney of the electricity generating station. To its left a taller chimney identifies the Corporation's refuse destructor. At the bottom of D is Holywell Farm. At the left of B are the carriage sheds for the coaches of the LMS electric railway. Of the track passing the sheds one line branches left out of the picture to West Watford and Croxley; that to right serves Croxley Mills and Rickmansworth. On the right-hand edge the silk mill premises in use as a laundry and across the road from works can be seen a few of the old mill cottages. The cultivated field in C is earmarked for the housing estate comprising Riverside Road and Colne Avenue, principally to house persons displaced from demolished slums. The wooded area, upper right, is the dell of Blackwell Drive and carries across Tommy Deacon's footpath and into 'Oxhey Park', though not then named as such; the road leading to the mill is masked by the line of trees but is shown on p33. The River Colne meanders past the carriage sheds and though Wiggenhall Bridge cannot be seen its reflection is there.

A	B	C
D	E	F

Flour Mill Fire

A disastrous fire occurred in the town, on Wednesday night, which resulted in damages, estimated roughly at £20,000, to the Watford Flour Mills, High-street, the property of Messrs. T. Bailey, Ltd., in which the interests are held by the well-known milling family of Messrs. Putnam, who have been associated with the industry in this part of the country for a period extending over half a century.

The mills constitute one of the oldest structures in the town, and have been in existence many generations. They consist of a pile of buildings imposing by their plainness, solidity, and commanding height, as, with their elevators, they tower right above any of the adjacent property. John Welbys, of Watford, seems to have laid a claim to the Mill Pond at Watford in 1431, but the result of the suit, which arose between himself and the Abbot, is not given.

In the time of Abbot John of Wheat-hampstead a sum of £41 3s. 6d. was spent on repairs to the mill. About the same time certain inhabitants of Watford began to erect a horse mill, but were successfully opposed by the Abbot.

"The Fishery and all the shops recently erected upon the waste at Watford were granted in 1579-80 to John Farnham, and the mill in 1609 to Edward Ferrers and Francis Phillips, the fee farm rent of £13 from the Mill

Below: The Mill, an uninspiring structure, was the centre of a considerable amount of business in the Lower High Street that served the carters, their horses and transport needs.

Right: The mill was ruined, the hulk stayed empty and 'Valuable Property' signs failed to attract a buyer. The Mill and water rights were eventually bought by the Council for £2,250, and the mill demolished in 1938.

paid by them being granted at the same time to Sir Christopher Hatton and others."

"Ferrers and Phillips sold the Mill in the same year to Sir Thomas Lord Ellesmere, who died seised of it in 1616-17, and it subsequently passed with the Manor to the Earls of Essex. The present Watford Mill is the representative of this old Abbotial Mill." *(Victoria History of the Counties of England, Vol 2, p.452.)*

The building up of the banks of the Mill stream above the Mill, which extends for more than a mile, is attributed to the monks. The present structure was built by John Guest in 1826 upon the site of the old Mill, but being larger, one corner of it encroached upon a piece of the Turnpike road, and amongst deeds is an interesting document conveying that small portion of the land from the Trustees of the Sparrows Herne Turnpike road to John Guest for the sum of 10s.

The Mill was installed with two breast water wheels and seven pairs of stones, together with the necessary dressing tackles. This machinery was the best that engineering skill could produce, and made Watford Mill one of the best in its generation, and was in its time the "talk of the county."

The engineers who dismantled this machinery bore testimony to its substantial and perfect design. The introduction of the Roller system made it necessary to destroy obsolete though magnificent machinery in order to make room for a modern system.

The Mill was remodelled in 1921, and brought up to date by the present proprietors, Messrs. Thomas Bailey (Watford), Ltd., under the managing directorship of Mr. Gilbert Putnam.

WO, December 1924

Recollections

I remember in the late '20s, much of 'Lower High Street' for that was where I spent a lot of time visiting my maternal grandparents. They lived in the first house one comes to in Local Board Road—where the Pump House is now situated.

After No. 1 came two cottages, then the larger house beyond which was an enclosed property we called the 'Waterworks' hence the name of the Pump House Theatre today. No. 4 was a smart place then, called the 'Red House'. It was owned by a bank manager and his family; their little boy Philip was my playmate and I used to call him my 'sweetheart'. But his mother was rather 'posh 'and would make it clear that she was not too happy with her precious offspring associating with a rather scruffy little girl whose socks were forever falling around her ankles.

My grandfather's house was an interesting property with two large gates to one side, opening into what we called the 'Cart Shed' for instead of a car it housed a pretty little trap to which Dolly the pony would be harnessed to take us on sunny summer evenings for leisurely rides around Watford's leafy lanes.

Facing Local Board Road was a large flour mill, and although only a toddler, I can remember the excitement with which my elders discussed the night when it was gutted by fire.

The shell of it stood for many years after

Where now is the entrance to Tesco's stood a public house called 'Leatherseller's Arms'. It had a nice little garden at the back where we kids could play while our elders took a little refreshment. I remember one occasion when we managed to place an upturned bench against one of the wooden tables to make a super slide, and the tearing of my best silk dress during the fun.

Travelling further to the rear of the pub we

came to a sizeable piece of land belonging to my grandfather where he grew fruit and vegetables and reared a few chickens and pigs—the latter he would sell to Dumbleton's, the family butcher next to the Leatherseller's. His 'garden' as I called it, was bordered on one side by a shallow but fast flowing stream—the mill-stream—(which runs through Tesco's grounds today). In the stream thrived an abundance of crayfish or 'crawley-bobs's we called them. They looked and tasted like miniature lobsters–delicious. There were several other small pubs nearby including the Fox and the Swan, now all gone.

My grandfather worked for Benskin's Brewery as did two sons. Looking back, he must have slaved, one way or another, for every hour that God made. After grooming those huge shire horses he would drive them to the outlying ale-houses to deliver the great barrels of beer, taking all of a long day on the journey that a modern lorry would accomplish in just a few hours.

I would run errands for my grandmother – perhaps to 'Archers' a little shop near High Street Station that sold hot faggots and pease pudding to take away in a basin; then a little further up, Lipton's of the tea fame. On the right hand side of the High Street, just before Queens Road was the forerunner of Marks and Spencer's, called the 'Penny Bazaar' '— a good source for buying Christmas presents from my meagre pocket money.

Further up still, on the left hand side, was the open market. I remember being taken there once after dark (or perhaps late one day as the nights were drawing in) and the stalls had naked flares lighting up their wares. But perhaps that may have been my childish fancy and they must have been gas-lights.

Right opposite was the 'Essex Hall' where my parents used to go to the occasional elegant dances, my mother in her fashionably short dresses. Too short, as some of my school-friends relayed to me. Apparently their rather more staid mums were quite shocked. I never knew whether to be proud of this information or acutely embarrassed. Thus far up Watford's High Street was the limit of my childish horizons.

The upper part featured largely in my teenage years.

(Joyce Franklyn was born in Watford and penned these notes in 1995; 'Archers' is shown on p187 and the High Street area of which Joyce writes would have been littled changed from that shown on pages 92/93.)

Metropolitan Line

The Metropolitan line extension to Watford, which was planned before 1914, was completed during 1925. The Watford Station was formally opened on Saturday 31st October, and full services provided from Monday 2nd November, 1925.

Above: The hospital nearing completion. The land in Rickmansworth Road was purchased soon after the war's end, the Council being determined not to let the opportunity pass; and the Chairman of the Appeal Fund, the Earl of Clarendon, backed by C H Peacock of the Watford Observer, the Treasurer, set about raising £90,000 by voluntary public subscription and money raising events.

The success of the campaign was apparent when in July 1923 the foundation stone was laid and in June 1925 the Princess Royal, Princess Mary, opened the Peace Memorial Hospital in Rickmansworth Road next door to the Elms. Its 87 beds soon proved inadequate and extensions costing £70,000 were added in 1937, providing a total of 154 beds.

Right: The Market Place is thronged to greet the Princess Royal on her way to the hospital.

In an attempt to cut unemployment a plan was made to build a road from Mill Hill past Stanmore and around Watford joining the Hempstead Road near Hunton Bridge. Started in 1924, the By-Pass was completed in about two years and when finished afforded considerable relief to Watford.

This shows the swathe down to Hunton Bridge where it cuts across Russell Lane (from top left from Leavesden to bottom right at the Hempstead Road). The photographs at the bottom show the High Street during its last years as a venue for the ancient street market. The cars are parked on the old 'Market Place' and when the market closed considerable disquiet was expressed at the use of this space as a car-park. After much discussion it was later taken into use as a carriageway as shown on p206.

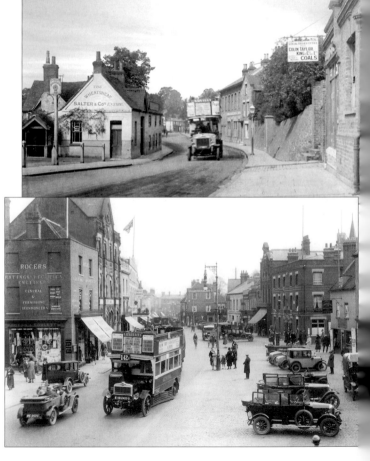

Ballard's buildings to go . . .

The buildings, in Court 8 *(right)*, had gained a reputation perhaps more unsavoury than deserved. Very old properties, they were in 1750 in the ownership of Mr. Dyson who had a small brewery at the end of the yard—the founder of Watford's brewing industry.

His son, and grandson, carried on brewing, and bought a house at 194 High Street, with attached grounds to where the brewery was moved in 1812. The last Dyson was a bachelor and upon his death the executors sold the brewery (then Cannons) to Joseph Benskin, a retired publican, in partnership with a local draper, Mr Bradley.

Benskins prospered, buying out Groomes (Kings Langley); Healeys,(King Street) and in 1923, Sedgwicks (High Street). (Water from the wells driven deep into the chalk provided water of exceptional purity—hence the name 'Watford Springs' for the swimming and leisure complex built in 1990 upon the brewery site. Benskins had by then been bought by Ind Coope in 1957, who were in turn bought by Allied Lyons in 1963 and brewing moved to Romford.)

But back in the 1830's the Ballard's Buildings housed a considerable number of railway workers from which spread the story that Ballard's buildings had been built for that purpose.

Most of the hamlet's courtyards consisted of a few dwellings, such as Meeting Alley which was just one row of cottages, but Ballard's buildings contained rather more buildings. Other more odious and dilapidated properties were demolished as slums much earlier but Ballard's buildings survived.

Because they were near to the Church and Market Place, and in the public gaze, they perhaps disturbed better-off residents' conscience not a little. Watford, as a town, had a better reputation than many for dealing promptly with property which did not meet sanitary and health requirements. Many tenants had lived long in some houses, were satisfied. and maintained them in spick and span order, and resisted the orders to demolish and move.

Above all they rightly resented the implication that THEY were the cause of the 'slum' in which they lived.

Leica

Above: *A camera using 35mm perforated cine film had for some years been the subject of development by the firm of microscope makers, Leitz. It was shown at the 1925 Leipzig fair with some degree of success. It had a focal-plane shutter with speeds 1/20th to 1/500 sec and was fitted with a non-interchangeable 50mm f/3.5 lens; a fantastic aperture for its time. At first this small camera was more a novelty but, improved, became a living legend.*

Right: *Both Archer's and Fowler's were small houses, just below High St Station, with modest conversions to open the front parlour for trade. They were demolished in the mid 1920s.*

The Strike.

There was great satisfaction that the 'Peace' had been built and opened with due pomp and ceremony, but the Mill fire was a huge disaster and Cassiobury House, sold and empty, still remained.

Otherwise, the economy appeared to be in a healthy state. The public demand for consumer goods was insatiable and confidence was growing—but suddenly the bubble of prosperity burst. Legislation was not then regarded as a tool by which the economy could be manipulated and as the money ran out so demand and prices tumbled.

Locally, the Watford Manufacturing Company, which at its Annual General Meeting of 1920 expressed optimism in all aspects of its manufacturing and trading outlets, reported also that its employees, through the Company's social welfare arrangements, received dental and eye inspections. This same company were to find themselves greatly overstocked with raw materials purchased at top prices and, worse, a new £300,000 factory partly completed. With bank overdrafts of £500,000, it went into voluntary liquidation in 1922. Compulsory wage cuts throughout industry were commonplace. Exported coal fetched only one-fifth of the price it had commanded a few years earlier. The payment of subsidies to miners was stopped following which the key industries of power, transport, printing, etc, went on strike in support of the General Strike called for 4th May, 1926.

With a year's prior warning of this possibility, the Government had made emergency arrangements to maintain essential supplies. With comparatively few homes enjoying the luxury of wireless receivers;

news was hard to come by. Some newspapers published a single-sided sheet little bigger than this page. The news sheets were eagerly purchased and read before being passed on.

The TUC called off the strike on May 12th as nothing appeared to have been achieved. The miners were forced to continue their struggle alone for another six months and locally John Dickinson & Co. banned unions and set up an in-house Union with a £50,000 grant.

World economic conditions, beyond the control and understanding of the man-in-the-street, generated long-lasting bitterness and strife. In 1929 America exacerbated the international problems with its own brand of economic depression.

Ralph Thorpe was made a Freeman of the Borough, and, apart from the many workers and families on the 'dole', prosperity gradually nudged its way back. The Street Market was removed to a site cleared of aged buildings and cottages; and a new Library was to be built. This was mooted to be in King Street but, fortunately, the premises were judged as unsuitable and the Hempstead Road site chosen. The increase in the size of the town dictated that sewerage, water supply and fire services needed to be improved. Two foreign firms decided to set up works in Watford and the Ministry of Labour set up a training centre for unemployed men … and the great debate raged on as to whether an indoor swimming bath should be built.

During the strike strong feelings were aroused; at the bottom of the High Street, at the bus garage, pickets and crowds awaited any driver who dared to take a bus onto the road. At Market Place, Market Street corner, on May 12th, a crowd gathered to see the first bus pass through, (next page). This it did without undue incident, signifying that the strike was over.
With no independent national or local papers some shops posted notices of bulletins heard over the wireless.
Here a small crowd gather around Trewin's window in Queen's Road to read such a notice.

Bus Windows Smashed

On Wednesday when the first National buses came out of the High-street garage, windows of three of the vehicles were broken by stone-throwing. News that the service would resume soon spread, and in addition to the strike pickets and a large body of members of the Transport and General Workers' Union, there was a considerable crowd round the garage.

The previous day there had been activity in the yard of the garage, and on Wednesday about half-past eleven, the first 'buses, labelled for Garston, drew up to the entrance gates. The first one, driven by a National 'bus driver who had gone back, came out. He was greeted with both cheers and jeers, and although the strikers were predominant vocally, many in the crowd shouted words of encouragement. This 'bus was manned by a volunteer conductor and a special constable. It got about seventy yards when a stone was hurled through a window.

This was the only damage done to it.

The second and third 'buses then came out and were subject to attacks.

The police immediately cleared the road and the path, and were reinforced by two more car-loads of officers.

WHP, May 1926

General Strike and Observer

The "Observer' of May15 was produced under very considerable difficulties. Though the general strike was called off on Wednesday, the printers were not given permission by the Typographical Association to return at once to work. Consequently, on Thursday morning they were very unsettled. They were torn between loyalty to their employers and to their Union. The typographical staff of this journal had responded to the call to strike with the greatest reluctance. They had no grievance, and left the office, at the call of their Unions, in dejected mood. Last Thursday morning they returned in a body to find all their places open for them.

But the tension was by no means over. The local Union officials were not prepared to see their authority upset. In the evening a note was delivered to the father of the "Observer' chapel, and the men were ordered to report at headquarters the following morning. If this order was obeyed it clearly meant that their unanimous promise to produce the "Observer," made on Thursday morning, would be broken. Consultations followed, and the men, who were working the usual extra hours on Thursday evening, announced their intention of continuing straight on. The men who went out on the rounds all returned with stories of the delight of the news-agents in receiving the paper. One shopkeeper, thinking that a further supply of the

London sheets had arrived, said she did not want any more papers, but when told that the parcel contained the week's "Observer," she snatched at it eagerly.

WO, May 1926

Overhauling a bicycle

Several days ago I decided generally to overhaul and paint my bicycle. At the time I did not realise the difficulties of such an operation, but I fully appreciated them later.

I soon discovered several pots of paint, with such curious names as Matt, Whitby Black, Transparent Lacquer and Ro-Mo. To make absolutely sure of painting the cycle correctly, I decided to use them all, and thus make certain of using the proper one. Thinking Transparent would appear very attractive, I determined to apply it first, as I did not know in what order they should be utilised.

After spreading several reams of paper across the floor I sat the cycle on its saddle, and proceeded. Unfortunately, I made several slight mistakes. I believed in using the paint very liberally, and when I had finished making the cross-bar appear transparent. I discovered that I had made the saddle transparent also. While painting the wheel rims the brush slipped once or twice and soon I had covered the tyres.

I also upset a large tin of Robbialac and converted the white washing copper into a Whitby Black copper. Upon being reprimanded, I logically pointed out that now there was no longer the need to whiten the copper, and although I had never seen a black copper before, I thought the colour scheme was very striking. Perhaps the art effect was somewhat marred when I spilt some Transparent Lacquer on it.

I then proceeded to paint with the Matt, and afterwards Ro-Moed the cycle. As I had not sufficient time, I did not allow each coat of paint to set, and soon the bicycle was covered with matts, lacquers and Ro-Mo. I was soon wading about in a morass of those various fluids.

My next move was to take the bicycle to pieces and oil it properly. I intended to replace the parts, but Dame Fortune decreed otherwise. As I unfastened nuts and bolts I deposited them into a small vase, and they were followed by small pieces of iron, lamp brackets, and, having well oiled the cycle—and myself (mainly myself)—I commenced to reconstruct the former. Again my plans went astray, for directly I found the correct bolt I lost the appropriate nut, and vice-versa. After securely fixing the wheels in the wrong places and the pedals on the wrong sides, I realised I had used the saddle bolt to secure the pedals, and I was obliged to take various parts to pieces again.

Eventually, the cycle was something—but not much—like its usual self. I was regarding my work with a feeling akin to pride when I remembered the steel balls of the free wheel still reposed in my hand, where I had placed them so that they should not be forgotten.

I immediately resolved to rid myself of that ill-fated bicycle, and as my brother firmly refused to accept such a present I placed it in the care of a cycle mechanic, who smilingly remarked that he could perhaps use it for spare parts.

I have not yet chosen my career, but this incident has convinced me that I am not fitted for the job of cycle repairing.

OLIVER E. GRIFFITHS, 5th year.

(Watford Central School Magazine, 1927)

Alderman Thorpe—the Freedom of Watford

After giving up farming in Lincolnshire Alderman Thorpe came to Watford where he started the Wells (Red Lion) Brewery, in St Albans Road. He did not marry, but worked hard to build the successful brewery. He took an active part in sport and, as Captain of the Fire Brigade, assisted at many fires. With his unique perception of what was 'right' for the town he took advantage of the sale of the Essex's estates. He made sure that much of the land was not developed but became public parks and lands in the ownership of the people of Watford.

In conversation with the Editor of the West Herts Posts he remembers:"I looked round for a site or premises. At first I considered some premises near the railway bridge in St. Albans-road, but they were not large enough.

"Then I bought some land next to the St. Albans-road Police Station. The 'Paget Prize Plate' proprietors had an adjoining site; they said their site was more level than mine, and eventually we agreed to exchange sites.

"Having decided on the site, of course, I started building, but only in a small way. The building was completed in 1890. As the trade grew, I extended until the premises reached their present size. "I had to do a bit of everything. I brewed in the early morning then I went up to London getting and seeing after business; and at night I saw the dray men in.

"I knew, from certain information that came to me, that the late Earl of Essex was placing some part of Cassiobury Park on the market, and I wanted the Council to buy it. What happened eventually was that certain people acquired a large portion of the estate, and it was from them that the Council bought 50 acres of the land they had acquired.

"Before we got this purchase through, I had to meet tremendous opposition, but since then everybody has recognised how important it was that we should get some of the park. What would have been our position now if we had not taken our chance at that time? There would have been nowhere for children to play. Watford without a park! It is unthinkable now".

By the unanimous vote of a special meeting of the Watford Borough Council, held at the Oddfellow's Hall, on Wednesday night, confirmed with enthusiastic unanimity by a large and representative town's meeting held subsequently, Alderman Ralph Alfred Thorpe, J.P., was made a Freeman of the Borough of Watford—the second honour of the kind which has been bestowed since the Incorporation of Watford as a Borough in 1922.

The occasion was unique in that for the first time a meeting of the Borough Council was held in a public place.

The venue of this gathering was chosen as a matter of convenience, and some 200 or 300 representative Burgesses of Watford had the unusual experience of seeing the Mayor and Aldermen of the Borough ushered into the Oddfellows' Hall, preceded by the Mace-bearer (Sgt-Major Maxted) and formal Council business transacted, under the Chairmanship of the Mayor (Alderman T. R. Clark).

At the request of the Mayor, the Town Clerk read the notice convening the meeting. The Mayor then formally moved the following resolution:—
(a) That this Council in pursuance of the Honorary Freedom of Boroughs Act 1885, do hereby confer upon Mr. Alderman Ralph Alfred Thorpe, J.P., second Mayor of Watford, the Honorary Freedom of the Borough as an expression of the high esteem in which he is held by the inhabitants of the Borough (b) That the Common Seal be affixed to an engrossment of the foregoing resolution.

The Deputy-Mayor formally seconded, and the Council carried the resolution unanimously. Alderman Thorpe signed the Roll of Honorary Freemen of the Borough. This concluded the business of the Council meeting, and the public part of the proceedings then commenced.

The Mayor said he considered himself extremely fortunate that evening, because, in his opinion, with which they would, he was sure, agree, no more pleasing duty could fall to the lot of the Mayor of the Borough of Watford than that of putting his hand to the resolution conferring the Honorary Freedom upon Alderman Thorpe. To attempt to enumerate the many virtues of Alderman Thorpe was an exercise which was as unnecessary as it was pleasant. They all knew him, and their presence there that night was a sufficient testimonial to his conspicuous and well-deserved popularity. *(Applause.)*

It might not be out of place if he briefly enumerated some of the matters which had specially received Alderman Thorpe's attention.

Six times was Alderman Thorpe elected Chairman of the old Urban District Council. He was named in the Watford Charter as substitute Mayor to the Earl of Clarendon; was the first Deputy-Mayor of Watford, and was the second Mayor of the Borough, serving in

that office for two years. As Mayor, he had the honour of receiving Princess Mary on the occasion of her visit to Watford to perform the opening ceremony of the Peace Memorial Hospital.

Alderman Thorpe was at present, and had for many years, been Chairman of the Watford Joint Hospital Board, and was also a member of the County Council and a County Alderman. For the Hospital, he was, at the inception of that undertaking, chairman of the town's meeting and a member of the original Committee.

He was Captain of the Watford Volunteer Fire Brigade for a great number of years, and he held the long service medal of the National Fire Brigades' Association. He had also been for many years a Governor of the Watford Grammar Schools, and had been President of many sports associations, and either president or vice-president of numerous societies and organisations. His donations made for public purposes, and his private benefactions must total a very considerable sum indeed.

Many of such as the Hospital, the Football Club, and others, had been known to the pub-

75 acres—one of the best investments Watford had ever made.

lic; but he ventured to say that Alderman Thorpe's private generosity, which on many occasions had been known only to himself, and guessed at by others, probably reached, or exceeded, the very considerable sum which, during those years, had been subscribed openly by him to any cause which had for its object the good of the inhabitants of Watford. *(Applause.)*

Some of them remembered the great struggle which took place over the acquisition, in 1909, of Cassiobury Park, and the strong fight put up by Alderman Thorpe at that time, in favour of securing to the public a park which, he ventured to say, was the town's proudest possession.

The attitude of Alderman Thorpe on that occasion would ever remind them of some of those qualities for which he was eminent in a marked degree—the qualities of fearlessness, foresight, and sound judgment. When such qualities as those were possessed together in a high degree by one individual, together with a most striking generosity of character, it was only to be expected that the result should be remarkable. In that sense Alderman Thorpe was undoubtedly a most remarkable man. He had been very fortunate in having the help of Mrs. Godson, especially in the performance of his many duties socially as Mayor, during his years of office. *(Applause.)*

The Mayor thanked Alderman Thorpe personally for the great assistance he had rendered to himself, both on the Council and in other directions, and also referred to their work together on the Tribunal during the war, to Alderman Thorpe's wisdom in grasping details and of his keen anxiety to see that nothing but justice was extended to all who came before him.

The Deputy-Mayor (Alderman H. B. Watkins) said that the Mayor had dealt so very fully with the many good qualities and the great services rendered to Watford by Alderman Thorpe that he had left very little new for him to say. He would like to refer to Alderman Thorpe's work for sport in the town. It was not generally known that he played cricket when he first came to Watford. He had been identified with the West Herts Club and ground and the football section of it from the beginning. At one time Alderman Thorpe carried the Watford Football Club on his back. *(Laughter and applause.)* Had it not been for Mr. Thorpe, there certainly would not have been any first-class football in Watford to-day. It had nearly petered out. The money he advanced for football at that time amounted to practically £2,000, and when the ground was bought by the late Mr. G. B. Dodwell and handed over to the town as a gift, Alderman Thorpe generously agreed to forego that debt which was due to him. *(Applause.)* Alderman Thorpe had never had full credit for the gift he made then. *(Applause.)*

Councillor H. Horwood said that was the most unanimous meeting he had attended for some time. He felt he could support that resolution both as a member of the Council and as Chairman of the Watford Trades and Labour Council. *(Applause.)* He did not know of any member of that Council or any member of the general public who would not agree that the honour they had just awarded had been well and truly earned. *(Applause.)* They know of his sterling work in connection with the Fire Brigade, and in the development of Watford's electricity undertaking, and the town's water supply. What had amazed him was how it was that Alderman Thorpe had managed in his spare time to put in so much public work when he was engaged successfully in another enterprise also connected with water—although treated in a different manner. *(Laughter.)*

The Alderman's Thanks

Alderman Thorpe, whose rising was signalled by loud and prolonged applause and the singing of "For he's a jolly good fellow" and cheers for Mrs. Godson, said it took him some time to collect his thoughts and think of what he could say on the numerous points made by the Mayor in his speech. Many of them seemed to come back like old times. Those had been rather hard times, but they were, he believed, for the good of the town. *(Hear, hear.)*

He had tried to do his best. Many times it had been hard work, but the people of Watford had always been kind to him, and he thanked them.   One of the times in which he had gone rather wrong in Watford was over the question of Cassiobury Park. Everybody had seemed against him, but he had stuck to it, and they got 50 acres, and the Corporation took another 25 acres before the option expired. *(Applause.)*

The Town Council was not satisfied with 75 acres. He did not know how many acres they had got altogether, but it was one of the best investments Watford had ever made. *(Applause.)* He felt that after all those years it was a great honour to be made the second Freeman of the Borough. *(Applause.)*

WO June, 1927

The Metropolitan Line

Watford had a double-sided 615ft platform, 30ft wide, capable of handling a full length main line steam train and sheltered by a 280ft wood and glass canopy supported on steel girders.

The platforms were lit from the traction current, the rest of the station from the local supply. A well-equipped seven-road goods yard contained a large shed, five-ton crane, horse and carriage dock and cattle pens, all reached by a new 40ft wide approach from the main road.

Watford Council has insisted on this, not wanting vehicular traffic along Cassiobury Park Avenue, as this was a residential road.

Management of the new branch was in the hands of the Watford Joint Railway Committee, reconstituted by the Metropolitan and the LNER in November 1925. Both companies provided a train service when the line opened to the public on Monday 2 November 1925.

Some consideration was given to moving the terminus closer to the heart of the town. Early in May 1927, J. M. Clark, who had been resident engineer for the branch construction noticed that premises at 44, High Street, with 2/ acres of backland extending to Cassio Road, were on the market. He sent a memorandum to Selbie in which he suggested that this property would provide adequate space for a small passenger terminus and outlined two possible approach routes, one in a tunnel for part of the way to avoid property demolition. Selbie took his usual positive attitude, getting the board to agree to purchase of the property 'in view of possible future eventualities'.

The transaction was made through a third party in October 1927, the LNER not being told until after the event. In 1928 the property was sold at a profit to the Metropolitan puppet company, N. W. Land & Transport Co Ltd, who leased it to a furniture retailer, ensuring it could be re-possessed without difficulty should it ever be needed.

But that it would be a railway station had now become much more unlikely.

London's Metropolitan Railway,

Alan A Jackson

44 High Street, The Empress Tea Lounge and Gardens' became Cedars Furniture Store, Grange at one time, and is currently 'The Moon Under Water' pub/come restaurant.

Water-Cress Losses

Nowhere is the aftermath of the floods being felt more keenly than among local growers of watercress. The recent floods have left more than one grower on the verge of ruin. The loss, locally, runs into thousands of pounds.

There are few greater cress-producing counties than Hertfordshire, and in the valley which runs between Watford and Berkhamsted, no fewer than nine growers have been affected by floods. One of the biggest of these is Mr. H. G. Sansom, of Cassio Bridge, from whose sixteen acres of "beds" goes out more water-cress than any other grower in the county produces.

His "beds," extending over sixteen acres, stretch from here to Uxbridge, a very big deposit being at West Hyde. The floods came, sweeping the tender cress from its "beds," and scattered it here, there and everywhere. In the corresponding week last year his output was four tons. This week there is nothing, and there will not be anything for a month.

The enormous demand which Mr. Sansom has to meet each year is illustrated by the fact that in a single week in a normal year, his output has reached twelve tons, which means 600 baskets. What Watford eats is practically negligible compared with Mr. Sansom's total output. The most he has ever had to supply in Watford is less than a ton, 40 baskets to be exact.

Whatever the price, the demand will probably be as strong as ever, for thousands of people look upon it as nature's own medicine. It holds a high reputation in the treatment of many kinds of diseases, such as consumption, gout, rheumatism, anaemia and constipation.

WHP January, 1928

Watford's £20,000 Library

On Saturday morning, Mr. F. J. B. Hemming, Chairman of the Watford Public Library Committee, laid the foundation stone of the new building, to cost, including the ground, about £20,000. The location is excellent—a site in Hempstead-road, not far from the Junction and the town's four main roads.

In August, 1911, the late Dr. Andrew Carnegie offered a grant of £4,750. In 1920, Mr. S. H. Timms gave a site, "Garfield House," in King Street, but this proving unsuitable was sold and the proceeds allocated towards the cost of the new site. Since the approval of the plans, the Carnegie United Kingdom Trust, which continues the work instituted by the late Dr. Carnegie, ten per cent. has been added to the original offer. The

Library Committee have also received the sums of £500 and £250 respectively as the result of a diversion of footpaths on the Munden and Bradshaw estates in 1919.

In this respect, thanks are due to the Hon. A. H. Holland Hibbert, J.P., D.L., and the Bradshaw Trustees, also to Mr. T. Moffet, a former Chairman of the Library Committee, who secured these gifts for the town, when acting on behalf of the Watford Fieldpath Association.

WHP March, 1928

Penfold—a new Industry

Chain-link fencing was started by the Germans; and works started in Belgium. The business of three factories is to be transferred to Watford where a new factory by the name of Penfold Ltd. is being prepared upon the Balmoral Road site. The machinery is being sent by rail direct to the site and as many as 100 local men will be found employment and training given; the new chain link fencing is expected to be in much demand.

WHP March, 1928

Historic Change at Watford

ALL WATFORD seemed to meet in the Market Place on Saturday, with the result that the crush on the narrow roadway and pavement was greater than ever.

Even those who, as a rule, try to wriggle out of the merry-go-round of cars, 'buses, prams and packs of people as quickly as they can, lingered on to have a last look at the busy scene.

The stream of vehicles through the High-street was like a tidal wave which threatened to sweep everything in its wake. How it is that more accidents have not occurred, goodness only knows!

A "Post" reporter who looked round the market found Mr. Henry W. Butler, popularly known as "Curly," selling fish just as he did nearly 30 years ago.

Mr. Butler's rent for his stall used to be fourpence. On Saturday it was 5s. Some, he said, paid as much as 30s. The price of his fish now is three times as much as it was 27 years ago. As a comparison of costs, he said that he pays as much for empties now as he used to pay for his fish.

WHP September, 1928

Cassiobury House has by now been empty for some years and the contents long gone. The valuable timber is sold, the bricks are carefully sorted; many went to the rebuilding of Monmouth House in the upper High Street as shops. There is still part left–of the stables, now Temple Close.

22nd September 1928 was the last day of the street market; this is a little earlier, the parade of shops next the Green Man is half built and there is vacant space between them and the Compasses for the remaining. This is not a busy moment and the open road is the width of the High Street for two-way traffic alongside the Market Place.

Opening the New Market

The Mayor, declaring the Market open, said that the opening coincided with the closing down of the old market across the road which had been in existence for 800 years. Watford at that time must have been a very small town, for only eighty years the population at that time was only five thousand. There was then practically only one street. Watford had developed and developed very rapidly since that time, especially so during the last decade when its development was such that the High-street was a great menace to pedestrians on market days.

Negotiations were opened with a view to the purchase of the market rights. A successful deal was accomplished about three years ago, thanks to the energy of Councillor F. Williams, then Chairman of the Market Sub-Committee of the Corporation. The result was that although they spent something like £20,000 for the purchase of the market rights, they were satisfied and able to go forward with a scheme for the removal of the market from High-street. The new market site and its equipment had cost £9,500, and all would agree that the eyesore of the slums of Red Lion-yard and Chequers-yard was a disgrace

and was better removed.

The new market occupied an area of 1,955 square yards. There were 187 covered stalls, including five for meat, eight for fish, and 174 general stalls. That meant an increase of 57 stalls and 400 feet frontage over the old market. The rents, including lighting, would be reasonable, compared with those of other towns.

At the conclusion of his speech, the Mayor was presented with a handsome basket of fruit, including a pineapple, grapes, oranges, and apples, by Mr. "Jimmy" Marsh, one of the largest stall-holders.

WO September, 1928

Loss of Banknotes

Announced that the Bank of England will in future undertake the printing of treasury notes, with the consequence that Messrs. Waterlows, of Milton Street, who have printed them since their introduction will lose a considerable amount of business. It is stated that several hundred men, women and boys will be affected. Questions were asked in Parliament but to no avail.

WHP March, 1928

Wesleyan (Methodist) Church

at the corner of Harebreaks and St. Albans Road, was officially opened by Mrs. Hunt, 22nd October, 1928. The new church and school cost £12,500. At the start of the opening ceremony it was announced that £2,000 was still owing; a collection raised £550 and later in the evening it was announced that the remainder was promised and the church free from debt.

Municipal Buildings

The Royal Institute of British Architects nominated Mr. E. Vincent Harris as assessor in the Competition for Best Designs. [With reference to the probability of building a new Town Hall].

New Library Opened

WATFORD'S new Public Library in Hempstead-road, the culmination of 17 years of effort, and erected at a cost of about £20,000, was formally opened yesterday by Sir Fredrick G. Kenyon, G.B.E., K.C.B., Director and Principal Librarian British Museum. In every way the town has secured a splendid home for its Library. Lieut.-Col. J. M. Mitchell, O.B.E., MC., M.A., Secretary of the Carnegie United Kingdom Trust (which contributed a grant of over £5,000 towards the cost), paid this high compliment "You have, on the whole, the best Library of its size in Britain."

WHP December, 1928

Top: *Jimmy Marsh presents the gift basket of fruit to the Mayor, Alderman Thomas Rushton.*

Left: *The group of statuary designed by Mrs Mary Bromet of which she said, in 1927, that she conceived them during the war, " I felt," she said, "that when a boy 'went out' he was either killed or maimed or to come home victorious. It was not for me to go to the Front and see our tin-hatted men in the toil and grime of the trenches. For most people at home it was the spirit of War they felt—the agony of the bereaved; the left-hand figure is dedicated to the dear ones who never returned. The right-hand figure is dedicated to all those who were maimed, especially the blind—for I have depicted him blind and groping. The middle one expresses Victory—he is waving his hand, shouting, 'We have won, it is over'". The Memorial was unveiled by the Earl of Clarendon in July 1928 and, after 1970's road widening, is in the Library Precinct.*
See pages 380/381.

The War Memorial is Dedicated; and the 'new' Market meets with complaints . . .

Memorial to War Heroes

At a ceremony noteworthy for its simplicity and the reverence of the large audience, the Memorial Cross, erected in Watford Cemetery under the instructions of the Imperial War Graves Commission, was unveiled and dedicated on Sunday afternoon. This Cross, which is 12 feet high, has attached a sword in bronze. On the base of the cross is an inscription, which reads:

"*This Cross of Sacrifice is one in design and intention with those which have been set up in France and Belgium, and other places through out the world, where our dead of the Great War are laid to rest. Their names liveth for ever-more.*

"*Erected by the Imperial War Graves Commission in Watford Cemetery, to the memory of members of His Majesty's Forces who gave their lives for the country in the Great War,* 1914-18, and who lie buried in the Borough of Watford."

When the shroud had fallen from the memorial, the Mayor said he regarded it as an honour, as well as a privileged civic duty, to unveil that memorial. It must be very gratifying to them all to know that Watford had been selected as one of the parishes in which the Imperial War Graves Commission had decided to erect a stone in memory, not only of those who had fallen in battle, but also to the memory of those who during or since the period of Great War had lost their lives through illness, due to injuries or wounds.

With marked significance to all assembled, but especially to men present who had gone "through the dust of conflict and through battle flame," there burst forth the martial notes of "The Last Post," sounded on the bugle by ex-Trumpeter S. J. Simmons who, after the completion of two minutes of silence, given up to the remembrance of those who made the great sacrifice, and solemn thoughts devoted to personal examination and the plea for peace, played "The Reveille."

The concluding prayer was said by the Vicar of Watford, who also pronounced the Benediction. At the close of the service all present joined in the singing of a verse of the "National Anthem."

WHP February, 1929

[*A book, 'In Memory', and containing the names of the war dead, was for many years exhibited in the Public Library in Queens Road, with a page turned each day.*]

Watford Market

Sir,—The Israelites of old were glad to be led out of Egypt, but as soon as something failed to please them they turned round on their leaders and said: "Why were we brought out of Egypt, let us get back there at once;" and recent letters to your paper show once more how difficult it is to please everybody, and how easy it is to criticise adversely. The old market was a constant source of complaint, but two correspondents have recently held up the new market to scorn, and have loudly cried: "Let us return to our old market!"

As far as I am concerned, and many Watford people agree with me, I am sure that the new market is a great deal better than the old one, though I do not say that there is not still room for improvement.

A market must be central, and where else was there a site in the centre of the town? The entrances may be narrow, but would the objector to them undertake to prevail on Messrs. Cawdell, Messrs. Kingham, or the Bank to remove part of their premises to permit of the enlargement of the market entrances?

The rain does drip down your neck, but so it did in the old market, and when a biting wind whistles down the high-street, the new

Above: At the Drill Hall in Clarendon Road the Watford Branch of the British Legion was presented with its standard by Lord Clarendon. After receiving the banner the procession marched to the Parish Church for a Service of Dedication; the Mayor and Town Clerk have just passed and representatives of other local Legion branches, with their banners, are following.
WO, March 1929

Left: The Memorial in Watford Cemetary, Vicarage Road, photographed April 2003.

White lines to be put down at dangerous corners ...

somewhat sheltered market is infinitely preferable to the old, entirely unsheltered one.

Moreover, a scheme is on hand for covering in the market entirely.

Unless you have a habit of walking in the road, the danger to pedestrians from cars backing out of the old market place is very slight, and the people who park their cars there have enough thought, if only for their own property, to see that there is no danger of collision with other vehicles.

The stalls in the new market are carefully arranged, and the actual tables are much cleaner and more hygienic than those in the old market.

The new market is not perfect, but it is a great improvement on the old one, which was dirty, dangerous, and a disgrace to Watford.

Yours etc. E. M. BRIDGER.
WHP February 1929

By-Pass Ice Rink

With sudden ice, as frost followed rain upon the By-Pass approach to Hunton Bridge, any driver brave enough to take the risk had more sport than expected A number of nasty accidents occurred, fortunately without serious injury; cars, buses and lorries all came to grief.
WHP February, 1929

Watford Motor Traffic

After many months of cogitation, the Watford Town Council have decided to put down white lines at dangerous corners in the Borough.

The first spot to be treated is the junction of Harwoods-road and Rickmansworth-road, where many accidents, some of a serious nature, have occurred. A great deal of comment has been caused by the fact that no sooner was the market cleared away from High-street than the available space was utilised as a parking-place.

Whatever objections may be taken to this practice, either by the shopkeepers whose entrances are affected or by the public who are inconvenienced, it appears that at present neither the police nor the Council can take action, unless obstruction, in a legal sense, can be proved, nor is it possible to collect any tolls.
WO March, 1929

The Market

THE MANY complaints that have been made about Watford's new Market are apparently producing results.

Among recommendations adopted at Tuesday's meeting of the Council was a proposal to borrow £4,200 for roofing the Market

The figures for the new Market make very good reading, from April 1st to June 25th this year, the receipts were £858 14s. 3d., compared with £481 1s. 3d. in the same period last year.
WHP May, 1929

Speed Limits

Speed limit on public highway must not exceed 20 m.p.h, Within any limits or place where speed limits have been granted by the Local Government Board or the Ministry of Transport the maximum speed is indicated in figures on the sign.

Liable on summary conviction, first offence, fine not exceeding £10; second offence, fine not exceeding £20; subsequent offence, fine not exceeding £50.

A person shall not be convicted for exceeding the speed limit merely on the opinion of one person as to rate of speed. He must be warned of the intended prosecution not exceeding twenty-one days after the offence.

Penalties.

Persons guilty of offences under the Motor Car Act, 1903, for which no special penalty is provided are liable for the first offence to

Above: *Parking in the Market Place at the corner of Market Street.*

Right: *Newsprint does not usually last very long; this is a copy of the original, very discoloured, 75-year-old cutting. "The line of the suggested Colne Valley road, mentioned in the Hertfordshire Regional Planning Report. It is stated that by improving the southern end of the High Street near Watford Bridge, particularly at the corner near the railway arches, and the construction of a new road leaving the High Street slightly north of this point, leading under the Five Arches alongside the Colne, a valuable connection will be provided with the Watford By-Pass south of Aldenham."WO 1928.*
(Plans were shown for the second time in 1987, and the road linked the By-Pass to Lower High Street and the Ring Road and Harlequin, by July 1993.)

Rubber hose to be made at Delectaland.   'A Big Man'; Alderman Thorpe dies . . .

a fine not exceeding £20; subsequent offence, fine not exceeding £50 or imprisonment not exceeding three months.

Taxation.
R.A.C. RATING OF MOTOR CARS.

The Rated Power of cars is determined as follows

(a) For Petrol Cars driven directly or indirectly by Internal Combustion Engines.—The rated horse-power of one cylinder of an engine is calculated as follows:—The internal diameter of the cylinder measured in inches is multiplied by itself (i.e., squared), and the product divided by 2·5. If the diameter is in millimetres, the figure 1613 is used instead of 2·5.

For engines with more than one cylinder, the rated horse-power of one cylinder, calculated as above, is multiplied by the number of cylinders of the engine.

(b) For Steam Cars.—The same calculation is carried out, with the exception that the rating is calculated for each cylinder separately when they are of different diameters, and the products added together, the result being the rating of the whole engine. In the case of double-acting engines this result is multiplied by two.

(c) Two-stroke and Two-piston per Cylinder Engines.—The ratings of these are calculated as under (a).

The duty payable on a car or cycle is based upon the horse-power of the vehicle, and is at the rate of £1 for each unit or part of a unit of horse-power. Any fraction over .1 is calculated as a unit.

Horse-Power.

Horse-power for the purpose of taxation is calculated in the same manner as for the R.A.C. Rating .

Diameter of cylinders in mm.	CORRESPONDING R.A.C. RATINGS for 1, 2, 3, 4, or 6-cyl. Engines.				
	6-cyl.	4-cyl.	3-cyl.	2-cyl.	1-cyl.
55	11·3	7·5	5·6	3·8	1·88
56	11·7	7·8	5·8	3·9	1·94
57	12·0	8·0	6·0	4·0	2·0
58	12·5	8·3	6·3	4·2	2·0
59	12·9	8·6	6·5	4·3	2·16
60	13·4	8·9	6·7	4·5	2·23
61	13·8	9·2	6·9	4·6	2·30
62	14·3	9·5	7·1	4·8	2·38
63	14·8	9·8	7·4	4·9	2·46
64	15·2	10·2	7·6	5·0	2·54
65	15·7	10·4	7·8	5·2	2·61
66	16·2	10·8	8·1	5·4	2·70
67	16·7	11·1	8·3	5·6	2·78
68	17·2	11·5	8·6	5·7	2·87
69	17·7	11·8	8·8	5·9	2·95
70	18·2	12·1	9·1	6·0	3·04
71	18·7	12·5	9·4	6·2	3·12
72	19·3	12·8	9·6	6·4	3·21
73	19·8	13·2	9·9	6·5	3·30
74	20·3	13·6	10·2	6·8	3·39
75	20·9	13·96	10·5	6·98	3·49
76	21·5	14·3	10·7	7·2	3·58
77	22·0	14·7	11·0	7·3	3·67
78	22·6	15·0	11·3	7·5	3·77
79	23·2	15·5	11·6	7·7	3·87
80	23·8	15·9	11·9	7·9	3·97
81	24·4	16·3	12·2	8·1	4·07
82	25·0	16·7	12·5	8·3	4·17
83	25·6	17·0	12·8	8·5	4·27
84	26·2	17·5	13·1	8·7	4·37
85	26·9	17·9	13·4	8·96	4·48
86	27·5	18·3	13·7	9·2	4·58
87	28·1	18·8	14·0	9·4	4·69

Above: *The list goes up to 165mm, 67.5hp for 4cyls.*

American Firm Coming to Watford

The £350,000 factory which was built at Delectaland six years ago, and has never been used, was sold last week.

An American firm has bought it—the Electric Hose and Rubber Company. There will be work for hundreds. The factory may open in September. This is, undoubtedly, the biggest industrial development Watford has experienced for years. Messrs. W. S. Weller and Son, the well-known local firm of auctioneers and estate agents, had the distinction of conducting the deal on behalf of Delecta, Ltd.

The story of the deal affecting the Watford factory has a strong flavour of American hustle about it. Only two hours before, Mr. Green had been talking on the 'phone to Mr. C. D. Garretson, of Delaware, U.S.A., who authorised him to make the purchase. They were hoping, he said, to open in September, but the process of converting the factory and installing machinery was being put in hand almost at once.

"As far as possible," he said, "the purchasers are going to use English machinery and fittings, but certain things will have to come from America." This great North Watford factory, has been a source of mystery to local people. For six years the massive pile of brick,

There is one thing in particular about the New Ford which no owner can grumble at, and that is the miles it does to the gallon — 30 m.p.g.

The NEW FORD TOURER

Strong as steel, because made of steel. Three speeds, four-wheel brakes, 14.9 engine, complete equipment (including bumpers). £170 at works, or delivered for first payment of

Left and above: *The Ford cars advertised have 77.5mm bore, rating 14.9hp and thus £15 Road Fund Tax. Later, to obtain more power with small cylinder bores (lower tax), the stroke length was increased leading to inefficient engines when compared with foreign engines having short stroke/larger bores. Eventually, decades later, the 'cubic capacity' rating was adopted.*

steel and concrete has remained silent. It is the biggest structure for miles around, a six-storey affair with a floor space of 158,000 square feet.

Mr. C. D. Garretson is the President of the Electric Hose and Rubber Company and was over here in March. He was impressed by the progressive atmosphere of the town of Watford. The class of workers appealed to him, as did the type of houses which were being erected in North Watford.

The Electric Hose and Rubber Company specialise in the production of braided hose, which they originated 30 years ago. There is a big market for this hose, which is rapidly becoming the understood thing in shipping and coal-mining, where it is used for the conveyance of air, steam and water.

The Colonies are big buyers, and they will be supplied from the Watford factory. That will mean a big saving to the company, for there is a heavier duty on American goods taken into British Colonies than there is on goods sent from this country.

WHP May, 1929

Watford as a Training Centre

The Ministry of Labour have acquired the large single storey building opposite Parkgate road School, which Delecta Ltd. have used for offices, printing and box factory, etc.

This will be converted into a training centre for 400 unemployed men, who will be drawn mostly from the distressed mining areas.

Among the trades which will be taught at Watford are building in its various phases; furniture making, upholstering, and cabinet making; motor manufacture work, body painting, etc.

WHP May, 1929

Death of Alderman R. A. Thorpe

WE regret to record that Alderman Ralph Alfred Thorpe died on Sunday at his home, "Lindum," Park-road, Watford. He leaves as an example to those who follow him in public service, a record remarkable alike for its quantity and quality. He was an Alderman of both the Hertfordshire County Council and Watford Town Council, a Freeman of Watford; a Justice of the Peace for Hertfordshire; on six occasions he was elected Chairman of the Watford Town Council; he was Deputy Charter Mayor and twice Mayor of Watford.

Fifty years hence there will have grown up generations to whom Watford's rulers in the earlier part of the twentieth century will be scarcely known, even by name.

Just occasionally, there will be people who, inspecting the handsome municipal buildings of those days, will, on reaching the Council Chamber, pause to read the names, inscribed in gold on oak boards, of the ladies and gentlemen who, through the long succession of years, have presided over the authorities responsible for administering the town's municipal affairs.

They will see the name of Ralph Alfred Thorpe occurring six times as Mayor of Watford.

The frequent recurrence of that name will cause this comment to flash to mind: "He was a big man!" The people in those far-on days will be using that expression to describe his high importance in the affairs of the town, but actually, though unconsciously, they will also be crystallising into a sentence the life and character of Alderman Thorpe.

He was a big man.

That can most truly be said of Alderman Thorpe. Could any man wish for a finer epitaph?

WHP June, 1929

Death of Mr. W. T. Coles

We regret to record the death, which occurred this (Friday) morning, at his residence, the Shrubbery, High-street, Watford, of Mr. W. T. Coles, who had reached the great age of 92 years. For over fifty years Mr. Coles had taken a prominent part in the public life of Watford.

In 1874 he was elected a member of the Board of Guardians, and was Chairman from 1895 to 1900. He was made a Justice of the Peace in 1894. He was a member of the old Local Board, and in 1896 was appointed Chairman of the Urban District Council, succeeding Mr. E. J. Slinn, the first Chairman. He was a director of the Watford Gas Company. Mrs. A. F. Broad, a member of the Watford Corporation, is a daughter of Mr. Coles.

WO June, 1929

Watford's New Cinema

Watford's magnificent new cinema, The Plaza, was opened on Monday by the Mayor of Watford (Alderman F. J. B. Hemming). He was accompanied by the Acting Deputy Mayoress, Mrs. M. Pearman, the Vicar of Watford (the Rev. Henry Edwards) and members and officials of the Corporation.

WHP May, 1929

The New Register

Yesterday, the new list of Parliamentary Voters came into operation. For the Watford Division the figures are:—

MEN	25,719
WOMEN	30,303
Total	56,022

Thus, women have a majority of 4,584.

WHP May, 1929

Baths at Watford?

Sir,—One can hardly expect your columns this week to be overcrowded with congratulations to the sub-committee which has been dealing with the question of supplying baths for the convenience of Watford's bathless, on their speed. That the sub-committee have awakened and presented a report must have really caused the main committee to have a severe shock. (How many of them have advocated 'baths' in their Election Addresses for many years?)

Does the sub-committee think that 24 baths, twelve for each sex, is enough? Their estimate of the number of people who would

THE PLAZA
WATFORD.

PROGRAMME *for* MAY.

Above: *The Central Hall in King Street 1926 before its conversion in 1929 to talkies and name change to the 'Regal.'*

Right: *A pre-opening illustration of the new Plaza, by the Pond, (later renamed Odeon.)*

Two Bridges

The Greyhound

The Fox

The Hare

The Rising Sun and Holly Bush

the Load of Hay

patronise public baths is amazing, considering the number of houses without that convenience has not appreciably diminished. It is to be hoped that the total number of slipper baths will be nearer 70 than 24; if only 24 is to be the number, how can the Mayor, if he publicly opens the building, ask the Corporation to have "one" with him if there are not enough to go round?

Yours etc.,
W. J. DAVIES

WHP, July 1929

•*On most important issues the local papers were in accord, but of 'Baths' the West Herts Post was definitely anti-. Open air baths were OK; covered baths a waste of money they labelled 'Squandermania'. This stance helped delay for years the building of the Public Baths.*

Council Houses in Eastbury Road

Sir,—I read, with some alarm, in your report of the Watford Borough Council meeting, that certain residents in the Eastbury-road locality have signed a petition, requesting the Council to reconsider their decision to erect 130 houses on a site abutting on Eastbury-road, and that other house owners in the district object to the Council's plans. I cannot help feeling how very selfish these people are, to come forward at this juncture and try to delay, and if possible prevent, the erection of only 130 new houses, especially in view of the urgent need for houses in the town. The present official waiting list is, I am told, over 900 families.

In your issue of 12th December, I read a heartbreaking case of a man, wife and four children living in one room in Gladstone-road, and I feel sure that no father or mother living in Woodways, etc., would like to live under those conditions. Judge Crawford gave this family

instructions to quit on 18th January, last Saturday, but where are they to go? Where is there a house to let within their means? Who wants a lodger with a wife and four children? These are the sort of cases the Council are trying to help. As the few houses they are building will only accommodate one tenth of the need in the town, they will, therefore, only be able to help the most necessitous cases.

If the petitioners only knew of the terrible overcrowding that exists in Watford, I feel sure they would never have signed such a petition. I hope the Council will proceed with the scheme as soon as possible, and bring a little happiness to 130 families, who at present have no home of their own to live in, and are anxiously waiting for one.

Yours etc.,
ARTHUR BENNETT.

WHP, January 1930

Gladstone Road

. . . the houses in Gladstone Road were originally quite grand; three storeys and basement. The basement leads to the garden backing onto th railway line. Many houses held three or four families; often a family of four or five in the base-

ment, and goodness knows how many in the rest of the house.

The main recollection is of the flickering gas lamps—the mantles didn't seem to last long or perhaps there weren't enough pennies to feed the meter, and in the winter, the problem of keeping warm. Thin threadbare blankets with layers of brown paper in between to aid warmth, which rustled and crackled; perhaps the noise made one feel warmer.

The tin kettles never lasted long, just something like the crying of the baby to distract attention long enough far the kettle to boil dry. Until a pot mender could be bought from Woolworths or Roger and Gowletts the hole would have to stay and a saucepan used in its stead. Nowadays, many of the houses are split into self-contained flats with all modern services.

Recollection 1987

A Word With Mr. F. C. Jarvis

IN my judgment, one witness for the opposition did not help their case. He was Mr. F. C. Jarvis of Oxhey-road, who, when the Inspector pointed out to him that his front door is a quarter of a mile away from the Council's estate, said: "Yes. But a housing estate means children, and they have a capacity for not liking their own roads."

The mentality behind such an observation in this twentieth century is amazing. I am not going to try to follow the gymnastics of Mr. Jarvis's mind, it will suffice if I say he has set me wondering whether, in the great hereafter, he hopes to dwell in a little heaven all on his own, with a notice outside: "Children must not pass this way."

It was not surprising that women at the back of the room applauded when the Town Clerk commented, "You don't object to sewage farms, but you object to housing estates and you object to children."

WHP, March 1930

[A sewage treatment works was at that time situated off Eastbury Road and opposite the proposed building site.]

Above: *Salmon's on the corner of Meeting Alley.*

Left: *Market Street, Camfield's next to the cattle market entrance. Postered wall is next to the small Post Office (see next page, the Compasses), later the Post Office site. The bus queue rails 'queue here for Garston, St Albans, etc' were introduced in June 1926 and removed one month later. At the 'Palace', Will Hay is playing.*

Queens Arms

Three Tuns

The Woodman

Three Crowns

The Dog

The Compasses

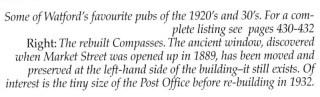

Some of Watford's favourite pubs of the 1920's and 30's. For a complete listing see pages 430-432

Right: *The rebuilt Compasses. The ancient window, discovered when Market Street was opened up in 1889, has been moved and preserved at the left-hand side of the building–it still exists. Of interest is the tiny size of the Post Office before re-building in 1932.*

The Geordies and the Taffies . . .

In the wake of the false boom years after the 1914-1918 war followed an economic depression on a scale the world had not previously experienced. As financial systems collapsed and America's Wall Street crashed, fortunes were lost as banks and businesses failed. Britain did not escape the depression although the light industry of Watford suffered far less than the heavy industries of the North East and South Wales After the General Strike of 1926 the unemployment level rose until, in 1931, it reached a figure of two million, at which level it stayed for a number of years.

(When comparing unemployment figures it must be remembered that today's insured workers include a great many wives, mothers and partners but that the workers of 1931 were principally male. Husbands and sons were then looked on as the breadwinners of the family— "a woman's place was in the home." The two million unemployed of 1931 represented approximately 20% of the country's workforce, the three million of 1986 represented about 8%.)

In 1931 unemployment benefit was cut by 10% and a 'means test' introduced for the long-term unemployed. Literally, any casual earnings, even a few shillings, were required to be declared and were deducted from the benefit received. Local relieving offices at Shrodell's (Union Workhouse), Vicarage Road, and at No. 1 Glencoe Road, Bushey, dispensed (after the hated 'means test') weekly meal tickets which were redeemable at local grocers and butchers such as Melia's on the corner of Carey Place, Lipton's and the Home and Colonial.

The high rate of unemployment meant that where a job became available it would often be filled by cheap labour, ("if you don't want the job there's others who do"). Consequently, a man's wage for a 48 or 50 hour week's labouring could be no more than 35 or 40 shillings.

In the early and mid 1930's many men would travel from the north of England, or walk from South Wales to seek work or attend the North Watford Government Training Centre in Southwold Road. The courses covered various aspects of manufacturing techniques, first and foremost that of engineering where the use of hand tools was applied to metal work. Drilling, milling and turning were included as was a working knowledge of micrometers and vernier gauges. The Training Centre carried out sterling work well into WWII and substantially aided the production of much-needed armaments. But back in 1930 that some of these men found jobs locally would cause annoyance among Watford men who had been unsuccessful, and the taunt of "Taffy go home" may have caused more than one local Welshman to cultivate a tactful change of accent.

Rowdy Street Scenes in Watford

A feud, which has already resulted in a certain amount of conflict between parties of Watford youths and Welshmen who are at the Ministry of Labour's Training Centre at Callowland, has caused a great deal of excitement in the town during the last few days, and the police have had to interfere.

Last night, there was a wild scene in the High street.

Razors and lengths of lead piping were flourished, and there were several free fights.

The police, who had been keeping close watch on the Watford party during the evening, acted promptly. They arrested two Watford youths and took them to King-street Police Station.

Although there have been exaggerated reports of casualties and the drafting in of extra police, actually only one injury has been reported, and the Watford police were able to quell the disturbance without assistance.

One of the leaders of the Watford youths told a "Post" reporter last night that the trouble started on Saturday evening, when the Welshmen set upon a Watford youth and hurt him. Since then, the Watford youths had formed themselves together and hunted the Welshmen down. On Sunday evening, he continued, two of the Welshmen were ducked in the pond in High-street.

A remark of another youth suggested that employment questions were connected with the trouble, for he said: "When the Welshmen go we shall get work."

WHP, January 1930

"The Parade," High-street

BUILDING development at the Pond end of High-street has led to much confusion over numbers.

The outcome is that the Town Council have instructed the Borough Surveyor to re-number the section of High-street from the Pond cross roads to Clarendon Corner with odd numbers.

The Council have also decided to call that section "The Parade."

WHP, February 1930

The Wheatsheaf Widening

The decision of Watford Town Council on Wednesday to carry out a widening scheme in Lower High-street, opposite the Wheatsheaf Inn, will effect a much needed highway improvement The opportunity arose through the Cannon Brewery Company, owners of this ancient hostelry, resolving to demolish the present building, and erect a new public-house on land at the rear, set well back from the new road. At this point the road has only a width of 32ft, and through this narrow thoroughfare an ever-increasing volume of traffic is poured from the roads which converge at Bushey Arches.

The Corporation Highways Committee, on learning of the contemplated re-building, approached the Brewery Company, and the negotiations have resulted in an agreement, under which the Company will make a gift of the land necessary for the road improvement conditional on the Corporation constructing a loop draw-up to the new inn.

Negotiations have been entered into with the adjoining owners and land acquired so that the street will be widened for a distance of 300 yards from the river bridge to Eastbury-road.

At the Government Training Centre a class is here learning the techniques of filing metal square and true.

The Wheatsheaf to be rebuilt . . . the Almshouses to go . . .

At the point opposite the new Wheatsheaf the road will have a width of 60ft. Here the present road dips, as the inn itself is low-lying, and it is proposed to raise the surface at this position.

The old Wheatsheaf has stood for well over 200 years, and is a link with the earlier Watford in the more leisurely age of the toll-gate and the pack-horse, before the coming of the trains and motorcars. The new building will be in modern style, and the work of construction is just commencing, but the road improvement cannot be effected until the business is removed and the old inn demolished.

WO April, 1930

The old Wheatsheaf was demolished in 1930/31 and the one shown alongside built. This was in turn demolished in 1995.

No exit

Another point was the proper planning of roads. Was any place so difficult to get out of as High-street, Watford? From the "Wheatsheaf" to King-street there was only one outlet—Farthing-lane. He was not throwing stones—he was a Watford man and loved the town. The poverty of concept in estate development was one of the most fruitful causes of depression.

A member said that when he came to Watford 7½ years ago he wondered whether there was any town planning. He saw a row of shops pushed up in front of the Parish Church, and learned that years ago the Council had an opportunity to buy them at a mere song.

WO, August 1930

The Ministry and the 'Buses

The Ministry of Transport have forwarded to the Watford Town Council their decision on the recent 'bus appeal. Three local proprietors of 'buses were refused a renewal of licences by the Council on the ground that certain conditions had not been observed. The proprietors took their case to the Ministry, who appointed an Inspector to hold an Inquiry. The proceedings extended over five days, and the upshot is that the licences are granted on condition that the services in question do not cover more of High street than the section between the cross roads and Clarendon-road.

The terminus is at Watford Junction. In their endeavour to restrict High-street traffic the Council may therefore be said to have gained their end. It was unreasonable, in the first place, to insist that services on the Hempstead-road route should carry their passengers no farther than the cross roads, and the decision of the Ministry seems a sensible compromise.

The extraordinary part of the whole business is that this common-sense solution was not reached in the discussions between the Council and the proprietors. We recognise fully that the Council has to assert their authority as far as 'bus traffic is concerned, and we appreciate the difficulties arising from uncertainty as to the extent of their powers. But to put the matter quite bluntly, they have only themselves to blame for the muddle which arose over licences.

At one time they had the proprietors working to agreed time-tables, and on a system of interchanging return tickets, but they permitted trouble which led to this agreement being

torn up. They have complained, probably with good cause, that they could get no guidance from the Ministry, but they have never attempted to take a strong line on their own initiative or manifested any real determination to get their own way.

Whether the position will be improved as the result of the recent Inquiry remains to be seen.

If the Council will only lay down certain lines on which they intend to act in future and adhere to them instead of losing themselves, as they have done in the past, in a maze of petty details, the situation may eventually be eased. The Council may feel some satisfaction over the Ministry's decision on the appeals, but regarding the subject as a whole there is certainly nothing upon which they can plume themselves.

WO April, 1930

By The Way . . .

To the memory of Alderman R. A. Thorpe, Deputy Charter Mayor and for two years Mayor of Watford, and his services for many years as Churchwarden of Christ Church, the parish propose to erect a Thorpe Memorial Hall in St Albans-road.

WO July, 1930

The Plight Of Eight Old Ladies

The eight old ladies who occupy the Essex Almshouses behind Watford Parish Church are wondering what is going to happen to them.

Their little houses are on the market, and they are in danger of being cast adrift on the world, with a contribution from the proceeds of the sale, to fend for themselves.

THE ESSEX ALMSHOUSES, THE OLDEST INHABITED DWELLINGS IN THE TOWN. BUILT 1580.

The fate of the Almshouses has become the topic of the town, consequent upon the keen debate which raged in the Council Chamber last week.

At that meeting, the proposition was made that the Corporation should consider the possibility of the purchase of the site for its use as a car park.

WHP, June 1930

The Almshouses.

The future of the almshouses in Church-street is still uncertain. The Town Council have decided to buy them, but whether they will be preserved or demolished is a matter left for further consideration. Whatever the outcome, the old ladies who live in this tumble-down row of cottages must be safeguarded. But the fate of the actual buildings should depend not on sentimentality as regards the past but on business reasoning and consideration for the future.

From what Alderman T. R. Clark said at Tuesday's meeting of the Council, namely that to renovate the property would entail probably a sum of £4,000, such a course certainly would not be sound business. We have come to the conclusion that as soon as some scheme has been evolved for the housing of the tenants, the almshouses should be demolished. They may be one of the last links with old Watford, but there surely is nothing very romantic or even picturesque about them. What is the proud Watfordian supposed to do— take a visitor to Church-street, point dramatically at the almshouses and say: "Old ladies have lived here for centuries?"

The whole position would be different if there were some historical link. But one might just as well take a visitor to a cornfield and say "This is one of our proudest heritages; corn has grown here for the last three hundred years".

WHP, October 1930

The Almshouses were founded in the 16th century, 1580, and, after enlargements of the cemetery in 1772 were substantially rebuilt as they stand today; the four original chimney stacks were embodied in the reconstruction.

Life carried on smoothly for the succession of inhabitants until disaster threatened in 1930 when Watford Council proposed to demolish them and purchase the land to use as a car park. The outcry caused reverberations which lasted for a year or so until a few volunteers offered £100 for each cottage for modernisation. When the total sum was almost raised the Council then expressed that they were no longer interested in the site; the almshouses were safe.

Danger was averted only to resurface in the 1970s when the relief road dictated that parts of their gardens were needed. This time sympathetic views held sway and further cottages were built behind the originals. The eight original Almshouses, whose doors faced onto the road, were again renovated; the 'front' doors being closed as 'false' doors and access made safer onto the gardens behind.

The Right Type Of Houses

A housing scheme in the Eastbury-road locality is reaching a definite state. There will be 80 houses for letting, and all are to be non-parlour, which means that the workers in the lesser-paid trades will stand a better chance of meeting the rent of a Council house without sub-letting.

WHP July, 1930

•*The Eastbury Road housing scheme was named 'Thorpe Crescent'*

PUBLIC MEETING

Essex Almshouses

A Meeting of townspeople will be held at THE LIBRARY, HEMPSTEAD ROAD, WATFORD, on THURSDAY, JULY 23RD, to protest against the threatened demolition of these Elizabethan buildings.

The Chair will be taken by

THE VICAR OF WATFORD, at 8.15 p.m.

The need for protest is urgent—the public is earnestly asked to attend.

WATFORD AMENITIES PRESERVATION SOCIETY. *President*—THE RT. HON. THE EARL OF CLARENDON. G.C.V.O.

Women's Idea of Ideal Homes

The 13 suggestions of the Ladies' Committee were as follows, the Housing Committee's decision being given in brackets:— A deep sink with a plug in every house. *(The Committee directed that deep sinks be provided.)* The copper placed near the sink to avoid the carrying of heavy baths and pails. *(This is always arranged where possible.)* The windows over the sink should all be made to open, thus allowing steam and cooking odours to escape more readily. *(The Committee recommended this window have push-out vent).* That gas cookers be placed away from draughts. *(This is done).* That larders, wherever possible, be built away from the sun, and one of the shelves to be of slate, for keeping food cool in the summer time. *(The Committee consider concrete shelves should continue to be provided).* As much cupboard room as possible, and a corner one in small bedrooms where space will not allow a square one. *(The Committee directed that provision be made for a corner hanging*

curtain and footboard). That doors be placed so that they open several inches away from the corners of the room, to avoid brushing the wall in passing. *(This is usual practice wherever space and planning permit).* A more liberal allowance of window than at present in Council houses, three or four casements at least, with two-thirds opening. *(The Committee agreed to a more liberal allowance of window, where desirable).* In the non-parlour houses, the kitchener should be convertible and economical and, if practicable, should heat the water for baths and so keep the house warm. The cost of gas for heating water by the gas copper method, as at present installed, works out at 6d. for a bath, and 9d. to a 1s. to do the weekly wash, which is altogether too heavy for small incomes. *(The Borough Surveyor will consider and report).* That the question of planting privet hedging in the back gardens be seriously considered. Lack of privacy is a source of much trouble in Council Housing Schemes. *(The Committee directed that Penfold or similar fencing be provided on the next scheme).* That a piece of wood fencing 6ft. high and at least 6ft. long be placed by the side of every house near the back door to prevent immediate overlooking. *(The Committee directed that where back doors face each other a fence be provided).* Wherever possible, lavatory and bathroom should be separate. *(The Committee state that this is done wherever practicable).*

WHP, November 1930

The Harrow By-Pass

Questions were invited, and Mr H G Howard mentioned the road across Batchworth Heath and said that the whole of the authorities concerned had petitioned the Ministry of Transport to preserve unspoilt this piece of country, but the Minister decided to proceed with the road across the Heath. He asked if that were a normal situation?

Mr Davidge, dealing with the broad issue of local authorities and the Ministry, cited the case of the Harrow and Watford by-pass which was to come from Harrow and terminate at Cassiobridge. The question was would it go further to Hunton Bridge?

At Hunton Bridge they came to the North Orbital Road, which would run at a radius of roughly 25 miles round London, coming from Tottenham through Chorleywood to Hunton Bridge, and going south by St Albans and Hatfield, and eventually to Tilbury Docks.

The question was should the road be continued along the Canal? (Several voices: *"No."*), He was not proposing to take a vote at that stage. *(Laughter.)* Or should it go via Rousebarn Lane: *("No")*.

The Harrow by-pass—to Hunton Bridge? . . . through Whippendell Woods?

Where ever it emerged on to the Rickmansworth-road some means would have to be found of continuing it. It was one at the most awkward conundrums, and, looking round on the representatives of the various local authorities, Mr. Davidge said, "Between you, you have to settle it." He thought it would be possible to find an ultimate road. "If it goes Rousebarn-lane, and Whippendell Woods there will be a row, and if it goes along the Canal there will be a row. It is a vital point, and may bring out hot feeling. You think it over, and, if necessary, I will come down again in a month or two's time, and we will thresh it out."

Councillor J. Evans asked why not an alternative route to Cassiobridge? The thing that had been troubling Watford Town Council for a long while was 'how to get through'. The only way he could see was to carry the road further west to the other side of the Canal higher up the Rickmansworth-road. It was originally suggested that the road should come through Cassiobury Park, but the Town Council blocked it, and they would block it going 'along the Canal or through Whippendell Woods. (Hear; hear.)

WO, October 1930

Sun Engraving

The photographic studios here remind one forcibly of a film-set erecting-room at Hollywood. They are immense. The customer's goods, for natural object photography, come into special storage rooms. And it does not seem to matter whether it is an iced birthday cake or an Axminster carpet, a dozen foulard ties or a tulip, when they have passed through these coldly staring, north-lit studios, wherein illusion cannot exist, their reproduction from an origin in fact to a facsimile in paper is not a matter of conjecture, but of cast-iron certainty.

The incontestable veracity of the camera is the basic element here. And the trained skill of the etcher paints the lily of the job thereafter. No man with a remnant of a conscience can say, when the colour printing of his object has come through in its finished state: "My original is better than this reproduction." The real and the printed copy placed side by side are as one.

The colour engraving of the "Sun" has always had a high reputation, but these new studios at Watford enable them to give their friends a better service in the future than, good as it has been, they have given in the past.

Colour-photogravure is one of their specialities, upon which they have spent many thousands of pounds on experimental and research work. It is the photogravure process before which the spirit of the average printer very naturally quails. Members of textile firms, requiring a high grade of smoothness on their cylinders for calico printing, have often expressed astonishment and envy, when visiting the works at Watford, at a photogravure cylinder surface of a perfection that they themselves can never attain.

The attitude of the makers and owners of their machine is always so amusing. In the presence of their "baby" they become quite inarticulate, or else volubly technical, which to a layman is much the same thing.

We stood in the shadow of a monstrous machine at Watford which is unique in all the world. An eight-colour photogravure machine, about sixty feet long, which does eight printings at once, and turns out seven to eight thousand complete coloured interiors of a magazine or a catalogue in an hour from the blank sheet which feeds into it at the centre.

"Where does it come from—Germany?" you shout in the uproar. "Certainly not'" they shout back. It appears to have been home-made—that is as to it specification: it was the result of the collective brains of the Watford men. Yet it is not all firms that give one this sense of stability in production, this rigorous cleaving to quality even when great quantity has to be handled.

One supposes it is that equilibrium in effort that only comes with continual self-testing through the years, and that a really great reputation can only be gained and kept by using the best methods and ignoring every other kind.

This, anyhow, seems The Way of the "Sun"—which has brought them to their present eminence.

Programme of the official visit of the Prime Minister (Ramsey Macdonald) to open the Trade Union Hall, Watford, 30 January, 1931.

High Street Improvements

An Order for the compulsory purchase of certain premises in connection with the Corporation street improvement schemes in Lower High-street and near the old Market-place, was the subject of a public inquiry held at the Municipal Offices on Monday morning by Mr. C. G. Mitchell, of the Ministry of Transport.

The problem of Watford High-street was very acute. Over 100 years ago, looking at a plan of Watford, one could see that the town simply consisted of one long street—the High-street.

Watford was a town or village on one of the main coaching routes to the North. About 100 years ago the London and Birmingham Railway was made, and the result was that traffic was shifted off the High-street to a considerable extent onto the railway, and the town spread out in a number of other directions. That being the case the problem of Watford High-street, which would no doubt have early become serious, slumbered for 100 years or so.

But after the war, owing to the advent—beneficent or otherwise—of motor traffic, the problem suddenly awoke, and awoke to some purpose. And the problem to-day was an exceedingly serious one. The Corporation

Church Street was an obvious danger with traffic entering and leaving the High Street. Though properties were bought, the lease of No. 98 was not available until 1939. Church Street was later blocked and some danger averted, but the narrow High Street remained an obstruction. Finally, c1959, the complete site came into the Council's possession. But instead of pulling the buildings down and opening both the High Street and the aspect of the church the road line was little changed, the pavement was widened and to partially meet the demand for shops the modernistic glass and concrete block was built. This in turn was pulled down in 1999 for the 2000 St Mary's Square.

from time to time as they were able had taken steps and had, so far as they could, taken time by the forelock, with the object of dealing with the very serious situation which had arisen.

The first step was after the war when the Corporation, with the help of the County Council, totally reconstructed the whole of High-street. The High-street up to that time had been what was called a water-bound road, and it was reconstructed with a foundation of nine inches of concrete, reinforced where necessary with steel mesh, and with a surface of asphalt.

Then, as various properties became vacant the Corporation took steps to acquire them. In 1923 the Corporation acquired No. 283, High-street Then in 1925 they bought Nos. 275 to 281, and also No. 289. All these properties were necessary in order to make an improvement which had been carried out so far as it had been possible, and for which the purchase of the properties Nos. 293a, 293b, and 293c, were necessary in order to complete that improvement to make it properly effective.

In 1926 the Corporation acquired a further property with a frontage of 20ft wide, extending to a considerable distance on the opposite side and immediately north of the proposed improvement, and a strip in front of Dalton House. In 1929 the Corporation, at considerable cost acquired, Nos. 96 and 98, High-street, and subsequently No. 100. These three properties with Nos. 92 and 94, which they were now seeking to acquire, formed the island site. In addition to the acquisition of these properties the Corporation in 1928 removed from High-street the old market, which had been held in the Market-place for many hundreds of years.

One of their main objects in acquiring the market rights and the new site was to relieve the High-street and make it more available for traffic.

In the spring of 1930 the Corporation faced a long and difficult inquiry before an Inspector of the Ministry of Transport, the result of which was that the Minister of Transport upheld the Corporation's view and imposed on the omnibus proprietors certain conditions which in effect prohibited them from running down High-street further than Clarendon-road corner.

Mr. W. W. Newman, Borough Engineer, confirmed the Town Clerk's statement, and said the traffic problem in High-street was getting worse. For the proposed improvement on the east side of the Lower High-street, just above the bridge, he considered that the acquisition of the properties mentioned was necessary.

The improvement was necessary because on one side of the road was the National omnibus garage and on the other side the entrance to the Gas Works. The road opposite Mr. Frost's premises was only 26ft. in width, and would not accommodate four moving vehicles.

Regarding Nos. 92, 94, 94a and 94b, High street, the acquisition of the properties was necessary in order to open up Church-street and to complete the Market-place improvement. This was the narrowest part of the High-street, and the worst spot for traffic.

Mr. Weaver: I take it that one of your objects is to enable traffic to come from Church-street into High-street?

Mr. Newman: It will allow that, but it is more advantage to High-street itself.

It would increase traffic into an already narrow street?—It would increase the number.

Where would that traffic go to?— Vicarage Road, I should think.

Is there not enough service at present down Whippendell-road and Market-street?— Market street is pretty congested.

And then you have King-street, an artery for traffic to come into High-street from the same direction?—Yes.

And the width of the High-street where King street joins is no wider that the width at the island site?—I cannot say from memory. It is

certainly more than 34ft. 5in.

The Town Clerk went on to say that Mr. Wilson seemed to be of the opinion that it was not worth while obtaining the Order unless the whole of the improvement ultimately projected could be carried out. That was not the view of the Highways Committee of the Town Council.

They were content with the Order as it at present stood, and were of opinion that it would give them what they wanted for the moment, and were content to wait if necessary for the falling in of the lease of No. 98 before absolutely completing the ultimate improvement that the town was entitled to.

Mr. Wilson: Then if the Highways Committee are satisfied I am quite content

The Inspector then declared the Inquiry closed.

WO, March 1931

Co-op Expansion

The Watford Co-op started in 1895 at No. 58 Leavesden Road, moving within a short while to St Albans Road; Market Street branch opened in 1902, Oxhey in 1906, Model Electric Bakery in Brixton Road in 1912, dairy depot in 1926 and the latest new store at 187/9 St Albans Road in 1928.

The Society employs 520 people, all of whom are members of a Trade Union, receive Trade Union wages and work under Trade Union conditions. The Society has 17,000 members in an area covering Wealdstone, Harrow, Oxhey, Watford, Bushey and Kings Langley.

Programme of the official visit of the Prime Minister (Ramsey Macdonald) to open the Trade Union Hall, Watford, 30 January, 1931.

Changing Watford

One half of the Watford Market Place improvement scheme is now nearing completion and it is anticipated that the whole scheme will be finished in about a month from now. As soon as the portion which was used as the old Market Place has been completed the traffic will be diverted to the new roadway for the old portion to be taken up, refaced, and relevelled.

The old Market Place used to slope down from the kerb to the roadway for drainage purposes, but as this will now be utilised for

The 'Island' site, shops 92, 94, 94a, 96, 98 and 100 was, for many years, cause for concern to the Council, here in 1956

Population 1931, 56,799

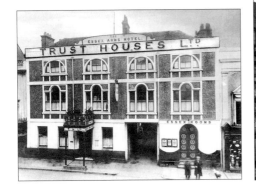

north-bound traffic only, it has been necessary to give the whole of the new roadway a new camber. This has necessitated a double kerb on part of the Market-street side of the Market Place.

When the new scheme is in operation all north-bound traffic will use what used to be the Market Place, and south bound traffic will travel on that part which is now used for the traffic both ways. Already two traffic signs indicating "one-way traffic," have been erected.

The centre of Watford High-street has now completely changed its appearance. The historic old hotel, "The Essex Arms," has entirely disappeared, and on its site Messrs. Timothy White, the cash chemists and household stores, have erected their big new branch which opens on Thursday next. Alongside is the reconstructed and greatly enlarged drapery establishment of Messrs. J. Cawdell and Co.

WO, May 1931

The Essex Almshouses

With reference to the recent letters from Colonel Healey and the Society for the Preservation of Ancient Buildings, it is interesting to note that at the last meeting of the Watford Corporation the Town Clerk reported that "Clause 16 of the Town and Country Planning Bill provides that a local authority who has passed a resolution to prepare or adopt a scheme may at any time make an order with respect to any building of special architectural or historical interest prohibiting the alteration or demolition of this building without their consent."

It is to be hoped that the first action of the Council under this provision will be an order for the preservation of the Essex Almshouses.

With the exception of the Church itself, those are certainly the most picturesque and ancient buildings yet remaining in the town.

One might be excused for saying that there is very little aesthetic beauty in this town to excite the admiration of of a casual visitor, but we still have a most restful pleasing relic of the past in the square surrounding the Churchyard; the side covered by these almshouses is certainly the best.

If we are too poor to preserve these from demolition for commercial purposes, one almost wonders whether the Church itself is safe.

Yours faithfully,

H. G. Howard, Cassiobury Park Avenue, Watford

WO, May 1931

Almshouses surprise

AFTER a discussion lasting three hours, Watford Town Council, at a special meeting, decided to inform the agents for the Essex Almshouses that they (the Council) were not interested in the purchase of the site.

The Deputy-Mayor (Alderman F. J. B. Hemming) proposed the adoption of a recommendation of a sub-committee that the site should be acquired for highway purposes, and that the

Almshouses should be demolished. An amendment moved by Councillor W. Bickerton, in what was perhaps the most eloquent speech ever heard in the Council Chamber, that the Almshouses should be purchased and preserved, was lost by two votes.

A further amendment, proposed by Alderman I. R. Clark (Chairman of the Highways Committee and a member of the sub-committee mentioned), that the Council "inform the agents that we are not interested in the purchase and we leave them absolutely alone," was carried by 15 votes to 7, and subsequently adopted as a substantive motion.

Reference was made to the starting of a voluntary fund to save the Almshouses, and the possibility of the Council becoming subscribers. It was also understood that the question of town planning the site as an open space will be considered.

WO, August 1931

Top: *The Essex Arms site transformation; the Essex Arms, centre of commercial life for decades, was demolished in 1931 and rebuilt, in partnership with David Greenhill, to house a James Cawdell shop, and Timothy Whites and Taylors, chemist and household goods. At the same time Cawdell's department store was rebuilt, and is shown here c1958 (was demolished in 1973 to make way for Charter Place).*

Timothy Whites and Taylors were bought by Boots; demolished, and the site again redeveloped, this time taking away part of the Charter Place entrance.

Right: *The Market Place in 1938 when the 'two-way' system had been in use for six years or so.*

The Essex Almshouses—a Public Meeting . . .

The Baths Spring Another Leak

For years now, Watford Town Council have been criticised for not providing a suitable swimming bath. When, at last, they really did decide to have one, there was another outcry against the amazing expense to which they proposed going and lately they have been subjected to further criticism for not making haste with the scheme now that they have decided on something definite.

WHP, August 1931

Essex Almshouses

THE response to the Mayor of Watford's (Alderman W. Bickerton's) appeal for funds for the repair and preservation of the Essex Almshouses has been quite generous, but if the desire to do the work during the coming summer is to be fulfilled, further support will have to be quickly forthcoming.

It is hoped to start the repairs and renovations early in the spring, and it is estimated that £800 will be required to do the work, £100 per house.

Three local gentlemen have offered to be responsible for a house each, and a fourth is covered by the £100 donation of Watford Corporation. The Mayor's appeal for the other £400 has so far realised £222, so that nearly £200 is still required.

WHP January, 1932

Housing Density

In connection with the new housing scheme of the Watford Town Council on the Leavesden Green estate, a discussion took place at Tuesday's meeting on the question of how many dwellings should be erected to the acre.

The Ministry of Health have fixed the density at 12. Councillor T. H. Simmons suggested 18-20, with a view to reducing cost and making possible a rent which is not an undue strain on the average working man. He proposed a resolution embodying his views, but was beaten on a division by two votes. The Ministry will not depart from their density regulation except under very special circumstances, and in their opinion, in Watford there is no case for exception. We think the Ministry are absolutely right No doubt the comparatively high rents charged for Council

houses are a hardship to many tenants, but the remedy is not to crowd small houses together, that would simply mean the creation of future slums.

The houses they erect must be a credit to the town and provide the amenities to which the tenants are entitled. The density rule is the outcome of experience, and lays down a standard that has been readily and generally accepted. The Council would only have been wasting time if, as was suggested, they had sent a deputation to the Ministry to press for a lowering of this standard.

WO, May 1932

Covering Watford Market

The work of covering Watford's market is now making progress, and a large part of the girder work is now in position. The whole of the work will not be completed, however, till the end of January. Operations started with levelling on September 19th. Twenty-one men are employed on the job at the present time, nineteen of whom are local, and it is expected that that number will be increased to thirty shortly.

WHP November, 1932

"To One Car Park—£15,000"

Sir,—With regard to the report of the last Watford Town Council meeting, and the comments of Mr. John T. Clarke, I feel that it would be well to enlighten him on modern methods. A municipal car park should be on the main road for entrance, and most certainly as central as possible. The proposed site I consider excellent. Our friend would do well to visit Rosslyn road, Upton-road, or the Parish Church, on a Saturday evening. 3,000 cars per week, at 6d. per car approximately £75 per week cash. Not a very heavy burden for the ratepayers, and then there is the sale of good frontage for shops, &c.

Watford grows daily, cars increase daily, and a central municipal car park is most urgently required. I have watched the development of this growing town for the past ten years. Can our friends find a better Council? I think they all take a real stand for economy. A visit to Windsor would give our friend a good idea of a municipal car park, perhaps our

friend is not a motorist, and therefore disinterested.

Yours faithfully,
PROGRESS, MOTORIST and RATEPAYER

WO December, 1932

Watford's All-Electric Baths Open

Watford's new public bath, erected at a cost of £37,000, and believed to be the first all-electric baths in the world, were in use by the public for the first time to-day.

The swimming bath presented an animated scene last night, for following on the official opening by the Mayor in the afternoon, a gala was held, and expert swimmers provided a display of grace and thrills combined.

Occupying a site just off the Hempstead-road, almost opposite the Public Library, the baths have an imposing appearance, and first impressions, coloured by a graceful approach and a dignified flight of steps, are not misleading. The building, with its wonderful system of heating and modern equipment, will certainly be one of Watford's show places.

Local pride is enhanced by the fact that the Borough Engineer (Mr. W. W. Newman, A.M.I.C.E., F.S.L, LR.I.B.A.) has been responsible for the design and carrying-out of the scheme, with the assistance of the Chief Electrical Engineer to the Corporation (Mr. A. W. Barham) in connection with the electrical heating and lighting equipment.

WHP May, 1933

• *A petition was filed in the High Court of Justice by the Westminster Bank against Messrs. North, of Whippendell Road and London. March 1933*

Pressing need became apparent after the Great War to provide the town with slipper baths and an indoor swimming pool. The Council could not easily make up its mind but when finally built, for an equivalent of £3.75 million, they were hailed as a success. Seventy years on they have seen upstart 'Watford Springs' (£12 million) come and go; but are under threat with plans for a vast 'civic centre' to be built upon the Baths, Library and Avenue Car Park sites.
The need for slipper baths (tubs) has decreased—from twelve there are now two only for each sex. This 1995.

The Almshouses are saved . . .

A Little Scene That Only Few Saw.

The bent figure of an old lady who lives in one of the Essex Almshouses sobbing quietly right through the service of thanksgiving and dedication, held to mark the restoration of the houses, on Sunday afternoon, was poignant evidence of how much these old homes mean to the dwellers therein. This sight was one that would have made subscribers to the restoration fund feel how greatly worth while their help has been. It was a pathetic little scene, this old lady tremulously happy that her home had been saved. Directly after the service she walked quickly back to her house, settled for many a day.

The service opened with the hymn, "O God, Our Help In Ages Past': the Rev. J. Napier Milne then 1ead in prayer, the Rev. F. J. Gould read a portion of the scripture, and the Rev. H. Earnshaw Smith solemnly dedicated the houses. The hymn, "Now Thank We All Our God," and the Benediction, pronounced by the Rev. Earnshaw Smith closed the simple, yet impressive little service. Mrs. L. O. Brewster accompanied the singing on a small organ.

The Mayor of Watford (Alderman W. Bickerton) told of how the almshouses came to be erected, and of the scheme for restoring them.

The almshouses, said the Mayor, were part of the circle of old Watford in the precincts of the Parish Church. There was also the Free School. These three antiquities—the Parish Church, the Free School, and the Almshouses—had now all been restored, the Parish Church in 1871, the Free School in the time of the Rev. Henry Edwards, who raised £400 for the purpose, and now the Almshouses. The three important sections had all been put into a fit condition for our generation to leave to posterity. The Almshouses were built in 1880 by Lady Bridget, wife of the Earl of Bedford.

When the Essex family came into being at Cassiobury, they maintained the houses in good and fine repair so long as their line lasted

and remained at Cassiobury. In 1922, the Essex family disappeared from Cassiobury. He would like to pay his tribute, not only to the pious founder of the houses, but to the generosity of the successive Earls of Essex, who had kept the houses repaired.

They all knew, continued the Mayor, what had happened since 1922—nothing.

The houses were left with nobody to care what repair they were in. In course of time, the houses had become damp and dilapidated, and in June of last year the houses were falling into decay. The Medical Officer certified that the houses were no longer fit for human habitation; either they had to be demolished or renovated and maintained.

The Charity Commissioners propounded a scheme to sell the almshouses, and the land on which they stood, and the land at the back. It was suggested at one time that the Council should buy the houses and land, and pull the houses down for road widening purposes. A further scheme was for a car park there.

Another suggestion was that a cinema should occupy the site. He wondered what old Watford people would have thought if that important link in the circle of old Watford had disappeared, and a car park or cinema had taken its place. It would have been a lasting reproach to the citizens of the town.

Continuing, the Mayor said that he and many others on the Council put their heads together to raise the money required. He became Mayor last November, and as soon as he got into that post he opened a fund to raise the £800 estimated to be required. Three generous citizens, Alderman Hy Brown, Col. Brigg and Mr. Alec Hicks, each offered to bear the expense of one house being restored.

A little negotiating by Councillor Evans and himself managed to get a little scheme through the Finance Committee and the Council, by which the Council subscribed £100. That and the offer from the three gentlemen already mentioned, meant half the money raised. They had a flag day which realised £104. By subscriptions, including £25 from

the Society for Protection of Ancient Buildings, about £130 was raised by the Watford Amenities Preservation Society. With other amounts, £894 had been obtained.

The Mayor went on to thank the local Press for their unfailing support to the scheme. Mr. Colbeck, who acted as architect, voluntarily, and the builders, who had carried out the architect's instructions well. The Mayor added that the drains were found to be blocked solid, and through this and other unlooked-for things, the total cost of the work would be about £1,000.

He was going on until the full amount required was raised. They had completed the work, and the houses were now a pride, pleasure and asset to the town. We of this generation had done our duty, and he hoped that generations to come would appreciate this, and do their duty when the time came.

A collection on behalf of the fund was made.

WHP, October 1932

Watford Slum Clearance

WATFORD CORPORATION'S slum clearance proposals were the subject of an Inquiry held by Mr. W. H. Cohn, on behalf of the Ministry of Health, in the Council Chamber on Tuesday and Wednesday. The Corporation asked for confirmation of Clearance Orders in respect of eleven areas, and Compulsory Purchase Orders in respect of three areas.

On the opening day the portion of the room reserved for the public was filled with tenants of the houses concerned, and on several occasions they made themselves audible with interruptions. The feeling of the tenants who attended was, judging by the applause, against the suggested demolition

Mr. Salter Davies in a general concluding statement, said that the slums in Watford were not of the appalling magnitude found in other towns, but he submitted that these areas were thoroughly slum in character. The only remedy was their demolition. It was proposed to rehouse the people on a very pleasant estate on the by-pass road in houses at 7s. a week, which were in the very strongest possible contrast with the houses mentioned in these Orders.

They would have amenities which would give them a decent standard of life and a chance of living such as they had never really had before.

The Inquiry then closed.

WO, May 1933

Traffic Lights

Watford's first traffic lights were installed at the junction of Langley Road, St. Albans Road and Station Road. The signals were worked by traffic-actuated road pads.

The second set of lights were at Queens Road/High Street and Kings Street. The installations cost £700.

WHP, June 1933

Following the renovation of the cottages a Service of Dedication was held.

The Lime Avenue is to be safeguarded . . .

Watford's New Fire Engine

The Watford Fire Brigade's new engine, which is now complete and ready for service, underwent exacting tests this week at the headquarters of the London Fire Brigade; and on Tuesday, after an extensive demonstration which included speed tests, it was formally christened by the Mayor of Watford (Councillor J. Evans), who broke a bottle of champagne over its front spring.

The fire engine is the first made by Messrs. Scammell, Ltd., the well-known firm of lorry manufacturers, of Watford West, and was designed with the close co-operation of the Watford Fire Brigade. It is the first fire appliance to be fitted with the Stone turbine pump which has hitherto been only used in liners and docks. This pump can deal with 400 gallons of water a minute, and with a 3/4in. nozzle the jet can reach a height of 139 feet. Two 5/8in. nozzles used together can send jets to a height of 115 feet.

The engine was taken to the Watford Waterworks on Tuesday afternoon, and in the presence of a large number of fire chiefs from the home counties and the Midlands, water tests were made. The hoses were run out and with the 3/4in. nozzle the jet of water reached the top of the waterworks chimney stack, which is 120 feet high. Tests were also made with two and four nozzles working at once, and the first aid extinguisher was also demonstrated.

At Messrs. Scammell's works the engine developed a speed of 50 miles an hour on the road. The design of the machine is of the most up-to-date character. It is fitted with one of Messrs. Scammell's famous four cylinder 40 horse-power engines, but can develop 85 h.p. A new escape and scaling ladder extending to 55 feet, foam generators, and gas cylinders are included in the equipment.

WO, January 1933

Cassiobury's Lime Avenue

THOUGH not a vestige of the noble mansion of Cassiobury exists, the magnificent avenue of Limes in what is known as the second park remains, and it is gratifying to know that its preservation has become the special concern of Watford Town Council.

Fear was recently expressed that some of the trees, from their great age, might be in a state of decay and prove dangerous to those seeking their shade. The advice of an expert, Mr. W. J. Bean, late curator at Kew Gardens, was therefore obtained, and his report, presented to the Council this week, is very reassuring. He does not know "a lime avenue of an age and size equal to this where the trees are in better condition."

Lopping need not be considered at present, it would be wrong to spoil the beauty and dignity of the avenue in this way. What could be done was to clear away from the base of the trunks the huge clusters of "adventitious" branches that in summer completely hide them, thereby robbing the spectator of the sight of a stately succession of tree trunks suggesting the columns in the nave of a cathedral.

Without loss of time the Council have commenced this work.

WO, April 1934

Top: *Although Watford's locally built fire engine was a source of pride it was not a commercial success, though serving the town well.*

Left: *Whippendell Woods, West Herts Golf Course and the Lime Avenue leading down to the canal. The main photograph shows the Avenue c1900 (with sheep keeping the grass under control) when the Cassiobury House was in use; the enlarged cut shows the distant house at that time.*

The 1994 colour print shows an autumnal scene with the distant green of the golf course crossing the pathway.

Architects for new Town Hall announced . . .

Proposals were submitted to demolish slum property in many spots including Red Lion Yard, Loates Lane, Grove Circus, Wells' Yard and Chater's Yard. Mr Cox, Medical Officer of Health, at an Inquiry, explained that premises were damp, lacked proper ventilation, some had no separate water supply.

Protests were received from tenants against the proposal to rehouse them at Leavesden Green in new houses, as this would entail them with considerable extra expense in travel costs amounting to, in some cases, 2/6d per week. Many of the demolition proposals were agreed, most notably that of Grove Circus (about where buses stop at rear of Charter Place).

When Thorpe Crescent was laid out the houses were rather more simple than the luxury Harebreaks site of a few years earlier. These were two or three-bedroomed and were of the 'non parlour-type'. (A living room and scullery and bathroom, a coal cupboard was indoors, under the stairs, and the toilet was outside the back door in the porch. Gas and electricity was provided, paid for by prepayment slot meters. The houses were modernised in the mid 1960s). But a 'new' house was not always a blessing. To uproot people from their lifetime's home, which

they had learned to afford, near work, near friends and near their religious centres, was for many a catastrophe. A larger dwelling needed new furnishings; electricity payments would be something new; their gas payments might be the same, or thereabouts, but their coal bill would be greater. Most new houses had a garden which needed upkeep and they had to find routes and expenses of travelling to work; to the town for shopping—in days before refrigerators; worse, loss of contact with friends and relatives. It is easy to understand why some tenants wanted to stay put for as long as possible when a future held terrors of the unknown.

If residents had problems, so did the council. There was a new town hall to be built for which the nearby road layout was to include a roundabout. A large tract of land became available, for an aerodrome?, but was bought and planned for playing fields; and a very pressing matter of solving the 'car parking problem'. Greycaine's were for years the largest producers in Europe of cheap novels; Odham's factory, a 'shadow' factory and a number of engineering works were built on the by-pass. Watford was busy.

North Watford Library

The question of providing a public library for North Watford was again before Watford Town Council on Tuesday, when a scheme to cost approximately £10,000 for the buildings alone was dealt with. The Finance Committee stated that they had deferred consideration of the question of the plan and cost, but approved of the purchase of the site.

An Aerodrome for Watford?

A definite proposal came before Watford Town Council on Tuesday, that they should purchase 118½ acres of land (the asking price being £25,000) for the purpose of a municipal aerodrome, subject to contract and the Ministry of Health's sanction.

WHP, July 1934

Watford Roundabout

IT is understood that work will be commenced shortly on a traffic roundabout at Watford High-street cross-roads. The estimated cost is in the neighbourhood of £12,000; 60 per cent, of this will be covered by a grant from the Ministry of Transport, and the balance will be provided in equal parts by the County Council and the Corporation.

There has been considerable delay over the scheme. It was put back because of the national financial crises, and revived twelve months ago when the County Council gave conditional approval; they expressed the surprising opinion that it was not absolutely necessary from a traffic point of view, but had been promoted by the Corporation for obtaining a layout on town-planning lines. As we said at the

time, a little appreciation of the volume of traffic at this spot and the absolute necessity for regulation at all hours of the day dispelled any idea of that sort. However efficient the A.A. patrols may be, the time has clearly come for the breaking up, by means of a roundabout, of the converging streams of traffic.

WO, May 1935

Watford's Municipal Offices

THE decision of the Assessor appointed by the Watford Corporation in the architectural competition for designs for the new Municipal Offices and Town Hall was announced at the meeting of the Town Council on Tuesday.

Mr. Vincent Harris stated that he had awarded the first place to Mr. C. Cowles-

Above: *A typical cottage interior; this a dining room of a 16th century Cassio Hamlet cottage in Hempstead Road—one of those to be demolished when the Town Hall was built.*

Left: *The Cross-roads in 1935. The foreground island includes the tree planted in 1887, a fountain and the AA kiosk. St Albans Road at the top.*

Voysey, of 14, Gray's Inn-square, W.C.1.

At the meeting of the Town Council in April it was stated by Alderman Hemming, who is Chairman of the Municipal Offices Sub-committee, that the assembly hall would accommodate 2,000 and the banqueting room 200. Each of the six competitors complying with the conditions is to receive a premium of 150 guineas.

WO. June 1935

Jubilee Tree Gets The Chop

The construction of the traffic roundabout at the junction of St. Albans-road, High-street, Rickmansworth-road, and Hempstead-road has caused the removal of some of Watford's oldest and most historical trees.

Of historical interest was the oak at the Rickmansworth-road end of the island at the junction of this road and High-street.

This was planted in June, 1887, by the Countess of Essex in commemoration of the jubilee of Queen Victoria. It could be neither moved and replanted nor included in the roundabout, so there was no alternative but to cut it down. The second pond at the Cross-roads, before it either dried up or was drained, on the Hempstead-road side of Little Nascot, is being filled in.

WO, January 1936

Death of King George V

TUESDAY bought to a close a week of unforgettable memories—the passing of a beloved king, the proclamation of his successor and, then, the funeral, with its mile-long procession through a crowded but silent London.

Only in the middle of the night has Watford High-street ever been so quiet and deserted as it was during Tuesday dinner-hour and the early part of the afternoon. Life seemed to have come to a stand-still in what is normally the busiest thoroughfare in the county.

At 1.30 three maroons boomed out—one in Cassiobury Park, one in Oxhey, and one in North Watford. It was the signal which had been awaited for days. For two minutes Watford stopped altogether. Silence prevailed, even the wind seemed to stop bending the boughs of the trees. It was the climax to events which had followed the death of the King.

Many Watford people had already attended some service of remembrance, though the official service was not until an hour and a half later. Councils had arranged, and some had held, meetings to pass resolutions of condolence with the Royal Family and loyalty to the new King, and declarations of the accession of the new King had been made.

Banks shut from 11 till 2; most offices closed from 12 till 5 or did not open at all, and cinemas were not opened till six o'clock. Many people went to London early—mostly by train—to pay their last respects as the funeral cortege passed through the streets; many, too, went to Windsor, mostly by car, to join the silent throng that waited in the shadow of the royal castle.

WHP, January 1936

Crematorium?

Watford Town Council decided on Tuesday to ask Watford Joint Burial Board to consider the installation of a crematorium on a site adjacent to the North Watford Cemetery. Councillor E. I. Baxter had given notice to move the resolution.

In doing so he said that cremation was the most sanitary and convenient way of disposal now in use. It had many advantages over other methods of disposal, and those which would appeal to the Council were that there was no paupers' corner, that the garden of remembrance could be used in perpetuity and became increasingly beautiful the longer it was used.

WHP March, 1936

Memorial to Lord Hyde

Lord Hyde, the son of Lord Clarendon, died aged 30, in South Africa during 1935, from an injury sustained when his gun was accidentally discharged as he put it down.

A corner of Lees Wood, on the Grove Estate, was formally opened in memory of the late Lord Hyde by his father the Earl of Clarendon, as a camping ground for the 1st and 2/1st South West Herts (Countess of Clarendon's Own) Groups of Boy Scouts. A Sarsen stone carries a tablet, cast by members of the 2/1st Group, to commemorate George Lord Hyde who had been a Scout and Rover of the Group.

The Service of Dedication was conducted by the Bishop of St Albans.

A Tour of Odhams

The type foundry comprises Linotype, Ludlow and Monotype casters and a fully equipped process studio to prepare coloured objects and artwork into film and supports and tissues for making the gravure cylinders. Odham's have flat-bed letterpress machines and three two-colour presses as well as perfecting presses which will print upon both

In sun, wind, rain and snow the AA man directs the traffic at the cross-roads—a task becoming increasingly difficult, and so a roundabout is decided upon. Across the road workmen are taking down part of Little Nascot in order to widen the road. At the other side of the St Albans Road is a large sign, behind Dixey's van and in front of the tree, advertising land for sale to build shops.
Mr David Greenhill, who built Faircross House, would later be interested, wanting to build fourteen lock-up shops, eight 3-bedroom flats, and sixteen 2-bedroom flats, over four floors. His plans were dismissed, the site remained undeveloped until c1957 when shops and offices were built.
Only minimal parking was provided for the shops. By 1980-90 the office use had ceased and by 2001 turned into accommodation.

Odham's large factory opens . . . takes work from Sun . . .

sides of the sheet. The output varies between 2,500 cph from the smaller machines to 1,700 cph from the largest.

Rotary Gravure is a fast printing method, needing large editions. The Goss Speedry Press, which we have, is the largest Gravure press in the world, and the fastest Gravure press in this country. It will print 64 pages, of 16 in colour, 8 pages in two colours, and 40 in monotone—at a speed of 50,000 copies per hour, folded, cut and counted. The total length of paper in the machine, when using all 15 units and printing 128 pages, is 634 feet; it can run through at up to 15mph. The ink is pumped from the ink department at the rate of 60 gallons per minute, per fountain. Surplus and vapours are sucked away through trunking and solvents reclaimed. Power for the press is supplied by 90 individual motors, needing in all some 26 miles of wiring to link all to the main switchboard.

Sheet-fed photogravure machines are used where versatility of differing types of paper and card stock may be used; printing in one colour at a time the run speed is up to 4,000cph.

In the course of building the factory service roads of more than a half-mile were built; two artesian wells with a capacity of 25,000 gallons per hour were sunk, and purification plant installed with a capacity of treating 8,000 gallons per hour by settling tanks and filters before being passed into the Corporation's sewers.

Odhams (Watford) Ltd, 1956 [Abridged]

Derelict Mill Purchased

Twelve years ago last December the Watford Flour Mill in Lower High-street was destroyed by fire. Even to-day, charred beams hang precariously from the upper storeys, while the wooden floor below is rotting away. Grass and weeds grow on the walls. The Watford Borough Council have approved a scheme to acquire the premises for £2,250. They will then be able to control the sluices. The Mill was one of the four mentioned in the Domesday Book. The "Observer" understands that the remains of the building are to be cleared.

WO, March 1937

Opening of Gaumont

Watford's newest cinema, the Gaumont, was opened on Monday evening by the Mayor, Alderman Henry Coates, J.P. He was supported by the Mayoress, Mrs. Coates; Cllr. C. E. Last, (deputy mayor), and Mrs. Last; Major A. J. Gale, I.B.E., (directors) and Mick Hyams (theatre controller). The guest of honour was Mr. Will Hay, the popular stage, screen and radio star.

The theatre itself is beautifully decorated and every seat in the building provides an excellent view of the screen and every sound can be heard without distortion. The proscenium is draped in a colour scheme of gold and brown and the curtain is of rich golden coloured velvet. Every seat is comfortably upholstered and ample knee room is provided.

The Mayor welcomed Mr. Will Hay, and said the British public appreciated good clean humour. Mr. Will Hay was received with prolonged applause. In his speech, he said that London might well be proud of such a fine cinema. Referring to the Mayor's remarks on British films, Mr. Hay said that a great deal of work and skill was being put into them and it was no longer true that America led the film industry. There was a time when a British cinema would be qualifying to have its doors closed if it stated that it would show British films, but all that had now gone.

WHP, May 1937

Sunday Games

THE Town Council have decided that they will not sanction games in the public parks on Sundays. This does not apply to games by organised clubs but simply to the throwing open of the parks for games for the general

Above: *A battery of 40 high speed letterpress machines at Odhams (shown c1950). Odhams (Watford) Ltd was started in 1936 to print many titles previously printed by Sun Engraving. Production also included a very extensive range of casebound books.*

Right: *Although the by-pass, shown here, had been built for several years the severe load and speed restrictions on lorries meant that any firm considering a site for a new factory would put rail links first.*
This shows Odham's new factory in 1936, next to the St Albans line with sidings running in from that line. At the front offices is space occupied by about fifteen 'senior management' cars, and alongside are about 20 cycles sheds for the workers. Other workers would walk or travel by bus.
At the top right of the view are the just built Westlea and Eastlea Avenues.

public. The discussion on Tuesday evening was conducted on a high plane, and both sides stated their case with dignity, sincerity and restraint.

The question of Sunday games, like that of the cinemas, is one that seriously exercises the minds of a large number of men and women who want to do the right thing. Where are we to draw the line? If it is right to open the baths for a portion of Sunday, can it be wrong to grant similar facilities to non-swimmers who want to play tennis or other games?

Again, if there is a moral or religious objection to public games, then there must also be the same objection to allowing games by clubs.

If Sunday games are allowed, then it will not be long before Sunday cinemas are permitted.

We have suggested on a previous occasion that this is a matter for a plebiscite. Both sides could state their case if this were done, and many Councillors who are now in doubt as to what the public really wants would have a definite ruling one way or the other.

Eventually, this will be found to be the only satisfactory way out.

WHP, May 1937

"Bigger Than Anyone Realises"

"Bigger than people yet realise" was the comment of the Mayor (Alderman H. E. Coates) on the proposed lay-out of the King George V. Recreation Ground, put before Watford Town Council at Tuesday's meeting.

The estimated cost of the lay-out is over £30,000, including:

Sixteen grass and four hard tennis courts.

Three bowling greens, three cricket pitches, and running track.

No 42 High Street was, in 1937, a building about 200 years old. It had been since 1887 the offices and works of the West Herts and Watford Newsletter. The premises were bought in 1917 by Mr G H Stratton who used the building as stationers and booksellers. In 1919 he had the front restored with a new supporting girder. In April 1937 workmen were engaged in making alterations to the rear of the building when the insides and front bulged outwards and collapsed, killing one workman and injuring two others. A family firm it remained as such until sold by 1966 when it was then trading as Universal Stationers Ltd.

Football, hockey and netball pitches.

A children's playground, and a £15,000 pavilion or a number of smaller pavilions, and conveniences.

The original estimate in 1935 was just under £20,000. Now the total cost, including the cost of the land, has reached £54,500, but the Herts. County Council has made a grant of £4,700, and a further grant will come from the King George V. Memorial Fund, and there is a grant of £1,000 from the Playing Fields Association.

WHP, July 1937

The 'Elms' (at the Cross Roads), and its paddocks behind, was bought in 1920 as a 'good bargain' at £12,250 though this caused much heart-searching of the Council's Sites Committee. The need was for a site to build a hospital as a Peace Memorial. The hospital was eventually built upon the stable land and ground in Rickmansworth Road, leaving the 'Elms' available for later use, perhaps for Council or other offices. Shown here, in September 1937, being emptied before demolition, The 'Elms' had for three years or so been used by the Treasurer's Department. Note that from pages 210 and 211 the roundabout has been built.

The Mill ruins to be demolished; a By-pass is proposed for St Albans . . .

New Town Hall

WATFORD Borough Council, at their meeting on Tuesday night accepted the tender of £146,471 by Messrs. Richard Costain Ltd., of London, for the new Municipal Offices.

The actual cost to the ratepayers may be either 4.21d. in the £, or 5.01d. in the £, according to whether the Council decide on a 60-year or a 30-year loan period.

WHP, September 1937

Sunday Cinemas

THE discussion at the Town Council on Tuesday on the question of Sunday Cinemas brought to a head a matter that has caused a sharp division of opinion for some time.

It is not a question whether the Town Council approve of Sunday cinemas, but whether the electors should be allowed to decide this matter for themselves. During the next few weeks we shall see a campaign by the "pro- and anti-cinema" people in the town.

It would be well if an effort was made to decide this question calmly and without bitterness. In fact, we believe most people have a pronounced opinion one way or the other on the matter, and it only remains for them to express it.

There is one difficulty, however, the single young people who are vitally concerned, will not have votes. For both sides there is much to be said. Those in favour of Sunday opening point to the fact that Harrow and other neighbouring towns have Sunday cinemas, and that the opening of the cinemas prevents a considerable amount of horseplay—and worse, in the streets and parks. In a town where so many young people are in lodgings, it is well that something should be provided for them.

Those against Sunday opening express concern at the desecration of the Sabbath and say that ample opportunity is provided for cinemagoing in the week.

They also fear that it is the "thin end of the wedge," and that Sunday labour will become more general if we give way on these matters.

Well, those are the main points.

We live in a democratic country, and there is no reason why the issue cannot be disposed of in the best of spirit.

WHP, January 1938

Many Families Benefit

No fewer than 826 necessitous Watford families benefited as a result of the Mayor's Christmas Appeal this year. A total of £342 was raised out of which subscribers to the "Post" Shilling Fund contributed £65.

At Tuesday's meeting of the Watford Town Council the Mayor (Cllr. T. Rigby Taylor) expressed his thanks to all those who had contributed to and worked for the fund.

He directed especial thanks to Mr. S. Jump who distributed the gifts.

The Mayor added that, as in previous years, there was a small balance left over which would be spent on coal for the most needy cases.

WHP, January 1938

Top: *Watford's last 'big cinema'—the North Watford Odeon— opened on 27th November 1937 (with Henry Fonda in the main feature "Wings of the Morning"), and closed in 1959.*

Left: *The roads are clogging up with parked cars; the speed limit of 20mph is not achievable in a mix of buses, pedestrians and cyclists and many are the suggestions to ease the problem. Unilateral parking is one favoured solution. Car parks are available but little used.*

Open Air Bath to be Closed

Watford's open-air bathing place at the Five Arches is to be closed, but the Baths Committee is to consider the possibility of providing other suitable facilities for open-air bathing.

It was revealed at the Town Council meeting on Tuesday that a report of the analysis of the water showed evidence of sewage and manurial matters. The Baths Management Sub-Committee recommended the closure following the analysis.

WHP, May 1936

Town Council and Unions

Watford Town Council at their meeting on Tuesday officially approved of the principle of collective bargaining for public employees through their Trade Unions.

The Council passed the following resolution:

"The Council, recognising that collective bargaining is in the interests of employers and workers, places on record its willingness to receive the duly accredited officials of the Unions at the appropriate Committee in connection with negotiations on wages and conditions of employment."

There was a time in the bad old days when employers imposed conditions on their workers. Now it was recognised that the worker was entitled to receive fair consideration, and that full and satisfactory relationships were obtained between employer and employee through collective bargaining. Most industries, and many local authorities, including the Herts County Council, recognised that.

WHP, July 1936

'Kodachrome'

16mm Kodachrome was Introduced, in USA, in April 1935, and Double-8 in Spring of 1936, followed by 35mm cartridges.

In Germany Agfa-color Diafilm was introduced in November 1936.

Leica

Since its introduction, the Leica has proved a formidable tool, and from 1932 has been available with a coupled rangefinder for automatic setting of the lens to correct subject distance. The shutter speed range is now extended from 1 second to 1/1000th.

The original f/3.5 Elmar was joined by the faster f/2.5 Hektor in 1931 to which is now added the 50mm f/2 Summar. The first wide-angle (35mm f/3.5 Elmar) was available in 1932, and the first long-focus lenses (73mm f/1.9 Hektor; 90mm f/4 Elmar) in 1931.

Thus the Leica is now a system camera.

In 1935 the Leica III, with 50mm f/2 Summar lens, cost £43. The model shown is with 50mm f/3.5 Elmar.

Large aperture lenses are needed to cope with black and white film which is of inherently slow speed. Kodachrome is approximately 8ASA (later 10ASA); Agfa films were 'Fine grain', 8ASA; 'Isochrom', 25ASA and 'Superpan' of 50ASA. By 1939 film had improved and speeds approximately doubled. Zeiss wide aperture lenses were more highly regarded for press and serious work than the Leitz.

Felix H. Mann, having started an illustrious career using an Ermanox plate camera has, like many other gifted German photographers, started to use and exploit the unique advantages of the small Leica camera—which would have a quite astonishing effect for Watford later in 1938 . . .

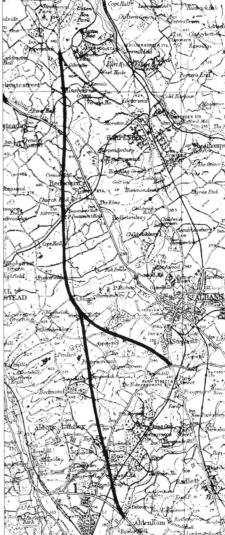

Proposed by-pass road for St Albans

"Through the courtesy of the County Surveyor (Lieut.-Col A. E. Prescott), we are able to publish this map showing the line of the proposed new by-pass road for St Albans.

The line proposed by the Ministry of Transport, as shown in the map, joins up with the Watford by-pass at Garston and, travelling due North and skirting Gorhambury on the West, intersects the Watling Street at Flamstead and links up with the Harpenden-road slightly south of Luton. Travelling South, the new by-pass forks to the South-East at Gorhambury, and links up with the North Orbital road at the point where it joins the old Watling street."

Herts Advertiser, August 1937

[The plan came to fruition when opened in 1959 as the 'M1' see also p227]

Left: Members of the Mickey Mouse Club queue for their Saturday show at the Odeon Cinema. The cafe retained the original name of 'Plaza' when the cinema was renamed.

Watfordians want nothing to do with ARP . . .

Watford's First Bus Driver Dies

Watford's first busman, Mr. George James Bence, of 46, Grover-road, Oxhey, Watford, died on Monday. He was 67 years of age.

The first bus was run in 1898 and the service was between Bushey Arches and the water-trough at Callowland, with Mr. Bence as driver.

The fare was 3d.; its very popularity led to disaster. Built to carry four passengers and a driver and conductor, people clambered on to the bus in such numbers that the bus often broke down. This happened so often that the service fizzled out and the bus was bought by the Standard Range and Foundry Company and was transformed into a lorry. The vehicle was an 8 h.p. Daimler.

Mr. Bence was one of the earliest motor drivers in the country. After his experience as a bus driver, he became inside driver for the Daimler Company. He then went into private service, and one of his duties was to make a journey a week to Margate. In later years, and until his death, Mr. Bence ran his own private hire service.

WHP, January 1938

Watford's Historic Mill

A TENDER for the demolition of the old flour mill in Watford High-street was accepted by the Town Council on Tuesday. The Council bought the mill and the water rights for £2,250.

They will now be able to control the flow and level of the water, thereby preventing, or at least reducing, flooding. The present mill was erected in 1826, and a short time before its destruction had been entirely remodelled. The structure was depressingly plain in character, and its final disappearance will be regretted by none.

WO, January 1938

Wanted—a Car Park

A MUCH-NEEDED improvement for the lower end of the town is being ridiculed in certain quarters. This is typical of the mentality which has been responsible for the neglect of Lower High-street and that has made this thoroughfare a cause of shame. In Lower High-street, Queen's-road and Kingstreet are traders who have been ratepayers for many years.

They have helped to lay the foundations of Watford's prosperity, and they should not now be penalised because the trend of commercial development is northwards.

Contempt has been poured on the scheme for a car park in Albert-street All sorts of difficulties have been raised, and it has been suggested that no car park is needed at this spot. The piece of waste ground it is proposed to convert into a car park is already being used by about 30 motorists a day. We have consistently urged that there is no need for an expensive scheme.

It is not even necessary to concrete the yard. So far as an attendant is concerned, he could be paid a moderate wage and take what he could in tips from motorists. This is done in other towns and cities not far from Watford, and would not make the Council responsible for the cars in any way. Three banks, two newspaper offices and several business offices, the police station, and the only railway station in High-street are nearer Albert-street than they are to the Municipal Car Park. One-way traffic could easily be introduced, even through Carey-place.

The High-street car park, useful though it is, is too far from the business centre of Queen's-road and Lower High-street to be adequately served by it A modest expenditure on levelling and improvement of the entrances is all that is required at Albert-street, and the business interests of the lower end of the town demand it.

WHP, February 1938

• *Albert Street was eventually cleared and demolished cl960 and the open space bounded by Derby Road, Queens Road and the rear of the High Street premises became better known as 'Sainsbury's car park' when Sainsbury's occupied the old library site in Queens Road from 1970-1986.*

A Dangerous Corner

Sir,—A serious accident at Garston on Sunday causes me to write this letter, as this occurrence is the latest of a great many which have occurred at the same spot I feel that the Borough Council's attention should be drawn once again to this very dangerous corner—the junction of the Watford-St. Albans main road with the North Orbital.

Surely the ratepayers' money would be better spent in the construction of a roundabout at this place, which is very dangerous and a disgrace to any town in its present state, than in widening a road which is already amply wide enough, and where accidents are almost unknown. I refer to the proposed widening of Horseshoe-lane. Yours truly,

S. GRAHAM WEALL

WO, March 1938

Compulsory Purchase

OBJECTIONS by various property owners to the application by Watford Town Council for a compulsory purchase order in respect of road widening and improvement schemes within the Borough led to the Ministry of Transport holding an inquiry into the proposals yesterday. Mr. H. Martyn Hooke conducted the proceedings. The case for the Town council was put by Mr. G. Salter Davies (assistant solicitor) and evidence was given by the Borough Engineer (Mr. W. W. Newman).

Among those who watched the proceedings were the Mayor (Councillor T. Rigby Taylor) and Alderman T. P.. Clark (chairman of the Highways Committee).

Mr. Salter Davies said it was intended to construct a new road commencing at Water-lane and proceeding along Lower Derby-road

SUNDAY CINEMAS WON
RECORD POLL
"WE BOW"—Opposition
"HARDEST FIGHT"—Proposers
FOR   9,565
AGAINST   6,908

A 50% poll was recorded.

WHP March, 1938

across Queen's-road into Beechen Grove and past the Clarendon Hall into Clarendon-road.

The object was to by-pass a portion of the High-street. Water-lane was narrow and very dangerous; it was considered that a 50ft. roadway would be necessary, but if traffic continued to increase it might be necessary to provide for 60ft. in the future. The only practical means of crossing the L.M.S. railway line to the north of Watford was by the main St Albans-road and the Corporation had had to consider the needs of providing a major road to connect the Watford by-pass road with the centre of the town. This could be done by widening and improving Bushey Hall-road and Aldenham-road.

Mr. J. A. Weller, representing the owners of other properties adjoining Water-lane, agreed that it was essential that the road should be widened, but said that certain owners would like to retain a portion of the back area for development Referring to the proposals for widening in Beechen Grove and Red Lion Yard, Mr. Salter Davies said it would become a main thoroughfare, and it was also proposed to provide car parking facilities at that spot.

Mr. Minton, Mr. W. Lawton, Mr. J .A. Weller and Mr. P. D. Lock, on behalf of adjacent property owners, objected on the ground that no more property should be taken than was necessary for street widening only.

Mr. Salter Davies pointed out that at present cars were parked in Beechen Grove, and when the scheme was completed there would be many more cars. Dealing with a further section of the Council's scheme, Mr. Salter Davies said it was proposed to reconstruct the junction of Wiggenhall-road and Vicarage-road which was a most difficult and dangerous corner, and carried most of the traffic from Market-street For this purpose a block of corner properties would be required. He gave an undertaking that as soon as the Order was confirmed the Council would acquire the properties; and Mr. Roper Cook, representing Mr. Hayter the owner, then withdrew his objection.

Mr. Salter Davies next dealt with the proposed improvements to Hempstead-road in the vicinity of the Russells Estate. He pointed out that it carried a heavy volume of traffic and said it was proposed to provide a 64ft. carriageway with a service road and preserve the fine belt of trees.

Mr. L. S. Woolf on behalf of Russells Estate, withdrew his objections on Mr. Salter Davies giving an undertaking that the land would be acquired as soon as the Order was confirmed.

Explaining the final part of the scheme, Mr. Salter Davies said that the junction of the Hempstead-road and St Albans-road was going to be the future centre of the town. The new Municipal buildings were in course of erection and there was the public library and the public baths. "Little Nascot" at present was used by the Council, but later it would be sold.

At present the road at this spot was not wide enough to cater satisfactorily for existing traffic and it would grow worse in the future. The Corporation proposed to widen the road to 80ft. and for this they desired the properties known as Cassio Hamlet. They did not wish to go ahead with the proposals immediately and did not see why the occupiers should be disturbed until the scheme came into force.

Mr. Wright and Mr. Weller, representing the occupiers of the properties involved, objected on the ground that the Council's proposals left things in the air and would result in hardship on their clients.

They did not agree that an 80ft. carriageway was needed.

WO, April 1938

Historian of Watford

IT is with deep regret that we have to announce the death, which occurred on Thursday last, of Mr. William Raymond Saunders, of "Uppershott," Toms-lane, Kings Langley, at the age of 67.

The son of a straw hat manufacturer in Luton, Mr. Saunders began his teaching career there, and in 1896 joined the staff of Watford Field School. He was for a time at Victoria School and was transferred to Callowland in 1922, retiring in December, 1930. He was a past president of the Watford Branch of the National Union of Teachers, and was particularly interested in schoolboy football. He is perhaps most widely known as the historian of Watford. When he saw old parts of Watford beginning to disappear and its old courts and alleys demolished, he decided to write a history of the town. He spent a number of years on this work, and his searches led him to documents in the British Museum, Somerset House, the Public Record Office, Watford Public Library and the registers of the Parish Church.

The result was a fascinating story of Watford's growth from Saxon times. His history was published first in serial form in the "Observer," and in 1931 as a separate book by Messrs. C. H. Peacock, Ltd.

Shortly after the war Mr. Saunders went to live at Toms-lane, Bedmond, and took a prominent part in the erection of the Village Hall, in which he retained his interest until the end.

Only two days before his death he was wheeled up to the hall and saw it for the last time.

WO April, 1938

Above: *Self-generating gas power plant, here with an LMS lorry; later extensively used by buses. Other alternatives were 'gas bags' on car tops.*

Right: *The High Street, looking to Clarendon Corner, in April 1939. The 'Parking Problem', which continually occupied councillors' minds, was solved by the onset of war, and the following ten or twelve years, before resurfacing with renewed intensity.*
The shops across the road, C H Fabrics and Perrings Furniture Store, (rebuilt) were, in the 1990's let as swag shops when traders moved into the Harlequin Centre.
The new millennium saw a new store for Woolworth's erected and opened.

Watford's Electricity Generating Station to supply the National Grid

Irresponsible

ON the other hand there is the problem of the irresponsible cyclist.

There are far too many of them on the road, and the worst are not the careless children, but the factory workers who flood the roads at certain times without the slightest consideration for anybody else. Not all of them behave badly, but a large proportion do. I have myself been ditched in a narrow road by a wild stampede of works cyclists, several of whom would certainly have been massacred had there been a car on the road.

The only possible remedy is some system of registration for all cyclists, so that prosecution and punishment are possible in cases of dangerous and careless behaviour.

This would necessitate some nominal tax, and unpopular though this would be, it seems to be the only fair way of dealing with the problem.

WHP, May 1938

Town Hall Foundation Stone Laid

Yesterday was a momentous day in the history of the town of Watford, probably the most important day yet.

The foundation stone of the new £150,000 municipal offices and town hall was laid, but to Watford people who are proud of their town there was much more in the ceremony than that

They hope it will be the first step in a new sense of civic dignity and interest, that it will be the means of breaking down that oft-expressed feeling that Watford is merely a dormitory town for London's workers.

WHP, May 1938

Watford's Cheap Electricity

TWO lectures on subjects of momentous importance to the town were given at a meeting arranged by the North Watford Ratepayers' Association held at the North Watford Methodist hall on Wednesday.

"The Watford Electricity undertaking" was the subject chosen by Ald. Henry Coates (Chairman of the Electricity Committee of Watford Town Council), while Capt H. W. Carter addressed the meeting on air raids precautions.

Ald. Coates pointed out that the electricity undertaking was the largest industrial enterprise in the town. It was run by the Council for the burgesses and primarily for those wishing to consume electricity.

The fact that Watford was such a smokeless town considering the large number of industries carried on in it was due to the fact that most factories used electricity as their motive power.

From an infant the Watford Electricity under taking had grown in 39 years to a lusty adolescent and Watford was the first town to have its streets entirely lighted by electricity.

The plant now supplied no less than 100 square miles with electricity.

Towns such as Hempstead and Bovingdon benefited from Watford's enterprise.

The people in Aldenham were causing some trouble and holding up the progress of the system in their area because they could not see that an extra charge for their current was justifiable. It was so because additional cables had to be laid, houses were further apart than in the town, and losses by transformers had to be taken into consideration.

In 1922 the plant outgrew the old building and the enterprise had to be extended. Three-phase current was generated instead of the old single-phase, and the voltage was raised.

In 1910 the undertaking had plant capable of generating 1,880 kilowatts; in 1922 there was 4,000 which supplied 4 million units a year, and in 1938 the plant could generate 36,000, which supplied 63 million units a year. Ald. Coates explained how the 1926 Electricity Act controlled the business of generating electricity.

When the Act was passed Watford was told that their station would be shut down; after a period Watford applied for a new plant and were told that they could not have it and they would have to take a supply from the grid.

The grid prices were higher than the charges made for Watford produced current and the town could not be forced to take its supply from the grid.

Watford was then asked to become a selected station to supply the grid, to which the committee agreed. Ald. Coates estimated that the town saved £10,000 a year by virtue of the fact they were using their own electricity and not that of the grid.

WHP, May 1938

Watford's Entrances

NOW that Watford Town Council have completed the work started by the fire many years ago, and pulled down the old mill in Lower High-street, this entrance to the town, once so dingy and dirty, is greatly improved.

The erection of new buildings on two sites there will also add to the freshness of the outlook, but it cannot yet be said that every aspect pleases.

The chief offenders to the view now are a number of billposting sites. If these could be altered or removed, this entrance to the town would give visitors a much better introduction.

There can be little complaint of the other main roads into Watford from the aesthetic point of view.

Hempstead-road will present a dignified appearance when the road works now in progress are completed, and with the imposing town hall dominating the town end of the road.

The entrance by St. Albans-road has also been improved recently by the laying-out of the roundabout on the same lines as the Pond roundabout

WHP, May 1938

18th May 1938; the speeches announce the importance of the occasion, the laying of the Foundation Stone of Watford's new Town Hall. in the entrance foyer. Mayor Councillor Rigby Taylor is seated left of dais, next to Town Clerk William Hudson.

More About Sunday Washing

Sir,—I am glad to see the subject of Sunday washing raised in your paper. At one time in this part of the town people used to put their washing out on Monday and Tuesday, and then no more was put out until the next Monday and Tuesday.

But now it is put out every day in the week, including Sunday. Surely housewives can do all their washing on six days of the week and leave us free from this disfigurement on Sundays. Sunday is so much more enjoyable if we make it different from other days.
R.L.K.

WHP, May 1938

Local Charities To Benefit?

Notification that the Home Office have made an order extending Sunday cinemas to Watford was received at the meeting of Watford Town Council on Tuesday.

The Town Clerk (Mr. W. Hudson) said that under the Cinematograph Act 5 per cent of the profits went to the Cinematograph Fund. The County Council were the licensing authority for Watford so that if any other conditions were to be laid down on the grant of the licences it would be for the County Council to formulate them. The Council could make suggestions to the County Council, for instance as to funds for charities to benefit in addition to the Cinematograph Fund.

In reply to a question the Town Clerk said that the amount to go to charities could be had up to the whole of the profits.

It was agreed that the Council ask the County Council to bear in mind the claims of the Watford and District Peace Memorial Hospital and the Watford and District Nursing Association.

WHP, June 1938

Cadet Flying Corps For Watford

With the object of creating a body of 20,000 youths familiar with aircraft and with flying, a new organisation is being started in the country. It is to be called the Air Defence Cadet Corps, and squadrons arc being formed in all big centres.

The "Post" has the privilege of giving first details of the scheme to be started in Watford. Watford has a great opportunity to make national history by being the first Corps organised.

It is hoped in Watford to raise two squadrons of 100 cadets each. Only 200 cadets will be enrolled, and this number will not be exceeded.

Cadets will be selected, approved and enrolled by a local Committee, consisting of the Deputy Mayor, Alderman H. Coates, Squadron Leader Burge, Alderman J. Evans and Mr. E. McGregor, and must be between the ages of 14 and 18.

They will be taught the elementary principles of aircraft

engineering and maintenance, the handling of simple work-shop tools and instruments, the general theory of flight, the identification of aeroplanes, the morse code, message carrying, meteorology, fire action, and model aeroplane making and flying,

They will be fully trained in air raid precautions, and be given an insight into the working of the Observer Corps, the Balloon Barrage Companies, anti-aircraft gunnery, searchlight and sound locator operation, and all other forms of passive defence.

WHP, June 1938

"Suitable and Wholesome Films"

The Council suggested that performances should start after the ordinary hours of church services and that the type of film shown should be suitable, wholesome and fit for people of all ages.

It also asked that the existing conditions that music be of a sacred or classical nature should be rigidly enforced.

WHP, July 1938

Garston House to be Demolished

Reputed to be one of the most ancient buildings in the county, Garston House is to be demolished to make way for a modern building estate.

The estate, comprising 55 acres of land adjoining Garston Park on the St. Albans-road has been purchased by Messrs. W. J. Rice and Sons and the lay-out of an estate to contain 500 houses has been provisionally prepared.

This 55 acres is the remnant of a huge property so old that its origin is lost in history. It is, however, certain that a house of some kind existed in the twelfth century while parts of the present house date back to the fifteenth and sixteenth centuries. With the sale there passed into the lands of Messrs. Rice a large number of interesting legal

Top: *Horseshoe Lane looking towards Watford.*
Centre: *Ganders Ash.*
Bottom: *Leavesden High Road. All c1938*

Picture Post—a New Weekly . . .

parchments of the reigns of Henry VIII, Queen Elizabeth, Charles II, right through to George Ill. These deal with such widely divergent subjects as the various sales of the estate through the centuries, tenancies, court proceedings conducted by the Earls of Essex and even marriage agreements. The seals of Elizabeth are exceptionally interesting and almost complete.

Penned in Gothic script, the parchments could only be deciphered clearly by an expert, and obsolete, intricate legal phrasing make the task even more difficult. Those of the time of Elizabeth are in Latin.

All have been presented to the Public Library, where expert assistance is being obtained for translations.

The earliest document is of the year 1542, recording a sale from Ruth Cartor to John Randall. From histories of Hertfordshire in the Watford Public Library and the documents the following facts come to light.

Nicolas, son of John de Garston, gave the tenancy of certain land at Garston in the 12th century and the manor was conveyed in 1368 from Bartholomew Blaket to John Curteys of Wymington.

In 1455 William Halle, of Schildyngtone, in the county of Bedford (Shillington) granted the manor to John of Wheathampstead, 33rd Abbot of St Albans. The Abbot and his successors continued to hold the manor till the dissolution of the monasteries by Henry VIII. On July 12, 1544 the Tudor King granted the manor to Richard Carter and Thomas Palmer.

Half the land was then sold to John Randall and his wife from whom that portion went to Michael Sayer of Marsworth, Bucks.

Meanwhile William, son of Richard Carter had died and his son, Richard, inherited half of the land and subsequently bought the other half again. In 1636 another William Carter

sold the estate to John Marsh, in whose family it remained till conveyed in marriage to Thomas Beech. Thomas Beech sold up in 1729 to Richard Capper of Bushey, a family name still surviving.

One of his descendants married Mary, the daughter of Robert Ord, then Lord Chief Baron of Scotland.

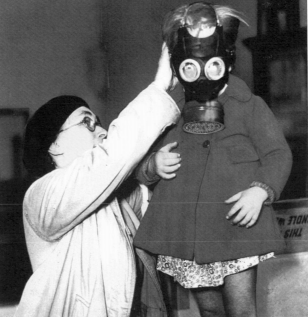

In 1816 the estate passed by sale to Stephen Moore, and thence in 1854 to Henry Cobb, and then to his widow in 1873. At that time the estate comprised 400 acres but in 1904 when Mr. Thomas Fames lived there the estate dwindled to 184 acres.

The sale of the estate by Robert Capper makes strange reading in the old document—
"I, Robert Capper, for the sum of 10s and for other considerations do sell, release and confirm unto the said Stephen Moore, the manors, lordships and reputed manors and lordships of Bushey, Bournhall and Garston together with the capital or mansion houses, buildings, gardens, farms, lands, tithes, etc." One wonders what the "other considerations" were. In another document, however, is mention made of a sum of £2,000 which Moore paid to Capper.

Messrs. Rice are conveying a portion of the land to the Corporation to be added to Garston Park. This includes a lake in the grounds.

With regard to the lay-out, Garston-lane is to be widened to a 50ft road and will go through in the direction of Munden.

WHP, July 1938

Above: Air raid precautions were started in 1938 on the advent of a war-scare. A sigh of relief was given when war seem averted but was short-lived with declaration of war in September 1939.
The year's grace had given the country a much needed breathing space to harness production and training to compete against Germany's might. Gas masks had been ready for some time, and were now being issued.

Right: *Scammell's, best known for their compact 'mechanical horse' and massive load carriers, adopted their three-wheeled tractors to be self contained fire-fighting units—to be much used in two year's time.*

David Greenhill's and Hulton Press' Picture Post's first issue from Sun Engraving Co Ltd 1st October 1938 delighted readers and stunned the sceptical trade. A sale of 250,000 was anticipated but 1/2 million were produced and 'forced' upon the trade. They all sold. Just ten weeks later the print run was a million and climbing. Picture Post helped change concepts of advertising. And, later, their campaigns spoke for the serving man and the shortcomings of his equipment.

November 5, 1938
PICTURE
POST
THE CRINOLINE COMES BACK
See Page 51
80
PAGES
HULTON'S NATIONAL WEEKLY
NOVEMBER 5, 1938
Vol. 1. No. 6
3D

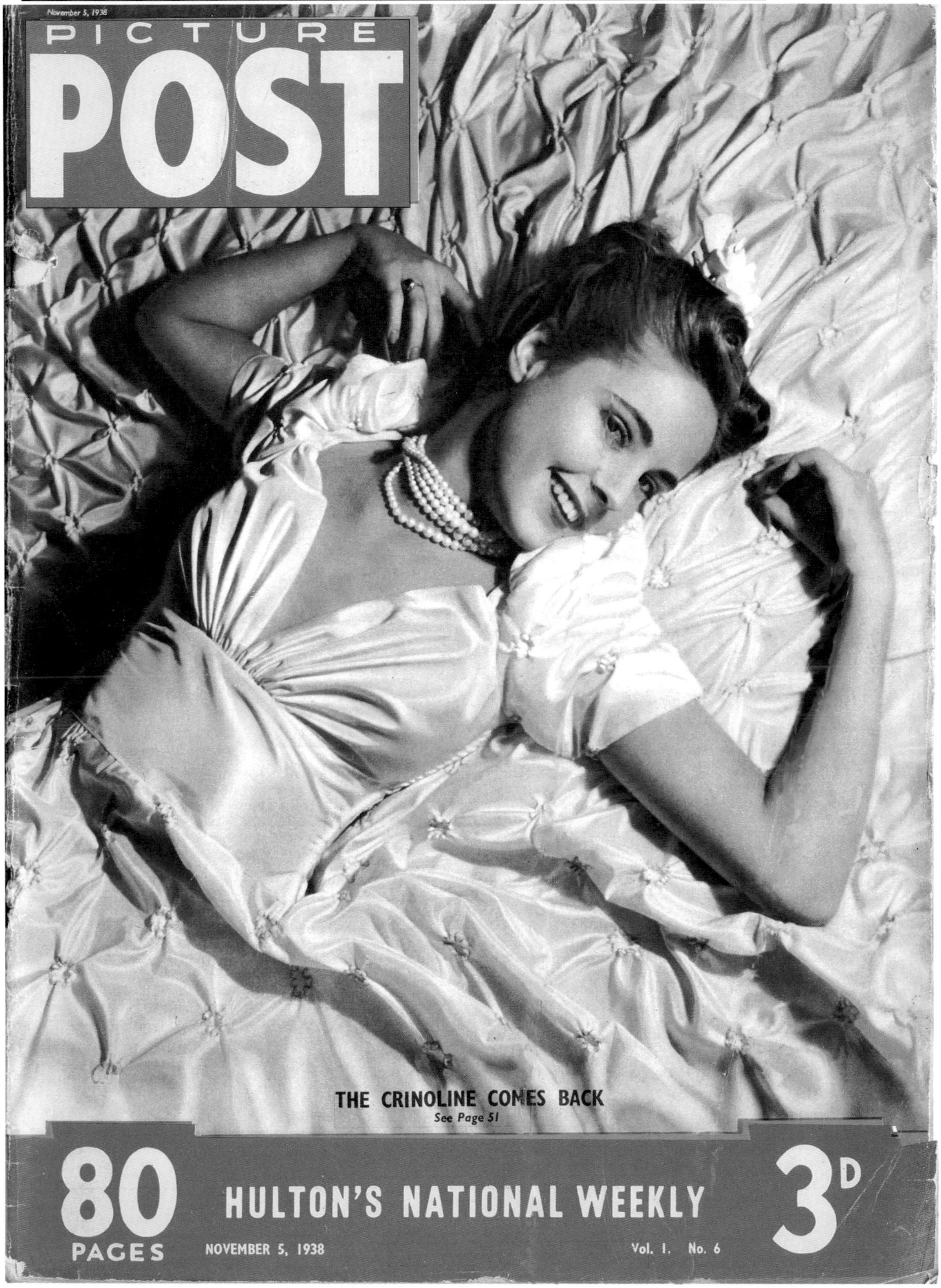

"This week, for the first time, 1,000,000 copies of PICTURE POST have been printed. This week, for the second time, the paper contains 88 pages. At this point in its progress PICTURE POST wants to answer a question many readers have been asking—why do we print advertisements?"

Readers liked the style, stories, photos and general make-up; they wanted more . . .

"Why should readers not get 80 pages of pictures and reading matter every week for 3d. There is only one answer. It is not possible to to do it at the price.

"The 3d you pay does not all go to the publishers of the paper. Wholesalers and newsagents receive approximately 1½d for their very necessary services. For the remaining 1½d, using the quality of paper and the same method of printing it would be possible for us to supply, without actual loss, a paper of only 25 pages each week.

"This is where the advertisers come in. The advertisers paid £100 a page for space in the early issues of PICTURE POST. So great however, has been PICTURE POST'S success—a million circulation instead of the 250,000 originally guaranteed to advertisers, that the rate has already been raised as from January 1 to £250 a page.

"It is the advertiser, therefore, who pays the greater part of the costs . . . he is *not* an enemy of the reader.
He is his friend."

Picture Post, December 1938

Fears of food hoarding . . .

Assembling The Respirators

A magnificent piece of work was put through in Watford in assembling the 60,000 to 70,000 respirators necessary. Authorities were not allowed to assemble the respirators until instructed.

Instructions were given first in Watford early on Monday morning. These were countermanded and then at 11 a.m. the order was again given.

The Mayor (Councillor T. Rigby Taylor) got into touch with the Sun Engraving Works, the Model Laundry, the Watford Steam Laundry, Millars Laundry, and Silverdale Laundry, and asked them to supply the staffs to assemble them. They agreed. Then it was found there were no jigs for assembling.

The Mayor and Councillor E. J. Baxter went to two regional stores and obtained jigs.

At 2 p.m. on Monday assembly started, and by midnight three hundred employees at the Sun and three hundred at the laundries had assembled 50,000 masks.

The others have been assembled since.

The Mayor wishes to make it quite clear that Watford was not behind in the distribution of masks, as some people have alleged.

WHP, September 1938

Fitting of Respirators

WE appeal to our readers to heed carefully the letter which we publish in this issue from the Mayor (Councillor T. Rigby Taylor) regarding the necessity for expediting all measures to be taken in the Air Raid Precautions Services within the Borough of Watford.

One of the most important of these is the fitting of respirators to all residents, and we ask that everyone concerned will do their best to make the gigantic task of fitting the population with gas masks as easy as possible by reporting to their respective polling stations when required to do so.

There is no need for alarm. The fitting of respirators is inevitable, and as a house-to-house visit would take many months, it is hoped by asking residents to attend for fitting. to complete this important work within three weeks.

The Authorities have done and are doing their part, and it is up to the public to assist.

WHP, September 1938

Inside the Drill Hall in Clarendon Road. The 343rd (Watford) Field Battery of the Herts Territorials was converted into an Anti-Aircraft unit on Nov. 1st, 1938. This is a training session in the use of height finder/predictor equipment.

A Message from the Mayor

The Mayor of Watford (Councillor I. Rigby Taylor) addresses the following message to the burgesses of Watford— "Though all necessary precautions are being taken in case of dire emergency it does not follow that war is inevitable. I would ask the population of Watford to be calm and to avoid panic.

I can assure them that everything has been and is being done for their protection.

I wish to thank all workers for their efforts."

WHP, September 1938

The Ill Wind, Food Hoarding

ONCE more the proverb of "the ill wind" comes to mind. The windy bravado of the Dictators during the past two weeks may indeed blow the English community a great deal of good—especially around London.

The past ten years has seen a growth of new and old towns around London proceed at an amazing pace. That growth has been so quick that outer London could be called little more than an agglomeration of dormitory building estates. Division between one district and another became purely arbitrary, for pride of town had not time to grow. There was no community spirit because, firstly, business interests were usually centred elsewhere and leisure pursuits were purely self-centred.

A.R.P. has probably done more than anything else since the war to change all that. By force of circumstances the new districts have of a sudden been welded into a unit of common effort to a common cause, and whatever wind may have blown the seed there, once implanted, must by the nature of things continue to grow.

Food hoarding was as prevalent in Watford during the crises as elsewhere, and the wireless warning that shopkeepers were not bound to take back inordinately large purchases found plenty of interested hearers.

In one instance a housewife had ordered 100 tins of condensed milk, accepted delivery and then wanted to send them back when the crisis had passed. Grocers in many cases were unable to make deliveries of orders within twenty-four hours owing to the tremendous demands made upon them.

It was mentioned at an A.R.P. meeting by Councillor Mrs. Armitage that a shopkeeper had said to her, "The women of Watford are thinking of nothing else except stocking their larders."

WHP, October 1938

Home Secretary to Inspect A.R.P.

The Home Secretary (Sir Samuel Hoare) and the Inspector-General (Wing Commander Hodsell) will be among those who will witness the Air-Raid Precautions exercises in Watford and Rickmansworth in the County black-out on Saturday.

The Black-out will be the biggest A.R.P. exercise held in the country. It will cover approximately 640 square miles and about 12,000 volunteers who have enrolled for the different services will be called upon to take part in the exercises.

All sections of the general public, including motorists, are asked to co-operate by extinguishing all lights between 11.45 and 2.30, and by remaining at home.

All of the regular services, the police, the St. John Ambulance Brigade, the British Red Cross Society, the railway companies, and the Post Office are collaborating.

WHP, November 1938

How PICTURE POST was started . . .

Felix H. Man (Felix Sigismund Baumann) was born in Freiburg im Breisgau in 1893. As a contributor to the Munchner Illustrierte Presse and the Berliner Illustrierte from 1929-1934, his photo essays covered all spheres of life. In 1934 in England he was the leading photographer with Weekly Illustrated when it first came into existence and, when Picture Post started in 1938, he was appointed Chief Photographer by the Editor. He remained with Picture Post until 1945 and returned as their colour specialist in 1948-1951.

His one-man shows have been exhibited in public museums and art galleries all over the world. His books on lithography and European Artists were published in the 1950s and the 1970s.

"In spite of the 'Ermanox' camera, with a lens with an aperture of f/1.8, if indoor photographs had to be taken by available light, or people such as conductors were to be photographed, it has to be remembered that negative sensitivities then were only a fraction of what they are today. The present-day photographer knows nothing of these difficulties, as all these problems have been solved mechanically—usually to the disadvantage of the eventual result.

In the early days, with the limited means at our disposal, it was nearly always the rule that the negative was under-exposed, and had to be reinforced after development, in spite of the fact that exposure times varied between one-half and one-eighth of a second. For this reason, all indoor photographs had to be taken with a tripod, as it was impossible to hold the camera steady. No light or distance meters were available. Distances had to be estimated, and only on rare occasions was it possible to look through the viewfinder, and never possible to control the picture on the matt-screen.

The number of photographs we could take was limited, as we had to work with glass plates in metal cassettes; as a rule, not more than 15 to 20 of these could be carried on an assignment.

We hardly ever exposed more than one negative of the same subject. We did not then conform to Bernard Shaw's idea that 'the photographer is like a cod-fish who lays a million eggs in the hope that one may hatch'—an idea which makes more sense today, when photographers may take 300-500 pictures for one story, of which perhaps 20 or so will be selected later by the editor who has encouraged these methods. The technical limitations of the early days demanded great concentration and creative capacity.

Each exposure had to be a hit.

I left Germany for good in May 1934.

I had to leave everything behind me and travelled with only a small suitcase, to avoid suspicion. I had been told that the best way into England was by Calais and Dover. Passport control took place on the boat, during the crossing. "How long are you going to stay in England," asked the Immigration Officer. When I replied that this depended on my work for various continental papers, my passport was stamped with an oval stamp, with the words 'Leave to land at Dover this day, 31 May, 1934, on condition that the holder does not enter any employment paid or unpaid while in the United Kingdom'.

As a journalist I could do free-lance work, even working for an English paper, provided I was not employed and paid a fixed salary or retainer, but paid separately for each job.

A few days after my arrival I met, by sheer accident, my old friend Stefan Lorant, the Hungarian former editor of the *Müncher Illustrierte;* he had been imprisoned soon after Hitler's takeover, but released through pressure from the Hungarian Parliament. "You are exactly the man I would most have liked to meet at this moment," he exclaimed, "I need you, as I am planning a new weekly illustrated paper with Odhams Press."

Neither of us had known of the other's presence in London before we met. For years we had worked together in Germany, he as editor, I as his principal contributor. We were a team, complementing each other. Was it coincidence, or fate?

At that time, photojournalism did not exist in England. The continental method of writing essays with a camera was unknown, and there were no illustrated weeklies of the continental type. The world's first illustrated paper, The *Illustrated London News*, published news photographs, pictures taken by scientists or explorers, or photographs of prominent society people.

Soon after his arrival in England in May1934, Stefan Lorant had learnt that Odhams Press were planning a reorganisation of some of their magazines. He made contact with the management, and suggested that they should publish a new illustrated weekly of the continental type. Odhams agreed, and their dying magazine Clarion was incorporated—in small type—with the new magazine, *Weekly Illustrated.*

The preparatory dummy was put together by Lorant in June 1934, in the continental manner, using a number of my old picture-stories. As time was short, I started, that month, to produce photo-essays for the new paper. When the first number of *Weekly Illustrated* came out on July 1934, the bulk of the picture stories were mine; Lorant had laid out, on the usual two pages each, four photo-essays of mine. I had worked on my own, as usual, with a personal assistant, also providing the facts for the captions and the brief texts. I was paid according to the number of pages of my work which were published; for several months the paper was largely dependent on my work, and I was earning from it between £40 and £50 a week.

This naturally caused some jealousy from others on the paper.

Maurice Cowan, thinking after a few months that he knew how to run such a paper, plotted how to get rid of Lorant and myself.

I was overworked, and my permit to stay in England was due to expire at the end of August. I decided to take a continental holiday, leaving about eight stories behind, to be used in my absence. Lorant only hesitantly accepted my suggestion that a German friend Hübschmann should take over in my absence; the latter and I agreed that he would fade away on my return. Later on Kurt Hübschmann changed his name to Hutton.

When I returned to Dover in October, the Immigration Officer again used the oval stamp, giving me another three months in England. In the meantime the squabbles at *Weekly Illustrated* were mounting. Lorant, fighting to retain his own position, was not able to give me sufficient support. A month after my return, I left the paper, predicting to Lorant that he too would be leaving within a couple of months, a correct forecast as it turned out.

Weekly Illustrated stumbled on without its founding fathers, until killed off by the overwhelming success of Picture Post in 1938; it was then reborn as *Illustrated.*

Until today, the importance of *Weekly Illustrated* as a picture magazine has yet to be assessed. It was through this paper that photojournalism was introduced into England. When Henry Luce was preparing the publication of *Life,* he came to England to study the back issues of *Weekly Illustrated.* I kept in close contact with my old friend and colleague, Stefan Lorant. When in the mid-thirties, he started to publish a magazine of his own, the pocket magazine *Lilliput,* it was only natural that I become a contributor at once.

In about June 1938, Lorant sold *Lilliput,* for

The Ermanox Press Camera was available from 1924 in 6 x 9cm, or 4.5 x 6cm sizes. Both versions could use film packs or plates in single slides. With no meter or rangefinder the extreme wide-aperture, for its time, made available light photographs possible. But even then most were taken using a lightweight tripod to give exposures of a quarter or halfsecond duration.

"I must arrest you . . ."

what was then a substantial sum, to Hulton Press, and then entered into negotiations with this young but financially very sound publishing house, about starting a weekly illustrated paper on the continental model.

The new enterprise, to be called *Picture Post*, was due to start in October 1938, so there was little time for preparations. When the first number of *Picture Post* went to press, trenches were being dug in Hyde Park to protect the civil population against air raids.

In contrast to this fatuous improvised protection, the first issue of the paper, which was intended to conquer England in a quick assault, was well prepared. This issue, of 750,000 copies, was sold out and had to be reprinted. By the spring, the circulation was nearly 1.4 million. Meanwhile Chamberlain had been and gone to Munich, the clouds of war had receded, the race for rearming was on, and the economy was prospering.

Many experts had forecast that a new picture paper could not succeed. Conditions in England were said to be completely different from the continent, and everything was against such a venture. The large editions of the Sunday papers would, it was said, leave no room for an illustrated weekly. Their large organisations and printing facilities enabled them to change words and pictures up to the very last moment, this was something that *Picture Post* would never be able to do, as this would involve changing a whole photogravure cylinder, covering sixteen pages, a long and costly business.

The phenomenal success of Picture Post made nonsense of all these predictions. Why, then, was the weekly such a smashing success?

There were a number of causes, but the most important of these lay in the conception and direction of the paper. Stefan Lorant, the editor, and the two principal contributors, Hutton and myself, were all experienced in our fields.

We had mastered our jobs and worked together as a team. Tom Hopkinson, the assistant editor, had learnt a lot in four years with *Weekly Illustrated*. His main job was to oversee the 'words' part of the weekly, while Lorant as editor and picture-expert held his protective hand over the whole project. The British public was, for the first time, introduced to abundant well-composed large-scale picture essays about ordinary, everyday things, which people were familiar with, but had never consciously observed.

In issue number one, published on October 1st 1938, there were 80 pages for what was even then a ridiculously low price of three pence. There were 39 pages of pictures, 22 of reading matter, and a four-page colour supplement on great British painters. The buyer needed several hours to go through the magazine thoroughly. Unlike the German weekly

illustrated papers, where essays or interviews were limited to two or three pages, *Picture Post* spread important pieces over six, even eight, pages. The accompanying text had to be much more detailed, so a number of journalists were taken onto the staff. Coming from a different branch of journalism, they tried to dominate the photographers.

As I resisted these attempts, I was not very popular with the journalists; I insisted that, when on a job, photographers came first, as we were, after all, an illustrated paper.

The leading political figure before, and at the beginning of, World War II was the Prime Minister, Neville Chamberlain. When he returned from his meeting with Hitler at Munich in 1938, did he really believe that 'Peace in our time' was secured by the famous piece of paper he waved at Croydon Airport? Or was it his intention to gain time for Britain, then largely unprepared, to re-arm?

A couple of weeks before the war started, I found a cottage in the Chilterns with vacant possession; anticipating what was going to happen, I installed myself there at once. 'The Old Forge,' my eighteenth-century cottage, was at Flaunden, a small hamlet of about 20 houses, with a church, a pub and the Flaunden General Stores, a tiny shop where cigarettes and postage stamps could be bought. The fear of the enemy within, the fifth column, caused me problems. As my time in Canada counted towards residence in Britain, I had been in a position to apply for naturalisation six months before the war broke out. My case was under investigation, but the outbreak of war stopped all naturalisation. I had become friendly with Sir Stafford Cripps, who tried to get me into the Ministry of Information.

But no alien could be employed at the Ministry; as the Home Office ruled that naturalisation could only be granted to aliens already working for a ministry, it was a vicious circle. 'Enemy Aliens' such as myself had to go before a tribunal. Before this took place, I could not travel more than six miles from my home. I could cycle the four miles into Watford, where the *Picture Post* offices had moved to, but my contributions stopped.

In June 1940, I was planting flowers in my garden at Flaunden, when the peaceful silence was broken by five men coming through my garden gate, four of them in uniform. The other said 'I must arrest you' and posted the uniformed men around the cottage to prevent any attempt to escape. This man, the Police Superintendent from Hemel Hempstead, gave me half-an-hour to get some things together, and then took me off to a single cell in Bedford Prison.

He managed to collect a fair number of aliens in this way, and after a few days, we were taken by train to Euston, and then marched across London under military escort to

Victoria Station, heartily abused by those we passed on the way, who supposed that we were dangerous spies. The M15 Colonel who interviewed me at once realised that a mistake had been made. He told me 'I cannot help you at present, but I can give you some advice. Be persistent in your efforts to get out. Try everything, and you will eventually succeed.'

He was right.

Three months later I was free, back at Flaunden and working again for Picture Post.

But the Police Superintendent evidently regarded me as a dangerous person still. One day I looked out of an upstairs window of the cottage and noticed somebody hidden in the bushes opposite. I went down and found the village policeman lying in the ditch. He was very embarrassed at being discovered. I said 'I am not going out today so you are waiting in vain—you had better go home.'

Stefan Lorant, though not interned, had suffered from a number of restrictions, one of the reasons why he had given up his position and emigrated to the United States in July, while I was interned. Tom Hopkinson had taken over as editor."

'Man with Camera,' Felix H Mann

Back to the Middle Ages

Later that day began the worst pogrom since the Middle Ages. Looting went on all over Germany and Austria. The houses of Jews were broken into, children were dragged from their beds, women were beaten, men arrested and taken to concentration camps. Foreign journalists were prevented, as far as possible, from gathering details, but it is known that in Berlin several Jews were stoned to death.

In the provinces, the number must have been higher. The police did not interfere. The fire brigades turned their hoses only on non-Jewish buildings.

All Jews in the streets or in wrecked shops, who were not manhandled, were arrested. In Munich, 10,000 Jews were rounded up and ordered to leave within 48 hours. This order was later rescinded, but not before hundreds of terrified Jews had run into the forests to hide from the mobs. In Vienna and the Sudetenland, Jews were made to crawl in the streets. On November 11, arrests were continued all over Germany. Many Jews, despairing, committed suicide. German shops refused to sell food to Jews.

Goebbels told foreign correspondents that he sympathised with the people in their desire to protest, denied that there had been looting or that he had organised the pogrom. "Had I done so," he said, "it would have been done more thoroughly." Not a single synagogue, hardly one Jewish shop, remained unwrecked.

Picture Post, November 1938

The sirens gave the signal for the 'blackout' . . .

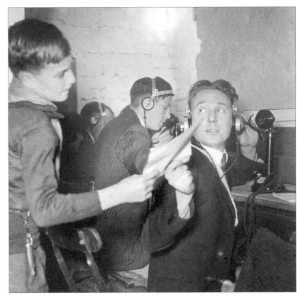

Preparations . . .

The Inspector General of A. R. P. (Wing Commander Hodsell) who was accompanied by Flight Lieut Eardley-Wilmot (Regional Inspector of the London Area), Major General Tindal-Lucas (Chairman of the Hertfordshire A.R.P. Committee), and Mr. Elton Longmore (Clerk to the Hertfordshire County Council), reached Watford Fields House at 11.40 p.m.

Here he was received by the Mayor (Councillor I. Rigby Taylor), and the Deputy Mayor (Alderman H. Coates), and was introduced to Councillor E. I. Baxter, Borough A.R.P. Chairman and other officials. As he was leaving Watford Fields House, the sirens in the town could be heard giving the signal for the "blackout."

The darkened streets, with red Hurricane lamps substituted for street lighting and even the traffic signals masked so that only small crosses of light could be seen, and all neon signs extinguished, gave the town an eerie appearance.

The first call by the Inspector General was to the air raid post at 14, Derby-road. Normally a gas meter testing depot it was sandbagged effectively and all the A. R. P. workers had tin hats—a surprise feature which caused one of the officials to ask how Watford had managed to get them! The post consisted of an operating room, which had a map of the two or three streets under the control of the post, and a rest room whose furniture included a bed for anyone off duty.

From there Wing Commander Hodsell went to Watford's "nerve-centre"—the control room behind the fire station, with eight telephones and elaborate maps dotted with small flags. He next visited the Car Park Attendant's office which was the centre of operations of the demolition squads. Operated by ex-Royal Engineers it presented a very business-like appearance, and the Inspector-General was particularly struck with a multi-coloured notice-board which showed at a glance where each section was.

In the car park were the ghostly figures of 100 auxiliary firemen with their four pumps, motorcycle dis-

Top: *In the Car Park the Car Park Attendants' Office shared the local public toilets building— here commandeered to form an ARP Post.*

Right: *The Ford V8 Pilot with fire pump trailer is drawn up alongside, and, top right, Scout runners are at hand to relay messages.*

Bottom: *Anderson shelters, in use during winter, were cold and clammy but effective against bomb blast.*

Working at a 'bomb crater'... Watford put up a very good show.

patch riders, and a Scammell 'mechanical-horse' fitted for demolition work.

On his way to the Car Park the Inspector-General had looked into the duty room of Watford Fire Station and had seen the switch which simultaneously sounds all Watford's air raid sirens; these sirens are all electrically connected to the fire alarm system of the town.

At Watford Fields he saw repair squads working at a bomb crater, and at Whippendell road he paid a brief visit to the depot where squads of workers of the Watford and St.Albans Gas Company and Watford Electricity Works were in readiness for emergency work.

Speaking to an "Observer" representative before leaving Watford, the Inspector General said "Watford put up a very good show. I was particularly impressed with the arrangements for decontamination and rescue work, and the notice-board I saw in the latter centre was the first I have seen in England. I was very impressed with the keenness of everybody. Watford is building up an excellent organisation."

The Watford Borough Control Room was in the Recreation Room of the Fire Station and was in charge of Mr. G. G. Crook (Deputy Borough Treasurer) and was fully staffed.

The Postmaster was an interested spectator.

This room was fitted with four telephones for incoming calls and four for outgoing calls and wireless.

Messengers were in readiness to carry the reports of the "casualties," etc., to the waiting ambulances and fire tenders. Members of the auxiliary fire service drawn up in the car park were inspected.

At No. 1 Whippendell-road an inspection was made of Rescue and Demolition Party and a Gas Party Squad.

WO, November 1938

Throughout the country air raid sirens have been installed. This is near the Bradshaw Post Office in Bushey Mill Lane. November 1938.

A New Incendiary Bomb

A new incendiary bomb has been invented. It is called the "kilo-electron" and makes use of the light and extremely inflammable metal, magnesium. It has been stated that the bomb burns at 1,300 degrees centigrade.

They will probably be released some ten or twenty at a time and owing to wind resistance will spread out as they fall It has been calculated that a bomber flying at 200 miles an hour at 5,000 feet or more and releasing 20 bombs per second, might be able to start a fire over 60 or 70 yards, providing the area was covered by 15 per cent buildings.

Experimental work has been carried out on methods of extinguishing this bomb, but so far the results have not been of any great importance. The use of the water spray is at present being developed.

One can stop the bomb penetrating a building by a quarter-inch mild steel plate, one layer of closely packed sandbags, or four inches of reinforced concrete.

The effects of the high explosive bomb, better known in the services as "H.E.," are the most terrible of all the weapons which can be used from the air. They have been known to weigh as little as 60 lbs., but only few over a ton have been dropped in the world's war zones so far. These bombs have a tremendous power of penetration downwards, and it is difficult to provide a measure of protection against this.

WHP, December 1938

New Town Hall

Sir,—I was a little concerned to see scaffolding erected round the tower of our new Town Hall, and to find that demolition has already started!

Certainly it is not a "Thing of beauty," but would have been useful as a factory (if permitted by Town Planning regulations), a block of flats (if not "too many to the acre"), or even a lodging house for Jewish refugee children! It seems a pity not to use it for some purpose, but if demolition is intended to be complete, the site

could be laid out as a pleasant public garden.

It looked quite nice before they put the building on it.

Yours faithfully, J. A. WELLER

WO, January 1939

The New Town Hall Critics

IT is time someone said a good word for Watford's new municipal buildings, and we are going to say it, though, to be candid, the clock turret cannot be described as a thing of beauty; not seeming to fit in with the general design.

But to ridicule the structure as a whole, as some of our correspondents have done, and to describe it as "something to shudder at and pass by," or as being suitable for housing Jewish refugee children, is to carry criticism to absurdity. The design was selected as the best in a keen competition, the adjudicator being a well-known architect of great experience.

It is not fair to judge the building in its present incomplete state. Tastes differ in architecture, as they do in most things, but it is something to be spared one of the ultra-modern monstrosities which some people admire and rave about. But we should like to see that clock turret reconstructed.

WHP, January 1939

Cattle Market and Car Park

THOUGH the site of the proposed municipal cattle market for Watford (the old Ballards Building area near Church-street) is not everything to be desired, the advocates of the scheme can certainly make out a strong case.

The original idea of the Council was to take a 999 years' lease from Messrs. Fisher at £300 per annum, but this has been altered to a 15 years' lease at the same figure, with an option to purchase for £7,500 at the end of that period.

The market would be let to an auctioneer on one day a week for something like £200 per annum, to which has to be added a similar amount for tolls. It may be mentioned that the cattle market at St. Albans practically pays for itself. The probability, therefore, is that the new cattle market will not be an appreciable burden on the rates. Tradesmen in the centre of the town will benefit from the country people visiting the Market, which it is presumed will be held on Tuesday. The only criticism of the scheme offered at Tuesday's Council meeting was that a nuisance would be caused by cattle and sheep being driven through the streets, but nowadays practically all the stock sold in the existing private cattle market held off Stone's-alley is brought in and taken out by carts and lorries.

This cattle market project would probably not have been put forward but for the possibility of combining with a car park available for six days a week. To provide proper access to Church-street the suggestion is to remove the existing mortuary building and to secure an option on the lease of the old National School, at present used for offices, with a view to dem-

olition. In time the whole row of buildings facing the Church may come down. This work, however, may not be undertaken for years to come.

WHP, January 1939

7 p.m. Curfew for Market and Shops

FAR-REACHING effects of a bylaw that Watford Town Council propose to adopt, in an endeavour to secure a uniform closing time for large numbers of shops, were discussed at Watford Chamber of Trade's quarterly meeting on Monday. With the exception of certain classes of exempted shops, the bylaw is aimed to secure a general closing time of 7 p.m., and in this category the Council will attempt to include the Borough Market, newsagents, and street vendors of newspapers, &c.

Strenuous opposition from the newsagents was forthcoming at the Chamber of trade's meeting, which was presided over by Alderman H. W. Beall.

The Secretary (Mr. B. J. Andrews) said that a deputation would, it was hoped, be received by the Borough Finance Committee on Tuesday. The four points they proposed to raise were: The effect on the market, street vendors; receiving offices; and exhibitions.

Alderman Beall said they would try to see that the order was carried out strictly in every

way. At present the hairdressers had kept out, but now they wanted to come in. He had had it more or less brought to him that the hairdressers would like to come in if possible.

He thought the earlier closing would help those who needed more time for A.R.P. duties in Watford. A member referred to confectioners who

kept groceries "under the counter," and said this scheme would give those people a good footing.

WO, March 1939

Proposed New By-pass Road

DETAILS of a huge road scheme for by-passing St. Albans, at an estimated cost of 1½ millions, were given at a Ministry of Transport Inquiry, conducted by Mr. H. Martyn Hooke, at the Town Hall, St. Albans, on Wednesday.

Mr. Rowland Hill (divisional road engineer), who presented the case for the Ministry of Transport, first dealt with the necessity of diverting traffic from St. Albans, through which the London-Holyhead trunk road (A5) and the London-Carlisle trunk road (A6) passes. Consideration was given to the loca-

tion of a bypass which would take through traffic from both A5 and A6.

The scheme commenced on the A6, just south of Luton. The Watford Spur left the route at its junction with the Leverstock Green-St. Albans road and took a southerly direction by Potters Crouch and passed over the North Orbital-road at Waterdale. It then passed west of Bucknalls, crossed the St. Albans branch of the L.M.S. railway from Watford, near Mutchetts Wood, and proceeded through the Munden estate to the Watford~bypass, which was utilised until it met the A5, south of Elstree. Consideration was being given to the construction of flyovers at several points. The length of new roads to be constructed was 16½ miles, while the North Orbital and Watford bypass roads were to be widened so as to provide duplicate carriageways and cycle tracks for a distance of 5½ miles. The length of trunk roads to be superseded was 26½ miles. The cost of the scheme was estimated at 1½ million pounds.

WO, March 1939
[The map on page 215 refers]

The Town Hall Critics

One correspondent, with heavy sarcasm, wrote that it was at all events "a very suitable building to house our worthy Council"! The Town Hall is now practically finished apart from furnishing, and it would be interesting to know if the critics are still of the same opinion For our part we regard the design of the building and its general appearance as admirable.

We make an exception of the clock turret, for which nobody has a good word, surely some improvement could be made here. The surroundings of the Town Hall have been planned with good taste, and altogether Watford has good reason to be proud of the new centre of its municipal life. Possibly the staff will move in before Christmas, but nothing has so far been settled about a formal opening ceremony; the matter is not likely to be discussed until it is possible to gain a clear idea of what the future holds.

WO, August 1939

A young lad, name of Nunn, living in Oxhey, had not long left school to start work at Apsley Mills, and had taken an interest in photography. These are from 6 x 6cm contact prints of, top, an up coal train approaching Watford Tunnel from the north; a John Dickinson longboat 'at Apsley' and, right, Cassiobury Park from the golf course; the paddling pool is behind the tree just right of centre. 1939. This book follows 64 years on!

Part VII   The Missing Years, 1939 to 1945

There was talk about Air Raid Precautions. The threat of war had been ominous for a long while. Picture Post had published an article, in November 1938, instancing the pogroms, including 'Kristallnacht', against the Jews and how, in Munich, 10,000 were rounded up and told to leave within 48 hours—an order later rescinded but not before overwhelming terror was caused. Air raid shelters were distributed. Of two types, the Anderson was of corrugated steel which was partly sunk into the garden soil and with sandbags or earth piled on or over; they gave excellent protection against blast. Morrison Shelters—less popular—were, in effect, re-inforced tables under which the shelterers could sleep; the construction would save them from the falling ceilings and roof, etc. Evacuees were brought into Watford from London and sent to to outlying districts, and ration cards were issued. War was declared on September 3rd, 1939 and the Borough Council made provision for providing allotments, and started a 'Dig for Victory' campaign. Apprehension indicated that something was going to happen—but as yet did not.

The Town Hall was opened in January of 1940, in the midst of the 'phoney war' when troops waited, and waited.

Hitler's blitzkrieg bypassed the French Maginot Line by overrunning Holland and Belgium and in a short time had forced the British Expeditionary Force back to the little resort of Dunkirk. From there some 330,000 troops were rescued by fleets of 'little boats'—a deliverance forever enshrined in our memory; the army was saved, but all equipment was lost.

The war became devastatingly real and was soon to be followed by capitulation of France. Much of Europe was now conquered and Great Britain, supported by Empire troops, stood alone, with trepidation. Invasion was feared.

Air Raid Precautions became a priority; buckets of sand and stirrup pumps were the standby equipment of the nightly 'firewatchers on the lookout for firebombs'. 'Home Guard' units were established. (They were later to be gently mocked in the humourous series of 'Dad's Army', written by Jimmy Perry, of Watford's Palace Theatre) but they had the merit of releasing younger men for active duty. Industry faced the problem that its skilled men were likely to be called up, and training programmes were started to teach women how to operate engineering machinery, which they did with every success. Women were called upon to serve in the Ambulance and Fire Services, and formed the ATS, WRENS and WAAFS, working closely alongside their 'senior' forces, often close to or in the front-line. They left their homes and formed the backbone of the Land Army where their work was vital in securing food supplies. Mobilisation was almost total but not all men were called to

arms; 'Bevin Boys' played their part as coal miners. There was a lull after May's Dunkirk debacle; it was thought that Hitler was preparing an invasion, with a motley collection of flat-bottomed barges totally unsuited to make a Channel Crossing. He needed first to destroy the RAF, which Goering boasted his Luftwaffe could do.

It could not, and did not.

Not all available RAF fighters had been sent to France in 1939, many were husbanded for Britain's defence. The need arrived; the German efforts to destroy the RAF bases was fought off, and in the September of 1940 the terror attacks on London and other cities started in earnest. Bombs fell in and near Watford where damage to housing was caused and lives lost. Pundits would say, knowingly, that 'they were after the railway viaduct' (to disrupt rail service to the Midlands) or that 'they were after such and such a factory'; we found out much later that the bombs dropped were completely indiscriminate, though not then seeming so.

There were drives to collect paper; iron and steel railings, and aluminium. For the first year ordinary products—camera films, stationery, clothing, furniture, household goods,—appeared with little outward change. But stocks were being exhausted and when gone could not be replaced. Savings drives came and went; magazines were available only by an order placed, there were no spare copies. They got smaller as did newspapers. Bananas and oranges disappeared and food was strictly rationed. The blackout caused hardships, torch batteries had to be used sparingly, razor blades scrounged and techniques learned to sharpen them for re-use. On the sparse rations the nation grew thinner, but fitter. War, and its effects, were to last far longer than anyone could have imagined. Women learned to juggle 'points' to buy clothing and make do without stockings.

The Kings George V playing fields were taken over for industry; Watford's diverse industry was harnessed in ways unknown until details could be revealed at war's end. The war started with biplanes and finished with jet planes, with aspirin and finished with penicillin, with rudimentary television and finished with radar. Watford made armaments, aeroplanes, and the penicillin. The news of victory by the Allies in Europe was received with intense relief tinged with horror and disbelief at the discovery of atrocities perpetrated by the Nazis. In August 1945, Japan surrendered under the additional pressure of the use of the atomic bomb.

After six years but a few days the war was over.

Evacuees from London change trains at Watford Junction for travel to Kings Langley, Hemel Hempstead and Boxmoor.   September 1939

Watford's Town Hall

IT is understood that Watford's new Town Hall will be formally opened, probably by royalty, early next year. The municipal staff may move in before that date. In the meantime it is announced that The Corporation, through a firm of London agents, are prepared to consider offers for a building lease of the site of the old offices, including the fire station, in High-street. The first idea was to sell the freehold, but, later, it was decided that leasing on 99 years' terms would be more profitable, taking the long view. Little Nascot, the building on the St. Albans-road corner of High-street, now used as public health offices, with a hut serving as a Welfare Centre, will also come onto the market, as a new Centre is to be erected on a site near the Public Library.

The Town Hall is costing Watford £150,000, so that a substantial set-off is very welcome.

Some idea of the value of High-street property may be gathered from the fact that recently Messrs. Rogers and Gowlett's shop fetched at auction £546 per foot frontage; even higher figures were realised a few years ago for other property.

WO, May 1939

West Herts Ready For Evacuation

FOLLOWING an announcement by the Ministry of Health yesterday preparations for receiving children and other "priority cases" evacuated from London were set in motion throughout West Herts.

The "Observer' understands that Hertfordshire is to receive 84,000 evacuees.

Watford and Bushey are the only towns in this area where there will be no billeting; they are officially termed "neutral zones." In every other town, village and hamlet London school-children with their teachers, and expectant mothers, are to be billeted.

Although not receiving any evacuated children permanently, Watford will be a "distributing" centre. Children will be brought to Watford Junction station and entrained from there to country districts. It is understood that they will come to Watford by bus, coach and tube, and in this connection a considerable portion of the bypass road from Finchley-road to the Elstree roundabout, will be a one-way traffic road for vehicles leaving London.

There will be no interference of early morning traffic from Watford stations, but during the day services will be curtailed.

WO, August 1939

The A.R.P. Problem

IT was reported at the meeting of Watford Town Council on Tuesday evening that £1,279 is being paid out in wages each week to workers in A.R.P. services in the Borough. This works out at over £66,000 per annum, or nearly £200,000 if the war should last three years.

Though this sum may not be so large as in some places, it is sufficiently alarming, and when it is remembered that expenditure on this scale is being incurred all over the country it will be seen what a vast drain on the national resources is involved. For the time being the Government will repay the whole cost on personnel to the local authorities, but that is little consolation to the taxpayers.

The wage bill at Watford includes £463 for the auxiliary fire service; and, as Councillor Baxter (Chairman of the A.R.P. Committee) pointed out, another six men are wanted before the Home Office requirements are reached. He said that the Committee were out to save money wherever possible, and no doubt in some cases voluntary service will be substituted for paid service.

WHP October, 1939

Council to Erect Shelters

OF the 12,000 "Anderson" shelters to be provided free to householders in Watford, the Borough Council estimate that 4,000 cannot be erected by the recipients owing to physical incapacity or other reasons, and at a special meeting of the Council on Tuesday it was agreed to exercise the necessary powers to enable the Council to erect these shelters at a cost that may run into nearly £30,000.

Of this some nine or ten thousand pounds will fall on local ratepayers.

The Civil Defence Committee and the Town Clerk were given exceptional powers in order to avoid delay.

WHP, July 1939

Now Do You Want a Shelter?

Only a few weeks ago the "Post" told the story of the delivery of the first Anderson steel air raid shelters.

More than a few people due to receive them refused for some reason or another—some did not want to spoil their gardens; others did not want the trouble of erecting them, and perhaps a few did not like to advertise the fact that their income was less than the prescribed amount

Most of those who refused are now regretting it and applying for delivery again. Some are even complaining of delay, but everyone wants a shelter now, and there is possibility that Watford Council may take away any shelters that have been lying about, not in position, for more than a week and deliver them to persons who require them.

Not until deliveries for the free list have been completed—and some 2,500,000 come into this category—will those who intend to pay be accommodated.

WHP September, 1939

Rogers and Gowlett's corner site in the High Street up for auction, April 1938, and was sold for £17,472; i.e. £546 per ft of a 32ft frontage.

Shock naval disaster . . .

Profoundly Touched

Sir.—As head teacher of one of the evacuated London schools, may I express on behalf of my colleagues and myself, our most grateful thanks to all the people of Kings Langley for the way in which they have received our children and their teachers.

We could never have believed that we should meet with so much kindness.

From the voluntary workers who took charge of our weary children so sympathetically on arrival—to the new "uncles" and "aunts" who opened their homes to them so willingly and spared no thought or effort to make them at once part of their own families—everyone seemed possessed with the same spirit of kindliness and the desire to help.

We shall never forget our reception here—we have, indeed, been profoundly touched.

A LONDON HEAD TEACHER
WHP, September 1939

When the Sirens Sounded

SUCH a complete surprise was the air raid warning on Sunday morning that in many parts of Watford the house-holders, instead of making for shelter as they had been instructed, congregated in the streets to converse with neighbours.

Some took little notice, fancying that the signal was just a rehearsal, but many in central Watford who took the warning more seriously were considerably alarmed when a warden in one area mistakenly rang a handbell for the "raiders passed" signal.

Realising that the ringing of a handbell had some connection with gas, but forgetting that it was the "gas all cleared" signal a number of persons rushed for their gas masks and took shelter.

WHP, Septembe, 1939

The Approach of Rationing

NOW that the National Register is virtually complete and the 40,000,000 rationing cards are being made out for distribution, we may expect rationing to be in force in the latter part of this month. In view of all the difficulties, especially in regard to transport, that war has caused, there has been remarkably little delay.

Nor has there been any serious shortage of any foodstuffs, except perhaps bacon in some districts.

If we remember the strain thrown upon rail and road traffic by the transport of an army of 158,000 men to France with all its modern equipment, to say nothing of the supplies required by the Navy and the Air Force, we may wonder that civilian life has been so little disturbed.

When rationing comes into force, we may count upon each household and each district getting a fair share of the foodstuffs, few in number, that will at first be controlled.

There is no need to suppose that the national stocks are inadequate—the contrary is the truth—but at the outset of what may be a long war the Government is right in taking full precautions against even a temporary shortage anywhere.

WHP, November 1939

Hertfordshire Police

After the Great War the trickle of road accidents became a flood. In 1927 fifty-seven people were killed on Hertfordshire roads, in 1936 this figure rose to seventy-five and in 1939 the total was 101.

Top: *At Chater School, one of the many groups undertaking the work of naming the ration books for issuing.*

Left: *HMS Courageous was built in 1917 and converted into an aircraft carrier to handle a complement of 40 aircraft. It was not at strength at the time of sinking on 17th September but its loss just 14 days after declaration of war was a huge shock.*
Walton's greengrocers on the corner of Clarendon Road have ample stocks of fruits, including those 'later-to-be-a-vague-memory', bananas.

£186,000 Town Hall officially open . . .

Town Hall opening

WITH befitting ceremonial, Watford's new Town Hall was officially opened on Friday afternoon, the ceremony taking place in the large assembly room.

The Municipal Buildings, standing at the corner of Rickmansworth and Hempstead roads, and costing about £186,000, have taken two years to erect, the foundation stone being laid in May, 1938. Based on a modernised version of Georgian tradition, the buildings are from a design by Mr. C. Cowles-Voysey, the contractors being Messrs. Richard Costain, Ltd.

The assembly hall has seating accommodation on the floor for about 1,300 people, and a further 300 in the gallery, while there is a capacious stage with seats in tiers.

It was a great disappointment that the Earl of Clarendon (Charter Mayor of Watford) was unable, owing to indisposition, to fulfil his promise to perform the ceremony, this duty being graciously undertaken in his absence by the Countess of Clarendon, who was accompanied by her daughter, Lady Joan Newman.

Representatives of neighbouring boroughs and other local authorities attended, and in the hall were representatives of all departments of the town's activities, with burgesses and many others from adjoining districts.

WO, 12th January, 1940

In a few short months Europe is over-run, Denmark, Holland Belgium and France conquered and occupied.

400,000 British and French troops are trapped in Belgium but by an unexplained act the German advantage is not immediately exploited and in ten days, with sunny weather and calm seas, a rearguard action halts the Germans long enough for 330,000 troops to be evacuated by 'little ships' off the beaches of Dunkirk.

Britain stands alone whilst the horrors of Nazi-dominated life start for the newly-conquered and vanquished. The Battle of Britain commences; every Spitfire and Hurricane is desperately needed and used sparingly.

Against overwhelming odds the 'few' repulse attack after attack against airfields in Hitler's effort to cripple the Air Force. When the Germans are almost to the point of success they change tactics and start to bomb London and other cities.

The airfields are saved to be patched up to continue the fight. Britain's solitary 'finest hours' had passed and Hitler had had his first defeat.

Dunkirk—May 1940
Battle of Britain—June to Sept 1940

Corporation as Pig-keepers

WATFORD TOWN COUNCIL are about to start a scheme for the collection of pig food. Householders are to be asked to keep in a receptacle separate from the dust-bin all sorts of food scraps, which will be collected by the dustmen.

The Council are buying two 60-gallon boiling pans, and intend to increase the number of pigs on the Corporation farm. Surplus food will be sold. The dustmen are to be paid 1s. per cwt. on the quantity they bring in, and it would seem that the experiment will have to be a big success if this outlay is to be covered.

At Tottenham the salvage is run on different lines. The dustmen have themselves formed a Pig Club. They have erected piggeries in their spare time on vacant land at the refuse disposal works, and have acquired a herd of 42 pigs.

For these they already have ample food and are selling tons of surplus. The vehicles are equipped with pig-food containers, and it is

Top: *The new Town Hall had been substantially completed for some time at the outbreak of war. Many buildings in the country not fully utilised were requisitioned for war use. It is stated that to avoid this happening to the Town Hall the Mace Bearer's flat was occupied. Some departments had moved in and the first Council Meeting, at which Alderman L H Andrews was elected mayor, took place on 9th November 1939. The 'official' opening took place on 5th January 1940. Here the Countess of Clarendon is speaking.*

Left: *Pig food collection, Holywell Farm, West Watford.*

B.E.F wounded arriving here in their hundreds ...

anticipated that the weekly surplus will soon be 20 to 30 tons. Watford Corporation have had a pig farm for many years. The Farm Bailiff has specialised in show specimens, and has been a very successful exhibitor at leading shows.

He knows his business and there is no reason why, in a short time, he should not have a large utility herd under his control, besides preserving the strain he has made famous.

WO, January, 1940

The Canal Towpath

FOR a considerable time negotiations have been proceeding between Berkhamsted Urban Council and the Grand Union Canal Company with regard to the public right-of-way along the canal towpath, and it is satisfactory to note that a compromise has now been reached. The Council agree to take no further action to remove the Company's notice boards prohibiting the use by the public of the towpath, and the Company, on their part, will grant an irrevocable permission of use.

WO, February, 1940

Urgency

There is a freshening spirit in the Government and the people of Britain. The first German bombs have fallen on English soil—the first drops of the shower of steel that Hitler has threatened. German troops are only 25 miles from the coast of Kent.

German parachutists must be expected at any moment from now on. Britain faces the most formidable trial in her history without despondency or alarm.

Picture Post, May 1940

B.E.F. Wounded Are Here

WE make an urgent appeal to everyone, not only in Watford, but in the whole of the district served by this newspaper, to come to the immediate aid of wounded men of the B.E.F., who have been arriving in Watford in their

hundreds since the gallant evacuation of Boulogne and Dunkirk.

Many hospital trains laden with their maimed and broken human freight have been arriving almost daily at the station. Here their field dressings, many of which are, of necessity, rough and improvised, are supplemented before the men are placed in the waiting ambulances which convey them to the various base hospitals distributed

throughout the county.

Owing to the very nature of their wounds, the importance of these heroes receiving immediate attention on their arrival cannot be emphasised too greatly, but such attention requires suitable materials for bandages, pads, etc. Here is where we call upon your sympathy and gratitude which can be shown in a practical manner by supplying these men with a few comforts.

WHP, June 1940

Watford's Century of Printing

AT a meeting of the Guild of Young Printers, in connection with the Watford Branch of the Typographical Association, held in the Oddfellows (Small) Hall on Friday evening, Mr. David Greenhill, of the Sun Engraving Company, gave a very interesting lecture on "Printing and its Development in Watford."

In the Public Library there is a poor-rate book, dated 1834, with the imprint "Peacock, Printer, Watford," and in the "Observer" office there is still an American hand-press dated 1820. The firm possess many specimens of work done in these early days.

John Peacock was followed by his son Samuel, who in 1863 established the "Observer," the offices then being in Queen's-road near the old Library. Samuel died in 1880, and his elder son, Thomas J. Peacock carried on on behalf of his mother. At the mother's death in 1893 Thomas sold his interest to his younger brother, Charles Herbert Peacock, who then be came proprietor, and ran the business very successfully till his death in 1930, since when his son, Kim Peacock has been director and manager.

Mr. Kim Peacock, who has taken a great interest in modernising the plant and in improving the "Observer," had been assisted by at least two, and possibly some other very

Top: *At the ARP Wardens' post at the corner of Loates Lane/Derby Road a Wardens' Corps Efficiency Presentation is taking place.*

Centre: *Wounded troops arrive at Watford Junction station.*

able men. The two referred to were Mr. F. H. Barnes, the editor, to whom he was indebted for the forgoing information, and Mr. W. J. Tamplin, who largely ran the works side of the business. When he came to Watford, some 35 years ago, Mr. Greenhill said, the "Observer" office was prominent among the small number of printers.

So far as he could remember there were:

Bemrose and Sons, who had the works at Milton-street, North Watford, now used by Messrs. Novobax Ltd. (Waterlows.)

Acme Engraving Co., process engravers and printers, who were in Acme-road, near Bemroses.

Mr. Edward Voss, in Loates-lane.

Mr. T. C. Warren, of the "Record" Printing Works.

Mr. Michael (who was father to Percy D. Michael, the Home Counties Alliance Secretary), in Queen's-road, and who later joined Mr. Voss.

Castle and Parker, of 151, High-street.

Mr. J. E. King, of 42, High-street.

Messrs. Curtis Bros., of King-street.

Messrs. Stone and Cox, who started about 1904/5.

André and Sleigh, of Bushey, who made a great reputation for fine engraving and later for fine colour printing, started about 1890.

There was also a **Mr. Ashworth,** who started in partnership with Mr. Meredith in 1901. He began at Bushey, and then moved to Clarendon road in 1906. In 1902 Mr. Ashworth made the first colour process engraving for the cover of "The Motor," and he believed he had continued to do them ever since. Mr. Ashworth still kept his flag flying in Fleet-street, London, and must be nearing the three score years and ten!

With regard to the more recent development of printing in Watford, Mr. Greenhill gave the following short summary of dates:

1914.—Sun Engraving Company Ltd. developed from Anglo-Engraving Co. and André and Sleigh, of Bushey, in 1914, and in 1918 took over the works in Whippendell-road, formerly owned by the **Menpes Press.** As you will probably know, the Menpes Press was a rather beautifully built and very well designed printing factory, planned by **Mr. Geo. W. Jones,** the eminent printer.

1918-1919.—Hudson and Stracey. Mr. Hudson was at the Menpes Press when the "Sun" took over.

1919.—Bournehall Press.—Mr. Lewis Blower now had a very nicely equipped plant doing very good work.

1919.—Gibbs and Bamforth Ltd. started in Watford by purchasing the "West Herts Post" and the "Watford Newsletter," and combining them into one paper.

1924-25.—Davey and Winterson started a small business in North Watford.

1926.—Messrs. Greycaines started in Watford.

1929.—Messrs. F. E. Blower and Co. took over Mr. Warren's business—the old "Record" office.

1935.—Messrs. Edsons (Printers) Ltd. came from Stoke Newington and built a very nice modern factory, very well equipped, and now doing a very good standard of work

1936.—The great firm of Odhams Ltd., came to Watford and started Odhams (Watford) Ltd.

1936.—The Chiltern Printing Works started in Clarendon-road.

WO, July 1940

CROXLEY ESTATES SUPERIOR HOUSES

1919

Per Week, inclusive
£635
FREEHOLD

3 double bedrooms. Tiled bathroom, coloured bath. Seperate lavatory. Beautifully fitted kitchen. Ideal boiler. Garage space.

The phenomenal growth of Croxley testifies to its excellent residential amenities. The outstanding value offered in our houses is reflected in their popularity. Our sales are definitely the highest. You are cordially invited to visit our Show Houses at Baldwins Lane and Frankland Road, Croxley Green.

New Printing Machine

Watford Town Council on Tuesday decided to buy a Multilith printer and accessories from the Addressograph Multigraph Co., Ltd., at a cost of £564 3. 5d., on which to print all the Council minutes and printing work.

In discussing the question of economy, Councillor E. J. Baxter suggested that it might be wise to ascertain how the operators might be affected by rules of the Typographical Association or any other printing union.

Council E. T. Warren replied that movable type was not used.

This was simply a duplicating machine. Councillor F. Williams stated that at first he thought here was the Council trying to economise and then they were going to spend £565, but looking further one realised that sometimes it was necessary to spend money to economise. Councillor Williams asked for an assurance that all the printing of each department would be done on the one machine.

The Committee had seen the machine working and it seemed to turn out very fine work They would make a considerable saving. At the present time the printing of the minutes cost £490 a year. They could duplicate them for half that amount.

The whole of the printing would be under the Town Clerk's department. The machine would pay for itself in a year or two.

WHP September, 1940

"Mr Percy Grillo, one of Watford's best known tradesmen, is, as our picture shows doing his bit as an ARP Warden. thus carrying on a tradition of which the firm of M Grillo and Son are justly proud. Four of the principals of the firm are British ex-service men."
With his cart in Watford Field Road

The Ministry of Aircraft Production purchases the King George V playing fields . . .

How Watford Hospital Has Grown

The last annual meeting of the Watford Peace Memorial Hospital as an unincorporated body was held yesterday. Although the actual incorporation took place in February, a resolution was required at the annual meeting to regularise certain matters arising from the incorporation and this was duly passed.

Sir John Caulcutt, the Chairman, commenting on the annual report, which has already appeared in the "West Herts Post," said that one or two useful comments could be made. The Peace Memorial Hospital was opened in 1925, and a report published in March, 1927, showed that at that time there were 87 beds in the hospital. In that year 1,126 in-patients were treated at a cost of £10,600.

Since that time, further accommodation was found necessary, and in 1937 the hospital possessed 154 beds, while the annual cost was by then £25,000. When the work now in hand was completed the number would be 308.

Up till 1937 the Committee had made both ends meet in regard to maintenance. But for the last three years there had been respective deficits of £1,908, £1,492 and £1,480. This was partly due to the increased cost of medical stores, which in many cases had gone up almost 50 per cent.

A total of £145,000 had been provided by people in Watford in order that the hospital might be built, furnished and carried on.

Since the outbreak of war, the Board of Management had been very much alive to its responsibilities towards the town.

They had been doing all they could to increase the accommodation with the result that two shell wards would soon be available.

WHP, July 1940

Slow Fund Support Criticised

Strong criticism of Watford's support of the Spitfire Fund was made at the meeting of Watford Town Council on Tuesday, and summing up his speech, Alderman H. Coates said: "If we don't get the amount required in the next three weeks or month Watford should be ashamed of itself."

Councillor S. W. Smith raised the matter. He said that the last amount published was £1,500. That figure, compared with collections in Watford in the past, would be considered stimulating, but when they compared it with the figure required it was a long distance off.

To raise the sum of £6,000 would mean a widespread, well-organised and highly concentrated effort with all possible initiative put into it. He had received letters disparaging the organisation of the scheme.

The Mayor stated that the total was now £1,650. The money was coming in slower than he anticipated, but it was coming in steadily.

There were several things they hoped would bring in reasonable sums. An auction at the Town Hall for which they required gifts, a dance, a boxing tournament, etc.

He did want, he said, more subscriptions direct from the public, and if possible some substantial ones.

Alderman Coates said that it was a very unsatisfactory response that only £1,650 should be raised in five weeks. It was unfortunate that Watford could not be aroused to the enthusiasm of many towns. It was a shame that this effort had not been considered worthy of the people.

Why are not the people of Watford ready to go out and say to their friends, 'Let us do something for the fund.' It should be sufficient that the Mayor is at the head of the Fund. Everyone should feel it his duty to get on with it"

Alderman Coates recalled that during his Mayoralty he made a special appeal for the Hospital He expected £5,000 at least. It was depressing to find that only £750 was given.

No matter what it was, there had been a lack of enthusiasm among the people of Watford. Watford looked upon itself as a dormitory town, and that the residents came here to sleep.

"I would like people to came here and wake up," he continued. He hoped, he went on, that a very big effort would be made.

WHP, November 1940

The New Police Court

ERECTED at a cost of £70,000, Watford's new Police Court was formally opened this week. For some 80 years the local Magistrates have shared the building in King-street with the County Court, the police headquarters being a short distance away.

Now, the administration, including that of the Magistrates' Clerk, is centralised in Clarendon-road. In quite a central position, the new building is a worthy addition to the public institutions of the Borough. It is admirably designed to meet a need that had become more pressing as the population grew. Fortunately the scheme was too far advanced to be affected by the outbreak of war.

There are doubtless older inhabitants of Watford who remember the primitive police station situated in one of the yards off Lower High-street.

The next move was to premises in Estcourt-road, later occupied as the Weights and Measures office. The King-street station was erected about half-a century ago, and had become just about as inconvenient and incommodious as the old Municipal building in High-street.

WHP, October 1940

£85 Expenses on Spitfire Fund

THE Deputy Mayor (Alderman L. H. Andrews), during whose Mayoralty the Watford Spitfire Fund was launched, is deeply concerned regarding the fact that the Fund having reached £5,001 has the not inconsiderable sum of £85 to pay in respect of expenses incurred. These include printing, postages and many other items which always accrue.

Alderman Andrews has appealed to us to give the necessary publicity to this fact, hoping that when once it is appreciated that Watford's own Spitfire is almost within grasp, the public will respond and see to it that Lord Beaverbrook has Watford's cheque for the full amount in his possession in the shortest possible time, particularly as it is now five months since the Fund was inaugurated.

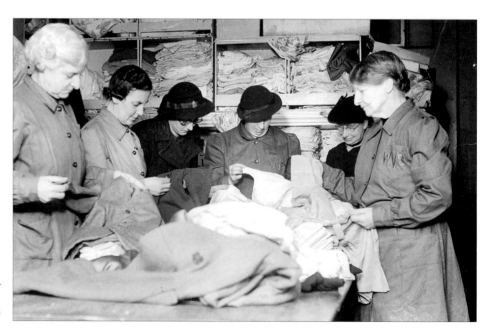

At Upton House, a WVS 'Clothing Party' sorting donations. 1943

. . . my pension; if the Germans win at least they can't touch that . . .

The Deputy Mayor might like to know that we have good reason for believing that if, say, £50 or £60 is subscribed by the public, a certain well-known local gentleman will provide the balance of the amount outstanding.

This is an extremely generous gesture, for we know that this person has already made a liberal gift to the Fund.

We have it on good authority that if the public make a good response to this final appeal, the Fairy Godfather will do the rest.

All subscriptions should be addressed:
Mayor's Spitfire Fund, Town Hall, Watford.

WHP, December 1940

Simple-Minded People

Sir,—A few days ago a man remarked: "Oh, well, if the Germans win, at any rate I have my pension and they can't touch that"

There is reason to believe that there are other simple-minded people in Watford who are similarly deceived. Can nothing be done to convince these that if so appaling a catastrophe as a German victory should overtake us, pensions and every other source of income would cease to be available.

We should simply be slaves, entirely under the control, in every department of our lives, of the Germans. Everyone would be compelled to work for whatever wages and during whatever hours the Nazi rulers might dictate.
C. CARR.

WHP, December 1940

Two Games on Christmas Day

It was decided on Tuesday afternoon that Watford and Luton will meet twice on Christmas Day. The match at Watford will take place in the morning at Vicarage-road, kick-off 11 a.m., and at Luton in the afternoon.

Watford and Luton are the first clubs to decide to play both fixtures on the same day. Many other clubs are likely to follow their lead.

The decision of Luton to agree to the double fixture is welcomed by Mr. William Findlay, Watford F.C. manager, who is responsible for the idea.

On Monday, when a decision had not yet been reached by the Luton directors, Mr. Findlay pointed out to me that the cancellation of Boxing Day football means that Luton would play Watford at Vicarage-road on Christmas Day, a large crowd would be certain to congregate—in all events the largest of the season—and Luton would derive half the gate-money.

On the other hand, had this return fixture in the afternoon not been arranged, Watford would not have had the opportunity of reaping in 50 per cent of the takings at Luton.

WHP, December 1940

Top: The new refreshment van presented by the American Red Cross is shown off in Rickmansworth Road, near the Park Gates.

Right: Tividale's was a small iron and brass foundry in Local Board Road, more used to making manhole covers and drain gratings. Here they have just cast a brass name plaque for H M S Watford, a vessel which was never commissioned.

The aircraft production at Leavesden . . . and bombs on Watford and district . . .

Watford acquired an airfield—though not in the manner first suggested back in 1936. The fields, 300 acres, known locally as Mile Field, were bought from the Council by the Ministry of Aircraft Production and a 1,000yd concrete runway provided. Also built were workshops, fitting shops and hangers. It was then leased by the Ministry to two Groups for aircraft production—the London Aircraft Production (LAP) and the Second Aircraft Group (SAG).

For those who enjoyed travelling by coach the odds were that the luxurious body they were sitting in was produced by Duple Motor Bodies whose works were in The Hyde, along the Edgware Road. They, with Chrysler Motors, Express Body and Motor Works, Park Royal Coachworks and the London Passenger Transport Board formed the London Aircraft Production Group. Handley-Page, based at London Colney near Radlett set up a satellite plant at Leavesden. The LAP made various sections of the the four-engined Halifax bombers at their individual works and transported them to Leavesden where they were assembled, flight tested and flown to their operational bases. The Halifax was large and heavy, weighing (without its 5 ton bomb-load) about 19 tons, Leavesden assembled 35 in their first year to July 1942, and made a total of 712 before production at Leavesden ceased.

In the meanwhile de Havilland were fully extended at Stag Lane and Lostock in making variable pitch propellors; Hatfield was extended with design for the new twin-engined wooden bomber, unarmed, which was to be faster than any fighter. The Air Ministry were not over-impressed though a trial order for 50

was placed. Work was not to interrupt production of Tiger Moths urgently needed for flying training.

The new wooden plane was named 'Mosquito' and development work carried on at Salisbury Hall, near Radlett with the first prototype flying in November 1940. A production line was started at Hatfield—where work was disrupted by enemy air raids on average once in every five days—and was soon to be found inadequate. A second line was started at Leavesden where the first models made were dual-control trainers; subsequently production was concentrated upon FIIs—these were day/night long-range fighters.

During the was 6,710 Mosquitos were built, of which almost 1,400 came from Leavesden, a production second only to Hatfield. Production carried on at Leavesden after the war when TR33s (torpedo/reconnaissance bombers) and T3 Trainers were made, making a grand total 1,476 before production finally ceased.

Of wooden construction, with parts made by the furniture trade, the use of wood—with which de Havilland's were very familiar—saved almost a year in production and prototype trials. The Mosquito could carry a bomb load of 4000-lb, they suffered fewer losses per thousand sorties than any other allied craft and were highly efficient at 'Pathfinder' duties. They destroyed one V1 bomb-site for every 39.8 tons of bombs dropped compared with 165.4 tons for the B-17 Fortress and 182 tons for the B-25 Mitchell.

As a fighter, or as a bomber, it had no equal.

The Air Raids

During the period of the blitz upon London, a considerable number of enemy planes crossed and dropped bombs upon Watford and the surrounding district. All incidents were recorded; many were of unexploded bombs which, nevertheless, had to be dealt with. Falling anti-aircraft shells added to the incident roll.

The main incidents during 1940 and 1941 were: 27th September 1940, fires started at Greycaine's and an unexploded bomb in Sandringham Road; October damage in Souldern Street; 31st October 1940, house wrecked in Cassiobury Park Avenue; 16th November 1940, house wrecked in Tudor Avenue; 5th December 1940, damage in St. Johns Road, five dead; 9th December 1940, damage in Eastlea Avenue, 4 killed and 2 injured; 2nd January 1941, incendiary damage to Trewin's store; 17th January 1941, damage in

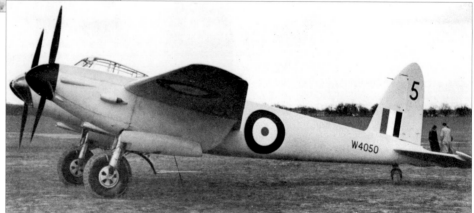

Above: It is stated that aircrews knew which Halifax was assembled at Leavesden for the green leather seat coverings were reminiscent of LPTB coaches; and that the smoother rivetting added 10-15 knots extra speed.

Right:. Mosquito construction at Leavesden concentrated on fighter variants.

Norfolk Avenue, four injured; 30th January 1941, three injured in Park Avenue; 15th March 1941, damage in Crossmead, 7 casualties. After this period of activity a parachute bomb was dropped near the top of Scots Hill on 17th February 1944; on 16th June 1944 a flying bomb caused damage near Rosecroft Drive and on 26th June 1944 in Oxhey Lane. The last incident was in the early hours of Sunday morning 30th July 1944, when a flying bomb damaged 50 houses beyond repair in Sandringham Road, 100 severely and 500 to a lesser degree. In this incident 40 people were killed and many more injured.

More bombs fell in wooded and open areas causing little or no damage. There is no evidence of 'planned' attacks upon the area or upon particular targets.

Top: *Eastlea Avenue; Cassiobury Park Avenue.*

Centre: *Tudor Avenue.*

Bottom: *St Johns Road;Rosary Priory, Caldecote Towers, Bushey.*

Death of Mr. James Cawdell

WE regret to announce the death, at the age of 73, of Mr. James Cawdell, of 17, Rickmansworth-road, Watford, who 37 years ago established the draper's business in High-street, which is still carried on in his name.

In 1904 he bought the business of the late Mr. George Langley in Watford, and, with the encouragement of his late wife, developed it from the days when Mr. and Mrs. Cawdell lived over the shop and had only 14 assistants, until 1924, when the turnover was six times greater and they had 50 assistants.

In the days when Mr. Cawdell was in business the cattle market was still held in the Marketplace, and occasionally sheep and cattle rushed through the entrance of his shop.

In 1929, in view of his rapidly increasing business, Mr. Cawdell bought from Trust Houses Ltd., the Essex Arms Hotel, one of the largest hotels in Watford, whose premises included the old Corn Exchange, which had been converted into a dance hall.

With the buildings he had to acquire the publican's licence of the premises, and for four months, until he allowed it to lapse at the next Brewster Sessions, he was actually a licensed victualler as well as a draper. In that year he converted the firm into a private limited com-

pany, and went into partnership with Mr. David Greenhill, under the name of James Cawdell and Co., Ltd.

The new firm demolished the existing shop and hotel, and on its site built the present large store in the Market-place.

WO, February 1941

War Weapons Weeks

THIS district of Hertfordshire is at length coming into line with other parts of the country in organising War Weapons Weeks.

A start was made at Bushey on Monday evening by the decision to make an effort from March 22 to 29, and a figure of £100,000 has been mentioned as the goal. Rickmansworth, on Wednesday, fixed as the period April 12 to 19, aiming at a similar amount. In each case the local authority is giving active support. Committees representative of local industries, banks, schools, British Legion, W.V.S., and Savings Groups have been formed and organisers appointed.

In Watford, which we should have liked to see taking the lead in such a vital movement, the date we have heard suggested is April 19 to 26, which appropriately enough, will include St. George's Day, with a quarter of a million sterling as the minimum. To ensure success a much more vigorous organisation will be required than that behind the long-drawn-out and only partially successful Spitfire Fund.

WO, February, 1941

Watford Grammar Schools

MRS. WHEELWRIGHT, a Watford member of Herts County Council, speaking at a meeting of the local Rotary Club, revived the Watford Grammar Schools controversy, which has been more or less dormant since 1935.

It will be recalled that when the Governors applied for a capital grant of some £18,000 for a pavilion they were told that such a grant could only be made on condition that the Schools were transferred to the County Council. The Governors would not forego their trust, and in this decision were practically unanimously supported by the townspeople, a public meeting showing how strongly local opinion had been aroused by the suggestion.

At that time Mrs. Wheel-wright ran counter to the general feeling in the Borough, and now talks about the Schools being left out of the post-war educational programme.

They have, however, gone along very well since the County ultimatum was presented and, in any event, the war has put any new building out of the question.

The County Council do not allege that the Watford Grammar Schools have been badly managed, or that the standard of education is not as high as that at any similar school in the country. They object to the Governors not being completely under their control in other words, they want to be sole masters. Local pride in the foundation they dismiss as mere sentiment.

To their standardised minds it is nothing that the Schools date back well over two centuries, that the founder, Dame Fuller, is a revered figure in Watford's story, and that generations have been brought up in the old Fullerian tradition. For no good reason at all they want to destroy Watford's pride in the individuality and historic associations of its Grammar Schools.

It may be that they want to be in control when Watford, with 75,000 in population, seeks county borough powers, so that their hands are strengthened if they decide to oppose. So far, fortunately, there is no sign that the Governors are in the least inclined to surrender their independence. They realise that if they tamely handed over the heritage of the Schools they would bring on their heads a great storm of protest.

WO, May 1941

Top: *A land mine dropped near the top of Scots Hill caused severe damage to All Saints Church, Croxley Green.*

Right: *Trewin's in Queens Road suffered an incendiary bomb attack.*

Watford Electricity Profits

WATFORD electricity undertaking made a net profit last year of £30,225, which was slightly less than for the preceding twelve months. The sum allocated in relief of the rate was £6,500.

It may reasonably be asked why this amount has not been larger, especially as the legal maximum is in the neighbourhood of £10,500, and Luton's transfer is £14,000.

For some years now Watford Corporation have been only making transfers from the income derived from the Borough itself, leaving out of account that from outside districts, whose objection to helping to "subsidise"

annual accounts (just published) of the Chief Engineer and General manager show what a vast volume of business is being done. An addition of 1,696 consumers during the year brought the total up to 31,832, and the tariff is among the lowest in England.

In its early days the undertaking did not show much promise of becoming a valuable asset to Watford. As a matter of fact, its sale to a company was seriously suggested, and it was only the determined stand made on the Council by the late Mr. I. C. Benskin, who was then chairman of the Electricity Committee, that saved the scheme. Though enjoying the

advantage of a monopoly, the undertaking undoubtedly owes a great deal to highly efficient and enterprising administration.

WO, May 1941

The Toll of the Road

ACCORDING to a police report presented to the County Council this week, 824 road accidents occurred in Hertfordshire last quarter. Of these, 23 proved fatal, as against 14 in the corresponding period of last year. Eleven people were killed by careless or dangerous driving, and seven pedestrians met their death through carelessness on their own part.

This toll of the road is very disquieting, and raises the question whether Magistrates are sufficiently severe on motorists whose guilt is clearly proved.

How far the returns are affected by the blackout in the winter months is not shown, but undoubtedly night driving in pitch darkness with war-time lights is a contributory cause.

Another factor is the recklessness to which some drivers of Army lorries are addicted. On the other hand the complaint of motorists about 'jay' walkers is proved by the statistics to be well founded. Pedestrian crossings are often ignored, and it is common for people to step straight on to the road without troubling to look for on-coming traffic, or, if they do look, to do so one way only.

The rules of 'safety first' are thus forgotten, often with lamentable results. The authorities will sooner or later be forced to take more drastic steps than any they have hitherto taken to deal with this question of road accidents.

WO, May 1941

Watford rates from profits to which they contributed became very vocal some time ago. There were several good answers to these protests—one was that outlying places had made no contribution to the capital outlay on the scheme—but to placate opposition the Council decided to adopt the principle mentioned. Despite the war, the undertaking continues to flourish. On the sales for public lighting there has been a drop of nearly a million units, but so small is the margin of profit in this branch of the business that the effect on the balance sheet has been insignificant The

Top: *Russell's Estate, bordering Hempstead Road opposite the Grove was used extensively for troop training; here a detachment of Home Guard. It was here that a young Jimmy Perry gained experiences to be later used in a show called 'Dad's Army'.*

Right: *53rd South West Herts (St Peters) Scouts Group, Bushey Mill Lane have a scrap metal collection ...*

Watford issues a challenge to Luton . . . a spy is parachuted in . . .

Thanks A Million

Watford and District War Weapons Week ended on Saturday and with the termination of this greatest of savings campaigns disappear any doubts—if there were any—that the public would rise to the occasion.

At the inaugural war weapons meeting held five weeks ago, a target of £500,000 was the aim. Most people were of the opinion that it was a modest sum, but despite optimism there were few who conscientiously believed that Watford's effort would reach the final enormous figure of £1,275,629, a sum equal to £12 7s. 8d. per head of the population.

WHP, May 1941

M.B.E. For Mr. George R. Bolton

Mr. George R. Bolton, Borough Librarian, of Watford, who was awarded the M.B.E. for his work as controller of 17 Group of the Royal Observer Corps, attended at Buckingham Palace on Tuesday when the King invested him with the honour. Mr. Bolton was announced by Lord Clarendon, who has so many associations with Watford.

WHP, July 1941

Change at West Herts Post

The copyright and goodwill of the "West Herts Post" have been purchased by Home Counties Newspapers Ltd., who have been in part associated with the management of the paper for the last twenty years.

With the exception of a few minor changes on the technical side, the paper will continue as usual under the editorship of Mr. W. Fleet Huson, supported by the present editorial staff.

Commencing with next week's issue, the "West Herts Post" will be published on Thursday afternoon instead of Thursday morning, and will appear in a much more convenient and handy form, a change that we are certain will be warmly welcomed by our readers.

WHP October, 1941

• *The West Herts Post from 1887, when it was founded, followed until 1919 the style of the Watford Observer in having the front page consisting of advertisements, mostly classifieds.*

Then, for a year, the West Herts Post cleared advertisements from the front page and ran news stories in their stead. This did not last and in 1920 they reverted to the 'Observer' style.

In the 1941 change the front page was cleared and given over to news stories, the page halved to tabloid size and the number of pages increased.

Layout is stylish, presentation snappy and stories are given good length and display.

A spy is parachuted in

19/20 September a German spy, Wulf Schmidt, is parachuted into Cambridgeshire. When captured he is found to have £132, $160 and a false passport bearing the name 'Harry Williamson'

Coal Must Be Saved

IT is as necessary in the home as in the factory that coal should be saved this winter. An appeal has been made by the Minister of Mines to all local authorities, urging the greatest economy in the use of fuel. All departments of Watford Corporation have been circularised to this effect by the Mayor, and doubtless industries not engaged upon war work will be recipients of a similar urgent appeal.

The bright autumnal weather of the past few days will have relieved many a housewife or maid of the task of lighting fires, and the equally disagreeable task of cleaning up the grates in the morning.

But with the vital requirement that the national war effort should reach its peak at the earliest possible moment, it is imperative that the domestic user should practise the greatest economy, not only in coal fires, but in the use of gas and electricity, and every other fueL

The employer and worker in business and the woman in the home must be linked in this great fuel economy campaign.

WO October, 1941

Pleased—And Displeased

Sir,—Congratulations to the new "West Herts Post!" Both for its make-up and content. On its present form it should be the medium for all progressive thought in Watford and district.

It is fitting also that it should seize on the question of production as the most vital one of the moment, and I venture to forward a few suggestions on this all important question.

First, we must have production committees in every factory, on which properly elected workers' representatives must sit, in conjunction with the owners.

All the cards must be laid on the table at conferences of these committees. Safeguards of living standards must be given, and guaranteed by mutual agreement. On the question of "hold ups" the workers must have equal access to all information relating to any given circumstance.

After supplies, comes manpower, and many of the Government's difficulties are due to their stupid handling of this question. At the moment we have enforced labour, with no proper sense of distribution. Some firms have too many workers, others not enough.

Under the present "cost, plus ten per cent" system, it is profitable to engage workers to do nothing. No wonder workers are cynical, and fed up.

The Production Committees could alter this. Amicable arrangements by voluntary agreement could soon be made to remedy these anomalies. Wages, too, lag behind the cost of living, and but for constant overtime would be insufficient to maintain proper living standards in these times of high prices. This is a source of great discontent.
John Bruce.

WHP, November 1941

5,000 Meals Daily

Plans for the opening of five or six British Restaurants throughout Watford will be under way shortly.

This encouraging statement was made by the Mayor on Tuesday at the official opening of the British Restaurant in the Baptist Hall, Leaves-den-road. When these restaurants are completed the Borough of Watford will be able to provide 5,000 meals per day. The Mayor pointed out that this scheme should to some extent remedy the "queue-epidemic" that is now rampant in the town.

Mr. W. Blackwood, Assistant Division Food Controller, who was representing Major C. R. Dudgeon, proposed a vote of thanks to the Mayor and in doing so praised the Mayor's power of oratory, a well-deserved tribute. He added that Watford's first British Restaurant was the most ideal he had inspected throughout the Division. (The Division includes all Hertfordshire and Essex.)

WHP, November 1941

Women wanted for training as engineers . . .

Training 8,000 Fireguards

ARRANGEMENTS are complete for the training of Watford 8,000 fire guards, and organisation is well forward. Eight thousand fire guard armlets and steel helmets have been ordered. All fire guards will attend a course of about eight lectures of about an hour each, spread over eight weeks.

The lectures will be given by the head wardens and the deputy wardens of the A.R.P. service, and will consist of two parts: (1) essential training, and (2) supplementary training.

The essential training is compulsory, but the supplementary training is voluntary, although fire guards are being urged to take the additional lectures.

The essential training will consist of lectures on incendiary bomb control.

WHP, November 1941

Watford Challenge to Luton

Watford is out to beat Luton once more—this time in the towns' Warships Week next March.

Watford's challenge to beat Luton's total each day, to reach one million pounds before Luton, and to exceed Luton's total both in amount and per capita was accepted last night (Wednesday) with the comment, "Your audacity can only be surpassed by our achievement."

The challenge was sent by the Mayor of Watford, Cllr. W. H. Price, after a meeting of Watford Joint Savings Committee at the Town Hall on Friday, in the following telegram: "Watford Joint Savings Committee issues the following challenge, which please convey to all workers in Luton Warships Week effort. We have chosen the weapons—each a light cruiser—for Warships Week next March.

Watford challenges in these terms:

"The citizens of Watford will beat Luton's total each day, will reach the million pounds mark before you, and, finally, Watford's grand total will be greater than Luton's—both in amount and per capita."

WHP, November 1941

Well Done, Chater Infants

An outstanding achievement in National Savings is reported from Chater Infants' School, who aimed at a target of £300 to buy an ambulance, and have raised just over £317.

WHP, December 1941

Women's War Work Inquiries

The two Government Training Centres in Southwold-road and Hempstead-road are anxious to fill every training vacancy available, and so enable them to send out qualified engineers to the many war munition factories in the Home Counties. One question which many women have been asking is: "Why, if I have got to register for essential war work, is an appeal made to me to offer my services?"

The answer is that registration necessarily takes some time to come into effect. If a woman who volunteers now is worth a score when registration day arrives, how much more

valuable is a volunteer who has already undergone a course of engineering training!

"That women have an aptitude for engineering," an official stated, "has been proved strikingly in many factories in Hertfordshire. While many employers are still a little reluctant to employ women on engineering work, this county has not been behindhand in trying out experiments.

"For example, two factories have gone so far as not only to employ women on men's work, but also to try out an idea of doing part-time shifts."

WHP, December 1941

History of the Last War Helps This

A HISTORY of the last war, extending to several large volumes, was proudly brought to the Mayor of Watford (Councillor W. H. Price) by a small boy, when he visited Watford Fields during his "paper-chase" tour of the Borough, on Saturday afternoon, in connection with Watford's paper salvage drive. The boy came struggling out of a house with them, and handed them to the Mayor, who put them in a civil defence league vehicle, which followed the loudspeaker car, and which was used as a touring collection depot.

"Wait a minute, I've got some more," said the boy, after the Mayor had thanked him, and handed him one of the lucky tickets which may bring him a prize. And into the house he went again and brought out the rest of the volumes.

The Mayor started from the Town Hall, and made a three-hour tour of the borough. With the aid of the loudspeaker he urged the people of Watford to make every effort to salvage paper.

His tour took him down the High-street, round Oxhey Ward, Watford Fields, Harwoods Ward, the St Albans-road, Bushey Mill-lane, the Harebreaks, and Kingswood.

One lady on the Kingswood Estate cleared the shelves of her bookcase of all the cheap sixpenny volumes she had.

WHP, January 1942

IMPORTANT

Government Announcement to Women

Ministry of Labour and National Service

There must no longer be any doubt in anybody's mind that every available woman in Britain will have to serve to win this war.

The Registration of age groups will proceed steadily. But this process, which necessarily involves interviewing, takes up precious time, and thousands of volunteers are needed at this moment in the A.T.S. for work that cannot wait. In the hour of their country's need, the Women of Britain have always responded, unselfishly and most courageously, to the call for service. The hour of need is upon us now.

You are being asked to volunteer to-day ahead of your age group. If you have already registered do not wait for your interview. Come forward, and say you want to help now.

There are many different ways in which you can serve, but the need of the AUXILIARY TERRITORIAL SERVICE is very great indeed. This service demands personal integrity, good intelligence and willingness to maintain a high standard of efficiency.

Members of the A.T.S. are working side by side with men in the Army and are also taking over vital work which releases men for the front line. Come forward now and help to build the mighty army that will lead a great country to Victory.

Post this to-day

Address it to The Auxiliary Territorial Service, AG18 99A, Hobart House, Grosvenor Gardens, London, S.W.1.
Please send me full story of life in the A.T.S. and details of the opportunities it offers. This does not commit me in any way.

Mrs/Miss_____ Age_____ (in confidence)

Address _____

Age limits, 17½ to 43. (Parents' consent needed under 18) Ex-Service women may volunteer up to 50. (Unsealed envelope, penny stamp)

Please call and have a talk at any Employment Exchange or A.T.S. or Army Recruiting Centre. They are there to help you.

200,000 ATS urgently needed

Mayor Councillor Price leads the town's waste-paper drive, starting, appropriately, at the new Town Hall.

241

Luton beats Watford on all three counts.

Trader's War Problems

WATFORD Chamber of Commerce has soon got down to the problems with which the second interim report of the Retail Trade Committee of the Board of Trade has confronted them, as reported in last week's "Post"

Though they have not yet decided what action they will recommend locally in regard to the main issues—the closing or merging of shops—the Executive Committee on Monday went into the difficulties arising from such action.

The Committee decided to send a resolution to the National Chamber of Trade, the Drapers' Chamber, and Sir Dennis Herbert, M.P. for Watford, pointing out that to safeguard businesses there should be some form of registration and licensing of premises so that those closed can be re-opened after the war, some reasonable compensation for any losses sustained through closing~ and some form of moratorium to protect the assets of a business, so that the owner can benefit now and not have to wait until the assets have disappeared.

WHP, February 1942

Soap Rationing

FROM Monday, February 9th, soap may be bought only against a coupon or buying permit The oils and fats used in soap manufacture occupy much shipping space, and some of this must be saved for food.

You will have 4 coupons in each 4-weekly period, and will be able to use these how and when you like within the period. There will be no registration, and you may buy from any shop stocking the kind you require.

Rationing will not apply to shaving soaps or dental soaps, shampoo powders, liquid soap, or scourers.

WHP, February 1942

H.M.S. Capetown Is Ours

THOUGH Watford failed to beat Luton in the Warship Week challenge their accomplishment in exceeding their aim of a round million pounds by over £200,000 was very commendable.

The cruiser, H.M.S. Capetown, can now be looked upon as another of Watford's tangible contributions towards the war effort, to be ranged alongside the destroyers paid for in War Weapons Week and the Spitfire donated by the Town.

The final total for Watford Warship Week, made known only yesterday, is £1,225,809. Luton's final, as announced on Monday, was £1,421,714.

Watford therefore ensured being able to adopt H.M.S.

Capetown, with nearly a quarter of a million to spare, but the effort, splendid as it was, failed to uphold the three-fold challenge to beat Luton on the aggregate, the day to day total, and the amount per head of population.

WHP, March 1942

2nd British Restaurant

The idea of communal feeding was carried a step further in Watford on Monday, when the new British Restaurant, at Alpha House, on the corner of St Albans-rd. and Balmoral-rd. was opened by the Mayor, Councillor W. H. Price.

The dinners served at Leavesden-road have been such a success that it is now proposed to start on teas at Alpha House, which is trying the experiment of staying open from 12 to 6.30, in order to serve an early evening meal to factory workers leaving about that time.

High teas of baked beans and welsh rarebit, or even an occasional egg can be obtained for 8d. while a more refined afternoon tea is only 4d. Otherwise the scale of prices remains the same with the main dish 7d., sweet 3d., tea or soup 1½d..The new restaurant which provides seating for 80 people at small tables, is to be served from the kitchen at Leavesden-Road.

The food supplies, travelling in special insulated containers which keep it hot for four hours, will be delivered by the two new Ford emergency food vans in time for lunch.

WHP, April 1942

Railings Will Go Soon

Quite a number of people in the last few weeks have put the question, "When are Watford's railings to be taken for scrap?"

Some have gone on to criticise Watford Town Council for not getting on with the job.

The railings are to be collected any day now, and let us take the opportunity right away of saying that the delay is nothing to do with Watford Town Council, and neither are they responsible for the collection, so don't blame them after the event for any damage that may be done. The removal and collection of these railings is undertaken directly by the Ministry of Works. The reason for the delay is that the Ministry are dealing with the job town by town.

WO, June 1942

Centre: *A 'ceremonial' queue of Councillors for the formal opening of Watford's second British Restaurant, on the corner of St Albans Road/Balmoral Road.*

War work

War work was obviously the thing and after a short course on basic engineering at the Government Training Centre in Southwold Road, the job to which I was directed was at Norman Reeves next to the High Street station.

Ford dealers? War work? As with most garages they had a couple of lathes, and any firm with machine tools was pressed into use. The work was for Scammell's, turning cast brass air filter covers for tank transporter tractor units. But, in mid-winter, with no garage heating except for a coke stove, it was no fun to operate a lathe clad for warmth in gloves and overcoat . . .

Cox's was a vast change from the lathes at the back of Norman Reeve's repair shed, a complete hive of industry by day, and to a large extent, night. Car, lorry and tank seats, aircraft seating, tank periscope assemblies—all among the perpetual crackle, smoke and sparks of the welders, and adjacent to the odours of the paint spray shop. Working in the machine shop were men and women producing a wide variety of small machined components. The women tended to stay longer as the men faced call-up and disappeared.

In the black-out all roads were dark but Aldenham Road with hedges and trees alongside was something else again—after all, a carefully-shaded and hooded cycle lamp didn't lose much light downwards, but what little light the dynamo gave wasn't much. Once at work the bright spots were the overhead gas heaters—welcome particularly on night shifts—and the 'lunch' break which would see a trek across road to the Busy Bee Cafe—open all hours!

Recollections 1987

None Were Idle

Saturday's registration in Watford of the 1900-class women yielded many fewer with young and dependent families, and should thus mean an increase in volunteers for factories and shops. There is plenty of opportunity for women workers, full or part-time, in Watford, and the "Post" is assured that all volunteers from this or other registrations could be absorbed locally at once.

Eighty per cent of the women who registered were married, and of these 60 per cent were engaged in household duties. The rest were fairly evenly divided between full-time and part-time work.

Of the single women, 85 per cent were working full time, and the remainder either doing part-time work or occupied with household duties.

None were unemployed.

WHP, July 1942

Dieppe Raid

SOME Watford men who took part in last week's large-scale raid on Dieppe will have thrilling stories to tell when they are free to relate their experiences during that exciting day.

Two who will have particularly exciting stories to tell are:

Top: Weapons Demonstration Week gives great fun to the youngsters

Right: Watford Junction Station, June 1942 Judging by the crowd awaiting to be served the news is grim; Rommel has been on the offensive in Africa and Tobruk fell on 21st June—the 8th Army were being chased to Egypt.

Note the direction sign to the American Red Cross Service Club.

243

Church bells to ring out for the victory . . .

Trooper Fred Craft, of 26, Home-way, Mill End, and Trooper Sid (Nobby) Clarke, of 240 Whippendell-road. Both are aged 22, and both were members of the small party which, not strong enough to capture a six-inch gun battery, worked round behind it, sniped the gunners to such good effect, that in desperation the Germans turned the guns on the snipers, and so could not shell the beaches, where the Canadians were landing.

The Watford district was also represented on the naval side of the operations by Ldg./Seaman Patrick Edgar, of 37, Lower Paddock-road, Oxhey, who was serving in one of the destroyers that took the Commandos over.

WHP, August 1942

More Women Needed

ALTHOUGH women in Watford and district have responded well to the call for workers in factories in the district, there is an urgent need for many more, both for full and part-time employment.

That need is growing daily and when the comb-out of young men, which Mr. Bevin promises, comes about the need will be pressing. Every woman who can offer her services can be placed locally. The shortage of women is holding up production of vital war requirements.

This is a call to you to come forward to help on the war effort in the best possible way. Watford wants to know why women are not coming forward.

WHP, July 1942

Tanks—£40,000 Short

Unless the small savings of Watford and district reach £40,090 this week there will be no tank-naming for the town. The position is that if Watford is to name ten tanks they must reach £253,000 by Saturday night. If they fail, then not even a small tank will go into battle carrying Watford and district's name.

Since the "Tanks For Attack" campaign started ten weeks ago the total had reached

£213,756 by last Saturday. The total for the week ending September 19 was £24,658, which must be nearly doubled this week.

Street group secretaries have toiled unceasingly, and the schools, social organisations and industrial groups have been no less enthusiastic, and they will do their utmost during these last few days to see that Watford does not suffer widespread disappointment.

WHP, September 1942

Offensive Inspires Workers

The great victories in Egypt and Libya have inspired Watford factory workers.

Now there is the feeling abroad that at long last the great Allied offensive is under way, the workers are roused to a new enthusiasm and a new solidarity. The first important task of the new Mayor of Watford will be to receive a deputation from Watford factory workers and Trade Union organisations, to hear about a suggestion that there should be a Libya Production Week in Watford.

The idea is to draw all Watford workers and citizens into the greatest effort ever to increase production, and economy.

When the lead for such an idea comes from those who will themselves have to make the effort, we know that the right spirit exists.

WHP November, 1942

Church Bells on Sunday

Church bells all over the country will ring out on Sunday in celebration of our Egyptian victory.

WHP, November 1942
• *This was to celebrate the victory at El Alamein where German forces were soundly defeated, setting the scene to be cleared out of North Africa.*

Restaurants to go?

The deficit for the period from the opening, October 29, 1941, to March 31, 1942, on British Restaurants and the cooking depot at Watford was £612, plus £95, being proportion of central administrative expenses, and also 2 per cent. in lieu of bank interest lost. In respect of the months April, May, June and July, the deficit was £10.

The Emergency Committee reported at the meeting of Watford Town Council on Monday that it was reasonable to suppose that some loss would be incurred in the future.

WHP November, 1942

Naming Ten Tanks

The Watford Savings Committee are now seeking to name the ten Churchill Tanks which is Watford's prize for collecting the magnificent total during the ten-week Tanks For Attack Campaign. Each tank will bear three names, meaning that thirty local names in all will appear on the tanks as they go into action. The following have been asked to submit names for the tanks: Ten street groups, six groups in the rural district, six schools, six industrial groups and two social groups.

In the rural district, Sarratt, Abbots Langley, Radlett, and Aldenham have been asked to submit names, and a further two will be named by groups in the Watford district

The Social Group and the Voluntary Services are also naming two, while the production, transport and commerce side of industry will also submit names.

The group in Kelmscott-close have given "Kelmscott," Kingsfield-road "Kingsfield," and Parker-street "Parker Group."

It is hoped that next week the "Post" will be able to give all thirty local names and also the numerous groups who narrowly missed naming a tank, but in the words of the Savings Committee were "highly commended."

WHP, November 1942

Another Million?

WITHIN the next few days Watford will announce its target for the "Wings for Victory" Week, which is to be held from Saturday, May 8, to Saturday, May 15. It is expected that the target will be at least one million pounds, the same as in Warship Week, but this may be affected if the Rural District does not join in Watford's effort.

At a meeting of Watford and District Joint Savings Committee on Monday, Mr. R. Mugford, Chairman, said, "I think this should be Watford's greatest effort of the war, even if we fail valiantly to reach our target." All targets are to be named in terms of aircraft. If Watford decide on a million, they will put it in the words of 50 Mosquito fighter-bombers.

These aircraft, stated to be the fastest fighter-bombers in the world, have distinguished themselves in actions against the Axis.

WHP January, 1943

Gas Buses

A new type of 'bus is to be introduced by the London Passenger Transport Board on routes No. 301 and 302, and as a consequence the position of the "Request Stop" signs are to be rearranged.

These buses will be driven by their own producer gas plants, instead of by petrol. They are much slower in acceleration, and the L.P.T.B., notifying Watford Town Council of the

The bargees survey the scene after firemen toil all night fighting a blaze at Croxley Mills.

A new Savings Drive—to buy 50 Mosquitoes . . .

introduction of this type of vehicle, stated that experience had proved the necessity of limiting the number of "request stops."

At the Council meeting, on Tuesday, the Highways committee reported that the Borough Engineer had inspected the points affected, and the police had been notified of the proposed change. It was agreed that the matter be left in the hands of Ald. T. R. Clark, Chairman of the Committee.

WHP, March 1943

New Cox's Production Drive

THE great example of Cox and Co's production drive has led Watford's Drive for Victory Campaign Committee to hope for a united town effort, which will stimulate the whole of Hertfordshire, if not the whole of Britain.

Mr. J. H. Price, Secretary of the Watford Drive for Victory Campaign Committee, has asked Cox and Co's Joint Production Committee to join with them in a scheme which will embrace all the local manufacturers. Cox and Co's campaign was introduced in December last as an inter-departmental production competition, arranged to cover the four weeks in the month, with prizes of National Savings certificates given to the winning department Interest was stimulated by means of speakers from the fighting services, and film shows. The competition was voted a definite success and resulted in an increase in output in nearly all departments.

This led to another campaign being introduced for March, and this time, in addition to the interdepartmental competition, prizes are also offered for individual effort among workers who excel. Full details of the scheme were reported in the "Post," and are now being circularised by the Watford Production Committee to upwards of 35 firms in the area, who, it is hoped, will inaugurate their own competitions in an all-out effort to increase production at this vital time.

WHP, March 1943

New Freemen Honoured

IN a ceremony which was simple, yet strikingly impressive, Watford on Monday honoured three of its most deserving public servants by conferring the Freedom of the Borough on Lord Hemingford, Alderman T. R. Clark and Mr. William Hudson, the former Town Clerk

The historic significance of the occasion was marked by the wide interest displayed and the number of county dignitaries present

There was scarcely a vacant seat in the hall, and the pageantry of the proceedings was followed intently especially from the balcony where there were a large number of schoolchildren, and American and Canadian guests.

The simplicity of the celebration was, perhaps, its greatest worth. There were no fanfares, no grandiloquent flights of oratory, but just straightforward, plain expressions of goodwill, carrying the convincing ring of spontaneity and sincerity as their hall-mark

"The boast of heraldry" was supplanted by a fervent good-fellowship, and a spirit of appreciation of sterling service fully rendered to the town, whose people were now saying a simple, yet unanimous, "Thank you!"

All who witnessed the ceremony were deeply moved, and the new Freemen more than any, and it was obvious that, like all of us, they recognised the event as the crowning joy of their careers, for what greater encouragement or reward can be expected by a public servant than a whole community's "Well done!"?

WHP, March 1943

"Coasting" Trains

BY planned "coasting," 8½ tons of coal are being saved every day on the L.M.S. Euston-Broad Street-Watford electric services.

In the operation of electric trains it is usual, in order to give economy in energy consumption, to accelerate rapidly, and then shut off power and coast to the point at which it is necessary to apply the brake for the next station stop. By calculation and experiment, the L.M.S. has determined the most economical points, and fixed a "coasting board" at these points for the guidance of drivers.

WHP, April 1943

Overcharging

Maurice Houtman, St Albans-road, Watford, who pleaded not guilty, was fined £25 with £7 costs at Watford Police Court on Tuesday for selling a second-hand table at an excessive price at Watford on September 30.

Mr. L. Jones, prosecuting for the Board of Trade, said the price of the table should not have exceeded the first-hand price plus purchase tax, which would have totalled about £7. Robert Kettle said that he bought the table as a solid oak one at £18 18s. He found that it was made of white-wood. Cecil Walker, a trade expert said that in 1942 the table would .have cost about £7, including purchase tax.

Houtman said he bought the table for £12 15s. at Hendon in 1943. He was of the opinion that the bottom of the table was oak. Plywood would not crack and was preferable to oak.

Before selling the table for £18 1 8s., he compared prices elsewhere for similar articles, and found they were selling at 25 to 27 guineas.

WHP, March 1943

50 Mosquitoes

WITH "Wings for Victory" Week opening on Saturday, the whole of Watford is on its toes for what promises to be the greatest small savings effort in the history of the town—the raising of £1,000,000 to build 50 Mosquitoes.

Everywhere there are signs that small savers are alive to the need for special exertion on their part, and the keen interest already being shown in the many R.A.F. novelty attractions in the course of erection shows the"Wings" Campaign Committee to have done its job in stimulating faculty.

WHP, May 1943

Giant Bomber on Show

Most interest so far is being shown in the giant Lancaster bomber, in the course of erection outside the Town Hall. The bomber, which is the same as was shown in Trafalgar Square during "Wings" Week, has been on 27 operation flights, including 13 over Germany and one over Berlin itself. It has also raided Italy, and has taken part in many daylight sweeps over Occupied France.

WHP, May 1943

A Watford Hospital closed through flies

Mrs. E. I. Allen described how she visited the hospital, and "could have 'dropped down dead' at the sight of the thousands of flies." It was only during the last eight months that the Borough had taken any action. Over one patient's bed there were between 600-800 flies on two or three fly-papers. Eleven fly-papers were dangling in one of the kitchens, on which were over 1,000 flies.

The Clerk to the Council (Mr. S Nicholson) read a letter sent from the Clerk to the Watford Joint Hospital Board, and referred to their letters connected with the complaint.

As long ago as January. 1939, complaints were made that the gravel pit opposite the hospital, belonging to the Watford Corporation, was becoming a nuisance. Since then this refuse tip had been sprayed, and refuse was being covered within 24 hours of being tipped.

The dump was also inspected by a representative of the Ministry of Health, who said that either the dump must be moved or the hospital. At the moment the hospital was closed as 21 patients and three of the staff had become affected by dysentery, which outbreak was directly caused by the fly menace.

Fresh cases of infectious disease and present patients were being sent to the St. Albans Isolation Hospital, and the Watford hospital had also to lend staff to nurse these patients.

The letter from the Clerk to the Hospital Board concluded: "My Board seem to have exhausted their powers of persuasion so far as the Watford Corporation is concerned, and apart from commencing legal procedings, there seems to be nothing further that the Board can do.'

WO, August 1943

The serious 'Fly War' rumbled on into October by which time the Council had received permission to run the destructor for 24 hours a day and only using the tip when absolutely necessary. Closed late August the Hospital re-opened in late October.

In 1949 similar complaints were levelled about the tip in Radlett Road being used, causing distress to Knutsford residents.

The Mosquito target reached and passed . . .

Crikey!—Mosquitoes

More than two years ago a silvery streak flashed through the skies, and from the lips of all who saw it there sprang the involuntary cry, "Crikey!"

That was the name by which the now famous high-speed reconnaissance fighter-bomber de Havilland DH.98 Mosquito, became known to R.A.F. and Observer Corps personnel during its experimental days. The only things known about it in those days were its amazing speed and almost incredible manoeuvrability, which, of course, gave rise to the exclamation, "Crikey!"

Since then the remarkable exploits of this plane over enemy-occupied territory and the heart of Germany itself, Berlin, have inspired many more exultant cries of "Crikey!" The Mosquito was reported in action for the first time in an attack on Oslo in September25 when it broke up a Quisling rally. It had been in service many months before that.

The Mosquito is unique in that it is one of the first all-wood aeroplanes to go into service with the R.A.F for many years, and its method of construction results in one of the strongest airframes yet designed, combining the qualities of lightness with perfection of streamlined form.

Following its amazing exploits over the Continent, the makers issued this description in the trade journals:— "Anopheles de Havilandus-offensicus. Characteristics: Furious and aggressive. Prolific. Flies great distances at high velocity to deposit eggs which are both distasteful and harmful. When molested shoots unpleasant streams from multiple probosci. Possesses penetrative and recording eyes. Habitat: Met in increasing numbers in Axia, where inhabitants are apprehensive of the imminence of a plague which promises to cause considerable inconvenience."

This also caused cries of "Crikey!" in trade circles. When it became known that during its "Wings" Week, which opens on Saturday, Watford aimed to raise £1,000,000 to buy 50 of these super planes, there were many more cries of "Crikey!" in the town, but we are confident that when the final result of Watford's "Wings" Week is declared there will be an explosive cry of "CRIKEY!"

More seriously, our "Wings for Victory" Week, more than any other previous savings effort, calls for a major effort. Its success depends on the small savings of the people. The astounding totals reached by Watford in previous efforts were a tribute to the willingness with which the wage-earner lent his savings to the State, but they also owed a great deal to the investments contributed by large firms and institutions like banks and insurance companies. This year presents a different picture.

The wage-earners of Watford are in many

This Lancaster had been on 29 operational flights, including a raid on Berlin, and was now relegated to the no less important task of drumming up interest in savings. Here being assembled on the green-sward in Rickmansworth Road, alongside the Town Hall, in May 1943.

ways fortunate in their circumstances. High wages are being earned, higher than ever in history. There is little on which money can sensibly be spent, and no one can deny the urgent need of the State.

The great thing to remember is that Watford must have an average of £5 from every man, woman and child if it is to equal the achievements of previous campaigns. Sixpence is not too little, nor £1,000 too much, to invest. The R.A.F. deserve more than the best we can do.

WHP, May 1943

"Wings" Well Earned

Watford's "Wings for Victory" Week total has now risen to £1,150,326, and may soar even higher when final returns are received.

With a target of one million pounds the organisers of the effort, and Watford residents generally, can take pride in this splendid result.

WHP May, 1943

HMS Capetown Plaque

H.M.S. Capetown, Watford's adopted ship, will now have a bronze plaque, designed in Watford, and made in Watford of gifts of old bronze by Watford people, to perpetuate the town's link with the ship. In exchange, Watford Borough and Watford Rural, associated in Warship Week effort, have each received a plaque bearing the badge of H.M. S. Capetown.

Following the adoption of H.M.S. Capetown in Warship Week, residents were asked to give old bronze articles to be melted down and converted into a plaque for the ship.

One donor gave his 1914 Mons Star.

The plaque, which weighs 40 lbs, was cast by Watford Iron Foundry, the design being sculptured by Montague W. Jackson, Watford School of Arts, and the finishing touches being applied by the Novobax Engineering Co.

Rectangular in shape, it bears the borough arms in enamel, and is inscribed: "To commemorate the adoption of H.M.S. Capetown by the Borough and Rural District of Watford, Warship Week, March, 1942."

The presentation of the plaque took place at a special meeting of the Town Council on Tuesday night and it was received on behalf of the Captain, officers, and ship's complement by Vice-Admiral A. L. Snagge, representing the Admiralty and National Savings Committee.

WHP, July , 1943

German Prison Ship

LIFE aboard a German commerce raider. men packed into the tanks of a tanker turned prison ship . . . running the British blockade... forty prisoners jumping from a train taking them to Germany . . . others tunnelling by night out of a hut, under the barbed wire and out beyond their prison camp to freedom.

These are some of the incidents in the thrilling story, which can now be told, of Seaman Jack King, whose return to Watford in July was described by the "Post"

Jack, aged 18,

Centre: *U.S. troops join the parade of troops in the 'Wings for Victory' parade. Mayor Alderman Simmonds takes the salute.*

Bottom: *This captured Messerschmitt 109 was on a 'pay to see' display on ground behind Cawdell's smaller shop.*

Oranges back on the menu—for the under fives . . .

believed to be the youngest prisoner of war, was a deck boy aboard the s.s. African Star, sunk in the Atlantic, but let him tell his own story.

Here it is:

"We were homeward bound from Buenos Aires when one morning we sighted a big steamer flying the Russian flag. She approached and fired a shot across our bows and signalled us to stop.

"We at once sent out an S.O.S. and continued steaming, but the raider then began to shell us. The first shot tore half our bridge away and more shells crashed into the ship, stopping our engines.

"We took to the boats, and the raider signalled us to come on board.

"Seventy four of us, including the captain and two women passengers, climbed on board the raider, which we found was a German."

WHP, August 1943

Italy Surrenders

Within a few hours of the news of Italy's surrender, Watford National Savings Committee had posters circulated all over the district urging people to celebrate by making a thanksgiving investment in War Savings.

First response to the appeal was made by a local Councillor, who invested £75. This was followed by a street group member who brought in £39.

Mr. R. Mugford, of Cawdells, who is Chairman of the Watford Savings Committee, went along to his Observer Corps savings group and invested £500 in 3 per cent, bonds.

WHP, September 1943

Oranges—New Quota

WATFORD has received its quota of oranges for the under-fives, and on Tuesday and again yesterday, pavements had little bits and pieces of orange peel as traps for the unwary.

Watford Town Hall steps were not immune, and one of our elderly councillors nearly came to grief through slipping. He righted himself with a rather comical effort, and turning to the "Post" reporter who witnessed the incident, he wagged an admonishing finger and said, "No names, now! No names!"

WHP, October 1943

Berlin Raid—D.F.C.

HELPED to shoot down a German fighter while rear gunner in a Lancaster during a raid on Berlin . . . while in great pain from wounds to both feet and in the leg subdued a fire in the turret with an extinguisher and finished it off with contents of coffee flask . . . remained at his post and helped to drive off two other fighters... unconscious . . . now the Distinguished Flying Cross.

This briefly sums up the experiences of Flying Officer Cyril Govier Pascoe, of 8, Vale-road, Bushey, on the night of August 31.

For "displaying a high order of courage and fortitude" is the official reason for the award of the D.F.C. The official citation states:

"When nearing the Dutch coast the aircraft was attacked by a fighter, but the assailant was destroyed by the determined and skillful fire directed by F/O Pascoe and the mid-upper gunner.

"Shortly afterwards the bomber was hit by fire from another fighter. The intercommunication system and the rear turret were rendered unserviceable. A fire broke out in the turret, but F/O Pascoe, although in great pain from wounds sustained to both feet and in the leg, obtained an extinguisher and subdued the flames, finally extinguishing them with the contents of a coffee flask.

"Displaying great fortitude he remained at his post and, later on, when the bomber was subject to interference from two enemy fighters, he assisted in driving them off before losing consciousness."

WHP, September 1943

● *Cyril Pascoe; to whose memory the first edition of 'The Book of Watford' was dedicated suffered the loss of a leg. He found employment in Cornwall and passed away there in December 1985.*

Jitterbugging at Dances

SHOULD jitterbugging be banned at Watford dances?

Cllr.. Mrs. Beall thinks it should, and said so at a meeting of the "H.M.S. Capetown" Comforts Fund Committee on Wednesday.

"In certain other places jitterbug dancing is being stopped and I think we should stop it here. Old-time dances are becoming very popular," she said.

The matter arose following a suggestion to organise a dance in aid of "Capetown" Fund and it was decided to book a provisional date to be confirmed later.

Looking ahead, the committee has arranged a whist drive for May 1, 1944, at the Town Hall.

It was announced that £450 had been sent for distribution among the ship's crew.

This left a balance of £48.

WHP, October 1943

Oxhey 'Plan'—Opposition

QUESTIONS may be asked in Parliament on the London County Council's proposal to settle 15,000 bombed-out Londoners on Oxhey Place Estate, which includes Oxhey Golf Course and Oxhey Woods, some of the most famous beauty spots in Hertfordshire.

A petition signed by more than 50 Bushey residents has been sent to Air Commodore W. Helmore, M.P. for Watford, protesting against the idea.

Bushey residents, who have for many years taken their Sunday walks on the Oxhey Estate, hope that the House of Commons will see their point of view and will veto the L.C.C.'s scheme.

WHP, November 1943

Satellite Town Protests

Sir,— Like charity, love of the beautiful can be a screen for other sins. The protests about the proposed satellite town seem to show a greater regard for personal pleasure and convenience than for the preservation of rural beauty.

The increasing encroachment of town on country, regarded from one angle, is indeed grievous, but nevertheless inevitable. The resultant losses, however, as Mr. Odell has indicated, need by no means be total if the

Embarkation leave

Sheila carries daddy's gas-mask,
Peter carries daddy's gun.
Mother's chattering on and laughing
As if parting were just fun.

She's put apples in his pocket,
He's got photos in his book,
When he isn't busy fighting,
He'll have time to have a look.

Dad is going to fight for England,
For a world where men are free,
Better times for all but — mostly
He'll be fighting for these three.

SALUTE THE SOLDIER

The soldier is giving up all he holds most dear. What can we do to show our gratitude? We can salute the soldier by saving. **SALUTE THE SOLDIER**

The L. C. C. want to build 15,000 houses at Oxhey.

new towns and settlements are intelligently planned. This is the point that most of the protestants appear to overlook.

Councillor E. I. Baxter has described the L.C.C. plan "as a good one, and better than any speculative builder could envisage."

A study of the County of London Plan, recently published by the L.C.C., also gives good ground for supposing that the authors of such a well-conceived scheme are hardly likely to botch a small cottage estate of 15,000 inhabitants.

The estate, presumably, is intended to accommodate a few of those who will need to be transferred from the slums if London is to become a city for our pride and not our shame, as much of it is at present.

And is there nothing to be said of the benefits accruing to the 15,000 fortunates who will be our neighbours? Is it to be pleasant Sunday walks for the relatively few, or health and happiness for the many?

And do Carpenders Park residents really think that the St. Meryl Estate is a thing of beauty and a joy for ever?

E. H. LARGE.
WHP, November 1943

Watford Pigs for Farms of Europe

ALTHOUGH they may not be aware of their role, the housewives of Watford are playing an important part in laying the foundations of Europe's future livestock herds. The scraps and kitchen waste which they assiduously put out for collection each week are being converted into flesh, blood and bone—in fact, the finest pedigree pigs—at Watford's own municipal farm.

Homesteads will have to be rebuilt, farms reestablished. And this, says Mr. Farquharson, the Borough farm bailiff, is where Watford comes into the picture. The breeding qualities of the Watford herd are known all over the world—so much so, says Mr. Farquharson, that many of the pigs that will become the nuclei of the Continental herds will be Watford pedigree stock. There will be Large

Fire watching

Whilst the drone of enemy bombers overhead kept many families for night after night in their cold and damp Anderson shelters, to emerge into an equally cold and dark dawn, volunteers were organised into fire-watching and fire-fighting groups. On a rota system, those on duty during an alert would be called upon to patrol a given area and to deal with outbreaks of fire should such occur. Promptitude with buckets of sand to quench the initial effect of an incendiary bomb; and follow-up with water from stirrup-pumps to attempt some form of control until greater help could arrive.

This study, taken on the roof of Cawdell's, shows the tower of St Mary's Church, and beneath it, the facade of the Kings Head pub.

'Whites, Middle Whites, and Wessex Saddlebacks of best quality, all bred at the Borough's own farm—Holywell Farm—which lies just off Tolpits-lane, in the south-west corner of the town.

The size of the herd at Holywell Farm has not only been maintained at its prewar level, but it is now 250 strong—bigger than ever before.

Sales of pigs, mainly from pedigree stock, at Holywell Farm during the nine months from April to December, 1943, brought in £2,500.

The best animals fetched anything up to 80 guineas. In December alone sales totalled nearly £700. Some of the porkers became somebody's tasty Christmas dinners; others are being used for breeding.

WO, January 1944

New Camera Club

TO-MORROW evening, at Watford Central Library, a number of Watford camera enthusiasts will meet to discuss the possibilities of forming an active photographic society in Watford.

It is felt that "leafy Hertfordshire," with its many beauty spots, provides wide scope for such a society, and Mr. W. Mitchell Bond, of 76, Harford-drive, Watford, the convener of the meeting, is anxious to hear from all who are interested in photography.

WHP, February 1944

L.C.C. Wants Oxhey Estate

The fate of the Oxhey Place Estate is now in the balance, the battle having reached its climax at Watford Town Hall on Monday and Tuesday, when Mr. W. H. Collin, ex-Chief Inspector of the Ministry of Health, came out

"D" Day.

of retirement to hear the London County Council's case for confirmation of a Compulsory Purchase Order and the arguments put forward by the opposition, including Watford Town Council, Herts County Council, Rickmansworth Urban Council, and the trustees of the Blackwell Estate. Defining the attitude of Watford Town Council, the Town Clerk, Mr. G. Salter Davies, said that although they sympathised with the L.C.C. in its problem of having to provide housing for 100,000 families after the war, they considered that there should not be one standard of accommodation for the wealthy and another for those referred to under the Act as "persons of the working class."

They did not want Watford drawn into the London maelstrom, but if the Order materialised Watford Town Council would do its best to make the people feel at home.

WHP, April 1944

Fourth Million

The town and district made a great last-minute effort, put in £232,605 that day, and so carried the total to £1,131,950. Even this was not the finish. The final balancing of accounts showed the total to be £1,142,058, or not far short of the £1,150,236 raised in Wings Week

A particularly bright feature was the great part played by small savers. They beat last year's figure of £12 7s. 2d. per head of population by 2s. 7d., much to the satisfaction of those responsible for this side of the effort

WHP, May 1944

Post-War Plans

Watford Town Council decided on Tuesday that as post-war expenditure will be restricted for the first three years, the town's five-year programme should be spread over eight years.

Schemes which have been prepared by the

various committees are estimated to cost £728,000 and the suggestion is that by delaying some of them the town will get better value for money, and it may be possible to finance them without increasing the rate burden in respect of loan charges.

Councillor Smith said he considered the committee had paid too much attention to the rate aspect. He added: "I do feel that the urgency of important schemes must over-rule the rate question. The citizens will want houses, and a very considerable number of them," he said.

WHP, May 1944

"D" Day

THE news that the Great Day had dawned was hardly credited in Watford during the earlier part of Tuesday. Scepticism at first followed the German broadcast. Then there was speculation that it might be just a feint landing.

When the B.B.C. announced a landing in force the mood of the people took on a noticeable change. There was visible excitement wherever groups of people gathered, and as bulletin followed bulletin, early excitement and enthusiasm gave place to a somewhat more sober mood, with a fuller realisation of what the great assault betokened.

The roar of the great armada overhead before dawn was the first indication that something unusual was astir, and throughout the day, as the planes streamed to and fro, eyes were lifted towards the sky—eyes that held a new light of hope and faith. Flying in a Lancaster bomber on "D-Day," Flight-Sergt. Hutton, of Watford, had a bird's-eye view of the start of the invasion of Normandy. Describing the scenes Flight Sergeant Hutton said, "It was an unforgettable sight, to be followed later on our

return journey by an even more imposing spectacle.

"Suddenly, stretched away as far as the eye could see, were two massive convoys, one on our port bow and the other to the starboard.

"These were no small fry, but big ships in line astern, with their escorts of destroyers and corvettes which fussed around them like chicks round an old hen. Some were flying balloons and the sight sent the pilot bouncing up and down in his seat and clapping his hands with joy. One of the crew counted 55.

"That was our big moment, for these two great convoys steamed steadily on course as if such a thing as war and opposition were out of the question."

WHP, June 1944

Top: *The invasion had been expected—the huge mass of troops and equipment could not hide the fact. Odhams'"Illustrated" of May 20th gave the probable line-up of Allied Commanders together with their German counterparts. US General Patton was not listed.*

Right: *'D-day' had come and gone; the Allied invasion of Hitler's empire was fact. But then, unexpectedly, came a new menace—that of the V1 flying bomb. Pilotless and with fuel enough to reach London or thereabouts, when the fuel ran out the motor would cut and the bomb descend. One such fell on Sandringham Road in August 1944 causing considerable damage and loss of life. Later Germany launched an even more deadly 'secret weapon'—the V2. This was a rocket which had a high trajectory and could not be tracked or shot down as could the V1. Advancing armies in France and Belgium quickly cleared V1 launching sites, but the V2's were from mobile launchers.*
Photos: Wulf Schmidt

V1 bomb falls on Sandringham Road . . .

Made Homeless by Flying Bomb

EARLY on Sunday morning a flying bomb crashed on to an area in Southern England. Deaths and injuries were caused and property was damaged. The most amazing thing was that Anderson shelters stood undamaged.

An A.R.P. worker on duty shortly before the bomb crashed told our representative that the missile dived. A fire followed. The N.F.S. and rescue squads were quickly on the scene. There was no shortage of willing helpers, prominent among these being Service men of all ranks and a number of American officers and men.

The work of rescue was considerably handicapped by scores of morbid sightseers, who in some cases even broke through the cordons.

The spot where the bomb fell is near where a bomb fell in the early days of the war.

WO, August 1944

District Mourns Flying Bomb Victims

A district's last tribute to victims of the flying bomb which fell on a housing estate was paid last week when a sympathetic crowd gathered as the funeral went to the cemetery.

Flags were at half mast, blinds were drawn and people gathered at street corners to watch the cortege pass. A reporter writes: On our way to the cemetery we climbed a steep hill, and came upon a small group of people standing outside a gate. We entered, and just beyond saw the robed figure of a clergyman waiting to receive the mourners. He walked to and fro in deep meditation.

"Silence, please," in a peremptory but sympathetic voice, caused all heads to bow, and the chief mourners in deep black walked slowly past and filed round the grave.

The coffins, draped with the Union Jack, were lowered, and a reverent hush fell as the clergyman moved to one side of the grave. He commenced to speak.

His voice, though sombre, was full of solace and reassurance. He said, 'I want you all to feel that you are supporting and sympathising with the bereaved.' He spoke of the victims, and muffled sobs were heard as he referred to an eight-years-old child. The sobbing stopped as he quoted a Psalm.

"I want all of you to feel that you are the mourners, that these people are our brothers and sisters," said the clergyman. He paused to pay tribute to the local Council for the manner in which they had arranged the burials.

"They have arranged it," he said, "that everyone of these people, though sharing a common grave, shall have their own funeral.

"They are not unknown," he said. "They are our brothers and sisters. They were sleeping in the same district as us. Some of them were very near to us.

"They lived their lives as we do, and their lives—in their own ways—were much like yours and mine."

The speaker was inaudible for a time as a fleet of aircraft roared overhead on their way to the battle fronts. Retribution was the keynote of those engines, and as the silver specks disappeared in the clouds the speaker continued:

"Let us pray for these people," he said, "that they may gain their eternal reward."

WO, August 1944

'D' day was June 6th, 1944. The flying bomb disaster occurred early Sunday a.m., July 30th, 1944

The "Halifax" production story—Official.   Wanted—8,400 homes in ten years . . .

L.C.C. to Build at Oxhey

BY his decision to confirm the Compulsory Purchase Order of the L.C.C. The Minister of Health allows practically the whole of the application—with some minor exceptions.

A little over 921 acres will therefore be acquired for development as a cottage estate to meet post-war housing needs. All the land is situate in Herts, and comprises the Oxhey Place Estate of Mrs. I. A. W. Blackwell. The Order apparently does not apply to 50 acres of land owned by the Artisans' and General Dwellings Company, which is within the Middlesex boundary. It will be remembered that at the Inquiry it was stated that the L.C.C. would be prepared to exclude the ancient Oxhey Chapel and to preserve a part of Oxhey Woods. It is by no means certain that the mansion of Oxhey Place will be demolished. Also of timely interest is the fact that the whole of the land which will be acquired by the L.C.C. is an area for which Watford Town Council are applying to be brought within the Borough boundary.

WHP, October 1944

A Forgotten Generation

Sir,—There is much talk of better education for children and I think most people will agree that it is desirable. One point, however, causes me a little concern. When the children have had the advantage of this new education, is it not likely that the relationships between parent and child will provide us with a ticklish problem?

The present parents of school children, and those young people who have left school and will be the parents of the future, must inevitably find themselves at a disadvantage with their children unless some opportunity is given them to at least equal the knowledge to be absorbed by their offspring.

How, I wonder, can this problem be solved, as the Education Act does not provide for the teaching of present or prospective parents.

T.F., Bushey

WHP, November 1944

Demand for 8,400 Homes in 10 Years

DEMANDS for the erection of 8,400 houses in Watford in the first ten years after the war, to relieve the housing shortage, are made in a 23-page memorandum to be presented to Watford Town Council. The memorandum has been prepared by a joint committee of the local Labour Party and Trades CounciL It is based on a survey which revealed that 4,271 Watford people are without adequate accommodation.

One proposal likely to cause much heart-burning is that a site of 112 acres in Watford's most "select" residential quarter—the Cassiobury Park estate—at present reserved for large houses, built four or six to the acre, should be used for the erection of 10-to-the-acre working-class dwellings.

The survey sums up its findings as follows: Dwellings required, 1,499; houses required (included in the above), 1,438; flats required (included in the above), 61; number of people expressing preference for a Council dwelling, 1,117; expressing preference for non-Council dwelling, 367.

Wishing to buy accommodation, 136; wishing to rent accommodation, 1,279; serving men and women requiring accommodation, 400; bombed-out families requiring accommodation, 69.

WHP, February, 1945

Firm's Merger Not Ominous

The "Post" learns that the amalgamation announced yesterday, of the printing firms of Messrs. Hazell, Watson and Viney, and the photogravure and letterpress printing business of the Sun Engraving Co., Ltd., will not result in any displacement of workers at Whippendellroad, Watford.

The transaction includes Rembrandt Photogravure Ltd., but does not include the process engraving section in London and Watford of the Sun, or the London typesetting section or any of the foundry departments.

WHP, March 1945

"London Pride"

WATCHED by hundreds of proud eyes, a Halifax bomber, streaming flags of the United Nations, zoomed gull-like over Leavesden Aerodrome on Monday afternoon.

It was a very special bomber, the 710th made by those who watched—employees of London Aircraft Production. It was also the last they would make before, with victory assured, returning to their peace-time jobs; and last, but not least, it bore the gallant name "London Pride" with the appropriate flower painted on it.

That was the end of the story, but perhaps it will be as well to leave the cheering, happy crowds for a moment and retrospect to a different scene—on December 15, 1941.

That was the date when Halifax No. 1 became airborne from the same field that saw the first flight of "London Pride."

Following an urgent appeal by the Minister of Aircraft Production, Sir Frederick HandleyPage—who witnessed Monday's ceremony—set about gathering his forces to produce "at the earliest possible time the largest number of bombers his resources would allow."

Reviewing this period on Monday, Lord Ash-field, chairman of L.A.P., said "It is unnecessary for me to remind you that at that time no employee of the Group (L.A.P.) had any knowledge of aircraft production." The Group consists of five concerns, among which is a section of L.P.T.B. Their deficiency of aircraft knowledge was soon a thing of the past for those who witnessed the culminating triumph on Monday. The ceremony took place in No. 3 hangar. As soon as the workers saw "the last of the many" bombers, they spontaneously broke into a loud cheer. Lord Ashfield read a telegram which he had received from Sir Stafford Cripps, Minister of Aircraft Production, in which the Minister offered his congratulations on the memorable occasion.

Lord Ashfield told the crowd: "To build 710 bombers has been a wonderful achievement and an experience none of us will ever forget."

After a tribute to Sir Frederick Handley-Page, Lord Ashfield said he would christen the aircraft in the knowledge that a gallant crew would make it play its part in helping to rid the world of a bestial and ruthless tyranny.

He then named the bomber "London Pride" while the band of Duple Bodies and Motors, Ltd., played the "Knightsbridge March" by Eric Coates. In the hands of the Chief Test Pilot, "London Pride" thrilled the watchers with an exhibition that proved it will be able to more than hold its own in the final routing of the enemy. Said an employee afterwards: "It gives one the impression of having completed a job well worth doing,"

WHP, April 1945

"News for the Troops" reporting U.S. Rhine crossing.

... a "lest we forget" account of the horrors ...

Drawing To The Close

WHEN the Allied armies were chasing a beaten and disorganised enemy back into Germany, and the Allied air forces were raining destruction on the Fatherland at a rate never before contemplated, even in this war, it was freely predicted that when the end came it could come suddenly. There was a general feeling that under this intensive attack from without and within, the battered Nazi edifice would crash, topple and fall almost overnight

Events have shown how wrong we were. The cracks appeared—the most ominous of the earlier ones was the attempt on Hitler's life last year— but still the Third Reich, against all the laws of nature, held together.

There have been other and wider cracks since then. The biggest ones, both within the last few days, have been Himmler's offer of unconditional surrender to Great Britain and the United States and the death of Hitler, the fanatic whose evil genius created and maintained the Nazi hegemony. The second event, which must in the end has, however, been made the occasion of an attempt to stave them off.

The appointment of Admiral Doenitz as Hitler's successor suggests a temporary suspension of the peace negotiations being carried on by Himmler, for how long cannot as yet be judged.

So we must, for the time being, remain on the tenterhooks which have kept us in suspense all this week In Watford, as elsewhere, the last few days have been memorable, if rather tantalising, ones. Everybody has been keyed up to expect the great announcement almost hourly.

WHP, May 1945

Thousands In Streets For VE-Day

HEAVEN'S artillery sounded its salvos as though to herald the dawn of VE-Day. For three hours a tropical storm, more violent than any since that which was the prelude to the day when we declared war on Germany, rent the darkness with vivid flashes, and torrential rain put out the pre-VE-Day bonfires. But the great day dawned calm and clear, the birds sang blithely, and Watford awoke to a glorious day—glorious in every minute of it!

Grey, soaked streets warmed quickly to brilliant sunshine; the bedraggled flags and bunting, in such profusion everywhere, flapped out the moisture, and soon Watford was gay again.

Then the streets filled—streets that were soon sun-drenched—and the hearts of the people warmed to the "King's weather." Lads of the Forces, especially those in hospital blue, received handshakes, even kisses, from perfect strangers.

Everyone was happy and glad to go to the Town Hall in the morning for an act of thanksgiving—but not all could be crowded into the great hall.

Then followed gaiety in its many forms—singing, laughter, street tea parties, illuminations, dancing, bonfires. Watford was determined to enjoy every minute of this great occasion.

WHP, May 1945

• *VE Day, Victory in Europe, 8th May, 1945. VJ Day, Victory in Japan, 14th August 1945.*

Lights Go On Again

With the exception of a few lamps which have been broken, Watford street lights will go up again on Sunday evening, following the putting back of clocks one hour to British Summer Time.

The Borough Engineer told the "Post" yesterday: "Everything is ready except for some lamps which are out of order but which we are to replace as quickly as possible.

WHP, July 1945

Victory-Joy Sweeps Watford

ALL Watfordians were tucked snugly in bed at midnight on Wednesday when Mr. Attlee made his momentous announcement that the world was once more at peace.

When they woke and learned the news yesterday morning it was with quiet thankfulness and subdued satisfaction.

Not until the afternoon, when the sun burst through the clouds, did it seem that full realisation that the war is over, the boys will be back, and life will return to its normal courses, burst upon the consciousness of Watford.

Then the shops closed, streets filled with gay, happy crowds, victory parties sprang up, bonfires were lighted, and the town gave itself over to a celebration appropriate to the historic occasion.

Watford did not really swing into celebrating mood until the evening, when old and young let their feelings go in victory parties which sprang up all over the district.

WHP, August 1945

The Hell of Belsen

A MEMBER of a Field Transfusion Unit with the B.L.A., whose wife lives in Gammons-lane, Watford, has been with the mercy mission at Belsen. What he has seen has so shocked him that he has written a "lest we forget" description of the horrors.

"This is the most tragic thing in my life, worse than any action I have been in." he says. "Since I have been away from home I have at times wondered what we were fighting for. I had heard yarns of seemingly exaggerated German atrocities, and had taken them all with a pinch of salt. But not now! Never has anyone on earth, other than the people responsible, seen anything like this."

Here is his description of a long, narrow building known as "The Human Laundry."

"Outside a long line of ambulances waited with their loads of living death. This building is appropriately known as the 'human laundry'. All along one side are benches, and to each one is an S.S. woman—a huge Amazon, callous and depraved. The patients are off-loaded by the few remaining German prisoners. There are men and women. They seem dead, but still breathing—a horrible sight. It's quite impossible to say how thin they are, only a covering of skin over the bones. To give you an idea: sometimes they bring two women in on one stretcher.

"Well, these S.S. women proceed to scrub them from head to foot thoroughly and powder the hair with anti-louse powder. They are then passed down to where they are put into clean blankets and sent to the Army hospital. I suppose this is their first wash in five years or whatever length of time they have been in the camp.

"We went into the concentration camp, which is full of typhus, TB., scabies, dysentery, and everything under the sun The awful stench is too over-powering for some.

"There are dilapidated old huts, rags, sacks, straw and everything conceivable which these people had tried to make out of nothing in order to provide some sort of shelter. The majority we saw were women. It was awful and hopelessly impossible to ascertain the ages. Girls of 18, 19, 20, looked like old wizened grandmothers.

"These women crawl out from under their roofing of sacking and attend to all needs of nature. Self-respect, decency, is all gone. They are lower than animals. Those who can walk shuffle along in faltering steps of six inches or so a time.

"We left the hut area and visited one particular place which had just been vacated. I do not know whether it was curiosity or a determination to see for myself, which compelled me and others to go inside. On the floor was a squelching mess about nine inches thick, and on top of that was such a collection of filth I can never hope to describe. Horribly stinking rags which just dropped off these people were strewn everywhere; tins, bottles, God knows what else, there was so much.

"At the end of this place three girls were still living! But the little room they had was more presentable. They looked reasonably well, having not been there long, and they had taken advantage of this room when the rest cleared out to go to hospital. I don't think they had been there more than a matter of months, hence their comparative good appearance, but their decency had gone even then.

"We went to the grave area. Huge pits of bodies alongside a heap of human bones 10 feet high. The most amazing thing was that there was a heap of boots and shoes stacked 15ft high, 30ft long, and 15ft thick. Thousands upon thousands. They had been taken off the dead and placed there as a reminder to the living of the fate which awaited them.

"We met these wrecks, wandering aimlessly around with an insane smile on their faces, looking with envy at the graves, hoping that they soon would find peace. On every building one saw the notice marked out in chalk. "Dead here. Will lorry please call." A few medical students were there, trying to straighten

253

The Horror of Belsen.

things out, but they had a hopeless task.

"That is very briefly what I saw. Fortunately, instead of going into a concentration camp to work, I am working with these patients after they have been de-loused and washed. We have 1,500 here; they are all T.B., typhus, etc. They are dying off rapidly. I suppose they cannot yet get used to receiving humane treatment, being fed at regular intervals, and a proper bed to lie in.

"At Belsen a squad of German Medical Corps personnel was sent there to help. When they met one of the S. S. Guards they set about him and practically murdered him. Yes, I am convinced that the blame is only on a clique, which so foolishly the German people have followed so blindly.

"These ordinary people are trying hard to make friends with us. They respect us, there is no doubt, in spite of the fact that they are compelled to do all the dirty work here. They are aware of the orders issued to us about no fraternisation, and I feel that they are trying to prove by their efforts to impress us, that they had nothing to do with this state of affairs.

"They did, I suppose, because they allowed the Nazis to rule them. I am certain, however, that they will not tolerate the Nazis again, and I believe they will become a democratic people, for they have been humiliated beyond description.

"Every word in this letter I have written is true, nothing exaggerated—rather understated. It is impossible to find the suitable words."

WHP, June 1945

"Squatters" in Langley Way Camp

THE "squatters" are here. Following the example of those in other parts of the country, local families, tired of living in pent-up conditions and tired of the futile trek and inquiries for a home of their own, have invaded the derelict American Army camp in Langley-way.

They came in force. Within a short while 50 families had staked their claims, and others had chalked their names on the few remaining huts. Dozens were turned away, but were not dismayed, and indicated they intended occupying some empty huts at Leavesden.

Some disquiet is being shown by those in the comfortable residential area of Cassiobury Park Estate, and by the Corporation, who have been approached to make water and electricity available.

WO, August 1945

Swift Switch to Peace Programme

WATFORD factories—managements and work-people alike—are straining at the leash to switch over to peace-time production, following the nation-wide cancellation of war contracts announced by the Government yesterday.

Several big local concerns have already begun the transition, and many others have their plans ready to put into operation.

Typical of this class is Scammell Lorries, Ltd., of Tolpits-lane, peace-time commercial vehicle makers, whose contribution to the transport needed by the Army, Navy and R.A.F. and essential home services during the war was colossal.

They produced for the Government 1,449 heavy breakdown and recovery tractors, 786 heavy artillery tractors, 6,074 four-wheel tractor conversions, 676 "mechanical horses," 4,268 trailer under-carriages and hundreds of other vehicles.

Government requirements for those types of vehicles and equipment will continue for some months, and as these taper off, production will be gradually switched over to supply the needs of the commercial work.

Example of a firm which did make a wide departure from its usual work is that of Dickinson's Paper Mills, who cut down on their manufacture of beautifully finished notepaper to produce anti-radar "black strips" and jettisoning petrol tanks for aircraft.

WHP, August 1945

Labour Gain Watford

Claimed to be the heaviest poll on record, 69,825 people representing 72.6 of the electorate, cast their votes. The final figures were:

Major J. Freeman (Labour)   32,138
Air Commodore W. Helmore (Con)   29,944
Major E. Harben (Lib)   7,743
Major Harben failed to poll an eighth of the total and thus loses his £150 deposit

WHP, August 1945

"Nachrichten" in its Millions

When in the late afternoons of last autumn Watfordians looked skywards and saw, high up a long procession of four-engined British and American bombers streaming towards the Continent they looked at each other with knowing glances and said, "Jerry's going to get another pasting today—a few more blockbusters will teach him his lesson."

Sometimes an employee of the Sun Engraving Co., Watford, was within earshot He could have told them that those planes weren't carrying bombs but newspapers—thousands of them.

He had helped print them at the Whippendellroad works, but he could not enlighten his acquaintances, for he was bound by the strictest measures of security silence. From July 14, 1944, to May 14, 1945, the Sun took part in a deadly type of psychological warfare which had as important a part in bringing about the German capitulation as

Belsen was not, as such, an 'extermination' camp; rather more a detention and labour camp. Towards the end of the war it was overwhelmed by vast numbers force-marched from camps in the east, to escape the oncoming Russians. Their privations on their long marches bred and fostered disease which Belsen was unable to cope with. There were many huts which needed to be destroyed and this was done by fire from flame-throwers, the large sized portrait of Hitler being a focal point. Belsen continued for some years as a staging and resettlement camp.

This photograph was taken by BBC recording engineer, R E Pidsley, who travelled with American and British Forces, filing the BBC's daily War Report. After setting up his disc-cutting apparatus he would use his Leica to photograph the action, from Cassino in Italy, through Natzviler to Paris, Belsen and Berlin.

Film was hard to come by; he 'scrounged' and used short ends of cine film cut and loaded into a Leica reloadable cassette; with this picture he had rare problems, hence the 'tramlines' across the negative.

Fairfield's at Aldenham ..."Ubend'em, Wemend'em" ...

bombs, shells and bayonets.

Every day during this important closing phase of the war the Company produced anything from a million copies of a propaganda newspaper in German—"Nachrichten Fur Die Truppe" (News for the Troops).

They were packed on the spot in special containers and dropped by plane the same day in the vicinity of German troop concentrations.

There came a time when the effect of "Nachrichten" was more devastating than bombs.

Reading of the good food and honourable treatment they would receive as prisoners, thousands of Germans, sick of war, rushed to give themselves up. Opposing armies that might have taken weeks to beat in the field disintegrated overnight Those newspapers, printed in Watford, helped to make the final, swift drive on Berlin possible.

WHP, September 1945

Sun's Atom Bomb Research

HAD it not been for extensive laboratory research work carried out at Watford during the past two years, the atomic bomb, conqueror of Japan, might not have been possible.

The work, carried out at the Sun Engraving Company's Whippendell-road works, was shrouded in such secrecy that even the "Sun's" workers engaged on it did not know until recently that they were participating in the construction of the atomic bomb.

After British and American scientists had carried out a tremendous amount of theoretical and experimental work into the possibilities of concentrating the energy of the split uranium atom to the point of a devastatingly explosive force, Imperial Chemical Industries were entrusted with the contract for the development of the "diffusion" plant essential to the construction of the bomb, it is recorded in a White Paper, "Statements Relating to the Atom Bomb." In this work they were assisted by two subcontractors, one of whom was the Sun Engraving Company as the leading experts on the deposition and electrolytic processes affecting metals. A small laboratory was set up at the Sun's Whippendell-road premises, and here research workers worked seven days a week.

Their particular problem was to discover a method of treating metal so as to make possible the building of plant necessary to the gaseous diffusion of the uranium isotope known as "U.235." A technical expert who had a considerable amount to do with the research at Watford told the "Post": "The work was very exhausting and at times taxed our ingenuity to the utmost. But we had the satisfaction in the end of being able to inform I.C.I. that we had found what they wanted."

WHP, September 1945

de Havilland's to Stay at Leavesden

SECRECY surrounding de Havilland's intentions regarding the future of their factory sited on the King George V Playing Field at Leavesden was lifted by Ald. T. H. Simmons at Watford Town Council on Tuesday when he revealed that the company wish to continue their occupation for the production of aero engines. He emphasised that De Havilland's were tenants of the Air Ministry, by whom the playing field was requisitioned in 1939, and that in any event De Havilland's would have to work to Air Ministry instructions.

Alderman Simmons was defending the action he took prior to the last Council meeting, when, replying to an enquiry from De Havilland's as to the Council's future intentions with regard to the site, he had informed them, through the Town Clerk, that the Council "favoured the retention of the aerodrome."

"I have had an opportunity of consulting with the managing director of De Havillands and his deputy," continued Ald. Simmons, "especially in view of the possibility of the firm going.

"There was the risk of the loss of employment for several thousands of workers there. If we had said, towards the end of 1944, "The Council wants the playing field back," what kind of a row would that have caused? I think I have a shrewd idea."

WHP, September 1945

Fairfield's Part In Air Warfare

WHEN a large, white-painted Wellington bomber, repaired and equipped with the latest Radar devices, took off from Aldenham airfield at midday yesterday, the Fairfield Aviation Company's last war job was done and the factory, employing 1,100 Watford workpeople, officially closed down. A grand "saved from the scrap-heap" task had been completed.

Jobs have already been found by the Ministry of Labour for practically all the displaced workers. They have been smoothly absorbed into other local industries.

Since August, 1940, when they came to Aldenham as a war-time subsidiary of Redwing Aircraft Ltd., Croydon and Wolverhampton, Fairfield's have repaired and refitted 1,809 fighter and bomber aircraft for the R.A.F.

A portion of Odham's factory was placed at their disposal. Their task was to rescue smashed-up aircraft from the scrap-heap and put them back into the air. This they achieved at the rate of practically a plane a day.

Working day and night, often at nerve-wracking pressure, they took badly shot-up Blenheims, Wellingtons, Hawker fighters and other types and made them airworthy again in a matter of hours. "Our employees worked wonderfully," Mr. Frank Collins, Fairfield's welfare officer, told a "Post" reporter.

"The majority, among whom were many girls and women, came to us untrained and entirely without technical knowledge. They proved remarkably adaptable and within a few weeks became amazingly skilled and efficient." Fairfield's speciality was the Lysander Intruder. To them, in conjunction with Wing-Commander "Freddie" Pickard, of "Target for Tonight" fame, goes the credit for the development of this specialised aircraft.

Developed from the old Lysander Army co-operation 'plane, the Intruder became a deadly thorn in the side of the foe. Painted dull black, it flew across the Channel night after night, transporting patriots and supplies to aid underground movements in enemy-occupied territory.

High spot of Fairfield's activity was during the Battle of Britain. As the struggle reached its climax so many 'planes were being shot down or seriously damaged that mobile squads were sent out from Fairfield's to repair them on the spot. These squads, who repaired a total of 693 aircraft and worked wonders at improvisations, became famous up and down the country for the motto stencilled on the back of their jerseys, "Ubend'em, Wemend'em"

WHP, October 1945

Getting the Houses Built

THIS is the problem confronting alike Parliament and the Local Authorities, and even more intimately many of their constituents. The bulk purchasing of housing materials and components, including complete factory-made houses, described by the Minister of Works in the House of Commons on Monday, when speaking on the Building Materials and Housing Bill, should, if operated with vigour and foresight, considerably assist in providing houses. For that is the vital need.

Briefly stated, a short-term policy this report propounded was for 350 dwellings in the first year and 550 in the second. A long-term policy involved 7,500 houses in ten years, including replacement of temporary houses.

If the new Housing Committee bring forward schemes for the speedy erection of dwellings we feel sure that support will be forthcoming from other Groups on the Council—for let it be remembered that the Borough has no mean record in respect of housing.

Meanwhile, the Mayor and Housing Chairman are appealing to residents for "spare-room" accommodation for urgent cases. A register is being prepared on the response to the appeal, which it is hoped will help to relieve the situation of some of the 2,500 applicants on the Corporation's waiting list.

While many smaller households have done their bit during the war years in billeting troops and workers in essential industries, there may be a good deal of accommodation available in larger houses.

WHP, November 1945

Penicillin made in Watford's BMH . . . H M King George VI visits Leavesden . . .

Kingswood is Exception

Watford Education Committee decided on Monday that although approval should no longer be given for the use of schools for social events such as children's parties and dances, an exception should be made in the case of Kingswood School.

Cllr.s. C. W. Tyrwhitt and S. W. Smith pointed out that Kingswood is a remote district with no other facilities for social events.

WHP, December, 1945

Watford's Penicillin

ON the fifth floor of a large Watford factory is an elaborately equipped laboratory in which a small army of workers— 60 per cent. of them local women— are working seven days a week to produce penicillin.

They make the new "wonder drug" at the rate of 1,000,000 doses a month.

During the latter stages of the war this laboratory was producing a very high proportion of all the penicillin made in Britain. At that time its activities were on the "highly secret" list, and although it is now possible to tell the story of its work, none of the 120 employees knows the formula to which he or she is working.

That is still a secret of the British Medical Research Council and the U.S. Office of Scientific Research.

Branch of a Greenford firm of manufacturing chemists, the laboratory was established under the auspices of the Ministry of Supply in the top storey of the British Moulded Hose Company's premises at Sandown-road, Watford, early in 1944. Delicate and costly apparatus was installed and stainless steel had to be specially diverted from armament production to provide some of the essential equipment.

A "Post" reporter who visited the laboratory this week saw girls deftly handling hundreds of flasks containing penicillin mould which passed slowly along on a conveyor belt.

He was told by the manager "Here you have intricate laboratory work carried out on factory production scale. Something like 90,000 flasks are growing penicillin mould here at any one time, and as a fluctuation of only one degree in temperature can seriously affect the growth, the care that must be taken can be readily understood."

WHP, December 1945

No Later Shopping

From now until March, 1946, Watford shops will have to close not later than 5.30 p.m.

Watford Town Council has made this decision under Defence Regulation 60AB, which continues to remain in force. Tobacconists, confectioners and newsagents are exempted from the Order, while barbers and hairdressers are allowed to remain open until 6.30 p.m.

WHP, December 1945

Spotlight on Cinemas

Watford Town Council is to ask Herts County Council for information regarding Sunday opening of cinemas in Watford.

Ald. Last, stressing that his question was not a criticism of the operation of Sunday cinemas in Watford, and that he had no grounds for believing that there were any irregularities, asked on Tuesday for details of the amounts paid to local charities, and also whether the cinemas were observing the conditions laid down regarding Sunday staffing.

Very stringent conditions were fixed regarding payments to hospitals and conditions of labour when the licences were granted, Ald. Last reminded the Council, and he had been asked to raise the matter. If he could be given an assurance that these conditions had been observed he would have nothing further to say.

WHP, December 1945

North Watford residents of the 1930's, before the advent of Odhams and the new estates, viewed the North Watford gasometer as an 'imposition' and 'hideous eyesore.' It was frequently complained of in the local newspapers, to no avail.

The car passing the gasometer has no number-plate; it carries HM King George VI and HM Queen Elizabeth on their way to Leavesden to visit the Canadian "Khaki University"; on their return they pass through Watford where it is noticed that the "King looked pale, drawn and tired" whilst the Queen, in a red coat, looked bright.

A spy above the town, and on the ground ...

"Harry Williamson"

Wulf Schmidt was born in the German province of Schleswig-Holstein in 1911; in 1919 the province was Danish and this gave Wulf Schmidt reason for claiming Danish nationality. Back in Germany in 1940 after a second trip of employment to Argentina he answered an advert seeking someone with knowledge of languages. He was recruited into the Abwehr as an agent and was dropped by parachute near RAF Oakington on the night of 19/20 September 1940. When caught he was carrying £136, $160; a passport in his own name and one in the name of 'Harry Williamson'; he had been sent to 'prepare the way for a German invasion'.

Taken to London for interrogation he realised that statements about 'devastation' to London were false. *[The blitz had started on 7th Sept].* His sense of self-preservation prevailed and he turned double-agent. He was handled by M15 and lived under control at Radlett. He was asked by the Abwehr questions about bomb damage, troop movements, factory and airforce installations and the like. His replies, manufactured for him and in his own inimitable style, contained enough truth to be believable, and much make-believe. After the devastating raids upon Coventry, *(14th Nov.)* he relayed lists of 'damage' and the 'facts' that he had heard that major manufacturers were moving to north Lancashire—beyond the range of German bombers.

He was believed.

He lived a life upon a knife-edge of fear of discovery by betrayal and treachery. As part of his cover he started employment in July 1943 with Greville's in Queens Road (who were then supplying the 'Watford Observer' with news photographs) and not long after was awarded the German Iron Cross First and Second Class for services to the Abwehr.

He relayed false information about areas supposed to be laid at sea with mines—thus saving convoys from attack in those areas; and fed extensive 'mis-information' about D-Day preparations to tie down German troops in the Pas de Cálais. He sent his 1,000th message in September 1944 and carried on until the end in May 1945. Remaining under MI5 cover he started work in 1945 for the 'West Herts Post', and in 1951 with the 'Watford Observer' until 1957 afterwards working for WEMCO until his retirement in 1975.

None knew, or guessed, his secret until it was published in 1991, the year before he died. True to his lifetime of secrecy his funeral was clandestine, and erstwhile colleagues and friends were denied paying final respects.

Taken in May 1939 this shows the centre of Watford from a German plane. The main heading refers to 'Watford, electricity works', a rather dubious honour for our Town Hall just being built!

He came for a few weeks and stayed, under a shadow, for the rest of his life; he served his 'adopted' country well and many of his photographs are used in this book and have enriched Watford's history.

J B N, 1996

Town Hall— Electricity Works?

The 1946 "Watford Observer" story:

Watford's escape is the more remarkable when it is now possible to reveal that the new Town Hall was not an administrative building, but the busy hive of war electrical equipment production. This mistake might have been very costly to the town—in lives, disorganisation and financially. For the benefit of those who doubt this gross mistake we reproduce a photograph of Watford taken by the Germans on May 24, 1939—a little more than three months before war was declared. This photograph was filed with thousands of other aerial photos of towns and villages of England in a Luftwaffe library at Lubeck, North Germany—used at one time by the crack "Luftwaffe 26 Gruppe." It was probably taken by a German passenger plane. Further aerial views of Watford were taken in August, 1941, and similarly filed.

The survey reproduced shows in black relief the Town Hall and the area between the Public Library and extending down St. Albans-road. This area was marked "A" and labelled to indicate electric equipment works. If this map was used it may have been responsible for the dropping in 1940 and 1941 of oil bombs, incendiaries and high explosives in the Highstreet, Queen's-road and Harebreaks areas.

WO, September 1946

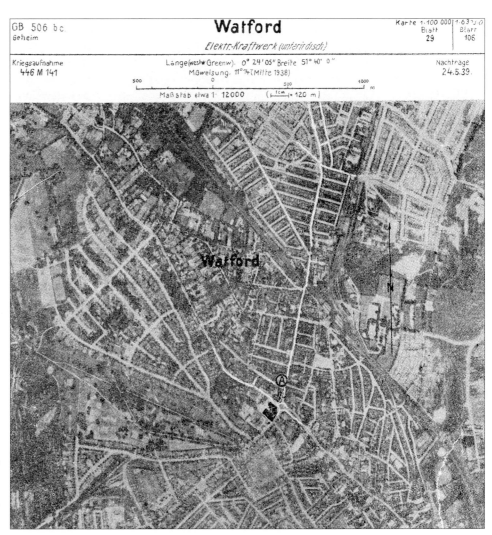

257

Watford—central area, has the characteristics of an overgrown village . . .

For planning purposes the centres of Watford, Rickmansworth, Kings Langley, Abbots Langley and Bushey (and to a great extent Hemel Hempstead as well) must be considered together and proposals must be drawn up for them regardless of local government boundary considerations. Watford is a good centre for industry and it is a prosperous railway junction, industrial, market and residential town; to some extent it is a dormitory for London black-coat workers, though less so than Bushey and Rickmansworth. Abbots Langley and Kings Langley are small independent townships with a smattering of London travellers, but now tending to become residential satellites to Watford. Watford is popular with industry owing to its excellent transport facilities. It is at a junction on the main London, Midland and Scottish Railway to Rugby, with a number of electric railways to London, served by the Watford By-Pass and the North Orbital Road (the latter will be of greater benefit still to industry when the section west of the Hemel Hempstead Road is constructed) and reasonably near to London. It also possesses a good labour pool and has flat land available for further industries.

The town exhibits something of the crowded town atmosphere which Londoners like, its shops are good and include the usual multiple stores. There is the further advantage of very attractive countryside near at hand, linked in one place right into the town centre by the splendid Cassiobury Park.

Watford is the natural centre for industry and already possesses a number of biggish factories which give it an impression of industrial importance and standing which is appreciated by industry and tends to attract further concerns. It is, therefore, proposed that any future industrialisation of this part of the Region should be concentrated here and not spread about Bushey, Rickmansworth and the Langleys. At the same time the town has already grown sufficiently large residentially for a place so near London and, unless checked, its urban sprawl will greatly impair the attractiveness of a large part of London's Green Belt Ring.

No population increase of Watford is, therefore, suggested, but substantial planned increases are proposed for Rickmansworth, Bushey, Abbots and Kings Langley and Oxhey; these centres will then function as residential dormitories to Watford and supply it with the labour required for an expanded industry. It is most desirable that they should not coalesce with Watford, and they must be planned with adequate local green belts, otherwise the whole area will become a magnified suburbia.

The Watford area is developing as a centre for paper production, printing, publishing, photographic paper and the manufacture of office equipment, such as duplicator machines and subsidiary specialised concerns related to printing, including ink manufacture; in addition there are firms manufacturing patent medicines, lorries, foodstuffs, etc.

Most industries will be able to change over quickly to peace-time production. The development of Watford as a printing centre with its subsidiary industries will give plenty of diversity of employment, and industrial expansion to meet the needs of the decentralised population could well be restricted to industries of this type, for which the available land should be reserved; other industries, such as general engineering, etc., are not needed, but there is great scope for new light clean industries such as cosmetics and pharmaceutical products giving employment to a higher proportion of women, in view of the tendency to expand industries which primarily employ men. Adequate areas are available for the industrial expansion, including part of the Cassiobridge Sewage Farm (when the Colne Valley drainage scheme comes into full operation), though the latter is rather inaccessible and lonely for industry, which normally likes to select locations near other factories. A population increase of over 50,000 is contemplated for the surrounding town centres, including Oxhey, which will look to Watford for work.

This should produce an occupied population of 25,000 and assuming half of this works in factories (a high figure, as only 31% worked in factories according to the 1931 Census), factory work will be required for about 12,500 persons. On the basis of 40 persons per industrial acre, an area of about 314 acres will be required. In practice less than this will be necessary as the expansion of existing concerns will almost certainly absorb a number of workers and the aerodrome and repair workshops (if they remain) will give additional employment. Excluding certain areas of low-lying or inaccessible land which are contemplated for industry, and lands on the Watford By-Pass adjoining the road to Aldenham (along which no further ribbon development of factories should be allowed) at least 314 acres are available for industry.

A suggestion has been made for an additional large industrial area of about 680 acres near Potterscrouch, but this is quite unnecessary to serve the contemplated population increase. It is in any case very badly sited, adjoining a projected arterial road, it has no railway facilities, most of the roads round about could never cope with the volume of traffic, both goods and passenger, that would be put on them; the development of such a site would stimulate a huge expansion of Watford up to the fringes of St. Albans and would break up good land and an essential part of the London Green Belt and also the local green belt between Watford and St. Albans. (This might lead to a 160,000 population increase in addition to the planned 50,000.)

Watford is one of the most congested towns in the Region (in spite of the by-pass) and wholesale replanning of the built-up area will be essential if the latter is to function successfully as an important industrial centre; the central area has in many ways the characteristics of an overgrown village and with the exception of one length of the Hemel Hempstead Road, its exits are narrow and tortuous. It is almost possible to watch the houses along St. Albans Road being converted into ribbons of shops. The only expansion of Watford itself which is proposed will be that needed to cover the internal movement of that part of its population which will be rehoused after rebuilding the central area.

The "Greater London Plan", by Professor Patrick Abercrombie, M.A, F.R.I.B.A, P.P.T.P.I.

Next page: A map of Watford in 1938. Little or no building took place during the war and so is substantially valid for 1945-1950.

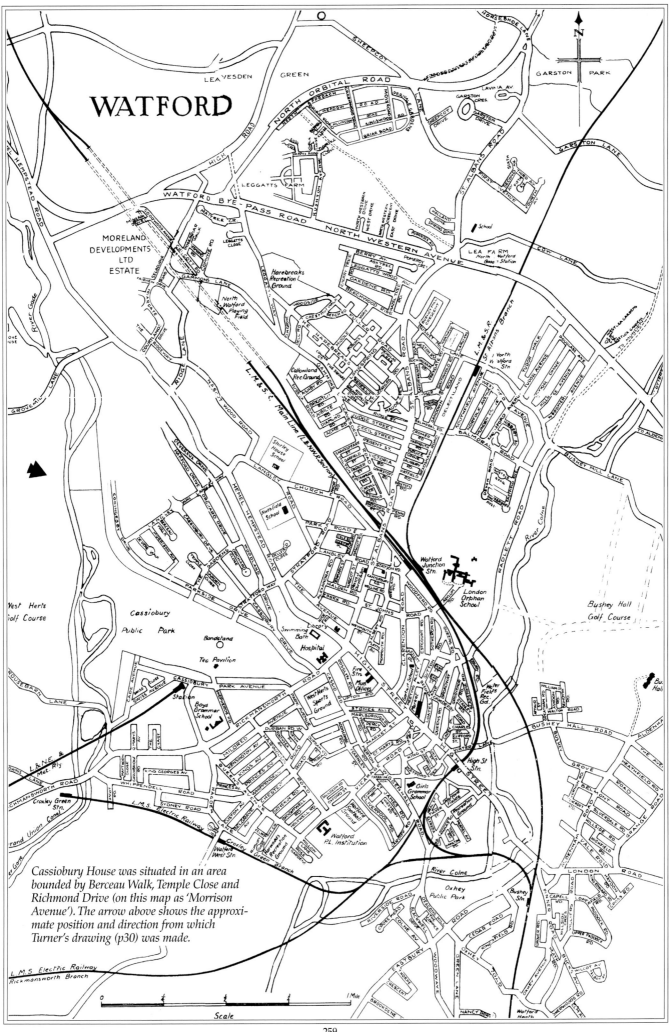

WATFORD

Cassiobury House was situated in an area bounded by Berceau Walk, Temple Close and Richmond Drive (on this map as 'Morrison Avenue'). The arrow above shows the approximate position and direction from which Turner's drawing (p30) was made.

L.M.S. Electric Railway
Rickmansworth Branch

0   ¼   ½   ¾   1 Mile
Scale

Part VIII

Picking up the pieces

The Plan thus prepared, with this multifarious guidance and collaboration, is now completed, so far as it is possible to say that a stage of finality can be reached by a living organism. There is now a chance—and a similar one may not occur again—of getting the main features of this programme of redistributed population and work carried through rapidly and effectively, thereby reducing overcrowding and locating industry in conjunction. The difficulties in normal times of moving people and industry are rightly stressed; but people and industry will go where accommodation is made available. Moreover, the war has made migration a familiar habit. Give a man and his wife a first-rate house, a community, and occupation of various kinds reasonably near at hand, within a regional framework which enables them to move freely and safely about, to see their friends and enjoy the advantages of London; add to these a wide freedom of choice, and they will not grumble in the years immediately following the war. The industrialist, if he be asked whether he is prepared to submit to the guidance of a Government official, will probably protest.

But if he is offered a choice of sites, with every modern facility (including labour) provided, and in addition a licence to build and access to building materials and labour, be will jump at the chance to get started as quickly as possible. Moreover, if Trading Estates are laid out ready for hire and actually a certain amount of building is done for small enterprises, these sites and factories will be eagerly taken up always, of course, provided they are sited in the most suitable positions.

The "Greater London Plan"

The Town's Borough Engineer, Mr Newman, had retired during the war, a Deputy having taken over until a permanent replacement could be found.

In 1945 the post was advertised; 37 hopefuls replied.

Frederick Clifford Sage, 38, won the post of Borough Engineer. From Wolverhampton, via Bilston, Birmingham, Gloucester, Harrow, Waterloo-with-Seaford (Lancs) and Ilford, he was to be responsible for the design and erection of new housing estates; roads, public buildings, design and construction of sewerage schemes, and the administration of town planning functions delegated by the County Council. He faced a bustling overcrowded town, short of labour and short of housing.

He faced huge traffic problems posed by Watford's one long street. He, and the Council, faced arguments with the County Council who wanted to restrict Watford's growth by limiting the amount of new housing which could be built. With workers who had come to Watford to man wartime industries, and who wanted to stay and get out of lodgings, and returning servicemen, now married and with young families started and wanting a home, he and his staff faced an uphill task.

During the coming few years he and his staff were to provide the spadework and bulk of information to County for framing the shape of Watford's future road network.

He worked within the constraints of small budgets and huge demand. He, and his team, attacked the problems with gusto; demolishing here, and planning tower blocks there. In the photograph on page 70 is 'Little Nascot' at the bottom of St Albans Road; it was demolished in 1959. Alderman Amey suggested a 'citizens' theatre with a parade of shop, exciting public imagination. Later, relief road plans were published).

Despite these plans, which showed huge road widening at the spot, the local newspapers and public still anticipated a new building to compliment and enhance the Town Hall approaches. A detailed analysis of buildings, density and usage, condition and access; of road usage—where vehicles left Watford after entering, and how many cars were parked and where—was made in 1954 and published as a draft plan in 1956.

The conclusion was that there should be an Eastern relief Road, from St Albans Road to Water Lane (which today we know as Beechen Grove). That property was involved caused an outcry, but the outcry did not ease the congestion. This plan, being too ambitious to be carried out within any foreseeable future, was the forerunner of alternative schemes. The Council wanted to widen King Street to lessen a very dangerous exit into the High Street; County said 'No', which left Watford's Council fuming until they decided that it had to be done—and did it.

In 1956 Mr Sage had broached the idea that the Clarendon and Station Roads be developed as an office centre: 'Why not a Threadneedle Street in Watford?' and of Clarendon Road as dual-carriageway. Of plans to develop the corner of Longspring and St Albans Road he spoke of the aim to make St Albans Road dual carriageway to the Cross Roads.

Of the Central Area plans (Feb 1957) he explained, in 1958, that car parks would be sited adjacent to the relief roads, and shops would be within easy walking distance and 'absolute safety of the shopping public can only be ensured by the complete segregation of pedestrians and vehicles'. In other words, a complete prohibition of all vehicles entering the shopping area.

He was in favour of high rise blocks of flats and suggested them for Sotheron, Sutton and Estcourt roads.

If Mr Sage thought that St Albans and Clarendon Roads could be 'dualed' he was either unrealistic about road widths, or over-optimistic about the amount of property which could be demolished to attain these roads. Of the 'pedestrian precinct scheme' he threw away the concept with "it would be difficult, though not impossible, to have a similar arrangement in Watford. The Central Plan does not provide for this . . . the new relief road will encourage its use by through-traffic, although still leaving the High Street accessible to all vehicles."

Of these plans Watfordians knew and cared little; they were far more pre-occupied with obtaining food and coal. It was a world of pre-fabs, rationing and acute shortages of consumer goods of all sorts.

They were not to know that a further ten years were to elapse before 'normal' times were to return.

Legless Hero Opens Carnival

When Group Captain Bader arrived, in a grey civilian suit, early in the afternoon, he was met by the Mayor, who escorted the legless hero to the platform and introduced him to the cheering crowd.

By coming to Watford on such a great day, said the Mayor, Group Captain Bader had done Watford high honour. They were privileged to have with them a man whose deeds had made his reputation international.

Declaring the afternoon session of the carnival fair open, Group Captain Bader said with a smile: "In spite of the nice things the Mayor has said about me, I would rather face anything than be facing you chaps on this rostrum.

"Nevertheless, I am very pleased to come to Watford, for Ald. Timberlake has been writing to me and telling me quite a lot about your show.

"I see that in 1943 you made a record 'high' for your hospital of £4,000. Today I hope the organisers will go one better and squeeze out of you at least £4,001."

The Carnival Queen, Miss Betty Saunders, called upon everyone to enjoy themselves, and reinforced Group Captain Bader's appeal on behalf of the hospital.

WHP, June 1946

Whitsun Downpour

NOT even so impressive a combination as Victory Day and the Whitsun Carnival in aid of Watford Peace Memorial Hospital could produce a day of "flaming June" for the double event, although everything else was organised with the utmost efficiency.

After Group CaptainDouglas Bader, "the legless wonder," had opened the Victory Day fete not even the torrential rain could separate holidaymakers from their revels.

Climatically, it was the same sad story on Monday. The gymkhana, highlight of the Whitsun carnival, suffered quick switches from sunshine to shower, but evening brought more settled weather, and thousands of visitors ploughed through the mud in search of pleasure—and found it, according to their varying tastes.

Children had a Victory concession. They were admitted free to the carnival and provid-

ed with tickets which were passports to the swings, roundabouts and other attractions.

Promptly at 10 am. Watford's Victory parade and carnival procession moved off from Hare-breaks, watched by crowds which thickly lined the four-mile route to Cassiobury Park.

Colourful and impressive came two open landaus, each drawn by a pair of prancing greys. The first bore the Mayor of Watford, Councillor J. Wright, in his red robes and glistening chain of office, together with the Mayoress, the Deputy Mayor, Councillor Mrs. Emily Beall, and the Town Clerk.

In the second landau travelled the Carnival Queen, Miss Betty Saunders, and her attendants, each carrying a gorgeous bouquet

Round the two carriages rode six outriders—four girls and two men—smartly dressed in military style costume.

After travelling down St. Albans-road into Station-road and Queen's-road, the procession turned into High-street where the excited crowds were thicker than ever. The long column turned into Market-st. and proceeded by way of Cassio-road, Whippendell-road, Harwoods-road, Rickmansworth-road and Shepherd's-road into the side entrance of Cassiobury Park.

WHP, June 1946

Council Workers Shocking Harvest

HALF A LOAF and 13 mouldy hunks of bread were the chief exhibits at Watford's Battle of Bread" Exhibition, which opened yesterday at the Kingham Hall, St. John Road.

They had been found by refuse collectors while clearing dustbins in one small sector of Watford on Saturday, and are typical of the shocking waste which is taking place in many parts of the borough every day, it is stated.

Mr. F. C. Sage, the Borough Engineer, told the "Post" yesterday that a special check had been made by his inspectors in the past few weeks and bread, potatoes, green vegetables and other waste food were often found in the van-loads of refuse.

It was hoped Ald. H. J. Bridge; local Food Executive Officer, would tell the Ministry of Food that Watford did not want bread rationing. If it

Top: The Mayor, Councillor J Wright, in the coach, passing the Police Station opposite Leavesden Road, in St Albans Road.

Bottom: The procession has turned from the High Street into Market Street.

was inevitable, that would be that, but if it was to be averted, the best means would be by avoiding any single scrap of waste.

Mrs. Gordon Spencer, a Ministry of Food speaker, outlined the causes of the present world food shortages, and the terrible effects it was having in the large Continental towns.

In the House of Commons Mr. John Freeman Watford's M.P., asked the Minister of Food whether he was in a position to make a further announcement about the likelihood of bread rationing,

Mr. Strachey replied that consultations with the bakery trade and others concerned were taking place, but if there were the slightest risk of grave consequences by not rationing bread, then unquestionably the decision would be to ration. Nothing had occurred since his previous statement on May 31 to make the introduction of bread rationing appear less likely.

WHP, June 1946

£150 Fines on Dairymen

FINES totalling £150 were imposed on a 73-years-old farmer, of Coldharbour Farm, Bushey, and his son-in-law, of the same address, for selling more milk than the permit allowed.

Mr. T. Anderson Davies, prosecuting, said the farmer was the proprietor, and his son-in-law the manager of a farm where a dairy business was carried on. A permit issued to the farmer on March 3, 1946, allowed him to sell 517 gallons of milk a week. For the five weeks from March 2 he sold weekly 676¾, 673¾, 676¾, 721¾, and 693¼ gallons.

From these sales he had made a total illicit profit of £37 8s. 5d. This position was discovered by an Inspector who examined the records at the farm.

Mr. Neild, for defendants, said the farmer had a farm of 180 acres, partly dairy and partly arable. He was 73 years of age and in poor health, and had never concerned himself with the milk records, which he left to the care of his wife. His wife was also in poor health, and at the time of the visit by the Inspector the books were being kept by Thomas.

Some of the milk which was sold was produced on the farm, and the necessary amount was made up by buying from a wholesaler. When the farmer was producing more milk, supplies should have been cut down from the wholesaler immediately. That was where the omission had occurred. The books were available for the Inspector to look at any time.

WHP, July 1946

Progress on Housing Sites

MEMBERS of Watford Housing Committee, anxious to see the progress in the town's housing drive, travelled round the various housing sites on Thursday afternoon last week.

The party was conducted by Mr. F. C. Sage (Borough Engineer).

The first site to be visited was at Riverside-road, where 44 permanent houses are to be

built. Work had begun on 40 of these, and ten were nearly completed.

It was explained by Mr. Sage that difficulty had been experienced here with regard to access roads. Special roads had had to be built, and the materials had been brought to the site without damage. The installation of electrical work was proceeding in some of the houses.

The idea was to keep a certain uniformity throughout, which was being done by using the same type of bricks, and a feature of these houses was the new type of concrete roofing tiles which were being used on all the houses.

The cost of the houses would be about £1,200 each, with some additional costs. This figure would not include the price of the land.

There were four old cottages, which would be pulled down when the tenants could be rehoused in the new houses now being built.

These cottages were the last of the "back-to-back" type in Watford, and some of the families had been living there for over 50 years.

WEST HERTS POST, Thursday, July 3, 1947—7

- - - CUT THIS OUT AND KEEP IT AS A GUIDE - - - - - - - -

How to get your new Ration Book

WATFORD BOROUGH

NAMES BEGINNING:	WHEN TO GO:	WHERE TO GO:
S — Z	Thursday, July 3 & Friday, July 4	Small Town Hall, entrance side leading to Car Park from Rickmansworth-road. Monday to Friday, 9 a.m. to 5 p.m.

WATFORD RURAL DISTRICT

ABBOTS LANGLEY and RADLETT SUB-OFFICES will be closed for normal procedure from June 7 until further notice.
Saturday, July 5, 13, Upton-road, Watford
Thursday, Friday, July 3 & 4, Carpenders Park, Church Hall.
Tuesday, July 8, Letchmore Heath, Village Hall.

RICKMANSWORTH

RICKMANSWORTH DEPOT, THE BURY, BURY LANE, RICKMANSWORTH
Thursday July 3 and Friday, July 4.
10 a.m. — 1 p.m. 2.15 p.m. to 5.15 p.m.

CHORLEYWOOD

CHORLEYWOOD DEPOT, CHORLEYWOOD HOUSE
Thursday, July 3 and Friday, July 4, 2 p.m. to 5 p.m.

WHAT TO DO

1 Fill up page 4 of your present ration book and leave it in the book.

2 Take your ration book and identity card to the distribution centre. (If your identity card does not bear your right address or if you have lost it or it is in a very bad condition, go to the Food Office instead.)

3 If you hold a green ration book as an *expectant mother* and you have to produce a fresh medical certificate to the Food Office before 20th July, you can get your new ration books at the same time.

4 If you hold a *temporary identity card* and have to renew it at the Food Office before 20th July, you can get your new ration book at the same time.

Food Facts will tell you what to do after you get your new Ration Book

MINISTRY OF FOOD

There were seven contractors working on the site, and on one particular block of houses there were eight carpenter trainees and eight bricklayer trainees from the Government Training Centre, with two instructors working. In all there were about 125 men working on the project.

The Committee members inspected some of the houses, and expressed their satisfaction with the work.

The next site to be inspected was at Leavesden Green on the Watford bypass. Here it is planned to erect 200 permanent houses, of which half have been started. The foundations have been dug, and in some cases building up to a height of three or four feet has been reached. It was stated that there were already 300,000 bricks on the site.

The last of the sites to be visited was at Garston Park, off the St Albans-road, where it is planned to build 280 houses. Here they have been busy cutting roadways, and the foundations of a few of the houses have been laid.

Altogether nearly 600 houses are being built in Watford by the Watford Borough Council at the moment.

WO, October 1946

£2,000,000 Herts Project

An Act of Parliament in 1937 gave the Colne Valley Sewerage Board the authority, by the Colne Valley Sewage Disposal Act, to construct a disposal works which would take the place of 24 small works all over the county. With their new scheme in mind they started a year late; but were forced to stop at the outbreak of war.

In May of this year, with the help of 165 German prisoners, they restarted.

"By 1948," Mr. E. A. Williams, deputy clerk of the Board, told our reporter, "we shall have finished the job."

"People may think that sewage is a distasteful subject, but it is all very necessary. In days not so long ago, when refuse was run into the fields and ploughed in to fertilise the ground for next year's crops, it was a distasteful thing.

WO, December 1946

Next page: top, *The young girl on the left is the author's youngest sister, Janet. Many years after this photograph she married and she and her husband were among the earliest to hit the emigration trail, to South Africa. Her husband, Alan, became a master builder, learned Afrikaans, got on well, and Janet for many years ran an antique shop.*
In 2002 the homeland called; the money they had saved could not be brought out of South Africa and a bank crash meant that they lost most of their life savings, though much has since been repaid . . .

Answers at Housing Exhibition

WHEN it is my turn for a house, what will it be like? Will it be easy to manage, and keep clean? Will it have any "gadgets"?

These are probably just a few of the questions the Mrs. Jones, Mrs. Smiths and Mrs. Browns, who make up the waiting list of 3,773 applicants for houses in Watford have been asking themselves.

They had the opportunity of finding out the answers to some of their queries at Watford Housing Exhibition last week, where main interest of women visitors was centred on the complete house, constructed on the middle of the ballroom floor in the Town Hall.

This house was exactly similar to one of the types of permanent prefabricated houses Watford Corporation is building on its sites.

This was no empty shell, but a fully furnished home, such as newly-weds, and couples sharing homes or living in rooms must often have dreamed of. Nothing had been forgotten. There were flowers in the vases, the clocks were ticking, and in the wonderland kitchen, there were all the necessaty pots and pans, and even packets of cleaning materials.

In the past kitchens have been treated as the "Cinderella" room of the house. Whether the women members of the Watford Housing Committee have brought their influence to bear or not, I don't know, but one thing is certain: in Watford houses of the future, that will definitely be a thing of the past, and the kitchen will take its rightful place, as one of the most important home features.

Nothing has been forgotten which will make for easy running.

Ample window space ensures maximum light and air, and correct placing of commodious cupboard units, and a refrigerator, leaves plenty of room to work, without wasting unnecessary energy. One typical housewife, who was looking over the model, spent most of her time in the kitchen. "I think it's wonderful," she told me as she opened and inspected cupboards, pleased with everything she saw.

WHP, April 1947

Despite years of rationing most children were well-fed and healthy, here leaving Watford-Field School.

NOT TO WOMEN IN GENERAL—BUT TO **YOU** THE NATION SAYS THIS . . . .

Britain's manpower is not enough to win back prosperity. We can't get on without the women. Many of you have your own household problems but the country is up against it. Whole-time or part-time we want *you* back to help Britain in the next strong pull.

Help to make the goods we want 🇬🇧 **Join your friends at work** 👥 **Put more money in your bag** 🛍

There are vacancies in important industries in most districts. GO, PHONE OR WRITE TO YOUR NEAREST MINISTRY OF LABOUR OFFICE.

WE **NEED** THE WOMEN BACK AT WORK AGAIN

1/3 on tick

We buy half our food, all our tobacco, cotton, rubber and most other raw materials from abroad. Since the war, instead of paying our way with exports, we've been getting one-third of all these things on tick. Now we're nearing the end of our credit. One day soon we must pay on the nail.

That means one of two things. Either we increase our exports by at least one-third, or we shall have to do without a lot of the things we now get from abroad. We are all in this together—and together . . .

WE WORK OR WANT

Issued by His Majesty's Government.

Above: *Two adverts which remind everyone of the need to save and work ever harder.*

Left: *The years of troop movements have passed; the Junction Station with stripped out canopy roof looks tired, tatty and careworn— like so many buildings and public places. Facelifting must wait; in mid-1947 lamp-posts still wear their black-out white bands, grey with age.*
In 1951 the canopy was still unrepaired.

Odham's new Goss 5 . . .

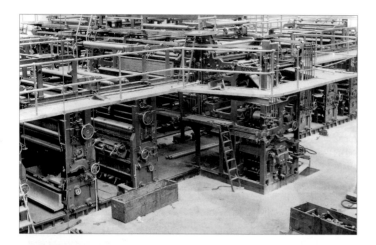

Town's Industrial Exhibition

WATFORD—sleepy market town at the close of the last century—has taken its place in the forefront of provincial industrialism.

Four decades of managerial drive and workers' craftsmanship put it there on Thursday, when the curtain was raised on the borough's own industrial exhibition, destination of overseas visitors and the shop window of the town's producing prowess.

The project brought from factory bench and technician's shop a sweeping, inspiring survey of the diversity of Watford's industry and wrote a new page in the history of Britain's industrial life, for never before has a town the size of Watford put its goods before the world.

This week—after busy workmen had won their fight against time to get over 60 stands ready by zero hour—the Town Hall has been the rendezvous of British and overseas buyers.

They saw what was described at an inaugural luncheon on Thursday as the results of the team work of local industry, and came prepared to negotiate large orders with local firms.

WHP, June 1947

Top left: *The installation at Odham's of the new Goss 5 in November 1947.*

Top right: *Copper depositing upon the gravure cylinders.*

Left centre: *Running up and first print trials.*

Left bottom: *Motor vans had been used prewar for milk delivery but the horse and cart still found favour with some dairies. The horse would know all the stops on the round.*

Next page: *David Greenhill.*

The Sun's achievements

Soon after The Engraving Co. established itself at Watford, David felt it important to introduce periodicals, which from a trading point of view was sound judgment as it established a regular turnover. A start was made with *The Draper's Organizer*, a weekly letterpress magazine which included a number of four-colour illustrations.

This development, however, made a great difference to the working conditions in the factory because it was not possible to produce such a book in a normal working week. Day and night work had to be introduced which has continued ever since, and this has enabled the firm to offer a service to its many clients which has been second-to-none in the printing trade. Before long other letterpress periodicals were undertaken and the department was kept very busy.

Nor was the expansion limited to the main factory. In 1932 an interest had been taken in Rembrandt Photogravure Ltd., a firm previously mentioned. In 1934 this firm was acquired by the Sun Engraving Company and it moved from Norwood to Watford where it continued to prosper until 1940 when World War II made it inevitable to close it down owing to the necessity for transferring the men to war work or the fighting services.

Although the development of special photogravure machinery was quite outstanding, David nevertheless had an equal interest in the machinery needed for other departments.

Mr. B. B. Bausch was the supply agent for the "Albert Frankenthal" machines in London, and apart from some photogravure machines made by this firm in Germany, David wished to discuss the making of a special twin-type of Letterpress Rotary in order to print economically *Weldon Ladies' Journal*. After many alterations and additions to the plans prepared, Herr Kurt Ganss came over from Germany to help reach a decision on the final specification.

David initialled the final plan and notes which Herr Ganss and Mr. Bausch took to 'the Chief" in London, who confirmed the order for the machine, which owing to its twin-character and the necessarily large number of guide-rollers, turner bars and spindles, gave the delivery-end of the machine a harp-like appearance, and the "Albert" designers and engineers always referred to this machine as the "Greenhill Harp."

Mr. Bausch and Herr Ganss met David over a period of many years between the two wars to discuss machines that for one reason or another British firms at the time seemed reluctant to make. David saw many changes in Germany between the years 1921 to 1937, and his comments on what he saw were of great interest. The essential fact stands out that orders went to Germany only because most British firms seemed more interested in repeating standard machines than experimenting with the new ideas which David and Mr. C. F. Cook discussed at length together,

and which the German firms were enterprising enough to interpret into blueprints and finally machines which gave the particular performance required.

In the early nineteen-twenties David first became interested in estate development

Sixteen acres of land were purchased at Garston, and the fifty houses eventually built there were the commencement of all development of Watford north of Harebreaks estate.

The land had a frontage to St Albans-road, and David was anxious to preserve the fine trees bordering the road, and in addition arranged tree planting along Garston Drive and Garston Crescent, which were constructed to serve the estate. David formed the company known as Watford Ideal Homes Ltd., of which his wife's cousin, Mr. R. Scott Willis was first secretary, becoming director in 1935. The earliest of the new buildings had been the Clock House, adjoining Messrs. Bucks Restaurant in High Street, Watford, in 1923, and this provided shops, offices and garages.

"Rutherglen," which had remained unsold when the family moved to Gade House, was converted into three flats. The next venture was more ambitious, as in 1934 he built a block of shops and offices to the designs of Mr. Hubert Lidbetter, F.R.I.B.A., and Mr. Henry Colbeck, F.R.I.B.A., on a site at the crossroads, Watford, opposite to the site on which was later built Watford's new Town Hall.

This building was the cause of a good deal of anxiety, as it was a little distance from the main shopping centre, and for some time it was probably more of a liability than an asset The site of Faircross House had been that of the house and garden of David's old friend Dr. Herbert Hall, who told him he wished to sell

this, and wondered what price he should ask for the property. David realized that Watford was developing so fast that ultimately the value of the site would appreciate, and named a figure that he felt Dr. Hall should obtain. However, no buyer came forward, and David decided to offer to buy at the figure he himself proposed.

Faircross House eventually became a reasonable investment, particularly since the building of the new Town Hall has brought added activity to the immediate neighbourhood.

David's last building venture before the war was the building of a block of flats in Clarendon Road, Watford, on the site of a large semidetached house known as "Grantchester" standing in a good-sized garden. This house was demolished and on the site the block of flats known as Grantchester Court was erected to the designs of his son-in-law architect, Mr. John Howard Leech, F.R.I.B.A. This block of flats proved a great success, and a drawing of them was exhibited at The Royal Academy Exhibition in 1938.

Some of the heaviest responsibilities came about through people asking his advice and help and then perhaps lacking the courage and capital to carry out the recommendations made. David had such confidence that his proposals were sound, that he found himself offering to make himself responsible for the necessary reorganization. To the family's amazement and concern (they felt he had more than enough responsibility in his printing career), they found that he had become involved in the affairs of a large drapery store, and later in a large farming estate, comprising four farms, three at least in a serious state of neglect.

David, whatever project he undertook, realized the importance of "key" men, and by appointing Mr. E. A. Corp of The Sun Engraving Company as secretary of the drapery store, and asking his advice on all the aspects of costs and expenditure on his various other enterprises, found he had not only a dependable associate, but a good friend and colleague, in whom he could confide many of his purely personal and private affairs.

Nineteen thirty-nine was the peak year for The Sun Engraving Company Ltd., who were printing and dispatching more than 1,500 tons of printed matter each week. The staff had grown to over 2,000 and was always a problem because of the highly specialized character of the work. These figures give some impression of the magnitude of the firm's efforts, and in order to accomplish the required output it was necessary for the factory hours to be continuous from 12 o'clock midnight on Sunday until 10 o'clock the following Saturday night.

Below is a list of some of the most popular publications which were produced by the company:
Ladies' Journal, Film Pictorial, Woman's Own, Good Taste, Weldons Bazaar of Children's

Fashions, Mother and Home, Good Gardening, Passing Show, Picturegoer, Weekly Illustrated, Pictorial Education, Farmer's Weekly, Mickey Mouse, Silver Star, Cavalcade, Everybody's, Picture Post, Supplement to Weekly Times, Vogue, Vogue Pattern Book, Vogue Knitting Book, Housewife, Country life, Christmas Pie, Summer Pie, Nursing Mirror, Pearson's Magazine, Today, Insets and Covers to Radio Times.

The weekly publications at one time had a total circulation of over 6,250,000. The monthly magazines totalled 2,600,000 and the quarterly and special editions amounted to approximately 6,000,000 copies. David had more than a cursory knowledge of all this work. Indeed, he would discuss the details with his executives, who had a great respect for his unbounded knowledge.

The volume of printed work had now reached enormous proportions and it was difficult to imagine that the output of the Works could be increased to an appreciable extent.

The Company was seriously considering expansion by building to meet the increasing demands, when one of the largest publishers with whom The Sun Engraving Company had a great reputation announced that they were building a photogravure factory of their own and would be taking away and themselves printing various publications. Although there had been rumours and the blow was not entirely unexpected, it caused much anxiety. The Company, if it were to make progress, had to replace this work very quickly.

There were two new publishers with whom David was in close contact, and it soon became evident that if contracts could be secured from them, these would more than compensate the firm for the loss of the other publications.

Before the last periodical of the old publishers was taken away The Sun Engraving Company was in the throes of preparing the new publications, one of which was *Picture Post*. In all the negotiations it was suggested that Picture Post would start at approximately 375,000 and fall back to 250,000 or 300,000 copies per week, but everybody was hopelessly wrong in this conjecture. Instead of falling after the first issue of 450,000 the second week's issue reached a total of 750,000 copies per week, and the number continued to rise rapidly until a total of 1,750,000 copies per week had been reached with a total of 104 pages per week.

Of all the work David handled, Picture Post was the finest achievement in photogravure, and the most remarkable example of his powers of organization, made possible by his ability to work as the leader of a team of specialists who shared his enthusiasm in this undertaking.

Although the purpose was not known until much later, it was about this time that The Sun Engraving Company Ltd. began to do the experimental work on a vital stage of the Atomic Bomb Development.

It began with an interview between David's colleague—Mr. Noel Hunter—and an official

of the Metals Division of Imperial Chemical Industries Limited; this firm was engaged on special work and thought the experience of The Sun Engraving Company might be used or adapted to assist them.

The production of the *Nachtrichten* newspapers was, perhaps unique; it started shortly after the Invasion of Normandy and continued seven days a week until May 1945. Formes were received at 5 a.m., stereos cast, and on machine by 8 a.m.; presses were running by 8.30 and 1,500,000 newspapers were delivered by 2 p.m. These newspapers (whose editors were Germans) contained the latest and most accurate information for the German soldier, and they were packed into special fused containers for delivery by the R.A.F. and the U.S.A.A.F. to the German Army by 5 p.m.

The firm's effort, the tempo of which constantly grew, kept pace with the steadily increasing demand, until even its enormous capacity was taxed to the limit. Taxed, but never beaten, as the staff worked long hours. Some men were recalled from munitions and from the Forces, and every means possible was used to maintain this important work.

The work for the Political Intelligence Department alone totalled 1,848,000,000 leaflets, many in four colours, weighed 4,400 tons and used 250 tons of ink.

The Sun Engraving Company's Engineering Department was constantly used to boost production in other factories and, particularly, those of high priority and in short supply. This breaking-up of bottle-necks meant that the plant and staff were being constantly changed and adjusted to meet a varying demand; nevertheless, the record is impressive:

679,000 bearings for Bren-gun carriers.

525 main-drive gears for Matilda tanks.

500 sprocket wheels for Matilda tanks.

975 stub axles for Hamilcar Gliders (including the prototype).

420,000 fuse timing rings for A.A. shells.

180,000 various parts for bulldozers, excavators and tanks, from screw bolts to major components. Much of the work was of a very difficult and specialized nature, and its success was a tribute to the high degree of accuracy achieved by the Company's Engineer—Mr. Donald Berry.

Early in 1942 the Company was approached by the Admiralty Signal Establishment to assist in making practical application of a scheme to improve inter-ship radio communication. The idea was that should a ship be in action the Signal Officer should have for his use a chart from which, with the aid of a code, he could determine what frequency of wavelength to use.

The work was of great operational importance and of the utmost urgency. Speed was essential, for the U-boat war was at its height, and yet the idea was a new one and production of its type had no precedent.

Furthermore, a completely new set of charts was required each month and in time to dis-

tribute to all the thousands of ships at sea, in every ocean of the world. How could this idea be committed to paper and be illustrated in such a way that ships' crews could easily understand and apply the knowledge under conditions which would permit no errors and with no loss of time? The firm's staff artists and production chiefs under David got down to this problem and devised a method of illustration and production which was completely satisfactory and thoroughly practical.

The production of these charts, a most exacting task, was continued for five years, and was later extended to include every Allied ship throughout the oceans of the world.

About the autumn of 1943, the Air Ministry, on the advice of His Majesty's Stationery Office, contacted David about some highly secret work which ultimately proved to be the most exciting that had been undertaken.

It was of the highest importance and had to be conducted under conditions of absolute secrecy and urgency.

It was, in fact, the "bible" of the Invasion of Europe by the Allied Forces.

The whole of the coast of France and Normandy had been photographed from the air and these photographs pieced together by experts. Vast areas were to be reproduced in the finest detail and thousands of copies printed and bound into book form for the use of the British Invasion Forces. So excellent were the results achieved that the Americans abandoned their own effort and the British scheme extended to cover all Forces.

The work was obviously of a highly confidential nature, and every production department had an area screened off; entrances were guarded and plates and copy transported between departments in locked containers.

David contracted to produce 60 units of a certain size per week, at the production peak this was extended to equal 480 of the original units. The work was of the highest possible quality, combining fine engraving and good printing. It was probably the largest process engraving order ever placed, comprising the etching of over 600,000 square inches of 175 screen plates, over 70,000 hand engravings of lettering and diagrams, also the make-ready and printing of over 1,300 separate sheets, 14,000,000 hand-folds and 27,000,000 hand collations.

Individual books weighed up to 7½ pounds, and to cover the operations up to and after "D" Day to the Rhine, 37 individual volumes were produced. The first work in the interest of security was called "Boxes."

After the invasion, as the Allied Forces swept eastward, so the demand for more and more production became increasingly insistent.

The next work was called "Cases," and made practical the gigantic strategic operations of Bomber Command and the American 8th Army Air Force. "Kartons" followed—covering tactical targets and ground operations in Holland, Belgium and France, not covered by the "Boxes" series.

Finally "Pakkets," code name for a further series covering the operations on the Rhine, the Ems and the Elbe rivers and also the Southern Redoubt on the Danube.

The tempo of work increased day by day as the campaign developed, and as demands appeared more impossible, so the response of the staff kept pace. The machine-room staff worked for forty-three Saturdays out of fifty-two in addition to late working on every day of the week. Girls in the warehouse worked for thirty weeks without a single day off.

David had shown qualities of leadership, organization and improvisation which have seldom been equalled, and had inspired his managers and staff to very great efforts. This period was a great strain on him, but he rarely lost the ability to look with confidence to the future, and time and again his mind would turn to plans for peacetime production and development. As early as 1941 he had asked for development plans and reports from his senior executives. His interest in the reduced periodicals never lapsed, and the work produced during the war years under extreme difficulty was of good quality.

It is not possible adequately to express the appreciation he and his co-directors felt for their staff, who spared nothing in effort, and put in long hours in order to meet every call for greater production required to meet the demands for special work for the Air Ministry, the Ministry of Information, the Political Intelligence Department and the Stationery Office.

Certainly the whole staff made a contribution of which they might be justly proud, to do their part, whether serving in the Forces, or doing urgent war work in the factory at home.

Miriam Leach

David Greenhill died in 1947 after a short illness.

At £22 3s 10d (including 30% Purchase Tax) this radio cost the equivalent of five weeks work to purchase. A 1987 comparative cost would be some £360. For a 'reverse' comparison a 1987 portable, with VHF, at approximately £20—would have been 90p (18/-) at 1947 prices.

In 2003 the low average wage is approximately £200 pw; more representative perhaps nearer £240, a ratio of 57x that of 1947.

This would make the 1947 radio cost at 2003 prices some £1268. A 2003 radio, with built-in CD player, costs £50; at 1947 prices equal to less than £1!

State-Owned Hospital

AFTER nearly a quarter of a century of fine service to the community as a voluntary institution, Watford Peace Memorial Hospital will, next year, under the National Health Act, become State-owned.

In the interim, the Board of Management is disposing of the hospital's free assets. The money is to be used for the benefit of the hospital, prior to nationalisation, in the firm conviction that "a bird in the hand is worth two in the bush." It will go mainly to meet the cost of extensions now in hand, and for repairs that were held up by lack of labour and materials during the war. Watford and district residents, whose generosity provided the money, will, no doubt, endorse the action of the Board of Management

Under nationalisation, incentive for voluntary effort, which it is the joy of many people to give to their local hospital, will presmuably disappear. But if the reorganisation will result in better salaries and conditions for hospital staffs, it will have achieved something really useful.

Nursing is a noble profession, but it is, generally, not well paid Small wonder that only those who love nursing are prepared to devote their lives to it

WO, October 1947

Diesels To The Rescue

AMONG 80 large firms in Watford Electricity Undertaking's area are now operating load transfer schemes, some have introduced staggered hours, others have begun night shifts and over 30 have installed auxiliary diesel or steam generating plant

Reduction of the load by $33\frac{1}{3}$ per cent between 7 a.m. and 7 p.m. is compulsory by a Government directive which came into force this month. Because of certain essential services and continuous processes which must be exempt it will be necessary, to attain an over-

all $33\frac{1}{3}$ per cent transfer, for industry in the Watford area to reduce daytime consumption by 40 per cent

Help in arranging this is contained in a pamphlet just issued by the Town's Electricity Committee, ten thousand copies of which are being distributed to local managements and workers.

It suggests that daytime use of electricity can be reduced by installing alternative types of factory heating or the transfer of machinery test running to night-time.

Firms have found that workers have readily co-operated in the new arrangements, Mr. F. W. Berringer, Watford district officer for the Board of Trade, told the "Post" "Both have shown a sympathetic appreciation of the position."

"So serious is the need that it is not a case hoping Watford's scheme will work—it has got to work. Otherwise nothing can prevent indiscriminate power cuts which will mean interruption or loss of production, and create unemployment"

WHP, October 1947

Oxhey Place Town Is Born

AT 3.30p.m. yesterday, Mr. and Mrs. W. A. Caldwell, formerly of Paddington, crossed the threshold of 50, Hayling-road, on the new L.C.C. Oxhey estate, and became the first inhabitants of a new town.

They had just been presented with the key by the Rt Hon. Lady Nathan, chairman of the L.C.C., who said the estate represented "a fine example of democratic planning to meet imminent means."

Lady Nathan made particular reference to the modern kitchens of the houses, which she described as "ideal workshops for the housewives."

They are four-roomed cottages, without parlour, but with kitchens large enough to dine in. Kitchen fittings and cupboard accommodation provide for perambulators, fuel and tools.

Ground and first floors each have a lavatory, and a constant supply of hot water is provided from the stove in the living room, which gives off background heating by means of ducts to two of the bedrooms. One bedroom is fitted with an electric fire, and the other two have points for fires. The linen cupboard is warmed by a hot water cylinder.

Typical of the foresight of the designers is the "one pipe" drainage system, which not only saves cast ironwork, but, being inside the house, is protected in frosty weather. Ample window space gives all the rooms a bright and cheery appearance.

These are the houses in which will live the first of an estimated 14,000 population, when the programme of 3,950 houses is completed.

WHP, November 1947

We Wish Them Happiness

TO-DAY we celebrate the marriage of Princess Elizabeth. From the hearts of all of us springs the hope that her romance may be one of long and unbroken happiness.

Princess Elizabeth holds a place of particular affection in the hearts of Watfordians. We shall not soon forget her youthful grace, vitality and charm, so abundantly evidenced when she visited the Hertfordshire Show in Cassiobury Park last year. Sincerely we trust that the Heir to the Throne may renew her contact with South-West Hertfordshire, and this time not alone.

Our thoughts to-day are particularly of two young, sublimely happy people.

But as the memory of this great day recedes into history, the Crown which one day the Princess will wear remains for us the emblem of stability, of unity, of continuity. It is a reminder of the principles and traditions which are the bedrock of our British way of life.

It symbolises our faith in our destiny, for which we fought on in Britain when all the odds were against us. Yet it was not the people of these islands who stood alone. Throughout the Commonwealth and Empire, men and women rallied unhesitatingly to the cause.

To them, too, the Crown is an unshakable emblem, and to its high service the Princess brings not only her own devotion, but our affectionate loyalty.

WHP, November 1947

Cycle Theft Epidemic—No Petrol

REMOVAL of basic petrol has increased the demand for bicycles, and an epidemic of cycle stealing has broken out in Watford. During the past week eight cycles have 'disappeared' from this district

WHP, October 1947

Sirens To Warn You

Air raid sirens are to be used in Watford as a last-minute warning of impending electricity cuts.

This decision was reached following complaints from industrialists that the cuts came so suddenly that they had no time to close down their machines or to prepare other methods of lighting.

Mr. A. W. Barham, chief engineer of the Borough Electricity Undertaking, told the "Post" that if the public also co-operates when they hear the sirens, the duration of the cuts will be substantially reduced.

Even with this method of notification, industrialists will have to move quickly as there will be only minutes, possibly seconds, to spare, as Watford electricity undertaking has no greater warning,

WHP, November 1947

The Parade, in 1949. Jays Furnishings and Lavell's premises were sacrificed in 1972 to build the flyover. It is a Sunday, when all shops are closed.

Overpriced Elastic!

PLEADING that he had lent his stall in Watford Market to a friend in order to repay a debt, Nanigopal Nandi, of Charlotte-street, W.1. was dismissed by Watford magistrates on Tuesday, when summoned for selling elastic at an excessive price and failing to display a price notice at his stall on July 8.

Mr. W. W. Dalziel, for the Board of Trade, said that Mr. Gover, a Board inspector, bought two yards of elastic from Nandi's stall for 10d.

The controlled price for this elastic—six stranded, flat grade—was 1½d. per yard. Nandi was not at the stall at the time, and Mr. Grover was attended to by Abdur Mohamid Asind Rauf.

WHP, December 1947

Future of Langleybury

Further representations to the Ministry for the requisition of Langlebury mansion for housing are to be made by Watford Rural Council.

Herts County Council want the house as a secondary school and seven flats.

Chairman of the Rural Council, Mr. G. Follet told the Council on Tuesday there was strong objection to children having to cycle along dangerous roads from Abbots Langley and Bedmond.

Watford Corporation was developing the district and there would be an increase of 500 children. Schools were being promised but it was doubtful when they would materialise. Schools should be going up at the same time as houses so that children go to schools "fit and proper, not hovels."

Mr. H. J. Harvey said the Council's proposal "looked rather like obstruction." It would be better to have a conference than to ask one Ministry to oppose the efforts of another.

The Clerk pointed out it was up to the Ministries to decide to which authority they would give way.

WO, January 1948

New Industrial Developments

HINTS of proposed new developments in and around Watford were given at a Public Inquiry held at the Town Hall on Tuesday. They included, apart from the already announced development of 'Kytes' as a paraplegic settlement, the zoning of Lea Farm for industrial purposes and the acquisition of the majority of the land there by Shell-Mex for research laboratories.

Another proposed development referred to was the use of Garston Manor and estate for agricultural research laboratories and a new secondary school.

The Inquiry conducted by a Ministry Inspector (Mr. S. G. Bulstrode) followed Watford Corporation's application to acquire by compulsory purchase 76 acres of land at Hillside, Hunton Bridge, for a new housing site. The objectors were the land owner, Mrs. V. Fisher, the lessee, Mrs. Lawson; and the farming tenant, a Mr. Norman. Mr. F. Thelfall, a Hunton Bridge resident, also registered an objection.

Watford Corporation's case was presented by Mr. H. I. Willis, and was based on the need for immediate acquisition of additional housing sites to enable contractors to carry on when work finished on the present sites. It was submitted that the Corporation had other sites, but these lacked roads and services, features which commended Hillside as an estate which could be developed speedily.

Top: *Moselle's shop on the Parade where they stayed for the next forty-one years, until the Harlequin Centre called in August 1990. Moselle's traded in Harlequin until 1998 when they withdrew into a store in Queens Road.*

Bottom: *It is much easier to stand and stare at the pond's water and fish if one has a railing against which to lean, but with the spate of changes in the 1970's an 'open-plan' approach was favoured.*

14 High Street; five minutes to study the proposals . . .

The Hillside estate, it was considered, had high amenity value and was in close proximity to the Abbots Garden estate now being developed. Provision for development there had been made in the Abercrombie Plan.

Although it was regrettable that agricultural land should be swallowed up, it was inevitable that there would always be hardship to someone, and in this case, the Ministry of Agriculture had not seen fit to over-ride a proposal to develop the estate.

WO, January 1948

"Old Town Hall" site

COUNCILLORS protested vigorously when they were asked to approve important proposals for the disposal of 14, High-street—the 'old town hall'—because they had had no opportunity of seeing them until arriving for Monday's Watford Council meeting. The Mayor, Ald. H. Coates, agreed to a five-minute adjournment to enable members to study them.

Eventually the Council accepted the proposals, chief of which was that Herts County Council should receive 12½ per cent, of the proceeds of the sale or lease, the remaining 87½ per cent, going to Watford Borough. A batch of tenders is being considered.

A report of the Acquisition and Disposal of Land Committee emphasised that the site, on which stands the Old Council Offices as well as the Fire Station and Ambulance Station now occupied by the County Council as fire and ambulance authority, should be sold or leased as a whole. If it proves possible for

development to be carried out on Watford Corporation's portion of the property before the County Council vacate their portion, this may be undertaken as a "first instalment" of the general development

The County Council is to be asked to agree to erect a new Fire and Ambulance Station on another site "at the first available opportunity."

While continuing to use the present site, they are being asked to concentrate their services in a smaller area of the property.

The Committee's chairman, Ald. H. J. Bridger, said "These tenders have now been opened, but I am not going to tell you the amounts offered because we are waiting for a report from our agents as to which, in their opinion, is the best to accept. The final decision will rest with the Council, but there is more to it than just the disposal of the land. There are several other important considerations."

Explaining how the County Council came to have a 12½ per cent interest in the land, Ald. Bridger said they were entitled to a proportion in accordance with the amount of the site held by the National Fire Service in 1939.

"We hope to be able to lease the ground on quite favourable terms. But it must be realised that it may be three, four or even up to 10 years before the Corporation will gain revenue because of the considerable building restrictions in force just now. For the time being, therefore, the lessees would only pay a peppercorn rent."

WHP, September 1948

Waste Paper Needed

IN every load of garbage valuable paper is mixed up with waste, and although the workmen salvage clean cartons and bottles, etc., they cannot be expected to sort out each piece of paper when fresh loads are continually arriving. In any case, once soiled its value is decreased.

If only each householder would scrupulously put aside, tied in a neat bundle, every piece of paper when the dustman calls it would save everybody a lot of trouble.

If housewives would watch the unloading of waste paper at the Tolpits-lane tip they would not ask dustmen to do an impossible job, but would make it easy for them.

Watford's paper collections show a steady increase over the past years, however (in 1945-46 421 tons were saved, in 1946-47 455 tons, and in 1947-48 507 tons in 11 months). A marked increase in paper collection since the new campaign has been shown, but there is still room for improvement.

WO, March 1948

Spy in the Sky

AN allegation that the outside wall of a brick building in St. Albans-road, Watford, had been treated with some material in order that it should not appear new was made by the Town Clerk (Mr. A. Norman Schofield) in the Watford Magistrates Court on Tuesday.

Mr. Schofield was prosecuting for the Watford Corporation in the case against a haulage contractor and builder, who denied that he was in the process of constructing a building without having the authority required by the Defence (General) Regularions, 1939.

In his opening summary of the prosecution's case, Mr. Schofield said that in March of this year a building inspector of the Corporation noticed that a building was in proces of erection in St. Albans-road.

On checking it was found that no plans had been submitted. It was also ascertained that no licence had been issued by the Ministry of Works for the building, which was estimated to have cost £269 0s. 8d.

Three wonders appeared following the war; pens which would write under water and in the air—Bic; electric light which was brighter per watt than any light bulb—fluorescent tubes, and nylon.

Watford High Street got its new lights quite early. On the left is the Midland Bank, next to it the Black and White Milk Bar. It is late Saturday evening; their door is still open.

"It is our contention that this building has been erected within recent months," went on Mr. Schofield. "I believe it is the intention of the defence to show this building was, in fact, begun at a date prior to that mentioned in the Defence Regulations. We have taken the trouble to obtain from a Government department copies of an aerial photograph of this site taken in 1946; we have here an expert on aerial map-reading who, I hope, will prove that these buildings were not there in 1946."

In fact, the aerial photograph was not shown to the Bench, it being held that it was not admissible evidence, there being no witness to prove the time and date at which it was taken, or that it was, in fact, a photograph of the area concerned. After the Bench had considered the case, the Chairman (Mr. Gordon Ross) said: "We accept the evidence that this work began before the material date, and although there was an alteration in the scheme, there was no alteration to the actual building." In these circumstances, he said, the charge would be dismissed.

WHP, September 1948

Mayor Gets "Switched On"

THE Mayor of Watford, Cllr. F. H. Vince, pressed a switch on Monday night, and in Watford Lower High-street the new fluorescent street lighting system blazed forth. It was greeted enthusiastically by the spectators lining the pavements, for a new milestone in the town's progress had been reached.

WHP, June 1949

Penalising The Press

WATFORD is the most renowned printing town in the country, and those thousands of craftsman who have added lustre to its reputation must be viewing with some misgivings the announcement that the stocks of newsprint have fallen so low that a return to war-time newspapers is a distinct possibility.

How long will it be, they must be wondering. before the periodicals and magazines, which Watford produces by the million every week, will also sustain a cut?

The Government, in addition to standing indicted for neglect in allowing the newsprint situation so sadly to deteriorate, may find itself accused of an assault on the freedom of the Press, to which it pays so much lip service in the intervals between condemnation by certain Ministers.

If, as is being alleged in some quarters, the newsprint famine has been deliberately engineered, is it fair that hundreds of independent local newspapers should be penalised along with the Party organs from out of Fleet-street, which are anathema to touchy Ministers?

WHP, July 1950

Seven Cinemas— (1948)

North Watford Odeon
The Plaza (North Watford)
Odeon (by the Pond)
Gaumont (the Parade)
Carlton (Clarendon Road)
Regal (King Street)
Empire (Merton Road)

Top: *Brandon's, mens outfitter's, on the corner of the approach to the church yard. New lamp post installed, the old not yet removed.*

Bottom: *Looking towards King Street Woolworth's windows are a pool of light; the shop has ceased to be a 3d and 6d store; across the road the lady looking in Jax's window may be wondering how many points of her clothing allowance she has left to spend.*

Londoners need homes . . .

The Capital had to work, function and stay put. When the night raids started on 7 Sept 1940 they continued without respite for 57 days; after a short break they resumed until the final large attack on 27 July 1941.

1,150,000 homes were damaged; 375,000 made homeless, 120,000 given new homes. The death and injury toll was huge. Swathes of the City were laid waste; but still life and business carried on . . .

Londoners had suffered throughout the blitz and most 'stayed put' under semi-permanent conditions of hardship. These problems were greatly increased with the V1 and V2 attacks in 1944 and 1945 and it was obvious that rehousing programmes would be urgently needed; it would not be possible to rebuild in London nor would it be desirable to rebuild to the same high overcrowded density as hitherto.

Land at Oxhey, in the ownership of the Blackwell family, seemed suitable for a partial solution. Mr Blackwell had recently died and it was supposed that the land would be offered to the 'National Trust' but this had not yet happened. The LCC wanted Oxhey's land. So many residents in and around Watford hated the idea of so much virgin ground being spoiled by housing that an enquiry had to be held.

It came to the conclusion, of course, that there was no reason why the compulsory purchase should not go ahead. In mitigation for the plan it was revealed that the land lay basically in a slight depression and could not easily be seen from the railway, and that the approach roads from Eastbury Road and Sandy Lodge would 'screen' the estate which would hold some 15,000 people. 4,200 houses were built.

For many who moved, the traumas of Oxhey, now called South Oxhey to distance it from its neighbours, seemed as bad as the worst days in London. There were no places of entertainment or worship; there were no shops until the first were built

in Little Oxhey Lane where at least six were occupied by the middle of 1949. The houses, of many varieties, were not insulated and had only a conventional fire in a living room; electricity proved too expensive to use for heating.

The first winters highlighted faults—burst water pipes were commonplace. Mobile shops made the rounds of the new streets—mostly unmade—and although welcomed there were complaints about the rather higher prices charged for groceries, vegetables and meats. For many the drastic change to a 'house' and quiet surroundings proved too much and meant a return to the London they knew and loved. They suffered in a similar manner to the handfuls of Watford residents earlier moved two or three miles from their so-called slum dwellings.

South Oxhey's shopping habits included, for many, a visit to Watford, amd seen, within the limits of great shortages of consumer goods, as a good place to shop.

But with Watford's own population steadily rising, the lack of shop sales-space became more apparent.

Above: *For some the pace in being allocated a new home was slow. For many there would have been pride at living in the start of a new town. Except that this was not a town but a housing estate, owned by the LCC.*
It was first administered by Watford Rural Council until control passed to Three Rivers Council.
The 'Totem Pole' near Hayling Road became the landmark pointer to find the roads and the 'Progress Board' behind and to the right showed the weekly tally of houses finished. Started in 1947 building the 4,200 houses was finished in 1950.

Left: *Hayling Road is behind the shortened golf Course.*

Next-door neighbour, South Oxhey . . .

South Oxhey—moving-in day

I was about four or five when we moved to Oxhey. I remember the moving van, something like alongside but more boxy; it took two days.

The kerbs were ever so high, but I was small. The house wasn't finished and if you know where to look you can still see the wheel marks of my three-wheeled trike from where I went gaily through the wet cement. The station is interesting; my mother used to tell me of my parent's visit of inspection. We lived in Bethnal Green and coming from Broad Street was no problem—she handled my pram OK.

When she got to Carpenders Park Station to go back she couldn't see any way to get across the track.

It was so long ago—a porter said: "Can I help you. Madam?"; "I want to get back to London, how do I get across?"; "I'll help you," was the reply, and the porter carried the pram and me across the track; my mother had to walk the boards. You can see, in the photograph (p271) where the white-edge line has been worn away.

A year or two later they must have built the footbridge. Life at South Oxhey was bad for the first few years; the roads were just being laid out—they weren't made, nothing seemed finished and it was miles to walk to the few shops. We had a horse and cart delivering to our part.

Recollections, (1987)

Above: *Two years on and pavements have been laid; the gardens would do any country village proud.*

Top right: *A family is moving in; the Co-op greengrocery van doing its round and,*

Below, *the August 1949 British Legion fete is in full swing against a background of building works and part-finished houses.*

New Hope In Lower High Street

FOR far too long there has been a lot of airy talk about the widening of Watford's Lower High-street, but out of the evidence at a public enquiry on Friday emerges the hope that a start will be made in about six months' time.

It will probably not be a very spectacular beginning. The proposal is to build two new factories 20 feet back from the new highway, which will have an over-all width of 64 feet, and will include 10-foot footways on either

Milk Five Days Old

MOST of the milk sold in Watford is anything up to five days old and may have been pasteurised twice. This was said by Mr. K. H. Marsden, Watford deputy Senior Sanitary Inspector, when a deputation from the Public Health Department on Wednesday addressed Watford Trades Council on food hygiene.

A member had complained that milk delivered to him in the mornings was 48 hours old and was "off" by tea-time. "It seems," he said,

"that the surplus milk is taken back to the milk people and dished out next day."

Mr. Marsden said most of the milk sold in Watford came from large distributive companies and was anything up to five days old.

It may come from the West Country or Bedfordshire. The milk is collected from the farms, taken to a collecting centre and pasteurised. It then comes by road tanker or rail to London and the surrounding towns, is pasteurised again and stored in a refrigerator for 10 to 15 hours. The milk is then delivered.

"There is nothing we can do about it," said Mr. Marsden. New milk regulations came into force in 1949 prior to which it was an offence to pasteurise milk more than once.

The Government recognised that it was impossible to enforce this law and amended it.

WHP, August 1950

"Fly-Bomb" Memorial

Witnessed by only a few members of the public, the stone erected at North Watford Cemetery in memory of the 40 people from the Sandringham-road area who lost their lives when the flying bomb fell in North Watford in July, 1944, was dedicated on Friday by the Rev. E. D. P. Kelsey, Vicar of Christ Church.

He was accompanied by the Mayor, Cllr. Mrs. M. E. Bridger, and members of Watford Town Council. The ceremony was simple to an almost Spartan degree. There was no unveiling, no wreath-laying, no hymn-singing, no flowers.

Mr. Kelsey recalled two things which stood out in his mind from the day on which the bomb fell. First was the noise of the missile.

side. If not a spectacular start, it will at least give an impression of the shape of things to come. How long it will be thereafter that the face of Lower High-street is completely changed is a matter of conjecture. To give a date for completion would, as the Borough Engineer puts it, be an entry into the realm of prophecy.

WHP, July 1950

Top: From the early days the station has now a footbridge to enable one to cross the tracks rather than 'walk the planks'.

Right: Shops at South Oxhey, in Little Oxhey Lane were the first—here in midsummer 1949 not all are yet occupied. The estate of 4,200 houses, when finished, covered a large area and these few shops left many streets and residents disadvantaged.

Soon afterwards there was a second noise—the sound of first aid squads and neighbours hastening to help the stricken. It was an enduring impression, exemplifying the eventual triumph of right over evil.

While the stone is a memorial to the 40 who lost their lives, it bears the names only of the 12 victims who are buried nearby in the Cemetery.

WHP, August 1950

Watford Store's £250,000 Fusion

A quarter of a million pounds was involved in recent negotiations which led to James Cawdell and Co. Ltd., the private company operating the town's biggest store, amalgamating with Macowards Ltd, which owns all its ordinary shares.

Under its new title of James Cawdell and Co. Ltd,—in which Mr. Robin Mugford, O.B.E., who was for many years managing director of the old company, will continue in that capacity—the company has absorbed Pocock's of Brighton, Dawson's of Sidcup and Macowards of Tunbridge Wells.

On January 1st last year the Legal and General Assurance Co. Ltd. bought for £260,000 the whole of the freehold store and arcade at Watford, which in February the Society leased to Macowards for 99 years at an annual rental of £13,500.

WHP, July 1950

£90,000 Railway Station

WORK on a £90,000 railway station at Carpenders Park will be started as soon as possible, state British Railways.

The present station was opened in 1914 as a halt to serve Oxhey golf course, but since St. Meryl housing estate was developed in 1935, and more recently the L.C.C. commenced building at Oxhey, railway facilities have been inadequate. British Railways said that any temporary relief by platform widening was out of the question, because of the nearness of the steam main lines.

They believed that a completely new station was the only solution.

Approval for the new station follows continual agitation from the Carpenders Park Community Association.

The two housing estates on either side of the line will be connected by a 12ft. wide subway, from which another subway will serve the island platform. Besides the usual station accommodation there will be space for 200 passengers' bicycles.

Central heating will also be installed. The new platform, 450ft long with provision for any necessary future extension to 600ft., will stand immediately south of the present station.

WO, June 1951

Top: *St Albans Road, the Police Station opposite Leavesden Road. It is a Sunday and patrons have just left the cinema*
Centre: *The Gaumont in the High Street (later Odeon) in April 1950*
Bottom: *The Carlton, Clarendon Road, Sunday 23rd April 1950—showing John Wayne and Anthony Quinn in 'Back to Bataan'*

Farewell to Derby-road

"The old order changeth, yielding place to new." Thus begins a supplement to issue No. 30 of "The Centralian," recording the fact that in September Bushey Grammar school will be a reality, and that Central School pupils would be moving there. The change will awake nostalgic memories in the hearts of the many Old Centralians who were taught in Derby-road.

After details of staff changes, and the efforts in the last term to keep up normal activities, the supplement (written by Mr. W. Hart) concludes:

"And so the time has come to record the passing of the Watford Central School. These notes are necessarily incomplete and leave unanswered many inquiries that have been made by present and Old Centralians during the last few weeks. The present pupils are proceeding tomorrow to fresh woods and pastures new. The old pastures are to be used for younger stock.

"During the last 23 years, your magazine has served its purpose. I have been associated with it since its inception, when Mr. Adkins, who was then headmaster, asked that it should be a really good thing and a credit to the school.

'The portrait of Mr. Adkins has been in the school hall since 1937 . . . ten years later than was at first anticipated, his vision fulfilled. On July 28 the Central School ceases to function; In September the Bushey Grammar School begins.

"The school is dead; long live The School"

WO, August 1950
(The Central School Magazine, Watford, was published from Spring 1927 until No. 39, Spring 1950)

Top: *the Blue Star Garage at Hunton Bridge in the 1950s.*

Above: *The meat ration is down to eight pence per week.*

Above right: *The studio was started in 1951 in the hopes that portraits and child studies would be in great demand; but the war-time era and demand had long gone (apart from the Christmas rush) and, soon, selling film, cameras, enlargers and slide projectors posed a bigger challenge.*

Right: *Remembrance Sunday 1949 and the Salvation Army lay a wreath on the Memorial outside the Peace Hospital.*

Council Wins Churchyard Fight

CANON Reginald James, "a parishioner of Watford for 81 years," has lost his fight to prevent the old parish churchyard being converted into a garden of remembrance, but has gained the safeguards he sought against its becoming "a picnic ground."

The local authority desired to improve the town, and it had been inspired by the Festival of Britain to improve the churchyard along with other sites.

The Council had submitted its proposals to the St. Albans Diocesan Advisory Committee, but the committee rejected them unanimously.

A hint of things of come was given by the Town Clerk when he said the Mother Church of the town was entitled to any improvements that might be made in the vicinity.

Herts Population Rise

HERTFORDSHIRE is now the home of more than half as many people again as in 1931—by far the largest percentage increase of any county in England and Wales. Over a third of this new population live in that area of the county of which Watford is the hub, and where the population has risen by nearly 90,000 to within sight of the quarter-million mark in the same 20 years.

Of the 43½ million population of England and Wales, one in about 70 are in Hertfordshire, and one in less than 200 are in the above-mentioned West Herts area,

It was the intention of the local authority, in the not too distant future, to remove the shops fronting the High-street, which at present obstructed the view of the Parish Church from the High-street.

Vicar of Watford, Canon A. St. John Thorpe, told the Court that he and his churchwardens had requested the Council to take over the maintenance of the old burial ground in 1943.

WHP, June 1951

Top: *Scammell's reign supreme with convenient and versatile transport for local short-haul work in congested towns.*

Centre: *Their eight-wheeled rigid lorries are successful but face competition from many other makers.*

Right: *The 100-tonner shown here in St Albans, is their largest vehicle, transporting a 70-ton 660hp Diesel-electric loco from the 1951 South Bank exhibition en route for export to Tasmania.*

stretching from Tring to Bushey and from Chorleywood to Elstree, which forms the main circulation area of the "West Herts and Watford Observer."

These interesting facts and those which follow emerge from the Registrar-General's preliminary report on last April's census, just published by H.M. Stationery Office.

WO, July 1951

Nylon Smuggling at Watford

LARGE-SCALE smuggling and evasion of import and export prohibitions on nylon stockings and currency were revealed in a case, which sounded something like an American gangster thriller, to Watford Magistrates Court on Tuesday. T. C. Fry, Jun., the American, of Sandringham-road, Watford, was charged with dealing in nine dozen pairs of nylons with intent to evade duty in April; dealing in 108 pairs of nylons with intent to evade duty in April; dealing in nylons at Brize Norton, Oxfordshire, with intent to defraud on duty for 72 pairs between February and April; deal-

ing in 72 pairs of nylons with intent to evade import prohibition; attempting at Ruislip to evade duty on 120 pairs of nylons with intent to evade the import prohibitions; and in March, contrary to export prohibitions, sending 35 £1 notes out of the country.

Fry pleaded guilty to all the charges.
WO, June 1951

Market Street Traders Losses

WATFORD Market-street traders, who met on Thursday to share their "considerable alarm" at the losses they have sustained through the thoroughfare being closed to traffic, wondered whether they could get com-

The 1950 procession started in the Harebreaks, passed through Station Road and the town to the Park, where the delights of the horse show and gymkhana and, in the evening, the fun fair provided the attractions. The procession was headed by the Carnival Queen's float and entries included those of Garston Youth Club, Kingswood Y C, Callowland Y C and Premier Y C (Parkgate), among many others. Premier Coaches usually entered a Vintage Coach whilst Scammell's invariably provided four mechanical horses and trailers for floats to be built upon.

pensation from the Corporation, enough to pay for fluorescent street lighting!

Their chairman, Mr. Russell Thomas, sen., said the Corporation had first to complete installing the new lighting for the whole length of High-street, and after that in St. Albans-road, and the question arose whether Market-street traders would be willing to raise the money for lighting their own street. He understood the Corporation were willing to erect the standards, but the rest of the work would cost £475.

Mr. Russell Thomas said that about 30 of the 70 traders in the street had expressed their readiness to help pay for the lighting, but if the others did not come in the scheme might have to be dropped. A trader then said he knew of a comparable case to the Market-street closing where the traders claimed compensation from the local authority—and got it. "Rebate on the rates would pay for the cost of lighting," commented the Chairman.

WO, September 1951

Watford Market Links On View

IN an effort to bring Watford industry and achievement to the notice of the world, and also to strengthen the links between the Commonwealth and the United States of America, Watford and District Industrial Exhibition opened with a flourish yesterday.

Industries, both large and small, had got together, and the result of their efforts was an exhibition unsurpassed in the history of the town. It remains open until June 27.

Crowds gathered at the Town Hall to welcome Commander Douglas Fairbanks, who opened the exhibition.

WO, June 1951

Duchess of Kent at Watford

WATFORD Town Hall entrance was thronged with people on Wednesday afternoon, eager to welcome the Duchess of Kent as she stepped from her car and

waved her hand before going on a tour of Watford's Industrial Exhibition.

Her Royal Highness, wearing a lime crepe de chine dress, white hat and shoes, and carrying a white handbag, was received by the Lord Lieutenant of the County (Viscount Hampden), the Mayor and Mayoress (Councillor and Mrs. L. E. Haines), the Town Clerk (Mr. A. N. Schofield) and Mr. G. R. Barclay and Mr. C. R. Greenhill (chairman and vice-chairman of the Exhibition Committee).

WO, June 1951

15,000 Visitors to Exhibition

WATFORD Industrial Exhibition closed at 9 o'clock on Wednesday shortly after the 15,000th visitor had paid to enter. Many thousands of pounds worth of export orders have been placed, including dollar export and sterling convertible export orders from South Africa, Australia, Indonesia, Portugal, etc.

One transformer, ordered as a result of the exhibition, will cost the purchaser over £5,000.

Hundreds of inquiries have been received from potential buyers, and many young people from Watford and the surrounding district have reviewed the various employments that will be open to them locally upon their leaving school.

WO, June 1951

Top: *The 142 and 158 services terminated and waited outside the Clarendon Hotel at the Junction.*

Centre: *St Albans Road looking townwards from the Railway Bridge.*

Left: *The Plaza cinema, April 1950.*

279

Twenty years ahead ...

100 years—Four Clerks

OFFICIALLY welcomed at his first Council meeting on Monday, Watford's fifth Town Clerk in 103 years, Mr. Gordon Hamer Hall, has been busy at work this week picking up the threads of his new job.

"I've spent most of the time in the Town Hall, and haven't been able to go out meeting many people," he declared to the "West Herts and Watford Observer," "but I've been delighted at the warm welcome I have received. I have been very much interested in the diversity of industry in the town.

"It is a fine shopping centre, and the Town Hall is magnificent—I don't think I have seen anything to equal it in my career in local government."

At the moment the new Town Clerk, like many a Watfordian, is looking for somewhere to live. He has two sons, Richard and Christopher, aged 12 and five, and they will probably be going to school in the district soon. Mr. Hall came to Watford from Ilford.

WO, February 1952

A Peep Into the Future!

Next week, at Watford Public Library, the public of Watford and Bushey will be able to see some of the results of careful, painstaking work on the part of the planners of County Hall, and what development is outlined for the Watford corner of the county in the years to come.

There, in easy-to-read graphs and maps, will be the main conclusions of the 192-page bound volume which is the analysis of the County Development Plan, a 1951 version of the Domesday Book in detail and scope.

How Watford must change to suit the times, yet still retain its best features, is shown. Suggestions include:—

HOUSING: About 6,400 houses to be built, 1,200 at Woodside, Hillside and Kytes estates and other sites between 1951 and 1953; 2,100 at Cow-lane, the Sewage Farm, etc., between 1953 and 1958; 3,100 at various sites and at Bushey between 1958 and 1973.

SHOPS: 60 new ones—20 (1953-58) and 40 (1958-73) at Cow-lane and the Sewage Farm.

SCHOOLS: 12 new ones, i.e., Woodside and North Watford, (1953-53); Cow-lane, Woodside, Gammons-lane (primary, infants), North Watford(R.C.), Cassiobridge Farm, Gammons-lane (primary), Gisbourne House (primary, infants), and Sewage Farm (secondary) (1958-73).

INDUSTRY: Set aside are 100 acres, mostly on the Cassiobridge Sewage Farm and the Station Estate, Radlett-road (1953-73).

ROADS: In addition to the main improvements the major proposals are—Horseshoe-lane, diversion to new junction with North Orbital-road (1958-73);

Radlett-road, new junctions with the Watford Bypass and Queen's-road (1958-73); North Orbital-road, extension beyond Hunton Bridge to Rickmansworth (1958-73);

Birmingham Radial-road, a new trunk road leaving the Watford Bypass north of Hartspring-lane (1958-73);

Aylesbury Radial-road, a new trunk road bypassing Watford to the West.

The last of these proposals is not likely to be carried out during the next 20 years unless the economic conditions change considerably.

Other projects: a new fire station in Whippendell-road; a police station in Leavesden Highroad; a telephone exchange in Stones-alley, Market-street, an extension to the gasworks in the High-street, and the new T.A. drill hall on the Sewage Farm.

Car parks, open spaces and other items are also contained in detail in the full report.

WO, February 1952

Keep Death off the Bypass

FOURTEEN Bypass firms, Watford Trades Council, and Leavesden Green and North Watford residents' organisations were represented at a meeting on Wednesday when the Watford Bypass Industrial and Residential Road Safety Committee was formed.

To keep death and injury off the busy and often fog-ridden bypass, the new committee

Top: *Gordon Hamer Hall, Watford's new Town Clerk.*

Left: *Commander Douglas Fairbanks, Jnr, KBE, DSC, after opening the exhibition in June 1951 toured the stands and showed a keen interest. Here he and the Mayoress Mrs L E Haines are examining the work of a colour-proofing press.*

The Plans unveiled . . .

decided to strive for a dual carriage-way for motorists, special tracks for the thousands of cyclists who use the road daily, safer crossings for pedestrians and better lighting for all.

A subway, fencing and pram-ramp at Leggatts-way, and a flashing red light suspended above the bypass at Cox's Corner (Hartspring-lane) pending a traffic roundabout at that point, were other suggestions, but by a majority it was decided not to press for a speed limit.

Formation of the committee was prompted by the recent fatal by-pass accident to an employee of Cox and Co. while he was cycling home. The firm's senior trade union representative, Mr. W. Slade, is chairman, and assistant personnel manager Mr. Frank Hampton, is secretary of the new association.

The latter quoted bypass accident figures which he described as "a black record which must be eliminated".

WHP, March 1952

Only the Best for Preservation

WATFORD Town and Country Planning and Plans Committee disagree with three of the buildings that the Ministry of Town and Country Planning suggest should be preserved in Watford as buildings of special architectural or historic interest.

The buildings concerned are Nos. 96 and 98, High-street, and No. 4, New-street. Objections will be made to the Ministry through the County Council, and the whole matter will be thrashed out before final decisions are reached.

Mr. F. C. Sage, the Borough Engineer, told the "Post" this week: "Just because a building is old it doesn't necessarily mean it's worth preserving. The buildings in the High-street, though old, have been spoilt by modern shop fronts.

We don't think these are worth preserving, and they are in the way of desirable improvements in the High-street and adjoining areas, so we have got to object to them," said Mr. Sage.

WHP, March 1952

The plans for the future of the town were comprehensive; many shops, many houses, new schools, new areas allocated for industry. There were not then, in 1951, many cars available. New cars were allocated according to priority— doctors and the like heading the list.

Not many may have noticed the road proposals—a road from Croxley Two-Bridges from Harrow to Hunton Bridge, and the Birmingham Radial Road.

The road-lines were planned pre-war (the St Albans By-pass/M1, though not then so-called, was in 1937, p215) and fifteen years is a long time to remember detail; who would be bothered in 1951 about something happening between six and twelve years hence?

For one, Town Clerk Gordon Hall spoke out most vigorously at the inquiry against the 'desecration of the Whippendell Woods and Green Belt'. Of the Park Gates, later, there was no inquiry; the Town Clerk was advised that they were of 'no historical interest' and in the interests of expediency down they came.

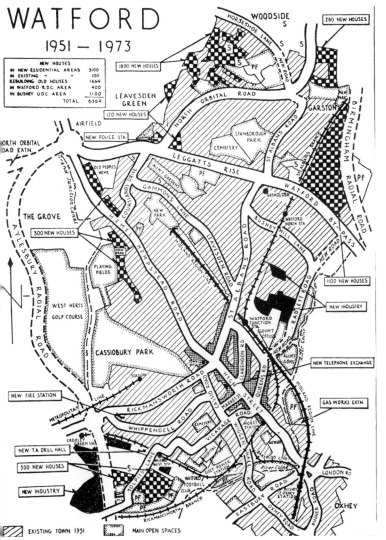

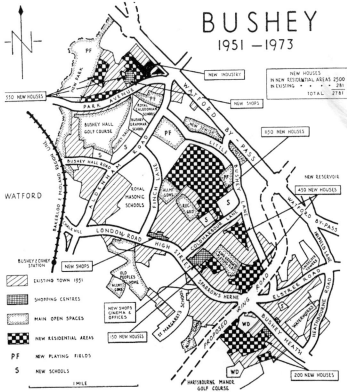

WHAT are your plans for 1958-73? Perhaps you have no very hard and fast ideas on the subject, in view of the distinctly unsettling world situation. Muddling through may be all very well for the individual, but communities must be planned decades ahead.

Next week, at Watford Public Library, you will be able to see some of the results of careful, painstaking work on the part of the planners of County Hall, and what development is outlined for the Watford corner of the county in the years to come. *WO, Feb 1952*

Prince Philip visits the B R S at Garston . . .

5½ Hours' Stay

LIKE most other people, the Duke of Edinburgh comes up against ordinary everyday problems which, though unimportant, arouse curiosity from time to time.

One of these problems was solved for the Duke by Mr. A. E. S. Wise during his visit to the Building Research Station at Garston on Monday.

Prince Philip had been taken into the experimental plumbing section, and was observing the flow of water through glass waste pipes when he asked Mr. Wise, the scientist in charge there, "Have you found what happens to make such a terrible noise when you are running the bath water away very quickly?"

Mr. Wise replied that they had, and explained, "It is the vortex drawing air into the flow."

The Duke's next stop was in the pre-stressed concrete section, where he stepped on to a pre-stressed concrete plank, springing it up and down under his weight to test its strength.

He next observed the effects of pressure being applied to a half-scale model concrete wall, and eventually saw the wall crack and crumble under tremendous pressure. In the same department, modem photo elastic methods of studying the strength of concrete were demonstrated and explained.

WO, May 1952

Free flights From Leavesden

THOUSANDS of visitors came along to Leavesden Aerodrome on Saturday afternoon for the de Havilland Engine Co. Ltd.'s sports and open day, and the first thing they did was to make a bee-line for the notice boards to see if their programme number qualified them for a free flight.

While these flights were being made in a two-engined blue and white "De Hav. Dove," Sir Geoffrey and Lady de Havilland flew in from Hatfield in a stylish red and white "Heron," a four-engined version of the "Dove."

WHP, June 1953

Left: *'Open Day' at Leavesden in 1951.*

Next page: *The Harrow signalman was aware of the first crash and threw all signals to danger—but the double-headed train from Euston had passed the track circuits and the second crash was a foregone conclusion.*
Many of the carriages were of wooden construction, including the two rear coaches of the Tring-Euston local train, with the remainder steel on wood frames. There were several newly designed and built all-steel construction coaches in the Liverpool and Manchester train, greatly contributing to that train's low death toll of seven.
K W Hewitt, Bristol, WO, October 2002

Watford families hit by Harrow train crash . . .

Harrow Crash

Watford and West Herts has been shockingly hit by Wednesday's triple train crash at Harrow Station.

Just before 8 p.m. last night, with the total death roll creeping relentlessly into the hundred mark, it was known that about a quarter of them were from local homes.

At 8 p.m. yesterday actual figures were: 19 from Watford, most of them from the North part of the town; Hemel Hempstead two: Tring two; and one each from Croxley Green and Kings Langley.

Many of the dead were teenagers.

In addition, anxious Watford families had reported seven persons missing.

Approximately two-thirds of the sixty injured in the Watford and West Herts district are Watford residents.

WHP October. 1952

Mayor Visits Bereaved

THE Mayor of Watford (Alderman L. C. Johnson) visited 13 of the bereaved families yesterday morning. He expressed to the relatives his personal sympathy, and that of the people of the Borough. "I felt it would be a far better thing to do than to merely sign a letter," he said.

The Mayor explained that he asked the relatives if there was anything the Town Hall could do to assist in the way of giving either legal or financial assistance to tide them over immediate difficulties. So far, he said, no assistance had been requested.

The Mayor was accompanied by his secretary (Mr. P. E. Judge) and the Deputy Town Clerk (Mr. G. Salter Davies) who was prepared to give what legal advice he could.

WHP, October 1952

The Harrow disaster, UK, 1952

The double collision on 8 October 1952 at Harrow & Wealdstone Station, 11 miles (18 km) north-west of London Euston on the West Coast main line to Scotland, was then Britain's worst peacetime railway disaster. Yet, just as at Newark six years later, the engine crew causing the disaster failed to act on a colour-light distant-warning signal which indicated 'caution' and that the driver should be prepared to stop at the next signal if it showed 'danger'.

It was a misty morning and the rising sun must have been brightly in the driver's face as the overnight sleeping-car train from Perth to London approached Harrow. That said, we simply do not know whether anything happened to distract the locomotive crew or whether the driver failed to see the distant signal's light against the bright misty background. The next signal, a mile (1.6 km) or so ahead, was at 'danger': a local steam train had crossed from the slow line to the fast line ahead of the Perth train to make its regular stop in the platform at Harrow.

The Perth express suddenly emerged out of the mist at about 60 mph (100 kmh) just as a host of commuters were boarding the local train, which was already well filled. The engine ploughed through the local's back three coaches and partly overturned. Within a minute or so another express, this one from Euston to Liverpool and Manchester and hauled by two engines—also travelling at about 60 mph (100 kmh) and with no chance of stopping—came the other way, and hit the shambles.

The two engines reared up as they smashed into the already damaged engine of the Perth train, carried away a span of the footbridge above the tracks, and turned on their sides across the adjacent platform and onto the tracks of the local electric line. . . where a fourth train was luckily stopped before it too became involved.

There was now a massive pile of wreckage: the remains of 13 coaches were compressed into a space about 130 ft (40 m) long, 50 ft (15 m) wide and 30 ft (9 m) high, with the Perth engine underneath. Including three of the enginemen, among them the crew of the Perth train, 112 people were killed and about 150 were injured, many of them seriously. Because many railway employees used the local train to get to work, some railway offices at Euston headquarters lost their entire staff.

Of those who survived, numerous people owed their lives to the rescuers, who included a US Army team that happened to be based nearby. We know what happened at Harrow, but the 'why' will remain forever a mystery.

This accident hastened the adoption of the automatic warning system (AWS) on British Railways.

Geoffrey Kitchenside, 'Great Train Disasters'
1997

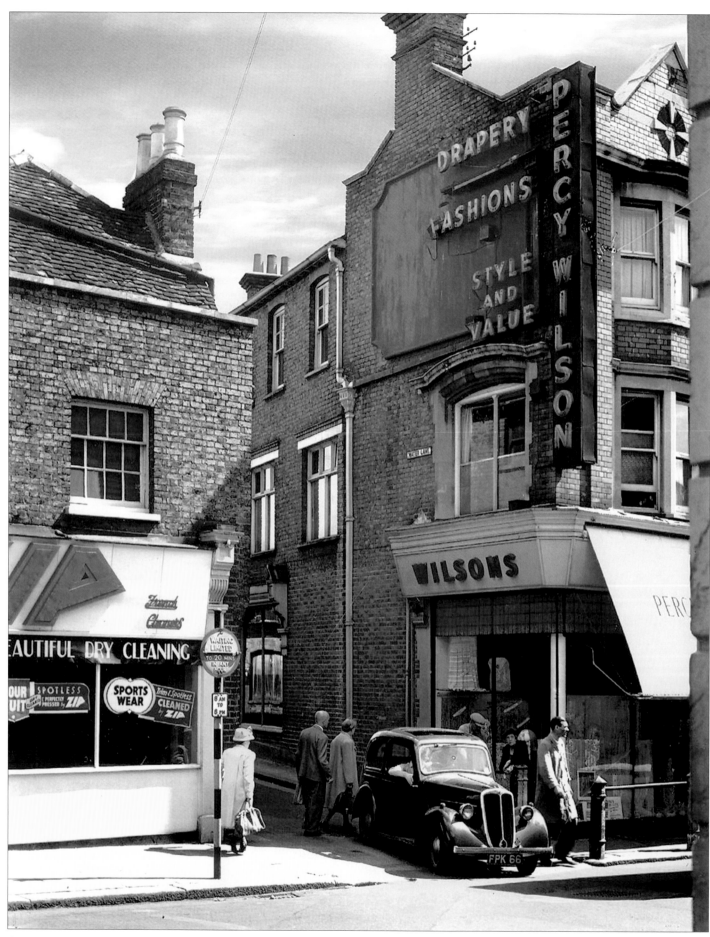

Water Lane Hill . . . the horses were thrashed unmercilessly . . .

Tom Simmonds was born, in 1910, in Whippendell Road but the family soon moved to Water Lane, No. 13. His life, through school days until conscripted into the army where he served until being invalided out in 1944, was centred around Lower High Street.

He recalled, 1988, that in his youth he worked at the family business of Simmond's, gentlemens' hairdressers; and at one stage he and his grandfather would go to the cottage hospital, the workhouse, and infirmary each morning.

"There we would shave and trim the hair of the inmates. At the workhouse the tramp ward was in the same block and the tramps—hundreds of them—would walk in from either Rickmansworth or St Albans, stay overnight and work next day in the vegetable fields at the back, throughout the day; stay overnight and be on their way early next morning. That was the law."

Of his earlier childhood days Tom recalled that the 'Hill' was an exciting place to live upon.

"Heavily-laden horse-drawn carts would take almost daily loads of export boot polish from the Watford Cobra Works; the horses were thrashed unmercilessly to make them gallop up the steep hill. Later, these were replaced by steam driven Foden wagons whose struggles up the hill were accomplished with a shower of hot cinders over the pedestrians."

The Five Arches Swimming Pool was well used; and the cold water held no terrors. The daily journey to school (Watford Fields) was along the footpath to the river Colne, past Benskin's Malt-House on the left, and Sedgwicks Brewery on the right of the river.

Just before meeting with the High Street he would pass a very small sweet factory, where he would always be enticed by the smells, as were swarms of wasps. He crossed the High Street to use Fox Alley and remarked that *"Farthing Lane, (now widened into Watford Fields Road), was then much too dangerous for pedestrians."*

Of Water Lane: *"The field upon which the College was built frequently flooded and was used by travelling fairs and circuses. The raised footpath used to have the handrail on the inside; if one fell into the roadway that was just too bad!"*

As a young boy he spent many happy hours standing on the pathway at the arch end recording the names and numbers of the monster steam engines as they raced their passengers northwards. After leaving school he first worked for the Sun Engraving Printing Works but joined the family firm in 1924.

The family by then had moved to Talbot Road, Bushey.

He recalls the anger there was in Watford when the Mansion overlooking the Park was sold and demolished. Every Sunday evening the family used to stroll up the High Street, have an ice-cream in Johnson's Ice Cream Parlour and then stroll to the Park where they would enter the bandstand enclosure and relax listening to the music for a couple of hours.

About the Mill: *"After the Mill was burned down there was no need to hold back the water to feed the millwheel. So the sluice gates were opened and straight way a broad river was reduced to a stream. So there was not enough water in the Five Arches swimming pool to use and we had to go to the new bath near the Town Hall and Library and pay.*

"We used to do our personal shopping at Messrs Oatley's, and Steabben's, both gents outfitters. These characters grew old, and no-one was prepared to devote their lives to their shops like these characters did. The houses in Water Lane were owned by a Miss Rodwell who lived in a residential house, adjoining the pub, opposite Water Lane. When she died the house was converted into a shop."

Tom came back from the army, and to the shop, shown below, but it was doomed by widening for safe access to the High Street, and he left to buy a business in Sidcup in Kent.

Tom Simmonds, 1988

Previous Page: *The corner of Water Lane in 1952; upon Percy J Wilson's site is now the Pyramid.*

Right: *Demolition of the two buildings on the corner of Water Lane, for road widening, revealed the antiquity of the timber-framed structure. Twenty or so years later, 1974/75, buildings a little further down were due to be demolished for Phase 5 of the road plans, and a minor outcry was caused when it was discovered that they were, in fact, Watford's oldest buildings of which the timbers dated back to the 15th century. Efforts were made to have some of the buildings taken to pieces to be rebuilt at the Chiltern Open-air Museum, but to no avail; they went and few Watfordians mourned their passing.*

Friday Market Starts

Last week, for the first time in its 24 years "under cover" history, Watford Market opened on a Friday, in addition to the usual Tuesday and Saturday. This will continue for a trial 12 months. About 70 new traders had stalls, presumably in place of regular Tuesday-and-Saturday holders, who were trading elsewhere.

Among the "regulars" who supported, however unwillingly, the first Friday opening was Mr. E. Evett, greengrocer and fruiterer, and secretary of the Market Stallholders' Association. He said that trade was not so brisk as it was usually on the regular opening days.

"If it keeps going for the year, the Friday market will be a success," he said. "But, quite frankly, I don't think it will keep going for a year." he added.

Said Mrs. Alice Canning, of 442 Gammons-lane Watford, "I think the Friday opening is a good idea, because the Market isn't so crowded as it is on a Saturday. Another thing is that we live a bus ride away from the market and it is a job to get on the buses on Saturdays; they, too, are so crowded.

"I shall certainly be here regularly on Fridays." Mrs. Constance Ralph, of Regent-street, Watford, said that she thought the Friday market was a good idea because it was less crowded than on a Saturday.

"On Saturday, too, I have my family at home, and have the midday meal to prepare, so I shall continue to come here on Fridays."

WO, October 1952

Planning Permission delay

One of the "most serious and alarming reports that has ever come before the Housing Committee" was how Housing Committee Chairman Councillor White described delays in the development of Kytes and Holywell Estates, speaking at Watford Town Council on Monday.

The Borough Engineer reported that delay in obtaining planning consent meant "there would be a temporary slackening off in the completion of houses." He also drew the Committee's attention to the delays attributable to the present practice of issuing separate authorisations for steel and timber allocations.

This, he felt, could be ameliorated by the Ministry of Housing and Local Government authorising local authorities to issue timber and steel allocations within specified limits. The Committee regretted the delay in obtaining town planning approval to the development of Kytes and Holywell, particularly in view of the repercussions of the provision of dwelling houses.

The Committee recommended that a request be addressed to the Ministry of Housing and Local Government for authority to issue within specified limits both timber and steel authorisatons. Councillor White said they had run across serious trouble over a long period with the Herts County Council over the Kytes estate.

Negotiations had proceeded since July, 1951.

"We still haven't got planning permission for that estate, and it has caused delay in the housing programme, as near as can be estimated, of four months," he said. They would feel the effect of that in nine to twelve months' time.

"Nothing will stop the hold-up in houses coming off the stocks in that time," he declared.

"In spite of not having formal consent we are proceeding with the Kytes estate," he said. "If they are going to pull the houses down afterwards, let them come and do it"

Councillors Edwards and Amey added their concern. The latter declared that of whatever political complexion they were, all councillors were deeply concerned with housing.

"I feel that the Herts County Council and the Planning Officer in particular are doing this Council a very great disservice," he said.

"This has been dragging on and on for months and months without the Borough Engineer getting anywhere at all. . . I think we should send the strongest possible protest to County Hall about the delays which will be caused."

WO, October 1952

Black Market in Sweets

WHEN two Ministry of Food officials saw a Watford man offering chocolates for sale from the boot of a car outside a public house, they hit on a black market trail which ended in Watford Magistrates Court on Tuesday. There, fines totalling £1,795 10s., plus 86 guineas costs, were imposed on ten defendants in respect of 84 charges involving nearly a quarter of a million personal points worth of sweets.

The "centre of the web of a system of illicit trading of very considerable substance," said Mr. B. M. Stephenson, prosecuting for the Ministry of Food, admitted 43 charges of supplying various retailers with a total of 212,562 points value in sweets, contrary to the Rationing Order, between October and August.

WHP, November 1952

Right: *Picture Post's enthusiastic cover.*

Above: *The Town Crier, in St Albans Road, reads the Proclamation announcing Princess Elizabeth as future Queen. For the eagerly awaited Coronation everyone had to get; or get to, a television set. And to celebrate, street parties were held wherever there was enough enthusiasm to organise one. The town's buildings were garlanded, and bunting, portraits and loyal greetings graced shops, civic buildings and homes. The souvenir issue of the 'Picture Post' (of 64 pages) had enticing adverts of 'things to come'; Agfa was advertising colour print film but for the average camera-owner it was 120/620 and 127 black and white roll films. What little colour was available was 35mm Kodachrome.*

Vol. 59, No. 11
13 June, 1953

Special
Coronation Souvenir
Number

1/-

God Save the Queen

Coronation, June 1953 . . .

Flats in the Centre of Town?

HERTS County Council had their own reasons for wanting Watford to close its housing list and stop expanding, hinted Watford Borough Councillors at their meeting on Monday. One way of keeping the list open was by building blocks of flats when the centre of the town was redeveloped, they suggested. A proposal mooted by Herts County Council that Watford's housing list should be closed was referred to the Housing Committee for further discussion and report.

Alderman Horwood commented: "I think to some extent the County Council are trying to lead us out into the wilderness on this matter, and we should not take the lead."

Councillor Amey said he proposed reference back because closure of the list would be doing a great number of people a great disservice and wrong.

"It will mean that people who have been on the housing list for two years or more—two years and 11 months even—will not be able to be considered for a house," he said.

Seconding, Councillor Hams suggested "While not wishing to pick any quarrel with the County Council," that the Borough Council was responsible for the government of the town.

"I think that the County Council do not want to see Watford grow, and I would suggest that we all know the reason for it," he said.

Supporting reference back, but for different reasons, Councillor Baxter said that closing the list was in the best interests of the people of the Borough. If they had nowhere to put people, they should not accept them on a list.

"When we have built up the whole of Watford we still shall not have dealt with all the cases on our housing list," he said. To add to it was giving promises they could not keep.

"The County Council should indicate to us where these people can be placed on a list, and not be put under handicap because they live in Watford," he said.

WHP, December 1952

Coronation Crowds Missing

In historic Cassiobury Park, once the estate of the Earls of Essex, holders of the title of Elizabeth I's famous favourite, preparations had been made for loyal Watford subjects of Elizabeth II to make merry in honour of their young Queen, who had been crowned only a few hours earlier.

But at the time the celebrations were due to start, many Watfordians apparently preferred to sit by their TV or radio sets while the great State procession threaded its way through London rather than brave the elements and weave their frozen way to the local park.

Nevertheless, a bright new Union Jack flew bravely in the centre of the festivity arenas, and, despite the cold and wet, sportsmen and sportswomen were limbering up for running track events.

An early arrival was the Mayor (Alderman A. G. Dillingham), who strolled round with his gold chain of office hung over a warm overcoat, and the few policemen had capes over their shoulders as if on mid-winter patrol. The Deputy Mayor and Mayoress (Alderman and Mrs. L. C. Johnson) and the Town Clerk (Mr. Gordon H. Hall) were also among the sparse gathering. The attendance was so small that

even in the beer tent, where loyal toasts might reasonably have been drunk in plenty, there were more assistants on the service side of the bar than customers on the other.

WHP, June 1953

Top: *At a street party in Church Road. Television has not yet taken over from the cinema—and the cinema has added advantage of colour, which television lacks.*

Right: *Here, local school children are taken to the North Watford Odeon to see the film of the Coronation.*

"Let us not be surrounded by a tarmac girdle . . ."

Harrow Rail Crash—Report

Automatic control of a warning type might have prevented, or mitigated, the Harrow triple train crash on October 8, states Lieut.-Colonel G. R. S. Wilson, Chief Inspecting Officer of Railways, Ministry of Transport, in his report of over 30,000 words published yesterday, of the disaster which cost 112, many of them Watford, lives.

Lieut.-Colonel Wilson also found that District Relief Signalman A. G. Armitage, of Harrow No. 1 Box, "should be exonerated from all responsibility for the accident."

The accident, the second worst in the history of Britain's railways, happened just after 8.15 a.m. The 8.15 p.m. Perth to Euston express, running late "at 50-60 miles per hour," in a patch of fog, passed the Colour Light Distance Signal at Caution and two Semaphore signals at danger, and crashed into the back of the 7.31 a.m. Tring to Euston "Local."

The "double-headed" 8 a.m. London to Liverpool and Manchester express, which was approaching "at not less than 60 miles per hour," crashed into the wreckage.

WO, June 1953

Situations Vacant

The engagement of persons answering these advertisements must be made through a Local Office of the Ministry of Labour or a Scheduled Employment Agency if the applicant is a man aged 18-64 inclusive, or a women aged 18-59 inclusive, unless he or she, or the employment is excepted from the provisions of the Notification of Vacancies Order 1952.

WO, June 1953

Road or Beauty Spot?

"The planners may wish to surround Watford by a green belt. Let us not be surrounded by a tarmac girdle."

So declared Watford Town Clerk, Mr. Gordon H. Hall, voicing Watford's objections to the proposed Aylesbury radial road, at the opening session of the County Development inquiry at the Small Town Hall on Monday.

He told the Inspector, Mr. R. B. Walker "The reason for our objection is that we consider the present line of the proposed road, as shown on the County Development Plan, would involve what we consider the desecration of this beautiful woodland, and we consider it would be to the very serious detriment of the amenities of our district, and also the enjoyment of many people from all walks of life, and from all parts of the county."

Mr. F. P. Boyce, deputy clerk to the Herts County Council, outlined the Council's view.

"It remains to emphasise that this is not a plan for all time, it is rather a prediction of the future in general limited for the next 20 years; a principal exception to that limitation being the trunk roads.

"The Plan has made that prediction with the first five of the 20 years particularly in mind. It is important that those who are concerned with this inquiry should remember that this Plan must be the subject of revision at five-yearly intervals, or more frequently if occasion demands." And:

"The County Council regard the preservation of the Hertfordshire section of the Metropolitan Green Belt, the Green Belt proposals shown on the plan, as the primary defence of the county against the continued spread of suburbia, and of fundamental importance."

The inquiry is expected to last into the New Year. Mr. Hall said that he was pleased to hear from the Inspector that the Minister would be giving the town's representations most careful consideration, and declared:

"If the Ministry of Transport do proceed with the proposals on their present line, I think I can promise them unmitigated opposition at every stage."

He told the Inspector that a few hundred yards from the hall where they were sitting was the entrance to the park, where Watfordians and others could walk for miles without thinking that they were near an urban area. It was this that would be disturbed by the proposed road.

"When negotiating for the purchase we had support from all hands. We had the Council unanimous on the proposal, and support from ratepayers' organisations and individuals. There was not one voice that said we should not purchase this land," he declared, adding "We obtained a contribution to the cost of it, not only from the Herts County Council, whose Development Plan this is, but also from the London County Council."

He produced the sealed deed relating to the purchase, and read the clause which stated that the land should be maintained and managed by the Corporation as an open space "for the public use for ever."

WO, December 1953

Top: *This car was built by Morris Motors in 1929 and bought in 1952 for £75. It had an MG badge upon the radiator and the wheel hubs. The 'tank' at the rear is false; the petrol tank being under the bonnet fastened to the dashboard bulkhead. Petrol was by gravity feed to the SU carburettor.*
Haskell's made a new hood and for the first year or two anti-freeze was not available. There was, of course, no heating or radio!
The simple 8hp side-valve engine gave a speed of about 55mph under the best conditions.
It was, it is thought, the first car in Cromer Road (right). Later the very large car on the left, seating a large family, was second. The other two are visitors.

. . . ten classrooms, each to accommodate 60 pupils . . .

Schools' 250 Years of History

In 1704, the year of Blenheim and the taking of Gibraltar, a school was built not far from the Parish Church of St Mary, Watford. Inscribed over its doorway were the words: "Anno Dni, 1704. This Free School was built and endowed for the teaching of poor children at the proper cost of Mrs. Elizabeth Fuller of Watford Place"

From this modest building, with its 40 boys and 20 girls, the first pupils, grew Watford Grammar Schools for Boys and Girls, who this week celebrate the 250th anniversary of their foundation.

Until her death in 1709, Mrs. Fuller herself supervised the affairs of the school, making provision in her will for its running after her demise. 40 shillings were laid out yearly for the purchase of wood and coals to be burned in winter. 20 shillings was paid annually to the Minister of Watford for preaching a sermon on May 1. 20 of the most deserving boys were to receive grey cloth coats with broad brass buttons and bands, and each boy was to receive a new grey bonnet.

If the revenues extended so far, the girls were to be clothed with linsey-wolsey gowns of the same colour as the boys' coats, Holland bands, quoives, or head-dresses, and blue aprons.

The last stage in the schools' history culminated in the building of the present girls' school, which was taken over in 1907, and the opening of the boys' school, in Rickmansworth-road (once again performed by Lord Clarendon) in 1912.

WO 1954

Death of Former Mayor

WE regret to record the death on Tuesday night at his Cassio-road home of one of the best-known, best-respected men in Watford—Mr. Thomas Rubython Clark, retired builder and former Mayor, Alderman, "Father" of the Council, and lay preacher. A widower for some years, he leaves two daughters. Mr. Clark, who was 86 at the time of his death, came to Watford as a small boy, and his long years of devoted public service will probably be best remembered through the reconstruction of the Borough's highways.

With the slogan "Vote for Clark and better roads" he was elected in 1910 to the old Watford Urban District Council. He became its chairman in 1916, and again from April to November, 1922, when he was succeeded by the Charter Mayor of the Borough, Lord Clarendon.

In was in 1921 that Mr. Clark was elected chairman of the Council's Highways Committee, in which capacity he gave the Borough unstinted service. Elected Alderman in 1922, he was elected Mayor of the Borough in November, 1925, and Councillor Bickerton justly observed: "If you want to see a monument to Alderman Clark, look at the roads"

In 1943 Alderman Clark was admitted an honorary Freeman of the Borough as, in the words of Councillor (now Alderman) Harry Horwood, speaking at the ceremony, one who had "devoted a lifetime of service to his fellow townspeople." Mr. Clark had been a member of the old War Tribunal and for some eight years was chairman of the local Burial Board.

As a builder he was concerned in erecting much local residential and other property.

WO, November 1955

Above: *Rickmansworth Road on a sunny spring evening showing returnees from an afternoon's promenade in Cassiobury Park. The curved In/Out road is the access point to the Assembly Hall (now Colosseum) over which the girls are just crossing.*

Left: *Arrival of Grammar School girls at Town Hall Assembly Hall, celebrating the 250th year of founding Dame Fuller's Free School. The boys had already arrived.*

Death of the Borough's Charter Mayor.   Mr Sage: 'offices for thousands . . .'

Death of Lord Clarendon

LESS than three months after a bronze statuette of a Boy Scout was passed by him to the 1st Abbots Langley Scout Group in memory of his son, the Earl of Clarendon, last remaining Freeman of Watford, died on Tuesday at his London home at the age of 78.

The Grove, the mansion now used as offices by London Midland Region of British Railways, was once the Earl's seat. Part of Lees Wood on the estate was given by Lord Clarendon to the 1st South West Herts and 2/1st South West Herts Scouts as a camping site in memory of his elder son, George Lord Hyde, who was killed in a shooting accident in South Africa.

In appreciation of his great assistance in obtaining for Watford a charter of incorporation, and for his services as the new Borough's first Mayor, the Town Council in 1928 presented him with his portrait in oils. This is now hung in the Town Hall.

He was made Freeman of the Borough in 1924. Following the recent death of Mr. T. Clark, he was the last surviving Freeman.

WHP December, 1955

Lord Clarendon, Watford's first Mayor

The "City" in Watford

OUR Borough Engineer, Mr. F. C. Sage, interested the experts at a national conference on housing and town planning with an idea he would like to see incorporated in The Design For Watford. It is a simple plan, just the establishment of a Threadneedle-street in the heart of the town.

But it is a good plan, and if it impressed outsiders with its simplicity, it will delight the citizens as a sound and very natural development of the business usage that has already taken control of the Clarendon-road, Station-road area.

That stretch is already a wing of the city. It is the administrative centre of many large firms and industries. But because they occupy the old houses, a lot of valuable space is lost. By tearing down those old buildings, Clarendon-road rebuilt could easily provide office accommodation for many thousands of white collar workers who now suffer the daily straphanging routine to London E.C. and so could play a big part in decentralising the City offices.

We could also help relieve the burden of

Mr Sage: 'two great disadvantages—smoke and noise . . .'

London Transport by employing here our neighbours from Harrow and Wembley.

Watford is not the only place that could help in this way but Watford is our interest. And, of course, Mr. Sage's design for Clarendon-road would bring in so much extra money to the rates without creating a new housing problem.

WHP, November 1956

Beehive Flats

Large blocks of flats in city centres were compared to beehives by Mr. F. C. Sage, Watford Borough Engineer, addressing the National Conference of the Town and Country Planning Association in London on Friday.

"I am not sure that a man housed in a beehive won't tend to become a bee—very efficient, very much like his fellow, and quite soulless." Mr. Sage, speaking during a discussion on housing densities, said he believed that in the large cities of Central Europe where housing took place in that way, it had proved to be the breeding ground of Communism.

Mr. Sage said he lived in a hamlet and would not like to go back to living in town, for there were two very great disadvantages in flat life in the centres of cities— smoke and noise.

"Until you tackle these two basic disadvantages, flat life in town will never be very popular."

WO, December 1956

Beehive Flats

I FEEL that the brief report in the issue of the "Watford Observer" of December 7, upon remarks which I made at a recent Planning Conference, are likely to give an impression I did not mean to convey.

It is true I stated that I preferred living in a hamlet but also stated that my daughter, who is a medical student at one of the large London hospitals, was practically obliged to live in town in a flat and thus within the small compass of one family the desirability for both house and flat accommodation was manifest. The clear inference was that a need for both types of dwelling was likely to be even more manifest in the larger "family" of a town.

The protagonist for flats in this session of the Conference was Mr. Sergei Kadleigh, well known as the designer of "High Paddington," a huge block of buildings intended to be built over railway lines in the neighbourhood of Paddington, and containing not only flat dwellings but also shops and commercial premises on a vast scale.

The project might truly be described as a Tower Town. It would be possible for anyone living in such a block to pass his whole life therein without the necessity of leaving it at all. I felt that such an existence, cut off from all contact with the countryside which God had given us, was not the type of life to be encouraged in our own country. It was to this building that I applied the name "Beehive" and not to the usual type of flat block, excellent examples of which have been included in many recent schemes in this country—F. C. Sage, Borough Engineer, Watford.

WO, December 1956

North Sea Gas

For some time gas has been obtained from wells drilled in the North Sea, near Norway. This gas is piped to both Holland and Norway where it provides a cheap and clean alternative to coal gas. This gas field is too far from Britain and so benefits are not available here.

Previous page, *bottom, shows Clarendon Road in 1936 looking towards the Junction. Clarendon Road runs from bottom right and Albert Street from the bottom left, across St Johns Road into Westland Road. The curved road from bottom left is Monmouth Street.*
Along Clarendon road on the right is St Stephen's Presbyterian Church and towards the end the last large house is of the G P O sorting office. On the left hand side is the Congregational Church on the corner of St Johns Road. Across St Johns Road from the church is Duddenhill, home of Mr Percy Fisher, before being sold and the ground, and that of the next undeveloped site, used for Magistrates Court and Police Station. An era of large houses, with tennis courts, and absence of cars, gives no hint of changes to come.

This page: above, *St Mary's Road chimneys offer a glimpse of what the whole town would once have looked like.*
Right: *A fire drill at the Clarendon Road Drill Hall and Fire Brigade Exhibition, June 1951.*

Part IX

"Chaos dictates earlier measures"

The memory of the stagnant, unrewarding, wearisome postwar years had faded. Door-to-door salesmen were offering water softeners and carpeting, Hoover were offering their washing machines and steam irons on hire-purchase. The prewar kitchen was hardly big enough to accommodate a refrigerator.

The housing programme was well under way but by no means complete. Almost all the sites shown in the plan on page 277 had been built or were in the course of construction; Kytes, Garston, Woodside, Hillside, Meriden, Hempstead Road, Holywell and Bushey.

The immediate postwar years were frustrating but the next few years were anything but. Watford, however, still had a Victorian road system with prewar parking facilities and an ever-increasing population. The traffic flow of work-days was severely disrupted by the numerous narrow and awkward road junctions; King Street/Queens Road, Market Street/High Street, Clarendon Road/High Street, Upton Road/High Street, Cassio Road/Rickmansworth Road, Derby Road/Queens Road, Vicarage Road/Merton Road/Wiggenhall Road, etc. Then, as now, car parking and its attendant problems worsened at week-ends. The burning question on everyone's mind was "Why don't they do something?" No matter the cost to the environment, the motor car must be given space.

With this in mind planning had taken place during the pre-ceding years including a vehicle count between April and September 1954. This estimated future traffic flows, destinations, numbers and where parked. The conclusions, together with land use recommendations, were published in 1956.

Among suggestions for car parks were: Church Street, 120; High Street Station forecourt, 10; Crown Passage, 20; Carey Place, 260; Meeting Alley (Roger's Timber-yard site), 330; rear of Clements, 130; rear of old YMCA in Clarendon Road, 130; Junction Station (Hotel garden), 40. These proposed car parks would give additional space for about 1000 cars.

The number parked 'on-street' on a normal week-day was in the region of 750.

An exit into Rosslyn Road was proposed to ease the bottle-neck of entrance and exit from Shrubbery Car Park into the High Street. Although this plan was more in the nature of a survey, recommendations for minor works were included. It also contained the basic concept for the relief Road (Beechen Grove) and the framework for Exchange Road.

Well before the plan was published shops built opposite the Town Hall were set back at a curve, to follow the future road line. *(When built they had greatly inadequate car space for the shop tenants.)*

While planners had been counting cars in tens and a few hundreds, right upon our doorstep the motorway planned long pre-war was under construction to speed traffic from London to the busy Midlands

The plans of 1937/39 for the St Albans By-Pass (p.211) were in advanced planning stages, paradoxically given the designation Ml.

At this time cars were still not freely available and so the pressure was bearable, but within a very few years car ownership became widespread. The road which could have saved Watford from the carve-up which was to follow in the early mid-sixties and early seventies—the Maple Cross to Hunton Bridge link—was obstructed at planning stages by environmentalists not resident in or near Watford, and then by lack of funds, owing to 'unexpected difficulties discovered on the projected route'. *That all traffic from the west (Slough) had to travel through Watford, meant constant jams at the Town Hall roundabout.* There was no way this traffic could be routed elsewhere; but traffic north and south, along the High Street to and from Hempstead Road—and suffering the hold-ups in the High Street—could be diverted along new 'relief road's which could be fairly easily built, and this was the plan proposed.

But before the 'master' plan could be put into operation, chaos dictated earlier measures and these came in 1962.

Left: February 1957 saw the first plan, which assumed that 140 houses were to be demolished, taking out Weymouth Street and many houses from Beechen Grove and Derby Road.

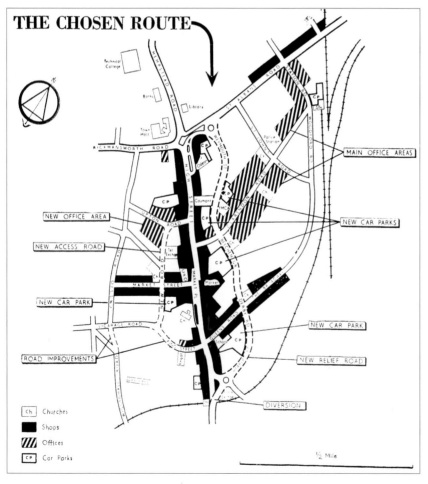

THE CHOSEN ROUTE

Ch Churches
■ Shops
▨ Offices
CP Car Parks

½ Mile

Left: *The M1, opened in 1959, here approaching Northamptonshire. Lack of commercial traffic would indicate that this is a Sunday.*

Below: *Just above the centre the St Albans Road runs across the picture. At the top of* **F** *the Plaza cinema, closed.*
In the top of **E** *is the two-lane railway bridge and above that blocks of maisonettes being built in Church Road. Towards the top right of* **E** *are the Railway Cottages, and below is Fishburn's works; to their left the railway engine sheds.*
The several lines of goods wagons in the sidings are mostly for coal. At the top right of **E**, *behind the hoardings, the original Watford Station*
In **D** *on the track nearest the bridle path is a stationary three-car Bakerloo-Line unit; The three wedge-shaped objects on the station platforms are the entrances and exits to the 'Callowland' side of the railway, and lead to the Bridle Path.*
In **F**, *Cassiobury Mills include Macmillan Foundries Ltd.*
Church Road, at this time, has still an entrance to St Albans Road. c1956

A	B	C
D	E	F
G	H	I

Benskin's merges with Ind Coope . . .

New Road Through Watford

THE most outstanding feature of the plan is the provision of a 72ft relief road which will take through traffic completely off the High-street between the High-street Station and the Town Hall.

The Borough Engineer (Mr. F. C. Sage) told the "Watford Observer" that the majority of houses in Herbert-street would have to go and some would be affected in Clifford-street and Charles-street. In Derby-road, the School, the Tabernacle and Standard Range premises would be unaffected, although the other side of the road would not be. The shops on the Queen's-road corners came into the line of the new road, and Horton's Garage would be affected to a considerable extent. Further along, Beechen Grove Schoolroom would make its contribution, but it was after the crossing of Clarendon-road that the majority of residential dwellings would eventually come down. Hardest hit would be Weymouth-street, the whole of one side of which comes out, but a number of properties would be affected in Monmouth-road, Platts-avenue, and Albert-road.

In moving approval of the draft plan, Councillor Buckingham said he was sure it was something for which they had all been waiting long. He recalled that it had been talked about for at least ten years and said, "It must be the most important development, in the physical sense, of our town since the happy day when we decided to acquire Cassiobury park." He emphasised, "These are draft proposals only."

At the proper time ample arrangements would be made for the hearing of objections, and added, "It must not be presumed it is a fait accomplii."

WO, February 1957

Mayor's Fund Over £300

Delight has been brought to 700 poor and needy folk of Watford this week who have received gifts—mainly food parcels and vouchers from the Mayor's Christmas Appeal fund.

At the week-end the fund topped the £300 mark and by Monday had reached £307 5s 9d.

WHP, January 1957

No Subsidy for £9+ Tenants

MORE than 96 per cent of Watford Council house tenants interviewed during the past 12 months have an income of over £9 a week.

This was disclosed to the Borough Council on Monday night, when the Labour Group attempted to get the rate subsidy for housing

raised from £30,000 to £35,500. It was defeated by 21 votes to 19. Tenants of council houses were not expected to pay more than one-seventh of their income; they had 4,611 houses, and some 3,476 were available on this basis to people with £9 or less a week. In a report on the rents of council houses the Borough Treasurer reported that the additional amount to be raised from the tenants was £21,000, and it was recommended that the rents of council houses should be increased. The suggestions are nil to 1s 9d. a week for pre-war houses (average increase 10d.) and nil to 3s. 6d. per week for post-war houses (average 2s. 2d.)

WHP, January 1957

Petrol Situation is Grave

WATFORD can expect more sackings if the petrol muddle continues.

After nearly a month of rationing, local firms which depend on petrol for production and distribution are realising just how much those coupons will mean to them and how much the shortage is hitting at the foundations of industry.

Commenting on the situation Mr. Kenneth McKell, of Penfold Wire Fencing Ltd. said: "The effect of petrol and fuel rationing, although expected to be fairly severe, is, in many instances, proving to be grossly inequitable in its effects on industry. In some directions unemployment is already threatened and unless some urgent action is taken to relax or redistribute some of the restrictions there is little doubt that it must become more widespread.

Factories cannot continue to work unless they receive their raw materials, frequently, according to their processes, to the dictates of a strict programme sequence, nor can they

continue to produce goods if they cannot despatch them from the factory.

WHP, January 1957

Benskin's Merger

WATFORD and the area served by Benskin's Watford Brewery will continue to get Benskin's beer if the take-over by Burton brewers Ind Coope and Allsopp is confirmed.

This is disclosed in a letter from Chairman and Managing Director of Benskin's, Mr. W. Kilkenny, recommending shareholders to accept the terms for the merger offered by Ind Coope. The terms of the offer—now in the hands of shareholders—are that Ind Coope shall take over the entire share capital of Benskin's in exchange for the issue of shares credited as fully paid by Ind Coope on the basis of eight Ordinary 5s. shares for every £1 Ordinary stock unit in Benskin's.

WO, February 1957

Families On Emigration Trail

DOZENS of families from all over South west Herts are selling-up and hitting the Empire and Commonwealth trail. And many of the emigration inquiries made through the last weeks have been from skilled Watford technicians.

Said Mrs. Russell, who has been handling the bookings for transatlantic air and sea passages at Pickford's Travel Agency in Clarendon-road:

"None of them seem to have any personal dislike for Watford. The majority of them are in good employment, good trades. They are fairly highly-paid workers. Their main reason for going is for the sake of the children."

A typical couple who confirmed this outlook were Mr. and Mrs. Ralph Kenny, of 17,

1957: St Albans Road, the Plaza Cinema is being demolished, the site not yet completely cleared; a garage/service station followed.

Albansview, Watford. A fitter at Scammell Lorries, Mr. Kenny declared: "At school I twice passed for special places at High School, but my parents just couldn't afford to send me.

"If my children," he said, pointing to seven-years-old Ralph junior and the toddlers, Theresa (3) and Lynn (2) "are bright they would automatically get a University Education in Canada."

WHP, February 1957

King Street Maternity

SINCE 1948 the local Hospital Management Committees have been at constant war with the Regional Boards, who are boss, fighting for no more than an adequate hospital service. In most of these formative issues it has been not so much what you want as what we can afford.

There is no such reason to back the Board's latest argument with Watford. They have conceded our need for more maternity beds. They had to. Mothers leave King-street too soon, others are being sent to Hemel Hempstead because King-street is so crowded. So something has to be done.

Watford points to land which the committee own at Shrodells and wants to build there for the mothers. The Board say they should extend by buying the property they need in King-street
We suggest to the Board that if they knew more of the King-street story they would not argue with the local people who know local problems as well as local needs.

King-street is going to be no

place for more maternity beds. It will soon be a really busy traffic thoroughfare. There are more reasons than the availability of land why the hospital should be extended along the Shrodells backwater.

WHP, February 1957

Goodbye Watford

HIT by petrol rationing, a North Watford decorator and his brother-in-law, an Abbots Langley carpenter, left this country on Tuesday to try their luck in Canada. And they are not the only people caught up in the emigration "snowball." The previous day, two middle-aged residents of Leggatts Wood-avenue emigrated to Canada and another family man whose parents live in that road is off to Toronto in a few months' time.

A young couple from the Kingswood area might go to Canada soon and a 27-years-old Abbots Langley man is going out in June to make a new home for his hairdresser wife.

WHP, March 1957

Watford's "Mainz Week"

Plans are afoot to run a "Mainz Week" in Watford later this year, Cllr. E. C. Amey announced on Monday when he spoke to Watford chamber of Commerce about the aims of the new Mainz-Watford Society.

He said an approach would be made to the Chamber and to Watford traders to run a "Mainz Week." Wine merchants would, if interested, be able to make a good show of the Rhine wines made in Mainz.

WHP, March 1957

The Regiment

"GENTLEMEN, the Regiment." That will still be the toast, for though the county regiment will disappear with the merging of the Bedfs. and Herts and the Essex Regiments, the spirit will never die. The Hertfordshire Regiment (T.A.) will in the true sense of the word become the county regiment. These are two of the considered opinions of members of the Bedfs. and Herts Old Comrades Association whose hearts are full of pride for their old regiment and who have the battle honours of the 16th Regiment of Foot at their finger-tips.

The new regiment will join the Royal Norfolks and Suffolks, the Lincolns and Northamptonshire Regiment to form the East Anglian Brigade.

The amalgamation of the Bedfs. and Herts. and the Essex Regiment is expected to take place well before the date envisaged. In a Special Order of the Day, Lieut.-Gen. Sir Reginald F. S. Denning, Colonel of the Regiment, intimates that the Regimental Depot at Kempston will cease to exist as a training establishment. "It is felt," he adds, "that the presence of a Regimental Headquarters will preserve the full regimental spirit, help our Old Comrades to cling closer together and continue to bring aid to members of the Regiment who may be in need." And from Hertford, Brigadier J. A. Longmore says he would like to make it clear that none of the Territorial units are affected by the re-organisation.

The Hertfordshire Yeomanry Artillery, the Hertfordshire Regiment, The Hertfordshire Company R.A.S.C., the Provost Detachment and the Hertfordshire Company W.RA.C. will continue their tasks and titles unchanged.

Top: in the 'covered' market, 1956

Left: Just across the road from the photograph on the previous page is the block of railway cottages, sound and in good condition, but soon to be doomed for rebuilding the railway bridge and eventual electrification of the main line.

... enabling Watford to face competition from Hempstead's modern New Town ...

They have recently reverted to a wholly voluntary basis, and in the few months that have elapsed since this was introduced they have gone a long way to recapture the pre-war corporate and comradely spirit which can only be achieved among genuine volunteers.

The 16th Regiment of Foot was formed in 1688 at Reading, and in its early years had such battle honours as Namur, Steinkirk, Blenheim (1704), Ramillies (1706), Oudenarde (1708) and Malplaquet (1709). Because of its service as Marines during the attempt to capture Cathagena in South America in 1740 the Regiment is entitled to play Rule Britannia in addition to its Regimental March.

It was in 1809 when the Regiment assumed the title of Bedfordshire and in 1881 the 1st and 2nd Battalions were affiliated to the Bedford-shire and Hertfordshire Militia.

During the Indian Campaign the Regiment added Chitral to its battle honours and this was followed quickly by South Africa, Mons, Ypres, Loos, Somme, Gaza, and Palestine.

Casualties during the First World War were 18,000 with 336 officers and 5,745 N.C.O.'s and men killed. Nine Victoria Crosses were gained. In 1919 the title was changed to Bedfordshire and Hertfordshire to create a closer link between the regiment and the two counties.

The Second World War brought a crop of battle honours starting with Dunkirk(1940), N. W. Europe (1940), Tobruk (1941), Tobruk Sortie, Bel Hamed (the only infantry regiment to gain this honour), Tunis N. Africa (1941-43), Cassino, Trafimene Line, Italy (1944-45), Athens, Greece (1944-45), Singapore Island, Malaya (1942), Chindits (1944), Burma (1944).

The Hertfordshire Regiment T.A. during this war gained honours at the Normandy Landing, N.W. Europe, Montorsoli, Gothic Line, Monte Gameraldi, Monte Ce Co, Monte Grand, and Italy (1944-45). With such a record behind them how can the spirit fail? Or as the Old Comrades say, "What's in a name?" And already they are devising badges for the new Brigade. Favourite is a simple laurel wreath with "East Anglia" scrolled across it.

WHP, August 1957

Whippendell Saved from Radial Road

VICTORY has come to Watford Council and local organisations who protested against the plan to drive the Aylesbury Radial-road through Whippendell Woods. The Minister of Housing, Mr. Henry Brooke, has, in effect, told the County Council to "think again," and has deleted the project.

In general, he approves the County Development Plan, and states that the upholding of the Green Belt in Hertfordshire is a prime objective. Of the Aylesbury Radial-road, the route of which was condemned as vandalism by Watfordians, he says:

"Although there is evidence of need for the section of this road proposed between Pinner and Hunton Bridge, the amount of traffic that would use it is uncertain, and much would depend on the effect of other roads proposals yet to be carried out. In view of the serious effect of this proposal on Whippendell Woods and the golf course at Watford, the Minister has come to the conclusion that further consideration must be given to this road, and he has, therefore, deleted the section between Cassio Bridge and the proposed North Orbital-road near Hunton Bridge."

WO, December 1958

Watford's New High Street

THE face of Watford is changing rapidly. During the next year bigger changes still are likely to take place. These will follow the pattern of making Watford streets more attractive, wider and safer. Three prominent "land marks" will go. Halsey House and the Fire Station in High-street and the old Brewery in St. Albans-road. Two streets will also disappear for a car park. Already No. 1 St. Albans-road is on its way down to dust.

Once the building is down the gardens fronting St. Albans-road will be extended

Above: *Oxhey Park, 1957, the river-side path between Wiggenhall Road and Lower High Street; the wartime defence pill-box has yet to be removed.*

Right: *Alderman Thomas F Harris, J P, Mayor of Watford, presenting the scroll conferring Freedom of Entry to the Borough of Watford to Lt General Sir Reginald F S Denning KBE, CB of the 3rd East Anglian Regiment.*
This grants the regiment the privilege of marching through the Borough, on ceremonial occasions, with colours flying, bands playing, drums beating and bayonets fixed. July 4th 1959.

This privilege was exercised in 1962 upon the return of the regiment from a tour of duty in Singapore and to mark the change of name to the 'Royal Anglian Regiment'. The presenting Mayor on that occasion was Alderman J R Hicks.

round the corner into Hempstead-road. Certain buildings at the back will be retained for the Parks Department and The Avenue car park will be left until something concrete is forthcoming.

Work is also to begin soon on the demolition of the Old Brewery in St. Albans-road and this site will be developed by Hille Ltd. with the erection of six shops which will be set back in line with the North Watford Post Office.

This development will allow a widening of the bottleneck at this point and construction of a wider pavement. A new railway bridge is to replace the present St. Albans-road one but the news at present is that it will be no wider.

WHP, May 1959

"New Look" for High-street

BLOCK up the very heart of Watford High street. Block up the High-street entrances to Queen's-road and King-street. Force all through traffic into a clock-wise stream on a central Watford "rim" road. In these drastic measures the Borough Engineer, Mr. F. C. Sage, sees the only chance of preventing the central shopping area of Watford from becoming completely choked in the next few years. In these measures he sees the only possibility of enabling Watford to face competition from Hempstead's modern New Town and retain its popularity as a shopping centre and continue to enjoy prosperity.

Designed to create safer and more comfortable conditions for pedestrians and to reduce congestion by increasing ease of traffic flow without increasing its general running speed, the scheme—it will cost £80,000—has been presented to the Highways Committee.

So has an interim scheme costing £29,000, which can be put into operation very much more speedily.

WHP October, 1959

Progress on Balmoral Bridge

AT last the long-awaited new Balmoral-road, Watford railway bridge is taking shape.

Work is now well in progress, and on Sunday, May 10, the old brick arch—for so long a danger spot for pedestrians and a traffic bottleneck—will be demolished and the new steel girder bridge rolled into position.

This will enable the local highway authority to widen the 12ft. road at this point to 45 ft.

The new bridge is being constructed by British Railways for Watford Corporation.

WHP, May 1959

Last Cattle Market

ON the last Tuesday of 1959 there were more cattle than usual, as well as pigs, sheep and calves on offer, and competition was keen.

In 1890, the market came into the hands of the late Mr. W. Hurst Flint, of Messrs. Humbert and Flint, then to the late Mr. C. H. Halsey, till Mr. Hodgson took over in 1936. Watford Corporation now holds the Charter rights.

Watford market continued a busy and important venue for many years, but the Ministry of Food took over control of slaughtering during the war, and by the end of the war Watford had only two slaughter-houses left.

At the same time Watford was progressively growing more urbanised and less agricultural, with the loss of farmland to the Hemel Hempstead New Town and other surrounding development.

So, with "the writing on the wall," Mr. Hodgson reluctantly made his decision to close the Watford market, but the goodwill of its business will be transferred to Mr. Hodgson's bigger market at St. Albans, which has been covered, provided with a car park and improved in various ways.

WHP, December 1959

Top: *The last Cattle Market, in the last week of December 1959.*

Right: *The Balmoral Road bottleneck. The bridge girders are in place enabling the remains of the old bridge to be removed, and the road, at last, widened; completion was in 1960. See 'Munitions', p158, 160.*

Mayor Explains High-street Scheme

COMPLAINTS about the council redevelopment in Watford High-street are answered by the Mayor, Ald. T. F. Harris, he writes: "I should like to clear up a misunderstanding which appears to exist in the minds of some people regarding the rebuilding of these premises. I have heard it suggested that the Corporation, having acquired these properties for road widening purposes, are allowing the developers to rebuild to the old line.

This is not so. In fact the carriageway is being widened by 7 feet to 30 feet at the junction with the Market Place and, in addition, along the whole of the frontage a pavement 15 feet wide is being provided in substitution for the old pavement which at places, was as narrow as 5 feet in width. The new pavement width to be provided is exactly the same as we ask other developers to provide on redevelopment."

WHP, March 1960
• *This refers to the block of buildings in front of the Parish Church, No. 92 to 100, and although the Corporation are correct in stating the foot-path-width, the upper storeys of the building overhang and do not present a sympathetic appearance. In keeping with the 'old' line of Church Street which opened onto the High Street, an open walk-through is provided between No. 92 and 94. The Council's plan of June 1951 to 'remove' the shops (which the Council owned) was forgotten until 1999 when they were demolished and St Mary's Square formed.*

£2 Million Idea

AT its next meeting the Watford Town and Country Planning and Plans Committee can expect a planning application before them which could radically change the face of Watford. The proposal to develop a 12-acre "shoppers' world" in Lower High-street is being put forward by the Blackpool firm of B. H. O. Hills, Ltd., retail store proprietors.

It is reported this week that negotiations have been completed to buy the site from Benskins. It is believed that the contract price for the sale of the land is about £200,000, and that the whole project will cost £2 million.

The site, which is on the opposite side of the High-street from Benskins, extends on the High-street frontage from the Watford Motor Company down as far as the old mill. It takes in all the land behind that frontage and over the river extends as far as Water-lane, including what is at present an undeveloped field.

WHP, May 1960

The Ever Rising Tide

Mr. Marples should cut the cackle and ease the traffic. He should be made to realise how important it is for the North Orbital-road from Hunton Bridge to join the Denham By-pass, a link so vital between east and west, a main artery flowing from the M. 1.

WHP, May 1960

Top left: *Water Lane, flooded, in 1960; at least the pedestrians had the benefit of a raised walkway whereas in modern flooding (2001, top right,) the road is impassable to pedestrians, and closed to motorists. The blue hoarding shields the construction of a motel upon the site. In the background will be noted the new bridge of Waterfields Way from the High Street.*

Right: *StAlbans Road rail bridge was the worst of Hertfordshire's five bad-road back-spots (the High Street was second). In a rush hour, back in 1954, 1,211 vehicles, of which 110 were buses, and 1,452 pedal cycles, would pass. An average hour saw 822 vehicles and 165 bicycles, perhaps 3,000 per day. In 1935 a week's census counted 24,105 cyclists, 3,445 daily. Part of the new dual carriageway, as far as Station Road, was built in late 1961, the old bridge removed and rebuilt in 1962/3 and the railway's electrification programme followed in two phases of April 1966 and March 1967.*

Dr Tibble's Vi-Cocoa factory was started at Bushey Mill Lane/Sandown Road in 1899; and three years later suffered a disastrous fire. As the 'Watford Manufacturing Company' they masterminded munition productions in the Great War. They expected great business thereafter, and had this factory built. It was a white elephant which bankrupted the company and remained empty until taken by British Moulded Hose (and who used the top floor during WWII for producing Penicillin). This fire in June 1961 gutted much of the building, which was later restored. BMH relinquished the site in 1977 and the building was demolished.

Meriden Tower Blocks

The Borough Council are just now weighing up the possibilities of projecting four 12-storey blocks of flats on the northern sky-line. The flats that will be built on stilts over the central car park will be only half this height. They're six storeys.

The dwarf-the-neighbours business block in Clarendon-road will be nine storeys. So these at Meriden are way up there on their own. Do not make the mistake of taking this scheme for granted.

I go no further than to say I would like to see the picture in bricks and mortar. I may only add that I am encouraged to be optimistic about that possibility by the Town Hall interest in the preliminary plans prepared by Mr. F. C. Sage, the Borough Engineer and Surveyor.

They could have turned down those first plans on the spot, but they did not do that. They were interested enough to want to know something of the cost, and they ordered sketches to be prepared. We have months to wait, several at least, but the result will be worth it.

I know 2,000 families who think so for certain. They are the people on the council waiting list for houses. The projected flats, four blocks of them, each 12 storeys high, will provide homes for 144 families. And that's a whole lot more than could be accommodated in houses built on the same site.

WHP, July 1960

•*The plans were duly passed, but two blocks only were built.*

Top: *Plans for the 1962 new road system.*
Right: *Visual of how the Meriden Estate could look.*

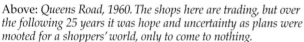

Above: *Queens Road, 1960. The shops here are trading, but over the following 25 years it was hope and uncertainty as plans were mooted for a shoppers' world, only to come to nothing.*

Right: *The morning after the snowfall of the last day of 1961 revealed a transformed wonderland; Rickmansworth Road deserted and New Year's day traffic and business stopped in its tracks . . . and the Pond looks like a fairyland grotto.*

Below: *Cassiobury Entrance Lodge (Park Gates), 1960.*

Blizzard

The last day of 1961 and the first few of 1962 saw many falls of heavy snow driven by northerly winds. The town on the Monday morning presented a deserted air as people faced unaccustomed difficulties in travelling

Along the Parade by MacFisheries, Garners and to Clement's, the snow was piled some two or three feet high upon the edge of the pavement; leaving just a narrow snow-bound passage for passers-by.

Film, 'Around Watford' 1961-62

Mail Held Up

Mr. A. K. Smith, Head Postmaster, said at the sorting office in Clarendon Road that normal mail had been cleared after the Union of Postal Workers' work-to-rule. But there was an accumulation of what was called 'deferred matter'.

Bad weather conditions and staff shortages meant that the strength was 60 staff short out of 200.

WHP, January 1962

Above: The Corporation snow ploughs had a busy time from 5am, but January 1st, normally a busy work day, was quiet. The snow and ice took several days to clear.

Right: The local branch of the Salvation Army holding their weekly meeting in the service road outside the Halifax Building Society premises near the pond.

Through the following pages of the High Street panorama (1994/5) the history runs from 1961 to 1988, at places interspersed with items and photographs to link older times with the modern High Street. There are many side-by-side comparisons as, for example, the 'Green Man' evolution on page 365.

1958
The Parade.

183/185	Cyril Power, Hair Fashions
181	Radio Rentals Ltd. Offices
179	Robinson Rentals Ltd
177	Faksim Supplies/ Faksim Foto Ltd
175	House & Garden (Watford) Ltd. Fancy Goods
171	The Continental Delicatessen
	169/167 Eastern Carpet Stores,
165	Lloyds Bank Ltd. (Executor & Trustee dept)
161	W J Elliott Ltd. Piano Tuners
159	Martins (Allied Retail Trades Ltd)
157	Derwent Television
155	Walkers, dry cleaners
153	Westminster Bank, Bank Chambers
153	Claude Barker & Partnrs.
153	Griffin—
151	Westminster Bank Ltd
149	Eastern Gas Board

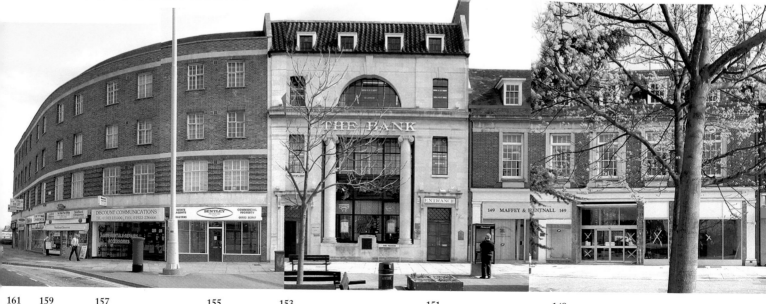

161   159   157   155   153   151   149

The gathered crowd, standing in silence for two minutes, before the lighting of the symbolic beacon

Monday 8th May 1995 was much like any other early May day, bright with sunny periods. But this particular day was distinctive, being fifty years since 'V' (Victory in Europe) Day 1945.

The generations involved in that struggle were thinned with the passing of time. Watford had no air base, nor was it a garrison town. Its involvement with the war was to provide manpower and that of an industrial manufactory. Many of the former never returned from service duty; more lost their lives as a result of enemy action over the town..

Of the remarkable and diverse range of products made much will not be known; the veil of secrecy over war production was tight although partially lifted at war's end when some firms were pleased to tell of their 'war-work'.

This day was of national remembrance; Watford had representatives from twin towns of Mainz, Nanterre, Pesario and Novgorod and in the evening a 'spirit of the years' singalong was led by band and singer.

The time of anticipation was 8.40pm when the symbolic Beacon was to be lighted, but, first, the lighting was preceded by a two-minute silence. Sharp at 8.38 the report of the maroon fired from the top of the YMCA building and the attentive crowd froze, standing in casual poses; in one instance with a hand poised over a bag of perhaps chicken and chips.

Silence reigned, only broken by the tinkling of the pond's fountain. Another maroon sounded to mark the end of the silence and with a buzz of sound activity resumed.

The lighting of the beacon, part of a nationwide chain of 2000, took place, lit by Mayor Cllr Maria Green, and merriment continued for another hour or so.

For many the day, and the era, was well and truly over. A section of Watford's public had remembered and done its duty.

Above: *The pond c1910 and, right, in 1962*

| 147 | 145 | 143 | 141 | 139 | 137 | 135 (EEB) |

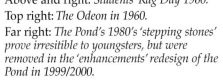

Above and right: *Students' Rag Day 1960.*

Top right: *The Odeon in 1960.*

Far right: *The Pond's 1980's 'stepping stones' prove irresitible to youngsters, but were removed in the 'enhancements' redesign of the Pond in 1999/2000.*

133   131   129   115   113

Fire Station Closes

THE name's the same, the faces are the same, and the telephone number is the same. But that is where the similarity ends. For as from 14.30 hours yesterday, Watford Fire and Ambulance moved, after 60 years, from Watford High-street, to its brand new £80,000 Station at the junction of Rickmansworth and Whippendellroads.

The bells for fire and ambulance will ring out no more from Watford High-street.

Instead it will be life in the ultra-modem, twin block station, with its 83-foot radio mast towering above, revolving around the watch room round a three-sided control console with rows of telephone switches, bells, buzzers, warning lights, factory alarm systems, and an impressive red emergency phone. The whole thing looks for all the world like the control room of a nuclear power station.

WHP, February 1961

•*Forty years on the problems of getting from the fire station to the rest of Watford presents problems difficult to overcome; a new station in lower High Street is suggested.*

113	The Parade Confectionery Ltd
111	Flats
107	Bunting's, cycle dealers
105	Tea & Coffee Specialists
99	W S Wellers & Son, estate agents
97	H Dresner, baby linen
95	Hugh Lloyd, chemists.
93	Cookery Nook
93,	Misses Driver, ladies' hairdressers;
93	Flat
89 & 91	Gwen Martyn, ladies' outfitters
87	Sun Insurance Office
87	Christian Science Reading Room
85	Radio & Electrical Equip. Renters Ltd
83a	Peter Spivey, sports outfitters
83	Sixty Minute Cleaners Ltd.
79/81	S Cole (Menswear) Ltd.
77	B Gunner Ltd, butchers
	Knightswood Coaches (rear of cinema)
69	M Bishop Kenyon Ltd, gowns.

GAUMONT CINEMA

Above: *The corner of Church Street and New Street (opposite St Mary's Church): the distant three-storey building was once Watford's Workhouse before new premises in Vicarage Road (the Union House).*
The Odeon poster features 'Ferry to Hong Kong'.
Right: *The ex-workhouse.*
This part of Church Street is under the greensward fronting Church car park.

Watford's Parking Solution

A bold multi-storey car park plan to save Watford from committing commercial suicide—"the inevitable fate of a town which fails to solve its parking problems"—was presented to Watford Town Council by the Borough Engineer (Mr. F. C. Sage) on Monday.

The plan looks way into the future—to the time when, it is estimated, parking facilities will be required for 3,500 vehicles.

It provides for meter street parking for 500 cars, surface car parks (possibly metered) for 642 cars, and multi-storey facilities for 1,996 vehicles.

Suggested sites for the multi-storey parks are the Central car park (Beechen-grove), at Carey-place, in Church-street and at the Shrubbery car park.

The fact remains that our roads are becoming so congested that they can no longer be used as free car parks," Mr. Sage told the members.

WO, January 1961

Changing Face of Watford

THERE are three more "pubs with no beer"—to borrow the words of a popular song—in Central Watford at the moment.

They are the three old "locals"— "The Greyhound," "The New Inn," King-street, and "King's Head" in Market Place—which closed their doors when the new "Robert Peel" was officially opened last week.

"The New Inn," meeting place of Watford and District Darts League, and A.E.U. branch, and other organisations, was at one time associated with Healey's Brewery, situated in George-street on the site of Pickford's depository, which was absorbed by Benskin's at the end of the last century.

Closing of "The King's Head" means that several organisations, including the Buffaloes, Watford Cine Society, another A.E.U. branch, and the local chess club have had to find alternative meeting places. It has been noted for its catering and, in particular, for "Kaye Aitch Night," which was introduced by a former manager for the serving of chicken in the rough.

WO, April 1961

Chop-Shop in the High Street

WE often hear talk about the changing face of Watford High-street. Do we ever pause to really consider the extent of those changes over the past ten years or so? There remains little more than the railway arches and gas works at one end, the Pond at the other, and the Parish Church in the centre, to identify it with the main thoroughfare that was Watford's in the early twenties. Demolition and reconstruction work in the central area of the town has been gradually gathering momentum in recent years, and today the town centre must surely be undergoing more changes than at any other time in its history. How many old Watfordians returning to the borough would recognise it from any of the views obtained by an "Observer" cameraman in a recent pictorial survey of the High-street?

The Gaumont cinema was built in 1937 and renamed the Odeon in September 1963 after the closure of the Odeon by the pond. This cinema went three-screen in June 1974 and was still trading profitably in 1983 when the site was sold for redevelopment, resulting in the nearby Sainsbury's supermarket. Removal day, 17th October 1983

81   79   77   69   Gaumont Cinema

Starting a journey down the High-street from the roundabout, we find ourselves completely surrounded by buildings which were non-existent when Watford received its Charter in 1922, and the extension to the parade of shops on the St. Albans-road corner has only taken place in recent years.

The pond, of course, has been a feature of the town since its earliest days: the Odeon (first called the Plaza) was the first large cinema to be built in the High-street, and the nearby Monmouth House will be remembered by some of the oldest inhabitants, although changed in general appearance.

It is the opposite stretch of the High-street (or The Parade as it is generally known at this point) that has either undergone or is undergoing the greatest change in recent years. Now nearing completion on the site of the original 'Halsey House', home of the Watford Conservative Club, is a vast new block of modern shops and offices matching in design the neighbouring block which stands on the site of the old residence known as 'The Woodlands'.

Moving further down we pass what remains of the old Watford Fire Station and, looking across the site of 14 High-street from which the affairs of the borough were conducted before the war, we get an unusual view of

The Parade, 1964, traffic entering the High Street from Upton Road/Exchange Road, where traffic is two-way to the Town Hall, but one way to Clarendon Road.

63	J P Taylor Ltd, ladies and gents' outfitters
57, 59 & 61	Moselle Ltd, ladies' outfitters.
55	Arthur East Ltd, corn merchants
53	Halford Cycle Co. Ltd. cycle dlrs
51	Barratt W. & Co. Ltd, boot dlrs.
49	Jas Wilson hairdrssr
49	Lewis A. & Co. (Westminster) Ltd, tobccn-sts.
47	H J Searle & Son, house furnishers
45	Samsons, clothiers
43	Double-Wear Ltd, shoe repairs.
41	Evelyn's, ladies hairdressers
41	F Rickards, photographer
41	Thomas Maggs, hairdresser
41	Gilflex Conduits Ltd.
39	Samson's, clothiers
35 & 37	Jay's Furnishing Stores
33, 31, 29,	Clements (Watford) Ltd

Exchange-road (formerly Upton Road). Continuing our journey we see few shops which have escaped vast structural alterations at some time or other since the war.

An outstanding exception is, perhaps, the building which "houses" a jeweller's, newsagent's and an old world restaurant, which is reputed to be over 300 years old. In the Market-place there still remains the "Rose and Crown", but the once nearby "Spread Eagle" has disappeared to make way for a modern shop, and the "King's Head" is destined for destruction very shortly. As we pass into the narrow section of the High-street, our attention is attracted by another new block of shops with its vista view of the parish church and the new car park opposite.

On the left are two more gaping "wounds" where, until recently, stood the premises of Kingham's and C. H. Peacock Ltd, both flourishing concerns, now moved to premises elsewhere, which still bear the names of the old Watford families.

The widened Water-lane turning (now nearing completion) will soon bring through traffic off the eastern relief road, and this brings us to Lower High-street which, though still, perhaps, the "Cinderella" of the town, has seen remarkable improvements and changes of late. The old mill, which stood a derelict eye-sore for many years following destruction by fire, has been replaced by a used car business with fountains playing in the foreground, and several similar business and modern garage premises have helped to bring a new 'look' to the area.

But all this is but a drop in the ocean of alterations and developments still in the offing.

Four multi-storey car parks, a street meter parking system, a vast shopping area on the old brewery site, all these are "on the books" to complete the transformation of the small market town that was Watford at the turn of the century.

WO, July 1961

*Upper High Street 1972.
The square **A** and **B**
shows Beechen Grove
remade and snaking past
Beechen Grove and
Clifford Street car parks
to Water Lane and the
High Street. In **B** the
light coloured new build-
ings are of Littlewoods,
Marks and Spencers and
British Home Stores.
Straddling **B** and **E** is
Watford Market and
below, in **E** is the
Beechen Grove car park,
behind the squat Carlton
Cinema and Palace
Theatre. In **H** Clement's
new extension, with a car
park upon the roof, sits
behind the conglomerate
1898 buildings.
In **F** and **I** road works
are taking place as is the
construction of the fly-
over from Upton Road to
the new Beechen Grove.
In the middle of **H** is the
bulk of the Odeon cine-
ma and in **I** is the
newly-built Gade House.
Moving upwards to **C**,
St Mary's Church may
be seen, together with the
new 'Church' car park.*

A	B	C
D	E	F
G	H	I

45   43   41   39   37   55   33   31   29

Clements to go? ... two tower blocks of flats, and shops, suggested ...

Despite the great affection for Clements store it has faced an uphill struggle against the diminishing popularity of the Parade and the lush verdant trees at the corner of Clarendon Road which hide shops and flyover. The quantitive parameter is 'foot traffic' and what foot-traffic there is has been passing from the top end to the town centre and Harlequin.

In face of falling trade Clement's management sought premises in Charter Place, only to find that the necessary basement area (for sales-space) could not be used; the projected move fell through and Alders took the space. In the meantime Westgate moved into Littlewoods old premises adding extra difficulty to Clements' trading.

The photographs of the scale model show the two-storey shopping podium to be as high as the adjacent Parade shops. Above are five storeys of flats; at the rear, abutting the ring road, two blocks of eleven storeys, 155 flats in all, with car parking for about 100 cars underground.

The model, on display during April 2003, was to obtain public opinion before plans go to Council for discussion.

33, 31, 29, 27, 25, 23,	Clements (Watford) Ltd
21	Sainsbury J. Ltd. provn merchants
17	Fuller's Ltd, confectioners. ,
11 & 13	Dorothy Perkins Ltd, ladies' underwear.
9	Barclays Bank Ltd.
7	J H Dewhurst Ltd, butchers
5	Willerby & Co. Ltd, .tailors
3	Mac Fisheries Limited
1	Garners Ltd, bakers.

CLARENDON RD/DUDLEY'S CORNER.

6, 7 & 8 John Collier (Prices Tailors Ltd)

Baptist Church

Green Room

Parade shops

Rigby House

| 29 | 27 | 25 | 23 | 21 | 19 | 17 | 13 |

Top left: *Charter Day 1922 procession, passing Clarendon Road.*

Left centre: *Looking towards the Pond in the early 1950's.*

Left bottom: *Window-gazing at Collier's, 1965.*

Above centre: *Changes in preparation for the ring road system meant extra traffic entering Clarendon Road in a 'race-track' fashion, hence the wary looks. Above right: the youngster would just like to push a button. 1962.*

Bottom: *Sainsbury's were still on the Parade serving from behind counters whilst, across the road in new premises Finefare showed a way forward in self service shopping.*

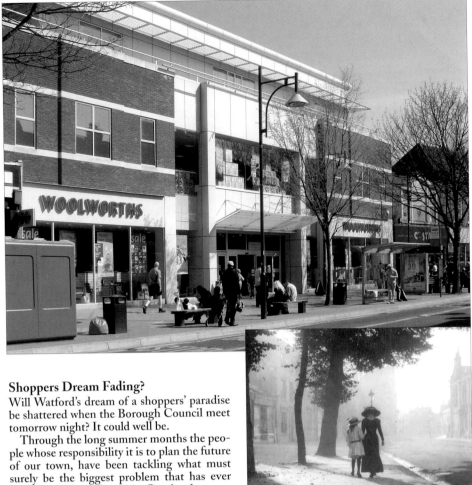

Above: *Following Harlequin Nos. 27-35 remained blighted until the block was rebuilt as a new Woolworth's store.*

Right: *The scene c1900 and, below, a Russian St Petersberg group entertain passers outside Woolworth's in spring 2002.*

Next page top: *The High Street in 1960, and the precinct in March 2003*

Shoppers Dream Fading?

Will Watford's dream of a shoppers' paradise be shattered when the Borough Council meet tomorrow night? It could well be.

Through the long summer months the people whose responsibility it is to plan the future of our town, have been tackling what must surely be the biggest problem that has ever confronted them. It was in October last year the Council first talked of the plans of R. H. O. Hills Ltd., the Blackpool firm, to build what some termed a paradise for shoppers off the Lower High-street. And the members gave an initial blessing to the proposals, providing matters like road improvements, siting of buildings, car parking, loading facilities and the culverting of streams could be ironed out satisfactorily with the developers.

But industry was alarmed. The feeling was that such a huge development would drain too much labour away for staffing purposes. A Ministry of Housing and Local Government Inquiry was called for. But in calling for it, the

DUDLEY'S CORNER

6, 7 & 8	John Collier (Prices Tailors Ltd)
9	Frederick Bateman & Co. Ltd, opticians.

HIGH STREET

29	C. & H. Fabrics Ltd, drapers.
31	William Perrings & Co Ltd, house furnishers
33 & 35	Saxone Shoe Co. Ltd
37	Charles Burt Ltd, house furnishers
39	W H Smith & Son Ltd, booksellers.
4d	James Walker (Goldsmith & Silversmith) Ltd.
41	Mrs N B Irwin, M.Ch.S. chiropodist
41A,	Meakers Ltd. outfitters
41A,	Wmn Jn Smee, dentist
43	Mac Fisheries Ltd, fishmonger.
43 (rear of)	Starling Displays (C. Starling) posters
45	Finlay & Co. Ltd, tobacconists

BUTCHER'S YARD

47	H Page (E. C. & C. E Last, proprs.), chemist.

Dudley's Corner 8   9   High Street: 27   29   31   33   35   37

During much of the 1950's Benskin's still made casks from staves and hoops by the old traditional method; likewise they maintained several drays, though, perhaps, used more for 'ceremonial' purposes.

Borough Council still let it be known that it smiled somewhat benevolently on the scheme.

But further thoughts came to their mind. This shoppers' paradise would have to tie up with the widening of the High-street, and the construction of a new roundabout. Car parking plans would have to be satisfactory. So would the provisions for the delivery of goods.

There was also a new theme, residential accommodation for at least 90 flats.

Talks went on throughout July. Out of them came the formula for a self-contained pedestrian shopping centre on American lines, covering seven-and-a-half acres and giving parking space for about a thousand cars to start with.

But it was also underlined that the Council had a plan of its own for the present central shopping area to be provided with relief roads to enclose it, and car parks for 3,500 cars. This present shopping space in the heart of Watford is increasing steadily to 28 acres.

Then came the million-dollar question. Did the 26 per cent increase in shopping floor space, provided by the proposed new shopping centre, reflect the true additional shopping potential of the area?

Would the potential turnover of the new shopping centre be matched by a comparable increase in the total turnover of the central area by attracting more people to the town?

Would the success of the new shopping centre come at the expense of the present shops to a large extent?

The experts called in, thought it would.

The setting up of a new centre to compete against the old shopping centre must be examined much more critically, they said.

So the experts have recommended that the Borough Council should oppose this proposed paradise for shoppers. As a place apart, although only a couple of hundred yards, from the present shopping centre, it would weaken, rather than reinforce the present centre.

Say the experts—our interests could be best served by expanding the shopping centre within the proposed relief roads.

And so tomorrow night the Special Town Planning Committee will recommend the Council to have a change of heart, despite the earlier enthusiasm expressed for the plan of R. H. O. Hills, the official view now is that the development would not be in the best interests of the Borough of Watford and should not be allowed.

WHP, September 1961

39   41   41a   43   45   Butcher's Yard 47

Left: Emma Oliver's evocative impression of a market day in 1866 would seem to owe much to Frederick Downer's capturing of the 1863 procession of schoolchildren photographed in the High Road (as then known) and the Market Place.

Top left: Meeting Alley corner, 1863; above centre: the cottages have been rebuilt and occupied by Freeman Hardy & Willis, and Child's, florists and above right Child's has given way to Salmon's (later Mence Smith's), later 'Burger King'. Below: Nos. 47 to 51 c1960

Next page: left hand column; top, 1863; centre: The Essex Arms c1922 before being demolished for rebuilding as a smaller Cawdell's shop, and Timothy Whites and Taylor's and the Market Arcade, and, bottom, Sheehan's premises at the top end of Red Lion Yard near Derby Road.

47	H Page (E. C. & C. E Last, proprs.), chemist.
49	A B Hemmings Ltd, bakers
51	Polyfoto (England) Ltd, photographers
51 (above)	Conways, tailors
51 (rear of)	Luca & Sons, fried fish shop
55	Freeman Hardy & Willis Ltd. boot mkrs
57	J Salmon & Son Ltd. grocers
MEETING ALLEY	
59	Government Surplus Stores
61a,	National Savings Committee (Watford District)
61	Findlater Mackie Todd & Co Ltd, Wine & Spirits
61	R Morris Leathercraft (Watford) Ltd, handbag mfrs.
61	Maypole Dairy Co. Ltd
63 & 65	Lloyds Bank Ltd
67	Cawdell James & .Co. Ltd. drapers
59	Timothy Whites, chemists
MARKET ARCADE	

Throughout the 'horse' era Sheehan's were the town centre stop for refixing, mending, making and fitting horse shoes, all custom sized and forged.

top right: Rogers' shop, Bucks & Oxon Bank, then alongside a yard entrance (signed Bull Head), shop, then the Essex Arms, c1880.

below: a long-lens view looking across the market place towards Clarendon Road where the wooded aspect is of Dr Brett's Watford House. c1880.

| 47 | 49 | 51 | 55 | 57 | Meeting Alley | 61 |

63   65   67   69   (Essex Arms)   Market Arcade

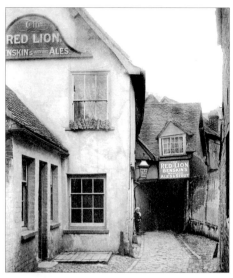

Next page: *The 'old' central Watford of 1962. In the bottom right of* **A** *Woodlands Parade block of shops is built, and the Odeon is by the Pond. The dark hulk at top of* **E** *is the Gaumont and top right of* **E** *a pair of new office blocks in Clarendon Road, In the centre of* **C**, *also Clarendon Road, is the high Melton House.*

At the top right of **D** *the empty space follows the demolition of the Fire Station while in the centre of* **D** *is the Post Office Telephone Exchange. Marlborough Road is at the bottom left of the square.*

At the lower centre of **E** *are the new-looking shops near the corner of Clarendon Road which house Perrings and Dolcis.*

In square **H** *Cawdells may be seen just above right centre and on the other side of the High Street the white wall of Fishers, Butchers. The small curve of narrow road is New Street and at this date, just above the parked cars, is three-storey house of the 1800s behind which is Fisher's slaughter house. Just above St Mary's Church, at the bottom, is the 'One Bell,' with public conveniences adjoining.*

At the bottom left corner of **G** *is the Salvation Army Citadel. In* **I** *Henry Kinghams store has gone and is due to be rebuilt as a BHS store.*

In the top corner of **I** *may be seen eight rows of roofs of the Market of which Red Lion Passage runs between and Kingham's.*

In the bottom left quarter of **F** *is Beechen Grove Car Park and entrance to which runs from Clarendon Road alongside the Baptist Church. Straddling* **F & I** *to the right of centre is Beechen Grove School of which the playground is visible. Above is the corner Sutton Road of which the white corner house is of Grillo's Ice Cream fame. Between Sutton and Estcourt Road next up, and the Beechen Grove Car Park, is 'triangle' of road once the site of the 'Circus' shown on p156.*

A	B	C
D	E	F
G	H	I

71, 71a   James Cawdell & Co Ltd
       ENTRANCE TO WATFORD MARKET

73   Midland Bank Ltd
75   Lennards Ltd, boot & shoe dirs
77 & 79 Isaac Walton Isaac & Co Ltd, outfitters
77 & 79 Sun Life Assuarance Society
77 & 79 Pearl Assurance Co Ltd.
77 & 79 Offices

       RED LION PASSAGE

83 & 85 Henry Kingham & Sons Ltd
87   Watford Academy of Dancing
87   Hilton S. & Sons Ltd, boot mkrs
89   Weaver to Wearer Ltd, tailors
91 & 93 Marks & Spencer Ltd, Dept. Store.

Left: *1890s entrance to Red Lion Yard (later a much frequented entrance to Watford Market).*
Top left: *The Red Lion.*
Top right: *Cawdell's, with a Market entrance between the store and Midland Bank.* above: *Henry Kingham's store with the arched entrance to the Market on its left. The modern vestige is alongside BHS, below.*

85   87   89   (George Inn)   91   93

Shop-Shape and Watford Fashion

THE good people of Watford are only just beginning to realise how lovingly the eyes of Britain's retailers linger on a town where the men in the main local industry (printing) average £1,275 a year, and the unemployment rate rests at a minimal 0.4 per cent

No sooner did Mr. Leslie Goldberg's R. H. O. Hills group apply for permission to erect a £2 million, 12-acre "Shopper's World" on the old Benskin's Brewery site at what is at present distinctly the wrong end of the High Street, than Mr. Arron Lermon and Mr. Saul Magrill, of Macowards, revealed that they had been negotiating for two years to put up something exactly similar on a seven-acre site right in the town centre.

They already own Cawdells, the rambling store which winds its way across a key half-acre, backed by the local market and a string of Corporation property in fairly urgent need of redevelopment, and they have the full backing of Mr. Walter Flack, the Murrayfield millionaire who now runs the shop side of the Cotton-Clore City-Centre set-up.

While Hills and Macowards growl, two other groups are acting. The Watford Coop, in partnership with the Jacobson brothers' fast-moving Montague Burton chain, are spending £500,000 in the New Year to put a store on the old fire station site, and Clements, a local business, are spending another £500,000 to double their present size.

The only trouble is, Watford is already one colossal traffic jam during shopping hours. So what happens when it becomes the most heavily-shopped high street in the country?

Sunday Times, November 1962

Expansion Plans for Watford Stores

On the heels of the £2 million "Shoppers' World" project for Lower High-street comes news this week of other big developments planned for Watford's central shopping area.

Clements and the Watford and Harrow Cooperative Society each have £2 million schemes, and Montague Burton Ltd. and Cawdells also plan to expand, although in Cawdells' case planning permission has not yet been sought.

The Co-op and Montague Burton Ltd. are jointly to develop the ex-fire station site in the High-street. They have offered the site free to the Corporation as a car park until Christmas shopping is over.

Director Mr. H. V. Hornsby, giving evidence at the "Shoppers' World" inquiry on Friday, said the project would start "in the next few weeks."

The first stage, he said, would add 40,000 square feet of floor space and parking for 110 cars. There would be roof as well as ground level parking space. The second stage would increase floor space by another 10,000 square feet.

WO, November 1961

see site pic, p370

91 & 93	Marks & Spencer Ltd, Dept. Store.	
95	John Lovibond & Sons Ltd.	
95	Pitty Frank W	
97	Geo Lewis Ltd, tailors	
99	Freeman Hardy & Willis Ltd, boot makers.	
LOATES LANE		
101	C H Peacock Ltd, Watford Observer & printers	
103	Waterman G. & J. Ltd, bldrs	
103	Jax Stores Ltd, hosiers	
105	D B Selgrove Ltd, jewellers	
107/107a,	True-Form Boot Co. Ltd.	

| 93 | 95 | 97 | 99 | Loates Lane | 101 |

atford's first recording medium, though not then seen as such, was the Parish Register, started in 1539. Dates of births, marriages and deaths were sometimes interspersed with details of the lives and times of the parishioners, and as such were much trawled over by earlier writers, notably Henry Williams c1880 and W R Saunders c1919-20 (their valuable extracts time and time again re-used!). Both used their researches in published histories of which the latter's 'History of Watford' (1931) was the most informative. The Registers are now in the care of Hertford's Record Office.

The 'Watford Observer' was started in 1863, in Queen Street; the 'Watford and West Herts Post' at 42 High Street in 1887, taking over in 1919 the 'Watford Newsletter' (1908 to 1919) printed in King Street. Mr C H Peacock acquired in 1896 the 'Herts Leader' and shop at the corner of Loates Lane where the 'Observer was henceforth to be printed. The 'West Herts Post' was first printed at 42 High Street, then in Carey Place, then from offices near the Pond, at Luton.

Thomson's Regional Newspapers introduced the 'Evening Echo' in 1967 and the introduction led to the closing of the 'Post' in May 1970 — at about the time the Park Gates went — so thus Watford lost two favoured landmarks. The 'Evening Echo' lasted until 1983 when it, too, folded.

Subsequently Watford was covered by the 'Review', a St Albans-based free-sheet. In later years the 'Watford Observer' and C H Peacock Ltd were absorbed into Westminster Press who in turn were absorbed into the Newsquest Media Group and who in 1999 further absorbed the 'Review'.

The 'West Herts Post' had been much appreciated, it being the first to employ its own photographers and use photographs extensively; it had a 'common-touch' which sometimes better gauged the feelings of its readers. It championed the causes of the 'common man' more loudly than did the 'Observer', but made a big mistake when, in the late twenties, it saw no need for the Public Baths (in Hempstead Road).

During the postwar years of development plans it joined with the 'Observer' on matters of importance and thus presented to the Council a united front which was hard to ignore. Now, for the first time in 112 years, Watford has only one newspaper albeit offering locally one paid and one free version, the 'Observer', and the 'Free Observer'. The 'Observer' is American owned being part of the Warner-AOL Group.

Above: *The 'Observer' newspaper office, 101 High Street, corner of Loates Lane, was centrally sited to observe and report the local news and, at its side, the original printing business to execute private and business printing needs. The news and gossip photographs on display were always much admired. Occupied by C H Peacock Ltd since about 1897 these shops, in 1960, are in their last months before being demolished in 1961.*

103   103   105   107, 107a

109, 111	Littlewoods Ltd, departmental stores
	QUEENS ROAD
115 & 117	Boots The Chemists
119/121	Woodhouse Ltd.
123	Shirley's, childrens' outfitters
125/127	Fantos Ltd, departmental store.
	ALBERT ST
129	S Grey & Co. Ltd, radio dealers

Above: Sunday 31st May 1992, just over four years since work on the Harlequin Centre started this Baldwin's 90m-(295ft)-high mobile crane is lifting out scaffolding and shuttering from the centre of the Phase 3 site. The NatWest Bank building was not to survive for long.

Left, top: Passing the Eight Bells, 1914.

Left, below, queueing for money, 1986

(Eight Bells) 109   111   113   Queens Road   115,   117

Above: *The domed building on the corner of Queens Road and High Street was built in 1914 for Watford's branch of Boots, here in occupancy of Ketts after Boots moved to new premises on the corner of Market Street. This is 1986; to the store's left can be seen the older houses/shops of Queens Road in their final years before Harlequin.*

Right: *The Crystal Palace beerhouse, 121 High St, c1898. The archway on the right is Court 11, Holts Yard.*

| 119 | 121 | 123 | 125 | 127 | Albert Street | 129 |

Above: *Shows Nos. 135 High Street, Carey Place entrance, 137, 139, 141 (Christmas' works). The tall building with dormer windows, No. 147, is shown on the right as Bratt Bros and is, from the opening of Harlequin, Boots' store and entrance to the Harlequin Centre. The photograph shows part of the reconstruction of the road in 1923; and the lower right shows the derelict remains of Christmas' coachbuilding era.*

The scene in 1960.

129	S Grey & Co. Ltd, radio dealers
131	Wm Riley, ladies' outfitters
133	Tucker & Co. (Tobacconists) Ltd
135	Keith Royle & Co. Ltd carpet dlrs.
	CAREY PLACE
137	Crown Wallpapers Ltd, wallpaper mfrs
139	Rossi's (London) Ltd. ice cream mfrs
141	F Meyers Ltd, fruiterers
143 & 145	Mac Fisheries Ltd, fishmngrs
147	Bratt Bros. Ltd, outfitters
147a	Dental Repairs & Laboratory
149	J S North, watchmaker
151	Lavell's Ltd, confctnrs
151a	Maxwells (Hosiers) Ltd
153 &155	G Gibson & Sons, pork butchers
157, 159	
	WATER LANE

Next page: *High Street/Carey Place, 1956*
A. New Road, Watford Motor Co Works, Benskins Brewery, (was Sedgwicks)
B & C. Benskins Watford Brewery
C. Extreme right, Watford Field School
D. Top right, the Labour Exchange
E. Water Lane; below, the Carey Place Works
F. Shops and houses remaining in 2003; include the Barclays Bank building at the corner of King Street
G. The road is Carey Place with Charles Street off to the left; above Charles Street is Clifford Street with Herbert Street leading into Water Lane
I. Queens Road, with Boot's on the corner and the Technical School complex backing from Queens Road into Albert Street behind. The cleared site abutting the High Street is of demolished Eight Bells, and Littlewood's store building.

| 129 | 131 | 133 | Carey Place | 137 | 139 | 141 | 143 | 145 |

A	B	C
D	E	F
G	H	I

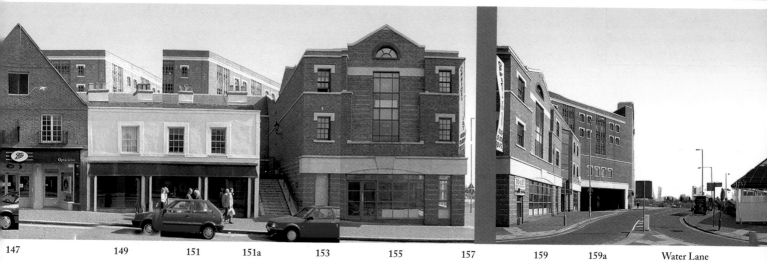

147   149   151   151a   153   155   157   159   159a   Water Lane

Carey Place . . .

The furore about preserving as much as possible of Watford's few remaining old buildings was justified as a study of the reworked fronts as photographs on pages 317, 318 and 319 show. When the Harlequin work commenced the old building's interiors and rears were stripped away and only the fronts remained to be carefully preserved and integrated into the new modern structures. There is now also a vestigial 'Carey Place' which acts as an emergency exit from Harlequin into the High Street.

Carey Place was a narrow road which ran from the High Street, from between numbers 135 and 137, to Derby Road at a point almost opposite Grosvenor Road. It was so named by a Mr. Carey who, it is stated, came to Watford to work as a plasterer on the old Beechen Grove Chapel. The road was unusual in that the numbering was consecutive rather than odd one side and even the other. The building above, was built for the West Herts Post in 1919/20; prior to that the site had an interesting history.

In the early 1800's the Petty Sessions were held in a room at the old Essex Arms Hotel in the High Street; then, for some years, both the Petty Sessions and County Court were held in the Carey Place building (which would later house the West Herts Post) until the Court in King Street was built (c1854).

After the Court was removed the building housed for sixteen years the Literary Institute, a substantial centre of educational influ-

ence, but which was outgrowing the premises. In 1871 Mr. Stephen Camp broached the subject of establishing a Public Library and Reading Room with the result that Mr. Thomas Clutterbuck presented land in Queens Road, and public subscriptions of £3000 enabled the building to be erected, and opened in October 1874.

The then disused Carey Place premises became, firstly, a Primitive Methodist Chapel around 1884 (Minister Rev. W Holland) and then headquarters for the Salvation Army before they moved to their new Citadel in St. St. Mary's Road.

Before the building, once Police Court, School, Library, and Chapel, was finally demolished it was last used by Messrs. Christmas & Co. for their coach-building business.

Meanwhile, the (West Herts) Post had been published from 42 High Street; and moved into the new building and started publishing from it in 1920. It continued as such until the Post moved to Luton.

Subsequently a number of printers including Hills & Lacey; Hudson & Stracey; Charles Straker and Wetherby were housed in the premises, and in the nearby locality.

Above: The earlier premises of the printing and publishing works of the West Herts Post. The Carey Place connurbation may be seen in better detail on page 321.

161, 163, 165 & 165a,	Percy J Wilson Ltd, drapers
167 & 167a,	Davant Ltd, house furnishers
167f,	Barringtons (Tailors) Ltd
169	Value Victor & Co Ltd, grocers
171	Reid Fleming & Co Ltd, hosiery stores
173	Bailey F. D. Ltd, radio dlrs
173a,	C W Swan, furrier
175	L A Leon Ltd, costumiers
177	Albert Morley Ltd, tailors
179	Domestic Electric Rentals Ltd.
179	Morley's (Watford), outfitters
179	Watford Tote Co. turf commission agts
179	Dr Scholl's Foot Comfort Service
179a,	Achille Sierre Ltd. dyers & cleaners
179b & 179c,	Anslow & Painter, cafe
179d,	Pet's Pantry, pet stores
179e,	Foster, Porter & Co. Ltd, who. clothiers
179h,	Bedford Refrigeration Co. Ltd
181	Miss Winifred Tunwell, ladies hairdresser.
181	The County Window Cleaning and Steam Carpet Beating Co
NEW ROAD	
183	J B Nunn, photographic dlrs
185	Vacant

161 163 165 165a   167 167a 167f 169   171   173a 175 177

Above: *A tale of progress, these intending revellers are making their way up the High Street to particpate in the Queen Victoria Jubilee Celebrations in June 1887. On the left side of the road the wall is of the bridge over the single track railway line to Rickmansworth.*

The three-storey house just beyond shows no sign of commercial activity but by 1893 the building is shop of Mr Oatley's to which his mens' outfitters business has expanded.

By about 1907 his shop has blossomed, right, complete with resplendant electric lighting, but was destined for a short life for the building being demolished in 1911/12 for twin track rail working. *The archway to the right of Mr Oatley's shop became New Road. In due course shops were built upon the bridge, below right. New Road was home to several businesses and, at one time, an abbatoir.*

The Bridge shops served well until their space was required for the ring road.

New Road is now a footpath to stores between the High Street and Tesco's and a roadway from a little further south acts as a service road. On the corner of Water Lane Wilson's drapery premises, long empty, were then occupied as Hammond's Music Centre, eventually being replaced by the Pyramid.

Top: 1893 (p95); above: c1907 (p119).
Below, left: 1986; right: Shops on the railway bridge, 1958.

179   179a   179b   179c   179d   181   New Road   183   185

Watford Example

"WATFORD stands out as an example to other towns." These words were spoken by Mr. Timothy Rootes, a member of the famous Rootes family who have built up a nationwide organisation in the motor car trade, so his praise is worthy of respect.

He was addressing a large audience at the opening of the new £50,000 showrooms built by Watford Motor Co. in the High-street and stated that figures proved our town to be one of the most wealthy areas in Great Britain.

The company opened in Lamb Yard, its present site, in July, 1921. And now it is one of the biggest motor engineering firms in the whole county. The staff is 40-strong and facilities are available for body-building, for painting and for welding, together with machine shops for any comprehensive work.

WHP, July 1957

Imperial Way

Imperial Way is extended by a new road called Colonial Way to Radlett Road and most of the 16 sites have been taken. Among them are Messrs. Keens, Dennison Manufacturing, I. Walls & Sons, British American Optical and McKay Transport. Five sites are vacant.

WHP, November 1961

Above: *Taken from the highest vantage point of Benskin's this shows, in the centre, the rear of Benskin House, currently Watford Museum. Beyond Benskin House, on the far side of the High Street is the distinctive form of the Three Tuns P H.*

At its left hand side is the entrance to the Watford Motor Co premises with the showroom on the left of the driveway.

Directly beyond the Three Tuns is the workshop building of Watford Motor Co, and to its right, the ramp leading to an upper service area.

The Bridge shops have been demolished (a hoarding can be seen on the corner of New Road to mask the corner). Nos. 183, 185 and 189 are empty. Weston's may still be trading as may Wren's and Stapleton's. Nos 209 onwards have all been cleared and landscaped with grassed area and hoardings marking their passing.

All the far High Street buildings were cleared by mid 1980 in preparation for a further phase of the road works.

187	Mrs W J Mailey, statnr. & post office
	CHAPMAN'S YARD
189	Westons (Watford) Ltd fried fish restuarant
191	S Murray, tailor
193	H A Swann (Watford) Ltd.. leather mchnts
193	Swann Denis
195	Stapleton's Tyre Services Ltd, motor tyre fctrs
195a	L Froud, coach repr
	WOODMAN'S YARD
197	London Drapery Stores
199	Gestetner Ltd. dupilcatling machine mkrs
201 & 203	The Watford Motor Co, Rootes dlrs
205	Three Tuns P.H
207	A T James & Sons, accntnts
209	Mrs Enid Wilshere, wardrobe dlrs
211	Jn Reginald French, confectioner

187   Chapman's yard   189 (Westons)   191   193   195   Woodman's Yard

Above: *The Three Tuns P H. To its left is the show-room of the Watford Motor Co Ltd (interior shown right) a subsidiary of Benskin's Brewery. The Watford Motor Co held the agencies of the Rootes Group of Sunbeam, Humber and Hillman.*

Top: *Weston's, No. 189 and Nos. 207, 209, 211*

197   199   201   203 (Watford Motor Co)   205 (Three Tuns P H/Yard) 207   209   211

New £380,000 College on Stilts

THE new South-West Herts College of Further Education has been designed as a college on stilts. This is because the £380,000 college is to be built on a four-acre site in Water-lane, Watford, where danger from flooding from the nearby Hillfield Brook has to be considered. In 1947 the site was flooded to a depth of four feet, and in 1960 it was also flooded to a lesser extent.

The centre block will be raised on stilts which will be both a safeguard against flood danger and also give under-cover parking space.

The architects of the County Architect's Department, under Mr. G. C. Fardell, who have designed the college, have based their space allowance for parking on the needs which have had to be met at Watford Technical College, where parking has presented a considerable problem. They have provided parking space for 176 cars and 100 motor-cycles.

The college, which will house 1,040 students in the first instalment, will have work-shops, science laboratories, 19 classrooms, a library, drawing offices, a dining room, kitchen, gymnasium and hall. It will have oil-fired central heating.

It is expected to be built by 1965.

WHP, January 1962

211a,	Jacob Frank, dining rms
213	Thos Doggett
215	Mrs Grace Martin, confectioner
217	D A Leefarr, radio dlr
219	Bramwell's Cycle & Motor Co. Ltd
221	Delroy Perfumery Co Ltd
221	Arnold Franklyn Ltd, mnfg chemists.
223	D Brum & Sons Ltd, tailors
225	J M Wren, saddler & lthr gds
227	Mrs M Blackwell
229	Douglas Shaw
229a,	British Cushion Supply Co. Ltd.
281	Hy A Williams
281	Dumbelton's (Hy. A. Williams), butchers
233	H & B Precision Engineers Ltd
public footpath to Water Lane	
235	Leather Sellers' Arms P.H
237	A E & D M Perry, antiques
237	W Edward Edwd
237a,	E Crane, refreshment rooms

High Street c 1956. Nos. 211 to 217

| 211a | 213 | 215 | 217 (Leefarr) | 217a | 219 (Branwell's) | 219a | 221(Delroy Perfumery) |

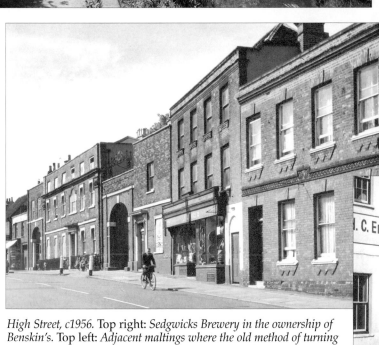

High Street, c1956. **Top right:** *Sedgwicks Brewery in the ownership of Benskin's.* **Top left:** *Adjacent maltings where the old method of turning barley into malt was by continuous heat from underfloor heating, a method which ceased when Benskin's was taken over by Ind Coope.*

Above: *Nos. 223 to 229.* **Right:** *Nos. 231 to the Mill site.*

Inset: *Dumbelton's c1900, p93.*

223   225 (Wren, Saddler)   227/229 (House)   231 (Dumbelton's)   233   path to Water Lane 235 Leatherseller's Arms)   237   237a

237	A E & D M Perry, antiques
237	W Edward Edwd
237a,	E Crane, refreshment rms
239 to 241	B G England (Watford Motor Cycle & Spares Service Ltd.),
	Devon Filling Station, petrol station
249	Elwin Matthews
251	Co-operative Funeral Furnishers Ltd
253	George Ausden, scrap iron mchnts

Top: *The Mill, from activity to dereliction and when, as a wasteland site it became a tidy used car lot.*

Above: *Perry's Antique shop was one-time home of Jimmy Perry of Dad's Army fame, the area a source of many sketches.* See p418.

Above: Glenne Motors and Devon Filling Station 1985

237   241 (Watford Mill)   Devon Filling Station   249

MARS shopping centre . . . a first-class hotel and ten-pin bowling alley . . .

MARS!

THE face of Central Watford will change drastically during the next five to seven years. By that time it is hoped that the Borough will have become the Croydon of North London.

Situated as it is on the perimeter of the Greater London Council it has a great potential. Planners have seen this potential.

First there is the Shoppers' World on which a public inquiry has just ended. This £2,000,000 scheme will result in the redevelopment of Lower High-street. Now comes the redevelopment of the area between Queens-road and Water-lane, extending back to the Eastern Relief road. This is a £3,000,000 scheme the Watford Borough Council will discuss at the February meeting.

Featured in the possibilities of the new scheme is a first-class hotel with assemby rooms behind. On the other side, under a six- or seven-storey car park, a ten-pin bowling alley is planned.

Another feature will be a pedestrian precinct from High-street near the corner of Water-lane.

The scheme, aptly called "The Mars Scheme," is being sponsored by Cubitt London Properties, Ltd. The architects are H. G. Huckle and partners. It will mean the redevelopment of nearly 8 acres extending along Queens-road to the Eastern Relief road and will include Albert-street and Carey-place, both of which will vanish completely.

The area, if the redevelopment goes forward, will be dominated by an 11-storey central tower block of 130 flats with garages for the tenants underneath the block

For the shoppers there will be a multi-storey car park. Access will be by the Eastern Relief road to the car park, from where the people will enter the pedestrian precinct to visit the shops.

There will be a rear service access to all the shops. Another feature will be the provision of overhead walkways. Cubitts also have in mind a ten-pin bowling alley for the scheme under the multi-storey car park, which will accommodate at the start 600 cars.

The Company already own a considerable number of properties in Queens-road and are actively negotiating for others in Queens-road, fronting, and in the rear of High-street

They have suggested that their holdings and the Corporation's holdings should be merged and the whole area redeveloped comprehensively.

The first phase, it is suggested, should take into account the pattern of acquisitions and take in the construction of the multi-storey car park and the Queens-road shops from Derby-road to, but not including, the College of Further Education.

It is also suggested that the Borough Council could to some extent control the development, as Cubitts would be willing to sell their freeholds to the Corporation subject to them being given a long lease at a ground rent calculated on an agreed percentage of the total cost to the Corporation of the purchase of their interests and the Corporation's interests.

The Company also proposes that such ground rent should be reviewed every 25 years. One of the suggestions is that the Company should build the multi-storey car park and sub-lease it to the Corporation, who would thus have absolute control of parking,

The surveyors, Rogers, Chapman and Thomas, have asked the Borough Council whether the scheme would be acceptable in principle, and have intimated they would be prepared to appear before the appropriate committee for further discussion.

The Borough Council have sought the views of the Corporation's consultants, Hillier, Parker, May and Rowden, and it is these views that the Property Committee will consider and pass on to the Borough Council for the February meeting.

WHP, January 1962

'Skyscraper' Staff Move In

"MELTON HOUSE"—the new Clarendon-road "skyscraper" office block—is now partially occupied.

Three hundred members of the staff of the Revenue Section of the Accountants' Department, British Railways, last weekend vacated the seven huts they have occupied at The Grove since 1939 and moved into the first five floors of this nine-storey building. Standing 92ft. high, "Melton House" is now the tallest building in Watford. The title was originally held by the British Moulded Hose factory (84ft) followed by the telephone exchange (75ft).

Other departments of British Railways are to occupy the remainder of the building, and it is expected that all will be in occupation by June.

They are: District Engineers (from St. Pancras), Superannuation Funds Office, and a small section of the Welfare Department.

In charge of the 300 already installed is Mr. I. Carr (Revenue Accountant), who said this week "After the old life-expired huts where we had to put on hats and coats to visit the next department, this is a very acceptable change. It is wonderful to be able to move around in complete comfort and in such clean surroundings."

WO, February 1962

Fine New School For Holywell

The huge Victoria Secondary Modern School in Tolpits-lane is nearing completion. It sprawls over several acres on a site opposite Scammell Lorries' factory, and is a necessary corollary to the Holywell Industrial Estate.

WHP, April 1962

• *(later Westfield Girls' School)*

Watford Cine Society

Formation of a cine society was mooted during early 1958 and a preliminary meeting was held on July 8th, 1958. Founder members were Roger Moon, Alan Campbell, Roger Nicholls and Bob Nunn. Alan Campbell was declared first Chairman and the first meeting was held

251   253

253   George Ausden, scrap iron mchnts

FROGMORE HOUSE.

on Monday September 1st and thereafter fortnightly on Mondays. This pattern continued during the winter of 1958/59 and weekly meetings started in September 1959—the meeting places moving from the Free School Hall to 14a High Street (whichis now the site of Gade House).

At an early date public shows were aimed at to bolster funds. The first show, in 1958, was at St Mary's Church Hall of a 'Ten Best' show. Ices were served in the interval! 16mm projectors used were Bell & Howell and Debrie.

From this it was decided to make up a mixed programme and so the first Film Festival was held at the Town Hall on 19th November 1959.

This included two Society productions, both on 16mm with striped sound. Unfortunately the hired arc projector could not cope with the edge stripe and sound 'wild' tape was run—the sync. being not too bad. The 2nd Festival was again a mixed programme with one Society 16mm film included. At the 3rd Festival the 1959 'Ten Best' programme was shown together with the innovation of telling the audience that at the end of the show a special short 8mm show would be shown at the side of the hall as an 'experiment'.

This was successful—the picture quality was good (Eumig with 6ft screen), and in fact better than the 16mm films because of the trouble with the borrowed projector. The 'home made' 8mm films were voted better entertainment than the 16mm 'Ten Best'!

So the decision was made. All future public shows would be of the members' own work and the first all-8mm show was in 1962. Eumig projectors have been used at each showing and the screen size is now 8ft.

In the meantime the Society's meeting places have included the 'King's Head' (now demolished); the 'Green Man'; 'Hertfordshire Arms'; and the British Legion Hall, Croxley Green (never to be forgotten by those who attended during the bitter winter!)

JBN, Cine Society History

Left: *In 1893 the Angel P H (No. 253) was still in business as such, until 1903. The house beyond is Grove Place.*

Top left: *The Angel looks serene in retirement, before being demolished, c1910.*

Top right: *Lower High Street, between Ausden's and Frogmore House. 1986*

253

Watford Gas Works (Eastern Gas Services depot)

The changes start . . . 'D-Day' is May 20th, 1962

The access roads of King Street, Queens Road, Market Street, Upton Road and Clarendon Road were all so narrow that a queue of just a few cars at each junction created a 'jam'. When added to the 'through' traffic which used the High Street — cars, buses, lorries, and the delivery vehicles stopped outside shops and stores, the result was chaos.

The plan announced in 1959 suggested blocking up the High Street and introducing a simple one-way ring-road. During the early part of Spring 1962 an apparently endless number of new traffic signs were erected and covered until the great day. The Sunday dawned fine and teams of workmen were busy painting new road direction signs, uncovering the new and removing some of the old. Traffic lights had to be altered. It was not long before the change had been made, and the local residents who had been up and about watching with great interest now had the sight of bewildered motorists finding that they could no longer travel their accustomed routes.

For example, it was no longer possible to travel from King Street across the High Street to Queens Road; King Street was now one-way leading *from* the High Street. Good humoured patience was much in evidence and by the end of the day the system was established.

As a temporary measure the Plan succeeded in easing some High Street traffic flow, although bus passengers had to learn new stops and there were unexpected problems at the Clarendon Road crossing, and between there and Upton Road. Lower High Street and the Parade/Pond stretch were little changed.

In the meantime through traffic did not have to face the congested stretch of road between Market Place and Water Lane. The High Street, Watford's backbone from time immemorial, had been broken at Market Street and Clarendon Road corner.

Forty-one years later and the town has an elected Mayor, whose task it is to sort out problems. One such which stares her in the face in 2003 is that of the ring road. It is fast, it jams easily, it is wasteful of time, fuel and energy. Is there a solution?

The High Street this day blocked at the corner of Market Street. 20/5/62.

Frogmore House

Eastern Gas Services depot

Frogmore Cottages, 1 to 4

Previous page: *In the top left corner of E are the High St houses and shops on the corners of Bridge Place. Those few places in normal dark tone remain. That greyed out is no more. Across A and B is the erstwhile garage of the bus companies. To the right in B Monaco Garage and behind Gazelda Works. Top left of D the Ever-Ready Works and top left of D the Watford Engineering Works.*

This page: *That greyed out is no more. Water Lane houses, High Street Station, the Museum (here, of course, Benskins), the few cottages in Watford Fields and Local Board Road, the Pump House complex and, in each picture, Ausden's premises, still remain. Straddling E and H is the George Stephenson College, on stilts, while at the top left of B Crosfield Business Machines works has not long been built.*

A	B	C
D	E	F
G	H	I

Eastern Gas Services depot
        Frogmore Cottages.
1
2
3
4

289   Bedford Products & Light Engineering Co. Ltd.
289   Eta Instruments Ltd.
291   Hy H Butterfield Ltd, mfng. chemists
293a Jn Laws F.R.H.S., seedsman
293b & 298c, Thirteens Cycle Depot (McIntosh & Worboys)

289   291   293 293a   293b

The 20-year plan revealed; link road to West Watford, eight phases . . .

Fluoride Opponents Still 'Anti'

SINCE fluorides have been added to Watford's water supply, the number of three-year-old children completely free from tooth decay has barely doubled. But despite the encouraging statistics revealed this week in the Ministry report on fluoridation studies in the United Kingdom, opponents of fluoridation remain unmoved.

Schoolmaster Mr. H. B. Foxwell, of St. Albans road, Watford, who led the local attack against the experiment, still collects all his water from outside the borough. And he says he will continue to do so. After reading the findings, he said this week:

"This is just what we expected. There probably is some apparent benefit, but it does cause mottling, and the benefit may be of short duration. Of the medical reports of no harmful effects, Mr. Foxwell said: "We know people who have made complaints to the Town Hall about stomach trouble following fluoridation, but these have been brushed aside.

"In one family I call on, three generations were affected. These things build up in our systems. Some people develop mysterious diseases, but we can never really put it down to fluoride. I am inclined to think something makes the 'soil' suitable for reception of the germs."

Mr. Foxwell said it was now believed that toothpaste with fluoride added was proving equally beneficial. This being so, fluoridation of the water was no longer necessary, and the actual "intake" could be reduced, he said.

As regards the statistics he declared: "They talk about a 50 per cent improvement at the age of five. I believe the average at that age was two decayed teeth per child, so for the sake of one tooth, they are taking away everyone's liberty to enjoy pure water." The average number of decayed, missing and filled teeth was 66 per cent less at the age of three years, 57 per cent less at four years and 50 per cent less at five years.

WHP, July 1962

293b & 298c, Thirteens Cycle Depot (McIntosh & Worboys)
Eastern Gas Board (works)
315   Jas Wm Shearman, Watford Gas Works
Social &   Sports Club

Shirley House College Plans

WORK on providing the new College of Further Education, proposed for the controversial Shirley House site in Watford, has been suspended—because of an unexpected legal complication dating back nearly 100 years.

Discovery of the snag has forced Herts County Council to send out some 300 registered letters to local residents asking if they would object to the lifting of the ban that this ancient covenant imposes on the erection of certain types of buildings on the site.

The covenant was signed in 1865.

It forbids the building of a public house, inn, beer shop or other shop or for any purpose of sale trade, manufacture or business or public establishment of for any purposes whatsoever which may in anywise be a nuisance to the neighbourhood or to the owner or occupier of any land adjacent without the previous consent of the owners, their heirs or assigns.

WO, October 1963

Graves Dug Up

HIDDEN from view by high screens, men are at work exhuming the remains of Baptist worthies who were buried in Beechen Grove Churchyard, Watford, over 200 years ago.

The screens were put up following complaints that the macabre work could be seen by people on the upper deck of buses in Beechen Grove. Mr. Bernard Cunningham, from St. Albans, said he and his men might find some gold rings or bracelets.

"There are 15 graves marked by stones, but there are also a lot unmarked. Some will be six feet deep, some 10 feet," he said. The oldest

grave dated from 1721, he said, the last was dated 1861.

The removal of the remains and grave stones is being done by the Corporation to provide an addition to Beechen grove car park in time for the Christmas shopping rush. The Council bought the old Schoolroom and adjoining burial ground for about £17,000 early this year and promoted an Act of Parliament for permission to remove the graves.

The Rev. Irwin Barnes, Minister of Beechen Grove Baptist Church said it had not yet been decided what to do about the headstones, some of which are now undecipherable.

The graveyard was the original burial ground for Baptist dissenters in Watford, but there have been no burials there for over 100 years now.

WHP, October 1963

Top: *Scammell's 'Contractor' range was introduced in 1964 and comprised seven models including recovery, heavy haulage and road train (162.5 tonnes). The previous 'Highwayman' range comprised GVW's of 24-52 tons.*

293b   293c

The Central Area Draft Plan, 1964 . . .

Following the 1956 Central Area draft plan, minor road improvements were carried out and in the meantime Hertfordshire County Council and Watford Borough Council had held 'informal' discussions on the shape the town should take. A new draft plan was published.

With the assistance of Chartered Surveyors and Estate Agents, Messrs. Hillier; Parker, May and Rowden, detailed analysis of shopping space and useage was made. Plans were made to turn Clarendon Road into an 'office' centre to save Watford residents travelling to London. (It also had the effect of attracting outside workers into the area.) Plans were similarly made for designation of factory and industrial areas.

Labelled a 'Draft Plan' this informal document carried detailed suggestions for a completely new system of roads, including a simple one-way ring road to provide access to the centre; an Eastern relief road; improvements to St. Albans Road and Rickmansworth Road which included a 'flyover' at a new junction at Weymouth Street; an underpass at Cassio Road; a major junction system to link with the Ml, a new road linking the southern end of the High Street with West Watford; and the eventual closing of the greater part of the High Street to vehicular traffic.

And at a later date the traffic flow was to be reversed in the system.

Regarding traffic density, the 1956 premise of a 75% increase in 20 years was reached within 8 years. The forecast was amended to 150% increase by 1980, i.e. 2½ times the 1959 level. The report commented that increase in vehicle usage 'will not cease at 1980 but will continue until a saturation point is reached in the year 2010.'

A number of shopping-site proposals were noted.

The 'Central Car Park site' took place and became known as Charter Place. The site bounded by High Street, Queens Road and the proposed Eastern Relief Road became known as the 'Mars' site. Arising from these various proposals was the question of whether the demand would be sufficient for the extra sales space created; and whether staff would be available, as, in the meantime, a number of established stores had already car-

ried out substantial extensions. Among the comments on the 'office survey' was noted the danger of 'reverse commuting' into Watford if the building of office blocks was not curtailed; and that those people who did so would eventually want to live in Watford.

The proposals put forward were designed to meet traffic requirements in 1980 and would have in general reached a limiting capacity and; to use the phraseology of the Buchanan Report; 'it is expected that the town centre will have reached its limit of accessibility'.

At the end of the Draft Report were listed the various phases for carrying out the works:

Phase 1 included Shrubberies car park. Charter Place, St. Mary's car park, and redevelopment of Queens Road for shopping.

Phase 2 was a new traffic gyratory system (Vicarage Road).

Phase 3, Cassio Road; Town Hall flyover *(changed to underpass)* and first stage of the Eastern relief road.

Phase 4, West Watford Link

Phase 5, completion of Eastern relief road Mars site; and commencement of residential development opposite High Street Station *(not done).*

Phase 6, third section of Eastern relief road to link with Ml connection, and to link with West Watford; redevelopment of Smith Street and Granville Road/King Street *(not done).*

Phase 7, dual carriageway in Clarendon Road between Beechen Grove and St. Johns Road

Phase 8, redevelopment of St. Albans Road/Langley Road; Park/Church Road/Nascot Road/Stamford Road; for residential use with some neighbourhood shops *(not done).*

These plans were prepared for the County Planning Officer, Ernest H Doubleday by Mr F C Sage, AMICE, MI Mun E, and his staff. Overlaid on these plans were to be the 'Mars' site (Harlequin); the Tesco site; the retail warehouses near Bushey Arches; the Watford and Croxley Business site; one ASDA, one Homebase and two Sainsbury supermarkets.

The overall result was that Watford became a vast building site for near twenty-five years.

In 1848 the Union Workhouse was moved from Church Street to a then somewhat remote building in Colney Butts. From there the inhabitants had a grandstand view of the wonder of the age, the steam locomotive.

From the high vantage point across the dip in the ground they could see, and hear, each train as it chuffed along the raised embankment between Bushey and Watford Station. In their spare time, with nail or broken knife, they scratched in the bricks their impressions. With passing of a century and half of weathering the images are indistinct, but nevertheless, expressive.

Nearby are a number of bricks carved with an obituary name and date. These are for the year 1857, the year before the graveyard was moved from the Parish Church to Colney Butts, which we know as Vicarage Road.

Last puffs of steam

The horse and cart was the accepted form of local carriage although being rapidly replaced by motor vans and lorries. Steam trains were supreme countrywide and the network of rail extensive. Scammells, by developing the three-wheel 'Mechanical Horse' and trailer; sounded the death knell of city-based horse traffic.

In 1921, to effect working economies, the old individual railways were merged into four regional groups comprising the LMS, LNER, GWR and SR. They continued to lose business and revenue up to the last war; and these losses paved the way for nationalisation in 1948, into British Rail.

In 1955 British Rail had a locomotive stock of some 19,000 steam engines—but diesel and electric locomotives were more efficient and modernisation plans were introduced. By the time the London Midland Region was electrified in 1966, the stock of steam locomotives had been reduced to 7,000. The networks of works sidings had long since been disused and most taken up.

Bushey Arches Facelift

THE secret of modern bridge building is pre-planning—and evidence of how essential this is was apparent during Saturday night and Sunday as the new bridge at Bushey Arches was placed on the reinforced concrete trestles that had been prepared for it.

Three weeks ago the old part of the bridge was removed. Officially it was known as the "second widening," for it was the second addition to the original bridge that Robert Stevenson, son of the famous George, had erected. This second widening was started in 1871 and by coincidence the contractor who signed the plans on August 28 of that year was himself a Stevenson.

This old bridge had a girder of 208 feet; it rested on concrete filled cast-iron columns that weighed nearly 30 tons.

The new bridge has been designed completely by British Railways. The designing engineer is Mr. C. F. Bonnett. of Berkhamsted.

WO, October 1963

Eastern Gas Board (works)	
315	Jas Wm Shearman, Watford Gas Works Social & Sports Club
317	A H Home Ltd, bldrs, (works)
317	S. & M. Trading Co. confctnrs
319	Southwood Alfd. C. beer retlr.

315 Watford Gas Works S S Club

Previous page, top: *Two of the 'train' bricks carved by workhouse inhabitants c1848 and below, one of several 'In memoriam' carved bricks;*

Bottom: *An up mixed goods passing through Watford Junction c1960.*

This page, top: *Tollgate 1871, (p59).*

Bottom: *c1930. Until at least the late 1930s all coal for the gasworks was transported from Bushey Station goods yard by horse and cart such as that coming into the picture.*

Bushey Arches in 1837, an object of awe and wonderment to the 3,000 population of the area. The Toll Gate presented a barrier to those using the road. In the foreground is the trackway which would become Eastbury Road. In the distance of the railway is the Bridge described by the Ordnance Survey as 'Colne Bridge' but colloquially 'Five Arches'.

In recent times developers, despite outcry, persisted in naming the nearby retail outlets as at 'Watford Arches', and the bridge over the river as 'Colne Bridge'. Popular usage favours Bushey Arches and not all that many people will know that 'Watford Bridge' over the river even exists.

Through the following pages of the High Street panorama (1994/5) the history runs from 1961 to 1988, at places interspersed with items and photographs to link older times with the modern High Street. There are many side-by-side comparisons as, for example, the 'Green Man' evolution on page 365.

Top: *One of Watford earliest industrial sites, that of Tidcombe, Henry Rogers and later Watford Engineering Works, and, of course, the wheat and chaff and local farriers.*

Right: *The beginnings of Watford's post-war industrial estate, here Greenhill Crescent, 1962.*

Eastbury rd
312   Wheatsheaf P.H.

Eastbury Road   Entrance to Oxhey Park   312 (Wheatsheaf P H

Banks to Computerise

A LINE of strange figures typed on the bottom of a cheque in magnetic ink marks a revolution in local banking—the Westminster Bank has brought electronic accounting to Watford, the first town outside London to join in what the bank hopes will be a nationwide computerlink among its branches.

The Watford Junction branch was the first to come into the scheme, 14 days ago. Last week the High-street branch switched over, and, from this morning (Thursday) the Cross Roads branch, at the Parade, joins in.

In addition to going over to computing procedures, the Watford banks are trying out a new system—the three branches will operate from a single set of machines at the Watford Junction office. The single line of figures printed across the bottom of personal cheques is the secret of the new system. It is a method that will reduce the time necessary to maintain individual accounts. no matter how active they are, and at the same time will relieve staff for other duties.

Though thousands of pounds have been spent on the new machinery required and on the training of operators, it is the everyday telephone that supplies the key link between Watford and the Central Computer System at the Bank's offices in Lothbury, London.

WHP, December 1963

Palace Theatre

The Palace Theatre, Watford and Hertfordshire's only live theatre, has, after a long and chequered history since its start in 1908, become a Civic Trust—a Theatre Trust supported by the Borough Council. The policy is to present straight plays, musicals and revues as part of a season of fortnightly runs.

Electrification

From March 1967 the suburban services between Watford Junction, Bletchley, Rugby and Birmingham will be operated by new four-car electric multiple-unit trains. Each train will have seating for 19 first-class and 319 second-class passengers. Two units can be coupled together to form an eight-car train. The frequent service to and from Euston will either be non-stop or calling at Harrow.

Watford Official Guide

Gade House

Gade House was officially opened on 28th January 1965.

George Stephenson College

The new college 'on stilts' in Water Lane has many departments installed; completion is expected in 1966.

More car space

Clement's car park, holding 350 cars, is now in use.

Princess Margaret at Palace Theatre

Princess Margaret and the Earl of Snowden paid an unheralded surprise visit to the Palace Theatre, May 19th, to see a performance of 'Macbeth'.

WO, May 1965

Compulsory Purchase Confirmed

THE Minister of Housing and Local Government has confirmed the Compulsory Purchase Order of the Watford Borough Council for 280, 282 and 284 High-street, Watford. The land, according to the Council, is needed for road improvement.

The order covers approximately 580 square yards of land and includes a motor-cycle engineer's, a cafe and a tobacconist's.

The public inquiry was held on May 7 when it was stated for the council that the dwellings were unfit for human habitation, and part of the land was needed for proposed road improvements. In the meantime it would be used as a car park.

WO, August 1963

New Kitchens

HOUSEWIVES living in Watford Borough Council houses are due for a big surprise—a Council scheme has started to give them modern, well-appointed kitchens and a hot water supply.

The Council plans to install "dream kitchens" in a further 396 dwellings. The houses under the modernisation plan are spread out as follows: 80 in Thorpe-crescent; 122 in Crossmead and Colne-avenue; 124 in Chilcott-road, Comyn-road, Desmond-road, Rosebriar-walk and Courtlands-drive; and 70 in Gammons-lane, Leggatts-way and Elm-grove.

Work on the Thorpe-crescent houses is due to start after Christmas. Crossmead and Colneavenue will be dealt with shortly, and the other areas will be treated later.

The scheme centres on the kitchens.

Bathrooms will be moved to give more floor space where possible—the baths themselves will be of modern squared-end style. Lavatories will be separate, and the coal cellars will be abolished. Instead concrete coal bunkers will be built outside the kitchens, in the back gardens, but adjacent to the house walls.

310 Watford Engineering Works

The Park Gates may be rebuilt . . .

Floors will be tiled, new sinks—the white sinks of the advertisements—will be provided and modern wall units and work-tops will be installed.

But perhaps the most important thing, from the householders' point of view, is the knowledge that modern boilers will be put into the kitchens—to supply hot water to sink, bath and newly fitted wash-hand basins—and hot water tanks put into the first floor bedrooms will be fitted into new airing and linen cupboards.

Front gardens will be separated from the pavement with new cement block walls and metal gates, and fences separating back gardens are to be replaced by plastic-covered wire fences. In the living rooms, modern grates, capable of utilising smokeless fuels, are to be installed.

WHP, November 1963

Rise of Odhams

In the 27 years since building in Watford the firm has several times extended. The factory employs over 2,700 people and produces over 7,000,000 magazines per week.

Following intensive research and development the introduction of pre-printed colour in national newspapers was accomplished in collaboration with Odhams Press Ltd.

WO Centenary Issue, 1963

Postal Codes

By next year is expected Watford will be one of the towns on the new 'Postal Code' system of mail delivery. Every house and business in the area will have its own individual code to enable more efficient sorting and delivery of mail.

310	Durant Melville
310	Maudwyn Ltd. tobccnsts
	Watford Engineering Works Ltd
306a,	Watford Sheet Metal Works
306	Cotterell & Pither Ltd.
304b,	Ever Ready Co. (Gt. Britain) Ltd. (print wrks),
304a,	Rich Ltd. finance company
304	Cowell Wm
302	Donegan Chas
300	Golding, Mrs. K

The system has already been tried in some parts of the country already and Watford is one of the towns to be included in the next stage. By 1969 it is hoped that 70 per cent of all addresses will be coded. This is a mammoth task since there are about 17,000,000 in the country. In Watford, too, it is a huge task.

A team of experts started work back in February and have spent months poring over maps and studying the present postal system. They have great trouble even finding some houses, because they don't have numbers and the new owners often change the fancy names.

The system at present in operation in some towns is for the first three letters of the town's name to be used in conjunction with three other figures and letters. Thus an address in Watford may have a code like WAT 2EF.

WHP July, 1967

'Rag' Van For Meals on Wheels

WATFORD College of Technology students on Saturday handed over to Watford Women's Royal Voluntary Service the meals-on-wheels van which was bought with money raised during 1967 Rag Week. Chairman of the Rag Committee, Mr. Ian Tarr, of 149 George Street, Berkhamsted, also presented a cheque for over £200 to provide holidays next year for old people.

WHP, July 1967

£1¼m. Bid For Wemco

A £1,250,000 takeover bid is being made for the Watford Electric and Manufacturing Company Limited.

The bid is being made by the British subsidiary of Harvey Hubbell, the American electrical wiring accessory giant whose sales last year were over 40-million dollars. Full details of the cash offer have only just been received by WEMCO and the board is to consider the bid in conjunction with its financial advisors, S. O. Warburg and Company within the next week.

Last week, WEMCO shares rose by 10½d. to 9s. 1½d. on the Stock Exchange, and some

observers are wondering if a counter offer will come from within the United Kingdom.

The offer, which the WEMCO board had little to say about this week, is for the Whippendell Road, Watford, factory and the subsidiary company in Northampton.

Altogether, about 650 men are employed, but Managing Director Mr. R. G. Smith seemed confident this week that a take-over would not mean any loss of jobs.

WHP, July 1967

Council House Sale

THE Tory plan to sell council houses to sitting tenants was given the go-ahead, in the face of Labour opposition.

One Labour member claimed that with rates and other expenses, purchasers would be faced with outgoings of over £9 a week for a £4,500 house on a 95 per cent mortgage. But Councillor John Charman, Chairman of the Housing Committee and "author" of the scheme, said if a tenant wished to buy a £4,000 house on a 30-year mortgage from the housing revenue account, he would be asked to put down a minimum 5 per cent deposit (£200).

With interest at 7 per cent in the £, it would cost the purchaser £4 4s. 7d net for the mortgage repayments. In addition, there would be rates, insurance and repairs. "Nobody denies this," he declared, "but even adding that lot on, it is a long way from the £8 and £9 a week we have had bandied about tonight." Ald. Amey said he imagined the only houses that could be sold for £4,000 were those at Harebreaks. "None of the post-war houses could be sold at this price,"

Councillor Peter Wilson (Conservative) said they were not depriving people on the waiting list. "The people who will want to buy their council houses are people who would remain tenants anyway so long as they remain in Watford."

WHP, July 1967

Watford Bridge over the River Colne

Park Gates

WATFORD's 19th century Tudor Lodge at Cassiobury Park gates, Rickmansworth Road, is likely to be resited and rebuilt as a cafeteria. Watford Borough Council is to be recommended on Monday to approve a scheme which is estimated to cost £54,000. As well as the cafeteria, it will include new public conveniences and a shelter.

It is hoped that the cost will be met by Government grants. If these are not forthcoming, it has been suggested that the council should pay for the work.

The site on which the lodge now stands is required for road improvements, but because of the historical and architectural interest of the building, the Ministry of Housing is against its demolition. To be re-erected with the same external appearance but adapted inside, the lodge would have to be dismantled brick by brick. Investigations show that the cost of dismantling and rebuilding the lodge with the necessary survey and adaptations would amount to £35,000. It is impossible, the council's investigators say, to determine in advance how much material could be salvaged and how much would have to be replaced.

Consideration has also been given to three other alternatives for the Rickmansworth Road frontage. They include a simple landscaping scheme costing £15,000; a shelter, refreshment kiosk, conveniences and store at £20,000, and a pergola type building with cafeteria, store and conveniences at between £20,000 and £50,000.

WHP, August 1967

Unions Fail in Cox Closure

"IT now appears inevitable that the manufacture of car seats and tubular furniture will finish at Cox of Watford's factory", Mr. Roger Homer, Divisional Organiser of the Amalgamated Engineering Union told the "Post" this week.

This was the outcome of a meeting on Monday between union officials and directors of Raleigh Industries, which recently took over Cox. The meeting has been requested by the unions to ask Raleigh's to reconsider their decision to transfer the activities of the Watford factory to the Midlands.

However, the Raleigh directors said they had considered for a long time retaining work at Watford, but their extensive research had led them to only one conclusion, that it was impossible on economic grounds, to do so.

District officials and senior shop stewards of the Boilermakers Union, the Transport and General Workers Union, the Amalgamated Engineering Union and the National Union of Furniture Trade Operatives, were present, with a senior shop steward of the Electrical Trades Union.

The best hope now, Mr. Homer said, appeared to be for some other manufacturer, who would retain as many of the staff as possible, to take over the Cox factory premises.

Union leaders intended to meet trades unionist Members of Parliament and Mr. Raphael Tuck, M.P. for Watford, in the near future, and this possibility would no doubt be raised then.

WHP, August 1967

Watford Census Results

THE picture of an affluent Watford and District, with thousands of two-car families, emerges from the Sample Census taken in April last year. As well as affluence, there is also a less prosperous side to life in this part of Herts. The census reveals nine homes in the borough and in Bushey, six in Rickmansworth and 21 in Watford Rural District that are without flush lavatories. And one in 10 homes in the borough still have no hot water tap and nine per cent, no fixed bath. Thirteen out of every 100 homes have an outdoor lavatory only.

There are more people with cars than without in Bushey, Rickmansworth and Watford Rural.

In Watford the position is reversed, and there are also comparatively fewer two-car families in the borough than in the other three areas. In the borough, nearly every other family—12,650 out of 25,200—has no car. Most homes in Watford borough, Bushey and Rickmansworth are owner-occupied. Those in the borough number 13,760 compared to the 9,360 rented homes. In Bushey about two thirds of the homes are owner-occupied.

At Rickmansworth there are 5,940 owner-occupied and 2,630 rented homes. In Watford Rural District there are more rented homes—8,790 compared to the 6,520 that are owned by the people who live in them. Women outnumber men in Watford. Out of a total population of 75,960, there are over 39,000 women and over 36,000 men.

Over 66,000 of the people in Watford were

Top: *Inside the Park gates, next to Rickmansworth Road, 1962*

new road, 1994: Dalton Way, leading to Century Park   304a   304   302

born in England and over 72,000 of them in the British Isles. Nearly 56,000 are natives of the South-East. The Irish form the next largest group with people from the North coming a close second. The Welsh outnumber the Scots by a short head. There are nearly 1,700 people from Commonwealth countries, Colonies and Protectorates.

These are the figures operating a year last April. The census shows that the population in Herts has risen by over 8 per cent since 1961 and now stands at over 832,000. There are proportionately fewer people over 55 in Herts than in England and Wales as a whole.

WHP, August 1967

300	Golding, Mrs. K
298	Penney Mrs.
296	Hart, Miss
	Bridge Place
294	Salmon David G.
292	Maison Joan,.
290	Sharpe Douglas E.
288	Bull Chas
286	Brown H. J. beer retlr
282	Rider Mrs. M. A.
280	Brooks J. W.
	London Transport Executive, motor omnibus depot
	Spurling Motor Bodies Ltd.

What Your Council House is Worth

These are the types of council homes Watford Borough Council is prepared to sell.

The three-bedroom 'semi' at Garston Park would cost £5,000 to £5,250. Four-bedroom Harebreaks house, £3,800 to £4,000. Three-bedroom Harebreaks house £3,600 to £3,750. Two-bedroom Meriden house £4,000 to £4,250.

WHP, August 1967

Chaos Continues!

PLANS for the critically-needed North Orbital Road, intended as a relief for the Ml traffic flowing through Rickmansworth and Watford, have once again been shelved. The Ministry of transport has announced that there is now no hope whatsoever that construction will be able to start in 1970, as originally planned.

This means that local car-using residents will now probably have to face at least five more years of mounting chaos on the already overworked A412 between Maple Cross and North Watford.

In a letter to Mr. Gilbert Longden, M.P. for S. W. Herts, the Parliamentary Secretary to the Minister of Transport, Mr. Neil Carmichael, says that due to "ground contours" on the North Orbital's proposed route, the estimated cost had risen from the original £1-million to at least £2½ million.

"All this means that the programming of the scheme has to be reconsidered," writes Mr. Carmichael. "We will press on as fast as we can, but at present, when there are still so many uncertainties, I cannot indicate when a revised scheme will start."

The news will come as a massive blow to all those who use the A412 to get to and from work. Already this year, there have been several instances of four-mile traffic jams, and rush-hour progress is often so slow in some parts that it is literally quicker to walk.

WHP, October 1967

No North Sea Gas until 1971

WATFORD gas users will have to wait until after 1971 for North Sea gas, the natural rather than the present manufactured gas.

Eastern Gas plans to convert all its customers to North Sea gas; the changeover is to start in April 1968 in the Hitchin, Baldock and Letchworth districts and will spread in the first year to Cambridge and parts of Norfolk.

The whole country is expected to take between seven to ten years to complete.

And the advantages to natural gas? It will be safer, cleaner and in the long run cheaper, say the Gas Board.

WHP, October 1967

300   298   296   Bridge Place   294   292   290   288

Lean Years Nearly Gone

AFTER nearly seven years of steady decline, Queens Road in Watford will soon become a busy shopping centre.

A row of twelve shops which have lain idle for the past few years, has now been completely renovated and two are expected to be open before Christmas. On the opposite side of the road, Littlewoods are preparing a new development which will continue their frontage from the High Street round into Queens Road.

The shut-down of the twelve shops started seven years ago when Cubitt (London) Properties planned a joint re-development scheme with Watford Corporation. The scheme fell through, however. The shops, all of which have been completely rebuilt within the existing shells, are the subject of negotiation. The proposed Littlewood development has encouraged interest from furniture, catering, electrical equipment and supermarket concerns. Trewin Bros., part of the John Lewis organisation, which has lasted out the depression, redeveloped their Queens Road premises two years ago. A Civic Trust type operation to brighten up the exteriors of the group of twelve shops is further planned.

WHP, November 1967

Coach Owners to Fight

SOUTH West Herts coach operators were preparing this week to do battle with Barbara Castle over her plans to takeover private coach companies.

At a meeting on Monday, coach operators from Watford and other areas of S.W. Herts formed themselves into a committee with Mr. Gordon Hewitt of Premier Coaches, Watford, at the head. This committee will co-ordinate with committees now being formed in North Herts, Bucks and other adjoining areas.

Through the Passenger Vehicle Operators' Association, who are organising the opposition to the Ministry of Transport plan, the South West Herts committee will liaise with coach operators all over the country.

Mr. Leslie Withey, of Knightswood Coaches, Watford, a member of the new committee, said:

"We know we have no hope of preventing the Bill. What we want to do is force amend-

ments. I don't think it will have an immediate effect, but in the long term we could lose our businesses," he said. Mr. Withey claims that

the nationalised operation would result in less satisfactory service to the public.

"Without the element of competition you won't get 100 per cent service," he said.

WHP, December 1967

Previous page: The flood of 1946. The right-hand view shows that from the river the flood extends about 250 yards/230m, an incredible distance to ford with no idea of where a firm path may be or of the likely depth!

This page, top left: Strikers in 1926 waiting see if any buses would be taken out. Story p189.

Top right: The 1960 flood add to the misery and even 2003 added its share!

Shown are two early post-war Premier Bedford OB's with Duple bodies. By 1967 Premier-Albanian were using Bedford Duple bodied Viceroys, and Continental travel was offered.

(Jolly Anglers)   282   280   London Transport Bus Garage

Lower High Street and the breweries . . .

This photograph, 1956, *(opposite)* shows Watford's age. At the bottom, a little way up the road, is a light coloured flank wall. It is all that remains of the old Watford Mill, destroyed by fire in 1924 with the remains demolished in 1938. The mill-stream's course is easily seen together with the seven-stepped sluice. In the days of the mill the water was always held back to give sufficient head to work the mill and until perhaps the early part of the 20th century the tail race flowed across the High Street as the small river that it was; Watford thus had two fords. When, after the fire of 1924, the water level was lowered, the swimming baths suffered greatly from loss of depth of water.

At the top right of the picture is the entrance to Water Lane. (The pedestrian crossing across the High Street helps place it.) In the triangle bounded by the High Street, mill stream and Water Lane were the oldest courtyards and houses of Watford. Stapleton's (No. 195) had a 15th century wagonway and was a 15th century town house.

Before demolition, in 1974, Nos. 177 and 179 were inspected (they were Oatley's menswear shops 70 years previously) and it transpired that parts of the building were also 15th century. Both were older than the almshouses. Borough and County Councils were made aware of this and it was hoped that timbers could be taken and preserved at Chiltern Open Air Museum, but this was not to be. Steabben's across the Street from 177 and 179, also a tailor's shop, proved to have been built in the reign of James I and was over 350 years old. This length of Street carried the 'Tun Inn' (1600-1740) (Benskin's House site), the 'White Hart' (c1600-1974), the 'Three Crowns' (c1600-1958), 'Leathersellers Arms' (1680-1960), 'Swan' (c1750-1997, with modern changes), the 'One Crown' (1750 -), 'Brewers Arms' (1839-1911), the 'Fox' (1854-1956), the 'Railway Tavern' (1854-1974), and the 'Rising Sun' (1854-1905).

Many of the buildings, small and compact, and ranged along the street, show their age. Of this photograph, all that remains are a few cottages in Local Board Road, Watford Field Road, the newer houses at top centre and shops beyond the 'One Crown'. The 'triangle', up to the railway and once containing Watford's oldest history, and many men's allotments, now lies under Tesco's.

In **A** Benskins are having built a new bottling plant; the white scar in **E** is where a run of old houses has been demolished exposing to view the Town Mission Hall behind. The gardens and allotments give an air of serenity that masks the fate that planners and developers have in store.

We're Proud of Our Role—Music Head

To the lilting music of Schubert's "Shepherd on the Rock" Watford School of Music's new premises in Nascot Wood Road became officially operational on Thursday afternoon.

The opening ceremony was performed by Mr. Claude C. Barker, Chairman of Herts County Council, which took over the school in 1955 at the request of the governing body. The new premises are in the extended and modernised ex-Gartlett School. The Principal of the school, Mr. Kenneth Leaper, spoke of how the school was founded in 1880 as a result of a musical society inaugurated two years earlier by the Rev. Newton Price, Vicar of Oxhey.

"Today, thanks to the foresight of the local authority, we now have this beautiful house," said Mr. Leaper, who is the third principal this century.

"Our primary aim is to try and give the best possible individual instruction, then opportunities for musical merry-making in groups under professional instruction. Now we must look forward to more expansion.

"The school is proud of the role it has played in the past and looks foprward to increased demands in the future," Mr Leaper concluded
WHP, 1967

New Gas

At last conversion is at hand; in many older homes the old original gas pipes are being replaced with new high-density yellow plastic pipes. Gas fires, cookers, water heaters, are all being fitted with new burners. The change-over to natural gas is not far away, and the days of the old gas works are numbered.

```
Dent, Allcroft & Co, lthr clothing mnfctrs
Gazelda Ltd.
Plaice Allan F. (Gazelda ho)
          Gazelda Villas.
          1 Jones Alfd.
          2 Childs Ronald
          3 Lannon Jsph
          4 Muir Wm

276      Keller Edwd. A
274      Palmer W. H; beer retlr Hit or Miss P H
272      Hearn Cecil —
270      Marsh Jn W
268a.   Banham, Mrs. Rosa
266
```

Monaco/Spurling Motor Bodies   Gazelda Villa/Gazelda Ltd, behind

A	B	C
D	E	F
G	H	I

tory road cossing High Street to Waterfields   276   274 (Hit or Miss PH)   272 (The Anchor PH)   270   268   266

We lose the 'Post', and the Park Gates . . .

Founded in 1887 some 24 years after the Watford Observer, the West Herts Post achieved an instant empathy with a readership more 'working class' than the farming and professional classes who were the the Observer's original readers. This distinction was marked in the late 1800's/early 1900's Post by the 'small-shopkeeper' type of advertisements carried.

Published first from 42 High Street a change of ownership took place in 1919 and the Watford Newsletter was bought and incorporated into the title. Upon a move to Carey Place new machinery was installed and the innovation made, in September 1919, of clearing the front page of advertisements and putting news in its stead. Perhaps because, in those days, a paper without the solid appearance of advertisements on the front page looked less than successful, it reverted to 'style' after one year. In 1941, when news of the town's activities during WWII was important; the Post again cleared the front page of advertisements, at the same time halving the page size and increasing the number of pages.

A brighter and more readable paper was the result and the Post grew in popularity and status. During the late 1960's a further change crept in when news stories were shortened to little more than 'bare bones' with catchy headlines. In November 1967 Thompson Regional Newspapers published the 'Evening Echo'—a daily paper based in Hemel Hempstead—and so the 'Observer' and 'Post' faced the competition of a new, bright daily paper produced by more modern methods than the older papers had at their command.

Without warning after issue No. 4306 dated May 21st 1970, the retitled 'Watford Post' ceased publication. Home Counties Newspapers Ltd. of Luton (name changed from Gibbs and Bamforth Ltd.) had withdrawn from the Watford area.

Upon closure, all photographs, plates and film negatives of people, places and happenings, made during the 'Post's' existance, were discarded without trace.

WATFORD
POST

135 THE PARADE, WATFORD. Tel. 26045
No. 4306   Thursday, May 21, 1970   6d.
Postage on this issue 4d.

'Just a piece of Victoriana; what did it mean?' Perhaps these were the thoughts of some of the Council when the time came to make a decision about retaining the gates. The gates were, by now, obstructing the plan to ease the Rickmansworth Road and roundabout traffic congestion. *As the Council owned the property it was not published in the list of properties affected.*

Watford's Town Clerk, who so vigorously opposed a road through Whippendell Woods and Golf Course and remarked upon the nearby park's beauty, was advised that there was no historical relevance to them.

True, there was no longer a mansion for the gates to give entrance to, and so it was expedient and cost-saving to knock them down. But since the struggles to buy the parkland for Watford, some sixty years earlier, Watfordians had accepted its acquisition with pride, and realised that the Council had then done a 'proper job' in completing the purchase. The gates were a fine entrance to a place of great natural beauty and it was deeply felt as an act of vandalism that they were demolished. An aftermath was that the Peace Memorial Hospital, now that the hospital was moved to Vicarage Road, was part demolished;

258   High St Service Station

and the remains were under threat. The outcry was such that efforts were made to incorporate the original front into future new buildings. And there the Peace Buildings (basically the original hospital) stayed empty.

Eventually it was realised that a need could be fulfilled and so the Peace Hospice project came into being.

The first stage of the Peace Hospice was opened in September 1996, nearly ten years after the hospital was closed.

Previous page, top: *Traffic queues in Hempstead Road replicated those from Rickmansworth Road in converging upon the Town Hall roundabout, right under council chamber windows! c1970.*

This page, top: *the Hit or Miss P H c1895, and in 1958.*

Right: *Taking down the Lodge—declared by many to be most outrageous act of vandalism perpetrated in Watford!*

Far right: *The planning notice left out any mention of park gates.*

Below: *There were not several lots of 'Bill and Ben' posters. The High Street montage comprises some 330+ photographs taken face-on at about 10 or 15 yards apart. Anything in the background, not obscured by a building front, will get photographed several times. Pylons are another example.*

Bridge over defunct mill stream course

256   254   252

Local Board Road; Crosfield Business Machines

Local Board Road, *below*, gained its named by being host to the 'Local Board' (of Health) formed in 1850; prior to that date there was no local 'government' as such—the Board being founded to effect improvements in the town's water supply and sewage disposal and general cleanliness.

Offices were established in Local Board Road in 1854. The Board gave way to 'Urban District Council' in 1895. In 1891 the town's population numbered about 16,000 and, typically, eight or nine board members would attend to deal with the town's affairs. (The Board meetings were held in one of the pump house upper rooms).

Local Board Road is notable for housing the beam pump which first supplied Watford's water. The supply was pumped from a depth of about 50ft and carried the length of the High Street via a 6 inch main to a reservoir in what is now Stratford Road. All the courtyards off the High Street were supplied via 2 inch branches; a 6 inch branch supplied the churchyards and on to the workhouse (Shrodells). By 1868 an additional 8 inch main was laid and this was in turn increased in 1881 to a 12 inch.

Pumping operations were transferred to a new pumping station at Watford Fields c1915; the pump house building remained and is now part of the 'Pump House Theatre.' Part of the theatre also occupies site and buildings of Tividale, an earlier local foundry of brass and iron.

In the High Street adjacent to Local Board Road was a small gatehouse type of building, No. 250 and alongside and almost up to

Right: *Shops on the corner of Local Board Road, 1956*

252	Martindale Mrs. G. H.
	Local Board rd...
250	British Cushion Supply Co. Ltd.
248	Coughtrey L. M. fire-wood mchnt
246	Coughtrey Mrs. W. E. boarding ho
244a,	Vallance Arth. Saml
	Watford Field rd...
242	Baker Antony G.
	Watford Town Mission Hall

Watford Field Road an imposing three storey edifice (top centre of *H* in the photo on page 345). By 1966 these houses had been demolished and the site that of Norman Reeves, Ford Dealer, dispossessed of their premises next to the High Street Station.

Crosfield Electronics were noted for their huge successes in making colour scanning equipment for the printing industry. Advanced electronics played a major role and this, with their mechanical expertise, led them to develop a bank-note sorting and counting machine. This was able to count 20 notes per second, and detect counterfeits. The counter had other uses—luncheon vouchers, lottery tickets, cashed Postal Orders.

To keep pace with their expansion a new factory was obtained; of 40,000 sq ft, in Watford's Lower High Street in 1970. By 1975 Crosfield had expanded considerably and more finance was to be sought by a stockmarket issue but a stockmarket crash negated this option.

The firm was sold to De La Rue and continued trading as Crosfield until it was sold (apart from the Press Controls Division) to Du Pont and Fuji Film in October 1989.

During the company's early searching for success in scanning they and Sun Printers cooperated extensively to their mutual benefits.

The Penny Drops

THE traditional British penny becomes redundant in February next year with the advent of decimal currency—it has grown old like human beings.

Although it will remain legal tender until 1973, its purchasing power will by that time be virtually nil.

WHP May, 1970

Trouble Again at Odhams

A DISPUTE between electricians and management at Odhams printers on Sunday led to a stoppage of work in the machine room of the production department.

"There was a difficulty between the management and the ETU chapel," said a spokesman. The dispute arose over the number of electricians to be engaged to do overtime work in the production department on Sunday.

As a result four presses were still throughout the day. It is not known whether the trouble will recur next Sunday.

It is understood that fewer electricians were required to do overtime work on Sunday than usual, and the men objected.

WHP, May 1970

Pumphouse

A BRAVE new venture in amateur theatre and arts in Watford and district will be hoping for a financial boost from a play which is being staged from October 4 to 7 at St. John's Hall.

The venture is the Pumphouse Theatre and Arts Centre, and the play "No, No, Nanette."

The Pumphouse Theatre and Arts Centre consists today of a Victorian pumphouse in Local Board Road, and a band of enthusiasts dreaming of a permanent amateur auditorium and studio facilities for Watford—and of the £15,000 or so needed to get the scheme really moving.

Among its current assets are some old seats, salvaged from a demolished theatre, and some offers of volunteer labour in the renovation work.

The Pumphouse has been leased by the Borough Council, and the original group interested in setting up the centre has been joined by the former South-West Herts Drama Council.

WOT, September 1972

Top left: *On the right hand side of Local Board Road Nos. 244-256 in 1956 are shown before demolition for business premises.*

Top right: *Crosfield premises in August 1986,*
and above: *Retirement flats under construction in 1995.*

Watford Field Road   242   (Watford Town Mission)   (Court 18)

Town Mission to Close

ALMOST 101 years to the month after it was founded, Watford Town Mission, in the Lower High-street, is to close because of poor attendance. When the Mission was started in October, 1856, that part of Watford was a poor and populous area. The only nearby school was the "Ragged School" in Ballards Building, which was filled to overflowing with poor children from the neighbourhood. It was from the school and from the alleys and back streets that the Mission drew its congregations.

WO, December 1957

Watford Town Mission Hall	
228	Turner Edwd. G. confr
	Swan alley
216	Swan Inn
214	Hertford Typewriter Service Ltd
212b,	Weightman Edwd
212a	Bannister Miss R.
212a	Card, Miss B.
212	David Hosker & Son, upholsterers
208	Kennedy's Publicity Service,
208	Tividale Tool Co.
	Fox alley
204	Harrison Wltr. Roy
202a,	Tomsett, Mrs. A
200	Benskin's Watford Brewery Limited,

Multi-million Scheme Starts Soon

IN something like three years' time, in place of the Central Car Park in Beechen Grove, there will be a massive shopping complex which should place Watford even more firmly in the top league of the country's shopping centres.

The new scheme—which will cost over £5 million—is centred around the overall plan for expanding and "pedestrianising" the shopping centre. The new project, which extends from the rear of the Palace Theatre to Red Lion Yard, and from Beechen Grove to the rear of the High Street's shops, will have underground servicing facilities for all its shops, and will allow rear service access to the existing shops on the north side of the High Street between Clarendon Road and the Midland Bank.

Under the scheme, the market will move into a new market hall where one link with the past will remain; stallholders will continue to

Top: *The town Mission Hall at the right of the cottages, the gates of which, with two young girls, is shown on p88.*

Next page: *top left, the new market, indoors, now open. Main benefit for traders is the vehicle and storage access from the basement;* top right: *The Fox P H*

'serve from the front' in the time-honoured manner.

Social needs have not been forgotten. The YMCA will have a new 175 study/bedroom block and in addition provision will be made for a restaurant, lounges and dining rooms, a gymnasium, squash courts, sauna and plunge bath facilities, and a conference room. All these facilities will be run by the YMCA, but will be available for the public. Above part of the shopping complex will be four car-parking decks with spaces for 800 cars. The car park will be served by lifts and staircases, and traffic direction to vacant parking spaces will be electronically controlled.

The entire site is being developed by Watford Borough Council, and the co-ordination work is being carried out by the Director of Technical Services, Mr. R. H. Brand. Consultant Architects are Messrs. Ley Colbeck & Partners, Consultant Engineers Messrs. Ove Arup & Partners, Consultant Quantity Surveyors, Messrs. Pritchard, Williams & Hunt, and Consultant Surveyors, Messrs. Hillier, Parker, May & Rowden.

WOT, May 1973

Pump House Success

AFTER just one full year in operation, the Pump House Theatre and Arts Centre in Local Board Road has reached an exciting turning point. In the past 12 months three full-length plays and two one-act play festivals have been staged. During the same period the centre has launched three club activities meeting once a week of folk, theatre and jazz.

These have enjoyed a remarkable season, collecting between them over two thousand members.

This means that in order to allow nightly events to prosper—and at the same time, to allow stage presentations a full week's run—there is a need for a second auditorium with its own bar, entrance, cloakrooms and so forth.

WOT, October 1974

| 242 | (Watford Town Mission) | 228 | 226 | 224 | 222 | 220 | 218 | (Swan Alley) | 216 (Swan Inn) | 214 | 212a |

Charter Place and new Market is opened . . .

Charter Place on Schedule

WATFORD'S biggest single redevelopment ever—the Charter Place Project between the High Street and Beechen Grove—is back on schedule. The three-day working week, steel shortages and other local difficulties combined to upset the programme of work. These problems have been overcome, however, and the help of good weather has enabled the contractors to get back on target.

WOT, October 1974

Shopper's Paradise Regained!

THE opening of the Charter Place Development means that Watford will be an even greater attraction for shoppers this Christmas.

Although there will be 800 additional car parking spaces at Charter Place, parking and traffic conditions will still be difficult in the Town Centre and to ease the problem a free "park and ride service" will again run on Saturdays between the Junction Station (British Rail Car Park) and the Town Centre.

Last year on nine Saturdays the service carried over 32,000 passengers to and from the Town Centre. It provided free car parking at the Junction Station for about 1,000 cars on each day, even though the car park was never more than two-thirds full. It also provided a free service for rail passengers arriving at the Junction Station.

WOT, November 1976

The box collectors

The market approach hadn't changed much since it was opened in 1928, except for the roof. What had gone though, from the early 1930s, are the several families who would arrive in the evening around 8 o'clock before closing time and wait along the Red Lion Passage wall. With home-made two- or four-wheeled barrows they'd be waiting for the traders to pack up, and then they'd be round collecting the apple and orange boxes. The wet, smelly, fish boxes they'd leave until last as make-weight if the evening's collection had not been good

The youngsters would be under the stalls as soon as possible for there'd be fruit thrown down there. True, the apples would be bruised, and the oranges soft in spots, but the bad parts could be cut out. And, perhaps, under one of the sweet stalls they could find a few toffees.

The parents would doubtless be on the lookout for last-minute food bargains; a joint of beef for a family could be bought late on a Saturday evening at Fisher's; across the Market Place, for around a shilling. The wood? That, after carting home, breaking up, removing nails and wire, would be sawn, chopped, bundled into firewood and sold to supplement a meagre income.

Recollections, (1987)

208   206 (The Fox P H)   Fox Alley   204   202   200

Museum Opens to Public

WATFORD Museum opened to the public on Saturday, March 14. A cavalcade of historic vehicles came down the High Street and was headed by the Benskins Dray carrying the guests of honour, the Mayor of Watford and Terry Scott. The Watford-born actor made a very amusing speech and unveiled a plaque. He later spent a long time in the Museum, signing autographs and chatting to the visitors.

Almost 1,000 people came into the Museum on the opening day, and in the following week a further 1,300 people visited the Museum. Apart from the permanent displays, there is also an exhibition in the picture gallery of portraits that will be on view for several months.

WOT, April, 1981

Vandals' Paradise

QUEENS Road pedestrian precinct, once a busy and thriving Watford shopping area, has become a desert of boarded-up windows, graffiti and torn posters, as traders have closed up and moved out in preparation for the Mars 1 shopping-development.

Michael Clewer, who runs one of the four remaining businesses, is preparing to follow suit. However, 12 years after opening in Queens Road, he is leaving with a bad taste in the mouth. "In keeping with other remaining businesses, we've had our shop windows smashed by mindless hooligans," he explains.

On two nights in early July, vandals smashed the windows of County Bedrooms, Abbey National Building Society and Habitat. On the first occasion, seven store-front windows belonging to Trewin Brothers, part of the John Lewis Group, were attacked. There is general agreement among the four remaining businesses in Queens Road that one solution would be an increased police presence at night.

A police spokesman comments: "Queens Road is patrolled regularly during the night. However, we are undermanned and given the resources available to us, putting additional officers on duty would mean neglecting other streets." Mr Clewer feels that crimes of this type are not connected with drunkenness. "In the case of Abbey National, there was insufficient time to have new glass fitted before the criminals struck again," he says.

Focus, July, 1982

Top: *John Wootton's painting of Cassiobury, 1748, was among those sold with other house contents in 1922 and last exhibited at Kenwood House in 1984. Up for sale by Sotheby's in New York, 2003, it was purchased for $120,000 (approx £80,000) by funding from the V & A, the National Art Collection Fund and local support. Now in the Museum's collection.*

Right: *The 'ring'road' view of the short-lived Watford Springs.*

200	Benskin's Watford Brewery Limited,
194	Benskin's Watford Brewery Limited,
184	Railway Tavern
182	Watford High Street Railway Station
	Finley & Co. Ltd. tobacconists, (kiosk)

entrance to Watford Springs   (Benskins Watford Brewery Ltd)   200   Watford Museum

Purchase Tax/VAT

Purchase Tax was abolished in 1976 and VAT introduced in its place. The first rates were 8% and 12½%; these were increased to one rate of 15% in June 1979.

Promotion

After 3 years in Division 2 and previous year in Division 3, Watford FC finally won promotion to the First Division in 1982.

This page, top: Watford Springs main block and interior, 1995.

Centre: Wood frame cottages demolished 1920's, 184 & 186 High St., just below High Street Station.

Right: High Street, burst water mains, 1957; right-hand side of the station, Norman Reeves, Ford dealers.

192   190   188   186   184   (Railway Tavern)   Watford High Street Station

Top left: *Watford Electricity Generating Station, much expanded, in the mid 1950's when it was coal fired and supplying the National Grid.*

Top right: *Becoming uneconomic against the larger, and nuclear, stations, it was in 1976 converted to gas turbines as a 'stand-by' station but demolished in the 1990's; the site, in 2003, the subject of plans to turn the area into small industrial units, with a link road to Wiggenhall Road to ease the strain on Cardiff Road.*

CEGB Employment termination

Dear Mr. Attwood
In accordance with the notice given, Watford Power Station has ceased to exist.

182	Norman Reeves (Motors) Ltd, Ford dlrs
180	White Hart P. H.
174,176 & 178	Wm. Steabben, tailor
172a & 172b	H G Cramer Ltd, toy & model dealers,
172	Davidson's, costumiers
170	Reynolds G.
170	Thos S Wood.
168	Butcher S. B.
168	Lawton & Wright F.A.I.
166	Davidson's, knitwear
166a	Garvey Jsph
164	Garland Ruby Ltd, gowns
162d	Thomas Kenneth
162a	Refuge Assurance Co. Ltd.
162c	Melfonte Ltd, oufitters
162	Art Wallpapers Ltd.
160	Three Crowns P.H.
	CROWN PASS
158	Knight P.

I am writing to advise you that, because of this closure, your service with the CEGB will be terminated on the ground of redundancy and you are hereby given one month's notice of termination, the first day of the period being 22nd August 1969.

... I would like to take this opportunity of thanking you for the many years of loyal service to the Industry and to wish you well in the future.

Yours sincerely,
E. P. L. G
Regional Personnel Manager
13.8.69

168	166	164	162c	162	160 (Three Crowns P H)	Crown Passage 158

The Odeon demolished in 1984 and the site cleared to make way for the Sainsbury store. An advantage in convenience shopping but a catastrophic loss of a town centre family entertainment venue, yet to be replaced.

THE FINAL **Echo**

No 2295   Wednesday, November 16, 1983   12p

The Evening Echo, 1967-1983

The Evening Echo was established in 1967 by Thomson Regional Newspapers Ltd., Mark Road Hemel Hempstead. Using new printing technology the wage and cost structure negotiated by the print unions at the outset was far higher than warranted. The E E covered a wide area from Luton to S W Herts and thus 'local' news was sparse.

Success in first years meant costs could be met but later periods of recession meant drastic cuts in advertising, particularly of situations vacant, upon which the Evening Echo largely depended, and huge losses of £2,000,000 in 1981/2 and £1,000,000 in 1982/3 could not continue. When the West Herts Post closed the final issue carried no special announcement; there was just no more. The Evening Echo in contrast provided a retrospect of their brief 16-year span.

Knighthood for M.P. Raphael

OCTOBER, 1980: Arise Sir Raphael! Watford's MP for 15 years on the day he got his knighthood. One of the best constituency MPs of his day, Sir Raphael Tuck served the town selflessly. His kindliness and sincerity transcended political barriers.

In November, 1980, Sir Raphael was made a freeman of the Borough of Watford, the town he loved and where he made his final home. Earlier this year Watford council decided to name five streets after him or some aspect of his life.

He died in 1982.

Final Evening Echo, November 1983

Sainsbury's new store

The recent start on the new Sainsbury's store on the Monmouth Arms site is the product of several years planning and negotiations by the Council. The development has been made possible by the Council initiating in 1979 the compulsory purchase of the land not already in their ownership.

Interestingly, the whole site had been in the ownership of the late Mr. Cox in the 1920s but he had sold off land from time to time, and by 1979 there were 15 different owners of parts of the site. Clearly, only the Council could hope to bring the site back into single ownership so that it could be developed as a whole.

It was expected that Tesco would be the Council's tenants, but after prolonged negotiations they withdrew in 1980. Fortunately, the Council had taken the precaution of requiring a very substantial deposit which, before its eventual repayment, earned thousands of pounds in interest.

This helped the Council take the courageous decision to press ahead with acquiring the site, even though there was no longer a definite developer in view.

168   166   164   162c   162   160 (Three Crowns P H) Crown Passage 158

By 1982, the national retailing situation had improved sufficiently for the Council to have detailed negotiations with a development cornpany and Sainsburys, leading to an initial agreement in March this year, again supported by a substantial payment.

Since then, the developers have successfully agreed to buy the Odeon cinema from Ranks.

This has enlarged the site to give a better-designed store, and four unit shops fronting The Parade, with a snooker hall above.

The promotion by the Council of this development reinforces the town's shopping facilities, adds to the available car parking, improves rear servicing and, not least, aids the rate fund by the payment made by Sainsburys for the site.

WOT, December 1983

New Development Brings Jobs

THE Borough Council has entered into partnership arrangements with the Carroll Group of Companies to secure a first-class extension to the Holywell Industrial Estate, which has been re-named Watford Business Park.

156	One Crown P.H.
152 & 154	Pearsons, house furnishers
150	Swallow Leonard B
150	Foster Bros. Clothing Co. Ltd.
148	Warren Chas
148	Dewhurst J. H. Ltd. butchers
146a,	Finlay & Co. Ltd.
146	Lipton Ltd. provision mchnts
144	Kasmir Alfd. Ltd., fashions
142	Currys Ltd. cycle dealers
140	Hepworths Ltd. outfitters
138	Wright S. L. Ltd. house furnishers
136	Walker, James Ltd. jewellers

1983: *End of an era and the largest job loss in the history of Watford. Odhams print works, one of the leading print houses in Europe for nearly half a century, closed.*

The aim is to provide high-class accommodation for industry, including new high technology industries. It is also envisaged that the existing Holywell Estate will be the subject of a concerted effort of environmental improvements to bring it into the '80s.

The extension of the Business Park will not only bring jobs to the town but increase the Borough Council's rental income, enabling it to cushion rate increases.

WOT, December 1983

'Junket' Jibe Over Councillors' Trip

WATFORD Council's ruling Labour group has been accused of "junketing" on the rates.

Tories are angry about a two-day visit to Sheffield to discuss twin-links with Russia. Deputy Conservative leader, Councillor Robert Gordon, said it was no surprise they were rushing off to the 'Kremlin of the north' for the junket. He told the full council meeting: "It is precisely expenditure of this type that compels the Government to take action before the Red Flag flies over our town hall."

Three Labour councillors will be going to the twinning seminar organised by the Socialist-controlled Sheffield City Council. Each will be entitled to claim attendance, travelling and subsistence allowances. Councillor Arthur Reynolds, one of the delegates, denied they were Left-wing extremists or that the visit would be all wine, women and song.

"The idea is to find out how other towns are conducting their relationships with the Soviet Union," he said. Labour leader, Councillor Fred Hodgson, accused the Tories of being hypocritical by supporting attendance at a West European twinning conference previously. He added: "If you ever get control it would be the Stars and Stripes flying over the town hall."

Final Evening Echo, 16 November 1983

Top left: *The Odeon by the Pond, when demolished and redeveloped, was home to Bailey's Night Club, and here, in 1984, Presto supermarket, soon to be outclassed by the newer Sainsbury's. Note the pre-scanning checkout where indivual prices were hand entered.*

Top right: *From the final Echo.*

| 156 One Crown P H | 154 | 152 | 150 | 148 | 146a | 146 |

The downfall of Odhams and the Sun . . .

If one picks up an old Guide to Watford the comment may be noticed that 'Watford is a print town; the largest in the country, possibly all Europe. It is a statement believed today by many but is no longer true for, although modern society consumes ever more printed material, Watford's share of large-scale printing has dwindled to a mere fraction of that of its heyday. It is not that the earlier magazines have been replaced by televtsion, for colour supplements, mail order catalogues and the like have provided alternative business.

The roots of print's downfall grew in the days of its early success. Sun Engraving and Sun Printers in the years before the last war were ahead of their time with quality rotary gravure colour printing and there was no shortage of customers requiring their services. The war reduced the demand for printing in general as paper shortages continued and even worsened in the post-war years. When paper became freely available again, there was still a huge demand for the products of Sun and Odhams but during the years of paper shortage, technology in Germany and the USA had caught up with and surpassed that in use in the Watford factories. An artificial printing boom in the late 1950's and early 1960's camouflaged later problems. Customers wanted colour printing, equipment was getting outdated; extra effort was needed to meet deadlines.

Unions were the first to appreciate that in the short term higher wages could easily be obtained from the employer by the threat of strike action with a consequential loss of production and late- or non-delivery. Management succumbed to these pressures. The increased costs had to be passed on to the customers who then turned to other print centres in the country that would only too willingly handle the work.

Watford's position was threatened unless costs could be reduced to be competitive. The years of escalating costs accepted by customers, with little alternative, had passed. To attempt to reduce costs, managements took the logical step of seeking to introduce new techniques and machinery which could be manned by fewer staff, a step bitterly fought by unions. The result was that machines were either over-manned, still continuing with high costs, or shut down.

Watford was acknowledged as a town of 'high wages of the printers'. In 1963, the Daily Mirror intended to start a colour supplement. Union branches circularised every print business, (large and small) within a large area, announcing that Odhams needed staff. With the attraction of high wages, the reputation of easy work loads and plenty of overtime, they had soon recruited and met their requirements. Scores of smaller businesses lost skilled and vital machine minders in the exodus, being unable, in commercial and jobbing print, to equal the high payments. At this time, 1963, the workforce of Odhams and Sun numbered some 3,500 each.

The Mirror supplement failed; Odhams became plagued with strikes. Resulting from one closure of many weeks a Royal Commission was held. The finding suggested that 'management and union should attempt to better cooperate'. A loss-making situation followed, leading to eventual closure.

At Sun Printers the trend of lower cost printing was quite clearly noted. Gravure produced high quality but took longer in preparation, and was more expensive. The Sun staff took immense pride in their achievements and, when the proposition was made to install the cheaper web-offset, the union's stance was that no members should suffer. In other words, the cheaper process should be, once again, overmanned and therefore, non-competitive. Multiplicity of unions meant quite severe and pronounced 'demarcation' problems. Web-offset was not installed at that time.

The years from the mid-1960's were traumatic for managements, unions and staff and it was not until very recent years that amalgamations started and demarcation restrictions eased. The damage had long been done; large print orders were placed elsewhere in this country and abroad.

Mr Robert Maxwell masterminded the Odhams closure, and merger with the Sun.

That is another story of disaster . . .

Grange Park to close

Alleged falling school rolls necessitated closure, or merger, of some schools. Plans in 1982/3 to merge Bushey Hall School (co-ed) and Grange Park (boys) were resisted.

The proposals were bitterly contested and much effort was expended by head teachers, staff pupils and parents in campaigning, protesting, fund-raising and petitioning. Leggatt's case rested upon badly sited alternatives; Grange Park that no alternative school places existed and that to close the boys' school restricted parents right to choose. The closure plans were not well formulated; parents worried that pupils would be left on dying sites; Herts County Council and 'new school' head teachers assured anxious parents that this would not be so.

In the event; closure orders were confirmed in the summer of 1985 and the pupils left on 'dying' sites. The closure co-incided with a long-drawn-out campaign of 'industrial action', disruptive tactics, by teaching staff in protest over pay and conditions, and despite the best efforts of some long standing dedicated staff the pupils did not receive the care and education that should have been theirs.

Grange Park boys' numbers dwindled from around 350 of September 1985 to around 135 in July 1987. Full integration with Queens School had not taken place and in the face of knowledge that Grange Park site was to be used for Bushey Hall School the remaining boys were intensely aggrieved at the treatment they had received. An attempt at integration was made two weeks before the end of the school year (when many boys had left) and had "nothing to do with rumours that an end-of-term demonstration of dissatisfaction was planned."

Bushey Hall School was closed and lay derelict for some years until the site was redeveloped for housing. Leggatts was also closed, the site transformed to a college campus taking students from the George Stephenson college (site sold), Callowland (Leavesden Road), and Ridge Street.

J B N

Grange Park School

SINCE the new proposals for the closure of Grange Park, Leggatts and William Penn schools have been announced, many reasons are, and will be given, as to why the above schools should stay open.

But while the fight goes on, please give some thought to the children who will have to try to maintain a high standard of work in a very unsettled atmosphere.

Most of the children, whether or not they show it, must be feeling as if their own little world is falling apart.

Is it not bad enough that we as a nation cannot guarantee them a job after all their studying? We are also unable to promise them that their schooling will be uninterrupted. Will the powers-that-be please remember statistics don't have feelings, but children do!—Mrs. G. A. Siggery, Maytree Crescent, Watford.

WO, March 1984

Well Done!

Even if the football club did not win the Cup their reception by the people of Watford could not have been warmer.

On Sunday May 20 Watford's Charter Place was crammed full and was a blaze of yellow and red.

The Borough Council was delighted to join with the people of Watford in saying "Well Done Lads—We Are Proud Of You".

The Wembley final with Everton (which Everton won 2-0) was described as the Friendly Final. In Watford the day after will be recalled as the happy homecoming.

WOT, June 1984

Above: *Two Specials on duty c1977.*

134	Watford Co-operative Society Ltd
132	Barclays Bank Ltd.
	King St
180	Rowe Alfd. King's Arms P H
126 & 128	Burton Montague Limited, tailors
118 to 124	Woolworth F. W. & Co. Ltd.
116	Broadmead Wireless Co. Ltd.
116a,	Salisbury A. L. Ltd. leather goods dlrs
114d,	Lyons J. & Co. Ltd, refrshmnt. caterers
114c,	S. & M. Fashion Shop, costumiers

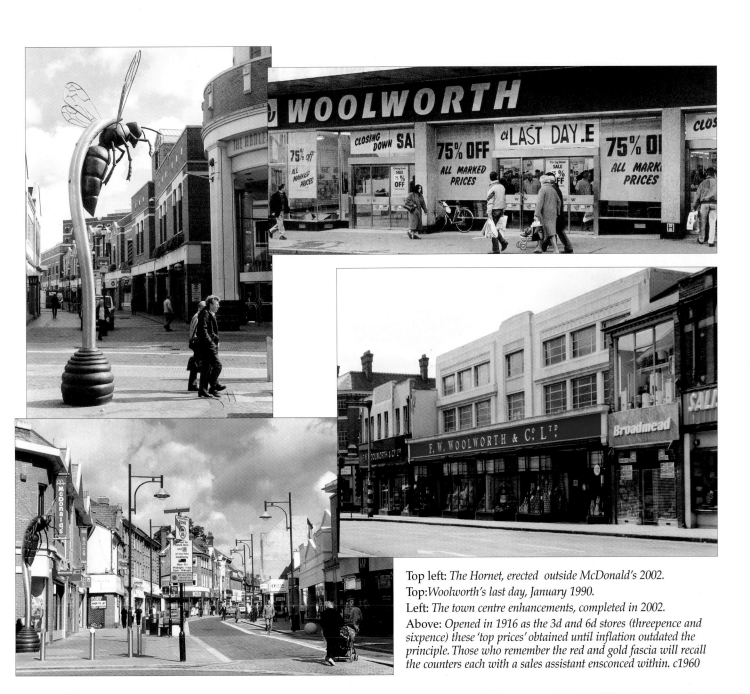

Top left: *The Hornet, erected outside McDonald's 2002.*

Top: *Woolworth's last day, January 1990.*

Left: *The town centre enhancements, completed in 2002.*

Above: *Opened in 1916 as the 3d and 6d stores (threepence and sixpence) these 'top prices' obtained until inflation outdated the principle. Those who remember the red and gold fascia will recall the counters each with a sales assistant ensconced within. c1960*

4   122 (F W Woolworth's)   120   118   116   116a   114d   114c

Sub Post Office to Close

Watford's Head Postmaster, Mr. R. H. Staines recently announced that he intends to close the New Town Sub Post Office in Langley Road, Watford.

End of an Era as Odeon Goes

The Council has decided to recommend that the new public highway serving the rear of numbers 47-115 The Parade and the Sainsbury's Store, be named "Gaumont Approach"; the Odeon was formerly named the "Gaumont".

WOT, December 1984

Palace Theatre's Cash Crisis

WATFORD'S Palace Theatre, probably the most successful regional theatre in the Country, is again facing a cash crisis. Its principal funding bodies, the Borough Council and the Arts Council, are both being hit hard by Government restrictions on public spending and are unlikely to be in a position to increase their grants significantly. Despite its superb record of attendances, audiences have averaged over 90 per cent for the past four years, subsidy has failed to keep pace with inflation.

However, a recent meeting of the Watford Civic Theatre Trust heard of a surprise of £4,000 from Equity, the Actors' Union, from a special fund. As a result of this, the Theatre Trust have decided to give serious consideration to continuing with its May production, which was in danger of having to be cancelled.

The Theatre is now launching an appeal to the business community for further sponsorship to ensure the May production proceeds.

The Theatre normally closes down during the summer period. Some profitable use for the Theatre during this period is being considered.

WOT, February 1985

Council Unveils New Estate

WATFORD Borough Council's Radlett Road housing estate was officially opened by Lady Monica Tuck on Friday 19th July 1985.

In her speech officially opening the estate, Lady Tuck thanked the Borough Council for marking the town's great affection for her late husband by naming the main roads on the

Top left: *Entrance to the Vicarage and Churchyard, 1914.*

Below: *The Churchyard entrance c1838.*

Right: *The Sensory Garden and Church, 2002*

114c   114b   114a   Entrance to St Mary's Churchyard   114   112

estate after him. The Mayor then proposed a vote of thanks to Lady Tuck and said: "The residents of Watford must give thanks to Sir Raphael Tuck, our Member of Parliament for so many years, to whom the town owes a great debt of honour."

She then complimented the speed and efficiency with which the contractors, Croudace Limited, had carried out the work so far on the estate. From the start in April 1983 the first properties were handed over in July 1984.

More than 300 additional homes are to be built on the site, which should be completed by March 1988. The northern section of the estate is now complete with 80 houses—69 of which are already occupied, and 93 flats, of which 33 are occupied. The final two blocks on this section are complete but have not yet been officially handed over.

WOT, August 1985

Educated English

If you are reading this in some remote part of the world, and there is a one in ten chance that you are, you are not going to believe a word of what follows.

It seems that Her Majesty's Inspectors for Schools (HMIs)—a body of men and women who plainly no longer strike the terror they once did into the heart of teacher and pupil— are getting a bit concerned about what children in England are being taught about the English language. So they fired off a pamphlet aimed at teachers outlining what they thought the little ones, from age five to age sixteen, should be taught about their mother tongue.

Here is the eyebrow raiser. So fierce was the response from teachers that the HMIs have had to redraft their contentious ideas.

No longer do they suggest that a child of eleven should know the difference between a vowel and a consonant. Altogether too demanding they now think, to suggest that the same kid might have been told by their teachers that in a sentence there is often a subject and a verb, and that it is a good idea if they agree.

No awareness of different tenses, by the end of a child's primary education, will be looked for. In the face of considerable criticism from teachers the hapless HMIs, intuitive spoilsports every one of them, have dropped from their original list of high attainment for eleven-year olds a knowledge of the rules of spelling, the functions of the main parts of speech, and the ability to tell the difference between statements, questions, commands and exclamations.

The HMIs are not the only ones in the education business who are bothered. They say that a consultation exercise they have conducted over the past eighteen months has shown that there is substantial agreement that children should learn something about their language and how it works. But even this modest concession to learning doesn't get anywhere, for no one can agree what it should be.

With the result, maintain the HMIs, that many pupils are taught nothing about how language works as a system.

Readers in the UK have long suspected it.

British Printer, August 1986

Above: *Shoppers in 1967 enjoy the High Street free from traffic. Later, when car ownership became more widespread, traffic re-appeared culminating in Orange Badge parking upon both sides of the road. Pedestrians, once again, had to stay upon the pavements until enhancements were in place.*

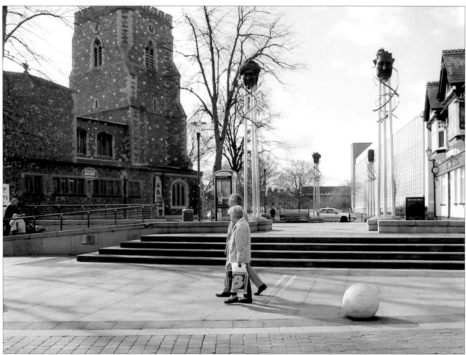

By 1999 the town had a hangdog and dejected air being the poor relation of the Harlequin centre, the road was a free-for-all for Orange Badge holders with that cause being given a poor name by many abusing the system. Enhancements had been on the stocks for some and great effort was made to complete the bulk by the end of 1999. Leader of the Council, Vince Muspratt, had set store on demolishing the disliked glass and concrete edifice fronting the Church and opening up space. To his credit, this he achieved, with Mayor Rosemary Bell cutting the opening tape.

Top: Pre-1888; Kings Head, 1962; Nos. 94, 92, 1956. Right: The 'Island Site', 1961.

100　　　98　　　96　　　Church Street　94a　　94　92　90 One Bell P H　　86　Kings Head Hote

Drop in Property Values?

Dear Sir,

The completion of the M25 has brought no less than five applications for major shopping developments within Watford's catchment area. Furthermore, there is the fallacy that surrounding every potential "green field" site there is a large untapped reserve of consumer spending power waiting to be put into the new shopping centre as soon as it opens its gates.

But little additional turnover is created—it is trade diverted from somewhere else—from local corner shops or from existing High Street department stores. And when trade drifts away from the traditional shopping areas jobs are lost, rateable values drop, services decline and town centres die.

The regeneration of the twilight area of Watford's Lower High Street under the umbrella of Mars 1, may appear a laudable project, but are we not merely relocating the shopping centre 400 yards back down the High Street and will not any increase in rates revenue from the new centre be counter-balanced by a corresponding drop in property values in the upper High Street?

R. E. H. Edmonds, The Parade, Watford.
WO, February 1986

100	Maddox (Mantles) Ltd, costumiers.
98	A E Spurrier & Sons Ltd, bakers.
96	Ford Service (Watford) Ltd, dyers & cleaners.
	Church Street
94a,	Kendall & Sons Ltd, umbrella mkrs
94	Shirt Manufacturing Co. Ltd.
92	Eastmans Ltd, butchers
90	One Bell P.H
86	King's Head Hotel
84	Henry Asher Ltd, rainwear rtlrs.
82	Spread Eagle P.H
80	Ryman (Counties) Ltd, stationers
78	Bewlay (Tobacconists) Ltd.
	New Street
76	F E Fisher, butchers

Proving town has a heart!

Dear Sir,

IF THE Mars 1 development of Watford is to take place, there must be a commitment to reopen the roads in The Parade and upper High Street. People can then see that a town exists; that it has a heart, that there is easy accessibility to a first-class theatre, places of entertainment and restaurants.

It must not continue to be a place which is alive with shoppers during the day and completely dead at night

If this scheme and other superstore developments are allowed to proceed without consideration to public amenities, then Watford, which geographically has probably the greatest potential of any town in the country, would just become another large clinical shopping centre.

S. Lipman, Gordon Hudson & Co.,
The Parade, Watford,
WO, April 1986

Create a clean, bright shopping centre

Dear Sir,

HOW pleasing it is that the shabby area to the south of Queens Road in Watford is to be developed. What a wonderful opportunity our council has to redeem itself and see that a shopping area that is bright, clean and attractive is created. We don't all want another noisy Brent Cross, nor even less another grey and soulless Charter Place, but a precinct that is a pleasure and relaxation to be in.

Do please let provision be made with affordable rents for arcades of small individual shopkeepers with their crafts and specialised merchandise.

Not just the big multiples.

Please make ample car parking easily accessible so that our roads are not clogged by traffic, and please create an area of beauty of which Watford can at last be proud.

M. Paterson.
WO, April 1986

Town Centre Art

For the town centre art enhancements carried out in 1998-2000 three main works of art were commissioned.

Largely funded through an Arts Lottery Grant worth £96,000 they include the **Spiral Sculpture,** next to St Mary's Church, which leads into the Sensory Garden. This, designed by Adrian Moakes, has 'the aim of softening the contrast between the commercial High Street, and the greenery and historical architecture of St Mary's Church'.

The **Hornet,** by Heather Burrell, at the corner of King Street and High Street, represents the importance to the town of Watford's Football Club.

The **Memory Wall,** by Carl Fielscher is at the upper end of the High Street beyond the Pond. 'It consists of 300 or so resin and glass blocks, semi-translucent, containing images important to people within Watford. Carl will be working to encourage as many people as possible to contribute to reflect the borough cultural diversity'.

At the time of writing these names seem not to have been decided. The edifice is lighted by spotlights within.

The Hornet is shown on page 359; the Spiral on page 360 and the Memory Wall on page 374. Above is one of the four Harlequin masks at St Mary's Square.

84	82 Spread Eagle P H	80	78	New Street	76 F Fisher (Butchers)

Victoria School goes

ANOTHER of Watford's landmarks bites the dust this week as bulldozers move in to knock down the old Victoria School in Addiscombe Road.

The site is being cleared to make way for the construction of the new Chater Junior School.

Built in 1897, it began its life as Fearnley Street School and was one of the first "board schools" of the period.

Previously all schools were private or church run until boards of elected local representatives were set up in each town to provide publicly-owned education for all.

In 1959 a decision was taken by the school governors to move the then named Victoria School to a new site in Tolpits Lane.

By 1963 the Addiscombe Road buildings were out of use and the new Tolpits Lane site was renamed Westfield School. Westfield School later became an all-girls school and the boy pupils were moved to Grange Park School in Bushey.

Although no longer a school, the Addiscombe Road buildings were back in use in August 1979 when they became a temporary police station while the present Watford station was being rebuilt. It remained the house of the law for 18 months.

WO, May 1986

16th-century houses go for new shops

ONE of Watford's oldest houses will be demolished to make way for a £100-million shopping complex because "it doesn't fit in with" the developer's plans.

Number 1a Carey Place is a timber-framed Grade II listed building dating from the 1600's and is superceded only slightly in age by number 22 the High Street—a restaurant and a jeweller's. St. Mary's Parish Church is the only building with parts which pre-date both.

The Mars 1 development means the flattening of almost all buildings bounded by Queens Road, Beechen Grove and the bottom end of Watford High Street. This week the developer's intentions to erect large shops, a shopping mall and a "food court" in the area have been branded as "unimaginative" by a leading conservationist who says the architects must alter their plans to suit the existing scene.

"The architects are not the slightest bit interested in the retention, preservation and refurbishment of this important listed building," says Stephen Castle, a member of a national architectural interest group and writer of a reference book called "Timber Framed Buildings in Watford. Their statement that the building is a sad and much modified version of the original and contributes nothing to the townscape of Watford is utter nonsense."

Mr. Castle says the right solution would be to expose the timber framing of No. 1a and the adjacent Nos. 137 to 139 the High Street for

74	Rose & Crown Hotel (Bass & Co. Ltd.),
	Market Street
72	Compasses P.H
68	(flat)
66	(flat)
66 & 68	Star School of Stage & Ballroom Dancing
54	Peter Lord Ltd, footwear
52	District Bank Ltd.
50	Green Man P.H
58	Offices
58	National Provincial Bank Ltd.

Above: *The Plaza/Odeon cinema closed in 1963 and was demolished in February 1964. In its place was built a groundfloor supermarket, Cater's, with a first floor night-club, Top Rank Suite. This gave way to Bailey's, Paradise Lost, Kudos and, to date, Destiny. The ground floor became host for a while to Kett's (after vacating its High Street store for the building of Harlequin) and Multiyork house furnishers. They vacated in 2002.*

Next page, top: *The 'Green Man' corner of the Market Place, c1900, c1970 and 1986.*

74 Rose & Crown Hotel   Market Street   72 Compasses P H   68   66

conversion to an attractive period restaurant and pub. Backing the alternative plans local archaeological society spokesman Tony Rawlins says a pub would be a good answer to the problem.

"I am opposed to its removal. It is a fine 16th-century building indicating what the alleys and courts of Watford once looked like."

The developers plan to take the backs off many of the shops in the bottom part of the High Street so that the old frontages, some of which date from the early 17th-century, are retained, although they would act as doorways to large stores and not be individual shops as now. But developers Capital and Counties say nobody in Watford cares or even knows about No. 1a's historic structure (it is a hairdresser's shop) and making it into a pub doesn't fit in with their re-development plans.

"We have offered to take it apart and erect it elsewhere, perhaps as a sports pavilion," said C & C's Anne Forster. "But as no site has been identified we have had to apply for demolition." The council looks unlikely to provide an alternative site. Development and planning committee chairman Les Cox says he's "not bothered about the building".

WO, May 1986

Destruction

Dear Sir, YOUR coverage, in the Watford Observer of May 16, of the proposed demolition of listed 16th- and 17th-century buildings in Watford's historic High Street/Carey Place is appreciated by those who are concerned about the retention of Watford's architectural heritage.

Nos. 129-131, 133-135, 137-139 and 141 High Street and No. la Carey Place were listed as Grade II in January 1983, as part of the Department of the Environment's resurvey of Watford's historic buildings to survive in the town. The DoE resurvey was prompted by the appalling wholesale destruction of the majority of Watford's historic buildings in the period 1950-1979.

This current application envisages not only the unnecessary demolition of the 16th-century No la Carey Place, but also the removal of the earliest part of No. 137 High Street, which dates from c. 1614—viz the mural depicting the Stuart Coat of Arms (Royal Arms of James I) removed to Watford Museum. As No la Carey Place and No. 137 High Street are statutorily listed buildings they cannot be demolished without the consent of the Secretary of State for the Environment. It is important to mention to Watfordians that sufficient representations to

the Secretary of State, on this and other aspects of the proposed Mars development, may persuade him to hold a public inquiry. In 17 years spent recording and campaigning for the preservation of Watford's historic buildings, I have received nothing but support from Watfordians.

Generally speaking they have mourned the passing of Cassiobury, Cassiobury Park Gates, numerous historic public houses and also the replacement of the traditional brick and timber-framed buildings of Watford's historic town centre with concrete muckheaps! The only opposition I have witnessed has originated from Watford Town Hall! Stephen A. Castle, member of the Vernacular Architecture Group.

WO, May 1986

D.I.Y. Observer

NEWSPAPER production at the Watford Observer and Free Observer has stepped smartly into the 20th-century and made a little bit of history in the process. The Observer has become the first weekly newspaper house in the country to go direct input with full co-operation from the unions involved. The transition from typewritten stories to single-keying on computer over recent weeks means that

62   60 Green Man P H   58 National Provincial Bank Ltd & offices

stories written directly on to computers by editorial staff, and advertisements from the tele-ads department, are sent directly to the photosetters, without further keying by the production department The change-over means that typewriters have been replaced by high-tech equipment and production facilities, leaving the field open for the area's leading local newspaper to expand its operation in South West Hertfordshire.

Following the signing of the Observer's new tech agreement, which has been negotiated at length by the National Graphical Association and National Union of Journalists, C. H. Peacock Managing Director Mr. Tony Greenan said: "Single keying has the effect of reducing the break-even point for publication."

WO, May 1986

Mars 1 plan angers local historian

A LOCAL historian, has accused the council of not preserving historic architecture.

Archaeologist Mr. Stephen Castle, a member of the Vernacular Architecture Group, said that the plans will add to the loss of the town's historic buildings from the 1950's onwards.

56	Palmers (Watford) Ltd.
54a,	Christmas A. & Co. Ltd. motor engineers
54	Stone J. & F. (Lighting & Radio) Ltd.
54	Ministry of Pensions & National Insurance
42 & 56	Palmers (Watford) Ltd, ladies' outfitters
48 & 50	P Buck Ltd, baker & caterer
46	W Wren & Sons, leather goods
44a,	London Kiosks Ltd. tobccnsts
44	Grange Furnishing (Watford) Ltd, house frnshrs
42	G H Stratton Ltd, booksellers,.
42	Motor Union Insurance Co. Ltd.
40	Lawley's (1921) Ltd, china & glass dlrs
38	International Tea Co.'s Stores Ltd, grocers
32	Mandley & Sparrow, est agnts

Renewing his earlier attack, he laid the blame squarely on the shoulders of the local authorities. "It has to be the attitude of local councillors. To my mind the council has not compromised, it has been demolition all the way with one or two exceptions," said Mr. Castle.

But as Mr. Castle gave his view and Three Rivers Council delivered its observations on the scheme, noting the loss of listed buildings, the chairman of the Borough's Development and planning Committee described at least one listed building earmarked for demolition as "an eyesore" and said he didn't care about the views of Three Rivers.

"My distinct impression is that other planning authorities in Herts seem very, very concerned about historic buildings and go to great lengths to ensure their preservation, and it seems quite clear to me that over the last 20 years or so Watford has done quite the opposite," said Mr. Castle.

He said that the resurvey of listed buildings by the Department of the Environment was deliberately brought forward because of the losses. "That was a conscious response to the appalling destruction of historic buildings in the town between the 1950s and 1979," he said. Among the losses he noted were the Leather-sellers Arms, High Street, dating from at least the seventeenth century, the sixteenth century Swan, the seventeenth century White Hart close to High Street Station, and the sixteenth century Eight Bells. "We are talking about dozens and dozens of buildings, some listed grade two, others not listed," he said.

Turning to Lower High Street, he said: "With the exception of Frogmore House and the Benskin Mansion and the adjacent coach

house and some small Georgian houses in a sadly dilapidated state, nothing has survived.

"That area which was once rich in historic buildings has been pretty well annihilated," said Mr. Castle. Last week Three Rivers Council considered the MARS 1 proposals.

The Planning Committee noted the loss of listed buildings, thanking Watford for the consultation. Three Rivers' main concern was the impact of additional traffic at Bushey Arches, themselves listed.

WO, June 1986

Rethink over plans for Mars 1 site

DEVELOPERS involved in the Mars 1 scheme in Watford have bowed to public pressure and submitted a new plan under which most of the listed buildings earlier set to disappear will be retained. A spokesman for Watford Borough Council said that most of the listed buildings would be retained "with modifications".

Top: *Mr Buck's bakery premises of 1872 (p62), recognisable below as 'Dixons'.*

Next page, top: *Arthur East and Mandley & Sparrow, almost the last of the earlier houses.*

Below: *The 'Peace' in 1972, just after the construction of the new road passing in front.*

56	54	54a Christmas & Co	52	50 & 48 P Buck Ltd	46	44a

The new plans involve improvement and refurbishment of the front range of buildings at numbers 129-151 High Street and 1A Carey Place. The rear sections would however be removed under the new scheme.

Number 1 A Carey Place has been described by conservationists as including features now unique to buildings in Watford, and the new plans follow only weeks after the chairman of the Watford Borough Council Development and Planning Committee described one listed building as "an eyesore".

Developers Capital and Counties confirmed this week that the bulldozers are unlikely to start in October as originally planned and the land agents have given shopkeepers an option to extend their lease until March 1987.

WO, June 1986

Mars one scheme gets a green light

A MASSIVE new development which will jolt Watford's shopping centre into the 21st century has been approved by Watford councillors.

They gave the green light to the transformation of the Mars one site at a meeting of the development and planning committee on Tuesday night. Members were told that a number of "minor" problems such as landscaping, lack of light to flats and effect on listed buildings in the High Street had been overcome. The plan is to construct a five level shopper's paradise on land between Charter Place and the Hammonds triangle site at the southern end of the High Street. It will provide 662,000 sq ft of shopping floor space and involve the relocation and extension of Trewins and an enlargement of both Marks and Spencer and British Home Stores. The entire development will be covered and closed at night and covered walkways will link the whole development with Charter Place.

The council are to enter into legally binding agreements to ensure that the scheme incorporates a leisure facility though exactly what form it will take has not been decided. Creche facilities are also to be included. The main stumbling block on Tuesday night proved to be what type of main entrance the shopping complex should have on the corner of Queens Road and the High Street where Ketts stands. It was decided that planning approval be given for the scheme with an entrance that retains the upper part of the distinctive Ketts domes. One group who are not happy with the scheme are members of the National Trades Union Council. They wrote a strong letter to committee members complaining of a lack of public consultation and said that even councillors got scant details of the plan. Secretary Dennis McGrath wrote "We are also concerned about the airey-fairey unconfirmed and uncommitted nature of the provision of any leisure facilities for the people of Watford." He said that the council had also failed to look at the question of public transport in the development though after reading his letter councillors agreed to pass the comments on to the bus services sub-com mittee for consideration.

Review, September 1986

Goodbye Peace

The Peace Memorial Hospital, Rickmansworth Road, was reduced to brick and rubble as it was demolished to make way for a long-stay geriatric hospital. The buildings had been empty since May 1985 when the hospital services were transferred to the Shrodells site.

WO, March 1986

30	Coachmakers' Arms, P.H.
	WELLS YARD
26a,	Brass Lantern, café
26	Stanley Pike, newsagent
22/24	Dan Jackson Dan, jeweller
22	Margt Lee, ladies' hairdresser
18/20	Provident Clothing Supply Co. Ltd
18 & 20	Offices
20	S & B Barnes Ltd, gowns.
18	Taylor Bros. (Grocers) Ltd
	Inland Revenue, H.M. Inspector of Taxes
(Watford	1st district)
14a,	Rigby House: offices:
14a,	W J Elliott Ltd, piano tuners.
	UPTON RD

Above: *Not since the building of the railway and Bushey Arches has a local enginering feat aroused so much interest—more so when the special Italian steel girders were subject to delays.*

Top: *When completed in 1986 the Gade Valley was split; in 2003 the M25 carries twice its designed capacity of vehicles.*

Maggie's one for the road!

Prime Minister Margaret Thatcher performing the ceremonial opening of the last section of the M25 motorway on Wednesday described the 117-mile ring around London as a £1 billion investment in Britain's future and praised the companies who built it.

The ceremony, conducted at a specially chosen site just east of London Colney, marks the end of more than two years of construction work on the £80 million section between Micklefield Green and South Mimms.

WO, October 1986

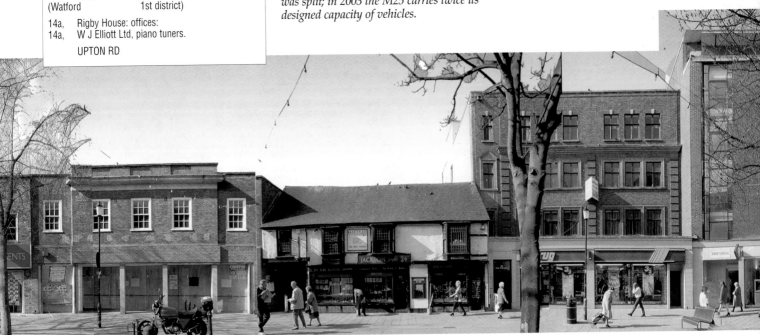

30 Coachmaker's Arms P H   Wells' Yard   26A   24   22   20   18

Traffic peace a welcome relief

A HUGE sigh of relief is being breathed by Garston residents following the opening of part of the M25 motorway last Friday.

They say life close to the congested A405 has been unbearable during the last year and are only thankful that the motorway has opened before one of their children is killed.

Forced to put up with a constant trail of high-speed cars and lorries during the many months of construction work, they have also been sickened by noise and fumes. But now the opening of the new five-mile motorway stretch between Micklefield Green and Bricket Wood has left the A405 virtually empty of vehicles.

"You could say that a weight has been lifted from our shoulders," said Kingswood resident Mrs. Jean James. Neighbour Mr. Laurant Parent of Meadow Road, said: "The traffic used to be shocking but the other day I went across for my usual walk and it was like a ghost town."

WO, October 1986

Upton Road corner from 1890 to 1968.

Charter Place facelift

A CONFIDENTIAL report has recommended Charter Place shopping precinct be refurbished by Mars 1 developers Capital and Counties who are part South African owned.

The outdated appearance of Charter Place will look even worse against Mars 1 when it is built and Watford Council's original plans were for another developer to undertake a revamp which is likely to cost about £20-million.

Above: 14a High Street, next to the Fire Station, was until 1939 the town's civic centre, of UDC and Borough offices.

14	Mrs. I. B Scott, duplicating agency .
14	Citizens' Advice Bureau
14	Watford & District Joint Fuel Office
14	Anglo & Italian Domestic Agency
14	(rear of) St. John Ambulance Brigade Head
14	Hertfordshire Fire & Ambulance Brigade

WATFORD CORPORATION CAR PARK

12 PrudentiaL Bldgs.:
(shop 1) The Three Keys Coffee Co Ltd, coffee mchnts
(shops 2 & 3) M Green & Son Ltd, costumiers
Prudential Assurance Co. Ltd.
(shop 4) Radio Rentals Ltd. wireless dlrs
(shop 5) Clara Reid Ltd, ladies outfitters
(shop 6) Watford Baby World Ltd. perambulator dlrs

14 High Street: Offices, C.A.B; Watford & Dist. Fuel Office   Hertfordshire Fire & Ambulance Brigade

But it is understood that a report which consultants Hillier Parker have written for the council recommends Capital and Counties undertake the work and take over the precinct's management. The Chairman of Watford Council's Development and Planning Committee and Mars I Special Committee said there are "a number of options" open to them over Charter Place but he denounced calls to shun Capital and Counties because of their South African connections. "We are forbidden to speculate on whether the refurbishers will be Capital and Counties or someone similar but it is our duty to look at the best deal for ratepayers," he said. "A bank loan to the council for £20-million would mean us taking all the risks and a colossal debt for ratepayers.

WO, October 1986

• *Charter Place market has more than 300 stalls of 6ft length. Let on a daily basis, singly or in multiples, the rent was £10 per 6ft per market day. There are also fifteen special-purpose fish and meat stalls. At the turn of the century stall rent in the market place was 4d and in 1928 5/-*

Twin-town mayors made freemen

THE MAYORS of Watford's twin towns in France and Germany were made Freemen of the Borough on Saturday in a ceremony that was marred by controversy over a defeated Labour proposal to include jailed South African Nelson Mandela.

The Chief Executive read the Resolution passed by Watford Council on August 18 admitting Herr Jockel Fuchs, Mayor of the German town of Mainz, to Honorary Freeman.

Council Leader Fred Hodgson said Herr Fuchs had supported the aims of the town friendship movement for the 21 years that he had been Mayor. "Herr Fuchs is Mainz's second most famous son," he said. "In a town survey he came second only to Gutenburg." The twinning of both towns has displayed 30 years of friendship which was forged in difficult times following the war. In his response, Herr Fuchs paid tribute to Edward Amey, the Watford mayor who made the first contacts with Herr Fuchs' predecessor. He referred to the appropriateness of the twinning.

Both were printing towns, Mainz being where Johannes Gutenburg invented moveable type. "I am proud of the great honour accorded to me. It is not just for me but for all the people of Mainz and I should like to extend greetings to all the citizens of our twin town Watford," he said. Councillor John Watts then welcomed Monsieur Yves Saudmont, Mayor of the French town Nanterre, praising his enthusiasm and determination for the twinning movement. In his response Monsieur Saudmont said 25 years after its creation the link was in "very good health."

Mr. Saudmont paid tribute to the late Councillor Arthur Reynolds and finished by saying: "Long life to Watford, long life to the friendship between Watford and Nanterre."

WO, October 1986

U.S. twin town

WATFORD NOW has a twin town in the United States. Wilmington, Delaware, became the town's fourth twin when Mayor, Councillor Paul Harrison, put pen to paper to sign the agreement. The historic agreement was signed before the annual Mayor's Reception at the Town Hall, Watford.

Appropriately, our colonial cousins were guests of honour at the celebration supper. For good measure, representatives from the Russian Embassy were also among the guests representing the people of Novgorod, Watford's twin-town behind the Iron Curtain. Watford is also twinned with Mainz, Germany and Nanterre, France.

WO, October 1986

Proud of our new hospital

Dear Sir,
I WAS sorry to see the letter from an old Watfordian in last week's paper, where she deprecated the loss of the old Watford Peace Memorial Hospital. I wonder if she ever worked or stayed there as a patient.

I, for one, am most grateful for the new wing at Shrodells. It may look like an air terminal but then it has to cater for so many of us. Falling ill recently I had occasion to use the Watford Hospital service. I found it excellent. All my appointments were kept to time and I was met with great civility and cheerfulness at every port of call. My stay in the Flaunden Ward was an education in how nursing should be. Nothing was too much trouble. There were many serious cases there but everyone was given the utmost attention. I don't think you could do better anywhere.

Six patients to a ward section was very spacious. (How many to a ward at the Peace?) We had the radio service, the papers and people to do our shopping. We had visits from the vicar and the priest. There are many good things about Watford and the Shrodells is one of them.

Jeffrey Higgins, Bushey.

WO, October 1986

Watford Corporation Car Park   Prudential Bldgs   1   2   3   flats   4   5   6

Storm

WATFORD and district is still recovering from the worst winds to have hit the area in living memory. As the rest of southern England reels under the full force of Thursday night's gales, people in South West Hertfordshire are also counting their losses.

No lives were lost but it will be a long process to clean up the trail of destruction left in the storm's wake. In just a few hours winds whipped up scenes of chaos as tiles were ripped off roof and trees sent tumbling. Commuters were stranded. Among the first to be affected were firemen who spent the early hours of Friday battling against the gales to answer emergency calls.

"The lads were working in quite dangerous conditions," said a spokesman at Garston Fire Station.

Firemen from Garston, Rickmansworth and Watford toiled through the night but for others the storm represented a day off work.

Commuters woke on Friday morning to discover all train services to London had come to a halt. With 20 wires down between Watford Junction and Euston, the situation was described by a British Rail spokesman as "pretty bleak."

There was frustration, too, for train travellers from further afield trying to get to London. The Irish Mail reached Watford from Holyhead, only to have to turn round and go back. Obstructions on the Under-gound's Metropolitan Line stopped trains to Baker Street for the morning although a limited service was back in operation on Friday afternoon. Main routes into London were open to motorists on Friday but fallen trees blocked some smaller roads in the county keeping council workers frantically trying to keep abreast of the workload.

"We have been inundated with calls to fallen trees," said a spokesman for Three Rivers District Council. "We have suffered along with everyone else and it has been all hands to the pump," he added. By mid-afternoon on Friday the council reported it had received 150 call-outs to trees that had fallen in 97 locations. Although the cleaning up was well under way by the weekend, fallen trees lining

the streets are a reminder of Thursday night's tempest. Among the irreplaceable losses are two of the biggest cherry trees in Hertfordshire which came down in Whispering Woods, Loudwater. Many of the trees in Watford's Cassiobury Park also came to grief and footballers had to abort their match in the Park on Sunday morning when they found a tree had fallen across the goalmouth. Cars were crushed and houses damaged by falling trees but as families now begin filing insurance claims, County police say they are thankful that Hertfordshire escaped as lightly as it did.

F Obs, October 1987

Woodlands Parade.
2, 4, 6   Finefare Ltd, grocers
8, 10   Times Furnishing Co Ltd, house furnishers
12   Co-operative Perm Bldg Society
        County Council)
(Nos.6 to 36 not built in 1958)

High Street

8a,   Youth Employment Office (Hertfordshire C C)
8   (Watford Conservative Club)
6   Cakebread, Robey & Co. Ltd, bldrs mchnts.

Woodlands Parade   2   4   6   8   10   12   16   18   20   22

Above: *Halsey House, home of the local Conservative Club, was sold and the land developed into shops, 1961/62, to extend Woodlands Parade, meeting new shops already built further along.*

Right: *The car queue is a result of the 1960 Carnival traffic jam at the roundabout.*

Lights could ease Dome nightmare

A WATFORD Councillor has called for traffic lights to be installed at the Dome roundabout to alleviate the "nightmare" for traffic, and pedestrians crossing there. Mark Oaten, Alliance councillor for the Stanborough ward, said "The roundabout is a well known traffic nightmare and is also dangerous for pedestrians."

"Many young mothers and old people have spoken to me about their fear of crossing there. I have even heard of some old people who catch the bus to avoid walking via the roundabout."

He feels a solution to the problems could be installing traffic lights. Mr Oaten's comments were echoed by local resident Ruby Morehouse of Spring Gardens who said it was "horrendous" trying to cross with her children aged six and two and a half. "It would be terrible if a child or elderly person were killed before something is done." The roundabout has been a source of local concern for over a decade and petitions have been sent to the council to try get action.

Peter Sanders of the county highways department said the council were currently having discussions with the Department of Transport about putting traffic lights at the roundabout.

Review, September 1986

New bus routes go into effect

London Country North West Buses have clinched the majority of Watford routes under the new Transport Act designed by the government to make bus companies more competitive by tendering to local authorities. It means there will be a change in services which come into effect on Sunday. One service to go is the 708 Aylesbury to London Greenline route.

Included in a package of improvements is a better South Oxhey to Watford service and new direct link between Watford and Harrow, via Carpenders Park. There will also be a better coordinated service along St Albans Road and more buses for the Meriden Estate. A feature of the new timetable is the service between Watford Junction and Watford Business Park, and Radlett Road—Watford Town Centre—Holywell Estate, which will now be operated by minibuses.

Other changes are to services W5, W6/16, Wl4, 212, 347/8, 349, 501, 719 and 749.

WO, October 1986

Green belt under attack

PROPOSALS that would mean the relaxation of the Green Belt as part of the plan to build 61,200 new homes in Hertfordshire by 1996 drew opposition from Three Rivers, Hertsmere and St. Albans' councils at the opening of the public examination of the Hertfordshire County Council Structure Plan Review. The structure plan policies have drawn fire from the districts' principals because of the proposal that Green Belt boundaries would be defined in terms of the degree of proposed long term expansion of the communities they surround. In some areas substantial amendments to existing boundaries are planned. The proposals follow the South Eastern Regional Planning Conference and have drawn criticism from the districts

26   28   30   32   34   36   High Street   8   6

who say that they have been foisted on the county by the Government.

The structure Plan envisages new homes within existing settlements—500 in Watford, 700 in Three Rivers, 1,400 in Hertsmere, 2,150 in St Albans and 2,050 in Dacorum.

But it also envisages major areas of new housing on the Leavesden and Abbots Langley Hospital sites, and the Hill End and Cell Barnes Hospital sites at St. Albans. In certain areas, such as Abbots Langley and the Woodside area of Watford, "green wedges" would replace the Green Belt. Totals for new homes envisaged by 1996 are Watford 3,400, Three Rivers 2,900, Hertsmere 4,000, St Albans 6,800 and Dacorum 8,600.

WO, October 1986

Scammell's seal huge MoD order

WORKERS at troubled Watford truck builder Scammell have got a £120m Christmas cracker from the army.

Just two weeks after the Leyland specialist vehicle maker announced 100 redundancies and short-time working in the face of falling orders the Defence Ministry has awarded them a massive order for 1,500 ammunition carriers. "It's the best Christmas present we could have," said one Scammell worker, summing up the jubilation of the workforce.

WO, November 1986

Faircross House

1	Watford Co-operative Society Ltd, grocers
2	Last E. C. & C. E, chemist.
	flats 1 to 13, inc
	Watford Ideal Homes Ltd
	David Scott (Builders)
3	Stan Pike Ltd, newsagts
4	J W Adams Ltd. F.B.O.A., F.S.M.C., opticians
5	Miss Marjory Ellen, ladies' hairdrssr
6, 10 & 11	Claridge (Watford) Ltd, gowns
7	Charrington, Gardner Locket (London) Ltd, coal mchnts
8	Stimpson Lock & Vince, est agnts
9	The Victoria Wine Co. Ltd, wine & spirit mchnts
11	10 & 6 Claridge (Watford) Ltd gowns

Scammells to close

NEWS of the Scammell closure has been received with surprise and anger by workers and union chiefs who dismiss claims made by Watford MP Tristan Garel-Jones that there are enough jobs in the town to cope with the 650 redundancies. The mood outside the factory gates was pessimistic this week, with many workers fearing the Leyland-Daf merger would mean the end of their working lives. "For the ordinary man working on the shop floor who is semi-skilled it is going to be very difficult to find work in this area," said chassis frame driller Andy Stevens.

"It's disgusting. We thought we were going to be saved," said rectification fitter John Bisley. There are some men who have been made redundant recently and they have applied for jobs and they can't find work."

The decision was also attacked by Peter Sweeting, joint shop steward for hourly-paid workers at the plant, who said it was nonsense to suggest that men who had been building trucks for 30 or 40 years would find new jobs in Watford.

WO, February 1987

Odhams ready for summer

Work is nearing completion on the first presses being installed at Odhams, Watford for the printing of the Daily Mirror.

A team of German engineers from MAN Roland are working round the clock on the installation of three two-unit Colorman 35s, printing on a 1.6 metre web. Sources within the factory say that the fitting will be completed in about two weeks, with a little longer needed for setting the electronic controls.

Experimental print runs will commence in four weeks.

Printing World, June, 1987

Fishburn plans to quit Watford

A move is in the offing for Fishburn Printing Inks, Watford. And while nothing has been settled yet, Fishburn is looking closely at two sites, one in the north and one in Sussex.

'We have been investigating the possibility of a move for some time,' says Paul Covell, head of oil inks sales, 'We looked at alternatives like Milton Keynes and others, but there's no decision yet'

The company is waiting for approval of

Faircross House: 1   2   3   4   5   6   7   8   9 10 11

development plans from BASF's board before pressing on. When Fishburn bought Croda last year, it had planned to redevelop Croda's nearby Harefield site. But Fishburn was itself the victim of a takeover by BASF, and the plans fell through.

Printing World June, 1987

Fishburn looks to the West

Favoured spot for Fishburn when it moves from Watford is Slinford in Gloucestershire *(sic)*. This has the advantage over the other possibilities because parent group BASF already has a site there.

The decision is not expected until the end of the year, and any move would not take place until three years after that.

Printing World July, 1987

Top left: The Scammell site in the 1960's. Shops have been built but the surrounding ground is host to many allotments.

Top right: Scammell's have 'closed' with caretaker staff only left.

Centre left: In the days of the Evening Echo and right, Fishburn's and the last to leave receives a friendly handshake.

Right: Fishburn's in its last year. One of Watford's earliest industrial sites— Cassiobury Mills, once a large and thriving sawmills and builder's merchants—Turner's, manufacturing croquet sets, cricket bails and wickets; house and building timberware; through a wide variety of uses and for around 50 years, Fishburn Printing Inks, recently absorbed by BASF Inks and Coatings. Behind Fishburn's, the Junction Station; the tall building to the right is Star House, Clarendon Road. 1986.

Demise of Fishburn's, John Dickinson's and the Isolation Hospital . . .

Cassiobury Mills and Fishburn's

Albert Fishburn was an ink technician of the American firm Ault & Wiborg; called up when the US entered the war he served in England in 1918. Upon his demob he stayed in England and in 1929 he, with Lt Col the Hon Bertram Russell, founded Fishburn Printing Ink Co Ltd, at Cassiobury Mills.

At that time there were printed nearby waxed discs for milk bottle tops, for which Fishburn's gained a contract to make the specialised ink. Packaging of food products, especially breadwrapping, cellulose wrappings (and later, polythene), corrugated cardboard cartons, all needed new inks of types and characteristics not previously made.

Tin printing needed new inks (and during WWII, inks had to act as a preservative layer to cans 'untinned'). Colour printing, prewar, was not common, but the art of direct-lithography for printing posters was highly developed and also needed special inks which had resistance to fading and industrial corrosion.

Fishburn's pioneered many innovations, but control passed to the Inmont Corporation of America, retaining the 'Fishburn' name.

'Fishburn's' was acquired by BASF in 1986 and finally vacated the site in 1990. Cassiobury Mills demolished is now 'Homebase'.

Skills shortage costs 80 jobs

THE lack of skilled labour is forcing an engineering company to quit Watford with the loss of 80 jobs. Watford Control Instruments is moving to Northamptonshire in a bid to find the skilled workers Watford cannot provide.

Said managing director Mr Alan Dover. "We have been very happy in the town but over the last four years we have found it difficult to survive here. We just can't get skilled labour."

It cannot attract people from outside the area because house prices in and around Watford are among the highest in the country. Company heads had hoped half of them would move with the firm. Now they admit that only 20 of the workforce of nearly 100 are likely to move to Corby.

Watford has not been able to keep up with the company's success. Over the last nine years Watford Control Instruments has grown by 17 per cent a year, increasing its business at home and abroad.

But success means the firm is outgrowing its Watford site. Watford Control Instruments was formed 35 years ago by the current chairman Mr Steven Brod. It was moved from London to Watford in 1961.

WO, November 1987
Watford Control Instruments was based in the Riverside Road Silk Mill premises.

New homes plan for first time buyers

A NUMBER of first-time buyers are to have a chance to buy property in Watford at a price they can afford. Watford Borough Council and a major building society are to build houses on the site of the former Holywell Hospital in Tolpits Lane.

Half the properties will be rented to council tenants, while the others will be sold on a leasehold basis, whereby the land will still belong to the council. Owner-occupiers of the homes sold will have the opportunity to buy the land from the council at a later stage. If building begins in January as hoped, the first homes could be finished as early as June 1989. The homes for sale scheme will consist of approximately 15 one-bedroom flats, 30 two-bedroom flats, 16 two-bedroom houses and 12 three-bed room houses. The one-bedroom flats will sell for around £38,500, with the price of the three-bed-roomed houses likely to be about £50,600.

Members of the council's Housing Services Committee said on Tuesday they thought it a good idea to offer tenants waiting for council transfers the chance to buy the new homes, as this would release council property for people on the waiting list. "It is OK meeting the needs of the transfer list but the real needs are on the waiting list," said Councillor Martin Rainsford. Committee chairman Councillor Mike Jackson later said many people could not afford to buy homes at Watford's inflated prices. The remaining two and a half acres of the old hospital site will be used for light industrial units.

WO, April 1988

This page, right: The Isolation Hospital in Tolpits Lane was demolished in late 1985 but at the time of the photograph, c1972, still in use. The rows of houses to the top right of the hospital site are in Croxley View and the buildings to the top are in Caxton Way/Greenhill Crescent.

John Dickinson & Co Ltd; Apsley Mills

Pre-1939 Apsley Mills employed almost as many as Watford's Sun and Odhams combined, drawing a goodly number of workers from Watford. So many that in 1938 a railway station was opened opposite the Mill's main entrance when Dickinson's were pre-eminent in manufacturing and selling stationery products.

The cycle sheds, here shown decorated in 1977, could house 1,200 cycles, and many more were stored near the north entrance.

Dickinson's once served the world, and the Empire especially. Post-1945 changed all that and instead of serving thousands of individual retail customers it contracted to serving fewer distributors. The onset of the telephone age lessened demand for the previous wide range of stationery products, and eventual mechanisation of the postal system following 'post codes' eliminated the profusion of shapes and sizes in which the mill once specialised. In 1966 Dickinson's merged with Robinson of Bristol making the Dickinson Robinson Group. By 1985 the labour force had shrunk from 5,000 to 2,000, and the Stationery Department and envelope departments moved to Belswains Lane leaving the Mill site available for redevelopment. Long before 2002 this had taken place and Apsley's landscape changed; later to followed by closure of the Belswains presence and its total conversion to housing.

In their heyday Dickinsons were paper-making inventors from the time they learned how to make paper from a web, rather than single sheets, embracing duplex boards, cartridge paper and, especially, envelopes when they became fashionable in 1835 following the 'penny postage'.

Dickinson's started in an era when canal transport made it possible; raw materials by barge, coal for power, and the despatch of the finished product to their London warehouses. Croxley Mill was the only one connected to a rail network, as well as the canal.

Back lands plans

BECAUSE Oxhey Hall and other areas in Three Rivers are considered desirable areas to live in, is it right that threats to where we live and our environment, by subtle pressures are being promoted, which set neighbour against neighbour and friend against friend, and is especially frightening to older residents, who are told that the planning which is before the council is a mere formality?

That was also said to me personally by one of the agents when I contacted them recently. It must be made quite clear to all residents, estate agents and developers that planning permission for housing on the back gardens in Oxhey Hall, is not a formality.

Estate agents who are, and have been currently involved in the buying and selling of houses in Oxhey Hall, have in a number of instances, when they have come to resell the houses, advertised them for sale with only 45-feet long gardens. This is an area where gardens generally average well in excess of 150-feet long. My investigations show that either fences are being erected, presumably by the agents, across the gardens of the empty houses and the land beyond is left to grow wild, or that incoming owners are being told that they don't own the ends of their gardens. Once developers obtain planning permission to develop on a particular desirable area, then in a short time that area quickly becomes undesirable.

- Roy S. Clements, Oxhey Hall Ward Councillor, Three Rivers District Council

WO, March 1988

From the top: *Working longboats in the lock alongside Nash Mills; the cycle sheds gaily decorated; both 1977.*

The Mill's main entrance; the time-office at the extreme right remains; the lower building towards the rear is the 1914 Stationery Department. The larger part-demolished building (1927) is the Envelope Department which, from the ground floor, housed box-making, printing, bag-shaped, banker's, and high-grade court and commercial envelopes. The older building on the left housed offices and the 'Work's School' (in which, earlier, typing was taught).

Right: *The 1933 'new wing' housed art, process and block-making, and production of cellophane bags, wages and small pocket envelopes for which Latex self-sealing flaps were introduced in 1937. Cellophane bags were being made in 1988 when the two lower pics were taken. The Card Department was north of this.*

The struggle to save the Peace . . .

After the end of the long and bloody Great War, Watford was not content in 1919 to have a piece of rusting captured booty or a grandiose stone cross as a memorial to the fallen. The Cottage Hospital in Vicarage Road had proved woefully inadequate in meeting its task of treating war-wounded in addition to more ordinary medical problems that arose. At War's end it was determined that Watford would have a fitting, long-lasting and totally worthy structure to mark their respects. It was to be a hospital; up-to-date and one of which to feel utterly proud. It was to be Watford's Peace Memorial.

The most suitable site was in Rickmansworth Road between the Cross-Roads and the Park Gates; the 'Elms' Estate. The estate was just over 10 acres in total size; the Urban District Council's Site Committee recommended the Executive Committee to 'acquire the site (the Paddock) for the erection of Watford's Peace Memorial'. Five acres was agreed to be more than needed; three acres was a figure suggested, but Mr Thorpe pointed out that, with five acres, there would be room for expansion as the town continued to grow. Purchase of the 'Paddocks' was dependent upon the purchase of the complete site and this was eventually agreed to as 'being a good bargain' and 'they were putting this hospital up for all time'.

The cost of the Memorial was to be £90,000 (at 1995 values about £8,000,000; renovation of the building in 1995/6 was put at more than £1,000,000) and was raised by an Appeal Fund. Donations, appeals, fund-raising events all contributed as did flag-days and collection of silver foil. The foundation stone of the Peace Memorial was laid in 1923 and the hospital, with its 87 beds, opened in June 1925. In 1928 a seal was set upon the Peace Memorial by the installation and dedication of a group of statuary of three figures representing the Bereaved; the Maimed and the Victors.

The 'Elms', as a house, stood for a few more years until, in 1938, it was demolished to make way for Watford's Town Hall that was completed in 1939, opening in January 1940. Its five acres of ground had cost £7,500. The extra five acres prudently bought for £5,000 (albeit unwillingly) proved their worth when extensions were carried out in 1937, bringing the bed total to 154. The Peace Memorial served as a voluntary organisation until 1948 when it, and the grounds, were taken from the Board of Management and into State Ownership under the National Health Act.

The 1960s saw Watford's traffic congestion rise out of proportion because its narrow Rickmansworth Road, meeting the Hempstead Road at the Town Hall roundabout, could not cope with the flow of traffic attracted by the M1. In planning the flyover, later changed to underpass, Rickmansworth Road would have to be widened for a considerable distance and in the way were the Park Gates.

If the Council were advised that 'they were of no historical value' those in power who were new to Watford may be forgiven for taking the comment at face value. That there were no local Councillors or planners with enough feeling for the well-known landmark is a burden with which the Council is saddled.

In the package of roadworks was the taking of part of the frontage to the Peace Memorial, the eventual blocking of the Rickmansworth Road entrance to Cassiobury Drive (which, to residents was a great relief after their road was used as a short cut for vehicles going to North Watford via Courtlands Drive), and the removal of the Statuary Group to a site facing the Library. To cater for the extension of Cassio Road, as an underpass into Rickmansworth Road in front of the Hospital, the road was substantially lowered and the frontage of the Peace

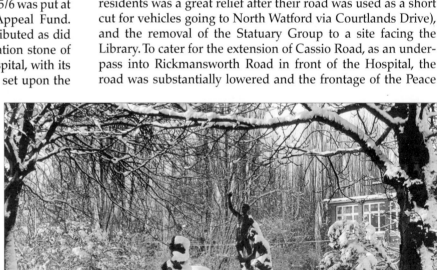

Top: The King Street Maternity Hospital building, used for many as years as offices for the Regional Health Authority. Demolished end 1995 for houses.

Right: The Bromet Peace Memorial Statuary Group in wintry dress in its designed place in Rickmansworth Road.

Memorial turned into a shrub-covered embankment with steps up from the footpath.

During 1968 the first stage of rebuilding Watford's hospital services —the opening of the brand-new maternity wing—had taken place. This replaced the old King Street Maternity Home.

Work started in 1979 to further enlarge the Vicarage Road site; this time with a six-floor general-purpose block. The first wards were opened in 1984 with the remainder following in 1985; the official opening, by H R H Princess Michael of Kent, took place during February 1986. The Victorian Wards of Shrodells, and the rather more modern wards of the Peace, were closed and all moved to the new 'Watford General'—an unimaginative, if descriptive, title totally devoid of personality.

If the hospital was to be saddled with an unappealing label, this was not to apply to the wards, where a competition was organised to find apt names. The winning entrant suggested that local villages and towns be chosen and the result is happily seen in the choice of Cassio, Heronsgate, Flaunden, Elstree, Radlett and Aldenham. In addition to the 250-bedded wards is a new Physiotherapy Department, Remedial Gymnasium and four operating theatres. The children's ward echoes the cheers—and groans, perhaps—of the nearby football stadium with the name 'Hornets'.

Watford Observer feature writer, Jean Groom, concerned with health matters and, passing the Peace Memorial Hospital site daily, enquired from the Health Authority officials what was planned for the site, with no sensible answers forthcoming.

When a sign proclaims 'site clearance' it is an open invitation for any number of youngsters to assist and the wonder is that anything was left of Watford's Peace Memorial. But for some reason or other the 'clearance' tackled only the later extensions, leaving the original 1925 building more or less intact. The 'site clearance sign' stayed long after work had stopped and so contributed much to subsequent damage.

That respect had been eroded was shown by the daylight theft of the clock; the front facade was unboarded, window panes broken and the building open to the ravages of rain, wind, snow and vandals. Jean Groome persevered with enquiries–which she renewed with greater vigour after the 1988 clock theft, but again to little avail. The curious fact of the clock 'theft' is that it was carried out by daytime workmen who had time and facilities for gaining entry to the building. They removed the clock and lowered it to the ground and van, and then carefully boarded up the resultant hole, all as if to an order, except that no-one admitted to giving such an order.

The thought is inescapable that the Health Authority considered the Peace Memorial, like the Park Gates, of no 'historic value' and that the site, so near to a town centre, could be sold for a very considerable gain. That the site had no access to a main road may have some bearing on events, but it may be comforting to think that the road developments that caused the loss of the Park Gates may have been responsible for the eventual saving of the original Memorial building.

Articles in the local press continued. They were spurred on by letters from readers asking for the retention of the Peace Memorial buildings for purposes connected with health care, expressing outrage that the fine buildings were allowed to fall into a bad state of repair.

The Health Authority, at last stung into action by what must have seemed to them to be local support on an unprecedented scale, announced that the original building, upon part of the site, would be repaired, refurbished, and converted to a 'Hospice', provided that the funds be donated from the public.

To this end, the establishment of a 'Hospice Appeal' shop at 1 72a High Street meant that members of the public could contribute without waiting for 'special events' which, of course, did take place.

More than £1,000,000 was raised within four years, with renovations starting during November 1995; the South West Herts Hospice openend in July 1996 to provide day care for about 15 patients on a daily basis of a five-day week.

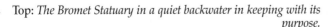

Top: *The Bromet Statuary in a quiet backwater in keeping with its purpose.*

Left: *When the Peace Hospice was opened in 1996 it was complete with donated facsimile clock to restore its dignity! A few years after the opening the Hospice was equipped with an eleven-bed care unit.*

The Peace Hospice:"Gently into the good night."

Peace facade to be retained

THE front part of the Peace Memorial will be retained when the hospital is converted to accommodate about 150 elderly patients. This information was given at Friday's meeting of the South West Herts Health Authority.

County Councillor Mrs Stella Meldrum said the Peace Memorial Hospital held a certain amount of affection as a place in the hearts and minds of the people of Watford.

Mrs Meldrum was told it was very much the authority's intention to retain the front building.

It is proposed to use the hospital to accommodate about 150 longer stay geriatric patients in purpose-designed new buildings. Holywell Hospital site is expected to be vacated by next January. "It is clear from inquiries received that a decision to dispose of this site would attract substantial interest," members of the authority have been told. The regional authority wants surgical facilities at Bushey and District Hospital to be withdrawn when the Phase Three development of the new Watford hospital opens at Shrodells.

WO, July 1984

Sell site of the old Peace

I REFER to your article in the Watford Observer on June 5, on the future of the Peace Memorial Hospital site; and am obliged to Mr Kemsley for his explanation of the delay in the profitable development of this valuable site.

If funds became available for redevelopment in June 1988 a further £200,000 must be added to the bill. Another surprising item of information is the possibility of using at least part of the site for health authority offices.

Why should the DHSS contemplate paying prime site rents for offices?

Surely secondary position offices are adequate, just as the Vicarage Road site was adequate for the Watford General Hospital.

Why can't the site be sold now on the open market and the profit put back into the Heath Service, preferably in Watford whence it originated? - N. J. B. 5, Pinner Road, Watford.

WO, June 1987

Care complex for old hospital site

A NEW concept in health care is planned for Watford on the Peace Memorial Hospital site. Work will start on the £9 million, 8,000 square metre development next summer if plans revealed this week get Department of Health and Watford Borough approval. The one, two and three storey configuration grouped around the courtyard and a pond, will take two years to build. It is to be of a domestic character and a scale to have a welcoming homeliness of an attractive residential scheme.

A casualty of the development could be the familiar frontage of the Peace Memorial Hospital. Mr David Kemsley, South West Hertfordshire health district strategy director said no promises could be made that it will be saved. The scheme is designed so that if it becomes necessary the old hospital can be used for sheltered housing, or some office schemes. The new development is one of four similar healthcare facilities planned for the district.

The others will be at Garston, Rickmansworth and Bushey. For the first time the DHA and Social Services will both be involved in the caring, and in the capital cost .

It is, says Mr Kemsley, to be a facility in which traditional community health facilities for the local population currently provided at the Avenue Clinic and 130 Hempstead Road, will be accommodated along with new facilities such as health promotion, medical loan services and a new child assessment unit.

There will be 72 beds for the continuing care of the elderly and a Social Services day centre with 40 places; facilities for 24 elderly mentally frail residents and a 15-place day centre, community clinics, child assessment facilities and child and family psychiatric services.

Mr Kemsley said that one of the reasons why planning the project had not been as quick as they had hoped, was that they were trying to provide something entirely new.

WO, October1987

Time we preserved a piece of history

IT'S the last straw - now even the historic clock made in 1924 by Watford clockmaker B. S. Morse, has been stolen from the front of the town's completely vandalised Peace Memorial Hospital.

For three years, since patients and staff moved to the new Princess Michael of Kent Wing at the Watford General Hospital Shrodells site, Watfordians and their visitors have watched with a fascinated honor as the well-loved building has taken scandalous hammering from vandals.

But the last patient had hardly moved out before the destruction began, and things have gone from bad to worse. The vandals have had a field day. All the windows have been smashed and this monument built by public subscription in memory of the gallant men who died in the Great War, is now in a disgraceful state of dereliction. It's hard to imagine that only three short years ago the "Peace" was centrally heated, with accommodation fit to be used by the health authority.

Along with Cassiobury Park Gates, it was an early casualty of the Rickmansworth Road widening scheme when the Peace Memorial [statuary] from which the hospital took its name, stood in the path of road changes and was removed from the hospital's front garden to a site beside the Town Hall opposite the library. Redevelopment work was originally scheduled to start early this summer, but plans for the site have yet to be agreed and an option to retain the familiar Peace Memorial front building has yet to be decided.

David Kemsley, South West Hertfordshire Health Authority strategy director described the theft last week of the hospital clock as sad.

The "Peace" is a focal building and the clock is a focal part of that building, he said. "To get it, someone, who knew what he was about removed the works from behind, and then went out onto the entrance roof with a ladder to remove the face."

What is amazing about the sorry story is that thieves had the cool nerve to work in full view of the busy Rickmansworth Road, overlooked by people living and working opposite.

WO, March 25 1988

Hospice gives hope

IN a country where death remains the last taboo, the word "hospice" conjures morbid and frightening images.

Often they are thought of as bleak places where terminally ill people live out their last days. Tears and despair are obviously very common in hospices, but those who work in them say there is also much laughter and joy. Much emphasis is placed on the quality of life for both patients and their relatives, and the staff's aim is to make the last weeks of life as comfortable and happy as possible.

Hospices are concerned with specialised care of patients with severe and progressive diseases—almost invariably advanced cancer. They are patients for whom radiotherapy and chemotherapy have failed, where a cure is no longer possible. Many of them are in pain, frightened and trying desperately to come to terms with the fact that they may not have long to live. Hospices aim to provide a high standard of medical nursing and spiritual care as well as support for these patients.

Patients are usually referred to a hospice by a doctor and the treatment they receive is free, although many make donations. The majority of patients who enter hospices are elderly, but the average age of hospice patients is getting lower and hospice staff have the relatively new problem of dealing with bereaved children.

There is no hospice in South West Hertfordshire at the moment, despite a huge need for one. Now there could be a hospice in Watford in a few years.

Hospices also normally have respite beds, used by chronically-ill patients such as Multiple Sclerosis or Motor Neurone Disease sufferers who come to the hospice for in-patient care for a couple of weeks while carers take a break.

A retired GP said attending to needs as well the symptons was at the very heart of hospice care. Dictionaries define a hospice as a "place of refuge on a journey." Real hospice care is about living and how to make the best of lives with the uncertainty of a serious and life-threatening illness.

"It is about how to go gently into the good night."

WO, November 1992

Works starts on the 'Mars' project . . .

Breaking ground for shopping complex

WORKMEN started up their bulldozers this week as clearance work began to pave the way for the £100 million shopping city which will change the face of Watford.

The Mars 1 development took its first steps forward as contractors set to work on the the now closed Clifford Street car park site.

WO, September 1988

Maxwell sells printing firm

PRINTING company Sun Printers has been sold by media boss Robert Maxwell to a six-man management buy-out team as part of a multi-million pound package. Plans by Mr Maaxwell to sell the factory were announced in October.

He said he would be stripping down the printing arm of his empire, the British Printing and Communication Corporation, which includes the Whippendell Road site. The West Watford works employs 200 staff and produces TV Times, Chat and Women Magazines. Company chiefs are confident of a bright future after the deal, agreed last month.

BPCC, comprising 48 factories, was sold to the management team for £265 million. Mr Maxwell's son Ian who is believed to have a 25 per cent stake in the company, and two other businessmen are non-executive directors of the firm. North Watford firm Odhams, that prints Mirror Group Newspaper titles, is not included in the deal and will stay in the hands of Mr Maxwell.

WO, February 1989

Sun land to be sold

SUN PRINTERS main premises in Whippendell Road, Watford, could be shut down and sold off to property developers by the beginning of next year. More than ten acres of land bounded by Whippendell Road and Ascot Road, was sold by print chief Robert Maxwell to a six-man management buyout team in January. This will leave almost 90 per cent of the site unused and the land, still owned by Maxwell Communications Corporation is expected to be sold.

The land is designated for industrial use and could be developed into a business park.

WO, June 1989

More traffic chaos likely

THE DEVELOPMENT of Watford and the greed of the "apparently" easy money may well prove counter- productive to the developers and local residents.

The roads in the town and all local roads in and out are already congested during peak hours and Saturdays.

Apart from the office and commercial developments in the town, the two major developments in the Lower High Street and the Dome roundabout must either take a major "market share" of customers out of the existing Watford stores and/or bring a massive influx of shoppers into the town and along the A41.

We must be talking about literally thousands more vehicles a week to make these enterprises profitable. The proposed link road can only partially alleviate the traffic problems leading in to and out of the town. What does the traffic do when it arrives in the already over congested roads in the centre of the town?

The unfortunate outcome will be paid for by a significant decrease in the quality of life of the residents of Watford and local outlying areas and a possible closure of other stores in the town as shoppers get fed up waiting for long periods in traffic jams to get into car parks.

C. R. J. L, Pine Grove, Bushey

WO, June 1989

Listed building is destroyed by fire

PARTS of an historic building in Watford were destroyed by a blaze, which took more than 30 firemen five hours to fight on Wednesday.

Classrooms were destroyed at the former Reed's School in Orphanage Road, more recently Department of Employment offices.

Part of the school was engulfed by flames in minutes. The roof and other parts of the building began to collapse and firemen had to fight the fire from outside, rather than enter the building. The development was to include conversion of the buildings into 168 flats, construction of 129 new homes and 176,000 square feet of office space.

WO, June 1989

Young leap housing queue by eviction

COMMITTEE chairman Councillor Mike Jackson (Labour) said people who had been evicted would very often go into a house that would have otherwise been let to someone already on the housing list. The queue-jumpers are creating such a problem that the council is investigating the idea of buying private homes and dividing them into short term hostels. "Perhaps if we had more hostel accommodation it would be better," Councillor Jackson said. Councillor David Barnes (Labour) said "We are not able to supply any more houses, although we should soon be doing some building in a very limited way. The whole problem is that because we have not got places to allocate, the whole thing is jamming for the people at the bottom. It's very frustrating. The sad thing is that, to some extent, we are remarkably powerless."

The council has two sites on which it intends to build council houses, in Garston (about 25), and on the Holywell Hospital site (about 140). They will know later in the year whether they are allowed to spend the £25 million they have from the sale of council houses. Councillor Vince Muspratt (Labour) said "Some of them are top of the waiting list and have been since way before Christmas."

WO, June 1989

Right: One of Watford's largest fires this at Kahne & Nagels warehouse in Imperial Way needed three hydraulic platforms to fight. Damage was estimated at £8 million. March 1989.

Next page: One legacy of some of the gangs who dug up the pavements and laid the cable are uneven pavements and badly levelled paving stones. The faults were not seriously manifest until responsibility could no longer be placed on to the contractors. .

Part XII

Mars 1 and Watford Springs

Watford people needed more shops. The town's structure meant that little 'normal' space was available. But although the Council knew that they had valuable land which could be redeveloped it is arguable that they realised the scale of project the developers suggested. It was so huge that not only would it increase the space enough to attract new trade but it would be large enough to suck in virtually all the bigger shops from the High Street. It was also lush and lavish; it had to be to attract people from a large catchment area. The money invested had to be returned, with a handsome profit . . .

Our problems start with Brent Cross. It was developed from land asset-stripped from an old-established firm making photographic chemicals, bought, the business closed down and the value of the land realised. It was cleared, and redeveloped into what we know as 'Brent Cross'.

In subsequent years 'going to Brent Cross' meant a shopping experience the like of which most had never met. Ample and convenient car parks; for those who did not wish to go by car there were regular and special bus services.

Doubtless the impact would have given a fresh urgency to bringing forward the 'Mars' plans but there will be very few who can recall the weekly 'West Herts Post' let alone an issue in January 1962 that carried a story of a project which 'would change dramatically the face of Watford within the next five to seven years' (p327). Perhaps the general public may be forgiven for their lack of interest, for how many times has something been announced, to be forgotten within days and not to resurface until perhaps decades later?

With a headline of MARS! the story told of a forthcoming February Council meeting at which would be discussed the projected plans for redeveloping the area between Queens Road and Water Lane into a shopping complex. To cost £3,000,000, the possibilities included a first-class hotel with assembly rooms behind, a tenpin bowling alley and an eleven-storey central tower block of 130 flats with garages for the ten-

ants underneath the block. The Council was looking at a plan which would ideally suit Watford people. Later, a new Council would be presented with a different set of plans; the hotel, assembly rooms, bowling alley and block of flats were gone. However, a leisure feature was included.

The 7½ acre redevelopment scheme would include Carey Place and Albert Road which would disappear completely. The Borough Council, it was stated, had sought the views of the Corporation's consultants, Hillier, Parker, May and Rowden and it was their views that the Property Committee would be considering.

The scheme fell through though the name stuck.

Years passed; steam power on the railway gave way to electric; manual accounting at the banks gave way to computer-

Above: *Queens Road still a vibrant shopping centre, c 1972*

Below, left: *Clifford Sreet was one of the several which had to go, but here leading to the cleared area known for a few years as 'Sainsbury's Car Park', the store then being in the rebuilt premises on the Technical College site in Queens Road.*

Below right: *Entrance road to the car park, from Derby Road.*

Residents' Associations . . .

power; shops in Queens Road were refurbished and given a new lease of life. Town gas (from coal) gave way to natural gas and our coinage went decimal. The Beatles and the swinging sixties evolved into only slightly more staid 70's. Watford lost most of its cinemas, found the High Street cut about and broken, lost the 'West Herts Post', the Park Gates, and, almost as unthinkable, lost Odhams as well!

The old market went as did Cawdells and after what seemed an interminable time Charter Place shopping centre—'Shoppers' Paradise'—finally opened at about the same time as Brent Cross. But a 'Brent Cross' it was not. The Mars plan had not, however, been forgotten. Developers and Watford Borough Council were biding their time; buying pockets and parcels of land against the day when action could begin. And, sure enough, in the early days of 1986—24 years on—the plans resurfaced.

The cost had increased to about £130,000,000.

A knowledgeable town trader ventured to state that there should be a commitment to revitalise the Parade and top end of the town and Councillors argued about what type of entrance it should have. . .

Behind the scenes, in Council, there were deeper rumblings. Although the council was well aware that the complex would close in the evenings, no night life, they wanted what had been originally promised; entertainment of some sort and a plunge pool was settled upon, though hardly 'evening entertainment.' Councillors wanted it within the complex; the developers knew it would not be viable to mix shops and swimming and wanted it separated . . .

At this stage of the story it is apposite to remark upon the rise of a relatively new force upon the local scene; that of the Residents' Associations. Watford Fields R A, was formed in 1974 at a time when Benskin's wanted to consolidate their brewery over ancient rights of way which were then separating their operations; later the WFRA were concerned that the Council wanted to build housing on Watford Fields (Lammas Land) in exchange for a couple of pitches on the by-now-cleared Benskin site. We owe to that group that we still have Watford Fields as open space.

Another early body, the Watford Heath and District Ratepayers Association, was actively involved with the 'Bushey Arches Traffic Management Scheme'. After years of involvement and campaigning the loss of key members hastened its decline. A little later (1972) the Oxhey Village Environment Group was formed to respond to potential disasters, primarily the concern to maintain the 'village' and conservation status, to inhibit infilling where covenants existed, and achieving considerable success in their aims.

Across the town other groups were formed, each in response to a particular threat or threats. These include Central Area Residents' Association; Lea Farm R A; Meriden R A; Leavesden Village Action Group, North Orbital Residents' Action Group (NORAG); a more complete list is on page 440. All have in common the concerns of their residents, in the main, of overcrowding, pressure of traffic or a very specific planning problem. In principle they aimed to re-inforce the efforts of their own local councillors where the councillors were unable to get satisfactory answers.

The Council's eventual answer was to set up in 1999 a system of 'Locality Managers' to act as go-between residents and council in some areas of the town. They, not surprisingly, identified problems, such as congestion and lack of open space, etc, about which the residents already knew. Over time, they found they were also unable to get answers and action and were, in effect, a further layer in-between resident and council. One of the first actions of 2002 elected Mayor, Dorothy Thornhill, was, in a cost cutting drive, the abolishing of Locality Managers .

Council had Benskin's old site across the road from the Harlequin project, and although zoned for industry (and changed to housing), it was found to be a suitable place to build a swimming complex, funded by payment from Mars' developers. But Capital and Counties would pay only £500,000 in lieu of the complex's space promised.

Below: *The 'Clifford Road' car park, colloquially referred to as 'Sainsburys', in its last days before clearance.*

The Borough's ratepayers would have to stump up the projected balance of £4,500,00. When finally finished Watford Springs was stated to have cost £10,000,000.

The first issue of the revamped Watford Our Town Magazine (October 1990) put the matter of cost rather quaintly; "The whole complex when complete will have cost the Council only 12 per cent more than it cost taxpayers to construct just one mile of the M25 motorway", the inference being that the Government took money from taxpayers for part of a road, but that, in Watford, the Council paid!

The housing that was to have been built upon the Benskin's site was built instead upon the old Isolation Hospital site in Tolpits Lane. The internal wrangling had split the local Labour group into two factions with one half trying to insist upon leisure within the Centre (despite the unsuitable mix) on the altruistic idea of forcing the centre to stay open 'so that there was life after closing time', the others recognising that a purpose designed and built swimming complex made better sense, albeit at a hugely increased cost.

The matter dragged on with plans being shown, and concerned Watford Fields' residents protesting, until Councillor Vince Muspratt told the meeting that "the complex had to be finished by March 1990 or it would never be built; Government restrictions upon spending mean that after that date the money will not be available and the much needed modern swimming pool will not be built."

'Watford Springs' opened on November 12th 1990, much later than expected and, it is stated, with considerable structural problems in its wake and unresolved.

In the summer of 1997 the Springs was closed for essential works, reopening on October 5th 1997. In August 2000 it was announced that repairs to the Springs were not financially viable; closure was inevitable.

'Watford Today' (October 2000) published some reasons: "Since its opening in 1990 there have been major structural design faults with the building which have resulted in on-going problems and short-term repair works over the past ten years. Problems have included the effects of humidity within the building and water leakage . . . it became apparent that a large investment would be required over the next few years to keep the building open.

"Watford Council have been advised that in order to keep the Springs open for the next few years would require an invest of £8,000,000. The Council has taken legal proceedings against the companies involved with the design of the pool and was successful in winning . . . the companies who were employed to carry out the building works went into liquidation and their insurance policies did not cover anywhere near close to the amount awarded to the Council, being just sufficient to cover our own legal costs."

And finishing up that residents could not be expected to pay; particularly as only 35% of those using the Springs were Watford Council residents; the remaining 65% coming from well outside the Borough.

Top: *The rear of No. 133 High Street, the subject of an archeological dig which proved unfruitful.*

Left: *1988 and the site cleared and extensive ground-work started. The whole sunken area is for the basement service area. Of the 'Harlequin Hole' it is substantially below street level to accommodate all services needed, including lifts, stairways, and a network of roads to allow goods vehicle service for the shops. The chalk, through which the foundation were dug, was once sea bed some 60 to 70 million years old. In more recent times the ground above was home to many streets and local businesses, all of which were displaced in one manner or another. At the top of the photograph the Derby Road Endowed Schools, opened in 1884.*

Though very popular it did little for Watford's evening life (which was the original intention) as would have been achieved if a leisure complex such as Woodside's Warner Cinema had been built upon the site.

As it happens, and not by any design of Watford's Council, the town does have in Harlequin an asset that is in some ways unique. Other towns in the country too have 'shopping centres'; Harlequin stands very high on design comparison, other centres may be converted large department stores, and the ancestry cannot be hidden. Even worse, some may be built out of town where shoppers forsake the traditional town-centre shops with even more dire results than we have seen in Watford.

Originally Watford wanted to build its centre further down the High Street where land could be more easily acquired. County Council vetoed those plans as 'making the shopping spread out too far' and so we have a centre that is actually in the town. The developer's of Harlequin went ahead; the Council's 'Watford Springs' was built, and demolished just ten years later as uneconomical to rectify faults or repair.

Near £12,000,000 was wasted.

There are three postscripts.

The first is a leisure complex at Woodside (Warners Cinema). Concurrently with Watford Springs and the

Left: *c1912, Queens Road, looking across Derby Road towards the High Street. The tall building on the far side of Derby Road was, at this time, Watford's Post Office (and later, Greville's).*

Below: *The premises 'A5' was once the site of an early Post Office. The modern building next along is that which replaced the Technical School after it was damaged by fire, leaving it available to be rebuilt as Sainsbury's supermarket. Here it is not long closed following Sainsbury's removal to Albert Road, near the Pond. This short stretch also once housed Mrs. Peacock's printing office from which was published the first Watford Observer in 1863.*

Below left: *A solitary figue enjoying the autumn sunshine is perhaps oblivious to the importance of the works just starting. Of the old buildings most had their fronts retained, but of the interiors much had to be rebuilt to meet modern safety and fire regulations. The wood beams of Nos. 139/141 were replaced replicating the originals.*

Below right: *As Watford's largest-ever civil engineering project gets under way shoppers are deterred from venturing along the High Street and the notice upon the site hoarding reminds shoppers that there are other shops further down . . .*

space, pin bowling, fast food, speciality pub design called 'City Dome'. The locals, realising many implications dubbed it the 'Horror-dome' and fought tooth and nail to get the drinks element substantially watered down. The plans went to the Department of the Environment; concessions won were swept away by Citygrove and Watford Borough Council and the enterprise opened in 1996. Some distance from the town's centre it is Watford's only cinema complex.

The second was that more land was to be available for development at lower High Street abutting Oxhey Park—11 acres in all.

The developers submitting plans, on Feb 14th 1992, were Zincarch/Citygrove.

Harlequin/leisure rumpus, land at Woodside was seen to be available which the Council advertised for development. It was valued at £800,000, for which the council is reputed to have received very little. A seven-screen cinema was mooted but leading figure Mike Jackson realised that that, alone, would not be viable and the remit should be widened to include 'leisure facilities'.

Citygrove, who masterminded Watford Springs, came up with a 720 car

They were aggrieved that they had not received an affirmative reply by early July, and tartly reminded the council the 'contracts' were on a 'minded to grant basis' dependent upon a resolution being obtained before July 31st. The developer's David Woolf jibed that Watford had only 150,000 sq ft of retail parks in the borough when a town of such size as Watford should have 1,500,000 sq ft. With reservations the plans were put to the Council in Chamber, with Mike Jackson pointing out that, in effect, 'If these plans be granted it will give leverage to County Council to fund a West Watford Link Road.' David Woolf's company promised many environ-

Top: At various points at the rear of the building site concrete mixing lorries were feeding the concrete pumps ...

Above right: Last stages of Phase I where the glass is being installed at the side of the High Street main entrance.

Below, left: A trio of cheerful floor layers/dressers pose for a memento photograph, with boarded-up units behind them. To the left of the picture is a unit reserved for 'Moselle' and, right, is shown the finished result.

386

mental improvements to the area but which were swamped with fast moving traffic. To add insult to injury his company renamed the area as 'Watford Arches' as Bushey Arches was not good enough. And nothing came of the forwarding of the West Watford Link Road.

The third postscript concerns a motel built in Water Lane during 2002. Local residents didn't want it and advised against it on grounds of frequent flooding. It was by our old friends Citygrove/Zincarch and the first flooding occured when building was in progress, which did not much interfere with the work. When, in 2003 the building was finished Water Lane was again flooded. Foot passengers could not access the building and it was inconvenient for cars. Water Lane was 'closed' for several months whilst remedial work was carried out.

There is yet another postscript.

Of the various occupants of the lauded 'Arches' retail park some disappeared, and in mid 2003 the whole site is now occupied as a Mercedes Dealership, ironically within 200 yards of where a 100 years or so ago the Watford Engineering Works were advertising what must have been Watford's first cars.

Above: *Queens Road is no longer. Trewins have moved into the first phase of Harlequin which saw units nearest the High Street finished and occupied. These included W H Smith's and Boots the chemists. Trewins retained their policy of not opening on Mondays, giving the centre a quiet appearance on that day. Sunday openings started on 23rd July 1995.*

Left: *With the Harlequin side of the High a veritable hive of activity, noise, dust or mud, the far side or the road suffered a constant crush.*

Below: *Once Trewins had removed their stock into their new home it was possible to demolish the many older buildings facing Derby Road/Beechen Grove and excavate the foundations and start building phase III proper, and its surrounding car parks. Here Trewins newer block, near the High Street, is still standing (seen through the 'arch' of the concrete pump). The building on the right is Marks and Spencer's store, which would be linked into the Centre.*

Cable TV . . . a chance to see yourself on screen . . .

Mars One leaves town 'no scope'

A SCATHING attack has been levelled at the Mars One scheme by a Watford resident who claims that it will leave no scope for "life after dark in central Watford." At this week's public inquiry Mr Roger Hillier also lodged objections to the threatened increase in traffic the scheme would attract and the loss of valuable town centre housing. To put it bluntly "what is in it for the residents of central Watford?" demanded Mr Hillier, of Gladstone Road.

"Watford already has more shoe shops than the average person needed, but it is impossible to buy a cabbage in the High Street," he claimed. "I am not sure that Mars One will remedy this shortfall," he remarked. Mr Hillier is a fierce campaigner against the link road, which was recently debated in detail during an eight-week public inquiry, which ended shortly before Christmas.

Watford council told this week's hearing, held at the Town Hall, that the Ml link was not a vital part of the Mars One project. "Of course, the Ml link assists the scheme but it's not essential to it," said Mr John Taylor, counsel acting for Watford Borough Council.

But Mr Hillier quoted evidence given by Watford Borough Council at the link road inquiry which stated that the Mars One scheme would be in jeopardy without the Ml Link Road, and he claimed that the council had considered them to be "inter-connected schemes."

WO, January 1988

New name for Mars 1 complex

WATFORD'S multi-million pound shopping complex—previously known as Mars 1—is to be called the Harlequin Centre. The name was chosen by a panel of judges after more than 250 people responded to a competition to name the shopping centre.

The winning name was sent in by Mrs Moyra Castle of Bushey who won a £500 shopping voucher to be spent at Trewin's, which is to be one of the major outlets in the redeveloped centre. The panel of judges were particularly impressed with the efforts of youngsters from Central PrimarySchool who launched a full-scale project on the centre.

WO, December1988
The choosing of the name 'Harlequin' proved to be very apt and brought the airy-fairy 'Mars project' down to earth. But before the work had started another outcry was raised concerning the impending destruction of some of Watford's few remaining listed character buildings; the start was delayed and many fronts and shells saved and incorporated into the High Street frontage.

The truth about Labour's rift

AS members of the Council's Mars 1 sub-committee our aim was to wrest for Watford people a bit more than shopping facilities and a small percentage of the rents from Mars 1.

It occurred to us that it was the ideal place for some additional leisure facilities in the town, being some distance from residential properties but close to car parking and public transport. Such a facility, we felt, would also be a means to avoid total shut down at night of that part of the town centre and possibly stimulate other leisure facilities nearby, such as restaurants and pubs. We were told not to upset the developer.

Although our time on the council meant that we had less experience than others of the Labour Group on the committee, we were experienced enough to know that good and forthright councils up and down the country, of varying political persuasions, had negotiated extra and quite substantial leisure facilities for their communities centred in such developments. With the Labour Party's support we pressed our point. The result was a negotiated agreement for a substantial site within the scheme for Leisure facilities and £4.5 million to equip the facility.

Although neither of us actually wanted a swimming facility, because we were looking for an addition to leisure in the town rather than a replacement or extension of an existing facility, being neither experts in the leisure field and feeling that we had done well to stand up to the Tories and pressure from some of those now calling themselves "traditional", we felt we had to accept this offer, as did the Labour Group and the Labour Party.

We both feel that had there been some will and more consultation with leisure consultants, we could have been looking at a facility currently missing in the town.

The deal we were presented with finally amounted to an extra £1½ million to vacate Mars 1 and a scheme for a comprehensive swimming facility to replace the Central Swimming Baths. What this entailed was a massive injection of ratepayers' money, again in millions, and a loss of vital housing land. In other words we would gain a better swimming facility than the Central Baths but at a huge cost and it would nullify the benefits won from the developers of Mars 1 for a completely funded new and extra facility right in the centre of the town. We were elected as Labour councillors to do our best for all the people in Watford, not to represent the best interests of developers and the powerful at the ratepayers' expense.

Councillors Veronica Conlon and Judi Jackson, Labour Group, Watford Borough Council, Members Room, Town Hall, Watford.

WO January 1988
Councillor Veronica Conlon, as Chair of the Development Control Committee, when Harlequin opened and the resultant exodus of High Street traders became painfully obvious, decided that, in pursuit of evening leisure, the Upper Parade should become a Cafe Quarter. Premises were converted into pubs, and night clubs . . . shops into cafes.

Every street could be dug up for TV

ROADWORKERS could dig up every street in South Hertfordshire if plans for cable television are given the go-ahead. The mammoth task of laying cables is expected to start next year and work could last up to five years.

A one-foot wide trench will have to be dug to lay the cables to pass every home in the area. A Watford Borough Council spokesman said highways and planning chiefs would need to have serious discussion with whoever runs the channel.

Once operational, the network will provide community-based programmes, entertainment and information channels and will allow all existing channels to be received without satellite dishes or aerials. A final decision is expected in November.

It is expected that viewers will pay an annual subscription fee for access to the cable channels. Guidelines set out by the Cable Authority require community based programmes to be given air time, so local people should have the chance to see themselves on screen.

WO, August 1989

In 1991 cable operators had merely 2000 lines installed; but by the end of 1995 this had increased to 1,200,000, and growing fast. At the same time BT had 21,000,000 residential and 6,000,000 business customers. Cable companies offered 'cheaper' phones but at a price—dependent upon accepting, and paying for, a package of cable TV options. To have and retain the telephone line a user was committed to accepting the cable TV service. Telephone connection fees could be as low as a fifth of BT's £115 and at such low prices, become very attractive to households who had not previously had a telephone.

Harlequin, finally complete.

Gorbachev sees the wonder of Watford

THE WORLD'S most powerful leader, His Excellency General Secretary Mikhail Gorbachev, headed straight for Watford yesterday in an important mission to find out what life is like for the town's workers. His 40 minute visit to CASE Communications on the Watford Business Park was in keeping with his trade theme of his two day trip to the UK.

Mr Gorbachev's personal wish to find out what life is like for the people behind the computers. How much did they earn, where did they live and where did they go on holiday were all questions the Soviet premier asked as he mixed with staff and gave them a day they will never forget.

Accompanied by Trade Secretary Lord Young and VIPs including Watford's MP Tristan Garel-Jones and Mayor Councillor Alastair Allan, Mr Gorbachev came to see CASE at work.

The job of interpreting for the Soviet premier, who speaks little English, went to CASE's Soviet Business Manager Mr Nick Applegarth who acted as principal guide for the afternoon. "I was absolutely delighted to be asked. It is an important day for all the people who have made this happen," said 28-year-old Nick, who last year spent five months in the USSR.

Before he left, Mr Gorbachev was presented with a special gift to mark his visit. Soviet aides had told CASE chiefs that the only thing he would accept would be something capturing the spirit of Watford. Watford Borough Council provided the perfect gift— the 'Book of Watford' by local historian Bob Nunn which features stories of the town taken from the pages of the Watford Observer.

WO, April 1989

Mikhail Gorbachev waves to waiting crowds when he visited Case Communications.

A community has been lost

I READ the article on the wonderful new shopping centre the town will have but wasn't there among the statistics about the number of bricks, etc., used, the number of houses that were pulled down?

In fact, a small community was lost.

I hope the profit from this venture salves the consciences of those who ordered it - or will it?
J. W. N. S, Sutton Road, Watford.

WO, August1990
The disappearance of the entire Carey Place complex and associated streets raised misgivings with some, but as the area had been systematically cleared over the previous ten to twenty years no-one bothered very much.

Harlequin centre poised to open for business

CUSTOMERS will be flooding into the Harlequin Centre next week when the first store of the multi-million pound shopping complex opens for trading. Appropriately the first shop to open, at 9am on Wednesday morning, will be Trewins, one of the town's oldest department stores.

By Christmas 40 new stores will have opened in the Brent Cross-style shopping mall which is costing in the region of £120 million.

The new Trewins store will be the biggest in the 11-acre shopping centre with 200,000 sq ft of shopping and storage space, doubling the floor space at its Queen's Road site. Trewins has been trading in Watford for more than a century.

It started as a tiny drapery business owned by a Mr Matthews in the late 1870s but quickly grew. In 1880 Arthur Trewin took over the store and by 1913 he had been joined by his brother Henry and had expanded to three shops in Queen's Road. After the Great War, Trewins was bought by Selfridges and was then one of 16 stores acquired by John Lewis Partnership in 1940.

The present site in Queen's Road was rebuilt in 1965 but the store remained, until now, the smallest in the John Lewis chain.

WO, August 1990

Not everyone has own transport

IN your July 27 issue you gave information regarding the Harlequin Centre, and the number of parking spaces, but no mention of bus services to there.

I do hope that the organisers of this development have not forgotten that there are still many people who do not have their own transport and have to rely on the bus service.

Unreliable as it is, we do get there — eventually!
R. B, Meadow Road, Kingswood.

WO, August 1990

The bus services were left unaltered (as being at Charter Place); traffic and bus lanes were altered to aid traffic flow, but with entrances and exits from the car parks crossing the flows, problems arose. Upon the Gartlett Road car park (flat land)

the Edward Hyde offices were built; the Shrubberies car park was renamed Gade and Harlequin's two new ones named King's and Queen's.

Phase II completed on time

Phase II of Watford's £100 million-plus Harlequin Centre has been completed on time. The £40 million final stage is due for completion next year and is being built on the site of the old Trewins store.

This store was completed four weeks ahead of schedule and enabled Trewins to begin trading there last August.

WO, June 1991

What future for shops?

SHOPKEEPERS in The Parade fear that soaring rates and rents will force up to half of them to close within the next six months.

That's the claim being made by one retailer who says the Harlequin Centre has created a Catch 22 situation for small businesses in other parts of Watford. Austin Rockman, who runs Sarnies Sandwich Bar in The Parade, says business has been lost to the Harlequin Centre but retailers like himself could not afford to move to the centre as the rents are so high. "I believe that we will see up to 50 per cent of traders moving out of The Parade within the next six months because they just cannot afford to pay the business rates and the rents. Trade has dropped off a lot since the Harlequin Centre opened and somebody has to do something about it soon or The Parade will be dead before the year is out.

"I have had to apply to the council to extend my opening hours just to try and keep the money coming in. I don't want to have to work 12 hour days but I haven't got any choice. If things don't improve soon I will seriously have to consider closing down altogether," said Mr Rockman. According to figures obtained by Mr Rockman from estate agents trying to lease units, the cost of a 218 sq ft shop space in the Harlequin Centre is £31,000 a year with a well positioned 233 sq ft unit available for £43,000. "There's no way businesses like mine could be able to afford those sort of prices but at the same time trade is so bad where we are we can't afford not to move," he added.

Review, June 1992

Centre opens — and that's final

MORE than four years of hard labour and planning finally came to fruition on Tuesday, when the third and final phase of the Harlequin centre was opened. Flanked by a leaping, twirling Harlequin and brass band and watched by eager shoppers, Watford's Mayor Councillor Peter Kiely revealed the plaque and declared the centre open.

A carnival-like atmosphere then filled the aisles of the two-floor mall with masks, balloons and flowers festooning staff and shoppers alike. Dominating the Watford skyline for miles around, the Harlequin Centre stretches from Queen's Road around the back

of the High Street, linking up with Charter Place.

Hailed as the major regional shopping centre for North London and the Home Counties, it boasts almost 150 shops and stores, both local, national and international. But traditional shoppers also have High Street favourites like British Home Stores, Marks and Spencer and Littlewoods, linking up to the mall.

Other stores expected to open in the near future include Hennes, Mothercare, Dixons and Miss Selfridge. Trewins was the first store to open as Phase One in August 1990.

Phase Two was completed in June last year, with the third and final phase completed on Tuesday. Managing directors of Capital and Counties and Sun Alliance Group Properties proudly declared that all deadlines had been met exactly to the day.

WO, June 1992

The opening of Phase II saw many desertions from the High Street including the showrooms of British Gas and Eastern Electricity. Elderly people who bussed into the town centre to pay their bills—and perhaps collect a prescription from Boots—found that all three had gone and they had to trek down the High Street to a then alien place.

Top left: *Naf-Naf on the corner of New Street* and top right: *Madhouse in Boots old store on the corner of Market Street.*

Right: *Harlequin was to be innovative in unit front design and in most instances a great deal of front gloss was put upon what was a quite small space behind. For a visitor to display a camera was to have a security man say "No photographs allowed", the reason given that 'store owners did not want pictures displayed in their trade press'.*

I love the Harlequin

REFERRING to the various letters and articles in the Watford Observer criticising the development of Watford, and in particular the Harlequin Centre, I thought I should write to assure you that many people including my family and myself, think a most wonderful job is being done. Of course we remember the old country town that Watford used to be, the cattle market, the High Street outside Cawdells with two-way traffic and parked cars. It seems incredible now, but there were not so many cars then, were there?

In the 1950s I worked at the Ever-Ready factory in Lower High Street and there were 120 of us with just three cars. Now I work in a factory in Leavesden with 96 people who come in more than 90 cars. That is an indication of the changes that have taken place in our lifestyles and we congratulate the council on keeping up with them. We love the Harlequin Centre and look forward to the next phase. We feel very pleased that we live in such a progressive area and we thank the planners for that.

F and G B, Duncan Way, Bushey.

WO, June 1992

Above: *'Auctions' attracted a bad press with buyers receiving rather less in their bags than expected. At an 'auction' in Wheelhouse, the ex-Times Furnishing store.* "I'm not here to sell you rubbish," *but perhaps thinks* 'You are here to buy it,' *and*, below, left: *Swag at 103 High Street, right: ex-Mothercare/ Habitat at 77/79 High Street.*

Top: *Harlequin presented warmth and cleanliness and freedom from street clutter, and, for those seeking the location of a desired store, the finder was essential.*

From Watford Springs in the bottom left-hand corner to the white wedge-shaped roof of Sainsbury's in the top right the road noose which constrains Watford's town centre is starkly visible.

It is the ring road which was deigned to have a reversed traffic flow—which is why the early multi-storey car parks had 'wrong-way-round'

entrances and exits. When the time came to reverse the flow is was deemed not practicable.

With the impossibility of making cross town journeys the increase in mileage must be incalculable. In this 1990 photograph Phase I of the Harlequin Centre is nearing completion but Queens Road has yet to be cleared for Phase III. The M1 Link Road has yet to be connected and

the Pyramid has yet to rise.

There is much building taking place in King Street. Watford Springs, though just built, will be gone within eleven years.

If one tries to follow the line of the High Street from top to bottom it disappears into and peters out at the mass of trees from Clarendon Road onwards.

Watford—34 accident black spots identified . . .

A terrifying toll on town's roads

A MILE-LONG stretch of St Albans Road in Watford has been identified as the worst accident black spot in Hertfordshire. In the last three years the stretch between Station Road and St George's Road saw a staggering 88 serious accidents. Now road safety watchdogs have asked Hertfordshire County Council to get back in the driving seat to improve safety measures for motorists and pedestrians.

They want increased spending on road safety measures—top of their priorities being improved street lighting to reduce the injury toll. They also want the causes of accidents to be monitored more closely.

Throughout Watford in the last three years there have been more than 780 accidents and 34 accident black spots have been identified.

Black spots are classified as stretches of road where there are more than 12 personal accidents within three years. County councillors were asked by highways officials to support work in improving street lighting, up-grading crossings, road markings and education to reduce accidents. As points where there have been fewer than nine accidents were not listed in the report road safety officers said the total number of accidents is likely to be much higher than the three-year total of 780.

The sub-committee heard that measures being taken were continuing to reduce the number of accidents and casualties.

Spending on road safety in Watford in 1989 was £29,500. This has been increased by 25 per cent this year to £37,350.

In Three Rivers, which covers Rickmansworth, South Oxhey, Chorleywood, Northwood and Sarratt, there were 233 serious accidents over the three-year period.

Spending in that area rose from £42,320 to £58,850 this financial year. In the Bushey and Radlett area, which includes one of the busiest stretches of the M1 motorway in the country, the injury toll for the last three years reached 154.

County council spending on road safety in Hertsmere has almost doubled from £43,850 in 1988/1989 to £82,520 until April this year.

WO, March 1990

The figures for money 'given to road safety' in 1990 were:

Watford	*£37,350;*	*780 accidents*
Three Rivers	*£58,850;*	*233 accidents*
Hertsmere	*£82,520;*	*154 accidents*

Time to tackle the defaulters

THERE are almost 17,000 people in Watford, Hertsmere, Three Rivers and Dacorum who have not paid a single penny in Community Charge.

In Watford alone, more than 500 people face the bailiffs after they failed to appear at Watford Magistrates Court last month.

Magistrates presided in six courts over three days and of the 996 summoned to appear, only 112 did so. As a result, 536 liability orders have

Top: *The mid-1930's congestion is well illustrated in this old cutting, showing the traffic leading up to the bridge from Station road in what was a bicycle age (3,445 per day).*

Above: *In 1994 County had the bright idea of reversing the traffic priorities at the junction of Leavesden and St Albans roads. All traffic northwards had to **halt** to allow southbound traffic to turn right into Leavesden Road. Chaos ensued and the resultant accidents caused a hasty rethink and return to normal 'straight-through' priority.*

Right: *It was safer for some cyclists for the St Albans Road line to ride in the centre of the road rather than kerbwise and have to cross fast turning-left-traffic at Leavesden Road.*

been served allowing Watford Borough Council to either send in the bailiffs or obtain access to wage packets.

The Clerk to Watford Magistrates Court, Mr John Clark, said "If the bailiffs find insufficient goods to pay the levy they can apply for that person to be committed to prison. I don't expect any of these applications to arrive before the New Year."

Watford Borough Council, which has continuously expressed opposition to the Community Charge, has approximately 56,000 on its register with 7,000 people not paying (12.5 per cent) and 500 cases pending decisions on rebates.

It has received £7.6 million (86 per cent) of the £8.95 million it expected to collect from the public by September 1, leaving a current deficit of £1.35 million.

A spokesman for Watford Borough Council said "We would expect the situation to improve. Although it looks like a £2.7 million deficit by the end of the financial year it would never get to that. I expect non-payment to drop dramatically by the end of the year."

WO, September 1990

Election shock

LABOUR swept back into Watford Town Hall for the 21st year running.

The biggest shock of the election came when councillor for 18 years and former Mayor, Mr Geoffrey Greenstreet, was ousted from his seat by Liberal Democrat Mrs Dorothy Thornhill by just 61 votes

WO, May 1992

Developers: cheap homes need

ALL new residential developments in Watford may soon have to provide extra housing for people on low incomes. The proposal being considered by Watford

Council's development and planning sub committee for more affordable housing in the town. An officers' report to the committee highlights the inability of low income households to find suitable accommodation because of the loss of rented housing stock and the right-to-buy policy. The committee backed a "statement of housing need" to assess the town's need for low cost housing.

The council then proposes to ask each new residential developer to make a contribution towards low cost homes—either by actually providing the homes or financial backing for homes elsewhere in the borough.

The homes would either be for rent or sale at "affordable" rates. Chair of the sub-committee Veronica Conlon said "We can only welcome any moves that help provide homes for everyone. If we can use our planning framework to try to assist the creation of more low cost housing and homes for rent in the borough then so much the better."

Review July 1992

Shameful legacy of media magnate

WHEN news broke last year that the socialist multi-millionaire Robert Maxwell had fallen from his luxury yacht and drowned off the Canary Islands, few suspected his parting would prompt the biggest pensions and investment scandal the country has ever seen.

After his death it soon dawned that the Maxwell empire was crumbling and that a huge proportion of his employees' pension fund had vanished. Hundreds of pensioners in Watford, former employees of Odhams and Sun Printers, were devastated when they heard that they could face losing the pensions they had relied on to keep them comfortable through their old age.

They are just some of 32,000 pensioners from all over the country who could find themselves facing poverty and destitution if their pensions are stopped. On Monday, while more than 2,000 pensioners lobbied Parliament and attended a huge rally in Central Hall, the Government was promising £2.5 million to keep the pensions going while it launched a thorough investigation into what had happened to the money.

More than £458 million went missing, £241 million of which is still unaccounted for and £217 million is still tied up in banks. But while the pensioners welcomed the payment at least as "a start" they still said it was inadequate. They are now determined to keep on fighting for the basic right to their pension. That fight began in earnest in Westminster on Monday and they vowed it would not end until the last Maxwell pensioner is guaranteed his or her pension entitlement.

WO, June 1992

It is arguable whether the Poll Tax was a good idea. That it spread tax among all instead of just the householder mean that young people, just earning and faced with setting up homes, were faced with large unexpected bills. That was a bad point. For an elderly single pensioner it meant a reduction. The Council were at considerable pains to note that it was a tax with which they were not in agreement, tacitly expecting many to not pay. Countrywide orchestrated demonstrations caused a rethink and reversion to a Rateable Value 'Council Tax'. 1991 Top, in the Clements precinct, bottom, Bridle Path.

Abbots and Leavesden Hospitals to go ...

Sympathy to family

I AM sure all the residents of the Harebreaks Estate would wish to offer their sympathy to the family of Councillor Bill Everett.

His sudden death was a great shock and he will be greatly missed. He was always ready to listen, always ready to help, always ready to give his time on our behalf.

It is a great pity that the community centre he fought so long for was not completed in his life time.

We hope that some part of this new centre will be named after him. He will be missed by us all. - Rose M. Steel Chairman, Harebreaks Residents' Association.

WO, January, 1990

Town Hall chief is to retire

TOP Watford council official Mr Bruce McMillan is leaving the Town Hall following a departmental shake-up.

Borough Councillors have decided to rearrange Mr McMillan's law administration and corporate affairs department. Legal issues and administration will be split from corporate affairs which includes public relations and equal opportunities.

Mr McMillan, aged 49, is to take early retirement after deciding that although the changes were a good idea, the corporate affairs role would not be challenging enough for him.

The news of Mr McMillan's departure has been greeted with disappointment by council leader Councillor Fred Hodgson who said he would be very hard to replace. Mr McMillan has agreed to stay on until the newly reorganised council departments are running and a new chief executive has been appointed.

He has been in local government since 1962 and became a chief executive at the age of 28.

He has worked for Watford Borough Council since 1973.

WO, March 1990

Hospital site homes plan turned down

PLANS to build 900 homes on the site of Leavesden and Abbots Langley hospitals have been finally dashed by Environment Secretary Mr Chris Patten.

He has accepted an Inspector's recommendation to uphold Three Rivers Council's refusal of outline permission for the North West Thames Regional Health Authority plans. The decision followed a three day public inquiry last year and vindicated Three Rivers' major objection to the scheme that it would all but eliminate the Green Belt boundary between Watford and Abbots Langley.

While accepting the health authority's proposal for a "countryside park" to replace the loosely defined Green Belt buffer zone of scattered hospital buildings, Mr Patten agreed the layout of the scheme was undesirable. He rejected the scheme not because of the number of houses proposed, but because it was unachievable satisfactorily.

WO, March 1990

Opening of town's new leisure complex

SPORT lovers will be able to enjoy a new leisure facility in Watford this autumn when the Everett Centre opens on the former Leggatts School site. The £1.5 million centre has been named after the late Councillor Bill Everett, who was a tireless campaigner for sport in the town. The centre, situated in Leggatts Way, will include the existing swimming pool, which now has upgraded changing rooms, a new modern sports hall and a new community centre.

One of the school buildings has been refurbished to form a youth wing. The sports hall offers badminton and basketball and will be run by the county council's education department as part of Watford College. It will also be available for joint use by the public. Watford Borough Council wants to ensure the centre fully represents the local population and its need and would like to hear from groups, clubs and local individuals who want to use it.

WO, July 1990

New homes for hospital site

A MAXIMUM of 840 new homes could be built on the Abbots Langley and Leavesden Hospital sites under new plans lodged with Three Rivers District Council by North West Thames Regional Health Authority. Plans envisage development of 56 acres at a maximum density of 15 homes per acre, giving the possible maximum of 840.

The Leavesden Hospital chapel, administration block and hall would all be retained. It was uncertain how large the countryside park would be. "The plan just shows the broad area of the countryside park from Langley Lane in the west, crossing College Road and running through to the open farmland to the north east. It is identifying the swathe of land to be free from development and to comprise the wedge of Green Belt land that will permanently preserve the Green Belt between Watford and Abbots Langley."

WO, June 1990

Abbots Langley Hospital started life as barracks for Canadian Servicemen, later being converted into use as a hospital having hutted wards off a main corridor. The hospital dealt latterly with aged patients needing both short and long term care. In the constant seeking to find money for the NHS the under-used site was sold for housing, being run down in 1993/4 and closed in 1994. Many remaining patients were transferred to two care homes; the all new Langley House, Garston at 698 St Albans Road, and Windmill House, Windmill Street, Bushey. The latter was previously the Bushey and District Hospital, but after closure as a hospital was refurbished for its present role.

Each home has facilities for about 48 and upon closure of Abbots Langley Hospital took 38 people; the homes each also have facilities for fifteeen day-care patients. Though Abbots Langley, and Leavesden Hospitals have disappeared many of the Abbots Ward names, Balmoral, Harlech, Dover, Stirling and Edinburgh are perpetuated as street names on the new estate.

Above: Leavesden Hospital.

Right: Residents in Edinburgh Ward. 1992.

Part XIIa

Maxwell, and Rolls Royce

*T*he Book of Watford covered extensively the story of the skill and flair of David Greenhill in establishing Sun Engraving and Sun Printers that proved to be the major part of his life's work. Also covered, but very briefly, was the downfall of Watford's mainstream printing industry. The part played by Robert Maxwell was then unknown.

In June 1923, in Slatinske Doly, an impoverished Ruthenian village, was born to Mechel Hoch, a son, Jan Ludvick. A hard life included watching and learning from meat smugglers and wheeling and dealing was to foster talents which businessmen, later, were to fear.

The boy's trait of inventing or telling a story to suit the immediate need is evidenced by varying accounts of how he came to arrive in France in 1940; he reached England and enlisted and in October 1943 joined the North Staffs Regiment.

He served with enthusiasm and as a Lieutenant, was awarded the Military Cross, given in person by General Montgomery; he survived the war; his family perished. He spoke eight languages and secured a post in the Control Commission in Berlin where his position led him into contact with a newspaper publisher where his position and knowledge were invaluable in helping get scarce supplies.

Post-war restrictions on free trading posed challenges that he was able to circumvent; he entered the world of book distribution. Robert Maxwell (Captain), as he had renamed himself, had launched himself on a controversial and meteoric career where acquisition of more and more was to be his goal in becoming a millionaire. Many of the businesses he bought and sold were merely pawns or stepping stones; his accounting methods suited the day's needs on the basis that 'they mean what I intend them to mean'. He successfully stood as a Labour

MP but was disappointed not have been selected for a Cabinet post in Harold Wilson's government.

Odhams, part of Reed International, in Watford were being pushed into bankruptcy by inept management and intransigent unions. Maxwell haggled a deal where he bought the Odhams factory, 23 acres of land upon which it stood, a print order worth £30 million and a £7½ million interest free loan for £1½ million. He was intending to sack the 1500 employees and transfer the print work to BPC plants, but instead he sacked half the staff and transferred half to Sun Printers site.

He wanted to buy Waddington's (board games) and during the battle for takeover claimed that BPCC had just sold a large property in Watford for £20million. This was an intention that had not materialised as Watford Borough Council had not given permission for Sainsburys to use the site (Odhams) as a supermarket. He had borrowed £26 million in 1982 to pay off 675 redundancies and to part fund investment at Odhams-Sun, West Watford.

He lost his take-over battle and the sale of the site fell through; his coffers were not replenished.

An early company he owned was Pergamon Press where, to interest an American buyer, he greatly inflated profits-on-paper by buying and selling to interrelated companies and overstating overseas sales of encyclopaedias. This led to allegations of fraud and inquiries that haunted him for years.

He disliked thrusting forceful attitudes employed against him that were similar to those he used. He had a complete disdain for union arrogance such that when he rescued Park Royal (then printing the Radio Times) all went well for about two years until a further bout of strikes lost 16 million copies. His

Top: 2002, The once proud company name on the ruins.
Left: The Odhams Sun Printers Ltd premises in Whippendell Road 1986.
Slated to be sold by Maxwell as a 'quick-fix', the downturn in the market and inevitable arising queries of planning consents meant that Watford contributed to his downfall.

response was immediate in sending in men with 14lb hammers and breaking the 50-year old presses.

He discovered that overmanning was rife at the Fleet Street Daily Mirror plant and negotiated a deal by which, when value of plant, building, and pension fund was calculated, gave him the paper for free, and to break the restrictive union shackles he installed new presses at the Odhams site in Watford. Even this was contentious as he had alterations carried out without planning permission; what he wanted he just had done.

There can be no doubt that the rapacity of some sections of staff and unions made his take-overs possible; each led to more, with the finality that financing needs led to raiding the pension funds in the 'certainty' that all would come right.

Robert Maxwell was an acquisitor; he had no eye or penchant for the 'doing-detail' nor did he trust staff. If he was again expecting a large sum for the sale of land, this time in Whippendell Road, the onset of recession and sharp downturn in the market is perhaps one possibility he had not included in his calculations. Allegations were published in November 2002 which claimed to cast light upon Maxwell's demise, that as a self-styled 'King of Bulgaria' he controlled the Bulgarian Cooperative Bank, which he used for extensive money laundering purposes. He had a computer manufactory making counterfeit state-of-the-art machines from stolen blueprints which were sold throughout the Soviet bloc (where Western products were forbidden to be available). The masterstroke was when computer software 'Promis' was stolen from the Americans. Promis was designed to track myriad documents through legal cases, being alleged to garner massive amounts of data with great ease, keeping track of accounts almost anywhere in the world. It could be the most superb spy tool ever dreamed of. This is what it became.

Promis was re-engineered with a hidden secret 'trap-door' which could be tapped into allowing those who subsequently sold it to unsuspecting clients to know and follow every minute detail. This was computer hacking on a vast scale, before such activities were used for such mundane tasks as spreading viruses and 'local spying'. Maxwell used his Degem Computers company to make the software, which he sold around the world, eventually to make the mistake of trying to sell the software back to the Americans.

The circumstances of Maxwell's fall from his yacht during November 1991 were shrouded with mystery, questionable autopsies and a full State Funeral in Israel.

Those who knew him ruled out suicide and the ship's rail was too high to permit an acidental fall. In January 2003 a suggestion was made that Robert Maxwell was the victim of his own making that, being involved in an espionage intrigue, he wanted a extraordinarily large sum of money to solve his immediate problems. His paymasters, Mossad, realised that Maxwell was proving dangerous and, if paid, could come back again; he knew too much. This his contacts were not prepared to face. They lulled him into believing they would agree, and would meet him on his ship to pay what he requested.

He left his cabin for the assignment but met his fate at the hands of his assassins, leaving a mystery for the world.

Back in 1935 Watford Council bought land at Leavesden known locally as One-mile Field and the plan was a grandiose complex of sports fields.

The war intervened and the land requisitioned for war needs; leased by the Ministry of Aircraft Production as an aerodrome, and aircraft factory complex, both to do sterling service. Post-war the aircraft factory stayed in the hand of de Haviland, to retain local employment, who turned from aircraft to engines. At Hatfield they turned from successful warplanes to a civil jetliner. The result, the Comet, was an outstanding success, until three were inexplicably lost. Faulty window design was blamed, but inherent was de Haviland's rush to be air-

Below: *The sprawling site occupied by Sun Engraving and Sun Printers, Whippendell Road to the left, lay derelict until demolished in 2003. Polestar Printers are housed behind in the white-roofed complex. 1990. Ascot Road is on the right; later a sensible road was made to access the Croxley Business Park.*

Leavesden: Rolls Royce bought the land for a reputed £30 million . . .

borne to the extent that fatigue testing was rushed and inefficient. And it was fatigue which caused components to fail. The lessons they were so bitterly to learn benefitted the American aircraft industry and the startling lead which Britain held for a short while was lost. From this catastrophe de Havilland's never seriously recovered and at Leavesden the engine business went elsewhere and the site acquired and bought by Rolls Royce. Rolls Royce too, in turn, went into liquidation but they still had the land which they later sold.

Although Covenants were written into the deeds that the grounds should be for sports use it suited Rolls Royce and the lawyers that the Covenants were, like the Park gates, of no value. At which stage an intense battle for development rights

ensued, and the idea of a Film Studios was sold upon the premise of huge number of extra jobs it would bring (targetted to be equal to the number of workers laid off when Rolls Royce closed but not the same); part of the land was zoned for housing and part as industrial office complexes.

By 2003 a substantial number of houses have been built together with a first phase of commercial development. It is a Three Rivers project, confirmed in February 2003, but local residents fear that the downside of extra traffic to fill the planned 3,000 car park spaces will become a Watford problem by overloading the local residential roads, despite a planned new access road to the A41.

Workers join dole as factory shuts

THE gates closed for the final time last week on the Rolls-Royce factory in Leavesden leaving behind over 50 years of historic aircraft industry. The 300 acre site has been involved in aircraft production since before the war.

The area was bought from the Ministry of Defence and the manufacturing of aircraft products started in 1939.

During World War II the Mosquito and Halifax aircraft were built at the factory. After the war, the de Havilland Aircraft Company took control of the 300-acre site, including the airfield, and by 1954 the production of piston and gas turbine engines was transferred to the new headquarters. The company produced the famed Gipsy range of piston engine, and by

the end of the 50's the Gnome gas turbine engine was produced, an engine that is still used in Wessex and Sea King helicopters.

The Leavesden plant and aerodrome has been the site of some ground-breaking industrial achievements and became a focal point for entertaining and crowd-pulling air shows.

The aerodrome is publicly licensed and operated by the company and is open to executive, commercial and private users of light and medium aircraft and the airport also has air-

Leavesden aerodrome, works and environs in the early 1970's.

1: *The A405 before dualling.*
2: *Courtlands Drive/A41 crossing.*
3: *No. 1 flight shed (Mosquito/Halifax).*
4: *M1 spur Maple Cross/Hunton Bridge, (in preparation).*
5: *No. 1 Factory, LAP Group, then de Havilland engines, now Leavesden Studios.*
6: *South Way.*
7: *Langleybury Church.*
8: *1000yd runway.*
9: *Hunters Lane.*
10: *No. 2 Factory, de Havilland Aircraft Co.*
11: *Leavesden High Road*

craft maintenance and paint-spray facilities.

In 1987 Rolls-Royce became a public limited company with a flotation of shares on the stock exchange. All was well until the shocking news that the site was to close was announced in May 1991. The fight for survival at Rolls-Royce was a long and painful one for workers and unions of the plant. Since the fateful day in May 1991, protracted talks and plans have attempted to save employees from the dole queue.

When the firm announced the intention to shed several thousand jobs, it was a hammer blow to the local workers but worse news was to follow—the Leavesden site would close by the end of 1992.

It later transpired that the total number of jobs at risk was over 1,600—all but a handful of the entire Leavesden workforce.

The resistance was immediate from the Trade Unions and local councillors feared the closure would hit the town very hard. Rescue plans were drawn up of many different sizes and ideals, and strike action was also threatened by the workers. People were angry the workforce had not been consulted in the process. Vowing to fight, union convenor Fred Hodgson said: "The best thing for us is that this site is kept open —not only for us but for our children and for our children's children.

That is the main battle we have to fight."

Anger erupted again, when Rolls-Royce announced it would be sacking everyone then re-employing them with new conditions—chiefly a pay freeze. At the time, Liberal Democrat group leader Mark Oaten said: "It is the most disgraceful display of industrial relations I have ever seen."

The unions fought the move strongly and successfully forced the company to back down. Rolls-Royce had bought the land for the site for a reputed £30m from the Ministry of Defence, and was hoping to sell it for a handsome profit. That has proved to be harder than first thought, as the land is designated Green Belt and residents were given a chance to air their views via a questionnaire.

WO, June 1993

Film plan is in the can

Plans to turn Leavesden Airfield into a multi-million pound film studio development, creating more than 3,000 jobs, are finally in the can. Millennium Group Limited announced on Monday it has purchased the disused airfield from owners Rolls Royce for £42½ million.

Watford and Three Rivers Councils have already approved plans drawn up by Third Millennium Studios on behalf of MGL to convert the 200-acre site into film and television studios. The scheme also includes 300 homes, a family leisure centre and the development of a nature site and open recreation areas. Angelika Brozier, joint chief executive of TMS, said: "We believe that Leavesden is a great site with enormous potential for the development project. It will reinforce Hertfordshire's position in the British Film and Television Industry and will generate substantial employment opportunities, with some 3,000 new jobs estimated."

The phased development of the site is expected to take three years with further investment from the company of more than £150 million.

The former Rolls Royce engine factory was converted into a temporary studio last year for the filming of the new James Bond movie Goldeneye, which finished shooting in May. Eon Productions, who produced the movie, said they now hope to make all future 007 films at Leavesden.

Watford Council have greeted the news of the deal's completion with delight. Council Leader, Vince Muspratt said, "This could be the biggest boost to Watford in decades, not only in direct employment terms but in the spinoffs which will benefit the town as a whole."

Review, November 1995

Right: February 1993. Leavesden, No. 1 Factory, virtually cleared before closure where this group commemorates the last engine serviced at Leavesden (a Gnome Helicopter Turboshaft engine), with some of the remaining employees, ending more than 50 years of aviation history on site. The site closed 11th June 1993; the airfield continuing until March 1994.

Below: Leavesden Park office blocks upon the site of de Havilland/Rolls Royce No. 2 Factory. Spring 2003.

Revelling into the small hours

LATE night revellers will be dancing with delight at the news that restaurants, winebars and even pubs in The Parade, Watford, have been given the go-ahead to stay open until 3am every night except Sunday. The decision for a six month trial scheme was made by Watford councillors on Tuesday, in a bid to inject some life back into the heart of Watford.

But central residents, who only learned of the move yesterday, are furious and have vowed to fight it all the way. At the moment all premises except the town's night club, reopening as Kudos, have to close by midnight. The move means that even pubs like The Artichoke will have the go-ahead to apply for an early morning liquor licence from the courts.

Chairman of the Development and Planning Committee, Councillor Ms Veronica Conlon, a member for Central ward, said after Tuesday's meeting "The decision to allow some late night opening in this part of town is a positive one and should silence the critics who say the council does nothing to bring new life into Watford. We hope to attract investment in the Parade in the shape of leisure time facilities, particularly for young people. The council will still be able to impose earlier closing times as part of any planning consent."

But members of CRAW, the Central Residents Association of Watford, are said to be furious at the news. Spokesman Mr Victor Lewis May said: "We will be taking legal advice and consulting with our MP. The council are intending to turn this part of town into a 'Reeperbahn' complete with brothels. Life is already in the Parade with us–the residents–but they have forgotten us again."

Watford Borough Council has stressed research and police evidence indicated new leisure developments in the town centre were unlikely to lead to any significant worsening in late night noise or disturbance in the area. The Chicago Rock Cafe winebar and newly refurbished Kudos are due to open in September.

WO, July 1992

Retail park

I REFER to your report in respect of the retail park to be placed at Lower High Street.

I note that Mr Toby Bains and Mr David Woolf have been telling the people of Watford how badly they need such a scheme and how wonderful it is all going to be.

Not long ago they were saying the same thing about the Horror Hutch at Woodside Playing Fields on behalf of Citygrove. It is good to know that developers have our best interests at heart but I wonder if the gentlemen mentioned live near either of the sites.
C. E, The Gardens, Watford.

WO, August 1992

Top: *The Warner Cinema complex at Woodside, a general view, and, right the foyer and popcorn bar.*

Bottom left: *The Public's interest in the Council meeting debating the pending closure of the Assembly Hall led to a full gallery and the opening of Committee Rooms to cater for the overflow meeting, to where the proceedings were relayed by loudspeakers. March 1993.*

Bottom right: *During 1994 the Assembly Halls were run under private management—here the new signs later being installed in the October of that year.*

Improved reception at Town Hall

A £300,000 facelift for Watford Town Hall's reception area will offer a "one stop shop" enquiry point for the public. Councillors gave the go ahead to the scheme at Monday night's management committee meeting.

Enquiries on services offered by the council will be dealt with in the new reception area and ticket bookings will also be taken. The reception area will also include a play area for children, exhibitions and an interview room to allow people to make enquiries in private. Wheelchair ramps and toilets for people with disabilities will be included in the new reception area. The last Town Hall facelift cost £2 million. Councillor Terry Lester, vice chair of the management committee, said: "The council recognises that in a time of financial constraint we have to make decisions on just how much we can spend on projects such as this."

Review, Aug 92
The One-Stop shop was opened in September 1993

New homes brings rail link nearer

A NEW 457-home development is to go ahead in West Watford bringing with it a substantial contribution towards the cost of the proposed Croxley Green Rail Link.

Fairview New Homes agreed to pay £350,000 towards the rail scheme as a condition of getting planning pennission to develop the 17-acre Scammell site.

Proposals put forward include demolishing existing buildings at the Tolpits Lane site, providing access roads and landscaping open spaces.

But concerns were raised when Watford Council met on Tuesday and gave the scheme the go ahead. Meriden Labour Councillor Paul Woodward said "With this development potentially there are going to be an extra 400 cars passing through our streets every day in the rush hour and that situation is disastrous. I support the scheme but it is important we put pressure in the right areas to bring traffic calming to West Watford."

Mike Jackson, leader of the council, said "The opportunity to have an efficient transport system which will take people into the heart of Watford is one of the brightest pieces of transport news we have had for a long time."

During discussions on the proposed housing development Stanborough Conservative Councilor Sheila Jones asked for an added condition that all dwellings should have individual water meters. This follows a recent Review report of a flat owner's complaint of unfair communal water metering at another Fairview Homes development in Albany Grove, Sandown Road.

All new homes in the Three Valleys Water region must be fitted with water meters, but the water company say the manner in which the bill is apportioned to individual units is the responsibility of the managing agents. Roger Carter, Watford's director of Technical Services, advised councillors it was outside the council's power to impose such a planning condition and it could only be made as a request to the developers. The issue of water metering is due to be discussed by the council's development control sub committee next month.

Review, January 1993

The face of Peace to come

SIX lorries will roll on to the Peace Memorial Hospital site in Rickmansworth Road, Watford, next month bearing the first part of the South West Hertfordshire hospice scheme. They will bring half a dozen sections of what will become an enormous portable cabin — large enough to provide a day care centre for the terminally ill, to be assembled behind the main frontage of the dilapidated old hospital building. And the day care centre will be ready to take its first patients by the end of March.

News that the first part of the hospice will soon go ahead came just weeks after South West Hertfordshire Health Authority decided to allow part of the site to be developed as a hospice. This delighted the thousands of local people who had put their names to petitions asking the authority to do just that. The new day care centre will open initially for two days a week, quickly building up to four days a week.

WO, January 1993

Land sale cash to boost college

COLLEGE sites in Water Lane, Watford, Greatham Road and William Street, Bushey are set to shut this summer with the land being sold and the proceeds being ploughed back into local education facilities. The Water Lane site in particular is expected to be lucrative land to sell because of its closeness to the town centre and its access to the M1 Link Road.

The William Street site may be more difficult to dispose of because it is on Green Belt

Top: *The Metro Centre in Three River's Tolpits Lane.*

Left: *Cox's specialised in making tubular seating and furniture—very suitable for office and factory environments—as an alternative to wooden products. They established a pre-war factory on the By-Pass where springs were provided by Chiswell Wire Company who were founded in 1932/3 in Sandown Road at the Balmoral Road end. Chiswell's main business was then supplying springs to High Wycombe furniture makers. Both firms were pressed into war production, as were others, and after the war reverted to their previous roles; but Cox's finished in the ownership of Raleigh Industries. In rationalisation Raleigh's decided that the Watford plant was not viable. It closed in 1967, the premises having been divided and let in small units.*
In the early 1980s, after Croxley Business Park was built, the Cox's site was scheduled for the same 'business park' treatment, but with the onset of recession came to nothing. The site was cleared, and is now 'Costco'.

land. Ridge Lane, where the art department is based, is a fourth site earmarked for closure—but the college is keen to try to retain this. Hertfordshire County Council owns all the land, but it agreed to lease the sites to West Herts College at a "nominal rate" until at least June 1994.

Activity at three sites has already slowed considerably and after June there will be no activity at all at Water Lane. College principal Dr Frank Baker said part of the Faculty of Visual Communication remained on the site, but this would be based at Hempstead Road from September. Engineering students currently based at Greatham Road will also move to another unspecified site after the summer holiday. And students from William Street, studying auto-engineering, will also be working at another site in September.

Money gained from the sale of college sites will be ploughed back into improving facilities at other college sites. Dr Baker said the new £9 million plus Leggatts Way building, which opened in September, was paid for from money raised by selling the former Courtlands Drive site. This building now houses engineering and computing facilities, management studies and the sports hall. "Further education has not benefited in that way in the past. The county council is to be congratulated for having the foresight to do that," said Dr Baker.

WO, April 1993

Hospital surgery record

THE day surgery unit at Watford General Hospital has treated record numbers of patients during its first month of extended operating hours.

The new service has produced a dramatic fall in the waiting times for patients needing a wide variety of surgical treatment health authority spokesman Mr Mark Purcell claimed on Wednesday. More than 120 patients have been called in for their operation

weeks and sometimes months before the date they were originally given for inpatient treatment, he said.

Ms Angela Gilmore, the day surgery's manager, said "One patient was booked to have his operation in November but actually came to us in June. Patients being brought forward are having their operations a month earlier on average. "The patients sometimes can't believe we are offering them earlier dates but they are certainly grateful."

The waiting times for day case surgery are now less than three months and still falling.

Mr John Crisp, consultant urologist and director of surgery at the hospital, said "The expansion of day case surgery at Watford General Hospital has been tremendously successful. "In many cases given dates in advance of when they were originally booked to come in."

WO, July 1993

Are we entitled to 'freebies'?

WE are a heterosexual family of five, no gays or lesbians, no one cheating the state with false claims, no unmarried mothers, or so that it sounds more respect-able, no single parents, with the result that there are no bastards in the family, nor are there any intentions of having any under the circumstances described.

Could you kindly inform us of our rights, entitlements or any freebies to which we may be entitled. We all pay taxes in, then sit back

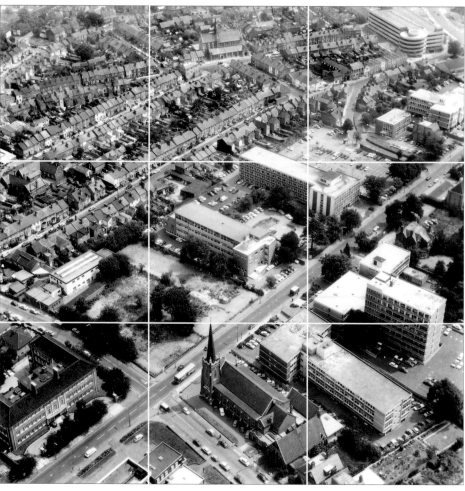

Top: *Labour Club Premises, Clarendon Road, 1999. Demolished 2002, rebuilt as office block, 2002/3.*

Right: *Clarendon Road, 1972. In C Gartlett School ground is a car park, straddling C and E is the new Oxford House and next to it is the cleared site of St Stephens Church. Straddling E and G is the cleared site later that of Sun Alliance offices. Crossing St Johns Road, in the bottom left corner are the Eastern Gas Board offices. In H is the Congregational Church; second office block right is Gresham House, once Oakley Studios.*

and watch it being handed out to those who claim incessantly, with no contributions being made. "We only want our rights", they claim, regardless of any responsibilities they may have for the position in which they find themselves, often much better than those of our elderly neighbours residing or existing around the corner. - C. M, Cecil Street, Watford.

WO, August 1993

Hospitals to merge
WATFORD General Hospital and Mount Vernon Hospital in Northwood are involved in negotiations that could result in them becoming a joint NHS Trust by April, it was revealed yesterday. A statement from the hospitals said a feasibility study would be carried out during the coming weeks to find if the new trusts would be "mutually beneficial for the local population and for both hospitals and community services.

Mount Vernon Hospital is already an NHS Trust. It was one of the first hospitals in the country to gain trust status. Watford General Hospital manager Mr Ian Campbell stressed one hospital would not take over the other. "It will be for the mutual benefit to both hospitals and for patients in the future," he said.

WO, August 1993

The name is different: Mount Vernon and Watford Hospitals NHS Trust, the grouping having taken place. Medical and care facilties at each differ and complement each other. It is to Watford's advantage to have access to Mount Vernon's expertise. Mount Vernon does not have an Emergency and Accident Department but does have a renowned cancer treatment centre.

Car parks have been extended; the bus stop is inside Mount Vernon's grounds—which are large—and there's an air of unhurried space. The bookshop and fund-raising shops are separate buildings as is the hairdressers; the coffee shop sports a decor not out of place in a good class High

Street shop. The hospital started as the North London Hospital for Consumption and Diseases of the Chest, a Northwood branch following. This hospital, with the surrounding land, was the gift of Charles Dunnell Rudd, for which the plaque in an entrance hall notes a date of 1901. Mount Vernon may lack the modernity of Watford's sardine-can block but it is set and spread in grounds about half the size of Cassiobury Park; the peaceful ambience must contribute to some feeling of well being. JBN, 1997

WATFORD GENERAL
- Total area of the hospital is 11 acres, on what used to be the site of the original Watford Union Workhouse.
- Building area on the site is 54,730 square metres, excluding Shrodell's.
- The hospital currently has 380 beds in use.
- Two percent of the hospital is said to be in Condition A, 92 percent in condition B, three percent in Condition C and three percent in Condition D
- Bringing all the buildings up to condition B will cost approximately £900,000

MOUNT VERNON
- Total area of the site is 69.711 acres, all of it designated Green Belt.
- The area of building is 45,861 square metres.
- The hospital currently has 350 beds in use.
- 12 per cent of the hospital is said to be in Condition A, 66 per cent in Condition B, 20   per cent in Condition C and two per cent in   Condition D.
- The estimate of bringing all accommodation up to at least Condition B is £1.5 million.

WO December 1993

DIY park planned for High Street site
A MASSIVE retail park for DIY, furniture, car pets and electrical goods is set to be built on a two-acre site off Watford's Lower High Street.

The scheme includes bulldozing the 200-

year-old pub The Wheatsheaf—and developers Zincarch have agreed to donate £25,000 towards adjoining Colne Valley Linear Park.

Last night Watford development councillors were due to give formal approval to 24,000 sq ft of retail space with 125 parking spaces on the site bounded by Lower High Street, the River Colne, Railway Arches and Oxhey Park.

Councillors will specify that only non-clothing and food stores can go on the site. "It is not considered that the town centre's vitality or viability would be adversely affected by the type and scale of retail development proposed," says a report to councillors. Developers Zincarch, based in Covent Garden, say they've already got potential occupants for the new retail park including Fads, Globus Office World, Carpetland, Essex Furniture, Tempo Electrical and Harveys.

Review, October 1993

Future Mayors to be political
FORMER mayors of Watford are dismayed the long tradition of the town's first citizen being "above and beyond politics" has ended. They say the decision to elect mayors only from the council's ruling group is deplorable and a "nail in the coffin" of the office of mayor.

Watford's ruling Labour group ended the tradition at Tuesday's meeting of the council, despite protests by Tories and Liberal Democrats. The socialists said the convention of a mayor being above politics had not worked well and past mayors had strayed into political issues. But former mayor Mr Geoffrey Greenstreet said changing the system was diabolical. "This is a nail in the coffin of this office. I think it's despicable and a very sad day for the town."

Another former mayor, Mr John Watts, said "It is the kind of thing you would expect from the British National Party. "This is not the socialism you would expect from a Labour council. It is very sad, I can hardly believe it has happened." Next year's Mayor would have been a Liberal Democrat. The present Mayor of Watford, Labour councillor John Horsfield, supported the move.

WO, October 1993

Allow free vote on next mayor
COUNCILLOR JACKSON is in error when he asserts that his proposal to monopolise the mayoralty is democratic. Only the system in the USA, where mayors are elected by the citizens, not just Councillors, can be said to be truly democratic—Watford, to its credit, and as a result of an initiative by the then Conservative-controlled council, devised a superior system more representative of the town as a whole.

The mayor sometimes represents the council but, at all times, the mayor would represent all the people of Watford including those who work here.

The office of mayor is non-party political

In 1993 the Cannon cinema in Merton Road is the town's last. Lasting for a short while after the Woodside's Warner complex it was closed, sold and left boarded up until the front was refurbished in 2003.

Dedication of the new Cross at Watford Heath . . .

and ought to be seen to be so. The points system is fair and demonstrates the impartial nature of the selection for mayor.

The method was the result of a gentlemen's agreement and, significantly, it is Councillor Jackson who seeks to break it. I wonder if he will bully all his party colleagues to vote with him when the next mayor is elected. If the office is non-political, why not allow a free vote? Watford's Labour Party rules the town on a minority of votes from the electorate so if Conservatives and Liberal Democrats agree on a nomination for next year's mayor it would be grossly undemocratic for Labour to reject it.

Councillor Alastair Allan, Councillor for Park Ward and former Mayor of Watford.

WO, October 1993

The Memorial Cross on Watford Heath

Erected in the Oxhey Churchyard in 1916 in memory of the 38 men of Oxhey who had already given their lives it was 'temporary', but names continued to be added until the end of the war in 1918.

Arrangements were made for a more permanent site and one of two plantations on Watford Heath were selected. Watford Urban District Council at first saw 'no object in re-erecting the wooden cross on Watford Heath.

The reluctant Council were finally persuaded 'provided that the Cross be maintained at no cost to the Council'. It was duly erected. With the passing of time the residents of Watford Heath adopted the Memorial and flowers were regularly placed at the foot of the

Cross. The Memorial lasted until 1951 when it collapsed.

At an Annual General Meeting of the Oxhey Village Environment Group in the late 1980's a proposal was adoopted that it be restored, and planning permission was granted by Watford Borough Council (at the going commercial rate) and an appeal launched.

The target of £1,000 was quickly reached and the new Cross dedicated by the Vicar of Oxhey, the Rev John Orme, accompanied by Rev Surat Hynd, Vicar of St John's United Reformed Church Northwood, and Honorary Queen's Chaplain, the dedication talking place on May 8th 1994.

Top: *Halfords on the Parade, Nov. 1989.*
Above: *Happy buskers on Christmas Eve 1992, Charter Place Entrance.*
Below: *Set in quiet surroundings upon Watford Heath a large number came to the take part in the short ceremony of the Dedication of the Cross. The men are outnumbered by the women and for those who suffered grief and parting from loved ones, mainly sons, brothers and husbands, during past conflicts, the replaced Cross has an especially emotive meaning. 1994.*

Rail Crash
A rail crash at Watford Junction caused one death and 68 persons injured. The crossover of the southbound train of empty coaches from the slow to fast up lines should have presented no problems; the 15.04 from Euston, a four-coach unit well loaded, was drawing into Watford, and is variously reported as having 'stopped' or 'slamming on the brakes'.

8th August 1996

Party Time
Watford's new MP, Claire Ward, claimed the constituency for Labour for the first time since 1979, polling more than 25,000 votes, and becoming the youngest female MP of 'Blair's Babes' in Parliament.

WO May 1997

New post to steer revamp
A new post has been created by Watford Borough Council to oversee the £60.5 million plan to revamp the neediest part of the borough. Ms Yvonne Fraying takes up the role of the Single Regeneration Budget from January 5th., with a seven-year contract by which time the project is scheduled for completion.

Another new post of Organisational Development Consultant has been created to change the way the council's estimated 800 staff are trained and assessed.

January 1998

Shelter for homeless
The Salvation Army Citadel has been bought earlier in the year by the New Hope Trust, for a sum of £185,000. The Trust hopes to turn the building into temporary accommodation for six months.

Long-term plans are optimistic that it can be turned into a permanent shelter.   *Sept 1999*

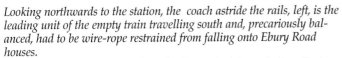

Looking northwards to the station, the coach astride the rails, left, is the leading unit of the empty train travelling south and, precariously balanced, had to be wire-rope restrained from falling onto Ebury Road houses.
The derailed coach on the right is the first unit of the train from Euston from which most casualties came. August 1966.

Right: Pickfords Repository, George Street, once the site of Healey's Brewery, shown here in 1990. With properties in nearby King Street a phase of redevelopment into office premises took place in the early 1990's.

People-power win crossing . . .

En route to traffic chaos

After 19 months of road works and near constant disruption to traders and residents the finished Green Route has been branded a failure by Watford Council.

Chairman of Planning and Highways Andy Head said "One problem is that buses have to join a single lane of traffic after passing through traffic lights. They are then stuck behind motorists which defeats the purpose of giving them priority."

The project Engineer at Herts County Council's environment department, Nick Gough said: "Unfortunately the Green Route is a long term scheme and it will probably be several years before the full benefit of this scheme is realised." Councillor Vince Muspratt said: "Most of the side roads have been reduced to one lane. Motorists wanting to turn left or right have to wait behind each other getting more frustrated. This is repeated at Garston Parade, and Langley Road."

WO, Oct 1999

One immense benefit was that phased lights at the crossroads of Station Road/Langley Road and St Albans Road at last allowed pedestrians to cross safely. The downside derives from Abbots Langley, Bedmond and Leavesden motorists being throttled by Leavesden Road/ Lowestoft Road and in consequence using Nascot Wood Road/Langley Road.

With no 'Right Turn' into St Albans Road from Langley Road traffic needing to get to Rickmansworth Road would make the short distance along Station Road to the junction roundabout to do a 360 degree turn to return to St Albans Road, join the Green Route bus blockage and thus add to congestion. This in turn helped bring forward a rethink of the Watford Junction road revision scheme, the effects of which have yet to be seen.

A more important downside, not immediately apparent, was that the scheme was sold on the premise that numbers of buses would be increased and that electronic time boards would be installed at major bus stops to indicate the expected time of arrival of the next bus. Both these improvements failed to materialise and hence the scheme is still only part installed as at 2003. Contrary to Nick Gough's assertation that 'time is needed', no improvement has shown itself.

The blight of the ghetto

Mrs Pamela Parmar, who runs 'Upstairs Dowstairs' hairdressers after working in St Albans Road for 25 years says HCC has let the residents and businesses down and: "We have been left with a ghetto, and who wants to come to a ghetto?"

WO, November 1999

Pedestrians dodge traffic to avoid subways

Mrs Phillipa Rees, of Essex Road complained to HCC about the difficulties the elderly had in getting from Essex Road and adjacent, to the High Street. In 1998 HCC carried out a survey and found that more than 1,600 people crossed the busy Beechen Grove Road to Albert Road (near Sainsburys) between 7am and 7pm, with just 40% using the subway.

The Central Town Resident's Association, had also been long campaigning for the crossing and, seeing it opened, Irene Adams, said: "The elderly, disabled and mothers with children do not use the subway because it is dirty, smells of urine, and is badly lit. Everyone feels vulnerable walking through it."

WO, November 1999
HCC took note and in May 2001 the crossing was built and opened.

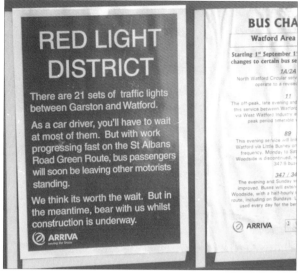

Posters in local buses promise misery for 'car drivers' as the buses 'leave you standing'. Unfortunately for the area it is not selectively 'car' drivers but also van, lorry, and utility-services drivers. It is also unfortunate that 'car drivers' rarely took their cars onto the buses and so missed this brilliantly worded warning. Seen on the 348 Kingswood-Mount Vernon route.

Inferno destroys school

On the last sunday of October an electrical fault caused a fire at Knutsford JMI School which in the course of a few hours defeated the efforts of firecrews and destroyed ten classrooms. In the classrooms were the results of months spent collecting memorabilia of the school's first sixty years.

A quick delivery of 12 mobile classrooms will enable a semblance of school to restart. Rebuilding is expected to take 18 months.

WO, November 1999

Above: *At the new pedestrian crossing Fred Hussey has cut the tape, pressed the 'Wait' button and now leads a mini-procession across in safety. 2001.*

Right: *Pre-'Green Route', 1991; to cross St Albans Road to Station Road was to risk life and limb; there were no safe phases until 1999.*

406

West Watford and South Oxhey granted £300,000 . . .

Run-down areas win £300,000

The funding was granted last week from the Single Regeneration Budget, which was set up to improve two of Hertfordshire's most rundown districts. West Watford Information shop is the biggest beneficiary at £80,000; Westfield Community School will receive £70,000; the adult education programme, £15,800; Harwoods Recreation Ground £26,000 to build a five-a-side basketball area and extension to football facilities; a £6,000 grant goes to Laurance Haines School for as computer room; £11,000 towards two community garden projects in South Oxhey; and £47,425 towards South Oxhey's library's lifelong learning centre.

WO, December 1999

Glass tower is favourite

A £3 million children's centre is to be built next to the Peace Hospice in Rickmansworth Road—a three-storey energy-efficient building made of modern reflective green glass.

The glass design received more than 60% of almost 1,000 people who voted for the project, to be called Peace Children's Health Centre. It will provide dental care, audiology suite, child and family clinic, and support for children with special needs.

WO, December 1999

Controlled Parking Zone

Many local roads near the Junction and town centre are used as 'long-term' free car parks by shoppers and commuters, to residents' great disadvantage. With pressure from several residents' associations the Council accepts the necessity for action and, after much consulation introduces CPZ. Residents buy a 'permit' for their car. Penalties for infringement were fixed at £40, increased in 2003 to £60, half price for prompt payment.

Below, left: *Lower High Street c1958. Percy J Wilson's drapery store, on the corner of Water Lane, has closed.*

Below right: *Harlequin frontages replace the earlier shops and the Pyramid the old store.*

Black and white suits me

Trying to give us a record of what the town looked like, Mr Nunn used computer techniques to convert black and white photographs into colour prints As one who dabbles with picture enhancement in my desktop publishing activities, I applaud his patience and dedication to this unusual project.

But I hope Bob Nunn will forgive me if I say I must question how genuine a representation of old Watford a book can hope to be.

Personally, I think the past looks better in black and white. I love old monochrome photos because they are more atmospheric and they represent the best at the time the pictures were taken.

Roy Stockdill

F O, September 1999

America and Germany had colour-print film during the WWII; postwar austerity prevented its widespread adoption in the UK until the late 1950's. Black and white was the norm for home darkroom work and newspapers; history has to be grateful for that fact. There was available 35mm colour slide film, but suitable cameras were then expensive to a public used to roll-film box-type cameras.

Kodak popularised colour slides with the Bantam Colosnap camera c1957, priced at £10 15s. 1d., half the price of a modest 35mm camera. It was not until Photo Technology introduced 'Photocolor II', simple chemicals for home colour processing, in 1975, that photographers could produce worthwhile colour prints in their home darkrooms. At this time the snapshotter was rather indifferently served, quality-wise, for colour prints and would remain so for some years to come.

The latest colour film printers, c2002 on, state of the art, are fully digital. The image is scanned, colour corrected and printed onto the photographic colour paper by high quality lasers; lenses are no longer used!

Daguerrotype photography, one of the epoch-making inventions in the history of mankind, was invented in

1839. It spread across the work; even to Leeds where the Mayor, Joseph Bateson, was photographed, and the result tastefully coloured. Painted backgrounds were introduced in Britain by Jean Claudet c1850 and the Daguerrotypes skillfully tinted.

Lumiere successfully produced 'Autochrome' colour plates and launched it upon the market in 1907 when it remained successful until the 1930's. When coloured postcards were the vogue a well produced colour card was far more enticing than a similar view in monochrome.

But, then, colour was a luxury and cost a little more . . .

Getting an art buzz

A giant hornet (Heather Burrell), spiralling Harlinesque steel sculpture(Adrian Moakes) and and a multi-coloured Memory Wall (Carl Fleischer) are three works of public art Watford has chosen to buy with a lottery grant of £95,000 as part of the new-look town centre undergoing a £5.5 million refurbishment.

WO, Nov 1999

Anger at invasion of new homes

Government plans to build 43,000 new homes in the south east of England every year for the next five years could change Hertfordshire's rural life for ever, according to county council leader Richard Ellis. The Governments wants at least 60% of the new houses built on 'brownfield' land and wants the homes to include large numbers of small, affordable properties.

WO, March 2000

Night bus to take trouble away from town

Didn't; shortage of funds.

1999

Airfield plan 'is rape of the land'.

Offices covering almost 40,000 square metres with more than 1,500 car parking spaces may be built on the former Leavesden Aerodrome site. Leader of Three Rivers Council said: "We are very aware of the serious concerns of residents about access, traffic and transport issues. We share the residents' concerns and we will scrutinise very carefully all details of the application with a view to minimising traffic impact."

WO, March 2000

Elected Mayor?

15,427 people voted for one of three options of which 651 papers were rejected, 69 as unmarked, uncertain, or identified the sender and 582 were not included because voters failed to complete the three-part requirements.

The result was a announced as a vote for an elected mayor and cabinet.

July 2000

Violence rages in High Street

Police used batons to break up a massed brawl and a teenager was left needing emergency eye surgery as violence raged at both ends of Watford High Street at the weekend. The trouble started outside Destiny nightclub; police quelled the violence and made one arrest but violence flared again about 4am at King Street.

A spokesman for the police said: "We are really at full stretch at the moment. There are up to 10,000 people coming into the town at weekends, and all we can do is try to keep the people in the town centre safe."

WO, August 2000

Recording studios to move in

CTS Studios, moving from Wembley, will begin recording orchestral work at the Colosseum in Rickmansworth Road in the autumn. A new control-room and large-screen digital projection facility will be created.

WO, August 2000

Incompetents or comedians?

The accounts of the Borough for 1999/2000 were not resolved: from page 1 of the WO April 13th Mrs Sharon Burd, finance director, said: "We did not always know exactly what money had been spent." But Vince Muspratt, Labour leader of Watford Borough Council, said: "However, no money has been lost." Clearly our great leader Vince knows more about accounting than Sharon—perhaps he should give her a helping hand.

For nearly 30 years I was MD of a number of companies. If my accountants had run books like Mrs Burd, I would have sacked them. If I had made statements like Muspratt, the revenue and probably enforcement bodies would have looked at me and my companies very closely.

Incompetents, or comedians—which?
S B

WO April 2001

Council's accounts fiasco

In what he describes as an extreme move District Auditor Mr Mick West said he had been forced to 'disclaim' the accounts for 1999/2000, a rare step meaning he cannot guarantee their accuracy.

July 2001

Watford Springs–astounding state of affairs

I am much obliged to Mr Odusina, communication consultancy manager of Watford Council, for his information of those who took responsibility for accepting the Watford Springs contract. I sympathise with his problem when he says: "I cannot say which councillors voted which way on the matters almost 14 years ago."

This is an astounding state of affairs for a major commercial undertaking, costing possibly £20,000,000 at today's prices. This loss of money is the equivalent to £250 for every man woman and child in the town.

The coming local elections provides an opportunity for the electorate to examine the commercial experience of the candidates and elect mature and qualified 'directors' to 'Watford plc'.   N S

WO May 2001

300 home estate planned

Linden Homes plan a 301-home estate on the former Metropolitan Station Approach site in Watford. Of the total there will 45 houses and the remainder will be apartments. About three quarters of the homes will be for private sale and the rest will be affordable housing for rent. The first phase is for for 113 homes, and the rest by the year following. £300,000 is to be paid in Section 106 money as contributions to 'local education, public open spaces and to finance road improvements'.

June 2001

Health role for MP

MP for Watford has been appointed parliamentary private secetary to the Minister of State for Health, the appointment being made by the Prime Minister Tony Blair.

July 2001

County council wants 4,400 homes built on your doorstep

A survey commissioned by Herts County Council identified 105 locations suitable for 1,300 new houses and flats. Included were allotments in Vicarage Road, the grass verge alongside Church car park, former Salvation Army Hall and grass verge in Beechen Grove near Albert Road South.

Councillors in Three Rivers joined Watford Councillors in an attack on the plan. While County Hall stress that the Urban Capacity Plan is theoretical the leader of Three Rivers Council has condemned at least 50% of the sites as unacceptable: "Nor will we agree to the cramming of our villages and towns with this preposterous proposition put forward by Herts County Council."

October 2001

Official: Green Route a Failure

Although changes look set to be made it would cost taxpapyers £1,000,000 to scrap the scheme.

A spokesman for the county council said: "The Green Route has not been entirely sartisfactory and it is because people have not been happy that we have reviewed it."

A report shows that although less cars used the route journey times have increased.

WO, October 2001

Theatre to receive cash boost

HALF a million pounds will be given to The Palace Theatre by Watford Council to help with a major renovation project. The sum will go towards restoring the Grade II listed Edwardian building and improving disabled access.

About £1,670,000 has been raised so far by the theatre to fund the rest of the scheme but the £125,000 to be taken from the council's Cultural Strategy reserves is urgently needed to fill a budget shorfall.

The remaining £375,000 will be given to the theatre in Clarendon Road in the later stages of the modernisation project and will be provided for in the 2002/2003 council budgets.

Administrative director of the Palace Theatre, Ms Mary Caws, said: "This money

---

Top: *An empty bus-lane forces a queue of vehicles to back up. On the northbound side of the road the clogged up road at the Homebase lights causes long tailbacks to the town hall.*
St Albans Road faces clogged up junctions at Balmoral Road; Longspring and the Dome Roundabout at morning and evening busy periods.
This is third fiasco put upon St Albans Road by County, the first being traffic lights at underpass roundabout, removed PDQ, the second traffic priority reversal, p393, also removed PDQ.

takes us a step closer to providing the people of Watford with the theatre they deserve."

The theatre is due to close in July when building work will start.

WO, Jan 2002

The scale of victory

LIBERAL Democrat Dorothy Thornhill became Watford's first elected mayor by inflicting a crushing defeat on Labour's Vince Muspratt. In the poll for post of Elected Mayor the final margin of victory was shocking in its scale. She won by 8,204 votes, 155 per cent more than her closest rival. And the Lib Dem only narrowly missed out on an outright victory in the first round of the double vote poll.

No one predicted such popularity.

She polled a total of 13,473 votes, after second choices were taken into account, trouncing Mr Muspratt, who won a total of 5,269. Tory candidate Gary Ling polled 4,746 in the first round just hundreds short of Labour.

Green candidate Steve Rackett took 851, Socialist Alliance candidate Paul Woodward 390, and Fat Cat candidate Tristram Cooke 330.

The 'missing £500,000' figured large in claims and counter claims as the candidates put their agenda to public meetings. Later, Mr Muspratt was to admit that an installation of an inadequate computer system, installed in 1999, led to the problems. At the meeting he disclaimed responsibility; from the Leader of the Council a fact hard to accept. Mr Muspratt left Watford after the election result, travelling to Norfolk where he settled, resigning his position as H CC Councillor for Meriden Ward in October 2002.

The election results saw significant gains of Lib Dem from Labour of Central and Holywell Wards where, at the latter, Councillor Steve Palmer, Vince Muspratt's right-hand man and executive member with responsibility for finance, was decisively ousted.

One of Mayor Thornhill's first promises was: "To deliver open honest democracy", and that all political parties would have access to documents which used to be restricted to the ruling Labour Party. Lack of access to documents was an oft-heard complaint from Councillors when trying to reply to queries from residents.

During the summer of 2002 the details of financial inaccuracy were stated to be from invoices for an extra £1,200,000 cost of town centre enhancement work having been 'not fully costed and reported'.

During the first half of 2003 the usually frequent notices in the local paper of Watford's 'Planning Applications' were noticeable by their absence, whereas Hertsmere and Three Rivers continued to appear. As a palliative it is promised that from September 2003 the applications will be posted upon a web site, shifting the duty from council to 35,000 households to frequently check.

This ignores the fact that by no means all households would, even with facilities, have the diligence to regularly check when it is far easier to scan the newspaper. It will surely be seen as a means to rush plans through without adequate safeguards.

New-site plans

The Allied Carpet store in Derby Road/Queens Road, once the site of the Wesleyan Church, has been empty since April 2000. A plan has been suggested to develop the site into 94 high quality homes and 316 square metres (3476 sq ft) of commercial units, and in July 2003 stated as "7-storeys."

November 2002

Round-the-clock drinks

Pub, clubs and bar may be allowed to open around the clock in biggest shake-up of licencing laws since 1914-1918 when 'hours' were introduced in an effort to get munitions works, especially, back to their work benches.

The proposals by the government are that landlords may decided their opening hours, that the Borough Council will issue licences, rather than the Justices; that it will promote trade and stop the closing-time run to 'drink-up and leave'. Locally the town centre residents are more wary with more than 20,000 revellers coming into the town centre and cafe quarter every Friday and Saturday evening.

WO, November 2002

Park and ride scheme scrapped

Hertsmere Borough Council approved a committee's decision to delete the controversial Stephenson Way park and ride site from their plans, also agreeing not to release land from the Green Belt.

It was said that: "Things have moved since the basic studies of seven or eight years ago. There is now a need to revist the transport study. Watford cannot hope to built to its heart's content and hope others use their Green Belt for its car parks."

WO, January 2003

£700,000,000 media park

MEPC, granted planning permission by Watford Council, now needs permission from Three Rivers. When finished in five to ten years time Leavesden Park will be set to host Britain's studio-complex, boasting a 50-acre back-lot. Up to 5,000 extra jobs could be created giving rise to residents' concern about the impact of traffic on congested local roads.

MEPC will give more than £20,000,000 in section 106 monies for local community projects. Councillors felt that '30% of Leavesden Park workers would travel by public transport were over optimistic'.

It was argued that £500,000 allocated for traffic calming would not stop motorists using St Albans Road and Hempstead Road as 'rat-runs', but it was stated that this would achievable with a shuttle-bus service, new cycle paths, footpaths and a car-sharing scheme.

The project would involve reworking surrounding roads including Junction 20 of the M25, Courtlands Drive, Hunton Bridge, Ashfields roundabout, Leavesden Green roundabout, and the Dome roundabout, which will made into two separate roundabouts.

WO January 2003

Sad to learn of Premier's fate

I WAS very sorry to read of the closure of Premier Coaches (The Watford Observer, January 31), after 80 years in business.

I have happy memories of safe, efficient and enjoyable journeys with them during the 1950's and 1960's, when living in the Watford area.

It is indeed sad to see the closure of such local firms. Progress may be all very well, but as an older member of the community, I find some things moving a little too speedily. — Mrs C., Cheddington, Leighton Buzzard

WO, February 2003

Floods–again

For the fourth time in five years some of Watford flood spots have been inundated. This recent flooding is stated to be the worst since 1947.

Many local road, including Lower High Street, Water Lane and Stephenson Way had to be cordoned off. Tesco's prepared sand bags, fortunately not needed.

Guests at the Premier Lodge Hotel in Water Lane had to be moved to accommodation in Kings Langley; Grant Ausden pinpoined some blame on the acres of concrete where once there used to drainage land; David Degan, ex-chairman of Friends of the Earth blamed the car for being too cheap and consuming 'about a billion gallons of fuel a day in the western world' and, later, it was noted that Water Lane remained closed for some months for 'remedial work'.

WO, January 2003

Council to launch planning web page

RESIDENTS in Watford will be able to access planning applications on line when a new web page is launched by Watford Council this September. The site will allow people to check on the process of an application, look at proposals and log any objections they have. The council hopes this will help improve the speed with which it deals with applications.

It believes that access to applications on the internet will prevent members of the public coming in to the town hall and asking to see individual plans, which is often time consuming and inconvenient.

The news follows fears that the Government could strip the council of its planning powers if its performance does not improve significantly. The council has been acting on advice of the office of the Deputy Prime Minister to improve the rate with which it deals with applications, but is having trouble recruiting and retaining staff.

FO, July 2003

Aphotograph of Clarendon Road Corner, taken near a half century ago shows the High Street and shops in High Summer. The vista is plain and uninteresting; the road functional. Consumer goods were becoming plentiful, and so were cars and traffic problems. They then seemed huge but not so bad as modern times. Traffic along the street kept the shops alive and vital.

The planners had to do something and that something was to route the traffic along a track overlaid upon the ancient Derby Road and the newer Exchange Road. A pedestrian precinct was the 'in' buzzword, a 'good idea'.

The artist's impression, 1964, below, gave a glimpse of things to come. Even, perhaps, persuading a landlord to agree redeveloping his property, and giving up a few hundred square metres of floor space over four floors to provide a canopy entrance. The flyover is lightly sketched in, the trees, in maturity, are small and see-through and the shoppers (minus bikes and buggies) are guided each side of the central features.

Artists' impressions are rarely of much use to lay persons and visual and reality rarely concur; they are designed to 'sell' the plan to officialdom.

The photograph, summer 2000, is a good average; there's no sight of road let alone shops and Watford's largest independent department store. It would be fair to argue that the subtle closing of the top end of the town in favour of easy pub night life has been no small contributory factory for Clement's impending demise in 2004.

When Capital and Counties masterminded the design of the Harlequin Centre; they knew how the comparison between

Top: *The 1950's and 60's Clarendon Road Corner;*

Lower: *The imaginative plan for the flyover and precinct; low trees and shrub beds, few people, no buggies, owners willing to redevelop, and no Clarendon Road (note the shrub beds). 1964.*

Bottom left: *Same spot, 1980, Clements visible in all its glory as well as other shops. The telephone kiosk and adverts are pointers . . .*

Bottom right: *2003 and the prominent curve of the road confirms that there's 'nothing up there'*

Next page: *Clarendon Road c1960 and the same aspect 2003 with traffic lights at St Johns Road.*

their gloss presentation and the drab street would work in their complete favour.

The Councillors were out of their depth with little idea of what was about be unleashed; their squabble was about entertainment instead of coordination. If they saw letters of concern in the press they would have been treated with disdain and ignored. The aftermath was that for nine years the High Street presented the appearance of a run down dump and while the 'visitors' were delighted with the Harlequin centre the thinking residents, the people who lived in the town and paid their rates,

"Our population in the day increases fourfold . . . to work and shop . . ."

were ashamed at what was left behind. It remained their despair; lack of town cinema and the installation of the inverted 'glass umbrella', and chrome and glass 'W' (both outside Gade House) did not help. The increased number of shopping and cafe quarter vistors meant that indiscriminate parking had to be avoided and to this end concrete balls were placed alongside kerbs. As it was impossible to see along the road extra signs were installed.

The Millenium gave Leader of the Council, Vince Muspratt, the opportunity to give the High Street a make-over, which he took and saw through to completion. The anomaly is that, despite the High Street from Queens Road to Clarendon Road being pedestrianised, it remains a bus route, with cars following, and from this there is a gradual rejuvenation of shops taking place—at the expense of the upper High Street which is so tastefully hidden.

Many planners and experts have had a hand in shaping Watford's environment with some leaving tangible benefits; but benefits usually bring unforeseen disadvantages and those who for some years are of an age to enjoy the benefits will, one day, ask—when their peace is disturbed—who allowed this to happen?

The cafe quarter's facilities prove so popular that at the weekend pleasure seekers arrive in coachloads. One or two clubs hold a 'membership' almost the equal of the Regal or Carlton cinema of old, at about 1,200 persons each.

The cinemas were family, with an ice cream in the interval. and closed in time to catch the last bus home.

The clubs and bars serve alcohol and are are open until 2 or 3am and several are seeking a permit to open until 4am.

CCTV cameras are needed to monitor the closing time, fracas are frequent and complaints made about the odour of the Pond—dubbed 'a septic tank'. Local residents are disturbed by turning-out time noise, damage to parked vehicles and by low-hovering helicoptors and police sirens. The cafe quarter may be 'vibrant' but, like the Harlequin Centre, serves mainly outsiders.

Statistics are interesting. In about thirty years the population has increased from about 70,000 to 79,792 in 2002. The loss of playing fields, infilling and new estates is out of proportion to the 3,000 or so homes that the increase represents. Much of the need for housing is from the increased number of elderly living on their own; a greater number are required for single-parent families who, at an early age, see motherhood as a step to housing and benefits. In the meantime there is genuine need for low cost housing for families with a low earned income. At the same time there are many houses coming onto the market being refurbished, and let. The result is that a victorian terrace house may have a letting price of £1,200 per month and as a consequence is let to several 'co-tenants' who may, or may not be car dependent.

The next interesting fact is that given in *About Watford,* Spring 2003, in which it is reported that 'Our population stands at 79,749 (National Survey, 2002) although in the day this increases fourfold with the number of people who come here to work and shop [to 318,996].'

With 224,247 people coming into, and going out of, the town each day it is a huge testimony to the engineering of our victorian main road structure that it copes. But for many of the town's 33,000 households it can, and does, present quite great problems of speed on unsuitable roads, instant gridlock following an incident and costs to residents in supporting the Controlled Parking Zones where it exists. It has to be accepted that buses are inadequate to cope with more than a desultory amount of this traffic while rail fares markedly increase living costs for those who are obliged to take the train. To balance this pressure the Council's newspaper talks about its commitment to 'raising the quality of life'. Any resident who is left hounded by the pressures introduced by those attracted to works and shops will wonder if any planners stand in the bus queues and listen to the raw comments?

It is into this scenario that a further two to three thousand homes are currently either in stages of building or actively planned. They are announced as providing 'benefits' to the town; and each developer will 'contribute' approximately £1000 per dwelling in 'Section 106' money to improving the local area, and road infrastructure. This 'tax' upon development is seen as a 'planning gain' and is primarily designed to enhance the area

Cardiff Road . . . SRB . . .

which remains after the cream is developed. It is also supposed to provide pocket parks, as play areas, but, again with all space used this effect proves sometimes controversial.

'Friends of the Earth' are notably absent at raising comment at this stage. But for an area that was in its prime in the days of generating electricity and destroying Watford's refuse and rubbish, and a hundred years later needs an access road to aid its regeneration, the 'Friends of the Earth' will be vocal, but not as Friends of 'People'. Cardiff Road is the area, and at the time of writing, the area is promised rejuvenation, hopefully not at the expense of the residents.

The Harlequin centre was announced as 'bringing shopping benefits' to Watford people. Of its 140 or so units few, if any, are run by local businesses. Almost, if not all, are franchises or branches of multiples or combines; loved by youngsters they take trade from neighbouring towns. There were in the glory days of the High Street many multiples; but also a greater number of individual businesses than the remaining few we have.

Despite its gloss and ambience our choice is limited and if the garments, fashions, shoes, jewellery and such-like are not to our choice there is not much left. Harlequin, like Watford Springs in its time, attracts about 35% Watfordians, and 65% out-of-towners. That 65% contributes most to Capital & Counties from rents and percentage of takings.

For a few years the Planning Department of the Town Hall has been working on the Watford District Plan. This sets forth in meticulous detail the sizes of dwellings, how near the cycle and car parking may be; the amount of 'green space', planning density, etc, and, when passed takes the town up to 2011.

Effectively eight years in gestation and of eight years life.

It is a planners' dream document.

Their legal and business experts will analyse their options and if any way can be seen to further maximise the return from a development their legal departments will be well in front of the Town Hall. To paraphrase an advert "Experience Counts." With current Government guidelines insisting that south-east England erect a huge number of dwelling Councils' hands are

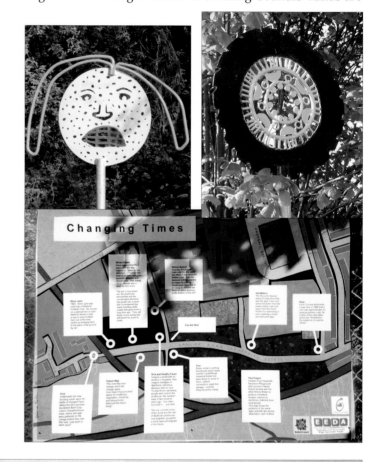

This page, above: *Councillor Robert Gordon faces an irate and anxious crowd of pupils who fear their school is slated for closure for housing and right: Bushey Hall School's pupils were moved to Grange School, London Rd, Bushey, and, after a while, housing built. See schools, p358.*

Above right:
The two painted iron-work motifs were designed by school children local to Holywell and Cardiff Road area. Funded by the SRB the face depicts the 'Pest House' in Willow Lane (for infectious diseases) and the Wheel and Tyre the car-breaker's establishments once nearby. The painted sign shows sites of other similar motifs and the dark mauve area astride Cardiff Road the site of the main area for regeneration. 2003.

Bushey Hall School 3/1990

the Sun Site . . . West Watford

tied. To object to a planning application is costly, and in almost all instances the result goes against the local council. From which it will be realised that local councils take flak by obeying Government guidelines.

The planning process sometimes involves consultations. In earlier years they were taken at face value. Plans were put up on a series of stands, viewers looked, some looked knowledgable; some saw further and wanted to ask questions of the two of three persons from the department concerned—usually County Council. Answers were usually vague but "We will note your concern, Sir". Sometimes a small detail would, indeed, be changed. Most times the plans went ahead. School closure have been a vicious source of angst. A closure would be announced, concerned parents worried, teachers organised protests, the affair dragged on and eventually the school closes. After a year or two, or more, lying empty, the demolition gang arrive, the debris carted away, and a housing estate goes up. For the parents a local school is no longer local.

Consultations don't take place when a site is empty; by some means unknown to those outside the few in office who sift the 'sensitive financial information', a plan is produced and announced to the press to gauge reaction. After a few tweaks a visual is produced and the project goes to 'consultation'; by that stage it is almost certain to proceed. *JBN*

Top: *This ground once held Watford's pride—its Electricity Generating Station; here cleared and awaiting a new future. 1998.*
Below: *2002 plans for the Sun site; left, on the old Ascot Road Corner looking townwards, and right, the town end looking towards Two Bridges.*
Bottom: *A sight unseen for 100 or so years, before Jones built his first print works on then virgin farmland. Latterly 'Odhams-Sun', 2003.*

Possibly coming to a car park near you—200-300 flats . . .

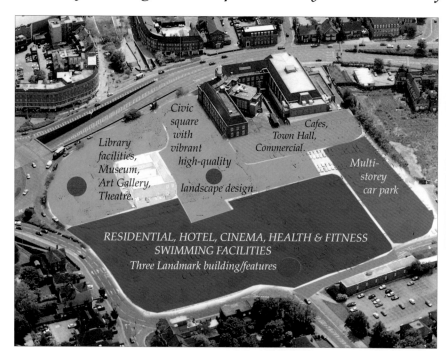

Library facilities, Museum, Art Gallery, Theatre.

Civic square with vibrant high-quality landscape design

Cafes, Town Hall, Commercial.

Multi-storey car park

RESIDENTIAL, HOTEL, CINEMA, HEALTH & FITNESS SWIMMING FACILITIES
Three Landmark building/features

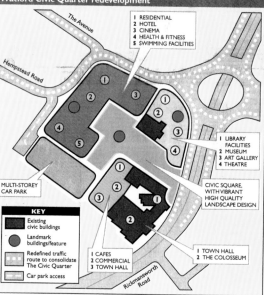

Watford Civic Quarter redevelopment

The Avenue

Hempstead Road

1 RESIDENTIAL
2 HOTEL
3 CINEMA
4 HEALTH & FITNESS
5 SWIMMING FACILITIES

1 LIBRARY FACILITIES
2 MUSEUM
3 ART GALLERY
4 THEATRE

MULTI-STOREY CAR PARK

CIVIC SQUARE, WITH VIBRANT HIGH QUALITY LANDSCAPE DESIGN

KEY
- Existing civic buildings
- Landmark buildings/feature
- Redefined traffic route to consolidate The Civic Quarter
- Car park access

1 CAFES
2 COMMERCIAL
3 TOWN HALL

1 TOWN HALL
2 THE COLOSSEUM

Rickmansworth Road

The plans make a degree of sense; the Town Hall would gain a 600-space multi-storey car park, hopefully with enough capacity to serve residents and visitors to the facilities, as well as town hall staff. As shown in the outline the Avenue roundabout would be abolished with the result that the feeder road would be able to access Watford via the Avenue and roundabout, and return to Hempstead Road; but not return to local roads without there being traffic lights or mini roundabout. Nascot residents would be obliged to join the 'green route' traffic and enter the village via Langley Road. Also to access the area will be residents from the 350+ homes in Rickmansworth Road area, 600+ from the homes in Whippendell Road and 155 from Clement's site. It is conceivable that there would be a knock-on effect at the roundabouts to the Croxley Business Park!

Top right: *'Civic Quarter area.'*
Above left: *The Avenue Car Park. 2003*

Below: *The 'Supermarket built on my old man's allotments' referred to on page 9. The vista extends at the left to the gasometer, lower High Street, to the Premier Lodge in Water Lane there hiding older buildings over which St John's church spire rises. 2003.*

. . . *and elsewhere* . . .

1550 new homes near town centre

Towards the close of press for this work the several new plans for development include:

Allied Carpet site, Queens Rd	96
The Clements site	155
The Metro site, Rickmansworth Rd	301
The Sun site, Whippendell Road	400+
The Springs site	300+
Leavesden Business Park	?
124 Rickmansworth Road (Observer Office site);	84+
Civic Quarter	250+

All will contribute monies to road and traffic management (a great increase in the number of sets of traffic lights?). Of these plans the Sun includes a health and fitness centre but otherwise there is no mention of schools, shops or doctor's surgeries. Nor extra roads.

It is admitted that the Civic Centre's are preliminary proposals*, (mainly to move the museum so that the Springs site may proceed; that houses may be built thereon), but at first sight the suggestions for the road layout smacks of the work of someone with little or no local knowledge.

* Though no further details have been made public 'Classic Concert Trust' wrote to their Friends, in Summer 2003, that "We have been assured that the inclusion of orchestral concerts certaily fits in the with plans for the new Civic Quarter in Watford . . ."

To get to shops within Watford's centre the only route for these 1550 dwellers is Rickmansworth Road, Whippendell Road and the Town Hall Roundabout.

Residents' Associations

Bradshaw Area Residents' Association
Callowland Triangle Residents' Association
Cardiff Road Residents' Association
Cassiobury Residents' Association
Central Area Residents' Association
Green Lane Residents' Association
Harebreaks Residents' Association
Harwood's Residents' Association
Lea Farm Residents' Association
Meriden Residents' Association
Nascot Residents' Association
North Orbital Residents' Action Group
Oxhey Village Environment Group
Railway Terrace Residents' Association
Rookery Tenants and Residents' Association
Tudor Residents' Association
Waterfields Residents' Association
Watford Fields Residents' Association
West Watford Residents' Association
This list is not inclusive nor does its assert that any association listed is still in being at the time of compiling during July 2003.

Top: *Razor wire at the Metro site and* above left: *an example of superb driving, but alas stuck, in trying to get a huge mobile crane, daily, to a block flats being built near the Town Hall. Both of Linden Homes, 2003, 2001.*

Left: *a reminder of Waterfields as a lake (looking towards Water Lane), 1903.*

XIV

Contemplation, and caring

MANY of the changes to the locality, reflected in this tome, have been wrought in the name of progress sparked by the explosion of population and the attendant vehicular traffic; some of of it at misguided hands—a case of council vandalism. A few, now precious, buildings apart, the only reassuring threads of consistency over past 100 years or so have been, in order of maturity, The Watford Observer, Watford FC and the even younger but no less important Palace Theatre.

The locality has grown to love and take pride in its club and the response to such as the 1999 Division I Play-off Final at Wembley, when 39,000 Watford fans bought tickets, would be beyond the imagination of the Hornets' founder, the retiring Henry Grover. It was he who successfully sought permission from the Earl of Essex for a group of young men to kick a football about Cassiobury Park, not far from the magnificent house itself, in 1881. Henry played 10 years for the club, which soon began to take part in organised matches under the name Watford Rovers.

They played in Cassiobury Park, then Vicarage Meadow and then Rose and Crown Meadow and won the Herts County Cup in 1888-89, with such notables as C H Peacock (proprietor of The Watford Observer) in their ranks. The club's first star was Freddie Sargent, one of three brothers who turned out for the team. Fred was a speedy and adroit goal-scoring forward but when the West Herts Club and Ground was formed at Cassio Road in 1890, overtures were made to Watford Rovers to represent the new organisation's football section.

After much resistance, Rovers were absorbed and became West Herts by name and the only other local side to rival Rovers was Watford St Mary's, drawn largely from working-class ranks. The rivalry between them and the 'Toffs' at Cassio Road continued but the spread of professionalism, initially rebuffed by West Herts in 1894, was such that interest in purely friendly matches began to wane. So, in 1897-98, both clubs adopted professionalism, West Herts having already sampled organised Southern League football the previous season, finishing ninth out of 13 in Division 2.

The third significant name in the club's early history, behind that of Grover and Sargent, was Benjamin Apps, who had voted for professionalism in 1894.

He realised the burden of paying players would be too heavy for the running of two clubs and successfully sought an amalgamation with Watford St Mary's, who played in Wiggenhall Road. The two clubs joined together at Cassio Road but elected to play under a name familiar to both camps: Watford FC.

The new club entered the 20th Century with what would prove to be a rare success: the clinching of the Division 2 Southern League title. Although sporting professionals, the club was distinctly amateur in concept, run by the West Herts committee and playing at a ground that utilised several temporary 'stands' for spectator use. Watford escaped relegation in 1901 when their opponents in the play-off, Grays, declined extra-time when the sides were drawn after 90 minutes, on the grounds they did not want to miss the last train home.

The club, which was to be known as the Wasps, Magpies,

Printers, Brewers and Blues over the next 60 years, escaped the drop by default. The following year they again struggled, lost the final play-off or test match and were relegated. There then entered the next two significant characters in the history of the club: the first was Ralph A Thorpe, chairman of the Urban District Council, and one of the key men in the making of the modern town of Watford.

Mr Thorpe, who was known as the Prince of Good Fellows, dug deep in his pockets to support the club, probably to the tune of £3,000, and appointed the club's first manager: one of the most famous players in the land, John Goodall, the former international. Goodall, at 39, was past his prime but steered the club back into the Southern League's top flight at the first attempt, without losing a game. While Watford have had their major financial crises in 2002 and 1952, the financial wolves have been sniffing at the doors for the best part of 100 years, for as I wrote in the club's official history: "In the unfolding story of Watford FC it is as if the community has nursed a particularly sick baby, which was not only fortunate to survive the ordeals of birth but suffered recurrent lapses throughout early adolescence and seemed haunted by the prospect of premature death. Delighting in those moments of apparent, flourishing health, the community has seen Watford grown stronger and come of age".

The first decade of the 20th century saw the club struggle in the Southern League Division I, become a limited company and then in 1914-15, a season over-shadowed by war, they clinched the Southern League Championship. This success was largely due to the second and longest-serving of the club's managers, Harry Kent, who was something of a transfer magician. He unearthed footballing jewels for little investment, sold them for a profit at the end of the season and then went in search of more. He managed against a background of problems with Watford forced to seek a new ground, for professional football was still regarded as tainted by some landowners, including the Dowager Lady Essex who owned Cassio Road.

There entered the sixth name: Benskins Brewery who were to help fund the club for the next 36 years, in effect buying Vicarage Road and equipping it for the club's move there in 1922. By then, Watford, with the rest of the Southern League First Division, had been absorbed into the Football League, joining Division 3 S where, in a manner typical of Watford's early history, they languished until the league formed a Fourth Division in 1958. There were hills and valleys, stars such as the goalscorer Freddie Pagnam and the darling of the 1930's, Tommy Boy Barnett, who served the club for over a decade, setting up aggregate appearance and goalscoring records.

The 1930's were remembered as a period of stylish failure, as the club went close to promotion in successive seasons but, after the Second World War, the dark days descended. Watford, then known as the Blues on account of the colour of the shirts they had adopted back in 1927, struggled but hope flared briefly in 1952. The Watford Observer called on the board to resign and played a large part in helping the club go to the town and form a new board with a fresh share issue. There was a period of brief promise with some good signings and the introduction of floodlights to the ground where the terraces had been concreted during the 1930's.

But following on from Kent, Benskins and Barnett, a new figure strode the turf at Vicarage Road at the end of the 1950's and, although his departure was to cause acrimony unmatched in the club's history, Watford's more fashionable and successful era that started 43 years ago, owed much to the signing of Cliff Holton. An almost legendary figure, a player in his prime and mentioned as an England candidate, the big striker came to Fourth Division club, as it suited his part-time intentions, and spearheaded Watford's rise from Division 4, with a memorable cup run to boot. Holton captured the imagination of the football public as no one individual player has achieved before or since.

The Holton Era sparked bigger attendances and a residue remained as Watford again hit lean financial times during which another significant individual emerged: Ken Furphy.

Forced to try and conjure a silk purse out of a financial pig's ear, he achieved in 1968-69, that which had eluded 12 of his predecessors, winning promotion to Division 2 of the Football League.

An appearance in the FA Cup Semi-Final was to follow before Watford again reverted to type and the success unravelled to see the Hornets, who had worn black and gold since 1959, plunge down to Division 4. Another era and another significant personality moved onto the Vicarage Road stage: pop-rock star Elton John who then helped to bankroll significant ground improvements and recruited the most popular and most successful manager in the club's history: Graham Taylor.

Success followed success with Watford winning the Division 4 championship, promotion from Division 3 the following year and, after three years making progress and recording some stunning cup successes, the Hornets achieved 'the impossible dream' of top flight football in 1982. A year later they finished runners-up to Liverpool, qualified for Europe, in which they played six games, and then won their way through to the FA Cup Final, where they lost to Everton in 1984.

Again the success turned sour, Taylor moved on and Watford dropped back, finally returning to the equivalent of the old Division 3 by the time the prodigal manager returned. Lightning did strike twice with Taylor steering

Watford to the Division 2 title and then, via the Play-off Final in May, to the top flight the following year. But football had changed since 1982 and Watford found the rarefied financial climes too much and fell back quickly to the First Division.

Taylor's record at Watford had included five promotions, three cup semi-finals and two visits to Wembley, but upon his second departure, it unravelled again. The board invested heavily in an ill-considered appointment of Luca Vialli as manager and, exacerbated by the collapse of the significant television revenues, the club faced a multi-million pound shortfall.

Once again the club went to the public and is now back on track, albeit with financial wings trimmed. The history of Watford FC has been a case of hills and valleys but supporters over the past 50 years have had considerably more ups to enjoy than downs.

Oliver Philips, 2003

Above: *Cliff Holton kick-started the successful modern era at Vicarage Road with goal-scoring feats without equal. He also took part in what would become a cornerstone of Watford's approach to the public; community involvement. Here Holton, (right) pushes over a pile of pennies with fellow goalscorer Dennis Uphill and Manager Ron Burgess (in the hat) at the Coachmaker's Arms.*

Right: *One of the favourite sons, Luther Blisset, home-grown England International, whose association with Watford F C coincided with the club's halcyon era in which he played such a key role.*

Dad's Army

The delivery entrance to Tesco's warehouse in the High Street sits squarely over what was once number 237 High Street; there's no place to fit a Blue Plaque or, indeed, any other reference to its history. Since 1922 the shop had been an antique dealers premises. Thomas Govett, who owned the business, was uncle to a young lad, Jimmy Perry.

Jimmy lived with his parents in Barnes, was mad keen on films and their stars. In 1940 young Jimmy at aged 16 was old enough to join the nearby LDV (Local Defence Volunteers). But Barnes being too near the blitz for comfort the family needed to move. Mr Govett died in 1940 and Mr Perry, Snr, running an antique business in Brompton Road, decided that 237 High Street made sense, and so moved his stock to Watford.

The smart Jacobean two-storey building nestled between the *Leathersellers Arms* public house, and Mrs Crane's refreshment rooms, whilst behind lay the remains of Watford Mill and a small stream ('the cut') which ran directly alongside the back of the large garden of No. 237. The Perrys decided to carry on using Govett as a trading name for the business as they presumably thought they'd be living in Watford for a only short while. In fact their home in Barnes did suffer damage during an air raid, and so they remained in Watford for the duration of the war and then for another twenty years.

Young Jimmy, now living in Watford, wasted no time at all in signing up with the local LDV (now Home Guard) in Watford which were the 10th Herts Battalion under the command of Colonel C K Cotton. They were based at Sedgwick's House just a few doors along the High Street at number 221. This imposing double-fronted Georgian residence was formerly the offices for the Sedgwick Brewery, however when the company was absorbed into Benskins brewery in 1924 the offices were vacated and the house was left empty for years and was supposedly haunted. Part was briefly occupied by the Royal Air Force Cadet Corps who took office in October 1938, however it was given over to the Home Guard in 1940 when the Air Corps moved elsewhere.

During this time the various officers, men, locations and incidents were making indelible impressions upon young Jimmy's mind and, some 20 years or so later formed the bedrock basis of a TV show called Dad's Army.

Unlike the platoon in fictitious Walmington, real Home Guard units were a lot larger and patrolled much smaller areas. In the show the size of the unit and the area covered were exaggerated for comic effect. In Watford Jimmy's platoon patrolled nearby Bushey Arches where the railway crossed the main road, as well as the River Colne bridge and the shops in the lower High Street. They often paraded in Watford Fields opposite the Perry's shop, and special training exercises were occasionally carried out in Cassiobury Park and at Russells Training Camp which was a large house and grounds situated to the north of the town (now an old people's home). By this point the Home Guard were well established, had got over their early problems and had become a fit, fully-trained fighting unit, or in Captain Mainwaring's words 'a smooth, well-oiled machine'. However, the 10th Battalion, being in town, were comparatively luckier than their country cousins in the 9th in adjacent Garston who notoriously had great problems in finding suitable head-quarters. Even when an empty house was found there was the problem of communication because the premises were not equipped with a telephone, and it was infested with cockroaches who proved to be a bigger enemy than the Germans!

In his time in the Home Guard Jimmy had to endure tedious lectures as well as demonstrations of home-made weapons which, although ludicrous, were a necessity because of the shortage of real weapons in the early part of the war

The platoon were eventually issued with real weapons in the shape of P17 rifles when the Americans sent the Home Guard two boatloads of arms, and Jimmy was put in charge of a Tommy Gun. "I took this Chicago Piano home to my Mother's horror", Jimmy revealed, "but we boys had no ammo." It seems that the commanding officer did not fully trust the younger members of the platoon with live bullets, and sent them down to the ammunition depot in Queens Road when needed. "So if Jerry had come we would have had to run back to get our ammunition", Jimmy said, revealing a situation which was ripe for situation comedy.

Jimmy's love of acting and the stage made him a good observer of character, and it seems that there were several people in Watford whom he remembered who were later to undergo transformation into residents of Walmington-on-Sea.

The pompous Captain Mainwaring was an amalgam of various people including Jimmy' s commanding officer who was also a manager of the local Halifax Building Society office.

There was an old soldier Jimmy served with in Watford whom he has referred to on a number of occasions who was the inspiration for Corporal Jones. Jimmy said that he remembers sitting in Cassiobury Park guarding a water-filled Vickers machine gun whilst the old man, who was in his seventies, entertained the younger soldiers with stories of the Battle of Omdurman and the enemy of whom he referred to as "fuzzie wuzzies".

"I knew the spiv too", Jimmy has said, and was referring to

a young Cockney soldier in the unit called Jim Sibthorp whom Jimmy remained friends with up until his death a few years ago.

A popular figure with bags of charm, he started a successful engineering business in Watford after the war which operated for many years and later relocated to nearby Leavesden. Of course Jimmy has also said that Walker was partly based on the spiv character created by Arthur English on radio in the 1940s, and in fact Arthur had been suggested to play the role before Jimmy Beck.

It also comes as no surprise to learn that Jimmy, 'the lean, keen killing machine', as he dubbed himself, was the inspiration for young Frank Pike (although Jimmy has also said that he was the joker of the platoon which suggests that he had something in common with Walker who he originally wanted to play). Although not a 'soppy boy' like Pike, he has admitted he was a little immature, his mum always made sure he wore his scarf on parade (Sedgwick's Yard was a chilly place to stand on a winter's night), and like Pike would often quote lines from his favourite films. It also seems that Dad's Army's most enduring catchphrase was originally directed towards the real Frank Pike, because whenever Jimmy expressed a wish to be an actor or comedian, his father would always reply with the words 'stupid boy'!

Interestingly Mr Perry's first name was Arthur which suggests that he was perhaps partly the inspiration for Sergeant Wilson.

Later Jimmy and many of the younger fitter members of the Battalion were chosen to form part of a special Commando unit called the Herts Sub Area Mobile Reserve. They undertook special training sessions and once a week were forced to endure an army assault course at the cricket ground in Park Avenue. They assembled at the Trade Union Hall in Woodford Road every Sunday. The hall, which was used for dances and other social occasions, became the unit's unofficial headquarters as it also had an office. Thus it was partly the inspiration for the church hall HQ in Dad's Army, and conflicts between other users of the hall, and Jimmy's commanding officer, doubtless inspired the on-screen friction between Captain Mainwaring and the vicar. Also, according to fellow Mobile Reserve member Walter Instrall, the unit regularly practised instruction in the hall and the Caretaker (their own Mr Yeatman) was obviously none too

pleased as the dance floor must have taken a real battering!

Suffice to say that Jimmy Perry was drafted into the real army, the Royal Artillery, in January 1944, where during his initial training he joined the Garrison Theatre—giving impressions and one-line gags. At the time of D-Day, June 1944, Jimmy was retained to help 'entertain the troops' which probably helped save his life from disaster in Normandy, but which led to him being posted to the far east, — in anticipation of a large push from Chittagong against the Japanese. But war ceased following Japan's surrender. A near-fatal burst appendix started another train of events which led to a tour of duty with the Royal Artillery Concert Party. As with so many troops sent to the Far East towards or just after war's end they were stuck there for a further two years or more. During this time Jimmy absorbed the atmosphere and characters which he and David Croft used to such good effect in 'It Ain't Half Hot, Mum'.

Demob in December 1947 was followed by a two-year RADA course, during which he found summer employment as a Redcoat at Butlin's, Pwllheli, north Wales where, once again, his experiences were being mentally stored, to surface much later in the series 'Hi-De-Hi!'.

Appearing at the Palace Theatre, London, in 'The Glorious Years', with Anna Neagle, he met his dancer wife-to-be, Gilda. They were soon married and enjoyed a busy professional acting and performing life. Jimmy's love remained with the theatre; he'd acted with the Melville players at Watford's Palace Theatre, where, in 1956, its leaseholder, Andrew Melville, put the lease up for sale. At this time the Council were considering demolishing the theatre to make way for an office block, but Jimmy and Gilda risked all by buying the lease.

After a brief period of redecoration they re-opened in September 1956; new seating was installed in 1958 and they had several years of succesful productions, even though they had to let the theatre out for pop concerts, wrestling and bingo during some quieter summer months.

They called time in 1965 and after producing more than 300 plays, eight musicals and nine pantomimes they sold the lease to Watford Council as a Civic Theatre, and went to live in Westminster. Jimmy Perry's contributions to TV comedy will long be shown and enjoyed as timeless classics. In the meantime the Lower High Street premises, shops, houses and Sedgwicks Brewery have all bitten the dust.

The Theatre, which they saved and kept alive for eight essential years, is currently undergoing a major rebuild and renovation.

David Noades, 2003

Previous page: *The Watford Trade Union Hall, Woodford Road, 1986.*
Above: *Against a background of an Anderson shelter in Watford's Museum in 1990, Jimmy Perry and James Sibthorp, at the opening of the Watford at War Exhibition, reminiscing over old times.*

The Grove: "... if coming by barge, allow 8 hours from London's Regent Park."

The Grove opened, officially, on 8th September 2003, sixty-four years and a week after it was invaded by 3,000 staff of the London Midland and Scottish Railway, moved out of London upon the outbreak of war. The house had been made ready as offices and a number of huts built in the surrounding grounds. Euston was no longer the LMS Headquarters; the Grove stayed their home until the end of the war when the main body of staff moved back to London. A few departments stayed until the early 1960's before returning; the Audit Department moved out and into Melton House in Clarendon Road.

Nationalisation took place in 1948, the British Transport Commission taking over; the Grove was used as a work study centre. When the British Railways Board was formed the Grove was again under railway control and as far as 1988 was used for training including a 'Management Training Centre.'

The house suffered years of decorative austerity but, unlike Cassiobury House, had succeeded in fulfilling a worthwhile role ... until in recent years when passers-by noticed the extent of landscaping to adjacent grounds and contractors' lorries coming and going with little or no clue as to what was happening.

The pre-opening 'open days' for golfers drew a full house for two days, when in mild late summer weather the 18-hole championship course, designed by Kyle Phillips, could be best appreciated. The house, as approached from the drive from Hempstead Road, appears unchanged. Behind has been built, in sympathetic style, a five-star hotel offering 211 rooms and 16 suites, three restaurants, three swimming pools, 25 meeting rooms, (all with ISDN and video conferencing facilties), a 500-person capacity ballroom, 400 parking spaces, 40 golf buggies, six WWII air-raid shelters (not stated whether functional) all in 300 acres of parkland.

Near neighbours of Watford, the Clarendon line started in 1608 with the birth of Edward Hyde who, in 1658 was Lord Chancellor to King Charles II and by 1661 gained the title Earl of Clarendon, which remained in the family until the 4th Earl died in 1753 with no male members of the family to inherit the title. A Thomas Villiers bought the Grove and married the heiress to the Hyde family. Cussans states that 'Villiers had been created Baron Hyde of Hindon, Wilts, in recognition of foreign diplomatic services and in 1776 was raised to the dignity of Earl of Clarendon.' He died in 1786 and is buried at Watford. He was followed by Thomas Villiers Hyde, *d1838,* and succeeded by George William Frederick Villiers ...

Two Earls of Clarendon.

George William Frederick Villiers, 4th Earl of Clarendon (1800-1870).

This distinguished member of the family so well known to the inhabitants of Watford by their interest in all that pertains to the welfare of the town, was born in London and was the grandson of Edward Hyde, first Earl of Clarendon, the friend and minister of Charles II. At twenty, he was an attaché to the British Embassy at St. Petersburg; between 1827-29 excise matters affecting Ireland and England were satisfactorily arranged through his efforts, as was a commercial treaty between England and France in 1831. These successes led up to the highly important post of Envoy-Extraordinary and Minister-Plenipotentiary to Madrid (1833), where his tact and impartiality gained him the G.C.B., on the recommendation of Lord Melbourne.

On the death of his uncle, the third Earl, he succeeded to the Earldom. In 1847 he was appointed Lord-Lieutenant of Ireland, an extremely difficult and dangerous post, owing to famine, Orange disturbances and the economic difficulties caused by the emigration of the peasantry.

"He carried Ireland through a period of conspiracy and revolution with little or no bloodshed" was the judgment passed on his conduct of Irish affairs. Royal favour was shown to him. Queen Victoria awarded him the Order of the Garter, and departing from her usual practice, desired him not to surrender the insignia of the Bath, as he had fully merited both distinctions.

Twice in his career he was Foreign Secretary, once in the Coalition Government of Lord John Russell and Lord Palmerstone ("England does not love Coalitions" was Disraeli's remark upon this Ministry), and also under Gladstone (1868-70).

His experience gained in his early days, his great ability and acuteness of judgement marked him out for further diplomatic honours. The Governor-Generalship of India was twice offered him and so was a Marquisate; these honours, however, he did not accept. In June, 1870, he died suddenly in London and was buried in Watford.

Left: *The east face of the old house is that seen from the road and drive.*
Right: *The Drive from Hempstead Road to the house.*
The reference in the heading to the time of travel by barge is from the sales brochure, 2003.

Edward Hyde Villiers, 5th Earl of Clarendon
1846-1914; he was the son of the preceding Earl. Like his father, he became a persona grata at Court, serving as A.D.C. to Queen Victoria and also to King Edward VII.

The Grove was his home; Watford and the County the scene of his public life. He became Lord Lieutenant of Herts, and for many years a member of the Herts C.C., being one of the original members of that body on its formation in 1880. The Herts Yeomanry, in which he held the position of Lieutenant-Colonel, found in him a warm supporter. On the occasions of the camp at Cassiobury, his was a familiar figure amongst his brother officers on parade in the Market square, and in the Park. He endeared himself to the townspeople by his unaffected interest in the progress and welfare of the town. His last appearance in public showed how wide were his interests and how faithful his expression of them.

During the Great War he visited the St. John Ambulance Brigade while at drill in St John's Hall. Though frail, he spoke a few words of encouragement and appreciation to the members, and then withdrew. A few weeks later he passed away and was laid to rest in a sylvan sanctuary of his own choosing, in his own grounds.

W R Saunders

George Herbert Hyde Villiers (1877 - 1955)

Became the 6th Earl. Whilst at Eton he broke his hip, spending a considerable amount of time in hospital.

It certainly brought an end to his promising athletic career. According to his obituary in The Times (1955), "he was an extra A.D.C. to the Lord Lieutenant of Ireland. A Conservative in politics, he was Chancellor of the Primrose League from 1919 - 21. He then became Lord in Waiting to the King, and was then appointed Parliamentary Under Secretary for Dominion Affairs, and Chairman of the Overseas Settlement Committee. From 1927-30 he was Chairman of the BBC.

In 1930 Lord Clarendon was appointed Governor General of South Africa and sailed there in January 1931 to take up his post. He lived up to every expectation, and made it his duty to know every part of the Union. He and Lady Clarendon identified themselves with beneficent works and social services of every kind. In 1935, he suffered a grievous loss in the death of his eldest son, Lord Hyde, as a result of a shooting accident.

When, in the same year, his term of office was extended, the result was received throughout South Africa with keen satisfaction. During his term of office he had seen the Union pass through a lean and difficult period, which followed the world depression. When he left it, in 1937, it was enjoying great prosperity. On returning to London he was created a Knight of the Garter.

On his return he became Lord Chamberlain and also Chancellor of the Order of St John of Jerusalem. During his term of office much of the ceremonial side of The Lord Chancellor's work was reduced by the outbreak of the Second World War. He performed his duty as Lord Chamberlain at the funeral of King George VI and resigned on medical advice shortly afterwards."

It was during the 6th Earl's lifetime that the Grove was sold. In 1922 he moved to Hampstead, London. This move brought to an end the family's long association with the Grove.
The Grove Story, BR Board.

When the house was sold it passed into ownership of The Equity and Law Life Assurance Company, from whom it was bought in May 1939 by Lineside Estates, a subsidiary company of the LMS Railway Co.

Top: *George Herbert Hyde Villiers played a substantial role in Watford obtaining its Borough Charter in 1922; this in 1950.*
Above: *The portico entrance to the Events Suites.*
Right: *The green at the seventh hole.*

Albert Dillingham, J P, Mayor of Watford 1953-1954, Hon. Freeman of the Borough

Albert Dillingham was Mayor in 1953/4 and to him fell the task of meeting many of the town's Coronation parties, here at Callowland; later I was asked to take a photograph of Council in session—to my knowledge the first time this had been done.

In 1987 I asked Mr Dillingham if he would write a foreword to *The Book of Watford*, to which he immediately agreed. The words he penned are as apposite today as then, which is why I again use them for this edition.

The happy colour picture was made in 1996; when at that time he was still self-sufficient enough to cook and 'do' for himself. He was born on July 3rd 1901 within the sound of Bow bells. As did so many others his parents moved from London to Watford, where the Dillinghams made their home in Bruce Grove, North Watford, in 1911. His working life started as railway clerk when he was 14, joining the Labour Party when he was 21.

In 1926–the troubled times of the Depression–he was made assistant secretary of Watford's General Strike Committee. With a sharp eye for detail, and lucid turn of phrase, he penned his own biography which was printed in the Watford Observer following the civic reception to mark his birthday.

The following excerpt describes the lanes and tracks:

"The Watford of my day ended a little to the north of Langley Road, and to the east of it finished at Harebreaks on one side of St Albans Road and Bushey Mill Lane on the other. The boundary was the St Albans Branch Railway line. Beyond this there was a delightful lane to St Albans with cornfields on either side. There was a footpath to Leavesden and Abbots Langley [at the Dome] through Gullet Woods, a galaxy of bluebells in the spring. Garston was a sleepy village having two pubs, a few cottages and an undertaker. It could be reached, if one was too lazy to walk

the three miles, by bus from the Junction Station—a bumpy ride!"

Mr Dillingham remembered the cattle market in the town and the Kinetic Cinema in the former Corn Exchange in the Market Place. In 1921 he became Secretary of the Bradshaw Labour Party and in 1926 was made assistant Secretary of Watford's General Strike Committee where he met Harry Horwood (who served as a Borough Councillor for 40 years and was also admitted a Freeman of the Borough).

When Mr Horwood stood down as President of the Watford Trades Council and Borough Labour Party to devote more time to his council work, Mr Dillingham succeeded him. He became a Magistrate in 1943 and later a County Councillor. He served as a Governor of a number of local schools and Cassio College.

He recalled, "I have also been honoured to meet so many local folk who gave freely of their time to organisations and charities without reward."

His wife of more than sixty years, Eleanor, died in 1994.

At the civic reception were his two sons, Paul, the elder, and John and daughter Celia, and their families. In thanking the guests Paul quoted Adlai Stevenson: "It is not the years in your life but the life in your years that count."

This, he said, was typical of his father. Albert Dillingham lived until a few days short of his 102nd birthday, passing away on June 21st 2003.

JBN, 2003

Gordon Rickwood and the changes

In 1924, 19-year-old Gordon Rickwood sat down and put pen to paper to write a charming lament for the town, which he felt to be altering beyond recognition.

Mr Rickwood, who was educated at Watford Higher Elementary School, died in 1988, and his son David, and daughter-in-law, Hilary, moved into his house at Frankland Close, Croxley Green.

While sorting through papers in the attic, Hilary came across Gordon's original manuscript, written in an elegant copperplate hand on paper which is now faded and yellowed with age. Mrs Rickwood thought his perceptive comments deserving of wider attention and in due course they were published in the Watford Observer in 1992.

Top: *Albert Dillingham in a happy mood in 1996;*

Centre: *With Mrs Dillingham at the Callowland School childrens' Coronation Party.*

Bottom: *In the Chair at a Council Meeting, 1953, from the left Rev'd Kesley, Chaplain; Gordon Hall, Town Clerk; Alderman Dillingham and on the right Alderman L C Johnson.*

1924 ... *laying pavement along the Rickmansworth Road* ...

Dated November 1924, Mr Rickwood's article is called "Changing Watford" and is deserving of thought in 2003.

"WATFORD as known to our fathers of 50 years ago was a pretty, country town, almost untouched by the hand of development. Today it is a bustling, industrial town as well as a favoured residential district, indeed, one might almost class it as a suburb of the great metropolis, so good are the travelling facilities, which even now are being added to.

Much as it has changed in the past, so it is still changing and will continue to do so in the future. Just for a moment consider the recent alterations in the High Street alone. Dudleys has transformed the corner of Clarendon Road and the two trees that are left—the sole survivors of perhaps many—look sadly out of place in front of the dazzling lights and the latest frocks. Just below, where used to stand the old buildings of the Eighteenth Century are now big, well-lighted shops of London firms, and opposite, the Clock House house, superseded others. Again, on the site of the Old Vicarage, more shops have been constructed and more are being built on part of the garden of Monmouth House. One wonders where they are all going to get their custom from. Thus, surely, are all the old buildings of the town disappearing, and the last to go, and the most picturesque of all, is the Green Man Inn.

Built perhaps 300 years ago, it has probably witnessed many strange sights and happenings in Watford and we cannot but regret that the old familiar place is no longer fit for modern requirements and has to be pulled down.

Cassio Hamlet, that quaint collection of old houses, especially charming when viewed from the pond, is slowly being modernised. Where used to stand two pretty, old cottages, there is now a huge garage and the "Horns" Inn is being demolished to make room for a more commodious building.

The borough council are at present laying pavement along the Rickmansworth Road as far as Cassio Bridge, which place once so delightfully rural, but now fast losing all its charm, and when the Memorial Hospital is finished and the proposed Town Hall is built, how changed the Cross Roads will appear!

So thus are time and progress making great changes here, and truly one can prophesy that Watford of 50 years hence, will be a very different place from the Watford we know now.

But however much progress is necessary, we cannot but feel a pang of regret that the old home of our forefathers is no more. Not only is Watford itself altering, but the neighbourhood around is undergoing great changes that almost threaten to convert our pretty Hertfordshire countryside into a vast, semi-urban district; and streets, however well laid, are but a sorry contrast to woodlands fields and hedgerows.

Cassiobury, that beautiful estate with such old mature woods and its stately park is being sold in building plots. The historic Moor Park estate of some 3,000 acres is being slowly

developed and as it embraces practically the whole of the land between Watford, Rickmansworth and Northwood; some day, I expect, we shall see, instead of smiling meadows and wood-clad hills and dales, one vast area of houses.

Garston, once so rural, is now quite a small town on its own. The new railway will be sure to have an effect on the expansion of Croxley and the Watford bypass road, (in the course of construction) will doubtless develop in time, the land through which it passes. This is a heavy list, but even yet another main road is contemplated which will cut right through the pretty country around Langleybury.

Oh, I wonder what this part of the world will be like when Progress has completed her ravishes. Surely a place very unlike a county noted for its beauty? Then the famous Hertfordshire Lanes and lovely woods will be things of the past, so is it not up to us to enjoy them to the fullest possible extent while they are here with us?"

Gordon Rickwood, November 1924

Gordon Rickwood's words evoke thoughts of sympathy for the changes he was seeing and describing with which we, facing similar changes, can well sympathise. The photograph of Blackwell Drive, below, shows the town he described. That of nearside Riverside Road (*p.33*) shows very well the lane which the inmates of Watford's workhouse (then near the Parish Church) would have to take to reach the Rookery Mill where they laboured in its silk-mill days.

A photograph of the Plaza (1932) showed the then new shop opposite as dealing in 'Pianos, Gramophones and Radios' and from a friend, who is a piano tuner, I learned that there was a connection between it and the old Rookery Mill. A request to the Watford Observer asking for information very quickly brought forth the desired result.

Mr John Crowley's daughter Margaret Lovely, now 89, phoned from an old people's home in Rock House, Doncaster, Yorkshire.

"My father started his piano factory in London just before the First World War.

"It was a new building with 100 men employed but the government wanted the factory to use for the war effort.

"So they bought him the old Silk Mill in Riverside Road by the River Colne in Watford. Most of the workforce joined the army, so the business was very small. Obviously there was not so much of a demand for pianos in that time but the factory at Watford contributed to the war effort by making parts for aeroplanes.

"I suppose they made and sold perhaps half a dozen pianos during the war. I learnt the piano and, at 89, I can still play. When I was married, we moved ten times if you can believe that. My husband was a geologist and moved round the country. Before that, the Crowley family lived in Coldharbour Lane, Bushey.

"I can't say exactly how long the factory lasted but we were still in business by the time of the general strike (1926). I think that put the end to the business coupled with my brother's death, who was only a boy, from blood poisoning. My father lost interest in the factory after that. He was very proud of his business but you could say the First World War really broke the back of the business. He did not employ 100 men after it as he did before.

"He had a shop in Watford High Street called 'For Most Matters Musical,' near the Pond. My father used to take me to the factory when I was a little girl. Later, I sometimes used to go with him down to the river where the old silk mill was. The demand for the pianos dropped off in the 1920s. Before then, we had sold pianos to New Zealand and America.

"It was a thriving business and my father was very proud that he received congratulations from the men who worked there for the way he ran the staff. However, the claim that they made pianos for Elliotts in the High Street was just a myth that has grown up."

WO, May 1996

An unmade-up Blackwell Drive c1924

A Message from Sheila Jones — 80th Mayor of Watford (2002-2003)

It has been my privilege to be the 80th and last Mayor of Watford in its traditional form. Government legislation has meant that, because we now have an Elected Mayor, a Chairman, not a Mayor, must undertake the civic role. My husband, Malcolm, was my Mayor's Consort for the year. He was the first Mayor's Consort that Watford had ever had, he refused to be a Mayoress, and the last.

During my 16 years as a Watford Borough Councilor, I have specialised in Planning. I have often been sad, angry—even appalled at some of the planning decisions made in the name of progress. Even worse, there are the big corporations who steamroller their plans through, sweeping aside what we all know and love. It can be very disheartening at times, although by no means all decisions are like that.

But being Watford's 80th Mayor has shown me a different side of my town. The Spirit of Watford is something very special. I didn't meet many "ordinary" people as I carried out my duties around the town. What I did meet is very many extraordinary people, all doing things over and above what could be expected

of them. My Charity for the year was "Carers in Hertfordshire", which is a Registered Charity. There are so many carers around—all unsung heroes. It includes adults looking after elderly parents or other relatives, husbands or wives looking after the other partner, and even quite young children looking after a parent. It saves the taxpayer a small fortune!

The Charity supports these carers in a variety of ways, giving them advice or a rest from what is often a harrowing task.

My theme for the year was "One Town, One Community". It encompasses all groups, regardless of racial origin, religious belief, gender, age or disability. It is not an easy task, but a great deal can be achieved by mutual tolerance, respect and understanding—and of course, humour.

The Mayor, because all groups hold the Office in high regard, can achieve much in this role. As Mayor, I was able to act as an enabler or catalyst to bring at least some of the many groups closer together. They are supported by Business and Fund Raising groups in and around the Town. At my Civic Reception over fifty Charities were represented, themselves representing over five thousand Charity workers, giving selflessly of their time and not seeking any thanks or recognition for themselves.

As I stated above, the Spirit of Watford is something very special. As my husband put it: "Watford fights above its weight". This is so true in so many aspects of life in the Town. It happens in Sport, the Arts (Music, Speech, Drama and Dance), and in Care—don't say it can't be done! We have Festivals, which attract participants not just from Watford, or even just from Hertfordshire, but have international recognition.

It has also been my privilege to have been Vice-President of Watford Football Club during my year in Office. The Club, aided by the Supporters Trust, plays an important part in the life of the town. Very importantly, it has for many years fostered a friendly and safe atmosphere, and again brings together so many people from the Town.

I was also fortunate this year in being able to contribute to the return of John Wooton's painting of Cassiobury Park as it was 250 years ago. In it is depicted Watford's first known black resident. The painting is an important part of Watford's Heritage, and has come home to Watford Museum.

I must not forget our very own firefighter, Russell Ward, hero of the Bali bombing. His selfless acts have given him world-wide fame. But he represents just the pinnacle of a huge number of unsung heroes in our Community—people who help others without a thought for them-

selves—people who do not see themselves as anybody special, just doing their job.

So if we look despairingly at the loss of things familiar from the Watford scene, and see some of what many would call 'monstrosities' that are replacing them, I see also not just a ray of hope, but a broad beam of hope, coming from the people of Watford itself. Watford's Spirit is the Spirit of the Town Motto 'Audentior'—'Yield not thou to ills, but go forth to face them more boldly than thy Fortune shall allow thee.'

I look forward to the future with great optimism.

Sheila Jones, 2003

Previous page: *There were fewer street parties in the Borough than in 1953; this time—with rather more cars—permission had to be sought and granted to close the streets concerned. The two larger pics are of Church Road; the smaller, Denmark Street. 2002.*

This page: *The Mayor's Reception, 2003: from the top, details from the Borough's Crest; arrivals; seated for the meal; Claire Ward, MP; Russell Ward awarded a Citation on behalf of the Borough.*

The Blaw-Knox connection . . .

Early transport depended upon the skill of the local smithy to make axles, wheels and wheel rims, to repair cart springs (and later, springs for cars and lorries). The unmade roads of the day took a heavy toll. With the advent of the railway, and an engine depot, Watford attracted a nucleus of engineers – mechanical engineers. When the Great War needed munitions Watford was not found wanting, and during that conflict the country's best brains were devising a method of producing forgery-proof bank-notes. The technicians of Watford's printing industry found an answer.

Watford was acclaimed the 'most scientific town in the County' and it attracted the industry which helped fuel the town's growth. Printing, in its two ego-towers, attracted reputation and kudos. The engineering industry provided a rich and diverse mix of employment and output; some names remain but the majority have faded under a relentless march of technology, mergers and relocations. One such is Blaw-Knox. Established in Bushey Mill Lane c1930 its main product is one which

Ault & Wiborg
Bedford Products
Blaw-Knox
British American Optical Co
British Moulded Hose
Buck & Hickman
Caird & Rayner
Chiswell Wire Co
Control Instruments
Cotterell & Pither
Cox & Co
Ealing Beck
Ellams Duplicators
Erinoid
Fishburn Printing Inks
Ilford Ltd
Intrama
LaPointe
Lee Bapty
Litholite Insulators
Penfold Fencing
Petro-Flex Tubing
Pictorial Machinery (Engineers)
Rolls Royce
S G Brown
Savage & Parsons
Scammell Lorries
Smiths Industries
Transformers and Welders
Watford Engineering Works
Watford Foundry
Waxed Papers Ltd
WEMCO

every driver in the land has at some time or another roundly cursed. We turn the clock back to the 1950's and 60's when our roads were inevitably single carriageway. There'd be a hold-up in getting through a town or village and when the open road beckoned the joy would quickly turn to frustration. The hold-up was one of three causes; an Austin A30, Morris Minor, or road works.

The A30's impeded progress for slow mile after mile, until they turned off. The road-works we learned to accept as a harbinger of relief. Inevitably leading the new road was an evil smelling dirty piece of apparatus laying the bitumous coating at a snail's pace. We weren't interested in its name or from whence it came. The Blaw-Knox pavers were made in Rochester, Kent and, because of Watford's proximity to the main-line station a depot was set up for spares, service manual production and field service.

The 'black-Wednesday' financial disaster saw the end of Blaw-Knox's independence for they finished in American ownership, but such is the reputation for the Kent-made machines that firms exist to make spares and refurbish machines to original spec.

A one-time good export earner it is little exaggeration to repeat the claim that near 80% of this country's non-concrete roads were laid by Blaw-Knox machines. The recent road works near the Junction made use of a B-K Paver, as did local roads in Nascot just a few years ago.

Top: *The forge from Leavesden dismantled and rebuilt at the Chiltern Open Air Museum.*

Above: *An early paver still in service resurfacing the less-demanding local roads. From the early 1930's through to the early 1970's Blaw-Knox had a service depot in Bushey Mill Lane, next to the railway and opposite the rubber works. The Watford depot housed a technical writing department and was a local base for spares and service engineers.*

Left: *A batch of refurbished models, 2003*

Left: *The list is that of some of the non-print, and non-food/chemical firms in Watford in the late 1950's early 1960's. A few of the firms are still in business.*

Listed Buildings; Honorary Freeman of the Borough

The Secretary of State for the Environment is required to compile "lists" of buildings of special architectural merit or historic interest. The administration of local and national conservation policies is, or should be, based on the lists which are themselves constantly under revision.

The guidelines observed by the Department of the Environment presume all buildings erected before the 17th century in original or near original condition are automatically listed.

The majority of the buildings of the 18th century and up to 1840 qualify on a selection basis. For the period between 1840 and 1914 the usually applied yardstick may be defined as the "principal works of principal architects." Due consideration is also given to buildings and structures that may be associated with our social and economic history. The "historic" factor may he defined as involving "known characters and recorded events". Then there is the all-embracing "group value" in the form of a terrace, square or village green.

In the selection process a qualifying building or structure will be graded and listed in the following manner:
Grade 1 —of very special merit
Grade II*~of highest general grading deserving special attention
Grade Il—of considerable importance and accorded to the majority of buildings.

The protection provided by current legislation offers safeguards only against unauthorised demolition and may be abused. A building is not necessarily sacrosanct because it is 'listed~

Address	Grade	Date Listed
lACareyPlace	II	7.1.83
14 Chalk Hill	II	4.8.75
St. Andrew's Church, Church Road	II	7.1.83
Gates to, and Salters Almshouses, Church Road	II and II	7.1.83
Nos. 1-8 Bedford Alms houses Church Street	II	26.8.5 2
St. Mary's Church (Parish), Church St. (off High St.)	I	26.8.52
Monuments in St. Mary's Churchyard	II	7.1.83
Free School, Church St.	II*	26.8.52
Beechen Grove Baptist Church, Clarendon Road	II	12.9.80
Palace Theatre, Clarendon Road	II	14.7.82
Baptist Tabernacle, Derby Road	II	7.1.83
Watford Central Primary School, Derby Road	II	7.1.83
St. Michael's Church, Durban Road	II	7.1.83
St. Matthew's Church, Eastbury Road	II	7.1.83
Holyrood House, Exchange Road	II	7.1.83
Cassio Bridge Lodge 67 Gade Avenue	II	7.1.83
Russell's, Greenbank Road	11	24.8.79
Canal Bridge, 200m N of Grove Mill (BWB) Grove Mill Lane	II	15.1 1.73
Heath Farm Court (formerly Heath Farm House), Grove Mill Lane	II	26.8.52
Canal Cottage, Grove Mill Lane	II	7.1.83
Dower House (ex Grove Mill House) Grove Mill Lane	II	26.8.52
Little Cassiobury (H.C.C. Education Office), Hempstead Road	II*	26.8.52
Garden Cottage, 129 Hempstead Road	II	7.1.83
Tollgate Lodge, 235 Hempstead Road	II	7.1.83
South Lodge, Hempstead Road	II	7.1.83
Manor House, 79-87 High Road, Leavesden	II	7.1.83
Watford Place, 27 King Street	II	26.8.52
Kytes House, Kytes Drive and Outbuilding to North of Kytes House	II	7.1.83
Holy Rood RC. Church, Market Street	I	12.9.80
Govt. Buildings, (former London Orphan Asylum) and Chapel, Orphanage Road	II	7.1.83
(Jacksons) 14-16 The Parade	II	7.1.83
Monmouth House, 85-89 The Parade	II	25.1 1.77

Address	Grade	Date Listed
91, 93, 95 The Parade	II	7.1.83
Nat. Westminster Bank, 151-153 The Parade	II	7.1.83
Nat. Westminster Bank, 58 High Street	II	4.3.74
Lloyds Bank, 63-65 High Street	II	17.6.80
Midland Bank, 73 High Street	II	25.10.77
97 High Street	II	7.1.83
129-131; 133-135; 137 High Street	II	7.1.83
141; 145; 149-151 High Street	II	7.1.83
The One Crown P.H., 156 High Street	II	7.1.83
158; 160; 166-168 High Street	II	7.1.83
172 High Street	II	15.9.83
172A High Street	II	18.9.82
Watford Museum 194-196 High Street	II	26.8.52
198, 200-202-202A High Street	II	23.1.73
Iron railings in front of former Benskins Brewery Site	II	23.1.73
Nos. 212-214 High Street	II	7.1.83
Frogmore House, High Street*	II	26.8.52
Bushey Arches Railway Viaduct, Lower High Street	II	7.1.83
All Saints Church, Leavesden, Horseshoe Lane	II	7.1.83
The Bandstand by Town Hall, The Parade	II	7.1.83
The War Memorial by the Town Hall	II	7.1.83
Former Holy Rood R.C. School, Percy Road	II	7.1.83
Former Convent of St. Vincent, Percy Road	II	15.9.83
Cassiobury Court, Richmond Drive	II	7.1.83
Watford Boys' Grammar School Rickmansworth Road	II	7.1.83
Master's House, Watford Boys' Grammar School, Rickmansworth Road	II	7.1.83
The Old Station House, 147A St. Albans Road	II	20.2.79
Benskins House (former Clarendon Hotel) Station Road	II	12.9.75
Watford Railway Tunnels, South entrance to West Tunnel	II	7.1.83
St. John's Church, Sutton Road	II	7.1.83
Shrodells Wing (former Watford Union Workhouse), Vicarage Road	II	15.9.82
Five Arches Railway Viaduct 200m N. of Water Lane	II	7.1.83

HONORARY FREEMEN OF THE BOROUGH

The Rt. Hon. George Herbert Hyde Villiers, Earl of Clarendon.	(Admitted 28th July, 1924) *
Alderman Ralph Alfred Thorpe.	(Admitted 22nd June, 1927) *
The Rt. Hon. Lord Hemingford.	(Admitted 22nd March, 1943) *
Alderman Thomas Rubython Clark.	(Admitted 22nd March, 1943) *
Mr. Wm. Hudson.	(Admitted 22nd March 1943) *
Ernest James Baxter, O.B.E., JP.,	(Admitted 1st September, 1959) *
Harry Horwood, Esq., O.B.E., JP.,	(Admitted 1st September, 1959) *
Edward C. Amey, O.B.E.	(Admitted 19th July, 1976) *
Hubert Buckingham Esq.	(Admitted 19th July, 1976) *
Albert G. Dillingham, Esq.	(Admitted 19th July, 1976) *
Sir Raphael Tuck, B.SC., (ECON). MA., I.I.M.	(Admitted 15th Nov.1980) *
Irene Tunstall Dunn	(Admitted 6th October 1997) *
Frederick Hodgson	(Admitted 6th October 1997) *
Elton John	(Admitted 6th October 1997)
Stella Meldrum	(Admitted 6th October 1997) *
Graham Taylor	(Admitted 25th June 2001)

* deceased

Holders of Civic posts

CHAIRMEN OF THE LOCAL BOARD AND URBAN DISTRICT COUNCIL

Charles W. Moore	1850 to 1872
Henry Catlin	1872 to 1873
Charles Francis Humbert	1873 to 1884
Lt.-Col. Copeland	1884 to 1884
Edward John Slinn	1885 to 1895

Urban District Council

Edward John Slinn	1895 to 1896
Walter Tidboald Coles	1896 to 1897
Charles Pryor Ayres	1897 to 1898
Joseph Clemson Benskin	1898 to 1899
Albert Edward Pridmore	1899 to 1900
George Potter Neele	1900 to 1901
Francis Fisher	1901 to 1903
Edward Kingham	1903 to 1904
Ralph Alfred Thorpe	1904 to 1906
George Longley	1906 to 1907
Sydney J. Ellis	1907 to 1908
John Andrews	1908 to 1909
Ralph Alfred Thorpe	1909 to 1910
Septimus George Mobbs	1910 to 1911
Ralph Alfred Thorpe	1911 to 1912
Joseph Southam	1912 to 1913
Walter Francis Goodrich	1913 to 1915
Charles Alfred Solomons	1915 to 1916
Thomas Rubython Clark	1916 to 1917
Ralph Alfred Thorpe	1917 to 1919
Frederick Hunt Gorle	1919 to 1920
George Longley	1920 to 1921
Henry Belcher Watkins	1921 to 1922
Thomas Rubython Clark	April to Nov., 1922

MAYORS OF WATFORD

The Rt. Hon. The Earl of Clarendon	1922 to 1923
Alderman Ralph Alfred Thorpe	1923 to 1924
Alderman Ralph Alfred Thorpe	1924 to 1925
Alderman Henry Belcher Watkins	1925 to 1926
Alderman Thomas Rubython Clark	1926 to 1927
Alderman Thomas Rushton	1927 to 1928
Councillor Francis Joseph Bache Hemming	1928 to 1929
Alderman Mrs. Amelia Florence Broad	1929 to 1930 (April)
Alderman Francis Joseph Bache Hemming	(April to Nov.) 1930
Alderman Frederick William Jeffs	1930 to 1931
Alderman William Bickerton	1931 to 1932
Councillor Joseph Evans	1932 to 1933
Councillor Charles Edward Griffin	1933 to 1934
Alderman Henry Jules Bridger	1934 to 1935
Councillor Ernest Charles Last	1935 to 1936
Alderman Henry Coates	1936 to 1937
Councillor Thomas Rigby Taylor	1937 to 1938
Councillor Harry Horwood	1938 to 1939
Alderman Lewin Halsey Andrews	1939 to 1940
Councillor Ernest James Baxter	1940 to 1941
Councillor Wilfred Harry Price	1941 to 1942
Alderman Thomas Herbert Simmons	1942 to 1943
Councillor Mrs. Martha Ann Ward	1943 to 1944
Alderman Herbert Waterman Beall	1944
Councillor Mrs. Emily Gertrude Beall	1944 to 1945
Councillor James Wright	1945 to 1946
Councilior Ransley William North	1946 to 1947
Alderman Henry Coates	1947 to 1949
Councillor Frederick Harold Vince	1949 to 1950
Alderman Mrs. Mary Edith Bridger	1950 to 1951
Councillor Laurence Edgar Haines	1951 to 1952
Alderman Leonard Charles Johnson	1952 to 1953
Alderman Albert George Dillingham	1953 to 1954
Alderman John Davies	1954 to 1955
Alderman Edward Cecil Amey	1955 to 1956
Councillor Albert Abbott	1956 to 1957
Alderman Harry Horwood	1957 to 1958
Councillor Reginald William Gamble	1958 to 1959
Alderman Thomas Frederick Harris	1959 to 1960
Alderman Ernest Henry Harrowell	1960 to 1961
Alderman John Richard Hicks	1961 to 1962
Alderman Henry William Lodder	1962 to 1963

Alderman George Wilfred Knox	1963 to 1964
Alderman Arthur Reynolds	1964 to 1965
Councillor Leslie Cyril Wright	1965 to 1966
Alderman Finlay Mackenzie	1966 to 1967
Councillor Miss Doris Mary Scawen	1967 to 1968
Alderman Alec Leonard Merrifield	1968 to 1969
Alderman J. Stanley Oliver	1969 to 1970
Councillor Ronald W. Jackson	1970 to 1971
Alderman Mrs. Mary Dodd	1971 to 1972
Alderman Robert I. Caton	1972 to 1973
Councillor Roger S. Homer	1973 to 1974
Councillor William G. Everett	1974 to 1975
Councillor Harry Price	1975 to 1976
Councillor Derrick Coleshill	1976 to 1977
Councillor Alan W. Bonney	1977 to 1978
Councillor Samuel I. Deakin	1978 to 1979
Councillor Norman H. Tyrwhitt	1979 to 1980
Councillor Sidney G. Reynolds	1980 to 1981
Councillor Edward Cecil Amey, O.B.E.	1981 to 1982
Councillor Edward Cecil Amey, O.B.E.	1982 to 1983
Councillor Geoffrey R. Greenstreet, A.I.I.M., M.I.P.O.M.	1983 to 1984
Councillor Mrs. M. I. Hughes	1984 to 1985
Councillor Mrs. I. Tunstall Dunn	1985 to 1986
Councillor Paul Harrison	1986 to 1987
Councillor Les Hughes	1987 to 1988
Councillor P. A. Allan	1988 to 1989
Councillor John Watts	1989 to 1990
Coucillor Veronica Conlon	1990 to 1991
Councillor Mohinda Chhina	1991 to 1992
Councillor Peter Kiely	1992 to 1993
Councillor John Horsfield	1993 to 1994
Councillor Maria Green	1994 to 1995
Councillor Norman Tyrwhitt	1995 to 1996
Councillor Paul Harrison	1996 to 1997
Councillor Sheila Rosser	1997 to 1998
Councillor Dorothy Thornhill	1998 to 1999
Councillor Rosemary Bell	1999 to 2000
Councillor Ian Brown	2000 to 2001
Councillor Sybil Tuckwood	2001 to 2002
Councillor Sheila Jones	2002 to 2003

ELECTED MAYOR

Councillor Dorothy Thornhill	2002 to-

CLERKS OF THE LOCAL BOARD AND URBAN DISTRICT COUNCIL

John Sedgwick	1850 to 1882
Henry Morten Turner	1882 to 1910
William Hudson	1910 to 1922

TOWN CLERKS OF WATFORD 1922 to 1974

William Hudson	1922 to 1940
Alfred Norman Schofield	1940 to 1953
Gordon Hamer Hall	1953 to 1974

CHIEF EXECUTIVE AND TOWN CLERK OF WATFORD

Robert Bruce McMillan	1974 to 1990
David Plank B.A., M.Sc	1990 to 1995
Carole Hassan	1996 to 2000
Alan Clarke	2000 to 2003

MANAGING DIRECTOR OF THE BOROUGH OF WATFORD

Alastair Robertson	2003 to

FREEDOM OF ENTRY

On the 5th July, 1959, the 3rd East Anglian Regiment (16th/44th Foot) were granted the privilege, honour and distinction of marching through the streets of the Borough on all ceremonial occasions with colours flying, bands playing, drums beating and bayonets fixed.

On the 26th May, 1983, this privilege, honour and distinction was formally extended to the 3rd Battalion (Bedfordshire, Hertfordshire and Essex) of the Royal Anglian Regiment as successors to the 3rd EastAnglian Regiment (16th/44th Foot).

An 'American' style of local government . . .

Councillor Ellie Burtenshaw is Watford's first Chairman (of the Council), and the post will continue the traditions started by the first Mayor, the Earl of Clarendon (Watford's Charter Mayor), in 1922, a campaigner who helped Watford gain its 'Borough' status, granted by King George V.

The Mayors from that date until 2002 were chosen from serving Councillors or Aldermen. The chosen mayor for each year was apolitical; that is, that the mayor's duties were carried out without political bias. In most years the mayors were chosen from a party which was not necessarily the majority party, and on this basis the mayoral system served the town well.

In 2002, Government changed the system. A referendum on a choice of how the town should be 'governed' resulted in an 'elected mayor ruling by cabinet'. In the vote for one of three candidates Dorothy Thornhill was chosen as Elected Mayor by a large majority. Also, in that year, Watford had a 'Civic Mayor', and Sheila Jones, following tradition, was chosen.

Two mayors did not make much sense and reference to Government meant that the post of 'Civic Mayor' should be abolished. This duly happened and the 'Chairman' takes over.

The Chairman has a number of duties and functions, one of which is to chair meetings of the Council. However, the main role of the Chairman is to act as official representative of the Council on civic and ceremonial occasions and to be a figurehead in the community which the Council serves. A chain of office is worn on all official occasions.

The Council's new political structure consists of an Elected Mayor with Cabinet, Overview and Scrutiny Panels and Area Committees. The full Council decides the Council's budget, Council Tax and its main policies, such as the Housing Investment Programme, the Cultural Strategy, the Community Safety Strategy and the Best Value Performance Plan. The Council also sets up the Scrutiny Panels, the Committees to consider and approve Planning and Licensing applications and the Council Functions Committee.

The Elected Mayor and Cabinet lead the whole Council. The Elected Mayor provides political leadership for the town, proposes the policy framework for approval by Council, proposes the annual budget and takes executive decisions within the policy framework for all areas for which the Mayor is responsible.

The Elected Mayor has Portfolio Holders and a Cabinet of six other councillors, which contains Portfolio holders and opposition Members. The Elected Mayor may delegate to officers or Members of the Cabinet some of his/her responsibilities to take executive decisions, or the Mayor may delegate some of the authority to the Cabinet as a whole to make decisions. Overview and Scrutiny Panels are an essential part of the new constitution and provide a counterbalance to the work of the Executive/Cabinet. The work of the Overview and Scrutiny Panels is to hold the Elected Mayor and Cabinet to account, to review policy and to contribute to policy development.

The new structure contains seven Area Committees for the following areas:

Woodside/Stanborough Wards; Meriden/Tudor Wards; Callowland/Leggatts Wards; Nascot/Park Wards; Vicarage/Holywell Wards; Central Wards & Oxhey Wards.

These Area Committees are led by the local ward councillors, with the community taking a full part, with appropriate officer support. Part of their role is to develop, deliver and monitor local action plans to meet community aspirations and needs and in due course will have delegated decision making powers on local issues with specific budgets.

Watford Council, July 2003

Rates of Personal Community Charge (Poll Tax) (1990) and Council Tax

These figures are given from the time of introduction of Poll Tax.

In introducing this new tax Watford Council adopted an unusually partisan stance: "While Watford Council is legally bound to send out Poll Tax bills to local people, it does so in full appreciation that poll tax is an unfair taxation system which takes little account of ability to pay.

"It is because of this problem that we have set up two special services to help. A special debt counselling service, available free of charge by phoning Watford 226400 ext 2636 will give advice on household budgeting and benefit entitlement. To help people avoid getting into trouble with poll tax bills in the first place, we also operate a poll tax 'Hotline'. We are here to listen and, in genuine cases of hardship, help out in whatever way we can.

"The number to phone is Freephone 0800 289230 between 10am and 4pm.

"As a last resort in the most dire cases of genuine hardship, the Council may ask the courts to investigate an individual's ability to pay. Only the courts can decide whether or not to reduce or write off poll tax debts."

Poll tax was payable for three years following which the system reverted to that based upon rateable value, with the name changed to Council Tax.

The following table shows the rates charged from 1993 to date:

POLL TAX, per individual	
1990/91	£403
1991/92	£403
1992/93	£314

Council Tax, Band 'D' per household	
1993/94	£570.00
1994/95	£609.25
1995/96	£610.65
1996/97	£666.46
1997/98	£700.73
1998/99	£768.29
1999/00	£831.51
2000/01	£875.38
2001/02	£926.49
2002/03	£1017.08
2003/04	£1173.91

Licensed houses closed prior to 1900; and existing since 1900

The information for this exhautive account has been drawn from several sources. They are, (1) The survey of Watford Manor in 1605. (2) The return of 1756 billeting facilities for men and horses. (3) The Manorial Records of Watford Manor. (4) Various deeds especially those of the former Sedgwick Brewery. (5) Early directories from 1792 until 1829. These documents are in Herts County Record Office, Guildhall Library, Watford Central Library, Public Record Office Kew, etc. I have also used the findings of the Watford Archaeological Society. In the period for which this information is valid, Watford was governed by the parish vestry and, to a decreasing extent, by the Manorial Court Leet which appointed constables for the 'hamlets' into which the parish was divided. These were Town Hamlet, Cassio Hamlet, Leavesden Hamlet, and Oxhey Hamlet. The High Street was not yet numbered, but I shall use for convenience the numbers given by 1871 and largely still in use today. These are some of the inns or public houses in Watford Parish founded before 1830.

An account of the Breweries of the district is given on pages 47 and 48, and a list of new licensed premises in the High Street, as of May 2003, is on p432

Artichoke, later **Hart**, High Street, c1730-c.1800. This was in a building lately occupied by the Oliver, and before that by Cakebread Robey, whose mock-Tudor showroom superseded the original 18th century house, on the west side of the Pond. In 1756 the landlord was John Crickmore; there was room for billeting one soldier and stabling two horses.

Blue Anchor, 242 High Street, occupied the building next to the Methodist Chapel and

its yard extended over the later Mary Smith's Almshouses. Here the Earls of Bridgwater changed horses when lords of the manor, had a thrift club; closed c1830.

Bull or **Bullshead**, 61 High Street, c.1680-1772. A large posting inn, bought and closed in 1772 by James Rogers, ironmonger. In 1731 it was owned by the Runnington family.

Chequers, Waterdell, c.1750-1900. Will Neale had it from 1840. Salter's.

Chequers, 73 High Street, c.1700-1865. Now the Midland Bank (HSBC). Thomas Cole kept it from 1820 to 1850. Salters.

Combes Beerhouse. In 1878 was attached to Tidcombes Iron Foundry, Lower High Street, Charles Lovers, tenant.

Crooked Billet or **Duke of Cumberland**, 164 High Street. c.1700-c.1800. Now occupied by Carousel*. In 1756 John Doggett had it with room for one guest. It was owned by the parish church and later became a shop.

Boot, (previously the **Cross**) 145 High Street, c.1750-1820. By 1800 it was renamed Boot. The building was retained when the Harlequin centre was built.

Fighting Cocks, Water Lane. c.1750-1856. This was kept in 1750 by William George but had no accommodation.

Fleur de Lys, 101 High Street. Scant information. It may not have held a licence. In 1824 Stewart Majoribanks presented it to the Morrison Trust as a home for the parish church Lecturer or Curate.

Ganders Ash Beerhouse c.1840-1880. Was kept by Mervyn Dollamore.

The Jolly Sawyers. Stood on the site of St. Huberts Lodge, 61 Church Road. It belonged to a Mr. Wright, kept by Tom Barrett, a sawyer, in 1849. Dem'd 1854.

Leavesden Beerhouse.
Of which the site is unknown, existed briefly in the 1840s and early 50s.

Little Oxhey Lane Beerhouse c. 1840-55 Kept by Mary Lawrence and James Gregory, farmers, in Storey's or Tooke's Farm, later S. Oxhey Library.

Maltsters Arms, 120 High Street. 1859-1880 It belonged to the almshouses and was kept by Will Norris. Demolished.

Nags Head, 146 High Street, c.1750-1821. Now Oscar's bread shop*. In the years up to 1821 when it closed to become the Church Infant School it was kept by Will Kemp, said by Henry Williams to have received bodysnatchers' parcels and to have sent them on to London by carrier. Then owned by the Parish Church.

The Railway Hotel or **Old Clarendon Arms**, St. Albans Road. Was in the yard of the old railway station from 1838 until 1858, when the station was transferred. It belonged to Calvert and Co., of Furnaux Pelham.

Three Horseshoes. 110 High Street. Even less is known of this which may have been merely the trade sign of the smith who is known to have lived there in the early 18th century. Afterwards it was a private house, later used as a shop.

Tun Inn, 196 High Street, c.1600-1740. Mentioned in an old deed, converted to private use and bought in 1773 by the mother-in-law of Edmund Dawson. Demolished and the present museum (Benskin House) built on the site in 1775.

Rising Sun, 206 High Street, early 18th cent. Later the Fox Beerhouse

Samuel Roate's Beerhouse. From c1850, 147 St. Albans Road. It remained a brewery with off sales until c1896. Later Victoria Brewery under F. Cocks.

Saracens Head, 85 High Street, was a major posting inn until 1780. Now beneath the British Home Stores. John Harding landlord. It became a private house, and late in the 19th century the shop of Henry Kingham, grocer extraordinary.

Six Bells, 100 High Street c.1700-c.1750. Little is known of this house, except that it

was closed by 1750 when the church peal was increased from six to eight.

Swan, 113 High Street, c.1660-1730*. This inn was bought by Thomas Hobson, and passed to his widow Dame Fuller, who placed a rent charge of £4 annually on it to support her Free School. It was run by the Brockett family. Became bank premises, latterly NatWest; now 'Gap' store.

Three early inns have not been located: **The Christopher** was owned by John Anderson or Potter in 1605. In 1662 Nicholas Colborne, Brewer, left an inn called the **Cock** near the market in his will, and in 1731 the Will of Will Runnington, landlord of the George, refers to the **Royal Oak**.

It should be noted that the modern premises suggested for some sites bear no resemblance to the lifetime of the olden pubs. The many photographs of older buildings throughout the book should give a better balance.

1. **The Anchor**, 272 High Street. c1750-1957. Demolished. Belonged to an actor, William Savigny, of Bridge Place, early 19th cent.; later a common lodging house.
2. **The Angel**, 253 High Street. Salters of Rickmansworth c.1700-1903. Originally the Maiden's Head then the Duke's Head. Demolished.
3. **The Arches**, formerly **Railway Tavern**, Chalk Hill. Clutterbucks of Stanmore. 1857-1973. Known as Luckett's after 90 years ownnership. Dem'd.
4 †**The Artichoke**, *see* The Oliver
5. † **The Badger**, Gossamers, Meriden Estate. 1961-.
6. † **The Beaver**, Courtlands Drive. 1963-.
7. † **The Bedford Arms Hotel**, Langley Road. 1869-.
8. † Blakes Free House,/**now the Pub on the Corner** 92-96 Queens Road. Recent
9. **The Brewers Arms**, 233 High Street. 1839-1911. Demolished.
10 † **Champions**, *see* The Leviathan
11. **The Clarendon Hotel**, Station Road. Brewsters 1862-1976; became Ind Coopes offices, now the **Flag**, with the former **Pennant** (No. 64) added on.
12. **The Coachmakers Arms**, 30 High Street. Started by George Ware, a coachmaker. 1850-. Rebuilt, enlarged in 1985 became a Wine Bar, by 1987 ceased.
13. **The Compasses**, 68 High Street. Smiths were the original brewers. When it was partly demolished in 1888 a fifteenth century window was discovered, still in the wall in Market Street. c.1725-1974; may have been the medieaval Christopher; *see* **The Joseph Benskin.**
14. **The Cricketers Arms**, Watford Fields. It was first called the Masons Arms after the first landlord, a mason. 1859-1967. Demolished.
15.†**The Crown**, St. Albans Road, Garston. Whittingstalls Brewery. c. 1790- 1980. Rebuilt as Calendars Licensed Restaurant, Allied-Lyons.
16. **The Crystal Palace**, 121 High Street. This tiny beerhouse doubled as a greengrocer's. Dysons Brewery. 1854-1908. Demolished.
17. † Caledonian Hotel/Dean Park Hotel, now **The Moat House Hotel**. Modern building. 1969-.
18.† **Daly's Bar**, 520 Whippendell Road. A new pub since 1984
19. **The Dog**, Hempstead Road. Smith's Brewery. A former haycarters' pub. 1720-1969. Demolished and now the car park for Watford College students.
20. **The Duke of Edinburgh**, 2 Aldenham Road. Originally the Colliers Arms. Healey's Brewery. 1860-1965.
21. † **Dunnings Bar**/ see The Stag
22. **Eight Bells**, 111 High Street. Was John Popes bakehouse; started as the Barley Mow, Sam Smith, brewer, bought it in 1753. The yard was rented from the former Swan next door. 1725-1954.Demolished; under Littlewoods/Westgate.
23. **The Essex Arms**, 69 High Street. In private ownership for many years but latterly Salters of Rickmansworth. Watford's leading inn and posting house for hundreds of years, the corn-exchange being a 19th cent. adjunct. 15th cent. to 1930 when it was bought and demolished by James Cawdell and David Greenhill. It became Timothy Whites and Taylors with the Market Arcade (The Corn Exchange site) between TWT and the rebuilt Cawdells. When Charter Place was built its entrance included the Market Arcade space. When the TWT site was later redeveloped the Arcade part of Charter Place was taken and added to the new shops. TWT is now JJB Sports; the Corn Exchange a jewellers
24.† **The Essex Arms**, Langley Way, Cassiobury Park. Old name, new site. 1975-.
25. † **The Estcourt Arms**, St. Johns Road. 1869-. named after the previous owner of this part of Watford (The Estcourt Estate).
26. † **The Estcourt Tavern**, Estcourt Road. 1869-. This road was originally called Beechen Grove from Grove Circus as far as Clarendon Road. Most of it is now called Gartlet Road, after a defunct girls' school.
27. **The Fox**, 206 High Street. 1854-1956 and demolished. The alley at the side was once called Rising Sun Alley after an inn which much earlier occupied the same site as the Fox beerhouse, and is not to be confused with the Rising Sun Beerhouse at 232 High Street.
28. **The George Inn**, 91 High Street. Smith's Brewery. 15th century-1935. One of the three leading inns of Watford. Demolished, part site of Marks & Spencers.
29.† **The Golden Lion**/ now Reids Bar, Estcourt Road. 1869-.
30. **The Green Man**, 60 High Street, Clutterbuck's. c.1730-1975. Demolished. This

was not a coaching or posting inn, but leased out gigs and stabling.
31. **The Greyhound,** 8 King Street. Owned by Bradshaws. Built in 1852 on Watford Place Estate, closed 1961 and demolished; originally The Freetrader.
32. **The Hammer in Hand,** Leavesden High Road. Was at the corner of Hunter's Lane. Originally a smithy kept by the Mallord family. Demolished in 1960. The smithy was removed and rebuilt at the Chiltern's Open Air Museum.
33.† **The Hammer in Hand,** Ganders Ash. 1961-. An old name on a new site.
34.† **The Happy Hour,** Eastbury Road. A large pub on the edge of town. 1958
35.† **The Hare,** High Road, Leavesden. Originally a farmhouse. Rebuilt. Long kept by the Downer family. Whittingstalls. c. 1790-.
36.† **The Haydon Arms,** Upper Paddock Road. Sedgwicks. 1862-. The name is taken from the nearby Haydon Hill. Recently threatened with closure.
37. **The Hertfordshire Arms,** St. Albans Road. Benskins. First new pub built in Watford since the late 19th cent. A large neo-Georgian house, with a music licence. 1935. Now a MacDonalds.
38.† **The Highwayman/(now The Jolly Friars).** Tolpits Lane. Nearly opposite West Watford Station. Originally named after a Scammell vehicle. 1959-
39. **The Hit or Miss,** 274 High Street. Started in c.1850 as the Carpenter's Arms by G. Clarke, a carpenter. Demolished late 1990s.
40. **The Hollybush,** 228 High Street. A small beerhouse from 1850-1903. Dem'd.
41.† **The Horns,** Hempstead Road. Clutterbucks. 1740-. Like the Dog, it was a call for haycarters. Rebuilt at the turn of this century.
42. **The Jolly Anglers,** 286 High Street. Started in 1860 by Healey's Brewery on or near the site of an earlier pub of the same name. Closed in 1964 and dem'd.
43. †**The Jolly Friars,** *see* The Highwayman
44. **The Jolly Gardeners,** St. Albans Road, on the corner of West Street. Built by John West who gave his name to the street. 1850-1958. Demolished.
45. **The Joseph Benskin,** 68 High Street. Installed in the old Compasses building in 1974 and closed in 1980.
46. **The Kings Arms,** 130 High street. Opened in 1852 in the former gate lodge of Watford Place. Groomes of Kings Langley. 1852-1961. Demolished.
47. **The Kings Head,** 86 High Street, Dysons. c.16th cent. to 1961. Demolished.
48. **The King William,** 319 High Street Dysons. c.1840-1959. Kept by the Lonnon family for many years. The building still stands by Bushey Arches. This pub, like those of the so-called Oxhey Village, was in Bushey Parish until the l890s.
49. **The Lamb,** 201 High Street Healeys. 1854-1902. Demolished.
50. **The Leathersellers Arms,** 235 High Street. Dysons. c.1680-1960. From 1820 to 1840 John Tookey, the landlord, was Watford's exciseman. Demolished.
51.† **The Leviathan Steamer,/now Champion's,** St Albans Road. Built by Henry Parsons, a St Albans brewer, in 1839, named after the new transatlantic steam-assisted vessels, 1839-. Name change 2003
52. † **The Load of Hay,** Watford Heath. In a cottage on manorial waste-land. c.1840-.
53 † **Mac's Place,** *see* the Oddfellows Arms
54. **The Malden Hotel,** Station Road. Ind Coope. 1865-1973. Demolished.
55 † **The Moat House Hotel,** see Caledonian Hotel.
56. **The Merton Arms,** Merton Road. Later an off-licence, c.1890-1938.
57. † **The Nascot Arms,** Stamford Road. 1869-.
58. **The New Inn,** King Street Healeys. Attached to Healey's Brewery buildings.1852-1961. Demolished to widen King Street
59. † **The Oddfellows Arms,/ now Mac's Place** Fearnley Street, Benskins. 1868-. Once kept by Barnabas Mendham whose family also had the Jolly Gardeners.
60. **The Old Berkely Hunt,** St Albans Road. This was on the corner of Weymouth Street opposite the Oddfellows Hall. 1869-1969. Dem'd for the roundabout.
61 OL Bier Gril/new name for The Rose and Crown, 9 Market Street
62. † **The Oliver/ now the Artichoke** by the Pond. Berni Inns. In Cakebread 63. † **The One Bell,** 90 High Street, originally 'The Bell' after the Market bell. This is the oldest existing licence of present-day Watford pubs, but the structure is turn of the century. Smiths. c. 1660-.
63. † **The One Crown,** 156 High Street Dysons. If the One Bell has the oldest licence the One Crown occupies the oldest building, dating in part to the 16th century. The first landlord was Jeremiah Friend, owning the building. 1750-.
64. † **The Pennant,** Station Road. Benskins. Started in 1978 in the former stables of the Clarendon Hotel, built in 1860. Named after Benskin's trademark, *see* No. 8
65. **The Prince of Wales,** 78 Villiers Road. Benskins. c.1868-1955.
66 † **The Pub on the Corner/** was Blakes Free House, 92-96 Queens Road. Recent
67. **The Queens Arms,** St. Albans Road. Dysons. Opposite the old railway station. Demolished to widen the bridge. 1839-1958
68. **The Queens Arms,** Queens Road. Sedgwicks. Originally belonged to John Kilby, former landlord of the Eight Bells. 1862-1968. Demolished.
69. † **The Railway Arms,** Aldenham Road. c.1858-. Dysons. The Lonnon family held it.
70. **The Railway Arms,** St. Albans Road. Dysons. By the railway bridge opposite the old station. 1839-1958. Demolished to widen the bridge.
71. **The Railway Tavern,** 184 High Street. Dysons. Acquired its name when the Rickmansworth branch was built 1854-1974. Demolished.
72. **The Red Lion,** Red Lion Passage (81 High Street). Healeys. Originally the White Horse, and later the Plough. c. 1600-1905. Demolished.
73. † **The Red Lion,** Colney Butts (Vicarage Road). Dysons. This was a smallholding called Colney Butts (Rabbit Strips) till 1800 when inherited by the Dysons. 1800-. Rebuilt c.1898.
74. † **The Rifle Volunteer,** 36 Villiers Road. Clutterbucks. c.1857-. Named after a local Volunteer Regiment
75. **The Rising Sun,** 232 High Street. A tiny beerhouse. 1854-1905. Demolished.
76. **The Rose and Crown,** 72 High Street. Vied with the Essex Arms and the George as Watford's leading inn. A stop for coaches with good stabling. Several times rebuilt c. 15th century-1968. Demolished.
77. † **The Rose and Crown,** 9 Market Street A new pub with no connection with the old inn except propinquity. 1968-. Now OL Bier Gril.
78. † **The Royal Oak,** Watford Heath. Like the Load of Hay built on manorial waste. c.1860-.
79. † Shakers Wine Bar,/ now **Mangan's,** Market Street. Recent
80. † **The Sir Robert Peel,** King Street. Opened in 1961 in the former Police Station and cells.
81. † **The Southern Cross Hotel,** Langley Road. Originally run by Australians. It is in converted houses and has bars. 1968-.
82. **The Spread Eagle,** 82 High Street, Clutterbucks. An early thrift club was held here. c1750-1958. Possibly the 1662 Cock. Demolished.
83. † The Stag, /now **Dunning's Bar,** St Albans Road, previously the Stag, originally the Bricklayers Arms, and later the Queens Bays. Dysons. 1850-. Partly rebuilt.
84.The Swan, 216 High Street Whittingstalls. Until 1800 was called the Hole in the Wall. c.1750-. Rebuilt in the 1930s and moved back from its street frontage. In 1984 it became Shades Wine Bar. Was Wag & Bone in 1995. Demolished.
85. † The Tantivy, **now the New Victoria** Queens Road. Built by Fred Sedgwick in 1873 to celebrate his revived Tantivy Coach to London. 1873-.
86. **The Three Crowns,** 160 High Street, Dysons. This was one of Watfords oldest pubs. It started life as the Bull, and later became the Crown. In 1750 it became the Three Crowns. The building and sign bracket remain. c. 1600-1958.
87.**The Three Horseshoes,** Garston. Originally a smithy. Rebuilt. c.1750/now a restaurant.
88.**The Three Tuns,** 205 High Street. Belonged to the first John Dyson. Closed in 1974. Demolished.
89. † **The Tudor Tavern,** Bushey Mill Lane. In a mock-tudor building on Rice Brother's Tudor Estate. 1943-.
90. **The Verulam Arms** or Hotel, Station Road. Dysons. 1860-1957. Demolished.
91. † **The Verulam Arms,** St Albans Road. A new site for an older name. 1957-.
92. †**The Victoria,** Chalk Hill. Salters. c.l858-.
93. † **The Villiers Arms,** 108 Villiers Road. c.1866-.
94. † **The Wellington Arms Hotel,** Woodford Road. 1869-.
95. **The Wheatsheaf,** High Street. By the site of the Toll house of the Turnpike Trust at Bushey Arches. Salters. It was a little low building with a garden at the rear where strolling actors performed. Rebuilt. c1750-1995. Demolished.
96. **The White Hart,** 180 High Street. This very old pub in an equally ancient building was demolished in 1974 to make way for the Ring Road. It was originally called the Maidenhead. Salters. c.1600-1974.
97. † **The White Lion,** St Albans Road. Weller and Co. 1850-. Partly rebuilt when the yard was filled in.
98.† **Wishing Well,** 188 St Albans Road. Recent
99. **The Woodman,** 25 Red Lion Yard. Healeys. Originally Toppins Brewery c1840. 1860-1968. Demolished.

All the above pubs are in Watford Borough, but the following are or were in Watford Rural Parish and are now in Three Rivers District.

1. † **The Cart and Horses,** Commonwood. 1840-.
2. † **The Clarendon Arms,** Chandlers Cross. Clutterbucks. 1840-.
3. † **The Dick Whittington,** Prestwick Road, S. Oxhey. 1957-.
4. † **The Grapevine,** Prestwick Road. S. Oxhey. 1967.
5 † **The Jet,** Hayling Road, S. Oxhey. 1959-.
6 † **The Partridge,** The Mead, Carpenders Park. 1969-.
7. **The Rose and Crown,** Bucks Hill. Groomes. c.1800-1964. Building remains.
8. **The True Blue,** Bucks Hill. Salters. c.1770-1914. Building remains.

† These premises are still licensed bars. The original brewers have been mentioned where known.

E. J Chapman, B.A. (Hons.) 1987 & 2003

Emigration, and immigration . . .

Wandering is, as we have seen, an old established trait. It is fostered by a need to better ones-self for either the need to live—food and work—or for a better climate or environment. It is the desire to maintain life which drives most people to move.

In the 1950s, days of depression and shortages and stifling restrictions, a considerable number of this country's younger people decided to emigrate. A main reason was stated as 'to give our children a better chance'. Their choice, for they then saw little future in their homeland.

From the late 1800s, within a century, the population had gradually moved from abject serfdom and excruciatingly hard working conditions into a more civilised era. This was hard won, largely by union power which fought for shorter hours and better wages, and by suffragettes who wanted, not equality, but better rights for women. Levering a population into better standards was long and hard, and when the standards had risen many unions wanted still more. Not for nothing was Watford known as the second richest town in the county, based on the biggest printers' wages. But high wages out of proportion make costs higher, and heavier to bear for those not so privileged.

Affordability and mobility in the form of the car enables many to travel further to places of employment; no longer were workers tied to a factory within walking distance or a cycle ride away, and so employers' domination gradually relaxed.

Workers had choice.

Pace of progress has been immense; methods of electronic communication mean that much work can be achieved swiftly and with less labour; and the end result is the greatest disaster of all in that machine and computer has reduced the need for people and many wake up to find that 'retirement' has struck some five, ten, or more years prematurely, leaving an empty life stretching ahead. If many of our friends and relatives sought a life elsewhere there are, equally, far more who see our climate, our land, our language and our way of life as more desirable than that of their own homeland, and Watford a desirable and thriving place in which to settle and serve. Over recent decades we have welcomed Caribbeans and Jamaicans who were invited by the Government of the day to come and work here (much as did the Australian Government when it attracted many from the UK). The immigrants found our winter climate hard to bear after their own warmth but most persevered; they spoke and understood English and soon integrated.

The ties with our 'Empire' were dissolved soon after WWII, but habit died hard and many of the colonies chose to remain connected as part of the British Commonwealth. Before, and after WWII, many from, for example, India chose to send their children to England for education, mainly in professions. Many chose to stay and second and third generations have been been born who are 'Indian' but have never seen India.

Partition of India in 1947 resulted in strife between the new India and the new Pakistan and since 1960 a great number of immigrants have settled from Pakistan. Without the 'reverse colonial' practice of seeking higher education here many have settled with a rudimentary command of English with which to start and many are, like our own 1960s emigrants, artisans seeking a better life than that which they left. Troubles in parts of Africa meant that many of Indian origin, who had settled and built businesses there, were forced out. They were welcomed here for their business acumen and industrious nature as were many 'settlers' of Irish and Italian extraction.

It is a far cry from the flint workers of 12,000 years ago; with a wide mix of racial origins, modern integration within Watford's communities has been peaceful and to everyone's benefit. But the new situation of 'asylum seekers' and 'illegal imigrants', in relatively vast numbers and in very short time, pose problems as yet unquantified, in ecomonics, health and integration. Watford, as does most of south-east England, faces an unprecedented demand for more houses with attendant problems in its wake.

1945; 22 pubs in the High Street . . .

On the north-east side were

Eight Bells,	**Three Tuns**
Leatherseller's Arms	**King William**

On the south-west were

Wheatsheaf	**Jolly Anglers**
Hit or Miss	**Anchor**
Swan Inn	**Fox**
Railway Tavern	**White Hart**
Three Crowns	**One Crown**
Kings' Arms	**One Bell**
King's Head	**Spread Eagle**
Rose and Crown	**Compasses**
Green Man	**Coachmaker's Arms**

By May 2003 only the **One Bell** and **One Crown** survive.
However the 'cafe quarter' boasts fourteen newcomers, including clubs which have licences.
* Even numbers, of the upper High Street shops, have been re-numbered but here the 'old' numbering is used to match the 1958 Kelly's Directory as used under the relevant strips.
At the time of writing two are refitting . . .

The north-east side has
Bodega is in ex-NatWest Bank at 151 The Parade;
Pane and Table in 135 The Parade;
Yates Wine Lodge in converted shops 115, 113 The Parade;
Bar-me is at 83/81 The Parade.

The south-west side has
Taylor's Cafe-Bar is at 134 High Street
Maximo is at 58 High Street (NatWest Bank)
Rat and Parrot at 48/50 High Street (Bucks)
Moon Under Water, 44 High Street (Grange Furnishing)
Chicago Rock in Gade House
Bar-Raka in Gade House
O'Neills in 5 & 6 Prudential Buildings, and 2 Woodlands Parade *
Lloyds No. 1 Bar is in 4 & 6 Woodlands Parade *
Bar Risa, 8 & 10 Woodlands Parade, * *(re-named)*
The Artichoke, 8 High Street *

Destiny (night club) replaces Kudos;
Area (night club) in Gade House
Jongleurs (comedy/night club) is at 1st Floor, 10 The Parade *
In addition a number of restaurants have drinks licences.

Subscribers

Presentation copies

Councillor Sheila Jones
 (last Civic Mayor of Watford 2002-2003)
Councillor Dorothy Thornhill
 (first Elected Mayor of Watford 2003-)
Councillor Ellie Burtenshaw
 (Chairman Watford Borough Council 2003-)
Peter Wilson-Leary
 (Editor, Watford Observer)
Oliver Phillips
 (Deputy Editor Watford Observer)
The Peace Hospice
Phil Burnish
Edgar Chapman
Gill Crowson
Roger Gagan
Patrick Hutchinson
Ross Jackson
Jonathan Lane
George Lorimer
Margaret Marshall
Bushey Museum
David Noades
Linda V Nunn
Paul O'Brien
Peggy Parrish
Simon Pascoe
Alan Pearson
Graham Simpson
Mike Stevens
Watford Central Library (five copies)
Watford Museum (two copies)
Grelle White

Subscribers:

Claire Abercrombie
Audrey Adams
Barry & Hazel Allaway & Boys
Mrs M A Allen
Anne & Alison Allen (for Bill)
Peter & Carolyn Allen
Mr Arthur E Amery
Ray & Margaret Andrews
Arnie, Julia, Zoe & Kyle Arnold
John Anthony
John S Ausden
Bill & Julie Ayre

Caroline Bagley
John S Ball
Dear friend Jean, love from Lucy
George Barnard
Angela & Zafar Basit
Mr John Henry Batchelor & Ms Rachel
 Batchelor
Ray & Carol Batchelor
Miss M Baxter
Julian & Judith Beardsworth
Hazel, David & Ritchie Bearfield
Michael & Jennifer Beck
Mrs Muriel Bell
Mrs Violet Bell
Mrs M Bennett
John Armstrong Benning
Eric Biggerstaff
Gareth & Margaret Bilson

Mr A Bishop
Mrs Rose Black née Landolfi
David & Valerie Blair
Richard Blake
Mrs Yvonne Boatright
Bas Boden
Peter W Booth
Ray Boscher
The Boskey family
Mrs E Bourne
William G Box
R & J D Bradbury
Ron & Doreen Bradshaw
David Bragg
Verdun & Freda Brain
Dennis & Kathleen Bridgewater
Lewis Brighton
Maurice & Sheila Brockman
Jon & Anna Brown
Simon J Brown
Kathleen E Brown
Brunswick Court Care Centre
Colin, Stella, Amanda and Angela Bullimore
Lynda D M Bullock
John Burchell
Bushey Museum & Art Gallery
Jean & John Burgess
Alan & Ellie Burtenshaw
Ann & Tony Butcher
Mrs Josephine Butler
Ian Butterfill

J E L Caldwell Esq.
Ken Campbell & family
Ralph & Marion Cannard
Madeleine & Peter Carpenter
John, Kath, Rob, Richard & Rachel Cassidy
Chantrey Vellacott DFK
Bryan & Hilary Chappell
Norman & Joan Child
Marie Clarke
Nick & Bridget Clarke
Ken & Elizabeth Clunie
Jessie & Brian Coates
Daphne Colbey
Stephen Colbey
Doris Collier
Susan Ann Collins
Elise & Holly Cooper
Gordon & Paula Cox
L E Cramer Motor Engineers Ltd
Mollie Cranwell
Fred, Cora, Alison, Ryan, Calum & Tommy
Paul & Sharon Croft, love always, Dad
Faye Cullan
Mrs Marjorie Cunningham

Judith & Keith Davies
Margaret A C Davies
Paul & Janie Davies
Robert Deering
In memory of Connie & Donald Deller
Kim Deshayes
Howard Dick
Judy Dick
Alan D Dickens & Mary O'Sullivan
Paul A Dillingham

Deirdre Dods
Janet Doherty
Mrs Pauline Dolling
Florence Donovan
Keith Dormer-Ainge
Ann P M Drucker
G Dryden
Stuart & Irene Duncan
Don & Pauline Dunham
Robert and Lesley Dunlop
Pamela Dyer

Mrs D M Elliott
Mr Rory Elliott
Stanley Ellis
Arthur & Christine Ellis
Paul England
Maeve England
Dylan, Katie, James & Rebecca Evans
Pamela Dorothy Evans, Peterborough

John & Yvonne Farrell
Jacqueline and Henry Fearn
Doris Findell
Patrick Fisher
James & Margaret Fitzpatrick
Roger & Mary Flint
Gordon James Floyd
Terry Flynn
Eric & Violet Ford
Daphne & Kenneth Ford
Mary Forsyth
Les & Marian Fox
Sean & Susan Francombe

Kenneth Gage
Sam Gardiner
Mr R A Garner & Mrs A M Garner
Garston Manor — O'Neill family
Jean & Roger Gibbs
Mr Manjit S Gill
R M Godman
Mr T A & Mr D J Godman
Mr & Mrs A J Godman
Penny Goodson née Miles
Bob & Pippa Gorman
Robert & Janet Grange
O E Grant
Ken Gravestock
John Gray
Margaret & Ron Gray
Mrs Agnes Greenwell
Stephen Greenwood & Gwen Seale
Ronald & Joan Gunton
Adam James Greenstreet
Margaret, Eric & Adam Greenstreet
John Barton Guy

Colin & Carole Hall, Peterborough
Ray & Carole Hall
Doreen & Donald Hallworth
Doris Handley
Mr & Mrs P J Harland
Anne I Harris
Donald Hart
Mr & Mrs J R G Hawes
Sally & Paul Hawkes
B Hayes

Subscribers

Daniel Haynes
Doris Ethel Hearn & Robert James Hearn
Maureen & John Heathcote
Doreen & Eric Hedges
Richard P Henderson 21/12/76,
Roger J Henderson 21/8/49
Scott M Henderson 11/5/73
Hubert H Henderson 12/6/26
Kai D Henderson 19/3/95
Nikolai K Henderson 28/3/97
John & Barbara Henderson
Miss D G Henry
The Hewitt family — Premier Coaches
Barry Hicks
Quentin and Lorriane Hicks, Mollymook,
    Australia
Delia & Gordon Higham
John & Maureen Hine
Philip & Linda Hobbs
Florence Hobbs
Alan Hobbs
Gerald Hodges
Mr & Mrs I P Hollins
Gladys Holloway
Peter Charles Hooper
Peter, Stefania & Alexander Horne
Nando e Giulia, Cerveteri, Roma
Jenny & Nick Horscroft
The Horton family
Mrs G M How
Mr & Mrs E Humphrey

Jim & Jean Innes
Barbara & Tony Izasars, commemorating
    their wedding 50 years ago (August 1953),
    when Bob Nunn took the photographs

Paul & Lynne Jackson
Mark Jacob
Linnea & David Janes
Mr R M Janes
Harvey Jaquest
Dr Tamas & Mrs Iren Jasko
J S Jephcote
Hilary & David Jones
Graham & Rosie Jones
Sarah Jones
Mrs J H Jones, for my two sons,
    Graham and Roger

John & Shirley Keable
The Kemsley family
Elsie Kennedy
Mrs C M Kerby
Peter & Alma Kiely
Ronald & Pamela Kilroy
Margaret Kinnear
John & Sheila Kirkham

George & Monica Lakey
Thanks to Don & Julie Lanstone
Agnes Lambert
Reginald Lambert
Mrs Rosemary G K Lancaster
Pat & Derek Lander
Bianca Maria Landolfi, in memory of
    Pasquale Landolfi
Mrs A J A Lane
Ann & Malcolm Larnach
H J Leach

Jock & Irene Learmonth
Neville G Lees
Bernard Lees
Mrs D M Lenham
Keith, Fiona, Katherine & Hermione Lester
Sarah & Catriona Lewis
Mr R J Liberty
Alan D Nicholson
Diane & John Lindeck
Sheila Lorriman

Shirley Macara née Bangert
Jean & Richard Machin
Brian Markham
Mollie & Martin Potter
Mary Machin
Christopher & Sharon Marchant
Doug & Joy Marriott
Owen Martin
Ann & Ed Martin (Leavesden)
Paul Maskell
W & J Mason
Bob & Mary Mayor
J F McCullagh
Bruce & Rose McMillan
In memory of Stella, Freeman of the
    Borough, from Tom
Alec & Beryl Merrifield
Roger & Christine Middleton & family
Tessa Miles
D Miles
Dave & Jackie Miller
Bettie Miller
Barbara Miller
Phyllis Miller
Nick & Mary Mills
Dorothy Moore
Agnes Moravszki 2001 - 2004
Bella & Ron Moulder
Mr P Mutum

Kenneth & Clodagh Nash
Michael K Neighbour
David & Sheila Niven
Shirley & Larry Noades
Mrs P Norris
Eric G North
Alan & Robbie Nunn
Ron & Edie Nunn
Colin & Nicki O'Brien
Margaret Ockenden, Tasmania, Australia
Joan Orton

John & Janet Page
John & Linda Page (Florida)
Terry & Barbara Page (Tandem TV & Film)
In memory of Bill (ex Blaw Knox) &Lily Page
Colin, Liz, James & Madeline Pascoe
Tina, Jamie-Leigh & Sean Pascoe
Ms Zara Peermohamed
Derek & Margaret Perks
Oliver Phillips
George & Kate Pickard
Paul Picton
Patricia & Graham Picton
Richard Picton
Charles Pinnington

Lal Pope, in memory of Jack (1913-1993),
    past Chairman League of Friends,
        Watford General Hospital
Arthur J Pott
Mrs E Potter
Peter W G Powell
Simon & Fiona Powell and family
Janet & Alan Power
Michael Pritchard
Alan & Lesley Pritchard
Martin & Doris Prizeman
Mrs Y Proctor & family
Mr John Pullen

Pam & Peter Quick

Sally-Anne Rafferty
Victor & Christine Randell
Doreen Ranscombe
Robert Ransom
Rosemary Reed
Mr & Mrs Colin Reeve
Gwen Reeve
Fred Richards
George & Janet Roadnight & family
Lisa, Neil, Thomas & Alfie Roberts
Peter & Rose Rowland
C & L Ryan

Brian & the late Inkas Sackville,
    in memoriam
Shirley & Brian Samms
Philip N Sampson
Elaine and David Sands
John Sargant
John & Elizabeth Sargent
Thomas George Saunders
Andrew, Mandy, Hannah and Owen Schutt
Mr & Mrs H G S Seaborne
Kevin & Ann Sharkey
Mark Sheldrake
Sylvia Shephard
Brendan G K Shilleto
RichardShort.com
Don & Daphne Shortman
Dave Sifleet & Duncan McKeich
Michael Simmons
Councillor Sheila Smillie
John Smith
Carol & Bern Smith
Beryl Smith
Holly & Heidi Smith
Raymond & Margaret Smith
Ronald C Spooner & family
Des Standen
Patricia Steeden, celebrating the life of her
    mother, Alice Otley,
    20th April 1902 to 5th July 2003
Gordon & Pat Stewart Trilogy
Susan Stone
A E & M M Stone
Linda Storey
Sylvia & Allen Stratford
C M & J W N Stratford
C A Stratford
Mrs Winnie Steggles
Val & Norman Sutton
John R Swain
Peter C Swain OBE

Watfordians . . .

Gerry Swinscoe
Malcolm & Terena Symes
Brian & Eileen Symonds née Carpenter
M Tamlin
K Tamlin
Peter Tapping
TMA Property Management (S Taylor):
   in memory of 100 years of the Great
   Rhodes Scholarship Oxford 2003
Stuart Taylor in memory of Colin Parry:
   Architect of De-Beers House,
   Watford 2003
Stuart J Taylor TMA Properties
Ken and Linda Taylor
David Tearle
Brian R Tearle, Parkside Drive
Peter & Cecilia Tearle, Ridge Lane
Richard & Jenny Thomas
Hilda & Howard Thomas
J D O & D J E Thomas
Rosina Thomas
Arthur & Daphne Tilley
D & T Thompson, Abbotsbury House,
               Greenfield, Beds

Graham & Alex Tooth
Barry, Sue, Taia & Kai Tunstall
Mrs Melita June Turner
Mavis & Norman Tyrwhitt
Terry Tyson

Kenneth Upson
John Upson

Molly Venn

Marie Cooper & Colin Waddell
Elizabeth & Arthur Waddell
Laura & Robert Waddell
Ann Waine
Pat Wakelin née Thomas
H Richard Walduck OBE JP DL
Phyllis & Joan Walker
Mrs B Walsh
Shirley Ward
C W Waters
Simon Watson-Picken & Alison Muir
Margaret & Dudley Watts
Reginald James Wedgerfield
T R Welch
David West
R & J Westcott
Lauren Marie Wheatley
K & F A Wicks
Christine & Clive Wightman
Pat & Ray Wills, Aldenham
J J F Wilson & M A Wilson
Diane & John Wise
Mr J Wolf
Kay & Malcolm Wood
Fredrick Murrell
B N D Wood
Audrey & Lionel Woodrow
Mr B J V Wright
Sue Horne
Maureen & Raymond Wright
Shirley A E Wright
Peggy Wynne

G T Young
F J Young

From top to bottom: *Baby Christine Collier, 1949; Cassiobury fair baby-in-arms 1988; girl with pram in the High Street, 1960; fisher boy, on the River Gade, 1994; pedestrian crossing, St Albans Road from Hempstead Road and the baths, 1960.*

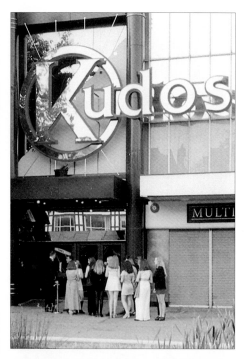

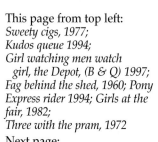

This page from top left:
Sweety cigs, 1977;
Kudos queue 1994;
Girl watching men watch
  girl, the Depot, (B & Q) 1997;
Fag behind the shed, 1960; Pony
Express rider 1994; Girls at the
fair, 1982;
Three with the pram, 1972

Next page:
Dancers, at Chef Corner,
  1960;
Caught in the rain, c1978;
Chatterers c1964; Sunseekers,
  St Albans Road near Town
  Hall, 1961;
Goodnights, the Parade, 1965;
Slippery slope, Avenue Car Park
subway, 1999.

A trio of twins . . .

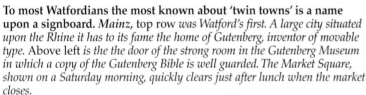

To most Watfordians the most known about 'twin towns' is a name upon a signboard. *Mainz*, top row *was Watford's first. A large city situated upon the Rhine it has to its fame the home of Gutenberg, inventor of movable type. Above left is the the door of the strong room in the Gutenberg Museum in which a copy of the Gutenberg Bible is well guarded. The Market Square, shown on a Saturday morning, quickly clears just after lunch when the market closes.*

Above centre is Nanterre's *'twin-town' sign and to the right L'Amadierre theatre, a focal point for the arts and below it an older part of Nanterre next to the town hall. A disastrous foreign policy in the late 1950s with their Algerian colony led to many Algerians making France their home. Nanterre became obliged to host some 14,000 in what became a 'bidonville', a shanty town. High-rise blocks of flats were built to cater for many when removed from the bidons. Nanterre has a very large University; it is noted for its students starting the riots in 1968 which spread throughout France and which, lasting for two months, led to better conditions/higher wages.*

Across both pages is a spread of **Pesaro's** *town square. At its left is Pesaro's Theatre; the imposing building across the square (right of centre) houses the town's Post Office, and at right edge is the Ducal Palace dating back to the 15th century. Pesaro is the birthplace of Rossini; his one-time home is now a small museum detailing his life, achievements and death. Pesaro is one of five small Adriatic ports whose history dates back to at least AD550.*

Below: *Watford's youngsters would love Cherbourg's skateboard park!*

Watford is also twinned with Wilmington, USA, and Novgorod, Russia, neither yet visited by the writer.

Nanterre's architecture is modern and functional. The top two photographs show Nanterre's Town Hall, surrounding by symbolic moat, and cheek by jowl with a nineteen-storey social and benefits building. To cater for a large immigrant population many high-rise blocks of homes had to be built. Nanterre, just six kilometres from Paris centre, is adjacent to the massive La Defense office & business connurbation.

Index

errata

p272 'an enquiry had to be held' should be 'inquiry'.

Bibliography, picture credits

As "The Book of Watford, 2nd Ed" is essentially an account of the past 150 or so years my main source of information has been the local newspapers.

In addition to excerpts from local newspapers I am grateful for permission to publish extracts from several books, and to have found others useful for reference. These included Britton's "Cassiobury", and the typescript of W. R. Saunders' "History of Watford". I am indebted to Major T. D. Sainsbury for permission to publish extracts from "Medals and Awards", and to Roger Culverhouse for assistance on matters dealing with the history of the Fire Brigade.

The main source of new material has been my own photographs, local news reports, publicity material from HCC and WBC and extra reference works. Unlike the 1987 book, which, in essence, stopped at about 20 years prior to publication, this work carries on up to date, September 2003.

The collection of illustrations in the Reference Library has been added to over many years and in periods of conservation many photographs have been remounted but, unfortunately, the authors' names, if noted, are lost. The earliest positively dated photograph is by Frederick Downer of the Wedding Day procession, 10th March 1863 *(p.55)*. His, and his sons work spans a period to 1919.

From about 1888 until 1926 William Coles rivalled Downer in quantity and quality, his business passing into ownership of Theodore Greville; many of his original negatives still exist in the care of the Library. Whitford Anderson was an architect who extensively photographed Hertfordshire's towns and villages; his record of Watford spans 1895 to c1905.

Jesse and Percy Landon, between 1895 to c1929 added views, as did Albert Warren (1902-1914).

A professional studio which produced town views was Couper Mathews, later Gregg Couper, c1906 to c1960. Mr. F. H. Haines, one time President of Watford Camera Club, c1905-1920; made many views of the town. George Bolton, Borough Librarian, contributed much material from c1922 to c1939, starting the 'local collection.'

Greville Studios, c1935-1943, were under contract to provide photographs for the Watford Observer and many negatives of this period survive, in particular of their 'war-time' series. Harry Williamson worked first for the West Herts Post and then for the Watford Observer; his work spans the years 1944 to c1956. His negatives made for Watford Observer survive. His extraordinary story is told briefly on p257.

It is due to the courtesy extended by the Watford Observer that I was able to research early years of their collection of photographic plates, and to use some felt to be of interest. A number of prints are by members of the Watford Camera Club, but carry no names, and also used are a number of 'anonymous' prints. Collections of old postcards exist, and I have been pleased to have used several donated by well-wishers. In many instances, copies have been made from newspaper prints, the originals having long since been lost.

The following list of credits is sequential, (exc) indicates an exception on that page listed.

Bibliography

Britain's Motor Industry, *1950, H G Castle*
British Bus Services, History of, *1989, John Hibbs*
Cassiobury, *1835, John Britton, courtesy Keith Seabrook*
Dacorum, Within Living Memory,*1988 Shipman & Jackson*
David Greenhill, Master Printer, *Miriam Leech*
DH, de Haviland Story, *1982, C Martin Sharp*
Domesday Book, Hertfordshire, *1976, John Morris*
Famous Bombers of WWII, *1957, William Green*
Famous Fighters of WWII, *1957, William Green*
Flint, Versatile Stone, the, *1992, H J Mason*
Greater London Plan 1944, *1945, Patrick Abercrombie, MA, FRIBA, PPTPI*
Grove Story, The, *1984, British Railways Board, Dennis Lovett*
Gutenberg Museum, Mainz, *1994*
Hertfordshire Illustrated Review,*1894*
Hertfordshire Photographers, *1839-1939; Bill Smith & Michael Pritchard*
Hertfordshire Police, Story of, *The Letchworth Press*
Herts & Beds Airfields, *1999, Graham Smith*
Kelly's Directories, *1949, 1958, 1966, 1970*
Last Complete Performance, *1989, Ivor Buckingham*
London & Birmingham Rly, *1840, Thomas Roscoe*
London, a Pilgrimage, *1970, Gustavé Dore, Blanchard Jerrold*
Man with Camera, *1977, Felix H Mann*
Maxwell, Assassination of, *2002,Gordon Thomas, Martin Dillon*
Maxwell's Fall, *1992, Roy Greenslade*
Maxwell, the Outsider, *1988, Tom Bower*
Old Roads of England, The, *1980, Sir William Addison*
Passenger Cars, 1924-1942, *1975, M Sedgwick*
RAC Handbook, *1927, RAC*
Railway Motor Buses and Bus Services, 1902-1933, *Vol 1, John Cummings*
Scammell, World Trucks, *Pat Kennett*
Seven Spies who changed the world, *1991 Nigel West*
Street and Place Names in Watford, 1973, *Alan W Ball*
Watford, Central Area Draft Plan, 1954, 1964
    E H Doubleday, OBE, PPTPI, FRICS, MIMssE, County Planning Officer, HCC
Watford, History of, 1884, *Henry Williams*
Watford, History of, 1932, *W R Saunders,*
    original typescript, courtesy of his daughter, Joan Saunders
Years Between, the National Story, *R J Crawley, D R MacGregor, F D Simpson*
Newspapers:
    Evening Echo   Focus
    ReviewWatford Illustrated   Watford Newsletter
    The Watford Observer   Watford Free Observer
    Watford Our Town/About Watford   West Herts Post

Photographic credits
Norman Davey, *11*   A Stafford Dupree, *13t & b*
George Bolton, *16, 180t, 182c, b, 186 cl, 187b, 199t & b, 210br, 211b, 213b, 320tl,*
Watford Central Library Collection, *21t, 25b, 26l, 32 (portrait), 34, 42, 43, 44, 52, 53t, 54, 53b, 61 main, 69r, 71r, 76, 77t, 93 c & b, 93t, 106, 107, 108t, 110b, 110t, 115t, 117 t & b, 122t, 122c, 125cl, bl,126b, 127bl, 130,*
131tr, 135, 136, 139t, 139c, 143t, 160, 162b, 172t & b, 175 t & cr, 179, 183tl, 185t, 186cl &cr, 187t, 192t, 197l, 204, 207t.209b,212t, 213t, 233, 236, 243b, 256t, 263, 264 t & c, 277t & c, 280t, 287b, 290t, 304c & T, 312c, 313tr, 314c, 325 mid l, 330tl, 334, 338, 347c, 367, 398, 399t
Author, *12, 13c, 21b, 45 insets, 47, 55 inset, 67r, 125r, 131bl & br, 132-134, 194b, 206tr, 207b 209cr, 227, 228, 264b, 268-275, 276c & b, 276c & b, 278, 279, 286t, 287t, 288, 289t, 293t, 294-296, 297b, 298tr, 298b, 299tr, 300-303t, 302cr, 303, 305, 306, 308, 309 exc tl, 310 exc cr, 311t, 313cl, 314tr, 317, 318 exc tl, 319 main, 320tr, 322, 323 mid l, 328 c & cl, 330t, 331, 336t, 338c, 341, 346, 349 tl, cr, 351tr, 352, 353tl, 353 main, 355-357, 360tr, 361, 362tl, 362 main, 362rc, 363-365tr, 367, 368, 369, 369cr, 373tr, 374, 375 exc tl, 377, 378, 379, 381-384, 385 exc top, 386-391, 393c & b, 394-396, 399b, 400-402t, 403, 404, 405 exc tl, 406-408, 410, 412-415, 420, 421 exc tr, 422, 426t&c, 438, 439, 448. High Street strips 301-374.*
Frederick Downer, *20, 55 main & top, 56, 57, 62, 63, 75b, 84, 85t, b86b, 88t, 90, 91, 99, 102, 109t, 109c, 112, 120t, 121t, 126t, 128, 129*
Postcards, *22r, 80, 121, 124, 127b, 139b, 141, 142t, 143b, 164 170, 175 cl, 178, 180c, b, 192b 219*
P. Heseltine, *23;*   Alan Fearnley, *36*
Watford Museum, *25t, 51, 59 main*
Britton's Cassiobury, *26r, 27, 28, 29 (exc portrait WCL), 30, 31, 32, 176, 177*
Bourne *31, 337*
David Spain Collection, *33, 423*
Heale Bequest, Camden Library, *39, 40, 41*
F. W. Haines, *45m, 120b, 123b, 127tr, 137t, 142c, 142b, 158l, 173*
Warren, A *59tr, 109b, 323tl*
Parrish, E, C, Collection, *61tl;*   Dunlop, Leslie, Collection, *62 main*
Newspaper pics *62t, 184, 195b, 256b (Wat Obs), 393*
L. I. N. *68c, 70*
William Coles, *69l, 71, 72, 74, 75t, 88b, 110, 118tl, 118b, 119, 122b, 159, 161, 165, 186bl, br, 188, 189, 190c, 195t, 323cr, 415c*
George Lorimer, Collection, *138*
Downer, F & Sons, *144-155, 157, 158r, 162t*
Newspaper, Daily Sketch, *158b*
Central Aerophoto, *168, 171*
Gregg Couper, *175, 193b, 210b, 218*
John Maltby, *214t*
Otto Brookman, *181cr, b;*   Hewitt Collection, *182t, 343c*
Aerofilms Ltd, *183, 186t, 212b, 290b, 307, 315, 321, 332, 323, 376, 393, 402, 414tr, rear end paper*
Greville Studios, *193t, 194t, 206b, 211t, 214b, 217, 222, 226, 229, 230, 231, 232, 234, 235, 237, 238, 239, 241, 242, 243t, 246, 247*
Watford Camera Club, *205, 350t*
Watford Observer, *19c, 289b, 291, 297t, 198tl, 311c, 325cr, 332 centre, 350, 370c, 389, 417, 419*
BarryAnthony, *291t, 291t, 323 mid r, 324t, 325, 326, 327exc cr, 328cl, 347tr, 348, 349tl, 359cr, 370tr, 373tl*
Tempest, Cardiff, *293b, 375tl*
Ray Mundy, *336cr*   Linda V Nunn, *372*
Ian Dellar, *426b*

The last page.

It was suggested in early 2002 that *The Book of Watford* be reprinted but that was not practical. Started in 1985 it was out-dated and only a new edition would encompass the changes of seventeen years; and there were comments that the print size was too small …

For this edition much of the original has been reset, in a slightly larger size, some items being carefully edited to retain sense but to save space. All captions are new. The physical technology has changed, the darkroom is replaced by computer and scanner. The framework is the first book; original photographs had to be found and scanned. The colour strips of the High Street scanned and edited to form two panoramas. (They were taken in the spring of 1965 and comprise nearly 350 separate photographs). New material had to be collated to come up-to-date.

The resultant two-year journey found difficult subjects, controversial opinions, but was spurred on by the wishes of those who expect to see a fair record, if that was possible.

As with any marathon there has to be a back-up team, but in my case it was more of a long distance solo runner where the team is, of necessity, very much smaller. My wife, Linda, watched in bemusement, with infinite patience (though frequently stretched), and it is to her that I owe the ability to complete the task. Her opinions steadied some of my wilder ideas and her immense amount of work in typesetting the original 1987 work formed the basis of the earlier part of this.

Ted Parrish, though passed away a few years ago, had been with me in spirit; he was an early campaigner against rash over-development and, once again, Edgar Chapman rose to the occasion by up-dating the pubs' list; a dauntless task for they nowadays change names so frequently. George Lorimer, though not now living in Watford, proof-read all the captions (and we disagreed on remarkably few).

Another who has left Watford is Barry Anthony whose comments start this work, and whose photographs of Lower High Street brought back memories of old shops and businesses of lower High Street.

David Noades reminded me that Jimmy Perry had played a significant part in Watford's history from his Home Guard and Palace Theatre days, and Oliver Phillips filled a lamentable gap in my own knowledge about the ups and downs of the lads at Vicarage Road. John Ausden helped with pub pictures, George Hewitt with rare pictures of Premier Coaches, and Ian Dellar went to considerable lengths to provide material for the story of Blaw Knox.

Arthur Ellis provided the link between the Ellis of lantern slide days of a century ago, through Ellis bicycles to their garage in Rickmansworth Road, now a Ford dealership. These and other contributors all had in common the fact that they offered far more material than space permitted using.

The Central Library's Reference Room, and Local Studies Cabinets, are the essential 'must' for any research about local affairs as are their files of local newspapers and, again, it has been a privilege to reprint excerpts from the Watford Observer.

Great effort was made to acknowledge the photographers whose work has been used but, inevitably, many photographs are unattributable but which command our thanks that they were taken.

My main contribution was to put it all together and, despite the best endeavours, the mistakes which remain are all my own.

On the technical side my PC had undergone several upgrades to enable programmes and storage to integrate efficiently; the ever-patient staff at SRS, on the Parade, gave answers to most problems during the various upgrades and rebuilds. When it came to transferring all the semi-finished work to a Mac (for final outputting), I found fresh problems and these Simon Pascoe solved.

There then remained the final hurdle of transferring the contents of my CDs to plates and then to press. During this time Alpine's staff were interested and concerned to get best result possible; how superbly they have succeeded is in your hands to judge.

Many 'histories' have to a certain degree to be sanitised to suit the paymasters who commission the work; for an individual the path is harder to tread for he can roam or digress at will, but one's opinions are not entirely one's own but are shaped by comments from generations who live in the town.

Sheila Jones, Watford's last traditional Mayor, provides the comment that "Watford fights above its weight." In the earlier half of the 20th century this was certainly true when we had caring giants of the calibre of Ralph Thorpe and David Greenhill who pushed from their position of business in a constructive manner. They were leavened by a good average of equally dedicated Aldermen and Councillors, who being in their day less political, had the town's interest at heart rather than party.

Those who now fight above their weight are not Watford's people but those who wish to take advantage of Watford's limited space, in a political climate which says 'build more and more houses'. The rules imposed upon the council tie their hands, and developers are only too happy to 'take' beyond their weight.

They are, of course, not in it for mere money, but are providing homes and work for Watford people who will, somehow, struggle through our overcrowded roads to shop, travel to work and take their children to an overcrowded school. Roads, to get about our lives and business, and hospitals to survive the pressures, are prime concerns.

The illustration above, reprised from page 412, has been modified to show the current hospital site, football ground, and the cleared site of the old generating station. It is this area which the editor of the Watford Observer, Peter Wilson-Leary, and Mayor Dorothy Thornhill, have suggested to the Beds and Herts Strategic Health Authority as suitable to be redeveloped to solve many of the problems posed by Watford General Hospital's cramped environment.

It would mean:
A front entrance in Cardiff Road
Hospital halt on the Croxley Rail Link
Health Campus for Auxiliary Services
New multi-storey car park
New link road to the hospital
Bus terminal in the grounds
New staff accommodation
A new medical block.

The Editor writes: "Option Two Plus promises to revitalise the town's general hospital by improving accessibility and delivering better facilities and services in a transformed environment. It would become a regional centre of excellence, to the benefit of us all." *12/9/03*

To which Ralph Thorpe, and the Watford Observer champions of the 'Peace cause' back in the 1920's, would doubtless agree …

J B (Bob) Nunn, 2003

Above: *The production credit to the map stated: "Children from Harwoods Adventure Playground and Laurence Haines School worked with artist Helena Roden to produce metalwork designs inspired by memories collected from local people. This map shows the position of the metal signs and the stories attached to each of them."*

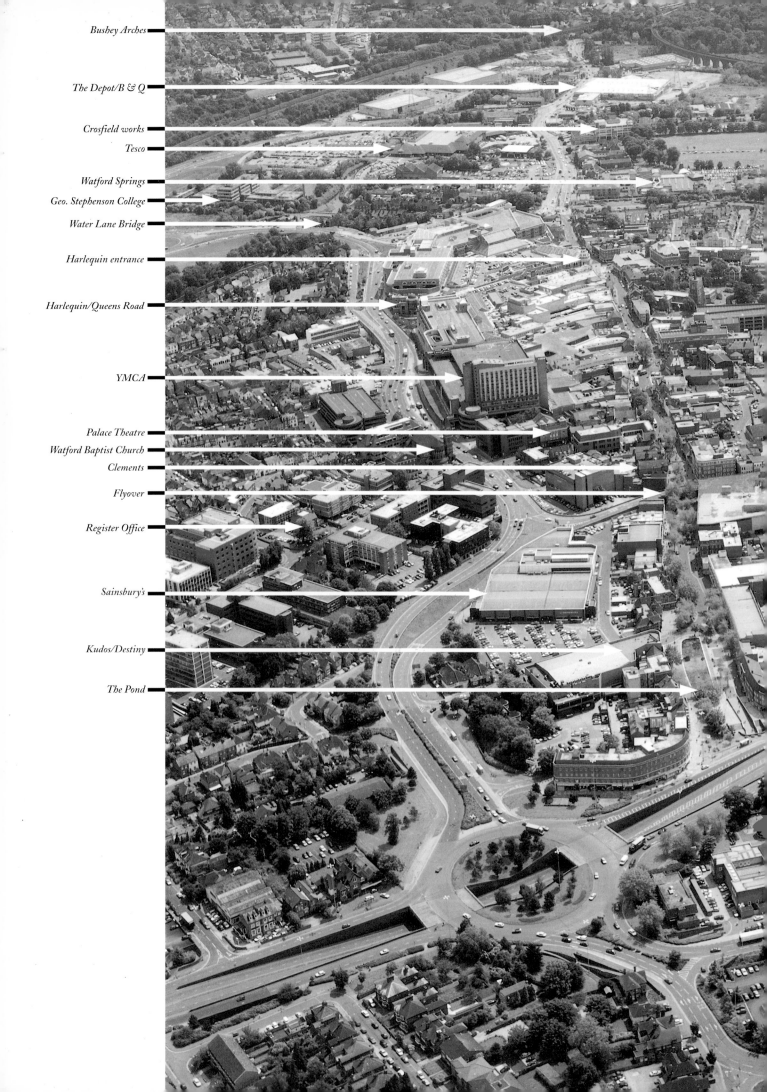

Bushey Arches

The Depot/B & Q

Crosfield works
Tesco

Watford Springs
Geo. Stephenson College
Water Lane Bridge

Harlequin entrance

Harlequin/Queens Road

YMCA

Palace Theatre
Watford Baptist Church
Clements

Flyover

Register Office

Sainsbury's

Kudos/Destiny

The Pond